Gustave Whitehead: "First in Flight"

*Hidden History of Gustave Whitehead
& the Wrights*

Figure 1: 1901: Gustave Whitehead and "No. 21"

Gustave Whitehead stands by his invention, the world's first airplane to make a successful, manned, powered flight.

Photo attributed to Stanley Yale Beach, Aviation Editor, Scientific American (spring, 1901)
Courtesy of Fairfield Museum, O'Dwyer archives

Gustave Whitehead: "First in Flight"

Hidden History of Gustave Whitehead & the Wrights

by

Susan O'Dwyer Brinchman

Cover design by The Paragon Agency

First Edition
Apex Educational Media, La Mesa, CA
2015

© 2015 by Susan O'Dwyer Brinchman

All rights reserved. No part of this publication may be reproduced, stored in a retrieval system, or transmitted, in any form or by any means, electronic, mechanical, photocopying, recording, or otherwise, without the prior permission of Susan Brinchman.

ISBN-10:0692439307
ISBN-13:978-0-692-43930-2

ADDITIONAL COPIES may be ordered from Apex Educational Media, P.O. Box 655, La Mesa, CA 91944-0655, for $24.99 each plus $5 postage; online at www.gustavewhiteheadbook.com; or your bookseller.

Figure 2: Gustave Whitehead circa 1901

Gustave Whitehead, "First in Flight"

Photo courtesy of Fairfield Museum, O'Dwyer archives

Table of Contents

Table of Figures 7
Acknowledgments 13
Preface 17
1. Intro 23
   - First Powered Flight 23
   - The Preparations 24
2. First Flights on August 14, 1901 33
   The Evidence 33
   Journalist Eyewitness Account 35
   - Richard "Dick" Howell 35
   - The "Flying" Article 41
   Illustrated with Earliest Aviator Symbol 47
   First Flight Locations and Conditions 49
   Later Flights of August 14, 1901 63
   More on Witnesses to the First Flight 68
   Newly Unearthed Local Articles Confirms Flights 74
   Herald Confirms Eyewitness Report 81
   Gustave Whitehead Confirm Herald Article 85
   Issue of Control 87
   Photo Questions 102
   Newspaper Coverage of First Flight 110
3. Next Steps 115
   Promises Flight to New York 115
   Whitehead and "No. 21" Go to Atlantic City 116
   First Flying Machine Factory 120
   - "No. 22" Improved Design 120
   - Problems Surface 143
4. A New Goal: The World's Fair Aerial Contest 147
   Whitehead First Entrant 149
   Early Planning of Aeronautics at the Fair 155
   The Aerial Contest 157
   Chanute, the Wrights, Whitehead, and the Fair 160
   News of Whitehead and the Fair 165
   Aerial Competition Problems 168
   The Eight Major Contests 169
   Criticism of Rules and Regulations 171
   The California Arrow and the Whitehead Motor 173
   Whitehead Prepares for the Fair 176
   Flying Machines at the Fair 182
   Whitehead at the Fair 183
5. Other Notable Whitehead Flights 189
   Significant 1902 - 1904 Flights 189
   - First Circuit: January 17, 1902 189
   - Milford Circuit 1902 193

    Earlier Flight Experiments, 1894-1901 196
- 1900-1901 Connecticut Flights 196
- 1899 Pittsburgh Flight 200
- 1897 New York/New Jersey Flight Experiments 204
- 1894-96/97 Massachusetts Flight Experiments 206

6. **Key Testimonies** **209**
    Eyewitnesses 209
- 1899 – 1902 Flights 210
- 1903-1911 Flights 218

    Scientific American on Early Flights 219

7. **Later Years** **227**
    1904 – 1908 Flight Experiments 227
    1909: A Falling Out with Stanley Yale Beach 238
    1910-1915 Helicopters, Lawsuits, Final Inventions 249

8. **Frequently Asked Questions** **263**
    Whitehead designs - Why did they change? 263
- Designs Timeline 265

    Why did Whitehead's much larger aeroplanes fail to fly? 266
    Why are there gaps in the historical record? 268
    Why wasn't Whitehead recognized from the beginning? 270
    Did Whitehead conduct scientific experimentation? 274
    Did the Wrights Visit Whitehead? 274
    What was Mrs. Whitehead's involvement? 281

9. **Funding and Finances** **283**
10. **Whitehead Historic Sites** **287**
    Where Whitehead Flew 287
    Whitehead Shops 292
    Whitehead Homes 297
    Whitehead's Gravesite 302

11. **Legacy** **307**
    The "Firsts" 307
    Whitehead's Main Accomplishments 309

12. **Kitty Hawk Revisited** **311**
    Kitty Hawk "First" Flights 311
    Wrights' Flight Problems 313
    Wrights' Flights Less Successful 314
    Wrights' Witness Statements 314
    Gaining Recognition as First in Flight – Who really was "first"? 316
    Little Known Facts About Kitty Hawk 317
    The Smithsonian-Wright "Contract" Crediting Orville Designed by Whitehead Detractors 318

13. **Conclusions** **333**
14. **Gustave Whitehead Timeline** **337**
    Endnotes **355**
    Appendix **391**
    Bibliography **423**
    Resources **425**
    Index **429**

Table of Figures

Figure 1: 1901: Gustave Whitehead and "No. 21" 2
Figure 2: Gustave Whitehead circa 1901 4
Figure 3: June 1901, "No 21" ready for summer flights 22
Figure 4: Whitehead stands next to "the Condor," with engine, spring, 1901 27
Figure 5: Front and Rear views of "No. 21," the "Condor" 28
Figure 6: "No 21" at 241 Pine Street, by workshop 29
Figure 7: Whitehead's airplane "No. 21," wings folded 29
Figure 8: Sketch of Whitehead's "No. 21" in flight, Aug. 14, 1901 35
Figure 9: Dick Howell, Editor for Sports of the People 36
Figure 10: Dick Howell as he appeared in 1928 36
Figure 11: Dick Howell, editor credit 36
Figure 12: Herald Sports Section Header 36
Figure 13: NY Times Sporting includes Aeronautics 37
Figure 14: NY Times Sporting Section Banner 37
Figure 15: Bridgeport Sunday Herald article "Flying," Aug. 18, 1901 41
Figure 16: Possible Dick Howell signature 47
Figure 17: "Flying" article had witch illustrated banner 47
Figure 18: Flying Witch – "The Original Aviator," Chicago Tribune (1909) 48
Figure 19: Herald reports two more flights made for Herman Linde in 1901 50
Figure 20: Bridgeport Evening Farmer reports flight made in 1901 "out near Fairfield beach" ... 51
Figure 21: Herald sketch of "No. 21" in flight thought to be over Turney farm 52
Figure 22: Ash Creek bridge en route to August 14th flying grounds (1900) 53
Figure 23: 1895 map showing elevations of Turney farm fields 53
Figure 24: Map of Fairfield, CT, shows Turney Fields flying site locations 54
Figure 25: Upper Turney field (1934) 54
Figure 26: Upper Turney field most likely Aug. 14th, 1901 flight site 55
Figure 27: Lower Turney field, alternate flight site (1934) 55
Figure 28: Map of Route on August 14, 1901 56
Figure 29: 1893 Map shows proximity to Fairfield Beach 56
Figure 30: 1912 map shows closeup of lower Turney field with house and trees 57
Figure 31: Access to lower Turney field shows elevation 61
Figure 32: Lower Turney field slight slope shown 61
Figure 33: Flat area on lower Turney field – ½ size it was in 1901 62
Figure 34: Stratford, CT beach areas 63
Figure 35: Road to Stratford Point, circa 1900 64
Figure 36: Lordship open space and beaches, Stratford, CT (1934) 65
Figure 37: Road to Lordship beaches, circa 1900 66
Figure 38: Anton Pruckner, circa 1901 67
Figure 39: 1910 US Census showing Whitehead family living next to Frederick Suelly 68
Figure 40: Bridgeport Directory shows Andy Celley living nearby 69
Figure 41: NY Sun article names Andrew Cellie and Daniel Varovi as investors 70
Figure 42: Named eyewitness James Dickie stands by "No. 21" in spring, 1901 71
Figure 43: James Dickie to Whitehead's left 71
Figure 44: Eyewitness Dickie in photo shoot sits by "No. 21" 72
Figure 45: James Dickie spring, 1901 72
Figure 46: Named eyewitness James Dickie closeup, 1901 72
Figure 47: Bridgeport Evening Farmer confirms August 14th flight near Fairfield Beach 75

Gustave Whitehead: "First in Flight"

Figure 48: Bridgeport Post article "Perfecting His Machine" (Aug. 26, 1901) 76
Figure 49: W. W. Cameron Trotting Park 78
Figure 50: Gustave Whitehead memorial fountain, Bridgeport, Connecticut (2014): "No. 21" 80
Figure 51: Gustave Whitehead memorial fountain, Bridgeport, Connecticut (2014): full view 80
Figure 52: January 26, 1901 Bridgeport Herald summer flight confirmation 81
Figure 53: Gustave Whitehead sketch 81
Figure 54: May 31, Bridgeport Herald "August 14, 1901 flight" confirmation 82
Figure 55: Whitehead triplane glider, photographed May 1903 84
Figure 56: Weisskopf's Flugmaschine (Ansicht von hinten) 86
Figure 57: Smithsonian-Wright Agreement of 1948 language directive (1) 87
Figure 58: Smithsonian-Wright Agreement of 1948 Label #1 88
Figure 59: Smithsonian-Wright Agreement of 1948 Label #2 88
Figure 60: Drawing by Paul Garber, Smithsonian, of Whitehead's rudder system 97
Figure 61: NY Herald illustration of Whitehead's "No. 21" 104
Figure 62: Bridgeport Daily Standard describes Whitehead flight photos 106
Figure 63: Scientific American reports 1901 Whitehead flight photos 107
Figure 64: The Scientific American of January 27, 1906 108
Figure 65: Aero Club Exhibition of January 1906, Whitehead photos 109
Figure 66: Collection of Pictures by Wm. J. Hammer 109
Figure 67: The World, Aug. 19th, 1901 – Latest Flying Machine Travels on Earth and in Air 111
Figure 68: Bridgeport Post announces Whiteehad to exhibit at Atlantic City 117
Figure 69: "Unrealized Dreams," Bridgeport Evening Farmer, April 5, 1902 122
Figure 70: Cherry Street shop, 1901 "First Airplane Factory," with "No. 22" prototype 124
Figure 71: Gustave Whitehead, fall, 1901 at Cherry Street shop 125
Figure 72: World's first airplane factory workers #1 125
Figure 73: World's first airplane factory workers #2 125
Figure 74: World's first airplane factory workers #3, Anton Pruckner leaning over plane 125
Figure 75: fits description of actor Herman Linde, Whitehead's NY sponsor 126
Figure 76: Cherry Street shop, 1901 "First Airplane Factory," photo #2 127
Figure 77: Cherry Street shop, 1901 "First Airplane Factory," photo #3 128
Figure 78: Bridgeport Herald illustration of first airplane factory 128
Figure 79: Bridgeport Herald front page feature Flying Machine Factory #1 129
Figure 80: Bridgeport Herald front page feature Flying Machine Factory #2 130
Figure 81: Evening World announces new airplane factory 132
Figure 82: Evening Telegram Announces "No. 22" and new factory 133
Figure 83: Sketch by John Whitehead of the likely "No. 22", seen April 1902 141
Figure 84: Bridgeport Farmer, Jan. 7, 1902 announces aerial competition at St. Louis Exposition 148
Figure 85: GW First Applicant, World's Fair Bulletin (Feb. 1902) 149
Figure 86: St. Louis Exposition Aerial Committee letter to Gustave Whitehead 151
Figure 87: GW and "No. 21" in 1901, photo #1 of 3 sent to Fair officials (Jan. 1902) 153
Figure 88: 1901, Sister-photo to Figure 87 154
Figure 89: "No. 21" in 1901, photo #2 of 3 sent to Fair officials (Jan. 1902) 154
Figure 90: "No. 22" in fall, 1901, photo #3 of 3 sent to Fair officials (Jan. 1902) 155
Figure 91: Distinguished Aerialists – World's Fair Bulletin, Feb. 1902 156
Figure 92: Professor Myer's Sky-Cycle 1 158
Figure 93: Prof. Myer's Skycycle 2 159
Figure 94: Aerial Contest course 160
Figure 95: Wilbur Wright's 1902 letter to Chanute shows knew of Whitehead 161
Figure 96: Chanute glider 168
Figure 97: Leo Stevens Letter to the Editor re: World's Fair contest 171
Figure 98: Baldwin's "Arrow" at World's Fair may have had Whitehead Motor 175

Figure 99: No Aerial Contest entries qualified. 176
Figure 100: Bpt Standard Article Whitehead 9.1.1903. 177
Figure 101: Whitehead Triplane 1903 First Tested As Glider 178
Figure 102: Two-Cycle Whitehead Motor, Sci Am (1903). 179
Figure 103: Gliding near ground, Sci Am (1903). 180
Figure 104: Gustave Whitehead shows he can fly ½ mile, Bpt. Daily Standard (Oct. 1, 1904) 180
Figure 105: Avery flies Chanute glider at World's Fair 182
Figure 106: East Entrance of the Transportation Building 183
Figure 107: Aerial View of Transportation Building, World's Fair 1904 183
Figure 108: Map of World's Fair Transportation Building and Aeronautic Concourse 184
Figure 109: Whitehead and his flying machine (1901), from official World's Fair report 1913 185
Figure 110: American Inventor Whitehead flight article 190
Figure 111: Circular route of January 17, 1902 flight. 191
Figure 112: 1902 Milford flight illustration. 193
Figure 113: Milford flight route to Charles Island (1902). 195
Figure 114: West End Flight Paths (1901-1902). 199
Figure 115: Whitehead in Pittsburgh article (1899). 200
Figure 116: Bates Street, Whitehead in Pittsburgh (1899) 201
Figure 117: Whitehead Pittsburgh flight trajectories 202
Figure 118: Whitehead Pittsburgh crash site (1899) 1. 202
Figure 119: Whitehead Pittsburgh crash site (1899) 2. 203
Figure 120: Louis Darvarich, Whitehead's Pittsburgh Assistant 203
Figure 121: Whitehead's Flying Condor (1897) 205
Figure 122: Whitehead's Triplane (1897). 206
Figure 123: Sci Am Whitehead Triplane Glider (1903). 222
Figure 124: Sci Am Whitehead Triplane Glider, rearview (1903). 223
Figure 125: Whitehead Triplane Glider w/operator (1903) 223
Figure 126: 12 H. P., two-Cycle Motor with Wire Flywheel; Weight, 54 Pounds. 224
Figure 127: Bridgeport Herald article Nov.22, 1908, GW to Outdo Wrights 228
Figure 128: Bridgeport Herald photo/sketch of 1908 glider. 229
Figure 129: Scientific American, Whitehead glider at Morris Park, NJ (Nov. 14, 1908) 231
Figure 130: Side view of Whitehead glider in free flight. Front view of Whitehead aeroplane making a glide. Scientific American (Nov. 14, 1908) 232
Figure 131: Transporting 1908 glider to Morris Park. 233
Figure 132: Stanley Yale Beach and Gustave Whitehead (Nov. 1908). 233
Figure 133: Howard Booth and Stanley Beach (fall, 1908) 234
Figure 134: Aeronaut Howard Booth at left, at GW's house (fall, 1909) 234
Figure 135: Aeronaut Booth in Beach's car, on way to Morris Park (Nov. 1908) 234
Figure 136: Howard Booth sketch in the Herald (Nov. 22, 1908) 235
Figure 137: Gustave (left) and brother John (right) at Ridgely Avenue home (1908) 235
Figure 138: Early morning milkman, Tunxis Hill (1908). 236
Figure 139: Large monoplane glider towing test, Lordship, CT (1908). 236
Figure 140: Whitehead runs alongside large monoplane glider towing test, Lordship, CT (1908). 237
Figure 141: Whitehead Beach Problems – Neighbors - Bridgeport Standard (1909) 239
Figure 142: Beach-Whitehead Biplane NYT (1909) 241
Figure 143: Beach-Whitehead Biplane – no wing coverings (circa Mar. 1909) 244
Figure 144: Beach-Whitehead Biplane with coverings (April 1909) 245
Figure 145: Beach-Whitehead Biplane, Aeronautics, April 1909 245
Figure 146: Beach-Whitehead design dipute (June 1909) 247
Figure 147: Stanley Beach's Flier - Monoplane (1910). 250
Figure 148: "Whitehead's Effort 1910" photo 1 by Arthur K. L. Watson 252

Gustave Whitehead: "First in Flight"

Figure 149: "Whitehead's Effort 1910" photo 2 by Arthur K. L. Watson 252
Figure 150: Whitehead's Helicopter (1911) 256
Figure 151: Whitehead's 3rd shop and helicopter at Ridgely Ave. (circa 1910-1911) 257
Figure 152: Whitehead – Burridge in Court, article (1912) 258
Figure 153: Draft registration documents for Gustave Whitehead, 1918 261
Figure 154: Whitehead will never give up practical, commercial flying machine (1903) 264
Figure 155: Lightweight monoplane "No. 21" made flights of up to 1.5 miles (1901) 266
Figure 156: Beach-Whitehead Biplane exponentially larger and heavier (1909) 267
Figure 157: Pruckner identifies (1901) photo 279
Figure 158: Orr's Castle, Whitehead flying site 288
Figure 159: Whitehead glider flight near Orr's Castle, Tunxis Hill, Fairfield, CT (1908) 289
Figure 160: Heavy Beach-Whitehead Biplane control center, by Ridgely house (1909) 290
Figure 161: Orr's Castle top left, viewed from Marlborough Terr. (1908) 290
Figure 162: Whitehead at Brooklawn Country Club (1910) 291
Figure 163: Beach-Whitehead Biplane at Tunxis Hill, Brooklawn Country Club (Jan. 1910) 291
Figure 164: Map of Whitehead's main flying grounds (1901-1911) 292
Figure 165: Whitehead's first shop at 241 Pine Street (June 1901) 293
Figure 166: Whitehead's 2nd shop, "The First Airplane Factory in the World" 293
Figure 167: Whitehead's 2nd shop at northeast corner of Cherry and Hancock, in West End 1 (fall, 1901-1902) 294
Figure 168: Whitehead's 2nd shop at northeast corner of Cherry and Hancock, in West End 2 (fall, 1901-1902) 294
Figure 169: Whitehead's 2nd shop at Ridgely Ave. (1910-1911) 295
Figure 170: Whitehead home and shop locations 1901-1906 296
Figure 171: Whitehead's first self-built home in "Holland Heights," now Tunxis Hill 298
Figure 172: A Whitehead shop at Ridgely Avenue (circa 1908) 298
Figure 173: Whitehead home and a shop (1908) 299
Figure 174: Diagram of two lots owned by Gustave Whitehead 1906/7-1914 299
Figure 175: Whitehead with his 1911 helicopter, on Ridgely Avenue property 300
Figure 176: Whitehead's last home, where he died, on Alvin Street, in 1927 301
Figure 177: Gustave Whitehead headstone, erected 1964 302
Figure 178: Gustave Whitehead's supplementary "footstone," erected 2014 304
Figure 179: Sci American - Wright witnesses only for later flights in 1905 315
Figure 180: World Almanac 1911 documented Orville's 1903 flights failures 316
Figure 181: World Almanac's "Chronology of Aviation" shows Orville's flights failures 316
Figure 182: Stanley Beach wrote Maj. Lester Gardner to check weather records 320
Figure 183: Beach Whitehead Statement draft edited by Gardner, p. 1 321
Figure 184: Beach Whitehead Statement draft edited by Gardner, p. 2 322
Figure 185: Maj. Gardner writes Earl Findley suggesting edits to Beach-Whitehead Statement 323
Figure 186: Asst. Secretary Smithsonian confirms Gardner and Findley planning label on Wright Flyer crediting Orville 325
Figure 187: Letter confirming Lester Gardner's involvement with development of Wright Flyer labels (part a) 326
Figure 188: Letter confirming Gardner participation (part b) 326
Figure 189: Gardner confirms working on label and agreeing to changes 327
Figure 190: Transcript of Paul Garber tells Earl Findley he represents Orville in the label planning 328
Figure 191: Telegram from Findley to Orville about "dynamiting" the July 1945 Reader's Digest pro-Whitehead article 329
Figure 192: Findley writes Orville blaming Dr. Albert Zahm for Whitehead claim (Nov. 1945) 330

This book is fondly dedicated to:

My loving family

My father, Major William J. O'Dwyer and my mother, Doris,
whose relentless 45 years of research brought further to light the flights of Gustave Whitehead
and unknown facts about early aviation;
for bringing to light the *Smithsonian-Wright Agreement of 1948* (aka "the Contract"),
with the help of then-Senator Weicker, in 1976

Gustave Albin Whitehead, his family, friends, and neighbors in the West End of Bridgeport and
Fairfield, CT, who envisioned powered flight and together, made it possible

Paul Jackson, Editor, Jane's All-the-World's-Aircraft, who took the courageous and correct
first step to recognize Gustave Whitehead as "first in powered flight"
Stella Randolph, whose original research in the 1930's began the preservation of
Gustave Whitehead's history for posterity

CT State Representative Larry Miller, of Stratford, CT, sponsor of CT House Bill 6671, signed into law by
Governor Malloy in June 2013, recognizing Gustave Whitehead as *"First in Powered Flight"*
CT State Governors 1963-present, especially Governors Dannel Malloy,
Lowell P. Weicker, Jr., and John N. Dempsey who all took important steps to
preserve Gustave Whitehead's legacy
CT State Senator Kevin Kelly, Sponsor of Senate Bill 772, to establish a
CT "Gustave Whitehead Day," establishing CT as "the birthplace of powered flight"
All members of the CT State Legislature, past and present
Fairfield County, CT Mayors and Selectmen

Stephen Link, of CT, grandson of eyewitness Elizabeth Koteles,
nephew of Whitehead assistants Bert and Andy Paap; and his wife, Regina Link
Jean Savage Collins, granddaughter of eyewitness Mary Savage
Ed Collins, Chairperson of the Gustave Whitehead Research Committee
Charles Lautier, Gustave Whitehead Research Committee
Andy Kosch, Whitehead "No. 21" Replica Pilot and Team Member
Gustave Whitehead Replica Teams in CT and Germany
The 9315th Air Force Reserve Squadron
Gustav Weisskopf Museum, Leutershausen, Germany
City of Leutershausen Mayors and Museum Directors
All FFGW (German Whitehead Research Committee) members
Fairfield Historical Society, Fairfield Museum and History Center
Discovery Museum, Bridgeport, CT
Connecticut Aeronautical Historical Association (CAHA) Founder, Harvey Lippincott and
members, who interviewed Whitehead eyewitnesses
Anton Pruckner and Junius Harworth, Whitehead assistants
Bridgeport and Stratford Public Libraries

© Susan Brinchman, 2015

Gustave Whitehead: "First in Flight"

To Gustave Whitehead, his family,
and all other aviation pioneers and their families,
who sacrificed so much ...
contributing their individual efforts
that humankind could fly for all future generations.

Thank you, one and all

Acknowledgments

"*Gustave Whitehead: First in Flight*" has taken over eighty years of research by many, three decades to plan, and several years to write. The people who participated in assembling information and kept alive the facts about Gustave Whitehead, despite the passing of time, are more than it is possible to recall or list. Many are included in the dedication at the front of the book.

To my father, William J. O'Dwyer, who has passed on, but leaves behind a vast collection of 45 years of Gustave Whitehead research at the Fairfield Museum in Fairfield, CT, and at the Gustav Weisskopf Museum in Leutershausen, Germany which he helped found … for all the guidance in how to find truth and research early aviation topics, obtaining little-known information; for his courage and persistence, I give the highest praise. Special thanks go to my longsuffering husband and family who, for years, have provided encouragement and gave me the time to do this work in addition to being "mom"; to my mother, who spent more than half of a very long lifetime, helping obtain and organize mountains of research, for her unflagging interest and support, and who passed away weeks before this publication could be held in her hands, I miss you, Mom, and hope you can look down upon us, still to enjoy our earthly pursuits. Much appreciation goes to the memory of the first researcher, Stella Randolph, for being persistent and having the pluck to take the bus many times to Bridgeport, CT, from Maryland, to interview witnesses, starting the entire process of preserving the Whitehead history.

In these past several years, there have been some exceptional people who provided invaluable assistance with various aspects of the research and writing process. "I could not have done it without you" is what authors often say – and now I know what that truly means.

Some of these are no longer with us; they also must look from God's company, to hear these thanks, given once again. To Ed and Jean Collins, Charles Lautier, Stephen and Regina Link, and their daughter, Regina, a very special thank you for your time and effort brainstorming, helping send me materials, and most importantly, for providing inspiration. Without your feet on the ground and *constant encouragement*, this book couldn't have happened. Ed, *you are the one who identified the exact location* of the first airplane factory in the world, in a photo of Cherry and Hancock streets that researchers never before understood. You took the time to walk part of the Turney farm location still left close to its condition a century ago, taking photos we could use. Charlie, you read through reels of microfiche for many months, to help locate some of the early, never-before-seen local articles on Gustave Whitehead. In memory and recognition of Ed Collins, Chairperson of the Gustave Whitehead Research Committee, Stephen Link, grandson of Whitehead powered flight witness Elizabeth Koteles, and Representative Larry Miller of Stratford, CT, who are, very sadly, no longer with us, I recall and so appreciate their ideas, inspiration, encouragement, and actions to keep the Gustave Whitehead history alive. They are greatly missed. Thank you, Pastor Josh, for your interest, and praying for me, as I engaged in this massive project! Douglas Westfall of The Paragon Agency, you are a saint, for you helped answer zillions of questions masterfully and selflessly, for several years and for your exceptionally fine cover design. Thank you for sharing your wealth of knowledge and providing so much help.

I am so grateful to the members of the Whitehead family, who have taken time to speak with me about their family's remembrances, giving a personal perspective that helped lend more understanding. I thank Andy Kosch for being such a dedicated educator of the public regarding Whitehead, and for sharing the first Whitehead replica with so many thousands of Connecticut residents, over the past three decades. Melanie Marks, history researcher extraordinaire, I really appreciate your time and valuable guidance in helping locate documents and historical facts. Dr. Elizabeth Rose, exemplary librarian at the Fairfield Museum, responsible for the impeccable organization of the O'Dwyer/Whitehead files therein, who took the time to see to it that I and other volunteer researchers had access when needed - I am most grateful to you. Thanks to the Bridgeport and Stratford library staff, for their helpful assistance. To Linda and Chris, for your vital help and suggestions – a million thanks. To Paul Jackson, whose singular courage "to tell it like it is," recognizing Gustave Whitehead as "first in powered flight" ahead of the Wrights, in the 100th anniversary edition of *Jane's All the World's Aircraft,* in 2013, and to IHS Jane's, for approving it, words are insufficient to express the gratitude of millions who wish to see accuracy in aviation history. Thanks are especially due to John Brown, of Germany, who realized there was an incongruity in aviation history, studied the existing Whitehead research, added more, and presented it to Jane's All-the-World's-Aircraft's editor, Paul Jackson, gaining more recognition and reopening the worldwide conversation about Gustave Whitehead, in 2013. I am very grateful to Joe Bullmer, USAF aeronautical engineer, whose technical study of the Wright brothers' documents and the aerodynamics of their aeroplanes led to his exceptional book *The WRight Story* – Joe, your questions, perspective, and comments about the Wright history and aeroplanes have been a great help. Mike Roer, expert on early baseball fields in Connecticut, so very glad you helped with sharing the history of the old trotting park was in the West End of Bridgeport and for your big heart in taking the time to work so hard to analyze historic factory building locations in a previously misunderstood Whitehead photo. Appreciation to the World's Fair expert and artist, Lee Gaskins, for your kindness and generosity in providing so many resources about the Fair. I thank all the unnamed people, from within and outside of Connecticut, intrigued by Whitehead's story, who helped in so many ways, including the sharing of materials inside numerous archives. Bless you all!

To Gustave Whitehead and his family, whose example shines on – you did accomplish "first flight," shared it, and *that* has helped make all the difference.

Susan Brinchman

Gustave Whitehead: "First in Flight"

An error does not become truth by reason of multiplied propagation,
nor does truth become error because nobody sees it. Truth stands,
even if there be no public support. It is self-sustained. ~Ghandi

Justice delayed is justice denied ...The Wrights were right; but Whitehead was ahead.
~Paul Jackson, Editor, Jane's All the World's Aircraft (2013)

I feel very confident that he [Whitehead] did make short flights from the
various interviews I have done. ~Harvey Lippincott, Founder and
President Emeritus, Connecticut Aeronautical Historical Association (1981)

The authenticity of these early street flights seems unquestionable.
~John B. Crane, PhD, Professor of Economics, Harvard University

[Whitehead] was a very able designer and developer of airplane engines and also airplanes and could well have been classed as a genius in that art...On examining the photographs and data of Whitehead's plane #21, I judge from my long airplane design experience it was capable of stable flight. ~Charles Wittemann

Those who expect moments of change to be comfortable and free of conflict
have not learned their history. ~Joan Wallach Scott

Truth is the only merit that gives dignity and worth to history.
~Lord Acton

On Feb. 18, 1998 an accurate full-scale copy of Whitehead's 1901 airframe,
powered with modern engines, flew a distance of one-half mile at the Luftwaffe Flugplatz
in Manching, Germany. ~Maj. William J. O'Dwyer, USAF, ret.

© Susan Brinchman, 2015

Preface

This book may change your mind about the credit for the world's first powered flights and who really invented the airplane. Within these covers are the secrets of early aviation history that long lay hidden. The author, a immersed in early aviation research for 52 years, explains and updates the historic record concerning Gustave Whitehead, increasingly recognized as "first in flight" and inventor of the airplane.

In 2013, Gustave Whitehead was recognized as "first in powered flight" by the governor and legislature of the State of Connecticut, and the world's renowned aviation authority, a primary reference for aviation history for over 100 years, the publication, "Jane's All-the-World's-Aircraft"[1], touching off an ever-growing firestorm of controversy, with no end in sight. Within these pages are found startling research discoveries that include:

1. All known evidence supporting Gustave Whitehead as "first in powered flight."
2. Why Gustave Whitehead was not credited with "first flight" earlier.
3. New confirmations of Whitehead's summer flights of 1901 by local press, in articles never before seen by researchers, long denied to exist by Smithsonian curators.
4. New details about Whitehead's flying and inventing years, with flights that continued through 1911.
5. New evidence showing why Whitehead's designs changed.
6. New evidence proving the *Smithsonian-Wright Agreement of 1948,* a contract crediting Orville Wright with "first flight," was planned with two of Orville Wright's close friends, longtime Whitehead detractors.
7. New evidence concerning the formal crediting Wilbur Wright as "first in flight" in 1911, arranged by a secret employee of Wilbur Wright and the Wright Company, to assist with their patent suits, skipping over Gustave Whitehead's accomplishments.
8. Comparisons of the "first flights" of Whitehead and the Wrights.
9. Discussion of Whitehead flight photos.

and much more…

2015 marks the 114th anniversary of Gustave Whitehead's first successful powered flights of 1901, which preceded those of the Wrights by over two years. Presenting comprehensive documentation concerning Whitehead's successful flights and experiments, this work reveals compelling new research and striking confirmations of his flights. It also provides a window into the most prolific years of this important early aviation pioneer, the first to succeed in "navigating the air" in a powered flying machine.

People all over the world are fascinated with human flight - its reality has changed the way we live. The incredible history of how flight came to be is still emerging. Much has been said, but more lies beneath the surface, waiting to be told. People want to know what *really* happened, and as the facts unfold, the evidence is presented for your interpretation.

This is a "work in progress," published using "print on demand" methods, with content updated, as new information is uncovered; the version (v.) with dates of publication/updates indicated on the title page of the book. If any errors occur in this book, they are inadvertent. Minor edits may occur on an ongoing basis, as they come to the author's attention. Due to the increasing number of discoveries possible concerning Gustave Whitehead's activities and flights, in part due to digitizing of information, with increased accessibility, it is likely updating of content may occur, from time to time, in a new edition. For instance, in less than the past six months, 16 new local newspaper articles about Gustave Whitehead, from 1901-1914, have been unearthed, in the course of writing this manuscript. The "new" primary source information confirmed that I (your author) was on the right track in relating events understanding how Whitehead thought and how the community perceived him. It was incorporated into the manuscript. Even if these had not confirmed my findings, they would have also been included. I am after "truth" and "historical accuracy," above all. As a longtime educator, I would not present this book without believing in its accuracy, based on all available documentation.

I will be up front about my perspective on whether Whitehead flew or not – after 52 years of close-range exposure to the research, witnesses, and participating in research myself, examining thousands of sources, *I am convinced that Gustave Whitehead did make successful powered flights multiple times, before the Wrights, and that he invented the airplane.* This book presents the available evidence for these assertions. It is up to the Readers to analyze and draw their own conclusions, which, no doubt, most will. My audience is posterity, especially. It is my intention to document the known evidence for current and future generations. We must keep in mind that whatever occurred from 1900-1903, whatever happened, happened independently of our opinions one way or the other. If Whitehead flew during those years, as witnesses and newspaper accounts said he did, then he did, and regardless of what we think, over 100 years later, those facts stand, independent of all "expert" statements. We are merely charged with uncovering those historic truths, to the best of our ability, without rejecting new information and without demanding that current or past interpretations of history remain "set in stone," forever. This is our mutual challenge, whatever our thoughts are now, on the topic of "first powered flight."

Without a doubt, there is more to find, with near daily revelations as one researches Whitehead - this book is written to establish the current state of "the Research" and the facts, as they are known today, concerning Gustave Whitehead's powered flights. Comparisons with the long acclaimed flight experiments of the Wrights and explanations of why Whitehead did not receive credit for being first in powered flight before now are provided, as these are an integral part of the story.

To study Whitehead's history, we must understand the man and his environment. - the realities and context of the period. We shall inspect what Whitehead and his contemporaries thought, said, and did. Examining the earliest flights of the 20th century has not always been possible to accomplish. Much misinformation contrived about Gustave Whitehead over the past century, particularly in the past 75 years, has muddied the waters, and still exists today. This book will offer authenticated proof, for all to examine.

Readers are about to embark on a journey into the past, one which may change viewpoints about early aviation history. Together, we'll view little-known events and documentation which occurred at the dawn of powered flight, hidden both in the hazes of time and in long-untouched archives. We will also listen to the long-stilled voices of Gustave Whitehead and the people who knew him, letting them be our guides. We'll hear their thoughts as they speak to us, emerging from over a century ago, telling us their story though what has been left behind "on the record," but out of sight, where no previous access has been readily available.

For over half a century, I have come to "personally know" Mr. Whitehead and his successful flights through the words of those who knew him, surviving photographs and documents of his work, and his own writings. In 1963, my father, Major William J. O'Dwyer, discovered photographs of a Whitehead aeroplane taken on the grounds of the Brooklawn Country Club Fairway, on the border of Fairfield and Bridgeport, Connecticut, in January 1910. Our mutual quest began then, to learn more about this humble but brilliant man who lived and flew in familiar places, whose history nearly passed us by. Eventually, my father was placed in charge of international research on Whitehead, becoming a world authority on his history. His research efforts would last

Preface

45 years, resulting in 18 linear feet of Gustave Whitehead files now residing at the Fairfield Museum, in Fairfield, CT, and the co-founding of the Gustav Weisskopf Museum in Leutershausen, Germany. Throughout that time, I was fortunate to be involved, functioning as a research assistant for the last thirty of those years. I have continued to move the investigation forward, since his death, in 2008. My training and experience in the classroom as a longtime educator has been helpful in this effort – I hope to stimulate discussion and more study of this crucial time in both American and world history.

Privileged to have been present for interviews conducted with Whitehead's contemporaries and eyewitnesses to flights, one is especially recalled, that of Anton Pruckner in the 1960's, as he earnestly described his experiences with Whitehead. I recall the instructions at the start of the interviews, those who had come forward as witnesses were told to be entirely truthful, "no matter what," as the records of their responses were being gathered to provide an accurate history for posterity. I see, in my mind's eye, their hands being placed on a bible to swear upon, to emphasize that they should tell only the truth. I remember aged people at windows pointing out how high a flight was, how far it went, telling what they saw and heard, and the later analyses of all that was learned.

Our home overflowed with Whitehead files and information; photos spread upon the dining room table and hutch. People lined up on the couches, coming to share their experiences, or to learn and carry the information to others. I was honored to meet the lovely Stella Randolph many times, the first Whitehead author and researcher, who'd conducted investigations for three years in the 1930's. I was present for a 1964 ceremony providing Whitehead, formerly buried in a pauper's grave, with a fitting headstone and grand tribute arranged. It was attended by what appeared to be well over a hundred, including officials, members of each branch of the armed forces, aviation pioneers who admired Whitehead, like Charles Wittemann and Clarence Chamberlain, and Whitehead's daughters and a grandson. Members of the Connecticut Aeronautical Historical Association (CAHA) and the Whitehead Committee, the 9315th Air Force Squadron (Ret.) which took this on as a project, people from Gustave's native town of Leutershausen, West Germany, and those who wished to learn more about Whitehead populated our lives for what seems like most of an intriguing lifetime.

Proof of the flights was abundant, even in the 1960's. Resistance to the information by the Smithsonian was strong and hard to fathom - that is, until "the Contract" with Orville Wright's heirs was unearthed by Maj. O'Dwyer, in 1976, with the assistance of Senator Lowell Weicker, Jr. (later, Governor), of CT, published in *History by Contract* (O'Dwyer and Randolph, 1978). The *Smithsonian-Wright Agreement of 1948*, between the Wright executors and the United States of America, stipulated that the Smithsonian would purchase the original Wright Flyer for $1 and other considerations, but that neither the venerable Smithsonian Institution *or its near-200 affiliated museums and research facilities* could recognize any other airplane or person as "first in flight," or the Wright Flyer would revert to the heirs. This "Contract" as it came to be called, finally explained the extreme reactions we had seen to documentation of Whitehead's successful flights by Smithsonian officials and their agents. This agreement is still in place, legally, today. Not until 2014, during the research conducted for this book, however, did it become known that *those who crafted the required labels for the Wright Flyer crediting Orville were the same friends of Orville Wright who had worked together for nine years to disparage Whitehead as "first in flight."* We have, unfortunately, received an incomplete and some think, misleading history of first flight and early aviation.

It is time to enter into the current record an *updated* presentation, with new historically significant evidence for Gustave Whitehead's first powered flights, and let the readers determine what they think. It is the hope of a growing number of citizens, that as soon as possible, the *Smithsonian-Wright Agreement of 1948* (recognizing only the Wrights as first in flight) or "Contract," as it is often referred to, will be withdrawn or nullified and early aviation history will become unencumbered, open to evaluation, and officially corrected at the United States' Smithsonian, the top history institution whose mission is "the increase and diffusion of knowledge."

© Susan Brinchman, 2015

Gustave Whitehead: "First in Flight"

The evidence for Whitehead's accomplishments includes authenticated newspaper articles; statements and affidavits by Whitehead, witnesses, and those who knew him; information from trade journals and reliable sources such as *Scientific American*; some, previously unseen.

I commend Governor Dannel Patrick Malloy, Connecticut's former State Representative Larry Miller (now deceased), and all the legislators of the State of Connecticut, as well as Jane's All-the-World's-Aircraft's editor, Paul Jackson (and IHS, Jane's publisher) for taking the first formal steps toward recognition of Whitehead's accomplishment as inventor of the first successful airplane.

At the time of this writing, it is apparent to a growing number of people that Whitehead *was first in powered flight and the inventor of the airplane.* The Wrights, afterward, *"improved upon the art of flying,"* to a significant degree, without a doubt. There is a specific place in aviation history for these great men, and all others who made significant contributions to provide all the elements of flight we enjoy today. They are best honored with the truth, all petty rivalries and biases put aside. History is not meant to be "contracted" to obtain an exhibit, history just happens and we should tell it.

Due to the highly controversial nature of the topic of who was "first in flight," this book has been intentionally structured to provide the Reader with as much primary source evidence as possible, with citations. It includes the full or partial text of key newspaper reports; portions of transcripts from significant interviews; and all documentation from the period that might shed light on the subject, with some gaps filled in and others waiting to be discovered. Readers will be asked to adjust to an era when language was used in a different manner; we are stepping back into an entirely different time period, to better interpret and, it is hoped, understand. In the interest of bringing forth this needed information on Gustave Whitehead, to aide in decision-making at governmental levels and for the sake of all those needing more accurate information for a variety of reasons, this book is being presented as early as possible. As a result, it is not in perfect form, the author considers it, as aforementioned, a work in progress, and asks the readers for their understanding and suggestions for future editions. An excellent glossary from the period may be found at "Navigation of the Air" by Victor Lougheed, an online book originally published in 1909, starting on page 465, archived at https://archive.org/details/vehiclesair01louggoog.

The structure of this book is intended to cover a complex topic, with key flights and experimental flight periods in Whitehead's life, while addressing the question of first flight credit. This book is intended to correct misconceptions and misinformation for the historical record, to help us understand Gustave Whitehead, his prolific inventing period, and what was happening that influenced him. Finally, it documents precisely the main questions many have had about Gustave Whitehead: "Why haven't I heard of him? Who is Gustave Whitehead? When did he fly, and did he stop? How could he have flown so early and well, and not so well, later? How do we know he made these flights? Was it just one or did he fly more than once? What was in his mind as he was working on his inventions? What about the Wrights? Didn't they fly first? Why wasn't Gustave Whitehead credited for that a long time ago?" There is a lot within these covers, but the topic is of such importance that any less than the most important evidence could not be left out. This is a condensation of 20 linear feet of research by William J. O'Dwyer and additionally, approximately the same amount by your author. This is not all that exists, but condensing the most important portions of that volume of materials has occurred in these pages, and additional light may be shed on the topic in the future.

The book's arrangement is somewhat unusual due to the need for extensive documentation and visuals for multiple topics. Some of the pictures are used more than once, relating to more than one subject. Some are similar, taken just a minute or so after the other, and hold historic value in certain respects. Some are of historic importance, having been sent to Germany for publication during 1901, or the World's Fair Aerial Committee in 1902. Rather than have readers hunting through the book for the one photo that covers several topics, these are placed within the sections they pertain to, and may appear again in another context. Evidence ties in together, like a tapestry, with threads running through that show up repeatedly. The story is told in chronological order

Preface

for the most part, within sections, though at times it has been necessary to present the most important events and work back in time from that point, to view what had just occurred. The complexity of the story of first flight credit which is part of Whitehead's story is also addressed, especially because it impacts our perceptions of who flew first, why the Wrights received credit, and how that could change, based on the information at hand. The main audiences I am attempting to reach are those with a strong interest in history, aviation history, and also, for the benefit of "posterity." In 500 or 1,000 years, there may not be access to the information available today, spanning the past century, concerning Gustave Whitehead and his achievements, but they may have this book. So I write to document everything pertinent to first flight and Gustave Whitehead, for both history lovers and those in the future. May I do justice in telling the full story of Gustave Whitehead, inventor, with abundant proof of his accomplishments, and show how the crediting for first flight has gone down a path that needs "righting." A less complex version of the proofs for his flights may be available in the future, but this particular book attempts to be more comprehensive. Reading "portions of interest", over time, may work well for today's busy readers.

Multiple dedicated volunteers, researchers, librarians, and those who documented Gustave Whitehead's life and accomplishments, over the past century, have made the contents of this book possible. To these many individuals, for their tireless and often, tedious work, this author expresses deepest appreciation. New information about Whitehead's life and inventions has poured in. due to the hard work of recent dedicated volunteers in Connecticut, and in part, to the increased accessibility of early reports via the digitizing of historical records.

Here is the true story of Gustave Whitehead, inventor of the first successful airplane, who made the world's first powered flights. I am pleased to offer this volume as a lifelong educator who loves history. *We simply want to know what happened.* It is our story; it belongs to all of us. No one can or should keep it hidden. An accurate history helps us know who we are and how we came to this point. That is, after all, *what history is about.* This is "*his story*," which is, quite literally, what "history" means.

May Gustave Whitehead, his family, his assistants, and all those who lived near them on Pine Street, Ridgely Avenue, and Alvin Street, believing in him and supporting these flights, rest in peace, knowing their efforts were not in vain. Thank you, one and all.

Susan O'Dwyer Brinchman, M. Ed
May 1, 2015
gwfirstinflight@gmail.com
www.gustavewhitehead.info

If anyone reading this has diaries from the era, local newspaper articles, documents, photographs, artifacts or information concerning Gustave Whitehead and his flights that they wish to add to this research effort, please contact the Fairfield Museum in Fairfield, CT and, if you wish, the author.

Figure 3: June 1901, "No 21" ready for summer flights

"The Condor," Whitehead's "No. 21" bird-like, twin engine, heavier-than-air machine made the world's first successful flights, first pictured in the *NY Sun* on June 9, 1901.

Photo courtesy of Fairfield Museum, O'Dwyer archives

Chapter 1

INTRO

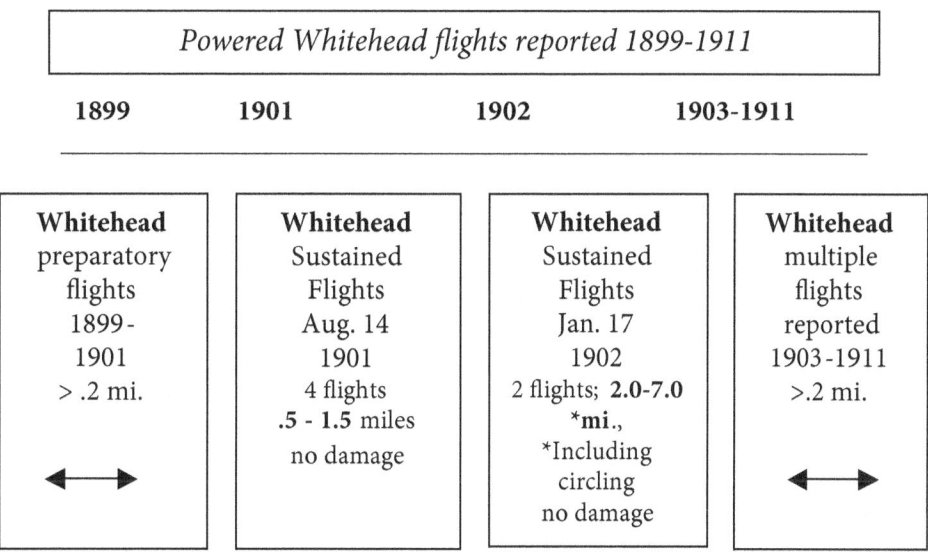

FIRST POWERED FLIGHT

Airborne over a long field "back of" Fairfield, Connecticut, the first sustained[2], powered, manned airplane in human history rose just before dawn on August 14, 1901.[3] This successful flight was independently documented by a trusted journalist invited to be an eyewitness.

The first in a series of several lengthy manned powered flights on that day, the "heavier-than-air"[4] aircraft was said to have flown a distance of half a mile, to an altitude of 50 feet, landing gently without mishap. Another half mile flight and a one and a half mile flight occurred in a second sortie, later that day, reported by multiple sources.[5 6 7 8] Gustave Whitehead, the airplane's 27 year old inventor, was at the helm, with a combination of emotions ranging from elation to an element of fear.[9] The plane, then referred to as a "heavier-than-air flying machine" resembled a large bird, in the Lilienthal fashion. It was the first seaplane, the first successful airplane to use wheels, and the first roadable aircraft that could be driven as a car - Whitehead's "No. 21" flying machine, nicknamed "the Condor" and "the Bird." Gustave Whitehead had designed, constructed, and flown the world's earliest airplane. These first flights took place two and a half years before the Wright brothers' famed experiments at Kitty Hawk. The flights made in August 1901, were not the only ones made that summer by Gustave Whitehead, but these were the first sustained flights from essentially level ground, with eyewitness documentation. Multiple successful manned, powered flights by Whitehead, throughout the summer of 1901 and up through 1903, extending into 1904, demonstrated significant control over his aircraft for the period, which will be shown to surpass the measure of control later claimed by the Wrights on December 17, 1903.

Gustave Whitehead, a German immigrant who settled in Bridgeport, Connecticut in 1900, received widespread, international credit and recognition for his numerous successful first flights in the early years of the new century, later becoming overshadowed by the feats of others, such as Glenn Curtiss and the Wright brothers. A Virginia newspaper commented three weeks later, on September 13, 1901, "To America May after all, go the honor of solving of the perplexing problem of aerial navigation … Gustave Whitehead, of Bridgeport, Conn., has invented an airship that will sail in the air… The whole country is greatly stirred by America's latest opportunity."[10] In the past 81 years, research about Whitehead's first powered flights has increasingly emerged; a growing number of authorities now consider Gustave Whitehead to be the inventor of the world's first successful airplane.

THE PREPARATIONS

Prior to making this lengthy, manned flight in his "No. 21" "heavier-than-air" flying machine, Whitehead conducted a number of preliminary, unmanned hops and tethered flights starting in May 1901,[11] following a period of systematic experimentation that began at least six years prior, when he lived and worked for periods of time in Massachusetts, New York, Maryland, and Pennsylvania. Whitehead would typically experiment first with models, then gliders, eventually adding power, and testing his flying machines with gradual further steps to ensure safety. Eighteen key witnesses later testified, the majority under oath, that they'd seen Whitehead make manned, powered flights from 1899 (when a flight was made that ended in a crash) through 1903. Constructed at his home, in the cellar, and at the backyard workshop at 241 Pine Street, in Bridgeport, Connecticut, the new flying machine, "No. 21," was an amazingly advanced invention for its time.

Interviewed and photographed for the previous several months by writers for multiple news and scientific print media, articles about Whitehead's latest invention, his "No. 21" flying machine, began emerging in June 1901. Gustave Whitehead began testing his aeroplane in May unmanned, graduating to manned powered flights throughout the summer of 1901, in a variety of locations. The flights, witnessed by large numbers of people at times, included "short hops" the length of a city block, and ending with longer, sustained flights said to be up to a mile and a half in length, starting and ending on level ground.

A lengthy account in the *New York Sun*, published June 9, 1901, examined the preparations for this particular flying machine, which began seven months earlier in Connecticut, in November of 1900. "No. 21" was underway not long after Whitehead relocated from Pittsburgh, Pennsylvania to the West End of Bridgeport, a city with 70,000 inhabitants[12]. *The Sun* interviewed Whitehead near the end of May 1901. He explained that the work was completed several weeks prior, whereupon it was tested in a hilly region near Fairfield, starting the machine "on the crest of a hill, right in middle of the road … When the machine begins to rise the upper engine is started and the lower engine automatically stops. It worked perfectly." The two unmanned trials were estimated at 1/8 of a mile and 1/2 mile. At the time of the interview, in late May the flying machine was "undergoing repairs made necessary by an accident which happened at the machine's [unmanned] trial flight on May 3 last. These repairs are nearly completed and at an early date the flying machine will again be tested. When and where the test will be made, Mr. Whitehead will not tell, because he does not want to be bothered with a crowd … the wings measure 36 feet … are made of muslin … the muslin, however, in the perfected machine will be replaced with silk, which was not used in the present case on account of expense."[13] *The Sun* revealed the accident occurred during

Chapter 1: Intro

the second of two unmanned tests with "220 pounds of ballast" onboard, the flying machine traveled up to an estimated 1/2 mile, then without a person to guide it, crashed "slanting downward and dashed bow on against a tree," ending the experiments till the machine could be repaired.[14] To make tests at this stage, Whitehead would typically set a timer to control the duration of the straight-line, unmanned flights. His flying machine design was inherently stable, easily settling down as does a bird, landing upright unless running into an obstruction.

A photo shoot of the new plane and its inventor had been held in the spring of 1901, in the West End of Bridgeport, in an open field along Cherry Street, made by Stanley Yale Beach, Aviation Editor of the *Scientific American*, a resident of nearby Stratford.[15] A number of these photographs were included in a lengthy article in the *Scientific American* in June describing Whitehead's preparations as of that date. They remain the best record of Whitehead and his soon-to-be successful "No. 21" flying machine, photographed several months before the plane made any manned tests. The condition of the ground, the clothing of those photographed, and the lack of leaves or buds on the trees indicate the photos were taken in March or early April 1901. The aeroplane's accident in early May precluded a May date for the shoot.

The *Scientific American* of June 8, 1901 contained the first of many articles about Gustave Whitehead's inventions, entitled "A New Flying Machine." It informed readers that Whitehead's "novel," bird-like flying machine was being tested a few miles away close to Fairfield, Conn., though not yet in "free flight," but nearly ready for some "preliminary trials." It described the flying machine, compared to "a bird or a bat," as 16 feet long, made with wooden ribs braced with steel wires and canvas stretched over the frame [of the fuselage], resting upon four one-foot diameter wheels, Its front wheels were connected to a 10 horse power engine to "get up speed on the ground," while the rear wheels were "mounted like casters," able to be "steered by the aeronaut." Large curved wings, called "aeroplanes"[16], were said to be on "either side of the body," "covered with silk," and concave, "resembling a bird in flight," which could be folded back against the body when not in use. Its ribs were made of bamboo, "braced with steel wires." The machine had a ten foot rudder corresponding "to the tail of a bird," also collapsible, which could be raised or lowered, to be steered for horizontal control. A "mast and bowsprit" ... "held all .... the parts in their proper relation."

Fixed "across the body" and "front of the wings" was a "double compound engine of 20 horsepower," which drove two propellers in *opposite* directions; *first* "running the machine on the ground by means of the [10 horsepower] lower engine" using the wheels - *then*, [at takeoff], when enough momentum was obtained, switched to an upper engine that "actuates the propellers so as to cause the machine to progress through the air to make it rise on its aeroplanes"[17] [wings].

The article described the wings of "No. 21" as "immovable," with steering to be done "by running one propeller faster than another," comparing this to how an "ocean steamer with twin screws" is maneuvered. Notably, Whitehead's plane was described as having "a special aeroplane being provided to maintain longitudinal[18] and transverse[19] stability," a concept still essential, at this writing, to control of an aircraft.

Details were provided for the motors and propellers ... "the lower engine is of 10 horsepower" ... the upper engine is a calcium-carbide based, double compound cylinder; and the propellers, which were six feet in diameter and turned in opposite directions[20]. The dimensions and weight of each component were detailed, showing the degree to which Gustave Whitehead had systematically and scientifically calculated the requirements for successful flight.[21]

With certainty, it may be said that Whitehead's "No. 21" flying machine, as described in June 1901, poised to be the first successful powered airplane, incorporated many attributes still in use in modern aircraft, over a century later – an inherently stable design with wings utilizing horizontal, curved surfaces; the use of a launching method employing wheels, the buildup of speed for takeoff through use of a ground engine; a seated pilot [22] [23](rather than one that reclined, as with the Wrights' flyers) in a cockpit with controls; two powerful (puller-style, located in front) tractor propellers which turned in opposite directions, pulling the airplane forward; use of a rudder for horizontal control, and a primitive means to control pitch and roll.

© Susan Brinchman, 2015

Gustave Whitehead: "First in Flight"

Gustave Whitehead's detailed descriptions were sent out to be read by the general public and all other prospective flying machine inventors, nationwide - and ultimately, worldwide - in the pages of the *Scientific American* and other popular print media of his era, while others were still experimenting with all manner of crude kites and gliders, oftentimes keeping their methods secret from the world. High interest in Whitehead's revolutionary concepts would help stimulate later aviation efforts, heavily influencing the infant industry, for all time, evidenced by Whitehead's pioneering features, still in use. Gustave *intended* for his discoveries to help develop flight for mankind. In that unselfish, most admirable respect, Gustave Whitehead's earnest wish was to advance human flight for the good of mankind. Soon after the publication of these articles, his pioneering efforts would result in that very important wish being granted – Gustave would repeatedly fly his successful invention, the world's first airplane.

357

A NEW FLYING MACHINE.

A novel flying machine has just been completed by Mr. Gustave Whitehead, of Bridgeport, Conn., and is now ready for the preliminary trials. Several experiments have been made, but as yet no free flights have been attempted. The machine is built after the model of a bird or bat. The body is 16 feet long and measures 2½ feet at its greatest width and is 3 feet deep. It is well stayed with wooden ribs and braced with steel wires and covered with canvas which is tightly stretched over the frame. Four wheels, each one foot in diameter, support it while it stands on the ground. The front wheels are connected to a 10 horse power engine to get up speed on the ground, and the rear wheels are mounted like casters so that they can be steered by the aeronaut. On either side of the body are large

aeroplanes, covered with silk and concave on the underside, which give the machine the appearance of a bird in flight. The ribs are bamboo poles, and are braced with steel wires. The wings are so arranged that they can be folded up. The 10-foot rudder, which corresponds to the tail of a bird, can also be folded up and can be moved up and down, so as to steer the machine on its horizontal course. A mast and bowsprit serve to hold all the parts in their proper relation.

In front of the wings and across the body is a double compound engine of 20 horse power, which drives a pair of propellers in opposite directions, the idea being to run the machine on the ground by means of the lower engine until it has the necessary speed to rise from the ground. Then the upper engine actuates the propellers so as to cause the machine to progress through the air to make it rise on its aeroplanes.

Chapter 1: Intro

The wings are immovable and resemble the outstretched wings of a soaring bird. The steering will be done by running one propeller faster than the other in a way analogous to the way in which an ocean steamer having twin screws can be turned, a special aeroplane being provided to maintain longitudinal and transverse stability.

The lower engine is of 10 horse power, and weighs 22 pounds. The diameter of the cylinder is 3 7-16 inches by 8 inches stroke. The upper engine is a double compound cylinder, the diameters being 2¼ and 3 7-16 inches with a 7-inch stroke. The engine weighs 35 pounds, and calcium carbide is used to develop pressure by means of explosions. The propellers weigh 12 pounds, and are 6 feet in diameter, with a projected blade surface of 4 square feet. With a drawbar test, the upper engine being run at full speed, the dead pull was 365 pounds. The weight of the body and wheels is 45 pounds. The wings and tail have 450 square feet of supporting surface, and the weight is 35 pounds.

"A New Flying Machine," *Scientific American*, June 8, 1901

Figure 4: Whitehead stands next to "the Condor," with engine, spring, 1901

Photo by Stanley Yale Beach, used with permission of Fairfield Museum

WHITEHEAD'S FLYING MACHINE, SHOWING ENGINE AND PROPELLERS.

WHITEHEAD'S FLYING MACHINE, SHOWING AEROPLANES.

Figure 5: Front and Rear views of "No. 21," the "Condor"

Upper photo: Gustave Whitehead and young daughter Rose
Lower photo: Whitehead at right of group, with Rose in his lap. Photos from *Scientific American.*

Left to right: Edward M. House, a renowned "American diplomat, politician, and presidential advisor"[24], and Whitehead's neighbors, investors, and assistants. Photos by Stanley Yale Beach Aviation Editor, Scientific American.[25]

The *New York Herald* also weighed in, visiting Whitehead at his shop during this crucial period, evidenced by photos of his shop and plane. The resulting, illustrated article in the *New York Herald* of June 16, 1901 further described Gustave Whitehead and his invention, soon to become the world's first aeronaut[26] to successfully pilot what the world would come to know as an "airplane." Whitehead referred to prior unmanned tests[27] of the aircraft in the interview.

Figure 6: "No 21" at 241 Pine Street, by workshop

"No. 21" in the backyard of Whitehead's home, next to his workshop
241 Pine Street, Bridgeport, CT. He built much of this plane in his cellar.
photo by NY Herald, June 16, 1901

Figure 7: Whitehead's airplane "No. 21," wings folded.
Illustration by NY Herald, June 16, 1901

(transcript, as published)

"Connecticut Night Watchman thinks He Has found out how to Fly"

Gustave Whitehead is a humble night watchman at Bridgeport, Conn. During the day, however, he is a scientist. He is devoted to problems of air navigation and is a compeer [Author's note: of equal

Gustave Whitehead: "First in Flight"

status or rank] of Maxim, Langley, Von Zeppelin and others equally well known in aeronautics. He has built fifty-six flying machines. The present perfected invention is his fifty-seventh and in it, he embodies his principles of bird flight as applicable to man. Mr. Whitehead is a Bavarian and a worldwide traveler. He has studied and photographed the flight of the albatross in the South Seas, the vulture in India and the eagle in the northern regions. He claims that what nature has done for ornithology, machinery can do for man. His ship has sailed the air for a distance of half a mile clear. He claims that airships on his plan will yet circumnavigate the atmosphere of the globe with a single load of fuel.

Whitehead's air ship is built of wood, canvass and steel. The body is sixteen feet long and is mounted on wheels propelled by a small engine in order to get up speed enough to cause the ship to mount on the aeroplanes, or wings. The latter are of silk, ribbed with bamboo. They are shaped like bat's wings and are stationary. Between these aeroplanes is an engine, which works a pair of propellers at the will of the operator, giving the ship its speed. This separate engine is twenty horse power and is run by force developed from calcium carbide, whose gas is exploded by electricity in cylinders. This is also Mr. Whitehead's invention. Aeronauts in America and Europe are watching the developments of the daring watchman-scientist's invention with increasing interest..."

[Whitehead was interviewed, stating:] ... "There are two engines in my airship. One is on the floor of the body proper for running the ship along the tracks til it acquires the necessary speed rise up the fixed aeroplanes, which are spread like wings on either side. The upper engines are placed between the aeroplanes giving swift rotary motion to the propeller blades which are six feet in diameter with a blade surface of four square feet. These are sufficient to keep the entire body in motion while suspended upon the aeroplanes, the weight of the body of the ship being about fifty pounds, the total weight of aeroplanes, engines, propellers, fuel etc. being about one hundred and fifty pounds.

The body proper is sixteen feet long, ribbed with light wood and steel, and covered with canvas tightly stretched over the framework. The wings are of silk, thirty-eight feet from tip to tip, with a ten foot rudder tail, all braced with bamboo and light steel, and capable of being folded up like the wings of a gigantic beast when at rest. A thin mast and bowsprit give additional firmness to the stationary aeroplanes and the tail, which can be moved up or down with a view to guiding the machine while on a horizontal course. The lateral steering is done by running one propeller faster than the other, while the body is suspended upon its 130 square feet of silk." [28]

According to Junius Harworth, a young associate of Whitehead's who helped Whitehead with his work on the planes, midsummer trials *were* conducted, with short hopping flights in the West End of Bridgeport, along the Bridgeport Gas Co. property, from Howard Ave., easterly to Wordin Ave. Then, at the eastern end of Pine Street, the plane was turned around, with additional hopping street flights occurring, returning to Howard Ave. Since there were houses and people around, and it was considered a risk, the plane was then transported (by pushing it) to Hancock Ave., where a flight was made at 5 feet in elevation. Multiple witnesses described preliminary powered, manned flights of Whitehead's aeroplane on level ground, during the summer of 1901, including one local newspaper, the *Bridgeport Evening Post*, which reported successful experiments in the first half of August.

"Mr. Whitehead ... finally commenced work on his present machine which he tested a few weeks ago in the old trotting park *[Author's note: then owned by P.T. Barnum]* in the West End of the city and which worked successfully." [29]

These events occurred prior to the longer *[more sustained]*, half-mile, manned, powered flights of Aug. 14, 1901 on essentially level ground.[30] The "short hop" street flights and experiments at various nearby locations,

Chapter 1: Intro

including P.T. Barnum's winter circus grounds at Bridgeport, in the summer of 1901, surpassed the December 1903 flights of the Wright brothers at Kitty Hawk in distance and were comparable in elevation. On multiple occasions, Whitehead claimed his manned flights had begun in June 1901, including a 1.5 mile flight early in the month[31], which could have been a manned, "combination power and soaring trial," from a steep hill, though no details or confirmations have survived. Witness statements gathered for most of the summer flights are presented in Chapter 6.

Based on all available evidence, the city of Bridgeport, and the nearby towns of Fairfield, and Stratford, Connecticut may lay joint, legitimate claims to the first powered airplane flights in the world, which occurred in rapid succession during the summer of 1901. Later successful flight experiments, which also preceded those of the Wrights, were made in those cities and in addition, Milford and Easton, Connecticut.

Chapter 2

FIRST FLIGHTS ON AUGUST 14, 1901

THE EVIDENCE

When he felt ready to conduct a sustained, manned test flight "for the record," Gustave Whitehead invited the popular, trusted, local sports editor Richard "Dick" Howell, of the *Bridgeport Sunday Herald* to be present; undoubtedly so the widely read weekly newspaper would publish the results in its sole weekly edition, documenting the event. Howell's article, "Flying," was published four days later, on Sunday, August 18th, 1901. *In hindsight, Howell's article became an exclusive eyewitness newspaper report of the first successful manned flight of an airplane.* At the time, the article was not seen as such, though the flight did capture public attention, worldwide. The story ran nationally, through Associated Press releases and as word spread, in close to one hundred additional newspapers, including the *New York Herald*[32] and the *Boston Transcript*; even making international news.[33] The *Bridgeport Sunday Herald*'s article and those derived from it were received well by the media and the public as an account of Whitehead's success and an example of ongoing experimentation with flying machines. The progress Whitehead was making encouraged the public to believe that effortlessly "navigating the air" and practical flight might be accomplished; thus, the broad international interest in the *Bridgeport Sunday Herald*'s coverage. It was an indication that what the public hungered for - the availability of public air transportation - was becoming increasingly closer to reality. At the time, no one was concerned with credit for "firsts," all of the focus was on the future practical development of flying machines for transportation and commercial use. In 1901, many of the general public doubted that man could *ever* fly, while others were in the process of just beginning to accept that this was to be possible. Some even thought human flight to be sacrilegious - to even attempt to go up into the heavens was seen as an affront to God, that those who tried to do so were invading "His realm."

On November 17, 1901, the *Bridgeport Sunday Herald* followed up this *undisputed* first story with a second, front page, feature article, announcing that Whitehead, "*the flying machine inventor*," had opened up a flying machine factory, and *re-confirming the successful powered flights made several months before*. "Flying Machine Factory, Latest of Bridgeport's Industries - *Gustave Whitehead, Inventor of Only Practical Air Ship*, Engaged in Building Soaring Carriages Which Will Be Placed on the Market in Spring" … "The shop is well stocked with steel and iron which is being used in the construction of a flying machine modelled after the one in which *Mr. Whitehead made two successful flights recently as described by the Herald* at the time. It was with this machine that Mr. Whitehead demonstrated the practicability of his invention during the season [summer] in Fairfield"… *Since that time two more flights have been made* for the benefit of the New York capitalist, whose identity is kept a secret."[34] Another, larger, feature appeared in its January 26, 1902 edition, portraying Whitehead as a man "working to perfect [an] airship that will not only fly but be of some use from a commercial point of view"[35], to be described more fully, herein. The *Bridgeport Sunday Herald* made an effort to consistently document Whitehead's distinctive progress in "the sport of" aviation, beginning in 1901, which also held significance for the region, in terms of jobs.

Andrew Cellie and James Dickie, described as Whitehead's partners, were reported as the other witnesses present for the first flight, both involved with the experiments. Of the three named witnesses, only the reporter, repeatedly confirmed by *the Herald* as Richard "Dick" Howell[36], popular local sports and feature writer, provided a detailed eyewitness account of that flight[37], reproduced below. Since that had been done, who would question it then, after all? As the tests and first flight occurred just before dawn, with the limitations of early photography, it is certain that a clear photo could not have been made. Since use of hand-drawn illustrations was the custom of this newspaper[38] - and most others at that time - a drawing of the plane in flight was included with the article. This illustration is thought to have been rendered by Mr. Howell, known to be an artist who illustrated his own articles at least through 1903 when another artist was hired. Richard Howell was named seven times as the eyewitness journalist by the *Herald Magazine* in 1937. Some researchers later theorized that the image might have been based on a photo, as it was reported through 1906 that at least one did exist of the "No. 21" plane in flight. An original photo of "No. 21" in flight has never been found, nor have any claimed photos been authenticated. There were additional flights made during daylight hours. According to witnesses, three more were said to have occurred later that day. At least several more were described in the following months by additional sources, in addition to the preliminary flights in the previous months leading up to that date. A photo may have been made during any of those daytime flights, if the rare person with a camera able to take photos was at hand, if Gustave Whitehead was concerned about documenting in that manner. Most definitely, it would be an indistinct photo of Whitehead's 1901 plane, due to the constraints of that era on photographing swiftly moving objects. A blurred photo of the *Whitehead 1901 "No. 21" in powered flight* is exactly what was reported to have been on display in January 1906, at the first exhibit of the Aero Club of America, witnessed by *Scientific American*'s Aviation Editor, Stanley Yale Beach (to be described in detail later in this book). If photos of Whitehead's early flights still survive, there are some indications these may be tucked away at the Smithsonian Institution, recipient of many of the photographs of that 1906 Aero Club of America exhibition and early flight. With the Smithsonian under longtime legal contract, signed with Orville's executors not to recognize any other contenders for the title of "first in flight"[39], or lose the Wright Flyer, full disclosure of its holdings may not been forthcoming. There is, also, always the chance that there is yet a legitimate photo of Whitehead's plane in flight, lying forgotten or unidentified, in an attic or basement, as these were known to exist, documented during those early years in multiple print media.

In March 2013, based on the preponderance of the evidence originally gathered over the prior seventy nine years, primarily consisting of Dick Howell's confirmed, exclusive, eyewitness newspaper report; additional journalists' accounts; and extensive numbers of witness statements, Whitehead was announced "first in powered flight" ahead of the Wrights, by *"Jane's All-the-World's-Aircraft,"* written into their 100th anniversary yearbook, an annual publication considered to be "the bible of aviation history"[40]. This proclamation was shortly followed by similar official credit from the state of Connecticut[41], where Whitehead invented and flew the first powered airplane. Both touched off a storm of controversy, especially amongst historians. Thus, aviation history has undergone the beginning of a drastic change, with these formal recognitions of Gustave Whitehead, increasingly seen as "inventor of the airplane," a humble but brilliant man who nearly became lost to the ages.[42]

Chapter 2: First Flights on August 14, 1901

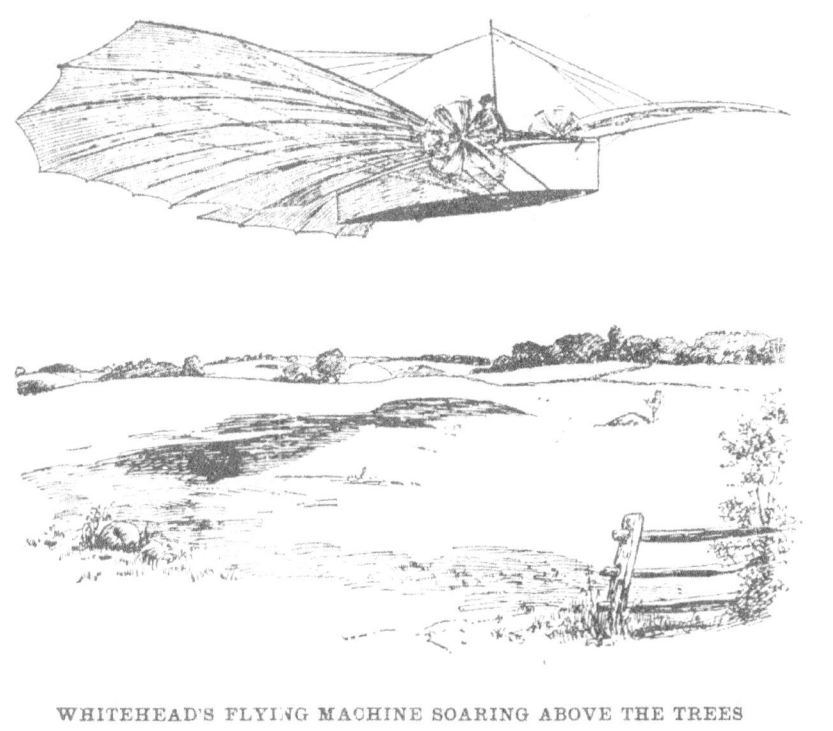

Figure 8: Sketch of Whitehead's "No. 21" in flight, Aug. 14, 1901

"WHITEHEAD'S FLYING MACHINE SOARING ABOVE THE TREES"
(Illustration with eyewitness account of Dick Howell, *Bridgeport Sunday Herald*, Aug. 18, 1901)[43]

JOURNALIST EYEWITNESS ACCOUNT

Richard "Dick" Howell

The sports section of the *Bridgeport Sunday Herald* of Aug. 18, 1901, a weekly newspaper, gave an exclusive, eyewitness account of that monumental achievement - "the first sustained, manned flight of an airplane with power and control" - written in the flowery style of the times. The detailed Herald article was conclusively confirmed to have been written by its "Sporting Editor"[44] and reporter, Richard Howell, later chief editor and publisher of the *Bridgeport Sunday Herald*. The *Hartford Courant* described Howell as "one of the most familiar figures in Connecticut public life, being prominent in sports, politics, and newspaper work for the past forty years" at his death, in 1930.[45] Howell was the perfect person for Whitehead to select as an eyewitness reporter; he was revered and trusted as an accurate journalist with a large following, particularly for sports reporting.

Figure 9: Dick Howell, Editor for Sports of the People

Bridgeport Sunday Herald **Section Header, February 2, 1902. Dick Howell, longtime Sports Editor for the Herald.**

Figure 10: Dick Howell as he appeared in 1928

dubbed "The Old Sportsman," the renowned journalist invited to document Whitehead's flight of August 14, 1901 as an eyewitness.[46]

Figure 11: Dick Howell, editor credit

Figure 12: Herald Sports Section Header

Chapter 2: First Flights on August 14, 1901

At the time, experiments with flying machines were considered to be an emerging sport, with past experience pertaining to "flight" involving sporting aircraft, such as gliders and balloons - much as hang-gliding is considered in the sports category, today. No commercial applications had yet been developed for practical use, as 1901 marked the first year in history when successful powered flights occurred. As a result, articles about aeronautics were typically found in the *sporting sections* of the print media for the era, including the *New York Times*, past the first decade of the 20th century.[47]

Figure 13: NY Times Sporting includes Aeronautics

New York Times **Sporting News Section carries aeronautics articles in 1909.**

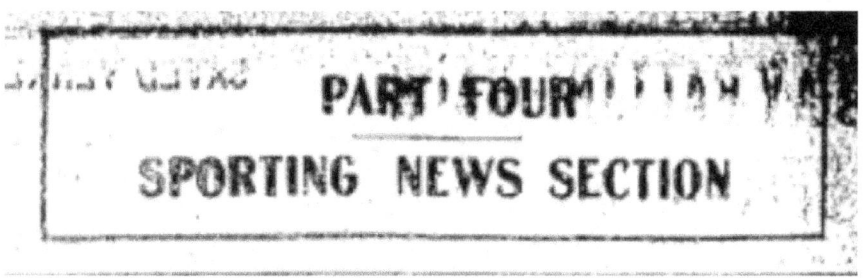

Figure 14: NY Times Sporting Section Banner

The *Bridgeport Sunday Herald*'s "Flying" article has been criticized for not being signed, though it was quite customary for the reporter not to provide a byline, and to refer to himself in the third person; for example, as "the Herald representative," when covering features.

There is little indication to show that either the reporter, Dick Howell, or the aeronaut/inventor, Gustave Whitehead, understood the full historic significance of what had transpired. Rather, it is obvious that the experience was interpreted as an example of unique and interesting progress with flying machine experiments. Public emphasis was on a practical application for flight, such as would not be seen for more than a decade, following intensive efforts by a host of inventors, including the Wrights, Curtiss, and countless others. A "short" flight of 1/2 mile was not viewed as extremely significant, because it was still considered to be impractical and under development. At the time, other "airships," namely, balloons and dirigibles, were flying distances of hundreds of miles and thousands of feet in elevation. Nearly three decades later, the significance of Whitehead's flights of 1901-1903 grew in stature, with more interest in who made "the first powered flight." It is doubtful that

Gustave Whitehead: "First in Flight"

Richard Howell, in his lifetime, understood the historic significance of his presence and resulting documentation of Whitehead's sustained, powered flight of August 14, 1901. In fact, Howell writes in his article, "Flying," "But while Mr. Whitehead has demonstrated that his machine will fly he does not pretend that it can be made a commercial success."[48]

Coverage of Whitehead's flights and activities continued sporadically, through 1914. During this time, Whitehead's early accomplishments and "firsts" were overshadowed by numerous other airplane inventors, worldwide, once the "secrets of flight" became known, who rapidly moved the art forward. Attention to aviation topics in "the Herald" was quite limited, with the exception of Whitehead's activities, in the first decade of the twentieth century. By 1908, the Wrights were mentioned, but only in an article mentioning Whitehead. On August 18th, 1912, when Howell was chief editor and publisher, a *Bridgeport Sunday Herald* feature article even bore this headline, "Aeroplanes Are Useless," referring to military maneuvers of a (non-Whitehead) plane that took off over Long Island Sound and returned, experiencing problems with wind and weather. This casual attitude towards the importance of airplanes, shared by many in the public and those in the United States government, was to change during World War I and in 1927, when Lindberg crossed the Atlantic.[49]The extent of local coverage is still unknown, due to incomplete archives, still stored on microfiche,with little manpower devoted to sifting through the reels.

The *Bridgeport Sunday Herald was a weekly newspaper*[50]*, never a daily*. This would become important when examined in later decades, as critics, including a defensive Orville Wright and several well-placed friends[51], rushed to point out that the story didn't break "the next day," claiming this proved it to be a hoax. *The Herald* expanded from covering stories about the Bridgeport region's news, its sports, industries, inventors, and "local color," to ever-wider areas of Connecticut. Bridgeport, known as a "city of inventors," provided topics of interest for a wide readership, telling of the "development and progress of the railroads, submarines, wireless, automobiles, and aviation"[52] within its pages. Sports was its specialty. "It devoted extensive coverage [to] sporting activity: baseball, football, bowling, tennis, golf, boating, and boxing." *The Herald included, in the early years of aviation, stories of local "flying" as both a sport and an emerging, fledgling industry*. Eventually evolving into the *Connecticut Sunday Herald*, the newspaper finally closed its doors in 1974, succumbing to a weak economy.[53]

At the time of Howell's death in 1930[54], even the Smithsonian refused to recognize the Wrights as "first"; rather, they were self-servingly crediting their own Secretary Langley with the glory of having developed the first plane "capable of flight." In the public eye, the Wrights *were* first, though, even in the 1920's, following heavy media coverage of their flights and lawsuits, with strong public relations efforts by the Wrights[55]. The highly competitive Orville Wright, last of the two brothers to survive, began to wage battle against all claimants considered to be contenders to the title of "first in powered flight," starting in the 1920's, right up through 1948, when he died. Not till after Orville's death, in 1948, was the matter of who was first in flight "settled," and then, by a *contractual agreement* designed by Orville's supporters, signed in a legal agreement with the Smithsonian.[56]
[57]

More than six years after Howell's demise, when Whitehead articles and research began to stimulate public awareness of the late inventor's achievements, the *Bridgeport Sunday Herald* provided conclusive proof to both the general public and the Library of Congress that Richard "Dick" Howell was, indeed, the eyewitness reporter for Whitehead's flight in August 1901.[58] In the *[Bridgeport] Herald Magazine*, "For the Week Ending Jan. 30, 1937," *the Herald* ran a full page article called "Forgotten Bridgeporter Was First Aviator," on page 4, explaining that they'd opened their files to the Library of Congress (where the article resides through this date) and to Dr. John B. Crane of Harvard. Dr. Crane, who was investigating Whitehead at the time on a small grant from Harvard, came to believe Whitehead had, indeed, made a number of flights before the Wright brothers. In their 1937 magazine issue, *the Herald* thrice confirmed Richard "Dick" Howell *was the eyewitness reporter on August 14, 1901*, with these published statements:

Chapter 2: First Flights on August 14, 1901

"It was a thrilling adventure for reporter Richard Howell, later publisher of the HERALD, to watch Whitehead's "No. 21" go soaring above the earth."

[After describing the story to the readers, *the Herald* again credits Howell ...]
"That is the story as reporter Dick Howell told it and as it lives today in the files of the HERALD." [59]

Then, on the next page (5) of the magazine, the Herald article about Whitehead, "Flying," from 1901, was reproduced with the title, "Here's Proof from the Files of *Bridgeport Herald*" with another statement crediting Dick Howell.

"The HERALD was one of the earliest papers to go air-minded, and this reproduction of a page from the issue of Sunday, August 18, 1901, shows *the story written by the late Richard Howell, then a reporter and later publisher of the HERALD.* The flight was made just after midnight [*Author's note: the manned flight actually took place near dawn*] on the Tuesday previous to this issue. Authorities are using other reproductions of this page in their effort to prove that Whitehead flew more than two years before the Wright brothers" [*appears at bottom of article*].

Even Stanley Yale Beach, a local who'd been Aviation Editor for the *Scientific American* and supporter of Whitehead's early flights for the first decade of the new century, identified Richard Howell as the eyewitness journalist who wrote the Herald article, nearly forty years later.[60] The statement appeared in his alleged "Beach Whitehead Statement." [61]

Fairfield resident, author and widely recognized world authority on Gustave Whitehead, O'Dwyer extensively studied the Herald's articles and Howell's writings on microfiche, in the 1960's.[62] [63] Letters from his readership were addressed to "Mr. Howell, Sporting Editor, Sunday Herald." The section of the newspaper he wrote sports articles for was called "Sports" or "Sports of the People," with Howell's name prominently listed on the masthead as Sports Editor (see above).

Major William J. O'Dwyer, observed, "By 1900, at the editorial room of the *Bridgeport Sunday Herald*, Richard Howell was already a feature writer. He was not simply a sports writer, though this was the only column he occasionally signed or was listed as Sports Editor for. In others he spoke as "this writer" evidenced by articles that includ[ed] naming his presence while representing the Herald."[64]

O'Dwyer notes in his 1981 research log[65] that in a July 15, 1900 article, Howell wrote about Connecticut inventor Simon Lake and his newly invented submarine, describing his own presence[66] during a documented test run. As with the Whitehead flight article, "Flying," Howell described what he saw; this time, being aboard when Lake's submarine made test dives in Long Island Sound outside Bridgeport harbor.[67] Howell embellished the Lake article with "liberal use of his drawings." According to O'Dwyer, as with the Whitehead article, Howell understandably displayed a lack of "technical accuracy," reporting what he saw from the standpoint of a layman. Another technology article of Howell's, which might have caught Whitehead's eye (and his later associates), appeared in the July 8, 1900 edition, concerning "Liquid Air"[68] just around the time Whitehead arrived in Bridgeport. Within that article it mentions that liquid air might be the solution to the need for a lightweight source of power, a means of solving "the aerial navigation" problem.

The *Bridgeport Sunday Herald* boasted on its front page, in 1900, to have "The Largest Circulation in the State." It is no wonder that Howell was selected by Gustave Whitehead to cover his long distance test flight of August 14, 1901. A relative newcomer to Bridgeport, if Whitehead consulted with the people in the area as to which newspaper and reporter might be best to invite to document this important test flight, they unquestionably would have recommended the *Bridgeport Sunday Herald*'s Dick Howell. As a trusted, popular journalist for the region, it is without question that Howell would have diligently reported the details, including accurately identifying additional witness participants - known members of the community. To do otherwise (as some have suggested) would have undermined his credibility with his widespread, close-knit readers. Fabrication of the story, while naming local citizen witnesses, might even have led to strong public objections or even legal action, of which there is no evidence. There is no record of James Dickie, a named witness who would later deny being present, objecting to the article. If there was an objection, he could have accomplished this through a letter to the editor or a lawsuit, which appear to have been plentiful during that period. At the time, powered flight was considered to be very controversial, many people saying, "If God wanted man to fly, He'd have given him wings." The article documenting Whitehead's flight would have had to be carefully and accurately written, in order to maintain the community's trust in this popular newspaper.

Francis Brennan, an associate of both Gustave Whitehead and Dick Howell, was interviewed by Major O'Dwyer in July 1969. Mr. Brennan, then 85 years of age and clear of mind, did not personally witness Whitehead fly due to his work schedule, but had this to say about editor / reporter Richard "Dick" Howell, one he viewed as a responsible journalist, highly regarded by his peers [69]:

> "I knew Richard Howell very well. If he said Whitehead flew, I would believe Dick. He was an honest man. We enjoyed everything about sports and those kinds of things. He was exceptionally reliable. Yes. If he said Whitehead flew a powered aircraft I would believe him. ... You had to know him to appreciate how honest he was. He was a good man, well-liked by all who knew him.
>
> ... "I can only say this. If Richard Howell said he flew, he flew. Howell was not one to start a hoax or lie. He was an honest newspaperman and well regarded and respected in Bridgeport. I knew Dick Howell quite well. Yes. I would accept what Howell wrote, anytime." [70]

Whitehead's "heavier-than-air flying machine," as early airplanes were called, was equipped with wheels and could also be driven as a car, in order to transport it to a desired location and as a means to provide ground acceleration for takeoff. At shortly after midnight, the "plane" was driven as a car, wings folded back like a bird's, rocking on its wooden wheels rimmed with metal[71], toward Fairfield (from Pine Street, past Ellsworth on Fairfield Avenue) to an unnamed field "back of Fairfield" along the highway, estimated by the Herald reporter at a speed of 20 to 30 mph. According to the newspaper account, Whitehead and "Cellie" occupied the seats in the plane, while the reporter and young James Dickie, aged 16 at the time, followed on bicycles. By the time Whitehead set up and ran tests on the plane and it was ready for its manned flight, dawn was nearly breaking. The first powered, manned airplane flight in the world was described in Howell's newspaper article in great detail, including its estimated altitude of 50 feet and the distance traveled, "fully half a mile." The plane successfully became airborne, controlled by its operator, and skirting some trees, landed gently in a level manner[72], without any damage.

When Whitehead went home, he reported to his wife, "Mama, we went up!"[73] He provided a description of his flight experience in the *Bridgeport Sunday Herald* article sidebar[74]: "*That was the happiest moment of my life, for I had demonstrated that the machine I have worked on for many years would do what I claimed for it. It was a grand sensation to be flying through the air. There is nothing like it.*"

Chapter 2: First Flights on August 14, 1901

The "Flying" Article

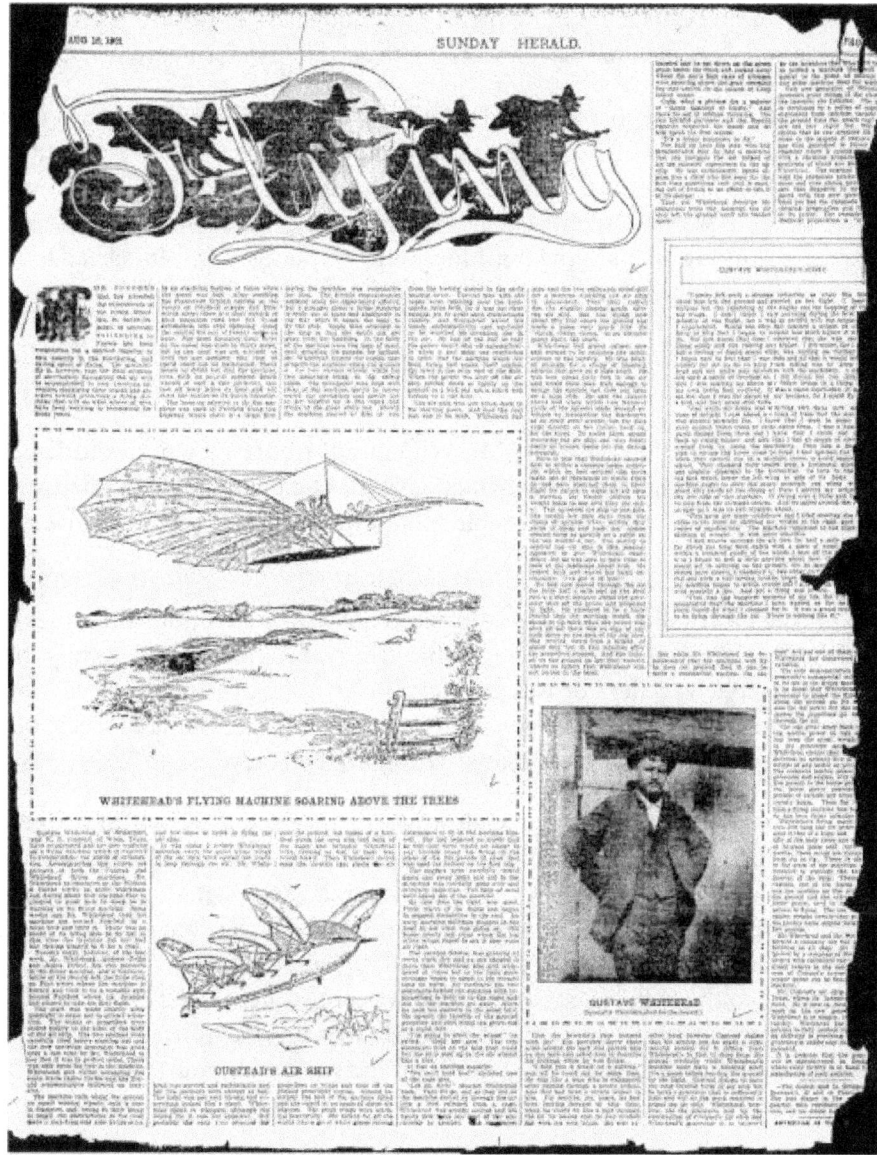

Figure 15: *Bridgeport Sunday Herald* **article "Flying," Aug. 18, 1901**

The article, as it appeared above, written in the flowery style of the era, gives us the feeling of being there, viewing the events as they unfolded, knowing what the participants felt.

(transcript)

Flying
(*Bridgeport Sunday Herald*, August 18, 1901)

"The success that has attended the experiments of the young Brazilian M. Santos-Dumont in scientific

Gustave Whitehead: "First in Flight"

ballooning in France has been responsible for a marked impetus in this country in the fascinating and daring sport of flying. The probability is, however, that the final solution of successfully navigating the air by two *American Inventor*s combining their brains and energies toward perfecting a flying machine that will do what scores of men have been working to accomplish for many years.

Gustave Whitehead of Bridgeport and W. D. Custead of Waco, Texas have co-operated and are now working on a flying machine which is expected to revolutionize the world of aeronautics. Accompanying this article are pictures of both the Custead and Whitehead flying machines. Mr. Whitehead is employed at the Wilmot & Hobbs works as night watchman, and during about half the time that is allotted to most men to sleep he is working on his flying machine. Some weeks ago Mr. Whitehead took his machine out beyond Fairfield in a large field and tried it.

There was no doubt of it being able to fly at that time but the inventor did not feel like risking himself in it for a trial.

Tuesday night, however of the last week, Mr. Whitehead, Andrew Cellie[75], and James Dickie, his two partners in the flying machine and a representative of the Herald left the little shed on Pine Street where the machine is housed and took it to a suitable spot beyond Fairfield where its inventor had planned to take his first flight.

The start was made shortly after midnight in order to not attract attention. The wings or propellers were folded tightly to the sides of the body of the air ship. The two engines were carefully tried before starting out and now the acetylene generator was gone over a last time by Mr. Whitehead to see that it was in perfect order. There was only room for two in the machine, Whitehead and Cellie occupying the seats while James Dickie and the Herald representative followed on bicycles.

The machine rolls along the ground on small wooden wheels, only a foot in diameter, and, owing to their being so small, the obstructions in the road made it rock from one side to the other in an alarming fashion at times when the speed was fast. After reaching the Protestant Orphan asylum at the corner of Fairfield Avenue and Ellsworth [S]treet there is a clear stretch of macadam road and the flying automobile was sent spinning along the road at the rate of twenty miles an hour. For short distances from then on the speed was close to thirty miles but as the road was not straight or level for any distance this rate of speed could not be maintained. There seems no doubt that the machine, even with its present common board wheels of only a foot in diameter, can reel off forty miles an hour and not exert the engine to its fullest capacity.

The location selected to fly the machine was back of Fairfield along the highway where there is a large field and few trees to avoid in flying the air ship.

It was about 2 o'clock Wednesday morning when the great white wings of the air ship were spread out ready to leap through the air. Mr. Whitehead was excited and enthusiastic and his two partners were almost as bad. The light was not very strong and everything looked like a ghost. Whitehead spoke in whispers, although the reason for it was not apparent. But probably the very time selected for trying the machine was responsible for that. The Herald representative assisted when the opportunity afforded, but a stranger about a flying machine is sadly out of place and absolutely in the way when it comes to the hour to fly the ship. Ropes were attached to the ship so that she would not get away from her handlers. In the body of the machine were two bags of sand, each weighing about 110 pounds, for ballast. Mr. Whitehead started the engine that propels the machine along the ground on the four wooden wheels,

Chapter 2: First Flights on August 14, 1901

while his two assistants clung to the safety ropes. The newspaper man kept well clear of the machine, partly to better watch the operations and partly not to get tangled up in the ropes and wings of the giant white bat. Slowly the machine started at first to run over the ground, but inside of a hundred yards the men who had hold of the ropes and inventor Whitehead were running as fast as their legs would travel. Then Whitehead pulled open the throttle that starts the air propellers or wings and shut off the ground propelling engine. Almost instantly the bow of the machine lifted and she raised at an angle of about six degrees. The great white wings were working beautifully. She looked for all the world like a great white goose raising from the feeding ground in the early morning dawn. The two men with the ropes were tumbling over the hummocks in the field for it was not clear enough yet to avoid such obstructions readily, and Whitehead waved his hands enthusiastically and excitedly as he watched his invention rise in the air. He had set the dial so that the power would shut off automatically when it had made one revolution in order that the machine would not keep flying and smash against the trees at the other end of the field. When the power was shut the air ship settled as lightly on the ground as a bird and not a stitch was broken or a rod bent.

The air ship was now taken back to the starting point. And now the real test was to be made. Whitehead had determined to fly in the machine himself. She had behaved so nicely that he felt that there would no longer be any trouble about his flying in the place of the 220 pounds of sand that was used for the ballast on the first trip.

The engines were carefully tested again and every joint and rod in the structure was carefully gone over and critically inspected. The bags of sand were taken out of the machine.

By this time the light was good. Faint traces of the rising sun began to suggest themselves in the east. An early morning milkman stopped in the road to see what was going on. His horse nearly ran away when the big white wings flapped to see if they were all right.

The nervous tension was growing at every clock tick and no one showed it more than Whitehead who still whispered at times but as the light grew stronger began to speak in his normal tone of voice. He stationed his two assistants behind the machine with instructions to hold on to the ropes and not let the machine get away[76]. Then he took up his position in the great bird. He opened the throttle of the ground propeller and shot along the green at a rapid rate.

"I'm going to start the wings[77]!" he yelled. "Hold her now." The two assistants held on the best they could but the ship shot up in the air almost like a kite.

It was an exciting moment.

"We can't hold her!" shrieked one of the rope men.

"Let go then!" shouted Whitehead back. They let go and as they did so the machine darted up through the air like a bird released from a cage. Whitehead was greatly excited and his hands flew from one part of the machine to another. The newspaper man and the two assistants stood still for a moment watching the air ship in amazement. Then they rushed down the sloping grade after the air ship. She was flying now about fifty feet above the ground and made a noise very much like the "chug, chug, chug," of an elevator going down the shaft.

Whitehead had grown calmer now and seemed to be enjoying the exhilaration of the novelty. He was

Gustave Whitehead: "First in Flight"

headed straight for a clump of chestnut sprouts that grew on a high knoll. He was now about forty feet in the air and would have been high enough to escape the sprouts had they not been on a high ridge. He saw the danger ahead and when within two hundred yards of the sprouts made several attempts to manipulate the machinery so he could steer around, but the ship kept steadily on her course, head on for the trees. To strike them meant wrecking the air ship and very likely death or broken bones for the daring aeronaut.

Here it was that Whitehead showed how to utilize a common sense principle which he had noticed the birds make use of thousands of times when he had been studying them in their flight for points to make his air ship a success. He simply shifted his weight more to one side than the other. This careened the ship to one side. She turned her nose away from the clump of sprouts when within fifty yards of them and took her course around them as prettily as a yacht on the sea avoids a bar. The ability to control the air ship in this manner appeared to give Whitehead confidence, for he was seen to take time to look at the landscape about him. He looked back and waved his hand exclaiming, "I've got it at last."

He had now soared through the air for fully half a mile and as the field ended a short distance ahead the aeronaut shut off the power and prepared to light. He appeared to be a little fearful that the machine would dip ahead or tip back when the power was shut off but there was no sign of any such move on the part of the big bird. She settled down from a height of about fifty feet in two minutes after the propellers stopped. And she lighted on the ground on her four wooden wheels so lightly that Whitehead was not jarred in the least.

How the inventors face beamed with joy! His partners threw their arms around his neck and patted him on the back and asked him to describe his feelings while he was flying.

"I told you it would be a success," was all he could say for some time. He was like a man who is exhausted after passing through a severe ordeal. And this had been a severe ordeal to him. For months, yes years he had been looking forward to this time, when he would fly like a bird through the air by means that he had studied with his own brain. He was exhausted and he sat down on the green grass beside the fence and looked away where the sun's first rays of light were shooting above the gray shrouding fog that nestled on the bosom of Long Island Sound.

Gods, what a picture for a painter of "Hopes Recalled at Dawn." And there he sat in silence thinking. His two faithful partners and the Herald reporter respected his mood and let him speak the first words.

"It's a funny sensation to fly."

For half an hour the man who had demonstrated that he has a machine that can navigate the air talked of his ten minutes experience in the air ship. He was enthusiastic, spoke almost like a child who has seen for the first time something new and is panting out of breath in an effort to tell it to his mother.

Thus did Whitehead describe his sensations from the moment the air ship left the ground until she landed again:

GUSTAVE WHITEHEAD'S STORY.

"I never felt such a strange sensation as when the machine first left the ground and started on her flight. I heard nothing but the rumbling of the engine and the flapping of the big wings. *[Author's note: this would likely be the silk between the struts since the plane was not an ornithopter. Also, propellers were often*

Chapter 2: First Flights on August 14, 1901

called "wings" in that period, and this comment may be referring to them.] I don't think I saw anything during the first two minutes of the flight, for I was so excited with the sensations I experienced. When the ship had reached a height of about forty or fifty feet I began to wonder how much higher it would go. But just about that time I observed that she was sailing along easily and not raising any higher. I felt easier, for I still had a feeling of doubt about what was waiting for me further on I began now to feel that I was safe and all that it would be necessary for me to do to keep from falling was to keep my head and not make any mistakes with the machinery. I never felt such a spirit of freedom as I did during the ten minutes [see p. 87] that I was soaring up above my fellow beings in a thing that my own brain had evolved. It was a sweet experience. It made me feel that I was far ahead of my brothers for I could fly like a bird, and they must still walk.

"And while my brain was whirling with these new sensations of delight I saw ahead a clump of trees that the machine was pointed straight for. I knew that I must in some way steer around those trees or raise above them. I was a hundred yards distant from them and I knew that I could not clear them by raising higher, and also that I had no means of steering around them by using the machinery. Then like a flash a plan to escape the trees came to mind. I had watched the birds when turned out of a straight course to avoid something ahead. They changed their bodies from a horizontal plane to one slightly diagonal to the horizontal. To turn to the left the bird would lower its left wing or side of its body. The machine ought to obey the same principle and when within about fifty yards of the clump of trees I shifted my weight to the left side of the machine. It swung over a little and began to turn from the straight course. And we sailed around the trees as easy as it was to sail straight ahead.

"This gave me more confidence and I tried steering the machine to the right by shifting my weight to the right past the center of equilibrium. The machine responded to the slightest shifting of weight. It was most sensitive.

"I had soared through the air now for half a mile and not far ahead the long field ended with a piece of woods. When within a hundred yards of the woods I shut off the power and then began to feel a little nervous about how the machine would act in settling to the ground, for so many flying machines have shown a tendency to fall either on the front or hind end and such a fall means broken bones for the operator. My machine began to settle evenly and I alighted on the ground with scarcely a jar. And not a thing was broken.

"That was the happiest moment of my life for I had demonstrated that the machine I have worked on for so many years would do what I claimed for it. It was a grand sensation to be flying through the air. There is nothing like it."

But while Mr. Whitehead has demonstrated that his machine will fly he does not pretend that it can be made a commercial success. On the other hand inventor Custead claims that his airship can be made a commercial success for it differs from Whiteheads in that it rises from the ground vertically *while Whiteheads machine must have a running start like a goose before leaving the ground for the flight.* Custead claims to have the most feasible form of airship but he lacks a generator that is sufficiently light and do the work required to propel the airship. Whiteheads however has the generator and by the combination of Custead's airship and Whiteheads generator it is believed by the inventors that will be able to perfect a machine that will come nearer to the point of success than any other machine thus far made.

This new generator of Whiteheads promises great things if the claims of the inventor are fulfilled. The power is developed by a series of rapid gas explosions from calcium carbide. At the present time the spark explosions are not very rapid but Whitehead claims that he can produce 150 explosions to the minute if required. The gas thus generated is forced into a chamber where it comes into contact with a chemical preparation the ingredients of which are known only to Whitehead. The contact of the gas with the chemicals produces an enormous and even piston pressure. It is said that dynamite is nothing compared with this new power. Whitehead has had the chemists inspect his chemical preparation and they marvel at its power. The chemists call the chemical preparation a "queer mixture" but not one of them denies that Whitehead has discovered something valuable.

The only demonstration of the new generator's commercial value has been in its use in the flying machine. There is no doubt that Whitehead used this generator to propel the flying machine along the ground on its wheels and also for the power for the engine that makes the propellers go when flying through the air.

The one great drawback is procuring motive power to run an airship has been the great weight required in a generator and engine. Mr. Whitehead claims that his motor will decrease by seventy five per cent the weight of any motor at present in use. The complete motive power including generator and engine will weigh about five pounds to the horse power. For a ten horse power generator twenty pounds of carbide are required to run twenty hours.

Thus far the longest time a flying machine has been able to fly has been thirty minutes. [*Author's note: likely referring to time spent flying in a circle, tethered, as this was one of Whitehead's preliminary tests*]

Whitehead's flying machine is sixteen feet long and its general appearance is that of a huge bat. From each side of the body there are wings made of bamboo poles and covered with muslin. These wings are thirty six feet from tip to tip. There is also a tail in the stern of the machine which is intended to regulate the accent and decent of the ship. There are two engines, one of ten horse power to run the machine on the wheels along the ground and the other, of twenty horse power, used to work the propellers in flying. The ten horse power engine weighs twenty-two pounds and the twenty horse engine weighs thirty five pounds.

Mr. Whitehead and Mr. Custead have formed a company for the purpose of building an airship. Mr. Custead is backed by a company of Southern gentleman with unlimited capital and they firmly believe in the commercial success of Custead's invention when a proper power can be found to run the machine.

Mr. Custead's airship is in Waco, Texas where its inventor originally lived. He is now in New York. The work on the new generator which Whitehead is to supply is progressing rapidly. Whitehead has applied for patents to fully protect it and expects no difficulty in receiving them as his generator is unlike any that have been patented.

It is probable that the generators will be manufactured in Bridgeport where every facility is at hand for the manufacture of such articles."[78]

(*end of transcript*)

The first flight was conducted in Whitehead's "No. 21" aeroplane, called a "heavier-than-air machine" at the time, to differentiate it from hot air or "gas" balloon driven airships. Like many of Whitehead's business partners, the Whitehead-Custead partnership did not last long. As with a number of other Whitehead business arrangements, it never materialized into the company the two inventors envisioned.[79] It has been said that a Whitehead motor was later used in a Custead ornithopter, in Waco, Texas, which reputedly was raised using the motor, under hawser restraint, utilizing four ropes of about thirty feet long each.

Chapter 2: First Flights on August 14, 1901

Major William J. O'Dwyer, Whitehead researcher, while the *Bridgeport Sunday Herald*, particularly Howell's articles and sketches, noted some appear to be signed, worked into the sketch itself. An area shown below, is one where O'Dwyer, viewing this page in microfiche, noted Howell may have signed the sketch, "Richard Howell" or "Dick Howell," under the left side of the fence. Findings were inconclusive. But signed or unsigned, the sketch is most likely attributed to eyewitness Howell, especially as it was so accurate concerning the location and "No. 21" in flight.

Figure 16: Possible Dick Howell signature

A later *Herald* artist, Andrew V. Barber, was incorrectly theorized by Whitehead detractors to have been the illustrator for the article. A front page press announcement covering his death on October 22, 1923 conclusively shows Barber joined the *Bridgeport Sunday Herald* as a cartoonist, artist, and writer, in late 1903. "He would have celebrated this year the twentieth anniversary of his connection with the *Bridgeport* and *Waterbury Heralds*…Barber came to Bridgeport in 1903… [80] Barber first appears in the Bridgeport Directory, in 1904, listed as [an] artist [for the] B. Herald, renting rooms at 243 Fairfield Ave., Bridgeport, CT. [81] Prior to that, through at least the census of June 1900, Barber was a resident of Los Angeles, listed as an artist, living with his parents and brother[82].

ILLUSTRATED WITH EARLIEST AVIATOR SYMBOL

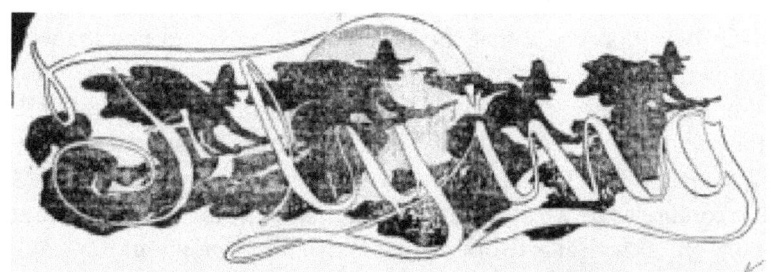

Figure 17: "Flying" article had witch illustrated banner

A banner of flying witches appeared behind the Herald's title for its "Flying" article

© Susan Brinchman, 2015

The detailed, full-page exclusive article was illustrated at the top with a drawing of witches on broomsticks, a depiction associated in that era with aviation. Perhaps, because before this point, the idea of controlled human flight was only found in supernatural legends

In articles from further into the decade, "motorized witches' brooms" or "flying broomsticks" were another description used by early aviators and the media for the crude aeroplanes of the era[83]. An Aero Club in Pennsylvania even adopted the witch on a broom as its logo, which it maintains through this writing.

Figure 18: Flying Witch – "The Original Aviator," Chicago Tribune (1909)

First noticed by researcher O'Dwyer, in 1909, the *Chicago Tribune* included this symbol of a flying witch as "the first aviator" to illustrate an article regarding Curtiss' performance at a ground-breaking aviation meet at Rheims.[84] "Curtiss had ridden witch-fashion astride a motor-driven broomstick (the age-old image of manned flight) as it were…"[85]

The imagery of "witches" as a parallel to man's flight is seen time and again during this period. In 1910, the New York Tribune ran an aviation article in which … Clifford B. Harmon, of the Aero Club of America, called the leading amateur aviator of the United States … *told how the witchery of ballooning through moonlit nights* had paled when he got a good look at an aeroplane…[86]

In 1945, Orville Wright would disparage the *Bridgeport Sunday Herald* article on the basis of its witch illustration, in a desperate attempt to "prove" the successful Whitehead flights had never occurred.[87]

Maj. William J. O'Dwyer, observed that the 1900 and 1901 Herald newspapers opened "almost every news item accompanied by the opening letter of the opening sentence with a delightful piece of artwork, far more decorative than simply a vine around a letter "T". It generally fitted the subject of the news item quite well [lending] Howell and the printers any given million choices of artwork. But who had flown in an airplane up to 1901, with power? Who made manned flight in powered aeroplanes? Only witches flew! It was undoubtedly the only image Howell could conjure as he wrote his article. He wanted something bold, undoubtedly, and did it to gain the reader's attention. Th[is] typical artwork format is prolific throughout the 1900 – 1903 editions of the Sunday Herald. It was simply a style."[88]

A further interpretation of the "witch symbol" may be its potential use as a virtual "double entendre," to help identify the area where Whitehead flew, for informed local readers; a second meaning, in addition to witch symbolism associated with "flight." It was locally thought, in the early 20th century, that a small hill above

Chapter 2: First Flights on August 14, 1901

Ash Creek was the site of the locally notorious "Witch Hill," where, in 1653, an unfortunate woman convicted of witchcraft was hanged. "The little hill that slopes down to Ash Creek is sometimes pointed out as the historic spot," stated a 1909 book by Frank Samuel Child, President of the Fairfield Historical Society.[89] This spot would have located on Turney's Farm, accessed by passing over the Ash Creek Bridge from Fairfield Avenue, then turning into what then constituted the main highway in Fairfield, the *Boston Post* Road. Richard "Dick" Howell may have cleverly provided this clue for those Fairfield readers who wondered about the flight location, despite the strong likelihood of a Whitehead request to keep the location out of the story, as was his habit, to preserve it for future use.

FIRST FLIGHT LOCATIONS AND CONDITIONS

The location of the first sustained, powered flight documented by the *Bridgeport Sunday Herald* has been called into question often, due to its seemingly vague description. This has confounded local efforts to establish a monument and added to the controversy regarding the authenticity of the Herald's report. However, to investigate history, one must dig deeply, while considering the everyday language of the region, the thinking of the people at the time, and other evidence which might be used to improve understanding. We must understand the context of those living in Whitehead's time, while searching for more evidence. That is the approach used throughout this book, which we will apply to the question of the location of "the first sustained, powered flight" of August 14, 1901.

The only eyewitness account of the first flight, found in the article "Flying"[90], written immediately afterward by the Herald reporter, did not precisely identify the *exact* location of the first flight. Rather, the powered flight was described using terms like "back of Fairfield along the highway where there is a large field" and "beyond Fairfield." Researchers theorized these terms indicated *the flight had occurred in Fairfield*, and that the site descriptions used by Howell employed local colloquial speech, understood by the Herald's readership. The terms were seen as merely indicating the location was in the outlying area of the center of town, still within the borders of Fairfield, beyond its small "downtown" business area, governmental buildings, and town green.

> The location selected to fly the machine was back of Fairfield along the highway where there is a large field and few trees to avoid in flying the air ship.

> Tuesday night, however, of the last week, Mr. Whitehead, Andrew Cellie and James Dickie, his two partners in the flying machine, and a representative of the Herald left the little shed on Pine street where the machine is housed and took it to a suitable spot beyond Fairfield where its inventor had planed to take his first flight.

Above, two mentions of the location of the first flight, from "Flying," an eyewitness feature article by Richard Howell of the *Bridgeport Sunday Herald*, published August 18, 1901.

The route and conditions at the site were more specifically described by Howell, used by later researchers to identify possible locations for the flying field.

However, statements in several other local news articles, including the *Bridgeport Sunday Herald,* apparently previously unnoticed by previous researchers, reveal conclusively that Fairfield, Connecticut *was* the precise location of the first flight of August 14, 1901.

In a follow up article on November 17, 1901, less than three months later, the *Bridgeport Sunday Herald* specifically names Fairfield as the location of the flights. (*emphasis added)*

> "The shop is well stocked with steel and iron which is being used in the construction of a flying machine modelled after the one in which ***Mr. Whitehead made two successful flights recently*** *as described by the Herald at the time. It was with this machine that* ***Mr. Whitehead demonstrated the practicability of his invention during the season*** *[i.e. summer]* ***in Fairfield****" [see below]...* [91]

Notably, the article also indicates Whitehead had made *two more* successful flights for the sake of his new (then-unnamed) sponsor, Herman Linde.

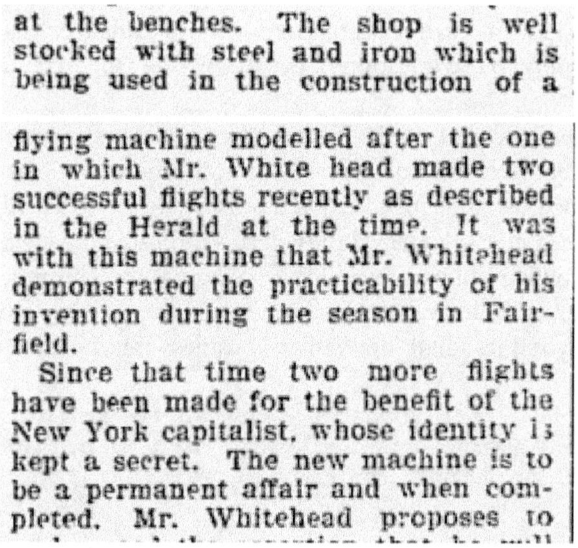
at the benches. The shop is well stocked with steel and iron which is being used in the construction of a flying machine modelled after the one in which Mr. White head made two successful flights recently as described in the Herald at the time. It was with this machine that Mr. Whitehead demonstrated the practicability of his invention during the season in Fairfield.

Since that time two more flights have been made for the benefit of the New York capitalist, whose identity is kept a secret. The new machine is to be a permanent affair and when completed, Mr. Whitehead proposes to

Figure 19: Herald reports two more flights made for Herman Linde in 1901

On Nov. 17, 1901, the *Bridgeport Sunday Herald* confirmed two successful flights reported previously by their newspaper, **in Fairfield "during the season" (a term used for summer)**, with two additional flights made afterward for the new sponsor.

A newly discovered local newspaper article from the *Bridgeport Evening Farmer* of 1910, gave a brief background of Gus Whitehead's history, referring to the "unheralded," sparsely witnessed flight of "1901" as "occurring out near Fairfield Beach," which undeniably is one and the same as that which Howell described, due to its date, location, circumstances, and noting of the few witnesses present.

Chapter 2: First Flights on August 14, 1901

> Gus Whitehead, as his friends best know him, is one of the most expert engine builders in the world. He has succeeded in turning out engines whose efficiency in proportion to their weight is marvelous. Years ago he was building engines for dirigible balloons. Back in 1901 he made a flight in an airship of the aeroplane type, out near Fairfield beach, when he soared through the air for one-eighth of a mile and astounded the few who were privileged to witness the unheralded trial.

Figure 20: *Bridgeport Evening Farmer* **reports flight made in 1901 "out near Fairfield beach"**

"Back in 1901 [Whitehead] made a flight in an airship of the aeroplane type, *out near Fairfield Beach*, when he soared through the air … and astounded the few who were privileged to witness the unheralded trial."[92]

The *Bridgeport Evening Farmer* article, written nine years after the flight, describes its distance as "one-eighth of a mile," a variation potentially attributable to the length of time which had passed, to be addressed later in this work. Witnesses to alleged later flights of the same day in Lordship were more specific concerning that location in their affidavits.

The first sustained, manned flight 'with power and control' of a heavier-than-air flying machine occurred on August 14th, 1901, in a field "back of" Fairfield, Connecticut, according to Howell's eyewitness description published on August 18, 1901. A second set of even more successful manned, powered flights took place later that morning, on August 14th, 1901, specifically described in witness affidavits as occurring at nearby Lordship Manor "on the sea beach," in Stratford, CT. These additional flights appear to be supported by several newspaper accounts in the fall of 1901[93].

After examining the evidence, Major William J. O'Dwyer, Whitehead researcher and international expert on Whitehead for 45 years, ultimately believed the "first flight" took place at a location called "Turney's Farm," about 2 miles from Whitehead's home and shop. This convenient site, in 1901, had several fairly isolated, raised, long pastoral fields accessible from what was then called "the highway." In addition, Turney's Farm was adjacent to Fairfield Beach, containing the only existing fields in Fairfield matching Howell's description and route, as well as the detail "out near Fairfield beach," found in the above-mentioned confirming 1910 article from the *Bridgeport Evening Farmer*.

An "upper" Turney field was located just a quarter mile west of the Ash Creek Bridge that still divides Bridgeport and Fairfield, where the "highway," the Post Road began; between what is now upper Riverside Drive and jogs along the Old Post Road, intersecting where today's Turney Road turns to the Fairfield Beach area. The upper field had an elevation of 26 feet above sea level, directly along the highway [94] [95], in the same directional position as the lower field, running east to west, with gently sloping fields and plenty of room for a half mile flight. There were divisions with apparent stone walls and lines trees at the perimeters, pictured in a 1934 aerial photo, below. Today, that area is called "Shoreham Village," a housing development bordered by the Post Road at the north; Shoreham Terrace Drive to the east; including Shoreham Village Drive at the center, where the former farm fields were located; with Turney Road to the west, and Turney Creek to the south. It is this area that seems to best fit all the criteria for the August 14, 1901 flight location.

The lower Turney field, more private, even in 1901, was on a then-high level plateau made of hard packed silt and sand, originally owned by the Penfields, and later, the Turney family. Near Long Island Sound, it was not far from present-day Fairfield Beach, close to Turney Road, alongside Ash Creek[96].

The "Turney Farm" location, indeed, is "back of Fairfield," as reported in the Howell article of August 18, 1901, near the then-existing highway, the Post Road[97], accessed by going along Fairfield Avenue to the Post Road, the Old Post Road and Turney Roads. Maj. William J. O'Dwyer, longtime Chairperson of the International Whitehead Research Committee, described why this location appeared most viable: "The route taken by Whitehead and his helpers to reach the flight site from Bridgeport (as described in Howell's article on August 18) … and the illustration drawn by Howell all combine to place the site at Turney's Farm, about a half mile north of the Long Island Sound … From all indications," said O'Dwyer, "Whitehead made his takeoff run diagonally across the farm, corner to corner, heading southwest into the prevailing wind. This gave him a potential flight course of at least a mile before reaching Fairfield Beach *[Author's note: Whitehead ended the flight in a field well before the beach]*. Howell's drawing depicts Whitehead aloft in Airplane "No. 21," a line of elms and chestnut trees atop a knoll in the distance, and two stone walls intersecting near the trees. Today, the walls are still there, easily found and identifiable as those that Howell sketched almost a century ago!'"[98]

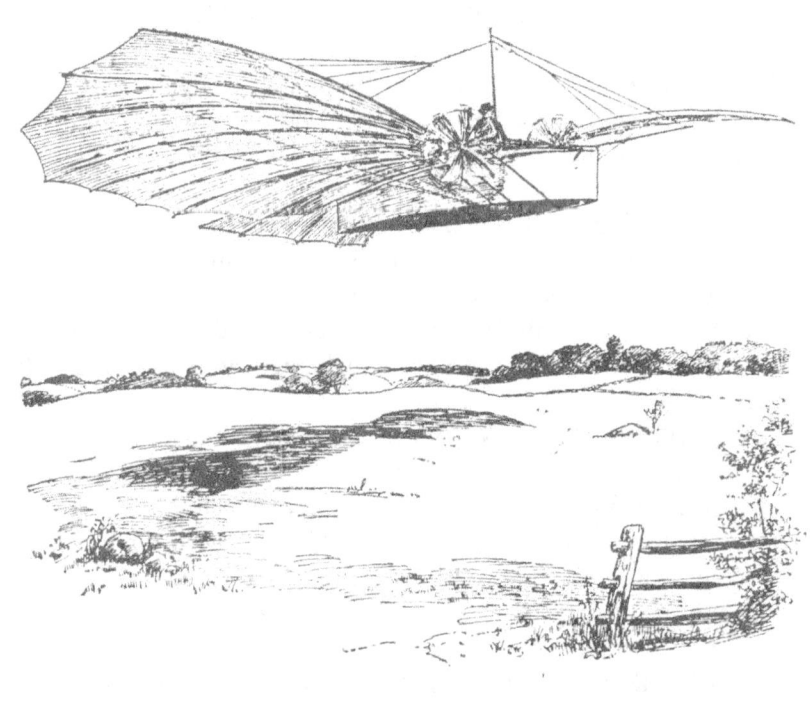

WHITEHEAD'S FLYING MACHINE SOARING ABOVE THE TREES

Figure 21: Herald sketch of "No. 21" in flight thought to be over Turney farm

Above: Sketch of first flight in "Flying" article by Dick Howell, *Bridgeport Sunday Herald*, Aug. 18, 1901, showing field where the flight occurred on Aug. 14, 1901.

Chapter 2: First Flights on August 14, 1901

Figure 22: Ash Creek bridge en route to August 14th flying grounds (1900)

The old Ash Creek Bridge[99], circa 1900, along the route from Bridgeport to Fairfield, traveled over by Whitehead on his way to his flying fields. This bridge is minutes from the Turney fields, along the Post Road and Turney Roads, pictured on the map, crossing over Ash Creek from Black Rock (western border of Bridgeport) to the upper Turney fields (Fairfield side), below.

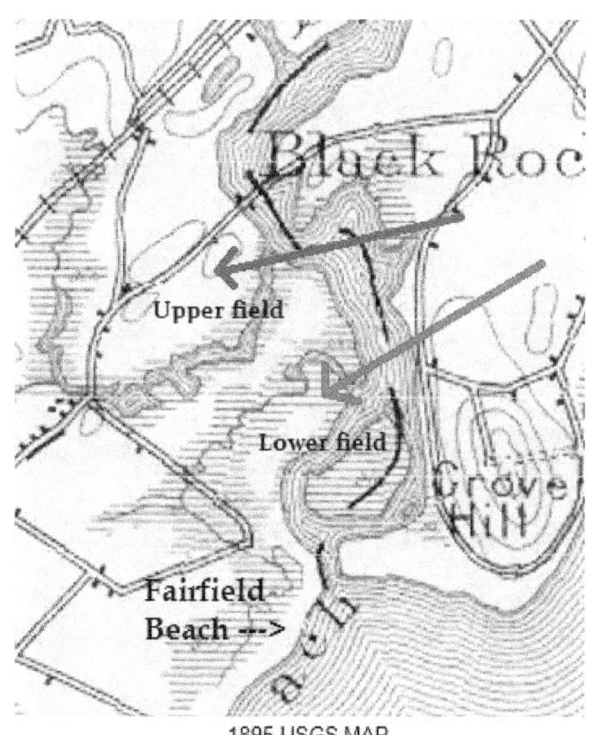

Figure 23: 1895 map showing elevations of Turney farm fields
Courtesy of CT State Library

1895 US Geological Survey map showing the Turney Farm, with "upper and lower" Turney fields accessible via the Post Road (along upper field) and the current Turney Road (lower field) at left, then known as "Creek Avenue." The fields were surrounded by "salt meadows," which would provide a soft landing, if needed.

© Susan Brinchman, 2015

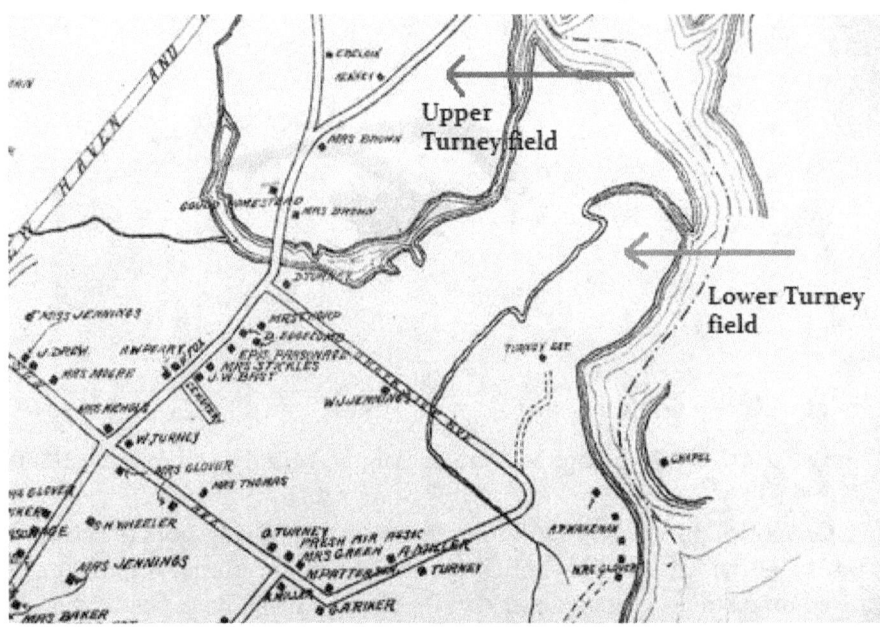

**Figure 24: Map of Fairfield, CT, shows Turney Fields flying site locations
Adapted from 1912 Fairfield Realty Co. map of Fairfield**[100]
Reproduced Courtesy of the Town of Fairfield, CT

Figure 25: Upper Turney field (1934)
Photo courtesy of CT State Library

**The upper Turney field(s) pictured in an aerial photo of 1934,
showing five fields with stands of trees and stone walls along them.**

Chapter 2: First Flights on August 14, 1901

This was "a large field" directly "along the highway" (the Post Road), could have been considered "back of Fairfield," meeting the criteria of the Howell description in his August 18, 1901 article, "Flying." This field existed in the early 1900's, shown on the 1912 map on preceding page. A flight in this field could easily have been 1/2 mile.

Figure 26: Upper Turney field most likely Aug. 14th, 1901 flight site
Photo courtesy of CT State Library

Close-up aerial photo of upper Turney field(s), 1934. This field could accommodate a flight up to ½ mile.

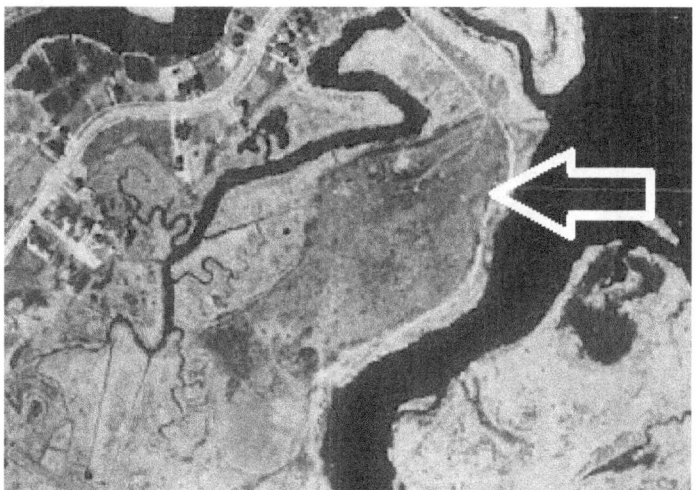

Figure 27: Lower Turney field, alternate flight site (1934)
Photo courtesy of CT State Library
1934 aerial photo of the Turney Estate "lower field." This field could have accommodated a flight between 1/8 and 1/3 mile.

© Susan Brinchman, 2015

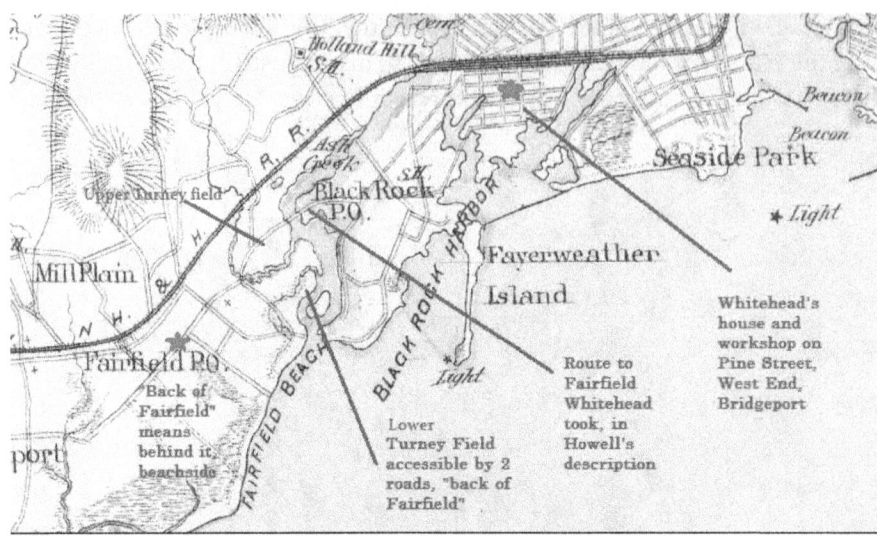

Figure 28: Map of Route on August 14, 1901
Map courtesy of CT State Library

This 1893 map (DH Hurd), shows the location of Whitehead's shop on Pine Street (red star at right) and the start of the center of the Town of Fairfield at left (red star). The map shows the Post Road that leads to the upper Turney fields and two roads that lead to the lower Turney field on its southeastern side (at left). These could both be considered, "at the rear or "back of " Fairfield, per Howell's article, and definitely both are "out near Fairfield Beach."

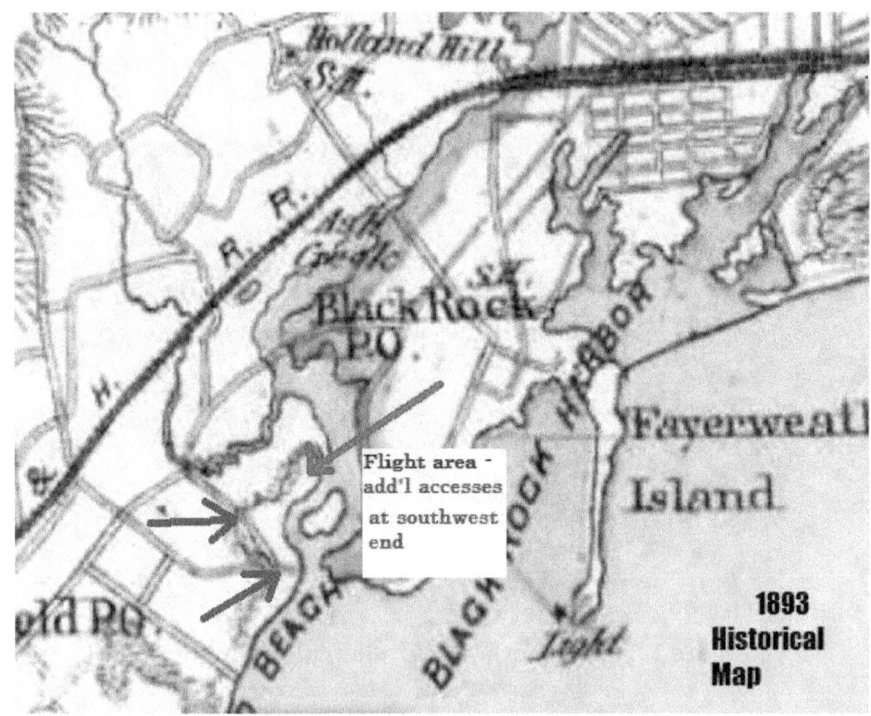

Figure 29: 1893 Map shows proximity to Fairfield Beach
Map courtesy of CT State Library

Chapter 2: First Flights on August 14, 1901

This 1893 map by DH Hurd shows longtime access to the lower field from both Turney and South Benson Roads, which existed in 1901. Note "Fairfield Beach" at lower left.

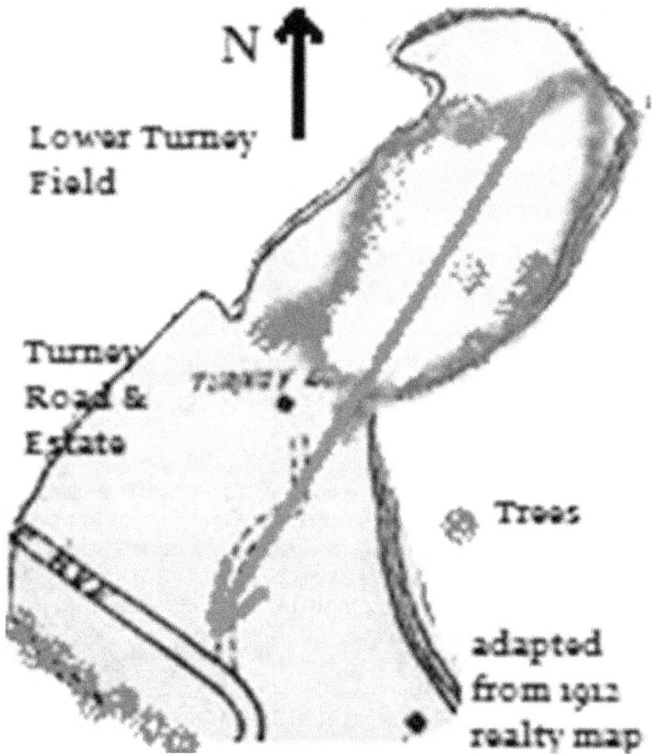

Figure 30: 1912 map shows closeup of lower Turney field with house and trees

"Lower" Turney field drawing adapted from 1912 map of Fairfield (Fairfield Realty Co.) and 1934 aerial maps.
Courtesy of Town of Fairfield, CT

To the right of the Turney house noted at top of drive, at "side of the inlet," was the ruins of the "First Mill"[101]. To make a full 1/2 mile flight here would have been difficult, but not impossible. A 1/8 to 1/4 mile flight would have been most likely, in this location.

The Route

Whitehead, his two helpers, and journalist Dick Howell began the after-midnight trek from Pine Street, in the West End of nearby Bridgeport, where Whitehead's shop was. According to Howell's account, "After reaching the Protestant Orphan asylum at the corner of Fairfield Avenue and Ellsworth street there is a clear stretch of macadam [crushed, broken rock, possibly including tar][102] road …The location selected to fly the machine was back of Fairfield along the highway where there is a large field and few trees to avoid in flying the air ship." [103]

The route from Whitehead's shop and home at 241 Pine Street to the upper Turney Farm field is 2.6 miles, traveling along the same surface streets. "The highway" in 1901 would have been considered the Old Post Road in Fairfield – also known as "the *Boston Post* Road," because it was *the highway* to Boston, long referred to as "*The King's Highway*" from colonial times – a vestige of which is still called such, to this day. At Ellsworth

Gustave Whitehead: "First in Flight"

Street and Fairfield Ave. marked the beginning of an open section of road, mentioned by Howell. The upper Turney Farm field runs right along the Old Post Road, or old highway. For more information on the location, with maps, visit www.gustavewhitehead.info.

The Flight Location

Howell described Whitehead's manned, powered flight of August 14, 1901, as *taking off from the slightly sloping grade of a field, flying 1/2 mile, and landing in the same field before the woods (trees) began*. This was a field, not a beach, as had been mistakenly reported in the CT media in recent years.

> **"I had soared through the air now for half a mile and not far ahead the long field ended with a piece of woods.** *When within a hundred yards of the woods I shut off the power* and then began to feel a little nervous about how the machine would act in settling to the ground, for so many flying machines have shown a tendency to fall either on the front or hind end and such a fall means broken bones for the operator. My machine began to settle evenly and I alighted on the *ground* with scarcely a jar. And not a thing was broken."[104]

Howell observed that Whitehead said, "I told you it would be a success," then fell silent for a time, appearing like a man who'd been through a severe ordeal. "He was exhausted and *he sat down on the green grass beside the fence* and looked away where the sun's first rays of crimson were shooting above the gray creeping fog that nestled on the bosom of Long Island Sound."

This tells us that they were near enough to the beach - which was about a half mile away - and in a slightly elevated position, so they could see the sun's rays breaking through the fog on the Sound. This is also confirmed by *the Farmer's* statement concerning proximity to Fairfield Beach.

The slightly sloping grade that the plane left from would indicate the northeast corner of the field ... landing in the southwestern corner.

Chapter 2: First Flights on August 14, 1901

> man and the two assistants stood still for a moment watching the air ship in amazement. Then they rushed don the slightly sloping grade after the air ship. She was flying now about fifty feet above the ground and made a noise very much like the "chung, chung, chung," of an elevator going down the shaft.

The flight was made in a one half mile long field ... "the field ended a short distance ahead."

> He had now soared through the air for fully half a mile and as the field ended a short distance ahead the aeronaut shut off the power and prepared to light. He appeared to be a little fearful that the machine would dip ahead or tip back when the power was shut off but there was no sign of any such move on the part of the big bird. She settled down from a height of about fifty feet in two minutes after the propellers stopped. And she lighted on the ground on her four wooden wheels so lightly that Whitehead was not jarred in the least.

One aspect of this night-time journey must be examined - on August 14, 1901, it has been pointed out that there was no moon[105], so one might wonder how might Whitehead have accomplished all this on such a dark night? The Washington Times of August 23, 1901 reported that Whitehead was asked why he didn't fly further than ½ mile on that date. Whitehead replied "… it was a dark night and I did not care to get outside of my bounds, as I was not familiar with the locality. I saw a good opportunity to descend in a lot, which I did, without the slightest accident." [106]

Gustave Whitehead: "First in Flight"

> "Since the feat of my half-mile flight was published I have been besieged by friends and have received many letters from inquisitive people all over the country. They asked me many questions concerning my machine and its flight. For instance, one man wanted to know why, if I traveled half a mile successfully, I did not continue. In reply I said that it was a dark night and I did not care to get outside of my bounds, as I was not familiar with the locality. I saw a good opportunity to descend in a lot, which I did, without the slightest accident. Besides, I know that if my air ship went all right for half a mile that it can go miles just as well.

From The Washington Times, "To Fly to New York." (Washington [D.C.]), 23 Aug. 1901, p. 2.

Gustave was resourceful and well accustomed to working at night with his experimentation. The stars would have been out, far brighter than in modern times, just as they are seen out in rural areas today, or the desert. Lanterns were available to him, as he often worked in his shop with these, according to Harworth's testimony[107]. He would have familiarized himself with the route and the flying field, as noted above in his statement to the Washington Times, following the roads using lanterns, just as some horse and wagons could have traveled at night in the area. Once on the open field, lanterns could have been set up to view the necessary flight path. As the actual manned flight was made just before dawn, there would have been some degree of light showing in the sky, to assist, in addition to manmade sources. In Howell's account, he mentions the light, which grew progressively stronger as the experiments proceeded.

> "*The light was not very strong and everything looked like a ghost...* She looked for all the world like a great white goose raising from the feeding ground in the early morning dawn ... The newspaperman kept well clear of the machine, partly *to better watch the operations* and partly not to get tangled up in the ropes and wings of the *giant white bat* .... The two men with the ropes were tumbling over the hummocks in the field, for *it was not clear enough yet to avoid such obstructions readily...*The bags of sand were taken out of the machine. *By this time, the light was good. Faint traces of the rising sun began to suggest themselves in the east.*"[108]

There is no sign that Herald readers were perplexed by the account, as both necessary travel and work at night were familiar to them.

The "lower field" at Turney Farm today is called the Ash Creek Preserve, a protected area that allows us to experience a bit of what Whitehead may have seen, in 1901. Below is the northeastern approach from Riverside Drive, which shows its elevation, above Ash Creek, an inlet from the nearby Long Island Sound. The photos below show the current approach to the highest end of the field, with the slight slope as one comes down the center of the field. All the trees and shrubs are less than a hundred years old. The open expanse in the middle of the field shows a view that Whitehead and the Herald reporter, Howell, may well have seen, the morning of the first flight.

Chapter 2: First Flights on August 14, 1901

Figure 31: Access to lower Turney field shows elevation

Figure 32: Lower Turney field slight slope shown
Note slight slope of "lower" Turney field from its highest elevation, 20 feet above sea level.

Figure 33: Flat area on lower Turney field – ½ size it was in 1901.
Above photos courtesy of Ed Collins (August 2014)

Note the wide open expanse of this field, with trees distant, ahead, as they were in Whitehead's day. There are a few trees in the middle, just as there were in the field described by Howell, that Gustave Whitehead avoided by flying around them.

Additional Locations Do Not Meet Criteria

Other locations where researchers felt Whitehead could have made the first flight of the day were fields located in the Holland Heights, or Gypsy Springs areas of current day Tunxis Hill, in Fairfield, about a mile northwest of his shop on Pine Street. These were some of his favored flying locations; however, the mention of Ellsworth and Fairfield Ave. en route, seem to rule that out, as do other elements of the *Bridgeport Sunday Herald* and *Bridgeport Evening Farmer* descriptions. Holland Heights and Gypsy Springs, are not located "out near Fairfield beach," and are miles away.

The reason why the flying site was left unnamed in the *Bridgeport Sunday Herald's* article may have derived from the frequent difficulties Whitehead experienced with finding places to fly away from crowds, sometimes conducting his experiments on private property, resulting in owners bringing the police to eject him. His plane was dangerous, with its large spinning propellers, as well as noisy and unusual, to say the least - so locating a place to conduct test flights while keeping both police and neighbors happy was always a challenge. Whitehead did not have the benefit of the isolation the Wrights sought and found at Kitty Hawk, North Carolina. It is probable Gustave requested that the name of the field be kept out of the newspaper. In an earlier interview with the *New York Sun*, in June 1901, he would not reveal the future site of his manned trials, in part, for these reasons.[109]

The Farmer's description of the location is clearer than that of the *Herald*'s. By adding the information that the flight took place "out near Fairfield beach," we are limited in choices for long fields in the area, with

Chapter 2: First Flights on August 14, 1901

sloping grounds, by the highway.

While it may never be known with certainty exactly where Whitehead made his powered flight in the early morning hours of August 14, 1901, we may rely on eyewitness Dick Howell's statement that the site was in a field near a highway "back of Fairfield" and "out by Fairfield beach," according to *the Farmer*. The upper Turney Farm field, along the Post Road, seems the most likely location, as it meets all the criteria.

Later Flights of August 14, 1901

Later that day, Whitehead was reported to have made at least several additional flights, according to several witnesses and a newspaper account derived from an interview in November of that year [110], Whitehead in a letter to the editor in the *American Inventor*, [111] and two eyewitnesses, Junius Harworth[112] [113] and Anton Pruckner[114]. The daytime location, according to Harworth, was at nearby Lordship Manor, an isolated point not far from Whitehead's shop, with open fields, a "sea beach" and a beachhead, jutting out into Long Island Sound, part of Stratford, CT.

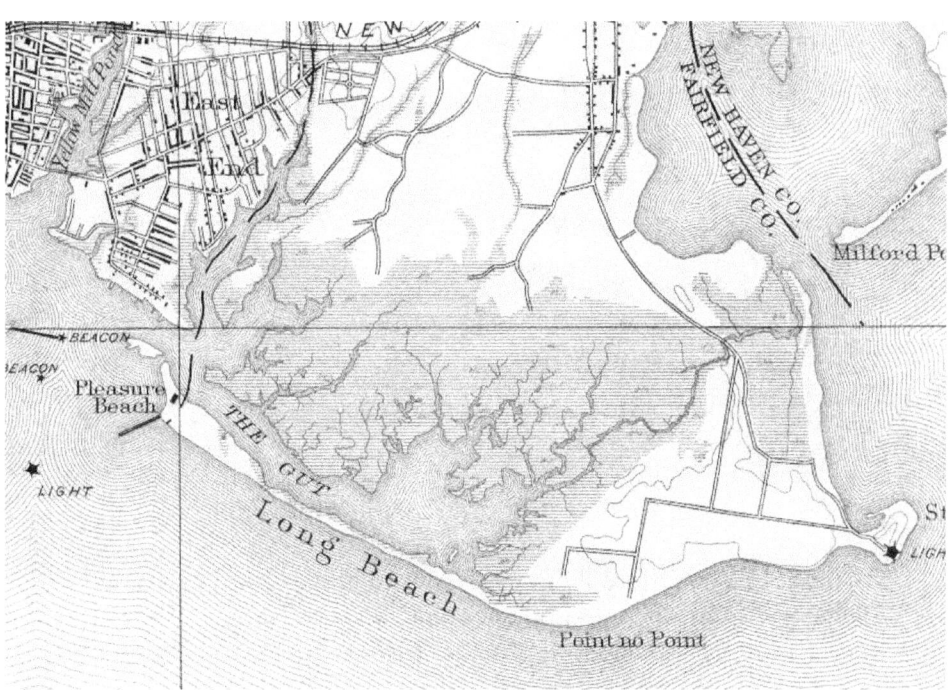

Figure 34: Stratford, CT beach areas
Courtesy of CT State Library

Junius Harworth told researcher Stella Randolph that the flights were concluded by late morning. While we do not have the specifics of why the change of location occurred, or even the exact location of the first flight of that day in Fairfield, we do know that Whitehead had to avoid hitting a tree in the field where the first flight was conducted, just before dawn. With daytime, landowners would also appear; Whitehead had a history of trouble with trespassing on private property and a desire to avoid police confrontations; the openness and isolation of Lordship, compared to Fairfield, would have provided the opportunity to continue his experiments uninterrupted, throughout the rest of the morning.

Gustave Whitehead: "First in Flight"

Junius Harworth reported, in a letter to Erik Hildes-Heim, dated Aug. 7, 1961:

> "G.W. [Gustave Whitehead] flights took place, early dawn, miles from the nearest habitation. Open exhaust noises were subject to prosecution, and a sesame for crowds to collect… G.W. wanted none of that, not to be arrested for operating an exhaust motor on a plane. He chose Lordship Manor, a vast open expanse save for shallow swells of seaweed, a fairly smooth road cutting through, no telephone poles or other obstructions; truly an ideal space for experimental flying."

Figure 35: Road to Stratford Point, circa 1900

The road to Stratford Point near the turn of the century (1900), showing the rural open spaces in Lordship.
Photo courtesy of Stratford Historical Society

According to Harworth, a horse-drawn truck took the plane to the Lordship location. "I recall distinctly seeing a large stack-truck, drawn by horse and may perhaps have belonged to Steves [Steeves] the trucker …" [Author's note: James Dickie, named by Howell as being present for the first flight in Fairfield, had a father who also owned a trucking business, said to transport Whitehead's planes at times.] "This truck had plane "No. 21" aboard and was about 6 AM, going to Lordship Manor. This trip was for the August 14th flights. At that time as well as now I was in the habit of arising early in the morning and pedaling many miles, this was on a Wednesday morning. I was not in school because it was during the vacation … The other flights, three, were all made before 11 AM, as I was home for dinner." [115]

Chapter 2: First Flights on August 14, 1901

Figure 36: Lordship open space and beaches, Stratford, CT (1934)
Photo courtesy of CT State Library

The open spaces of Lordship in the early years of the century, pictured above in 1934. An airport is now located near where Whitehead is said to have made numerous flights.

Sunrise was at 6:04 AM on August 14, 1901.[116] Dawn, the twilight period when, before sunup, the sun's rays barely begin to appear above the horizon, occurs about 30 minutes before sunrise[117]. Twilight was at 5:27 AM on August 14, 1901.[118] The first flight was said to have been completed just before dawn, perhaps about 5:00 or 5:15 AM, taking no more than ten minutes from start to finish (which may have included the preliminary help from the men holding the aircraft with ropes). According to the article, Whitehead relaxed and was interviewed, afterward, for at most, a half hour. There was time to drive the plane back the 2.3 miles back to his house on Pine Street, which could take perhaps a half hour even at 5 mph (and he could easily go 20 mph, according to the article in the Herald), and load it up, to be hauled 6.5 miles to Lordship Manor's beach in Stratford, leaving Pine Street between 6:30 and 8 AM. Harworth's estimate of 6 AM might be more of an estimate, not able to be exact. It is therefore quite possible that the young, energetic, enthusiastic Whitehead flew in both places on the same day, as reported by multiple sources, with time to do both. Then, he likely went home, leaving at noon, to finally get some sleep, exhausted but elated.

Harworth reported, in an affidavit (below), that one of the powered flights of that first day reached an altitude of about 200 feet and traveled about 1 1/2 miles, lasting four minutes (estimated distances and times). At least one newspaper account confirmed this in November 1901.[119] Pruckner reported a flight of 1/2 mile at 50 feet "in the air."

In a letter to the editor written to the *American Inventor*, published in April 1902, Whitehead said, "No 21 has made four trips, the longest one and a half miles, on August 14, 1901." [120]

Figure 37: Road to Lordship beaches, circa 1900
Photo courtesy of Stratford Historical Society

Open land looking south to Lordship, Stratford, CT in 1900, near where Whitehead reportedly made a second set of flights on August 14, 1901

Junius Harworth, young assistant to Whitehead, 33 years later signed an affidavit that he had been present for at least one of the flights on August 14, 1901. He was 12 years of age at the time of the flight.

" … On August fourteenth, Nineteen Hundred and One I was present and assisted on the occasion when Mr. Whitehead succeeded in flying his machine, propelled by a motor, to a height of two-hundred feet off the ground or sea beach at Lordship Manor, Connecticut. The distance flown was approximately one mile and a half and lasted to the best of my knowledge for four minutes.

The machine used was constructed entirely by Whitehead with my assistance, was known as a monoplane having a four cylinder two cycle motor located forward and using two propellers. Ignition was of the make and break type and used Columbia dry batteries. The gas tank was gravity feed and held two gallons of Petrol as then called. The body of the machine was constructed of pine, spruce and bamboo reinforced with Shelby steel tubing and piano wires. The wing coverings were of Japanese silk, varnished and fastened to the bamboo struts with white tape. These wings spread out behind the propellers and were supported with wires running to a central mast. The entire machine weighted approximately 800 pounds. Mr. Whitehead weighed around 165 pounds."[121] (Junius Harworth, August 21, 1934, then Assistant Foreman at the Packard Plant.[122])

In a letter to Whitehead researcher, Stella Randolph, Harworth wrote, "….8/14/1901… this date found us at Lordship Manor and made several flights including the 1 ½ mile flight. These flights proved to Whitehead that he could fly but to a limited distance, so he immediately set about to build a new motor …"[123]

Anton Pruckner, Sr., a machinist who'd attended engineering school in Hungary, worked with Whitehead from 1900 – 1901, and again after an absence of two years. Mr. Pruckner signed an affidavit in 1964, read to him in both his native-Hungarian and in English, that he'd witnessed a successful flight made on August 14th, 1901, when he was 18 1/2 years old.

Chapter 2: First Flights on August 14, 1901

"I did witness and was present at the time of the August 14, 1901 flight. The flight was 1/2 mile in distance overall and about 50 feet or so in the air. The plane circled a little to one side and landed easily with no damage to it or the engine or the occupant who was Gustave Whitehead."[124] (Anton Pruckner, 1964)

Figure 38: Anton Pruckner, circa 1901
Photo courtesy of Fairfield Museum

In a letter written on September 3, 1934, John Whitehead, Gustave's brother, named Anton Pruckner as an associate of and worker for Whitehead, "at the times those flights took place ..."[125] This verifies Pruckner's and Harworth's statements concerning the time period Pruckner was associated with Whitehead.

At 81 years of age, in a 1964 interview, Anton Pruckner indicated that he thought the flight of August 14, 1901 may have occurred at Seaside Park, rather than Lordship – though he admitted, at that time, it was hard to recall those specifics from 60 years ago[126]. Anton mentioned many successful Whitehead flights had been made at Seaside Park, out over the water – in the 1901 time frame, and he said, as early as 1900, with a single-prop earlier model he dubbed "No. 20" – these then stood out in his memory most, at that time. He described landing in the water with the powered craft, when necessary, and rowing back to land.[127] [128] Due to the sheer number of flights made by Gustave Whitehead during his constant experimentation, witnesses had a tendency to describe many different flight experiments. The passage of sixty years made it challenging to identify every location, especially when multiple locations were involved. Dates and the time of year were more readily recalled, paired with other events in their lives. Mr. Pruckner was not in good health, but was able to recall most of what was asked about his years with Gustave Whitehead, during the last three years of his own life. Pruckner could confirm the August 14th, 1901 flight and others in the 1901 time period, but could not corroborate the location being Lordship.

Anton Pruckner died in 1966, just ten days after his third formal Whitehead interview, that time, attended by Paul E. Garber, prominent Smithsonian National Air Museum founder and curator, at the time of the interview, Garber was the NAM's Asst. Director of the Education and Information Service. Pruckner was survived by two sons, including Anton A. Pruckner, a graduate of the Massachusetts Institute of Technology (MIT), Class of 1929[129], first trained in engineering by his father, during school vacations. [130]

Junius Harworth, younger than Pruckner by about six years, insistently asserted his own statements concerning the August 14, 1901 flights as having occurred in Lordship, through the end of his life, when unexpectedly, death arrived to claim him in October 1962, at the age of 73.

Interviewed by a Waterbury, CT reporter in 1964, while attending a ceremony held at Whitehead's grave, Anton Pruckner had this to say, "You are the ones who worry if he [Whitehead] ever flew – I *saw* him fly, so why should I be worried if any reproduction of his craft flies or not ... yes, I *know* he flew!"[131] [Note: Two decades later, several reproductions of the Whitehead "No. 21" aeroplane have successfully flown – one of these, for ½ mile [132].

© Susan Brinchman, 2015

Pruckner provided vital details of "No. 21," in the 1930's and 1960's, which only an assistant to the builder of the original could have known.]

Conclusive statements about the numerous powered flights made by Whitehead between 1899 and 1903, with their exact dates, times, and locations, have been eclipsed by the mists of time. Due to the passage of years before witnesses were interviewed, the most substantial evidence for the flights of August 14, 1901 derives primarily from the eyewitness statement for the flight at dawn on that date by the trusted local newspaper reporter, sports editor, and later chief editor, Richard "Dick" Howell, of the *Bridgeport Sunday Herald*, who described the flight in the next edition of his weekly newspaper, in a large feature article, four days after it occurred – the earliest date the newspaper could be issued. Preliminary flights, further flights of August 14th, and later flights on other occasions were mentioned in subsequent interviews with Whitehead and by numerous witnesses. The recent discovery of another local newspaper article from the *Bridgeport Evening Post* of August 26th, 1901, corroborates successful Whitehead flight experiments were being made with Whitehead's powered "No. 21" machine, by mid-August 1901.[133] What is abundantly clear is that a preponderance of the evidence, based on eyewitness testimonies and interviews, reveals that Whitehead was experimenting and succeeding with powered flight during a four year period (1899-1903), surpassing and predating the December 17, 1903 efforts of the Wrights.

MORE ON WITNESSES TO THE FIRST FLIGHT

The eyewitness article that appeared in the *Bridgeport Sunday Herald* on August 18, 1901 was confirmed by the editor of the Herald's January 30, 1937 magazine as an authentic account written by reporter Richard "Dick" Howell. In addition, *the Herald* explained, in that same edition, that its files were opened to the Library of Congress, to help verify the account. On February 17, 1935, the Herald republished portions of the 1901 news story.[134] On several other dates, November 17, 1901, January 26, 1902, and May 31, 1903, *the Herald* referred to its coverage of this important flight. There is no reason not to trust *the Herald's* account to be authentic, and accurate in its details.

Dick Howell named two witnesses to the first of a series of flights of that day, Andrew Cellie and James Dickie. Cellie could not be firmly identified or located *three decades* later when the Whitehead research began. Mr. Suelli (whose name was pronounced "Sully"), Whitehead's friend and frequent helper, who later was said to live next door to him on Ridgely Avenue in Holland Heights' housing development called "Lenox Park," was thought to likely be the "Cellie" (aka "Sully") of the newspaper article. However, Mr. Suelli's first name was not Andrew, but Frederick, on the 1910 Census, and he died before he could be interviewed by researchers.

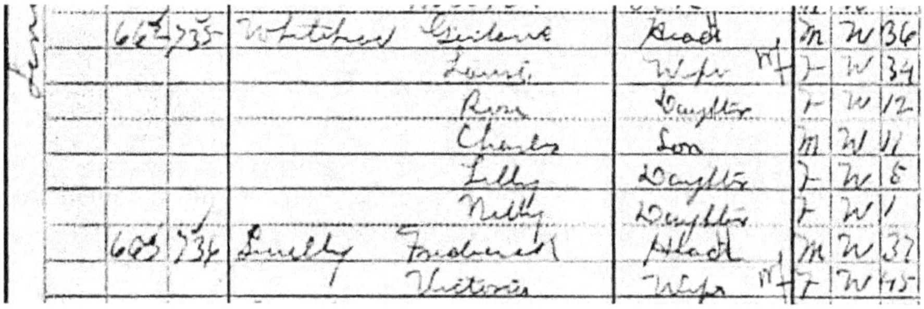

662	235	Whitehead Gustave	Head	M	W	36
		Louise	Wife M1	F	W	34
		Rose	Daughter	F	W	12
		Charles	Son	M	W	11
		Lilly	Daughter	F	W	8
		Nelly	Daughter	F	W	1
663	234	Suelly Frederick	Head	M	W	37
		Victoria	Wife M1	F	W	45

Figure 39: 1910 US Census showing Whitehead family living next to Frederick Suelly

Above, the 1910 Census shows Whitehead living at Lenox Park, transcribed incorrectly as "Whitaker." According to the Census, his next door neighbor *was* named *Frederick* Suelly, a 37 year old Swiss machinist who then worked in a shop. It is unknown if Frederick was ever known as "Andrew," and if he knew Whitehead in 1901. He had entered the country in 1893, so it is possible.

People in the West End neighborhood in Bridgeport, immigrants who were eager to live in houses rather than apartments, saved their modest earnings for this opportunity. They often moved to the very close Holland Heights (now, Tunxis Hill) area of Fairfield, where modest single-family homes were being built. It was within walking distance of the West End. A sense of community and ethnic ties kept this community together. It is possible that "Cellie," the witness, was Suelli, as many of Whitehead's friends were still in association with him seven years later, some living in the new neighborhood. O'Dwyer was told that the neighbors believed Mr. Suelli "always said" he was present during that flight. But with all the flights Whitehead made, and the evidence above, it is most likely this was not the right candidate, even with a similar sounding last name and having helped Whitehead, likely just in later years.

A better alternative to first flight witness Suelli for "Cellie" is Andy Celley, employed at the nearby W. & H. Manufacturing Company, the same factory where Whitehead worked for a time, who lived at 308 Wordin Ave., three blocks away from Whitehead's Pine Street shop, during 1901. He was listed under Alexander Celley's address, in the 1901 Bridgeport City Directory:

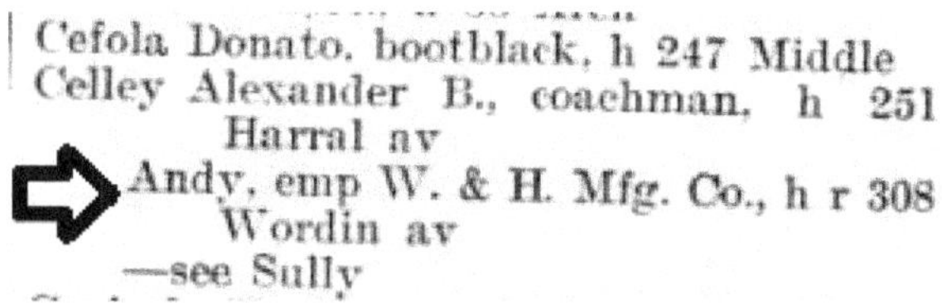
Cefola Donato, bootblack, h 247 Middle
Celley Alexander B., coachman, h 251
Harral av
Andy, emp W. & H. Mfg. Co., h r 308
Wordin av
—see Sully

Figure 40: Bridgeport Directory shows Andy Celley living nearby

Note how the Bridgeport Directory confirms that Celley was close enough to "Sully" to refer to that spelling as well

In 1900, there was also an Andrew Celey, of Spruce Street in the West End of Bridgeport, living 2 blocks from Whitehead (who may be one and the same as the 1901 Andy Celley). Names often were misspelled, or changed, from year to year, in the old records. Andy Celley moved to Leechburg, Pennsylvania the following year, according to the 1902 business directory, and has not been traced further, though Major O'Dwyer did make inquiries of the Leechburg Public Library in December 1982. The librarians wrote him back, indicating they have "gone through every avenue of approach to find the name in question but to no avail," including "the borough, Armstrong County Courthouse, and many other avenues."[135] It is certainly possible that he is the third witness of the first flight, mentioned in the *Bridgeport Sunday Herald* article. Since his name was pronounced similarly to "Sully" as was Suelli's name, and Suelli was also affiliated with Whitehead and his flights, it is easy to see why the first researcher, Randolph, in the 1930's, could not firmly identify nor locate the "Andy Cellie" with certainty, nor could future researchers. Interestingly, "Andrew Cellie" was also referred to as a minor investor in the project several months before the sustained flight of August 14, in a *New York Sun* article about Whitehead's plans to fly, published June 9, 1901, on p. 2, repeated in several other newspapers for the next few weeks [136]. The *New York Sun* was a prominent newspaper in the region of Bridgeport, CT, only an hour from New York City by train. Thus, we may be certain that an eyewitness with a name phonetically similar to "Andy Cellie" existed in 1901, despite the fact that he could not be located in 1930's. Cellie was involved and present during the development of the "No. 21" plane and its flight, having been mentioned twice in this capacity, in several different major regional newspapers. The spelling of names used by individuals, especially those of immigrants who Americanized their names, and in records of the times which varied from place to place, and year to year, as is evident in genealogical research, confounded later research efforts.

Gustave Whitehead: "First in Flight"

Whether "Cellie" was Celley or Suelli, *there was such a person in 1901 closely involved with Whitehead's inventions*, the third witness named in Howell's eyewitness account.

> About a year ago Mr. Whitehead came to Bridgeport, his interest and his faith in flying machines in no wise abated. He is a marine engineer by trade but as building flying machines is his serious occupation in life he got employment as a night watchman in a steel manufactory near his home here so that he might have some part of the light of each day in which to work on the problem in which his whole heart is enlisted.
>
> Having interested Andrew Cellie and Daniel Varovi in the subject they supplied him with the small amount of money he required and last November he began work on the present machine which was completed several weeks ago and is now undergoing repairs made necessary by an accident which happened at the machine's trial flight on May 2 last. These repairs are nearly completed and at

Figure 41: NY Sun article names Andrew Cellie and Daniel Varovi as investors
NY Sun, "Improved Flying Machine," June 9, 1901, p. 2

16 year old James Dickie,[137] one of Whitehead's occasional teenaged helpers in 1900 and 1901 (15 and 16 in those years, respectively), was named by Howell, in the August 18th article, "Flying," as both "a partner" and a witness to the August 14, 1901 flight. When interviewed in 1937 by the first Whitehead researcher, Stella Randolph, after being pursued *for several years* to provide testimony, Dickie finally produced a confused[138] and negative statement in which he denied that Whitehead had flown or could have flown and that he did not witness the flight of August 14, 1901. Randolph asserted that during her interview with Mr. Dickie, he exhibited "bitterness in his heart" about Whitehead, an attitude that she further described as "surly and belligerent," though at the time she did not understand the reason.[139] Randolph indicated in a letter to Junius Harworth in 1937, that on one earlier occasion when she spoke to him during the summer of 1936, Mr. Dickie appeared "surly" and "perhaps," as if he had been "drinking."[140] *Interestingly, this was the first time on record that Dickie ever objected to being named as a witness to the world's first flight by the most popular local newspaper, given the passage of thirty six years.* Junius Harworth, a close associate of Whitehead for 14 years, knew Dickie. He described him as "slightly scurrilous," having to be reminded by Whitehead not to bother other workers with his stories [when helping out]. Harworth later said Dickie often showed resentment, he felt that Dickie's statements in the affidavit reflected this, being "quite pronounced to date" [in later years].[141]

Four to five months before the August flights of 1901, a teenaged James Dickie was (later) identified in a photo, standing next to Gustave Whitehead (second from left), in a group which included a renowned inventor closely associated with Hiram Maxim - presidential advisor and diplomat, Edward M. House (1st on left), according to K. I. Ghormley. Ghormley was an attorney briefly hired in 1948 by C. D. Hudson, Stella Randolph's

Chapter 2: First Flights on August 14, 1901

first publisher, to investigate living witnesses to Whitehead's early flights. Ghormley said this of Dickie: "Mr. Ford [friend of Col. Ernest La Rue Jones, aviation historian]… assisted me in locating James Dickie, who was a close associate of Gustave Whitehead during this period in question. He stands third from the left in the picture opposite page 16 of "Lost Flights [of Gustave Whitehead]," and second from the left in the picture opposite page 44." [142] [*both, pictured below*]

**Figure 42: Named eyewitness James Dickie stands by "No. 21" in spring, 1901.
Left to right: Edward M. House, Gustave Whitehead, James Dickie (age 16),
with unknown fourth man, whose hand rests on wing.**
Stanley Yale Beach, photographer
Photo courtesy of Fairfield Museum, O'Dwyer archives

**Figure 43: James Dickie to Whitehead's left
James Dickie standing next to Gustave Whitehead, circa March 1901,
identified by Attorney K. I. Ghormley, 1948**
Photo courtesy of Fairfield Museum, O'Dwyer archives

© Susan Brinchman, 2015

Gustave Whitehead: "First in Flight"

Figure 44: Eyewitness Dickie in photo shoot sits by "No. 21"
Dickie is second from left.
Photos courtesy of Fairfield Museum, O'Dwyer archives

Figure 45: James Dickie spring, 1901
James Dickie seated second from left, next to Edward Mandel House, under wing tip of Whitehead's aeroplane "No. 21" with Whitehead (at right, with daughter Rose on his lap), **circa March/April 1901**
Stanley Yale Beach, photographer
Photos courtesy of Fairfield Museum, O'Dwyer archives

Figure 46: Named eyewitness James Dickie closeup, 1901.

James Dickie in cutout from photo above. Dickie, in later life, held a financial grudge against Whitehead, which he apparently addressed in 1937 and on several other occasions, by claiming that Whitehead's plane never left the ground. [143]

© Susan Brinchman, 2015

Chapter 2: First Flights on August 14, 1901

In a 1948 statement to Attorney Ghormley, made at the age of 64, Dickie said he was 16 or 17 years old when he worked with Whitehead for several years making pistons and "helping otherwise." He admitted to having "put up money for material, etc., but would not state how much." Dickie told Ghormley that Whitehead's plane "got off the ground when attached to the end of a 30 foot pole, travelling around in a circle," powered by "a steam boiler set up near the pole, conveyed to the plane in a flexible hose ... on the circus lot near Pine Street." Dickie gave a description contrary to that of others concerning the final material used for wing coverings and use of the propellers, opining that the plane was too flimsy to fly. Peculiarly, in his earlier (1937) affidavit, Dickie did not even describe the same aircraft or engine that Whitehead used for the actual flight, according to researchers O'Dwyer and Randolph. [144]

The plane, "No. 21," that he is pictured beside, was described by Dickie as it appeared several months before in a photo shoot by Stanley Yale Beach, Aviation Editor, *Scientific American*. In early trials, Whitehead used canvas, for the latter trials, silk. He was known to work on improving his engines right up to the point of flight. Dickie, from a large Irish/Scottish family in the locale, was listed as a "teamster" in the 1900 census, a chauffeur in 1910, and later, a well-known gravel contractor.

In the early 1960's, Dickie was interviewed again, this time by phone, by Major William J. O'Dwyer, a local Whitehead researcher who, it turned out, had been acquainted with him all his life. Dickie then admitted to O'Dwyer that he was upset because he felt Whitehead had never paid him money he owed him, and he did not wish to credit him for anything.[145] Whitehead had little funding and relied upon sponsors, small investors, and volunteers. Dickie was, indeed, admittedly an investor when interviewed by Ghormley in 1948, and named as "a partner," albeit a very young one, in the "first flight" project by Howell, the Herald reporter, in 1901.

"...Andrew Cellie, and James Dickie, his two partners in the flying machine ..."[146]

John Whitehead also named James Dickie as a young investor, in a letter to Stella Randolph, written on September 3, 1934:

"Two others, and this are the only ones I know of that helped my Brother before I came to Bridgeport was a young fellow by [the] name of Dicky [Dickie], about 18 years old at that time, who's [whose] father had a trucking business at that time. It was in Bridgeport out in Black Rock, at the first side street to right after you go through the Railroad bridge tunnel on Fairfield Avenue…The other man was Mr. Miller… a German American Machinist and Diemaker…… Mr. Miller [who lived nearby at Mountain Grove Cemetery] was also associated with Mr. Linde or rather was mechanical foreman at the time of [their] association."[147]

John Whitehead further explained, in a letter written November 5, 1934, that his brother Gustave often offered shares to those assisting him.

"As to my knowledge in order to get [funds] to work on his [all-consuming] desire to work on the problem of Aerial Navigation, he signed away many shares on any proceeds therefrom, I know of at least three cases, I myself had a pro rata share contract / long torn up for one particular machine."[148]

This is *not* the only case we know of where a person associated with Whitehead grew bitter at not being paid, as investors often demanded a quick return on their investment - lack of funding was a permanent condition that continued to plague Whitehead. It caused many problems for Whitehead and the loss of Dickie's support was but one example - however it is the only example we know of regarding an associate from the neighborhood who reacted this harshly. Money was scarce where Whitehead lived, but in general, his neighbors and coworkers were the most supportive people in his life, outside of his family. His troubles usually came from those who were wealthier and who made unreasonable demands, without providing enough funding to accomplish the results they desired.

For 35 years, the *Bridgeport Sunday Herald* eyewitness report naming the two witnesses, Cellie and Dickie, went unchallenged by either man, according to the public record. James Dickie lived in the area and must have known of the article - in fact, he had to have been contacted by many people who read of the astonishing flight that the newspaper reported he invested in and helped with. There is absolutely no indication that Dickie denied the August 14th, 1901 flight he was described as present for, published in the most popular newspaper in his immediate neighborhood and throughout Southern Connecticut in those early years, or that he demanded a retraction. Neither does this anomaly seem to have been covered in the 1930's nor 1948 interviews. Cellie [may have actually have been spelled Celley], as aforementioned, moved from the area shortly afterward, and was not heard from again, nor could his new residence be located by past or present researchers. We do, however, know that "Cellie" did exist, mentioned to his own community in their favorite newspaper, a witness to the successful experimental flight of Gustave Whitehead.

The Whitehead flights came to be documented beyond any other "first flights" laid claim to, including those at Kitty Hawk, despite the interference of "time" passing, as we shall see.

NEWLY UNEARTHED LOCAL ARTICLES CONFIRM FIRST FLIGHTS

Articles by several competing Bridgeport newspapers confirming Whitehead's flights of August 1901, have been newly discovered by this author and assistant researchers, during the writing of this manuscript. These are very significant because, while the local editors were not all invited to be eyewitnesses to Whitehead's sustained flights of August 14, 1901, their independently written local articles verify Whitehead's flights were credible to their staff and readers. This is a fact long denied by current-day, often Smithsonian-based, detractors. Whitehead's contemporaries said that *many* local newspapers carried articles about him, but these have been difficult to locate due to incomplete local newspaper archives and difficult-to-search microfiche files. With the advent of digitized newspapers, more is able to be located each year, which essentially substantiates all that the witnesses and the *Bridgeport Herald* Sports Editor, Dick Howell, testified to. There should be many more articles to find, with additional searches in local archives.

The most stunning local article to be uncovered, published by the *Bridgeport Evening Farmer* in 1910, newly discovered on April 2, 2015 as a recent addition to the *Library of Congress' Chronicling America* digitalized newspapers collection in the course of research for this book, presents a revealing history of Gustave Whitehead's experimentation with flying machines. In a paragraph devoted to proving Whitehead was a gifted builder of lightweight engines, *the reporter specifically credits Whitehead with an aeroplane (thus, powered) flight in 1901, for a distance of more than the length of two football fields (1/ 8th of a mile, or 660 feet).* Its content also provides more clues to the exact flight location, long sought by researchers, saying *that the flight occurred at an area near Fairfield Beach*. Therefore, the article undeniably refers to the successful "first powered flight" experiment during the early morning of August 14th, 1901, witnessed by Dick Howell, James Dickie, and Andy Celley. While *the Farmer* article does not credit Whitehead with a one-half mile flight (a recollection which likely is a detail in error, as nearly ten years had passed), the 1/8 of a mile distance it does mention, even if correct, *is still 660 feet, which is 5.5 times longer than the so-called "first flight" of 120 feet credited to Orville Wright 2 1/3 years later*, in 1903.

Chapter 2: First Flights on August 14, 1901

> Gus Whitehead, as his friends best know him, is one of the most expert engine builders in the world. He has succeeded in turning out engines whose efficiency in proportion to their weight is marvelous. Years ago he was building engines for dirigible balloons. Back in 1901 he made a flight in an airship of the aeroplane type, out near Fairfield beach, when he soared through the air for one-eighth of a mile and astounded the few who were privileged to witness the unheralded trial.

Figure 47: *Bridgeport Evening Farmer* **confirms August 14th flight near Fairfield Beach**
Bridgeport Evening Farmer, June 20, 1910

(*transcript*)

"Gus Whitehead, as his friends best know him, is one of the most expert engine builders in the world. He has succeeded in turning out engines whose efficiency in proportion to their weight is marvelous. Years ago he was building engines for dirigible balloons. *Back in 1901 he made a flight in an airship of the aeroplane type, out near Fairfield beach, when he soared through the air for one-eighth of a mile and astounded the few who were privileged to witness the unheralded trial.*" (*Bridgeport Evening Farmer*, June 20, 1910)[149]

(*end of transcript*)

The same newspaper, *Bridgeport Evening Farmer*, on March 12, 1912, *credited Gustave Whitehead with the invention of an airship which gained him national standing* – the flying machine referred to is without any doubt, "No. 21," the first airplane to successfully make a powered flight, recently shown to have been covered in over a hundred national and international newspapers at the time, making Whitehead instantly famous in 1901. The reporter further describes Whitehead as *well known to the citizens of the area.*

"The defendant [Gustave Whitehead] is well known throughout this section and attained national reputation by inventing an airship a few years ago."[150]

In addition, on August 26th, 1901, an article entitled "*Perfecting His Machine: Gustave Whitehead Improving Flying Apparatus – Takes Out Two More Patents. To Exhibit at Atlantic City for Next Two Months at $150 a Week*" appeared in the *Bridgeport Evening Post*, on page 1.

port Evening

BRIDGEPORT EVENING POST
PAGE 1

NEWS BY ASSOCIATED PRESS DIRECT TO THIS OFFICE OVER SPECIAL WIRE.

BRIDGEPORT, CONN., MONDAY, AUGUST 26, 1901.

Masthead for *Bridgeport Evening Post* article of Aug. 26, 1901
"*Perfecting His Machine*"

PERFECTING HIS MACHINE

Gustave Whitehead Improving Flying Apparatus—Takes Out Two More Patents.

To Exhibit at Atlantic City for Next Two Months at $150 a Week.

Chamberlain & Newman, patent attorneys have in hand the task of securing two more patents which are desired by Gustave Whitehead, of this city to be utilized in perfecting his latest flying machine. The success thus far attained by the inventor shows that perseverence wins invariably, despite the obstacles confronting the student.

Inventor Whitehead has been 20 years working on air-machines. One of his friends declared this morning that Mr. Whitehead when he came to this city a few years ago had to have his car fare advanced by co-workers that he could reach here and accept a position with the Wilmot & Hobbs Co.

Mr. Whitehead had made thousands of dollars but it was all expended on his invention. He left this city a few days ago to exhibit his flying machine at Atlantic City during the next six months for which he is to receive $150 per week.

Mr. Whitehead was one of the first inventors to risk operating an air-machine and experimented with a soaring machine which he sailed from the mountains to the level about Johnstown, Pa., for a number of years.

He also built an air-machine which he sailed about at the Pittsburgh fair a dozen years ago and finally commenced work on his present machine which he tested a few weeks ago in the old trotting park in the West End of the city and which worked successfuly. The inventor now has all the financial backing he needs and from present indications his flying-machine promises to attract world-wide attention.

Figure 48: *Bridgeport Post* **article "Perfecting His Machine" (Aug. 26, 1901)**
(Courtesy of the Bridgeport Public Library, Bridgeport, CT)

Chapter 2: First Flights on August 14, 1901

(transcript)

"PERFECTING HIS MACHINE
Gustave Whitehead Improving
Flying Apparatus –Takes Out
Two More Patents.
To Exhibit at Atlantic City for
Next Two Months at $150 a
Week.
(August 26, 1901, Bridgeport Evening Post)

Chamberlain & Newman, patent attorneys have in hand the task of securing two more patents which are desired by Gustave Whitehead, of this city to be utilized in perfecting his latest flying machine. The success thus far attained by the inventor shows that perseverance wins invariably, despite the obstacles confronting the student.

Inventor Whitehead has been 20 years working on air-machines. One of his friends declared this morning that Mr. Whitehead when he came to this city a few years ago had to have his car fare advanced by co-workers that he could reach here and accept a position with the Wilmot & Hobbs Co.

Mr. Whitehead had made thousands of dollars but it was all expended on his invention. He left this city a few days ago to exhibit his flying machine at Atlantic City during the next six months for which he is to receive $150 per week.

Mr. Whitehead was one of the first inventors to risk operating an air machine and experimented with a soaring machine which he sailed from the mountains to the level about Johnstown, Pa. for a number of years.

He also built an air-machine which he sailed about at the Pittsburgh fair a dozen years ago and finally commenced to work on his present machine *which he tested a few weeks ago in the old trotting park in the West End of the city and which worked successfully.* The inventor now has all the financial backing he needs and from present indications his flying-machine promises to attract world-wide attention."

(end of transcript)

This significant article, recently unearthed from local archives by C. Lautier, a member of the *Whitehead Research and Advocacy Committee,* is quite important for a multitude of reasons. First, because it confirms that more than one local newspaper credited Gustave Whitehead with success in August 1901; that his "No. 21" powered airplane *did* make successful flight experiments several weeks earlier – and more than once during the month. Past critics had pointed out that *local* competitive newspapers allegedly did not carry pre-Wright, Whitehead flight stories but this was quite the contrary, as the *Bridgeport Evening Post* article illustrates. The latter even names a new, specific location in which some recent, successful experimentation occurred - "the old trotting park" in the West End of the city of Bridgeport, an area of level ground a few blocks from Whitehead's shop on Pine Street, near State Street and Fairfield Avenue, used for light carriage races in the mid-19th century, owned by P.T. Barnum as part of his circus' winter quarters in the early 1900's. One of many convenient sites for Whitehead's flight experiments, the land was open, flat, and was bordered on three sides by the waters of Burr Creek in 1901.[151] Interestingly, the site was not far from the Fairfield border, on the western side of Bridgeport, but would not be considered Fairfield nor close to Fairfield Beach, so it is describing yet another set of summer trials. Today, the area is industrial, located between Fairfield Avenue, Spruce, Pine, and Wordin streets, with the waters filled in.[152]

Gustave Whitehead: "First in Flight"

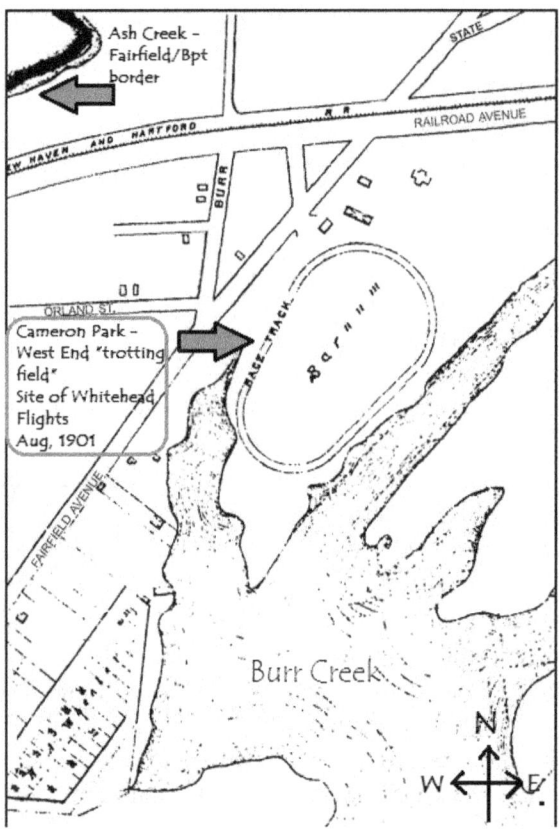

Figure 49: W. W. Cameron Trotting Park
– The "old trotting park" racetrack, then owned by PT Barnum,
**was a few blocks from Whitehead's shop and home; the site of successful testing of
Gustave Whitehead's "No. 21" flying machine, in the first half of August 1901.** [153]
*Atlas of the City and Town of Bridgeport, Conn.; Published by G. M. Hopkins, 1888.
Historical Collections Department, Bridgeport Public Library, adapted by Mike Roer. Map used with permission,
courtesy of Mike Roer*[154] *and the Bridgeport Public Library*

Bordered by water, a "softer" landing could be made with the boat-like aeroplane, built for that very occasion. *The Post* reveals very specific information researchers didn't have before, very importantly confirming some of the Whitehead flights witnesses had described in the area of the Barnum and Bailey winter quarters and street flights in the immediate area. Since Whitehead reportedly made frequent flights when testing his machine, in a variety of convenient locations close by, this does not rule out the sustained flight also made in "a field back of Fairfield" on August 14th, as reported in the *Bridgeport Sunday Herald* by Richard Howell, eyewitness, and later, in the *Bridgeport Evening Farmer* of 1910. The trotting park, only two blocks from Whitehead's home and shop, could not be the site reported by Howell, as it does not fit in with either the route he described, which continued far past Ellsworth Street on Fairfield Avenue, or the details of the flying field along a highway (main road), which bordered upon a woods, starting with a row of trees one half mile away from the starting point, with a slightly sloping hill and clump of trees in the middle. In fact, this newly discovered *Post* article adds an additional location within days of that flight, from a second primary source, another well read, popular local newspaper. One more specific level, open area is added to the abundant list of Whitehead flying grounds to consider for this time period. It is confirmation of the many successful powered flight experiments leading up to his sustained flights of August 14, reported by numerous sources for that summer of 1901, starting in June.

Chapter 2: First Flights on August 14, 1901

The article shows that Whitehead had thought about patents and was working on obtaining them as early as Aug. 26, 1901, as it named the attorneys he was using. Critics have claimed Whitehead did not know enough to apply for patents, but this evidence shows he *was* working on these, early on. The article reads "patent attorneys have in hand the task of securing *two more patents which are desired* by Gustave Whitehead, of this city to be utilized in perfecting his latest flying machine." Whitehead ultimately may not have sustained adequate funds to see these patent applications to completion, as there have been none from this period found in the record. However, preparing for patents as early as August 1901 would have caused a change in Whitehead's outgoing behavior earlier in 1901 and later, to begin protection of his inventions. He would have avoided giving specific details to newspapers, perhaps avoiding sharing photos of the plane in flight with newspapermen, or performing for crowds, when possible, as did the Wrights in both cases, advised by attorneys to keep their secrets until fully protected.

Whitehead had very bad luck with financiers; they never lasted long enough to give him the large amount of capital needed, which his modest jobs could not provide.

The *Bridgeport Evening Post* article, "PERFECTING HIS MACHINE" explains this means "perfecting his latest flying machine." It refers to Gustave Whitehead's multiple consecutive inventions and desire, consistent with what the general public desired, to be able to fly about "at will" and carry passengers commercially, to New York City, and beyond. Helpers Harworth and Pruckner said that Whitehead no sooner finished flying one aeroplane than he was working on improving it, often reusing the parts.

As previously indicated, Whitehead's trip to Atlantic City was known of and investigated by several prior researchers, including Major O'Dwyer, but this article reveals he was initially set to go for several months, and be paid to exhibit his plane there, a new disclosure. There is a discrepancy in the article concerning the length of time Whitehead would remain in Atlantic City. Evidence gathered previously indicates the two month period indicated in the subtitle is most accurate; whereas a six month period mentioned in the body of the article has to be an error on the part of the reporter. Whitehead's aeroplane was being examined at Atlantic City during the weekend of September 21st, by an emissary for his competitor, Smithsonian's director, Samuel Pierpont Langley; then he was back in Bridgeport, signing an agreement with a new sponsor, Mr. Herman Linde on October 1st.

Details about Whitehead's financial difficulties during the trip from Pittsburgh, said to have first started on bicycles, are revealed by the Post article. He may have borrowed money from Darvarich, the friend he was traveling with, in order to continue on by train, or from multiple coworkers in Pittsburgh.

A prior "soaring" flight with a glider is described. This took place from a high mountain, reported in earlier articles concerning his experimentation in 1897 and 1898, while in Baltimore and New York.

This local article states Whitehead has found financial backing, one of the earliest to report this, following the press coverage of the previous weeks.

Lastly, the journalist is quite correct in stating Gustave's flying machine will bring worldwide attention – it has done so for the past 113 years, with no end in sight.

While making a few minor errors related to Whitehead's general history – notably that "a dozen years ago" (1889), he was not in Pittsburgh and had not yet entered the USA until 1893, according to the US Census of 1900. Whitehead had been in Bridgeport for about a year at the time of the writing of the article, rather than several.

One of the flight witnesses, a "regular" Whitehead assistant, Junius Harworth, years later stated that the *Bridgeport Post* had carried many articles about Whitehead. However, the early *Post* articles are not readily accessible – these are only available on microfiche, in a limited fashion. This newly surfaced article proves there is much more "gold" still waiting to be found, concerning the flights of Gustave Whitehead.

Fittingly, today, a few blocks away from the "trotting field" flight experiments location, a "Gustave Whitehead Memorial Fountain," near the busy intersection of Commerce Drive and State Street Extension, honors Whitehead and his successful street flights, which occurred in Bridgeport in the summer of 1901.

Gustave Whitehead: "First in Flight"

Figure 50: Gustave Whitehead memorial fountain, Bridgeport, Connecticut (2014): "No. 21"
(Photo by Ed Collins, used with permission.)

Gustave Whitehead "No. 21" sculpture and fountain is located near his home, first and second shops, and the "old trotting park" where Whitehead practiced flying.

Figure 51: Gustave Whitehead memorial fountain, Bridgeport, Connecticut (2014): full view

The Gustave Whitehead memorial fountain inscription reads:
"**FIRST IN FLIGHT**
Gustave Whitehead
Bridgeport, Connecticut
Born 1874 Died 1927"
(Photo by Ed Collins, used with permission.)

HERALD CONFIRMS EYEWITNESS REPORT

The *Bridgeport Sunday Herald* confirmed its report about Whitehead's flights on *at least five separate occasions*, beginning several months later, in November 1901; January 1902, and again in May 1903. In the 1930's, the *Herald*'s editor reconfirmed the eyewitness account in 1935 and 1937.

On November 17, 1901, the *Herald* ran a long front page feature article about Whitehead, *referencing his summer flights in Fairfield,* and announcing the establishment of the world's first flying machine factory, in Bridgeport's West End.

> "The shop is well stocked with steel and iron which is being used in the construction of a flying machine modelled after the one in which ***Mr. Whitehead made two successful flights recently as described by the Herald at the time.*** *It was with this machine that Mr. Whitehead demonstrated the practicability of his invention during the season [summer]* ***in Fairfield****"... Since that time* ***two more flights have been made*** *for the benefit of the New York capitalist,* whose identity is kept a secret."[155]

On January 26, 1902, the *Bridgeport Sunday Herald* ran a large update about the new flying machine factory and Whitehead's views on flying. The article, located on page 4, *confirmed that Gustave Whitehead had been flying the previous summer,* in the article's fourth paragraph. It was, as was customary for the Herald, illustrated with sketches, like Howell's eyewitness article of August 18, 1901. (*emphasis added, below*)

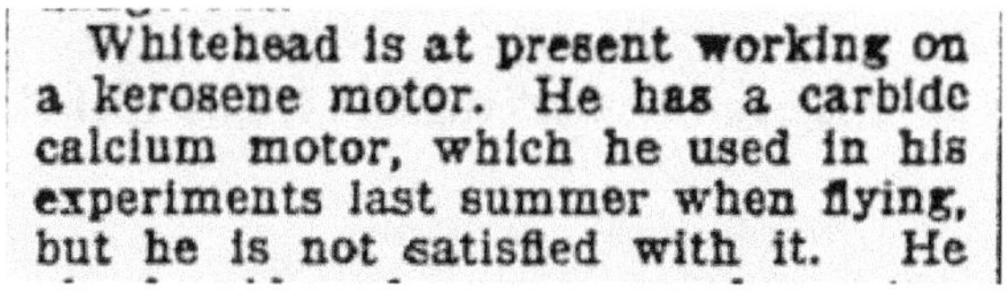

> "Whitehead is at present working on a kerosene motor. *He has a calcium motor,* ***which he used in his experiments last summer when flying***, but he is not satisfied with it."[156]

Whitehead is at present working on a kerosene motor. He has a carbide calcium motor, which he used in his experiments last summer when flying, but he is not satisfied with it. He

Figure 52: January 26, 1901 *Bridgeport Herald* **summer flight confirmation**

Bridgeport Sunday Herald **reconfirms Whitehead's flights of the summer of 1901, in a January 1902 feature article.**

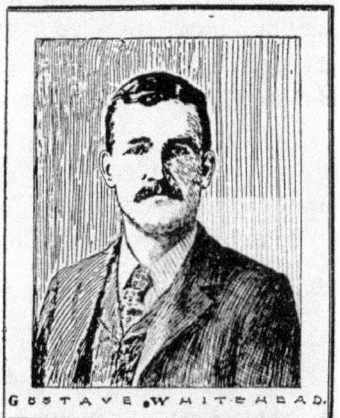

Figure 53: Gustave Whitehead sketch
Bridgeport Sunday Herald **January 26, 1902 and May 31, 1903**

Gustave Whitehead: "First in Flight"

On May 31, 1903, the *Bridgeport Sunday Herald* ran another feature article about Gustave Whitehead, referencing his flights of several years before: "two years ago the Herald printed an article descriptive of one of Mr. Whitehead's flying machines. That machine was shaped like a boat ..." [157] The 1903 article covered daytime test flights of a triplane glider at Holland Heights, getting ready to be fitted with a motor that Whitehead predicted would allow him to fly to New York. This time, there was a daytime photo taken of the slowly moving glider flight "by the Herald photographer," published in the article. Again, the article was written in the third person, with "the Herald representative" present and given a short test flight.

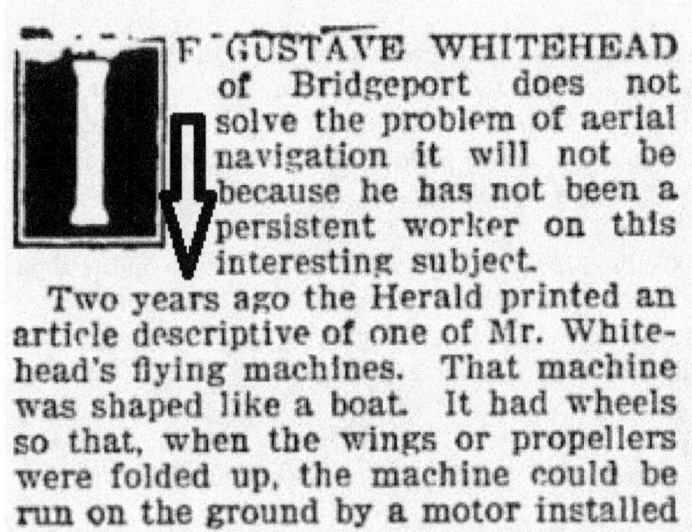

Figure 54: May 31, *Bridgeport Herald* **"August 14, 1901 flight" confirmation**

(partial transcript)

"If Gustave Whitehead of Bridgeport does not solve the problem of aerial navigation, it will not be because he has not been a persistent worker on this interesting subject.
Two years ago the Herald printed an article descriptive of one of Mr. Whitehead's flying machines. That machine was shaped like a boat. It had wheels so that when the wings or propellers were folded up, the machine could be run on the ground by a motor installed in the body or boat for that purpose.
But the motor for the boat shaped flying machine was not all that Mr. Whitehead expected of it, and *he laid aside that machine and turned his inventive genius to another form of machine and also to the development of another motor.*
...[Triplane glider pictured] The test was made on Holland Heights, a beautiful spot overlooking Long Island Sound, about a mile west of Bridgeport. As Mr. Whitehead's new motor is not yet finished the tests of the machine's ability to fly were of necessity limited but so far as they could be determined were satisfactory ..."

(end of partial transcript selection)

In the article, Whitehead is said to be working on a motor which he expects to install in two months' time. A follow up article was done in the fall, in the *Scientific American* of September 19, 1903, reporting that the motor had been installed and successful manned, powered flights made.

Chapter 2: First Flights on August 14, 1901

Whitehead openly discussed his lifelong focus on the future of practical, powered, commercially viable flying machines. His goal was then to be able to fly to New York in an hour and a half.

> In talking with a Herald representative Mr. Whitehead said:
>
> "I will never give up trying to make a flying machine that will be practicable and of commercial value. It is easy to make flying machines that will fly, but they are toys and of no practical use. I feel certain that some day people will step into their flying machines at their doors the same as they do now in their automobiles. It may not be in my day but it will come sometime. Fifty years ago people would have pooh-poohed the idea of the automobile, but the sight of an auto is common on our streets to-day. So it will be with the flying machine some day. But we have yet to find a motor that is light enough and will furnish sufficient power. That is the

(partial transcript)

"In talking with a *Herald* representative Mr. Whitehead said: I will never give up trying to make a flying machine that will be practicable and of commercial value. It is easy to make flying machines that will fly, but they are toys and of no practical use. I feel certain that someday people will step into their flying machines at their doors the same as they do now in their automobiles. It may not be in my day but it will come sometime. Fifty years ago people would have pooh-poohed the idea of the automobile, but the sight of an auto is common on our streets to-day. So it will be with the flying machine someday. But we have yet to find a motor that is light enough and will furnish sufficient power ..."

(end of partial transcript, rest of article at endnote link) [158]

Figure 55: Whitehead triplane glider, photographed May 1903.

The May 31, 1903 article unmistakably demonstrates how Whitehead's mind worked - he was never satisfied, he always wished to improve on each model, oftentimes casting aside successful planes that flew (such as the "No. 21" and 22 models), but were, to Whitehead, "not practical enough," to experiment on other ideas, such as triplanes or helicopters. He wanted to fly long distances, with commercial applications, but had not fully developed the technology for this feat, though he was working on it for at least a decade and a half. He was not interested in flying as a sport, though it was to be considered mainly in that category for most of the decade.

Significantly, the *Herald* of May 31, 1903 quite conspicuously demonstrated their point of view toward Whitehead's flight of August 14, 1901. Deemed worthy of occasional mention, the 1901 powered flight was not recognized as exceptionally important from a historical standpoint. It was still more of a curiosity, a local event that had gained world attention for a time. The newsmen of their time were fixed on anticipating, along with the inventors and the general public, far more practical flights of the future - with greater distances flown, and flying with passenger and freight transportation capabilities.[159]

This was not much different from the way the Wrights were treated by the press, though Gustave Whitehead was given more credibility at the time of his flight in 1901 – undoubtedly, due to the journalist being present. Whitehead had the foresight to invite the *Herald*'s popular sports reporter to his long flight. This helped ensure confidence at the *Sunday Herald* that Whitehead had actually flown, and also, in the world press receiving the report picked up by the Associated Press.

By comparison, it took the Wrights *five* years, until 1908, to be taken seriously by the world press, for many reasons. The Wright brothers had no reporters present on December 17, 1903, during their very short, low altitude "first flights," and failed to demonstrate additional flights in May 1904, given several days to perform before a large gathering of press. [160] [161] The Wrights were considered to be frauds, even called "liars" by the

Chapter 2: First Flights on August 14, 1901

newspapermen of their day - both implied and directly, for years. [162] Famously, in 1906, it was said of the secretive Wrights "They are in fact either fliers or liars" in the Paris edition of the *New York Herald*, because there had been no demonstrations for the press and by then were increasingly secretive, to protect their patents, with no proof of any kind, nor any photos released, up through 1908. Immediately after their first powered flights at Kitty Hawk, when the Wright family attempted to get the Dayton, Ohio newspapers to cover Wilbur and Orville's flights of December 17, 1903, one editor adroitly replied that the 52 second, longest flight of that date (made by Wilbur) might be of interest to a parent, but was simply *too short to be of interest to his readers*.[163] Orville's flight of 12 seconds, now credited contractually with Smithsonian as "the first powered flight," wasn't even thought to be worthy of mention at the time. Much of their eventual news coverage was inaccurate, provided by those who'd not seen it – one widely disseminated early announcement originating from the Virginian Pilot erroneously described the Wrights' flights as going three miles[164], when the actual claimed distances for their four flights ranged from 120 to 852 feet.

"To see was to believe" in the case of "man flying." Hundreds had seen Whitehead fly, by May 1903, with factories and schools emptying out to watch; with many friends, neighbors, and complete strangers hearing about the flights and coming out to witness what most had previously thought to be impossible; the press was not always present.

There is evidence that Whitehead was not taken entirely seriously, similar to the Wrights, by local press "who did not see with their own eyes," though due to the "common knowledge" of his flights in the close-knit community, most of the local press were supportive. A competing local paper, the *Bridgeport Evening Post*, though not invited to observe flights up through April 1902, was initially supportive, reporting on successful August 1901 flight experiments at the trotting park in the West End of Bridgeport. [165] The next spring, the *Farmer and the Bridgeport Post* issued articles covering a rather dull minor lawsuit involving Whitehead's former sponsor, Linde, who'd not paid a bill at the lumber company, using it as an opportunity to write more amusing fare, poking fun at Whitehead for not realizing all his dreams or flying high – undoubtedly alluding to his promised flight to New York and development of a commercial airline, given less than a few months before Linde ran out of funds.[166] The *Bridgeport Daily Standard* of October 1, 1904, forthrightly supported Whitehead's flight capabilities; for they had seen the proof, two photos of Whitehead in flight "20 feet from the ground and sailing along" displayed in a local hardware store window. *The Standard* reported at that time, Whitehead was frequently making flights of half a mile.[167] In 1910, the *Bridgeport Evening Farmer* showed its backing for the validity of the 1901 flights in an article referencing Whitehead's flight experiment history.[168]

In any case, it is clear that Gustave Whitehead's early, successful, powered flights – *only later to be considered as an important first step by mankind* - were perceived as authentic by those who saw them, but impractical and thus, of occasional attention-grabbing, but not historic, impact.

The *Herald* would again confirm their 1901 article, in two issues of the 1930's. By then, the historic value of Whitehead's accomplishment was starting to be recognized. "Portions of the [eyewitness] story [of Aug. 18, 1901] were also republished in the *Sunday Herald* of February 17, 1935."[169] On January 30, 1937 the entire eyewitness article of August 18, 1901 was reprinted in the *Sunday Herald Magazine* entitled "*Here's Proof From the Files of the Herald*."

GUSTAVE WHITEHEAD CONFIRMS HERALD ARTICLE

After completing the first flight of August 14, 1901, Gustave Whitehead, being a German immigrant, wrote the Illustrirte Aeronautische Mitteilungen (Illustrated Aeronautical Record) in Germany, about his successful experiments. In his letter, he confirms that he made a half mile manned flight following a test flight with ballast, just as described in the *Bridgeport Sunday Herald's* "Flying" article, by Dick Howell. Whitehead says, "I'll never forget the feeling I had." He goes on to say that his motor ran the entire day at full speed, using 10 pounds of fuel, and did not heat up nor was it very noisy. *This firsthand account by Whitehead, sent to the largest aeronautical journal in Germany, agrees with the Howell account, making it another validation needed to authenticate the eyewitness Herald account of August 14, 1901- particularly that describing the flight and Whitehead's experience.* It is probable that this description is in Whitehead's own words, being more accurate due to being taken from a letter, rather than being interviewed and quoted (or misquoted). For instance, *this description places the duration of the flight to be 1.5 minutes, vs. 10 minutes in Howell's article.*

In its October 1901 issue, the Illustrirte Aeronautische Mitteilungen published an article concerning Whitehead's experiments and quoted his letter. An English translation, found in O'Dwyer's files at the Fairfield Museum, is as follows:

(translated transcript)

The Flying Machine of Gustav Weisskopf (Whitehead)
(Der Flugapparat von Gustav Weisskopf)

"Gustav Weisskopf, a German from Ansbach, Bavaria, has sent us from Bridgeport the following description of the flying machine he constructed there several months ago.

This machine follows in essence the outlines of a bird, has a body of 16 feet in length, 3 feet high, and 2 1/2 feet maximum width. The body rests on 4 wheels. The diameter of these wheels is 1 meter. The front wheels are started by a 10 horsepower engine, while the rear wheels run free. On each side a lifting surface has been attached, made of stiffened [bamboo] cane covered with silk. The wing spread is 36 feet and the surface area of the lifting surface is 450 square feet.

Figure 56: Weisskopf's Flugmaschine (Ansicht von hinten)
Translation:
Whitehead's Flying Machine (view from behind)
[Note: The journal is mistaken; this is the view from the front]
Photo provided by Gustave Whitehead to 'Illustrirte Aeronautische Mitteilungen' is now located at the Fairfield Museum, O'Dwyer archives, and is reproduced herein with its permission.
This photo was also sent to the St. Louis Exposition authorities, with his application, in Jan., 1902. It is the sister-photograph to one seen in Figure 4 of this book, showing tree and other images in the distance, above the wings of the flying machine.

"The lifting surfaces are strongly concave on their undersides and show absolutely no slack.

Chapter 2: First Flights on August 14, 1901

Standing diagonally across the body within the height of the lifting surfaces, a double expansion engine of 20 horsepower drives two propellers in opposite directions with 700 turns a minute. To preserve the stability of the machine in its length, an automatically functioning machine has been installed. The power fuel is calcium carbide and acetylene gas. The motor weighs 2 lbs. (1 lb. = 453 grams) per 1 horsepower and is a marvel in xxxxx construction. The 30 horsepower engine uses 60 lb. of fuel in 6 hours; that is, 2 lb. per horsepower and 6 hours (?) which must be described as a very good result. ... My motor produces at the propellers a power of 350 lbs., which is 85 lbs. more than the weight of the entire machine. [*emphasis added*] I made the test flights with my machine. In both flights the machine landed without the slightest damage. On the first flight, 220 lbs. of ballast were carried, so that the total weight was 500 lbs. After the motor had started, the machine traveled about 30 yards, then lifted and flew about 1 1/2 minutes. On the second flight test I made an hour later, I removed the ballast and boarded the machine myself. I will never forget the feeling I had. The result was the same as with the first flight. The duration of the flight was 1 1/2 minutes and the distance covered was 2800 feet [½ mile] [Author's note: the length of the flight, in Whitehead's words, was 1.5 minutes not 10 minutes per Herald]. My motor ran the entire day at full speed and used 10 lbs of fuel. The motor did not heat up nor did it get very noisy; it shows a mechanical efficiency as good as any steam engine." (The illustration shows a rear view of Whitehead and his machine.) [Author's note: the illustration actually shows a front view of the "No. 21" flying machine.]

THE ISSUE OF CONTROL

Some aviation historians, such as those at the Smithsonian, have increasingly pointed to the issue of "control" over a flying machine as one of the central themes in determining credit for "first powered flight," especially as the evidence for Whitehead's earlier powered flights mounted. Discussions have even occurred in preparation for the day Whitehead might have to be credited for being "first in powered flight, in order to prepare arguments to prevent him from being credited as "inventor of the airplane," to preserve (contracted) titles for the Wrights.

Upon examination by experts, the Wright brothers demonstrated enough control in late 1903, to allow them to fly "straight and level"[170], with difficulty. Their "first flight" currently credited by Smithsonian at 12 seconds, previously was considered "unsuccessful," with zero evidence for having made turns of any kind. Aeronautical engineer and author, Joe Bullmer, has conducted an extensive study of the Wright aeroplanes, making this observation of the Wrights, "Indeed, as they found out in 1904 and 1905, none of their earlier vehicles were even capable of executing turns."[171] Even NASA has described the Flyer as "maneuverable" but not controlled, (*see* following section on *Stability, Balance, and Control*).

Based on the evidence presented in this book, it can be said that Gustave Whitehead clearly made successful, sustained, powered flights multiple times, making "straight and level" flights, with some changes of direction, and even turns and flights in circuits (circular, or returning to the starting point), ahead of the Wrights, for further distances and higher elevations. Whitehead was also unmistakably first into the air, with power.

The *Smithsonian-Wright Agreement of 1948,* a legal agreement herein referred to as "the Contract," requires the following label on the now so-called "Wright Flyer," using these contractual words [172] (discussed at length in Chapter 12) (*emphasis added*):

> "There shall at all times be prominently displayed with said aeroplane a label in the following form and language:"

Gustave Whitehead: "First in Flight"

Figure 57: *Smithsonian-Wright Agreement of 1948* **language directive (1)**

"The Original Wright Brothers' Aeroplane
*The World's First Power-Driven Heavier-than-Air Machine
In Which Man Made Free, Controlled, and
Sustained Flight*
Invented and Built by Wilbur and Orville Wright
Flown by Them at Kitty Hawk, North Carolina
December 17, 1903
By Original Scientific Research *the Wright Brothers Discovered the Principles of Human Flight
As Inventors, Builders and Flyers They Further Developed the Aeroplane
Taught Man to Fly and Opened the Era of Aviation*
Deposited by the Estate of Orville Wright."

Figure 58: *Smithsonian-Wright Agreement of 1948* **Label #1**

Further, "the Contract" requires this second label, with this exact language displayed with the aeroplane:

"The first flight lasted only twelve seconds, a flight very modest compared with that of birds, but *it was nevertheless the first in the history of the world in which a machine carrying a man had raised itself by its own power into the air in free flight, had sailed forward on a level course without reduction of speed, and had finally landed without being wrecked.* The second and third flights were a little longer, and the fourth lasted 59 seconds covering a distance of 852 feet over the ground against a 20 mile wind."

Wilbur and Orville Wright

(From Century Magazine, Vol. 76 September 1908, p. 649.)

Figure 59: *Smithsonian-Wright Agreement of 1948* **Label #2**

Label #2, above, comes from a paragraph written by Orville Wright, with his sister Katharine, submitted to Century Magazine as if he and his brother wrote it. Wilbur was in France, at the time, having left directions for his brother to follow in writing the article. However, rather than follow Wilbur's directives, Orville, always "the lesser brother," gave himself credit for the "first flight" on Dec. 17, 1903, ahead of his brother.[173] The now famous article was published in September 1908, in Century Magazine. Even in 1908, Orville was beginning to finagle a way to be recognized as "top dog" in the race for "first flight" glory, a passion which consumed him for the rest of his life.

Chapter 2: First Flights on August 14, 1901

Credit for the first powered flight was given to the Wrights by the Smithsonian Institution in 1948, with the following ostensible criteria found within the Flyer's mandated labels:

1. first
2. power-driven, heavier-than-air machine
3. manned
4. free flight
5. sustained
6. sailing forward on a level course without reduction in speed
7. landing without being wrecked
8. controlled

Each of these will be examined in this section, to attempt to determine which of the two, Gustave Whitehead, or the Wrights, should best be given credit for the first powered flight. All documentation for the Wright flights came solely from the Wright brothers. Documentation for Whitehead's flights included an eyewitness newspaper feature, notarized witness statements, witness interviews, multiple local media articles supporting the flight(s), and statements by Gustave Whitehead. Photographs of Whitehead's "No. 21" flight of 1901 were described by the editor of the *Scientific American* who'd seen them, after being displayed in 1906 at the first Aero Club of America exhibition in New York City. A photograph claimed to be of Orville in the Wright Flyer, at an altitude of two feet was finally issued by the Wrights five years after their claimed flights, in 1908. At the time, the brothers were positioning for world patent rights and complete control of world aviation, while they were focused on sale of their aeroplanes for many millions of dollars to multiple world governments.

Overview:

"Being First"

There is ample proof that Gustave Whitehead was "first in powered flight," based upon all evidence presented in this book. One may pick various dates and time periods when Whitehead flew, 1899 - 1903, especially those attested to by witnesses, before the Wrights made their flight experiments on December 17, 1903. The Whitehead flights during the summer of 1901 with "No. 21" are within his most prolific, successful, early time period, verified by local media and multiple witnesses. These predate the Wrights' flights by roughly two and a half years. "No 21" will be used, therefore, as the primary flying machine whose flights will be compared to those of the Wright Flyer, though there are others to choose from, up through September 1903, which predate the Wrights. There are several other inventors, often-times mentioned as "first" into the air, with power, but in each case, it is for mere inches, definitely not anything even approaching the true flights of Whitehead in terms of elevation and distance.

Use of a Power-driven, Heavier-Than-Air Machine

All of Gustave Whitehead's aeroplanes meet this criteria, with the exception of his gliders, intentionally built and tested, prior to adding power. His "No. 21" was a power-driven, heavier-than-air machine. This is supported with documentation, including witness statements, newspaper reports, and photographs. The Wright Flyer was also a heavier-than-air machine, similar to a man-carrying box kite with power.

Manned Flight

During the flights of summer, 1901, "No. 21" was manned by Gustave Whitehead, according to media, witnesses, and Whitehead's self-reports. The Wright Flyer was self-reported and self-documented, manned, alternately, by Orville and Wilbur, for its four flights of December 17, 1903.

Free flight

Gustave Whitehead's "No. 21" made numerous street and open field flights, in untethered "free flight," in the summer 1901. The Whitehead flight of August 14, 1901 was, at first, hand-tethered, then released, as the propellers were activated. The Wright Flyer was in free flight, according to their own reports, after launching from a track, guided by the hand of Wilbur to keep it steady, before liftoff.

The "No. 21," as with today's airplanes, was able to make a manned takeoff using wheels attached to the under-structure of the fuselage, employing a ground engine to build up speed till it could be switched over to the two engines used for powering the puller (tractor) propellers, which would lift it into "free flight." As with today's airplanes, Whitehead could use this launching method on level ground to make flights, such as on the city streets and in open spaces. "No. 21" was not dependent on the wind for lift, it could operate in still air or moderately windy conditions. Alternatively, when on a slope, he also employed men to pull the plane forward, at an angle, till it caught the air and lifted, whereupon the propellers were then turned on.

On December 17, 1903, the Wrights used a track for their pusher-propelled flying machine, which ran downhill onto the beach off a sloping dune, and had at least one man running alongside to keep it moving and on the track, requiring a 22 (+) mph headwind to raise off the track. When they returned to Dayton, Ohio after that date, quite famously, the Wright brothers could not get their flying machine airborne without designing other launching mechanisms, such as a catapult, or by September 1904, a "derrick launcher," a system utilizing a 20 foot high pyramid-shaped tower utilizing ropes, pulleys and weights . Their pusher propellers were less effective and became obsolete, as did their launch mechanism.

Comparing the two, one might ask, which was more like today's airplanes? Which lasted the past century?

Sustained Flight

In the summer of 1901, Whitehead's "No. 21" plane made a number of sustained (i.e. longer) flights, estimated to cover a distance of from several hundred feet up to 1.5 miles. An eyewitness journalist documented Whitehead's *half-mile flight* on August 14, 1901. The flight credited to Orville Wright by Smithsonian *is* for an *estimated 120 feet,* made on December 17, 1903. (Wilbur Wright made *the only measured, and longest flight of the day at 852 feet,* which still falls short of the Whitehead distances.) The Wright flights are based entirely on self-reports for distances.

"Sailing forth on a level course without reduction in speed"

Gustave Whitehead's "No. 21" met these criterions, "sailing forward" until just before landing, and from a place with a slight "sloping grade" in a field, according to the account by the eyewitness journalist, Richard Howell, for the flight of August 14, 1901 and Gustave Whitehead's self-reporting. The same day, later flights were said to be made by witnesses, in Lordship (Stratford) on level ground. Whitehead street flights were made prior to these, and also, flights on the beach, that summer and fall, all on level ground. The beaches in coastal Connecticut are narrow and essentially level, with a gentle slope leading to the water, similar to that pictured near the water at Kitty Hawk.

The famed photo of Orville's flight of December 17, 1903 shows a definite slope to the takeoff point, the Flyer running along tracks placed at the side and base of a steep sand dune. Technically, this could not be considered flat, or entirely level. Orville Wright credited himself with having accomplished all these criterions in his statement published in Century magazine, above, for a 12 second flight, lifted by a 27 mph wind (according to "*How We Made the First Flight,*" published in *Flying*, December 1913, by Orville Wright). He reported that his aeroplane was darting ten feet, up and down and side-to-side, in the wind. It is hard to imagine that there was not a reduction in speed with this difficult, brief flight. There is additional self-documentation about the Wright Flyer's first flight of the day that confirms a short hop and control problems, in William J. Hammer's and Hudson Maxim's 1911 "*Chronology of Aviation,*" a description vetted by the Wright brothers and later officially approved

Chapter 2: First Flights on August 14, 1901

by Orville, to be explained further, in Chapter 12.

Landing without being wrecked

Gustave Whitehead's "No. 21" landed without being wrecked, as it was inherently stable, "pancaking" – settling gently to the ground, upon landings. This is documented by the eyewitness journalist's report for August 14, 1901 described in Chapter 2, and by multiple witnesses and Whitehead's descriptions of the sustained flight and others he made between 1901 and 1903, in Chapters 2-6. On the other hand, three of the four (demonstrably unstable) Wright flights on December 17, 1903, crashed into the sand, with damage. Perhaps Orville meant, in the Century magazine article now immortalized as a mandated label at the Smithsonian, that his plane was not completely wrecked, but then, neither were Whitehead's.

"Controlled" Flight

This criterion is the most-hotly debated of all of the above. It will require closer examination, but should not impact whether Whitehead was "*first* in powered flight." The Smithsonian also questions what "flight" means, and what it means to be called "inventor of the airplane." But our focus, herein, is whether Whitehead (or the Wrights) really had "controlled flight." For this section the author has consulted with an aeronautical engineer, who is also an author with expertise in both modern and early aircraft, and another expert, a highly experienced United Airlines pilot trained at the "Harvard of the Skies," Embry-Riddle Aeronautical University. In addition, the author has located and presents that which previous teams of engineers and experts had determined about Whitehead's flying machines, for a variety of purposes, including, to build several replicas/reproductions. Whitehead and his contemporaries described, wrote about and photographed his aeroplanes, yielding important information for use in current-day evaluations. Though scores of others, including pilots and engineers, have informally considered the airworthiness and control elements of Whitehead's "No. 21," some constructing working "copies" which have flown impressive distances, it would be interesting if *neutral,* currently qualified aviation experts would conduct further formal aerodynamic evaluations of Whitehead's powered aeroplanes.

The Smithsonian has signed a legal contract, an agreement with Orville's heirs, to require the labels seen in the previous section in this book in *Figures 59 and 60*, and within the full *Smithsonian-Wright Agreement of 1948* in the *Appendix*, to be placed on the Wright Flyer, which will be discussed in more depth later in this book, particularly in Chapter 12. The label is full of misinformation about what the Wrights accomplished, herein revealed to have been designed by friends of Orville who were prominent "Whitehead detractors," working on derailing the Whitehead claims for the past nine years. The "Contract" has been used to deny Whitehead recognition as "first in flight"; for instance, it is currently claimed by Smithsonian historians that the Wrights had control and Whitehead didn't. But the Smithsonian goes farther than that – quite absurdly claiming, at this current date, that not one of Gustave Whitehead's powered flying machines even left the ground, implying or even stating (at various times) that all eyewitnesses and local press during these years (from Connecticut) including Whitehead, were either mistaken or lied. "Supporters of the claims have been arguing in favor of Whitehead for many years, while the critics, like me, have been vigorously refuting their evidence." (Tom Crouch, Head Aeronautics Curator, Smithsonian National Air and Space Museum, March 2013) [174]

The "issue of control" came up in a discussion at the Smithsonian about Whitehead's claimed flights, held with Smithsonian's Aeronautics Curator Tom Crouch (of Dayton, Ohio, the Wright brothers' home town, educated at Wright State University) and Connecticut Aeronautical Historical Association (CAHA) Founder & President Emeritus, Harvey Lippincott (who'd been present for multiple interviews with Whitehead eyewitnesses and contemporaries still living in the 1960's and 1970's), filmed in 1981 for German television, by producer Spannenberger:

>> LIPPINCOTT: I feel very confident that he [Whitehead] did make short flights from the various interviews I have done.

Gustave Whitehead: "First in Flight"

>> CROUCH: The only area in which Mr. Lippincott and I really have even minor disagreements is the fact that I am not at all sure in my own mind that there is evidence for the short hops. I think he and I agree that the hops, even if they did occur, as Harvey believes they did, *can't be qualified as flight in the sense that they were either sustained or honestly controlled in the air.* And I think that both of those are important criteria when you are talking about flight.

>>LIPPINCOTT: *I think that the Whitehead machine of the 1901-1902 period had control up to a point.* We're not sure exactly how much lateral control he had – he may not have had lateral control actually built into the machine, but he had sufficient dihedral that he might have been actually ... in still air, he might have been able to fly laterally without disaster. In rough air he might have lost control. We know he had elevator control. We know that the propellers, by speeding one up and slowing one down would turn you, not quickly, but would turn you. But I have not found anybody who really gave any evidence that he made any major turns in his flights.[175] [176]

Good questions for Smithsonian curators are: If you believe Gustave Whitehead never left the ground, how could you know that he had no control? Or if you think Whitehead did leave the ground, why is he not receiving credit for that? On the basis of what independent evidence, for instance, *consultations with qualified aeronautical engineers*, do you believe the Wrights had control or that Whitehead did not? Why have the so-called "replicas" or "reproductions" of the Wright Flyer failed to fly, despite all historian claims? Lastly, how can an aviation historian determine that a plane could not fly – does he have an aeronautical engineering degree and experience? Curators at the Smithsonian and many professional and amateur "aviation historians" have been shown to be very wrong about the Wright history, for lack of technical background and inattention to existing evaluations of Wright aeroplanes.[177] The main areas of investigation by qualified experts - not historians, particularly those with vested interests - should be whether a particular flying machine made flights, what the independent evidence is to support the flights, the airworthiness and aerodynamics of the aircraft in question, and scrutiny of the replica/reproduction projects, all leading to examination of whether the aircraft could have flown. However, with the *Smithsonian-Wright Agreement of 1948* in place, it is doubtful that Smithsonian could ever pay an expert or group of experts to neutrally evaluate the Wright Flyer OR the Whitehead flying machine(s), since the results could lead to loss of the Wright Flyer, under the terms of the Agreement ("Contract"). It is safe to say that Smithsonian curators can merely postulate in favor of the Wrights as first, but not examine the evidence, *for fear of what they might find.* This summarizes the past 67+ years of resistance, since 1948, to finding out more about Whitehead's flying machines and flight claims – which may be described as a combination of avoidance and denial. Before that, for twenty years, the Smithsonian sought to obtain the Wright Flyer from an angry Orville Wright, and that was no time to be investigating Whitehead for "first flight" claims, either. Prior to that, Smithsonian was busily claiming that its own Secretary should hold the laurels for inventing the first plane "capable of flight." Suffice to say, Whitehead has not been given "a fair shake," to date, by our nation's most prominent history center.

So, which inventor(s) demonstrated "control"?

Currently, according to NASA, control indicates whether the pilot was able to direct the movement of the aircraft with particular reference to changes in attitude and speed. Attitude is defined, by NASA, as the orientation of an aircraft with regards to three dimensions which may be described as the three axes involving pitch (lateral, or up or down movement of the nose), roll (longitudinal, or the up or down movement of the wing tips), and yaw (vertical, or the side to side movement of the nose).

Critics have questioned whether Whitehead met a strict definition of "control" for his airplanes. In Whitehead's flying machine, the pilot stood or sat in the cockpit area, at the front of a fuselage, as with today's airplanes. His monoplane was said to be "inherently stable;" it would not pitch or roll. It was not dependent on

Chapter 2: First Flights on August 14, 1901

wind. In order to navigate multiple powered flights down city blocks, over a city neighborhood, and country hills without damage to himself, onlookers, or surrounding buildings or trees, the use of at least a fundamental system of controls would have been necessary. Whitehead's shorter street flights in Bridgeport remained in the road with few exceptions. An occasional test resulted in an accident, which was to be expected, as the aircraft and controls were under development. It is a fact that Whitehead employed first, a tail rudder that could be remotely manipulated up and down by the pilot, then a four-sided rudder that could be manipulated up and down and side-to-side, in flight, according to some witnesses and descriptions. The wings of his 1901-1903 aircraft were said to be fixed (did not fold down at the sides till he wished, when on the ground) but flexible, made of bamboo poles covered with canvas and/or silk (at various times), wired so that the pilot had some potential for additional control. Yet whether or not this was consciously employed in the summer of 1901 is unknown. We do know Gustave Whitehead was working on improving controls and was said to have made some circular flights in 1902. These were accomplished through use of running one propeller faster than the other, applying methods used by ships. The bird-like structure of the flying machine may have added to its ability to be controlled for Whitehead's many successful flights before December 1903. Some of these features are still employed – to mention just a few, the use of horizontal and vertical tailrudders, tractor propellers, and certainly, flexible monoplane wings are vastly the rule, rather than the exception (*See Chapter 11: Legacy*.)

The Wrights, on the other hand, made a box-kite-like "biplane" glider, and added power, using pusher propellers, with a pilot lying prone on the center of the lower wing, to fly it. Their aeroplane was entirely dependent on the wind to rise up, for without a strong headwind, the first "Wright Flyer" could not leave the ground. Once in the air, the wings could theoretically be controlled through a twisting mechanism, known as "wing-warping," providing controls intended to keep the aeroplane straight and level[178], which rapidly became obsolete, overtaken by improved methods, before the end of the decade. During the flights of December 1903, by the Wrights' own written documentation, they did not have actual control of their flights, as their "flyer" plunged into the sand and uncontrollably bobbed up and down in the wind. It is a myth contrived partially by Orville, five years later, on the eve of their patent lawsuits - which required proof of a pioneer invention - that they had actual control, then. Any successful rudimentary controls established by the Wrights were to come years later, and are not used in today's airplanes.

As the old saying goes, "the proof is in the pudding," concerning controls and successful flights. Whitehead's powered flying machines performed better, during the years in question, 1901-1903. Many elements of his flying machines are used in today's airplanes. Neither the Wrights, nor Whitehead employed flawless controls, nor the exact methods of control used by today's airplanes. Both parties were experimenting with how to perfect control during these years. Neither the Wrights nor Whitehead would ever accomplish perfect control, though their experiments allowed them to make limited powered flights. It would take many more years of experimentation for others to perfect the means now utilized to fly modern airplanes. However, Whitehead was clearly first into the air with power, using adequate control which allowed these multiple early flights, before the end of 1903.

By January 1902, Gustave Whitehead was publicly describing how to employ wing-warping of a sort that may have been viable in use with his flying machines. Whitehead described a form of wing-warping, during a time when he was allegedly visited by the Wrights, *(see Chapter 8)* and knew Stanley Yale Beach, an associate of the Wrights. It was not a new science, either, as Octave Chanute so famously pointed out to an angry Wilbur Wright, years later:

> "I did tell you in 1901 that the mechanism by which your surfaces were warped was original with yourselves. This I adhere to, but it does not follow that it covers the general principle of warping or twisting wings, the proposals for doing this being ancient. …. Please see my book, page 97, for what d'Esterno said of the laws of flight; the 3d being torsion of the wings and the 6th being torsion of the tail. Also, page 106, Le Bris, rotary motion of the front edge of the wings…

Gustave Whitehead: "First in Flight"

When I gave you a copy of the Mouillard patent in 1901, think I called your attention to his method of twisting the rear of the wings. If the courts will decide that the purpose and results were entirely different and that you were the first to conceive the twisting of the wings, so much the better for you, but my judgment is that you will be restricted to the particular method by which you do it."

Whitehead's 1899-1904 experiments show ever-increasing control of his aircraft in these three dimensions, using methods that were the first of their kind and worked for him. These controls were successful enough to produce numerous manned, powered flights before and shortly after those of the Wrights of December 1903, during his most successful and prolific flying period.

Stability, balance, and control

By all accounts, Whitehead's "No. 21" airplanes, and those which followed, were known to be "inherently stable"; his aircraft would remain horizontal, avoiding nosedives, settling to the ground gently when the power was shut off. [179] [180] NASA defines *Aircraft Stability* as "the property of an aircraft to maintain its attitude or to resist displacement, and if displaced, to develop forces and moments tending to restore the original condition." (*NASA Thesaurus*, Washington, DC: National Aeronautics and Space Administration)[181].

The account by eyewitness Richard Howell may not describe fully what might have been available to Whitehead during the flight of August 14, 1901, though it would appear Whitehead employed, on that occasion, the *shifting of his weight*, using the center of gravity, to "steer" around a clump of trees, as do the birds of the air, for the world's first successful sustained powered flight. This was an accepted means of lateral control (also known as pitch or vertical control) for gliders of his era and later varieties of gliders and powered "ultra-lights," in the present day. What Whitehead used was a primitive means of "*banking*" the airplane, which worked to adjust his course, to avoid disaster. His flight of August 14, 1901 was, apart from that adjustment, "straight and level." He did have the capacity used in early 1902 for completing "circuits," by running one propeller faster than the other, to make wide circular flights. It has been suggested that this may have been the precursor to what is now called "differential thrust," which creates "banking" (changing direction), such as the "thrust vectoring" used in fighter aircraft today. Whitehead's "No. 21" aircraft may meet the NASA criteria, as its structure provided longitudinal (roll), also known as *horizontal stability*, as the rear horizontal rudder could be moved up or down with wires that ran to the cockpit, accessible in flight to the pilot..

To land, Whitehead would simply shut off the "puller-style" [tractor] propellers, to settle down gently upon the ground, according to the Whitehead interview in the *Bridgeport Sunday Herald*. [182]

Whitehead described how to accomplish this type of control in a series of articles and letters to the editor, by the end of 1902, in the popular press and trade journals. A device Whitehead invented for stabilizing the craft horizontally was mentioned as early as June 1901[183].

A *Scientific American* article of June 8, 1901, entitled "A New Flying Machine" (p. 357), as aforementioned, described the "No. 21" plane as having a controllable horizontal rudder, as follows:[184]

> The 10-foot rudder, which corresponds to the tail of a bird, can also be folded up and can be moved up and down, so as to steer the machine on its horizontal course.

Steering was also to be accomplished using the twin six foot diameter propellers which turned in opposite directions.

Chapter 2: First Flights on August 14, 1901

> The steering will be done by running one propeller faster than the other in a way analogous to the way in which an ocean steamer having twin screws can be turned, a special aeroplane being provided to maintain longitudinal and transverse stability.

On August 22, 1901, the *Boston Daily Globe* reported Whitehead's steering mechanism as follows in this comment:

> "I have perfected my steering apparatus and regulated my twin screws so that one can revolve enough faster than the other to cause it to steer. The principle is the same as twin screws worked on an ocean liner."[185]

According to a *NY Herald* interview with Whitehead in June 1901, describing "No. 21":

[Author notes inserted]

> "There are two engines in my airship. One is on the floor of the body proper for running the ship along the tracks [*Note: did not refer to rails, at times boards were used or a clearing*] til it acquires the necessary speed to rise up the fixed aeroplanes, which are spread like wings on either side. The upper engines are placed between the aeroplanes giving swift rotary motion to the propeller blades which are six feet in diameter with a blade surface of four square feet. These are sufficient to keep the entire body in motion while suspended upon the aeroplanes, the weight of the body of the ship being about fifty pounds, the total weight of aeroplanes, engines, propellers, fuel etc. being about one hundred and fifty pounds. "The body proper is sixteen feet long, ribbed with light wood and steel, and covered with canvas tightly stretched over the framework. The wings are of silk, thirty-eight feet from tip to tip, with a ten foot rudder tail, all braced with bamboo and light steel, and capable of being folded up like the wings of a gigantic beast when at rest. A thin mast and bowsprit give additional firmness to the stationary aeroplanes *[Note: another word for wings]* and the tail, which can be moved up or down with a view to guiding the machine while on a horizontal course. The lateral steering is done by running one propeller faster than the other, while the body is suspended upon its 100 square feet of silk."[186]

> [Author's note: the wingspan of Whitehead's "No. 21" was 36 feet from tip to tip[187], and the fuselage was 16 feet long[188]. The silk needed for the wings was 360 sq. feet for the first "No. 21" reproduction made in 1986, at Bridgeport, based on the same dimensions.[189]]

It is likely Whitehead continued to improve and work on "No. 21", in his customary fashion, till the sustained flights occurred in August 1901. Additional flights were reported in the fall of 1901. It is probable that Whitehead began work on what would become "No. 22" between late August and October 1901.

In a letter sent to Stella Randolph dated August 6, 1934, Whitehead's brother John recalled the "No. 21" or nearly identical "No.22" airplane which he had later seen (in April 1902, when he arrived in Bridgeport), though not in flight, due to a broken motor. Gustave briefed John about his most successful flight with this machine, at a height of up to 40 feet with this plane, in [over] Long Island [Sound]. Based on the information given to a journalist from the New York Evening Telegram who interviewed Gustave Whitehead in November 1901 at his shop[190], the machine John viewed was most likely the *next version* of "No. 21," the very similar but more powerful "No. 22'", as it was "No. 22" which was later described as having a broken motor. The motor of "said machine," estimated at "20-25 horsepowers" was a "4 cylinder 2 cycle motor of an opposed type, resembling a 2 cycle motor" built in Bridgeport "for speed boats."[191]

Gustave Whitehead: "First in Flight"

The bird-like wings of Whitehead's "No. 21" were "fixed" in place during flight (did not flap as with an ornithopter, or fold back, as they could on the ground), but *could flex*, being made of bamboo, with wires running from their tips to the cockpit area. This presented the availability of wing-tip control for the pilot, used by Whitehead, according to Anton Pruckner, his assistant. Today's modern airplane wings must also be able to flex, to fly under windy and other conditions experienced during flight. Air passengers often look out their windows to view the phenomenon of wing movement, which airplanes have built into their basic design.

Whitehead's brother John, reporting on the abovementioned flying machine ("No. 21" or "No. 22'", which were very similar) sitting in his brother's yard, in April 1902, said, *"For steering, there was a rope from one of the foremost wing tip ribs to the one opposed, running over a pully [pulley] in front of operator a lever was connected to pulley; the same pulley also controlled the tailrudder at the same time."*[192]

The Wrights employed their own, undeveloped form of "wing-warping" controls which, in reality, didn't work well to control their aircraft, as the "Flyer" bucked up and down, carried primarily by the wind on December 17, 1903. That day, the Wrights rode their kite-like flying machine in a straight line for some very short hops that crash-landed into the sand, launched from a rail, from a slope. Their particular type of "wing-warping" methodology was not designed to make turns possible, till much later. Their controls, according to the record, didn't work well for at least three years, till they improved their methods, and even then, were considered unstable and "uncontrollable," killing off a large number of their own pilots and forcing them to close their flight school for a time. Later, with the development, by others, of the more superior ailerons and "spoilers," the Wright design and control methods became obsolete.

Interviewed on May 20, 1964, Whitehead's mechanic and assistant, Anton Pruckner answered questions about the balancing and control of the aircraft, using the rudder, adjustment of wing surfaces, and propellers. Notably, Pruckner also indicated that his main work with Whitehead was *before* 1903, when the Wrights made their famed flights.[193]

> [Pruckner]: "You could move it one side, and you could move the other side to balance it" [in flight]. You didn't need much of it for them two big wings was spread out, you know. It would be hard to go down, the pressure would hold you up...
> [O'Dwyer]: Could you ... possibly recollect whether any part of the wing or the tail surface was movable, or was it rigid? Which way was that?
> [Pruckner]: From the beginning we didn't have anything to move, but after we found it out, so we had a tail to move... It went sideways, only sideways we had. [a rudder] ... on the back. Then, after, we changed it. We put a universal joint on it so we could go up and down the same way.
> [O'Dwyer]: Now, this tail surface that sticks out in the back. Which direction did this move?
> [Pruckner]: Well this move up and she moved this way.
> [O'Dwyer]: How about the wings? Was there any way of moving those wings?
> [Pruckner]: Well from the beginning we didn't have anything.
> [O'Dwyer]: Not when you first started?
> [Pruckner]: ...when you are going straight, you got to have a little wings so you can keep on going up, so we made a universal joint, and moved it, to keep the angle.
> [O'Dwyer]: Was that adjustable in flight?
> [Pruckner]: Why, yes. You fly it, you can adjust it yourself.
> [O'Dwyer]: Even while you were in flight?
> [Pruckner]: While you fly it, yeah.
> [O'Dwyer]: How about the propellers? Were the propellers a fixed position pitch, or were they adjustable?
> [Pruckner]: Well, yes. They were screwed right in there and you could change your pitch any time you wanted but not when you're flying, or anything like that. Only thing, you'd have to stop and adjust your pitch" [not when the engine was running][194].

Chapter 2: First Flights on August 14, 1901

In an interview conducted in 1966 with Anton Pruckner, with Paul Garber, Assistant Director of the Smithsonian present, an undated vertical rudder and control feature was described by Pruckner and sketched by Garber, as Pruckner spoke. The functioning of this rudder, located "*beneath* [the] tailplane" was described by Garber in a letter to Major O'Dwyer, dated November 9, 1966: "As I understood Tony, - there was only one control, - steering to right and left by means of a vertical rudder which was manipulated by a U-shaped line extending from the rudder's pintle along the sides of the fuselage and around pulleys at bow so that the right or left or both hands of the pilot could pull or push fore and aft on either side to swing the rudder." [195]

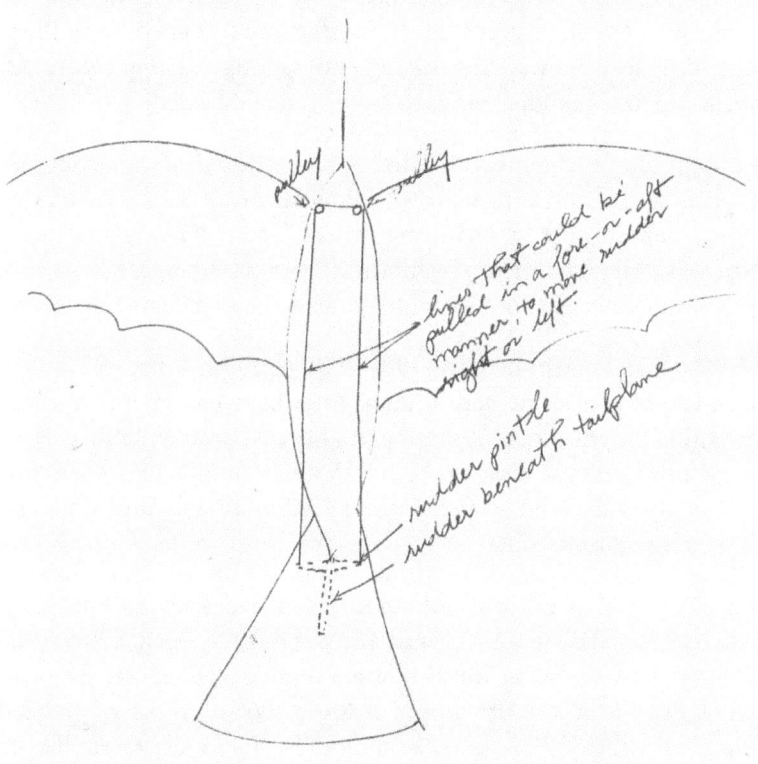

Figure 60: Drawing by Paul Garber, Smithsonian, of Whitehead's rudder system
Courtesy of Fairfield Museum

Above, sketch of Whitehead's "No. 21" vertical-rudder control feature, by Paul Edward Garber, Asst. Director, Smithsonian, following interview with Anton Pruckner, Whitehead's assistant. The diagram notes by Garber are as follows: "lines that could be pulled in a fore-or-aft manner, to move rudder right or left, and rudder pintle, rudder beneath tailplane." With the vertical rudder located beneath the tail, it was not visible in known photographs of this section of the flying machine, on the ground. Paul Garber wished to ask Pruckner more questions about whether there was horizontal rudder control, but Tony Pruckner died within ten days of that interview.

Major William O'Dwyer, Whitehead researcher and expert for four decades, a former United States Army Air Force flight instructor and longtime USAF Reservist, describes Whitehead's wings and rudder:

"His entire 20, 20a, 20b, and 20c series evolved into the craft we identify as "21." 21 was, remarkably, a forecast of things to come. It had a semi-delta wing surface which resembled the "Clam" built later by Sikorsky aircraft in the late 1940's. Twenty One had a controllable tail surface which was controlled by adjustable leverage along with spring tension, the forerunner of today's booster controls. This same ingenious and primitive concept was applied to his wing wires to maintain camber, while at the same time it left them semi-flexible as with a bird's wing in flight. At one time, he designed and tested forward controls (elevator) ... with counter weights for automatic leveling - the forerunner of automatic flight equipment.

The entire aircraft included a complete fuselage with relative ratio sizes to the wings - as those of today...The pilot stood or sat as required and had a cockpit area with accessible throttle, steering, and miscellaneous controls conveniently located. The craft could be taxied along the ground on wheels. One of the more outstanding features were the folding wings, designed long before our giant aircraft carriers and aircraft storage which demanded wings to be hinged and folded."[196]

As for wing warping, Harvey Lippincott, Director Emeritus of Connecticut Aeronautical Historical Association (CAHA), explained in a 1981 interview with Popular Mechanics, "When the wing edge of a model of "No. 21" is bent, there is a definite aileron, or warping effect - *so he did have control.*"[197] During an interview conducted at Smithsonian for German television by filmmaker Spannenberger the same year, CAHA President-Emeritus Lippincott again emphasized that he thought Whitehead had a degree of control:

"I think that the Whitehead machine of the 1901-1902 period had control up to a point. We're not sure exactly how much lateral control he had – he may not have had lateral control actually built into the machine, but he had sufficient dihedral that he might have been actually … in still air, he might have been able to fly laterally without disaster. In rough air he might have lost control. We know he had elevator control. We know that the propellers, by speeding one up and slowing one down would turn you, not quickly, but would turn you."[198]

Major William J. O'Dwyer, in an undated summary of research findings of the late 1960's, stated: "The most remarkable discovery today about #21 and #22 aircraft has been the possibility he controlled this craft through means of wing warping. Wing warping was not an accepted science or a word - it first was an experiment - without a title. Prior to Anton Pruckner's death in 1966, CAHA's Whitehead Research Committee recorded his recollections over a period of 3 years. Among these, he made statements concerning their ability to control the wing surfaces by wing warping - by pulling on the wires attached from the ribs to a central pole or mast. This was immediately located in front of the pilot's station. The wires were within easy reach...While designing the CAHA plans for Whitehead's #21 craft, Irving Berger of Sikorsky's engineering department, and senior draftsman for the firm, offered his opinion that Whitehead was able to control the wings by pulling on the same wires. This theory was advanced without his ever having heard Pruckner's testimony. Descriptions offered by claimed eyewitnesses to his early experimental flights and hops testified the craft turned - as if controlled. They described Whitehead as being able to fly his craft - purposely - in any predetermined direction ... In the summer of 1966 one of Germany's master model builders began building a replica of #21 for the purpose of a radio controlled powered model. Later it was covered and flown ... While constructing the craft, Herr Leinert, its creator and builder, accidentally brushed one of the wires leading down to the wing. He immediately discovered the wings were warpable through this process. It was demonstrated conclusively to O'Dwyer."[199]

Unlike Whitehead's plane, *which by its design was inherently stable*, the Wright Flyer was *naturally unstable*, as is shown in this description:

"The absence of a fixed vertical fin, a fixed horizontal tail and of wing dihedral made the 1903 Wright Flyer an aircraft with no automatic or "built-in" stability; the pilot had to control the machine

Chapter 2: First Flights on August 14, 1901

manually and continuously during flight, and this was in accord with the brothers' original design intentions"[200] ("Wright Flyer," *Flight*, Dec. 1953.)

NASA's Glenn Research Center has analyzed the Wright Flyer of 1903. It has this to say of the Wrights' design: *[emphasis added]*

"… [the Wright brothers' 1903 aircraft] was the first piloted aircraft that was heavier than air, self-propelled and *maneuverable*." [Author's note: NASA does not say the Wright Flyer had *control* and is obviously unaware of the earlier flights of Whitehead.]

"Each of the four flights was marked by an instability in pitch; the nose, and consequently the entire aircraft, would slowly bounce up and down. On the last flight, hard contact with the ground broke the front elevator support and ended the season's flying."[201]

In descriptions provided for the *Evening Telegram* (NY) of November 1901 and the *American Inventor* of April 1902, (see below), Whitehead confirms making improvements to his design by building and successfully flying a new heavier-than-air machine, "No. 22". In Jan 1902, he flew "No. 22", taking off from Lordship Manor, CT, out over Long Island Sound, describing how he used both the rudder and propellers to make a wide turn, to accomplish a a long, circular flight.

In an article written by Gustave Whitehead for the *Bridgeport Sunday Herald* of January 26, 1902, he explains how both a horizontal and vertical rudder may be used to control a flying machine. By January of 1902, Whitehead was already indicating this improvement would help effectively "steer" the plane.

> So it is also with the flying machine. Suppose there were a horizontal rudder in front of our flying machine, which could be set at any angle up or down, now if the machine was in motion and the air stationary, and the plate set at an upward angle, then the corresponding upward thrust would certainly cause the machine to raise at an upward course until the same plate is again set horizontal. It will also cause the machine to descend, if you set the plate at a downward slanting angle. So there we have a very effective way of steering a flying machine up or down, and also provide for longitudinal stability, providing the speed of the machine is high; and as for steering on either side, a vertical rudder may be used wth the same effect.

Bridgeport Sunday Herald, **Jan. 26, 1902**

(transcript)

".… So it is also with the flying machine. Suppose there were a horizontal rudder in front of our flying machine, which could be set at any angle up or down, now if the machine was in motion and the air stationary, and the plate set at an upward angle, then the corresponding upward thrust would certainly cause the machine to raise at an upward course until the same plate is again set horizontal. It will also cause the machine to descend. If you set the plate at a downward slanting angle. So there we have a very effective way of steering a flying machine up or down, and also provide for longitudinal stability, providing the speed of the machine is high; and as for steering on either side, a vertical rudder may be used with the same effect." [202]

(end of transcript)

In the trade journal "*The Aeronautical World*" of December 1902, an article described "W.G. Whitehead's

Gustave Whitehead: "First in Flight"

New Machine," No. 24, a design with controllable wings, tail, and propellers. It was a model based on "No's. 22 and 23," set for upcoming trials by January 1, 1903. It had two sets of wing surfaces for the purpose of determining *"which of the two are best, movable wings, or adjustable aeroplane surfaces, and thus settle for all time this important point...the set or angle of the aeroplanes will be altered and controlled by levers, which will regulate the force of compressed air which actuates them in order to deflect the aeroplanes so as to incline or steer a circular course without shifting the position of the ballast or aeronaut. The tail or rudder will likewise be lowered or raised by means of compressed air controlled by levers...The screw blades [propellers] will be made adjustable so that during flight their set or angle may be changed at will to any desired degree. The machine will run on the ground as an automobile, as illustrated in cut of the old machine above"* ["No. 21" is pictured]. [203]

Whitehead's advanced knowledge, shared with his fellow inventors, worldwide, gained from eight years of testing and many experimental powered flights during the period when the Wrights were still building bicycles and only gliding, is astonishing by comparison. Successful powered flights by Whitehead were reported during 1901, 1902, 1903, up into 1904 and even through 1911. The lack of newspaper coverage for each of them is understandable. He was not seeking fame but successful experimentation. Still, Whitehead's newspaper coverage exceeded that of the Wrights by at least several hundred times during the years of his successful flights. There is no reason to believe that he did not implement the control methods described in the *Aeronautical World* of December 1902, in 1903, or earlier.

As has been pointed out by past researchers, the Wrights applied for their wing warping patent in March 1903, three months *after* this article appeared. In later years, Wright patent applications were submitted for movable rudders, and were expanded to cover use of ailerons, and all horizontal surfaces - much of which Gustave Whitehead had successfully pioneered and shared information about, a decade earlier. These essential components of flight, demonstrated and described by Whitehead several years earlier, were to be later forbidden to him and all others, unless under the control of the Wrights. Aviation development in the USA, by the Wrights' competitors, was shut down tight.
[Emphasis added]

> Wilbur Wright to Orville (July 10, 1908):
> "It might be well to write to [Glenn] Curtiss that *we have a patent broadly covering the combination with wings to right and left of the center of a flying machine which can be adjusted to different angles of incidence, of vertical surfaces adjustable to correct inequalities in the horizontal resistance of the differently adjusted wings... Say that we do not believe that flyers can be made practical without using this combination* and inquire whether he would like to take a license to operate under our patent for exhibition purposes. I would not offer any manufacturing rights."[204]

Curtiss commented on the Wrights' attempts to establish a world monopoly on flight, in Nov. 1912:

> "Their exploitation as the first to fly has been used in an effort to get the Court to enlarge the scope of their patent."[205]

The need for the Wrights to establish being "first in flight" to expand their patents was eventually accomplished in Court with the help of a subrosa employee, as shall be shown. But these legal maneuvers cannot dispel the fact that Whitehead invented and successfully flew multiple powered aircraft well before the Wrights' Kitty Hawk trials.

As "No. 21" (and its successors) was a roadable airplane, steering was necessary when it was running along the ground, as a car. The steering controls for ground travel should not be confused with those intended for use during flight, but we may consider the extent of Whitehead's early genius. Junius Harworth describes this

Chapter 2: First Flights on August 14, 1901

system:

"The rear, or steering wheels, were of the same construction as the front. The shaft however was pivoted from the center of the floor and to the outer edges of the shaft we had brazed a quadrant of flat steel or shoe which slid along another quadrant fastened to the bottom of the floor. When the machine had to be turned the wheel shaft shoe ran or slid along easily. The steering cord was fastened to the outer ring of the shaft as shown.

The plan view of the drawing [Harworth drew plans for Stella Randolph to illustrate this] shows a rope drum having an arm with two spools or knobs attached for gripping while steering the craft. This entire assembly was secured to the mast. The drum had a 3/8" rope wound around it in the same manner as on board ships. From the drum the rope ran thru pulleys located, one on each side, next to the wing cradles, the rope continuing on down the outside of the [fuselage] to the shaft rings."[206]

Whitehead's heavier-than-air flying machines had enough control to make a number of successful sustained, manned powered, flights, from 3 to 50 feet in elevation, according to witnesses, and for reported distances of from one-half a mile to an alleged seven miles, as well as shorter flights of several hundred feet, according to witnesses and reports, *in the several years that preceded* those of the Wrights. Whitehead was publicly describing, developing, and experimenting with the use of moveable vertical and horizontal rudders and methods of wing-warping during these years. He was prevented from fully patenting his far-sighted ideas in time, limited primarily by finances.

Whitehead arguably invented and flew with a significant measure of control, successfully, on many occasions, involving both sustained and street flights, in 1901-1902 and beyond. His comparatively lengthy flights of that period did not end in accidents. His aeroplane designs did not require wind to takeoff or fly.

The Wrights flew shorter hops, without control, unsuccessfully, in Dec. 1903. Their flights, requiring use of a track placed on a sloping surface, relying on a strong headwind, ended with dives into the sand. It would be several more years before they had mastered even moderate control of their plane, and more than a decade before pilots stopped being killed in Wright aeroplanes, due to their well-known tendency to stall. Wright replicas and reproductions still have problems flying – famously made apparent to the world during the "100th Anniversary of Flight" events at Kitty Hawk, North Carolina, on December 17, 2003, despite years of preparation. The "painstakingly accurate reproduction" of the Wright Flyer, built "at a cost of $1.2 million," traveled down a 200 foot long wooden launching track and lifted six inches into the air for one second before twisting and ploughing its right wing into the sand, causing the large crowd assembled to groan.[207] Not one person was ever killed in a Whitehead flying machine during the ten years of successful flights and experimentation, nor in any of the Whitehead "close reproductions"[208] which have been shown to be airworthy. In fact, a Whitehead "No. 21" reproduction based on detailed information from Whitehead's assistants, and use of careful photographic analysis, was *successfully flown for half a mile* in 1998, on October 4, 1997. It is pictured in a test flight by Horst Philipp at Manching airport, in Bavaria, Germany, documented on film, available at this writing to view on "YouTube."[209]

Which machine demonstrated more success and control in the initial years? Which inventor was earliest? Which contender has multiple witnesses with affidavits? Manipulation of the bar will not change the fact that Gustave Whitehead was first to execute manned, powered flights, on both level and elevated ground, in a variety of geographic terrains and conditions, with sufficient controls to accomplish those unparalleled feats safely; nor will it diminish Whitehead's unlocking of "the secrets of flight" and the elements he first utilized, many still employed in today's aircraft. The wording of the Century article written by Orville and the current labels on the Wright Flyer are false and misleading, unfortunately written to glorify Orville, rather than being based on reality. Thus, it can be said that truly controlled flight was in its infancy in the early years of the 20th century, and it would be left to others to accomplish.

PHOTO QUESTIONS

One of the major criticisms of the evidence for Gustave Whitehead's early flights is the absence of photographs of these powered flights, to substantiate the claims. In today's world, and for the past fifty or more years, "in-flight" photographs of Whitehead's aeroplanes have been demanded by some and expected by nearly everyone who hears about the flights. Why is this? Is it because we have always documented historic facts using photography? Have inventions always been documented with photos? The answers to both are "No." However, having been raised with the famous photograph of Orville Wright "in flight" on December 17, 1903, it just seems logical that we should also have a comparable photo of Gustave Whitehead in flight, if he actually did fly. So why don't we? Or, does one exist? If so, why was one never published?

Seeing is believing, for feats like flying. We have become accustomed to expecting photographs of these and all other sorts of events. Photojournalism was just beginning to be used during the turn-of-the-century period when Whitehead began his successful flights. The Wrights were badgered to produce photo proof, from 1903-1908, especially because they could not reproduce the flights for the press the following year, and because, due to patent concerns, did not wish to, for five years. The press began demanding photos of the Wrights, perhaps because man in flight was so unbelievable to them and the public back then. Most people today don't realize it was five long, secretive years later, in 1908, when the Wrights finally produced the photograph we have become so familiar with – showing Orville several feet high in the Wright Flyer, lifting off the track.

Cameras Not Common

Cameras were just becoming available to the average person, with the Brownie camera introduced a year before Whitehead's 1901 flights. It cost a dollar, which was equivalent to half a day's pay for Gustave, out of reach for the millions of poor, who struggled to pay rent and feed their families. By 1901, a quarter million people in the United States had purchased Brownie cameras, but it is doubtful that they were considered plentiful. In the coming decade, cameras would become more common, but still, a luxury affordable only for the upper echelon of the middle class, such as the Wright family, or the wealthy. Whitehead and his neighbors were not in that category. To film a Whitehead flight, therefore, one would have to be invited – members of the big city press or wealthy patrons would be amongst those with cameras. None of these were present for the August 14, 1901 flight, but it is possible some were, later, for the others known to have been photographed. Stanley Yale Beach conducted a photo shoots in spring, 1901 with his extensive photographic equipment, as Aviation Editor for the *Scientific American*. Whitehead did not invite Mr. Beach to his August 14th demonstration. Beach was neither liked, nor trusted by Whitehead and his assistants, according to several of those interviewed – a feeling that bore out to be quite insightful, in the future. Dick Howell, of the *Bridgeport Sunday Herald*, was considered trustworthy and he was invited – but apparently, without a camera or the light needed to photograph the results.

Missing Whitehead Flight Photos

At this writing, *there is no known, authenticated, surviving photograph for any of Gustave Whitehead's powered aeroplanes "in flight,"* despite occasional widespread claims to the contrary. One Whitehead photo claim emerged, rather recently, in 2013, but has been attributed, by a number of investigators, to be a blurred photo very similar to another view of a John Montgomery glider, strung between two trees, taken in 1905. Researchers have keenly sought the corresponding, but missing Whitehead powered flight photos, known to exist in his time, for the past 80 years, to no avail, to date.

At least several Whitehead powered flight photos *did exist,* including for his 1901 "No. 21," reported on by the *Scientific American* in 1906, and for a later 1903/1904 model, by a Bridgeport newspaper, the *Bridgeport Daily Standard*. The smaller, less sophisticated, local newspapers operating on small budgets in the area of

Chapter 2: First Flights on August 14, 1901

Connecticut where Whitehead lived did not appear to use photographs to accompany their articles in 1901, except for occasional still portraits. Drawings illustrated newspapers in the 1800's, with photographs starting to be used in the 1890's, but not fully incorporated, likely due to costs, in 1900 and the earliest years of the century. Instead, artists' sketches or lithograph-style illustrations accompanied their articles. The use of photography by journalists in the greater Bridgeport area, and in much of the nation, to document powered flights was still several years away. It does not appear that any Whitehead powered flight photos were published in the newspapers, but since many old newspaper archives are still not digitized, archives are often incomplete and remain on microfiche. It is still possible that a Whitehead photograph may yet surface, with the most likely source being private ownership, rather than located in a newspaper or magazine.

First Sustained Powered Flight Was a Night Flight Which Could Not Be Photographed

The first sustained powered flight of "No. 21" on August 14, 1901, though made in the presence of a reliable local newspaperman, was not documented with published photographs, but rather, with a sketch of the scene, as was customary for this newspaper. The flight witnessed by the journalist was made in the dark early morning hours just before dawn, as was Whitehead's custom, to avoid crowds, and take advantage of early morning weather conditions. There had been one incident reported of nearly running over a small boy who got in the way of the plane[210], a time when a group of boys grabbed onto it and were lifted twelve feet up into the air, and another account of many children following the plane[211]. When Whitehead did fly before crowds, the police sometimes were required for crowd control. [212] With a plane that had six foot propellers running and an excited populace not used to seeing flight, with no controlled airfields in existence, it was no wonder Whitehead would choose the isolation of nighttime for his demonstration. In 1901, night-time conditions were not suited to picture taking, nor was it easy to photograph swiftly moving objects, especially in very low light, without a blur - day or night. Junius Harworth, Whitehead associate and helper for many years, including 1901, said, "... no films were in use which could be used at dawn ..."[213] There was no moon on the night of August 14, 1901, and the lanterns described by Harworth as used during experimentation would have been of no help for obtaining photographs. During the daytime, even with a camera, a rapidly moving object would be hard to capture. That would change, over the course of the next decade.

Documentation Considered Accomplished

Whitehead's invited a major local sports editor to be present to document "No. 21" in a sustained flight with an article that would inform the public of the results. In 1901, in Bridgeport and surrounding towns, the written word, not photographs, informed them of events. Those present had their minds on the matter at hand, which was attempting a long flight, to learn from, while staying safe - not proving a flight (which seemed self-evident at the time due to the journalist's presence), for future generations. Whitehead considered the flight a success, but was eager to improve upon it. His goal was not to seek fame or fortune, but to eventually build a practical airplane that would be useful to travel in from place to place, transporting people commercially. A photo, albeit blurred, may have been taken of the plane in flight as the basis of the sketch on August 14, 1901, but there is no proof of this, and it remains unlikely, due to the hour the flight was made.

Whitehead's flights on August 14, 1901 are well documented through the eyewitness journalist report and later witness affidavits, despite the lack of photo-evidence.

Gustave Whitehead: "First in Flight"

Figure 61: NY Herald illustration of Whitehead's "No. 21"

depicted *as it would appear in flight*, from a sketch in a June 16, 1901 article
two months prior to his sustained flights

Whitehead's Documentation Vs. the Wrights'

The Wright Brothers did not invite *any* journalists to be present for their December 17, 1903 flights, which took place during daytime hours. All Wrights flight documentation is based on their own records, reports, "diary entries," and a few conflicting statements in interviews and letters made decades later by several witnesses; none made sworn affidavits. Their flights took place on a very isolated beach in North Carolina, to be away from crowds, but for additional reasons, wanting to protect their work from prying eyes. Journalists had trouble believing the Wrights' flights had occurred, as a result, for years. Three of the five Wrights' witnesses were from the local lifesaving station. They had been asking the Wrights if they could watch for months. They were finally given the date. A young boy, Johnny Moore, happened to be in the vicinity.

> "Those who did arrive were John T. Daniels, Willie Dough, and Adam Etheridge of the Lifesaving Station, lumber merchant W. C. Brinkley of Manteo, and Johnny Moore, a 16 year old boy from Nags Head." [214]

Four of the five witnesses to the Wrights' flight on December 17th, 1903, [215] reportedly invited themselves (lifesaving crew and Johnny Moore) and produced no written statements for this date till decades later. The famous photo by Daniels was set up by the Wrights for him to snap the photo when the plane lifted from the track, which he did. [216]

> "We inquired what day they expected to fly. Finally they told us the day. Finally, on this day, the 17th of December Daniels, Dough and myself were out there helping to get the machine out of the camp out on the track." [217]

It should be noted that the famed photo of Orville Wright "in flight" technically proves only that the

Chapter 2: First Flights on August 14, 1901

plane lifted 18 inches off the ground, in a strong wind. Further, the record shows that purported "flight" was in reality a brief hop that ended in damage. We have been told that the Wright photo proves powered and controlled flight, but it, in reality, it does not. A Whitehead photo of a plane in powered flight would be helpful, but should not be considered necessary.

Whitehead, by inviting a respected journalist who wrote about sports, showed foresight in documenting the first official trial of "the Condor." Aviation was seen as a recreational sport at the time, as no commercial applications had yet been possible. Neither the Wrights nor Whitehead thought to have their witnesses sign affidavits at the time of the flights. We can be certain that their minds were on testing their craft and staying alive, never imagining that in the future there might be questions about the validity of the witnesses' statements, nor other claims of first flight. Their common goal was to perfect a practical heavier-than-air flying machine. We have evidence that both had photos taken, or attempted, of early trials of their powered, manned aircraft, yet not all survived. Those that did, as we will learn later, are not necessarily of successful flights, in the case of the Wrights. Regarding witness affidavits, *none were ever* taken of Wright witnesses to the powered flights at Kitty Hawk. Nearly a score of Whitehead witnesses to manned, powered flights before 1903 were located and affidavits taken, in the 1930's, 1960's, and 1970's. Even in the 1980's, people who had known Whitehead were found, oftentimes around a century old, and in nursing homes – but they still remembered him and his flight experiments.

Whitehead Attempts to Photo Gliders and Powered Aircraft

It is well documented that Gustave Whitehead was aware that photos and other illustrations were important, and that he (and some of the press) were interested in providing some examples of the flights being made by both his gliders (without power) and powered aircraft. On January 17, 1902, Gustave attempted to make photos "which didn't turn out well" of his circling flights made over Long Island Sound, described in a Letter to the Editor of the *American Inventor* in their April issue. Written during the winter, Whitehead said he'd try to make photos again and invited the editor to be present and take pictures of his next set of flights in the spring. There is no evidence that the trade journal contacted him back to come and make photographs.[218]

There are a number of press and other photos of Whitehead gliders on the ground and in flight at very low speeds, with powered heavier-than-air planes on the ground, taken during the period 1901-1909. During one of the photo shoots of a Whitehead triplane glider in flight over a field, a few years later, it has been well-documented that the photographer became so frustrated by blurring of the photos from even the low speed of the glider that a static photo had to be taken of how it would look in flight. The glider was slung hanging from a tree by wires.[219] [220] Photographs of rapidly moving objects was difficult, if not impossible, in 1900's - this is an example of the problems Whitehead was having with photographing his flights.

Whitehead Flight Photos in the Press

Whitehead continued to develop multiple designs, making powered flights through at least 1910, according to a score of witnesses. The *Bridgeport Daily Standard* newspaper reported, in its Oct. 1, 1904 issue, that (undated but recent) photos of Whitehead in successful powered flight were being displayed in the local Lyon & Grumman's hardware store window, in Bridgeport, for all the public to see.[221]

Gustave Whitehead: "First in Flight"

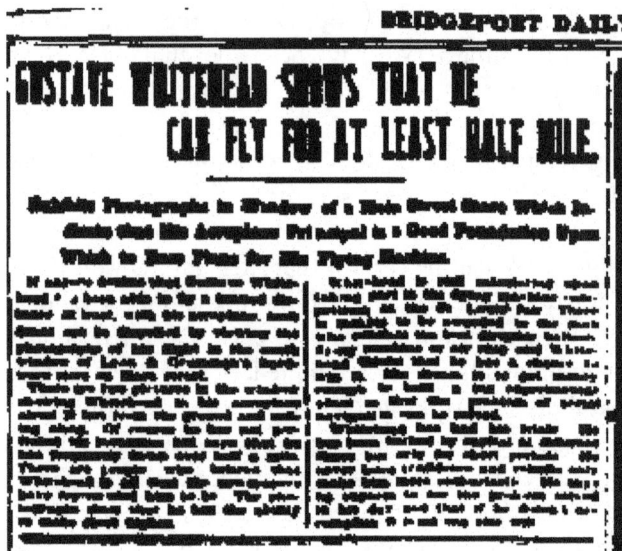

Figure 62: *Bridgeport Daily Standard* describes Whitehead flight photos

(Transcript of the article:)

GUSTAVE WHITEHEAD SHOWS THAT HE CAN FLY FOR AT LEAST HALF MILE

"Exhibits Photographs in Window of a Main Street Store Which Indicate that His Aeroplane Principal is a Good Foundation Upon Which to Base Plans for His Flying Machine.

If anyone doubts that Gustave Whitehead has been able to fly a limited distance at least, with his aeroplane, such doubt can be dispelled by viewing the photographs of his flight in the south window of Lyon & Grumman's hardware store on Main Street.
There are two pictures in the window showing Whitehead in his aeroplane about 20 feet from the ground and sailing along. Of course he has not perfected his invention but says that he has frequently flown over half a mile. There are people who believe that Whitehead is all that the newspapers have represented him to be. The photographs show that he has the ability to make short flights.

Whitehead is still calculating upon taking part in the flying machine competition at the St. Louis World's f[F]air. There is $100,000 to be awarded to the man who exhibits the best dirigible balloon, flying machine or air ship and Whitehead thinks that he has a chance to win it. His dream is to get money enough to build a big experimental plant so that the problem of aerial navigation can be solved.

Whitehead has had his trials. He has been backed by capital at different times but only for short periods. He never loses confidence and rebuffs only make him more enthusiastic. He says he expects to see the problem solved in his day and that if he doesn't accomplish it some one else will." [222]

A blurred photo of the 1901 "No. 21" plane in flight was said to be exhibited at the First Annual Show of the Aero Club of America in New York City, written up in the *Scientific American* of January 27, 1906.[223]

Chapter 2: First Flights on August 14, 1901

> inventor prefers to keep secret. No photographs of this or of larger man-carrying machines in flight were shown, nor has any trustworthy account of their reported achievements ever been published. A single blurred photograph of a large birdlike machine propelled by compressed air, and which was constructed by Whitehead in 1901, was the only other photograph besides that of Langley's machines of a motor-driven aeroplane in successful flight. In order at least partially to substantiate their claims, it would seem as if aeroplane inventors would show photographs of their machines in flight. This has been done by Mr. Maxim

Figure 63: *Scientific American* **reports 1901 Whitehead flight photos**
Scientific American, Jan. 27, 1906, pp.93-94

Text of the photo description:

"A single blurred photograph of a large birdlike machine propelled by compressed air, and which was constructed by Whitehead in 1901, was the only other photograph besides that of Langley's machines [Author's note: these were *models* of Langley's machines] of a motor-driven aeroplane in successful flight."

The blurred photo of Whitehead in flight was carefully investigated by Whitehead researcher, Major William J. O'Dwyer, in the early 1980's-1990's, but without access to the full-sized photos hanging on the wall or conceivably located elsewhere in the exhibition hall, it was not possible for Major O'Dwyer to definitively identify which photo Beach had referred to. As aforementioned, a photo of Whitehead from the same 1906 exhibition was allegedly identified as "a photo of Whitehead in powered flight," in 2013, which touched off a brief, worldwide media flurry of excitement and controversy, but did not prove to be a Whitehead plane in flight, after all.[224]

The original glass plate negative of the blurred photo of the 1901 plane described in the *Scientific American* of 1906 has not yet been located, nor have any subsequent prints made from it, despite extensive searches; these and the other in-flight photos known to exist in 1904-1906 due to multiple journalists' eyewitness accounts, may have been lost over time. Since the photo of Whitehead's "No. 21" airplane in flight appeared to be part of hundreds of photos exhibited with an extensive aviation collection of William Joseph Hammer, aviation enthusiast and Consulting Engineer (later Wright proponent and employee), donated to the Smithsonian in 1962 by IBM, there is conjecture that the Whitehead powered flight photo may now reside buried deep in the Smithsonian archives - perhaps, it has often been said, deliberately so.

Gustave Whitehead: "First in Flight"

Figure 64: The *Scientific American* **of January 27, 1906**

Scientific American **of January 27, 1906 described a blurred photo of Whitehead's 1901 plane in powered flight**

seen at the Aero Club of America's First Exhibit of Aeronautical Apparatus that had just concluded. There is no record of a challenge to this statement from the many hundreds that poured through the exhibition.

Chapter 2: First Flights on August 14, 1901

Figure 65: Aero Club Exhibition of January 1906, Whitehead photos

Arrow at left shows location of some Whitehead photos on display, near William J. Hammer aviation photo collection.
William J. Hammer Collection, Smithsonian Institution
O'Dwyer Archives, Fairfield Museum

Figure 66: Collection of Pictures by Wm. J. Hammer
Sign on wall under bottom line of photos

There were numerous flights reported by witnesses in the period from 1900 - 1903. Photographs of gliders in flight existed and at least several were reported for the 1901 "No. 21" aeroplane in flight, in possession of at least one of Whitehead's contemporaries, but appear to have all been lost.

Photos were mentioned by the daughter of a Whitehead associate, Mr. Miller, according to Major William J. O'Dwyer, Whitehead researcher, who, with the 9315th US Air Force Squadron (Ret.), conducted a project to identify remaining witnesses and photographs in the 1960's and 70's. John Whitehead, Gustave's brother, named a "Mr. Miller" as the (Cherry Street) shop foreman, recollecting which people were most influential in their associations with Gustave Whitehead during the 1901 flight period. A Mr. Miller was also mentioned as an earlier sponsor, who apparently died around the time Mr. Linde sponsored Whitehead, in the fall of 1901, and could not have been the shop foreman. In the 1960's, O'Dwyer researched and located the person who was likely the daughter of the sponsor named Miller, then quite elderly, who told him that her father was given photographs of Whitehead's flight experiments and told to save them, as they were important. Following this discussion, she entered a nursing home, where she died soon after. O'Dwyer was not able to obtain the photos as Miller's granddaughter could not find them in her mother's house. She did recall playing with them as a child, having no understanding of their importance. The granddaughter recalled seeing photos of aircraft in flight, as well as engines and aircraft under construction.[225]

Another photo has been said to have been taken by a ship's captain as the plane flew overhead, but this has also not been found.

One thing appears certain - a number of photos of Whitehead's early powered flights were taken at various times. It is still possible some still exist, in archived materials, or in the homes of people who may not realize their significance. We still have the testimony of multiple journalists who saw them, and others who said they had existed.

NEWSPAPER COVERAGE OF FIRST FLIGHT

Close to a hundred national and international newspaper articles, in addition to the many eyewitness statements, have been located by Whitehead researchers, covering the Whitehead "first flights" of August 14, 1901. Initial, key articles published by local press in Connecticut, New York, and Boston, Massachusetts, now placed within a collection of at least 50 additional newspaper and magazine articles at Whitehead archives[226] in Fairfield, Bridgeport, and Stratford, Connecticut were identified prior to the use of the Internet, due to painstaking research through local archives and libraries by early researcher Stella Randolph[227] and later, Major William J. O'Dwyer, Whitehead researcher[228] with the help of the local historical societies. These spanned the time period from August 18, 1901 (when the *Bridgeport Sunday Herald* broke the story to the public) through 1902 and continued for the next decade, including mention of Whitehead's first flights in publications such as *Scientific American*. Additional articles are now available through Internet searches of digitized newspapers.

Many of the local, national, and international newspapers described the flight and gave the names of the two witnesses, with variations on the spelling of Andrew Cellie (ex. Collie) and James Dickie, causing them to become local celebrities, no doubt. Some of the newspapers sounded just a tad doubtful, as with the Wrights announcements several years later, it was hard for the press, as well as the public, to believe that man could fly "unless they'd seen it with their own eyes," as did eyewitness journalist, Dick Howell, of the *Bridgeport Sunday Herald*. Perhaps the fact that a highly respected, well-known, fellow newspaperman, like Howell - later renowned as the top newspaperman in Connecticut -was an eyewitness led credence to this manned flight, which had seemed to most everyone, an impossibility in 1901. The New York City newspapers were regional, just sixty miles away. Closer yet were the surrounding Connecticut cities of Danbury, Norwalk, and New Haven, which ran the story and updates on Whitehead's activities, in the following weeks. One other Bridgeport newspaper, the *Bridgeport Evening Post*, revealed additional flight experiments that preceded "the final test" Howell had witnessed, with new information on what Whitehead was planning next. *Particularly of note, not one local newspaper, nor one person, including those named as eyewitnesses, challenged the Bridgeport Herald's account, throughout the late summer of 1901 and into the winter of 1902*, though the opportunity to ridicule the story would have been readily available, if untrue. No other Bridgeport newspapers ran Howell's exact account, conceivably by mutual agreement within the collegial atmosphere of the city's press, as he had landed the "exclusive" for that local readership. The region's broad coverage, with descriptions of other flight experiments, shows the degree of confidence in Whitehead's (and Howell's) statements that the flights had, indeed, occurred.

Chapter 2: First Flights on August 14, 1901

These article headlines and selections below are but a small example of the news coverage of Whitehead's final "No. 21" flight experiments, which resulted in the half mile flight.

The *New York Herald* (NYC, NY) ran a prominent account on August 19, 1901,

> "INVENTORS IN PARTNERSHIP TO SOLVE PROBLEM OF AERIAL NAVIGATION
> Gustave Whitehead Travels Half a Mile in Flying Machine Operated by a New Acetylene Chemical Pressure, Lessening Motor Power Weight Seventy-Five Per Cent
>
> BRIDGEPORT, Conn., Sunday – With the purpose in view of perfecting a flying machine that will solve the problem of aerial navigation to the point of commercial success, Gustave Whitehead, of this city …..last Tuesday night, with two assistants, took his machine to a long field back of Fairfield, and the inventor for the first time flew in his machine for half a mile. It worked perfectly, and the operator found no difficulty in handling it. Mr. Whitehead's machine is equipped with two engines, one to propel it on the ground, on wheels, and the other is to make the wings or propellers work…In order to fly the machine is speeded to a sufficient momentum on the ground by the lower engine, and then the engine running the propellers is started, which raises the machine in the air at an angle of about six degrees… the hopes of the inventors for success are placed on a new pressure gas engine which Mr. Whitehead has invented…He has applied for patents… "

The *New York World* (NYC, NY) of Aug. 19, 1901 reported,

> "LATEST FLYING MACHINE TRAVELS ON EARTH AND IN AIR; INVENTOR, WHO HAS NEW MOTOR, MAKES SUCCESSFUL TEST.

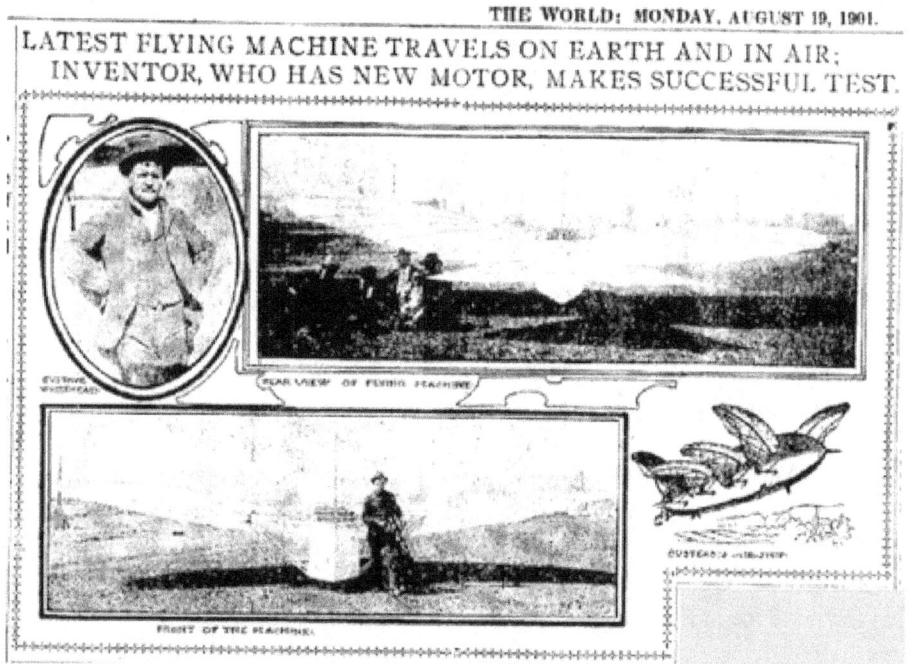

Figure 67: The World, Aug. 19th, 1901 – Latest Flying Machine Travels on Earth and in Air

Gustave Whitehead: "First in Flight"

> WHITEHEAD FLIES IN HIS AIRSHIP
> MACHINE RUNS ALONG THE GROUND AT A HIGH RATE OF SPEED, THEN FLAPS ITS WINGS, DARTS UPWARD, AND SOARS LIKE A BIRD
> AT INVENTOR'S WILL ALIGHTS WITHOUT JAR
> EXPERIMENTAL TRIP MADE AT BRIDGEPORT WITHOUT ACCIDENT, ALTHOUGH MACHINE AND MAN HAD A NARROW ESCAPE FROM COLLISION WITH A CLUMP OF TREES
>
> GUSTAVE WHITEHEAD CAN FLY …"

(The rest of this long article is a rendition of the *Bridgeport Sunday Herald* feature.) It does report that "Custead is now in New York."

The *New York Sun* (NYC, NY), which had carried news of Whitehead's unmanned flight experiments in May in their June 9th, 1901 edition, announced Whitehead's successful manned, sustained flights in an article in their August 19th, 1901 issue, on page 2:

> "WHITEHEAD MACHINE FLIES. BRIDGEPORT INVENTOR SAYS HE'S MADE ANOTHER TRIP
>
> Took It in the Night Last Week and Went Half a Mile Fifty Feet Above Ground – He Dodged a Clump of Trees by Tipping the Machine to One Side.
>
> BRIDGEPORT, Conn., Aug. 18 – Gustave Whitehead, the mechanical engineer of this city, who has been experimenting with flying machines for a decade, has made a final test of his invention. It is said to have flown a distance of half a mile with Mr. Whitehead at a height of fifty feet and to have descended safely…"

The New York Evening Telegram (NYC, NY) weighed in, also on August 19, 1901, with,

> "HALF A MILE FLIGHT IN AIR
>
> Connecticut and Texas Investors Give a Successful Exhibition of Their Flying Machine
>
> [BY TELEGRAPH TO THE EVENING TELEGRAM.] …."

The Brooklyn Eagle (NYC, NY) of August 19, 1901, pronounced,

> "Whitehead Has a Flying Machine.
>
> BRIDGEPORT –With the purpose in view of perfecting a flying machine that will solve the problem of aerial navigation to the point of commercial success, Gustave Whitehead of this city and W.D. Custead of Waco, Tex., have formed a partnership. Both men are inventors. Mr. Whitehead last Tuesday night, with two assistants, took his machine to a long field back of Fairfield, and the inventor for the first time flew in his machine for half a mile. It worked perfectly, and the operator found no difficulty in handling it."

The New Haven Palladium (in nearby New Haven, CT) recounted, in a full column article,

Chapter 2: First Flights on August 14, 1901

"New Flying Machine Bridgeport Mechanical Engineer Sails through the Air at Pleasure
Bridgeport, Conn., Aug. 19 – Gustave Whitehead, the mechanical engineer of this city, who has been experimenting with flying machines for a decade, has made a final test of his invention. It is said to have flown a distance of half a mile with Mr. Whitehead at a height of fifty feet and to have descended safely… The flight was made at 2 o'clock on Wednesday morning in Fairfield with Andrew Collie [Cellie] and James Dickie, who have been furnishing the inventor with capital for the past year, as spectators. If their versions of the flight are true, Whitehead has a real flying machine…"

[Note: Actually, the unmanned test flight was made about 2 AM, and the manned flight, just before dawn. Some of the near hundred rewrites of the *Bridgeport Sunday Herald*'s Associated Press article mistakenly set the time for the manned flight at "just after midnight or 2 AM."]

The Boston Transcript reported in a half column article, on August 18, 1901,

"AN AIR PARTNERSHIP
Whitehead of Bridgeport and Custead of Texas Expect Much from an Acetylene Motor

Bridgeport, Ct., Aug. 19 – With a view to perfecting a flying machine for commercial purposes Gustav Whitehead of this city and W. D. Custead of Waco, Tex., have formed a partnership…last week Whitehead flew in his machine half a mile…The company is capitalized at $100,000."

The London St. James Gazette wrote,
An Acetylene Air-ship.

Mr. Gustave Whitehead (says the New York correspondent of the "Daily Mail") has invented a combination air-ship and automobile. The complete motive power, including an acetylene generator and engine, with fuel for twenty hours, weighs five pounds per horse-power. In a test at Bridgeport, Mr. Whitehead ran along a macadam road at twenty miles an hour, and short distances at the rate of thirty miles. He then opened the throttle of the machine, which spread its wings and rose 50 feet. After sailing half a mile, Mr. Whitehead alighted safely. The machine is 16 feet long. Its general appearance is that of a huge bat. While Mr. Whitehead has demonstrated that his machine will fly, he does not claim that it can be made a commercial success. He says, however, that his invention will decrease by 75 per cent the weight of any motor now in use. He regards his machine as in the experimental stage, and will try to make further improvements."[229]

Whitehead later referred to the flights of August 14, 1901 in subsequent interviews, like the one with the New York Telegram, three months later, where he explained that he had flown a mile and a half in the machine then lying in his yard, abandoned, as he was already engaged in building an improved model made with aluminum. "With all his knowledge, Whitehead is a modest man. When I surprised him in his shop, he at first refused to talk about his invention at all, saying he would rather wait until the new machine was completed. He declared, however, there was no secret about what he was doing and to prove it pointed out a window and said, *"There is the machine that I flew in. You can go out and look at it. It is abandoned now as junk for the new one I am making will be much lighter and stronger and will contain better material. The old one taught me my lesson, and that was enough for it to do."* [230] Whitehead would take to the skies again, successfully, two months later, in January 1902, with the new and improved model, "No. 22"

Gustave Whitehead: "First in Flight"

Chapter 3

NEXT STEPS

PROMISES FLIGHT TO NEW YORK

Following his successes of the summer of 1901, Gustave announced, within a week of his August flights, that his next project would involve building a new, improved, commercial aircraft that he would attempt to fly to New York, with at least one other passenger. Exhilarated by the summer flights, he enthusiastically made the "Will Fly to New York" declaration, undoubtedly somewhat embellished by newspapers running the story.

The announcement, published in a wide round of newspapers, including the *Boston Daily Globe*, included the news that Gustave Whitehead had begun to make modifications to "No. 21," described as "a rough model," which would allow it to be stronger, with improved steering, the "new machine will be large enough to accommodate half a dozen persons and my foreman [who will] accompany me on my trip to New York… Visitors are barred from the Whitehead workshop and sentinels keep all those who are curiously inclined at a reasonable distance…"[231]. Thus, "No. 22" had begun to be constructed, with the world informed, with animated plans (if underestimating, of the time and financial investment it would take) for commercial applications, within a week of his successful experiments of mid-August. This renovation continued, after a month-long trip to Atlantic City with his flying machine, now under construction to improve it, once again. The local "*Bridgeport Evening Post*," "*The Norwalk Hour*," "*The New Haven Palladium*," and "*The Danbury News*" were some of many local newspapers across Connecticut, with numerous others in New York, Massachusetts, and across the entire nation, which enthusiastically ran versions of these Associated Press stories, with updates on August 23, 1901, and throughout the fall and early in 1902. Newspaper coverage of this sort was often incomplete, focused on one topic, as the account by the *Norwalk Hour* mentions only one of the summer flights. The promised flight to New York ran similarly to this article in at least a score of newspapers. Custead, the airship inventor from Texas, his backer of several weeks before, was no longer mentioned in any accounts, though new sponsors were emerging.

The *Norwalk Hour* of August 23, 1901, announced,

> **Will Fly to New York**
>
> "*Gustave Whitehead Declares He Will Make the Sixty-Mile Trip.*
> Gustave Whitehead, of Bridgeport, who has made one ascension in his flying machine, promises to make another flight in his winged craft, from Bridgeport to New York, sixty miles, and says confidently that he has solved the problem of navigating the air. His machine, in which he made a half mile trip at a height of fifty feet, Mr. Whitehead says, "embodies all the principles of aerial navigation. It has large

wings attached to a body with the outlines of a sailing craft. Mr. Whitehead does not know how soon he can complete the machine which he has in process of construction expressly for the trip to New York, and which will include improvements of the original machines. "My machine, " said Mr. Whitehead, will be large enough to seat half a dozen people, and I shall take one of my machinists with me when I make the trip to New York. I am as confident that I can successfully fly to New York in it as I am that I can ride my own bicycle."[232]

The *Washington Times* of Washington, DC, of August 23, 1901, carried a long article about Whitehead setting a goal of flying to New York City and mentions his next step – an exhibition trip to Atlantic City.

"TO FLY TO NEW YORK.
Whitehead Certain that His Airship Can Make the Trip.
BRIDGEPORT, Conn., Aug. 23 – Gustav Whitehead, the flying machine inventor of this city, who one night a week ago is said to have flown a distance of half a mile in his machine at a height of fifty feet, said today that his next flight will consist of a trip to New York City and return. *For this purpose he is having a new machine built on his premises. The only difference in the two, he says, is that the new one will be built stronger and large enough to carry half a dozen persons*…Since the feat of my half mile flight was published, I have been besieged by friends and have received many letters from inquisitive people all over the country. They asked me many questions concerning my machine and its flight…"

WHITEHEAD AND "NO. 21" GO TO ATLANTIC CITY

Following the successful sustained, manned, powered flights of August 14, 1901, Whitehead exhibited his flying machine, early in the process of reconstruction following the final flights of "No. 21," at Atlantic City, New Jersey, leaving Bridgeport at the start of the last week of August. The *Washington Times* reported on Friday, August 23, that "during the latter part of the [coming] week" Gustave was headed for Atlantic City, to exhibit it publicly, at the invitation of an unnamed "Philadelphia gentleman." [233]

> During the latter part of the week Whitehead is having his present machine to Atlantic City, N. J., where he intends to exhibit it publicly. There is a Philadelphia gentleman interested in Whitehead who has asked him to bring the machine with him to that place. He will not divulge his name.

A popular local newspaper, the *Bridgeport Evening Post* of August 26, 1901[234] informed its readers that Whitehead "left this city a few days ago to exhibit his flying machine at Atlantic City during the next six months [said to be two months in its subtitle] for which he is to receive $150 per week."

Chapter 3: Next Steps

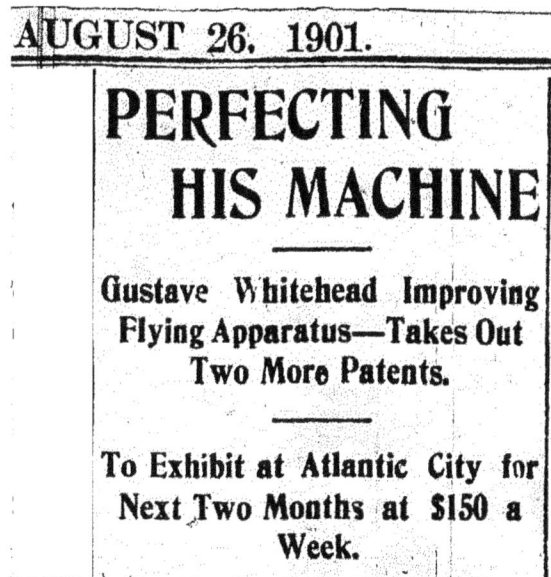

Figure 68: *Bridgeport Post* announces Whitehead to exhibit at Atlantic City

Bridgeport Evening Post, August 26, 1901, p. 1
Courtesy of the Bridgeport Public Library newspaper archives,
Bridgeport, CT

For an average wage earner with $600-$800 yearly, $150 weekly would be enticing, indeed – it was the equivalent of $4,300 weekly, in 2015. The reporter further indicated, "The inventor now has all the financial backing he needs and from present indications his flying-machine promises to attract world-wide attention."

During the Atlantic City exhibition, Whitehead was visited by a Smithsonian representative, F.W. Hodge, a clerk in the office of Charles Matthew Manley. Manley was a mechanical engineering student (later receiving his degree *in absentia* from Cornell University) and chief assistant to Smithsonian's third Secretary, Samuel Pierpont Langley, providing the latter help in building a "man-carrying airplane," including an aero engine.[235] Manley was busy redesigning an automobile engine originally invented by Balzer, hoping to increase its horsepower from 8 to its eventual 21. Whitehead's two-cycle aeroplane engine had four cylinders, with 20 horsepower and 700 revolutions per minute; widely recognized (worldwide) as making a successful flight of ½ mile in August 1901. Shortly after, inspecting the lightweight Whitehead aeroplane engine and obtaining ideas from it became a high priority for Manley. Whitehead had "beaten Langley and Manley to the punch," having designed an aeroplane and engine that successfully flew. The Smithsonian was mainly interested in fulfilling *its* goal of developing an aeroplane and engine, already generously funded with major grants from multiple sources, including Congress. Apparently, the best they could offer Whitehead in the fall of 1901, after his successful "summer of flights" was strong interest in "borrowing" his ideas. Later, when writing his memoirs, Manley failed to provide Balzer credit for the original design of the motor – which further substantiates Manley's self-centered attitude.[236] Charles Manley apparently also failed to credit Gustave Whitehead for a successful aeroplane motor of similar horsepower, which predated what is now known as the large "Balzer-Manley engine," though Whitehead's engine was carefully and systematically inspected, and may have influenced his designs. Mr. Manley was definitely not above "the *lifting* of design ideas" from others, on record as later crediting these entirely to himself. Whitehead exhibited his airplane at Atlantic City so the world and interested parties or potential sponsors might take a look, naively setting himself up to have his ideas stolen – unlike the self-funded, more business-oriented Wrights, who knew enough to be ultra-secretive to protect their inventions and future patents from theft, being less trusting, and having the benefit of better legal advice.

Charles Manley wrote Mr. Hodge, who was in Atlantic City, staying at the Albemarle Hotel, a letter on September 20, 1901, requesting him to surreptitiously gather measurements of Whitehead's "No. 21."

> "Mr. Traylor has just told me this morning that Gustave Whitehead, of Bridgeport, Conn., who has built a full-sized flying machine in which he claims to have flown a distance of half a mile, has his machine on exhibit on Young's Pier at Atlantic City. When Mr. Traylor saw it, which was only a day or so after Whitehead arrived at the Pier, they had not finished assembling the various parts of the machine, and he was consequently not able to get some information which I would like to have regarding it…"

Mr. Traylor was the private secretary to Secretary Langley.

Interestingly, the next paragraph expresses duplicitous statements, doubting Whitehead's machine could have flown; calling it "flimsy" for use with Whitehead's 20 horsepower engine, *yet wishing to gather extensive information on its construction that could be used for only one purpose, that which Manley was then engaged in, building an aeroplane and engine for Langley.* This, from a would-be co-inventor who, with government financing, given five years, failed to produce anything save several embarrassing public "flops" of the later Langley "Aerodrome," the last of which nearly drowned him in the Potomac, in 1903. Langley, with Manley's assistance, had been trying to develop a workable aircraft for the United States Army for several years, fated to be hopelessly unsuccessful, making Langley a laughingstock of the media, in the fall of 1903.

Manley continues, wanting Hodge to provide him with very specific information about Whitehead's flying machine, attaching the clipping with photos of Whitehead's "No. 21", from the *Scientific American*, June 8, 1901, p. 357, with parts hand-labeled by Manley, pertaining to letters referred to in his questions[237]…

> "…If it will not be too much trouble, and you can find time, will you be good enough to make a visit to Young's Pier and find out for me the following points about the machine:
>
> In order to make my questions more clear, I enclose a clipping which was published some months ago regarding the machine, and prior to the time that Whitehead claims to have flown in it. Referring to the diagram on the clipping, I would like to know how the brace rods are joined to the frame of the machine at the points marked xxx; what these brace rods are made out of, and their approximate diameter if they are round…"

The letter then explains Mr. Traylor thought the brace rods were nailed, which could not stand the strain from an engine – this was proven false from examination of photos of Whitehead's plane[238] and a 1963 interview with Anton Pruckner, Gustave Whitehead's assistant in 1900-1901, who explained that bolts, not nails, were used.[239]

> "…I would also like to know what the spread from tip to tip, marked z; the width of tail at the inner end, marked s; the length of the tail marked t; the width of the propeller blade marked y; and any other dimensions which it may occur to you to take after seeing the machine. These dimensions which I have asked for will be accurate enough if the longer ones are made by stepping it off, and the shorter ones by some such method as stretching ones arms and noting the point from the tip of one finger to some other point on the other arm.
>
> What I am more interested in than anything else, however, is his claim for his engine, which I understand is run by acetylene (or calcium carbide) gas, the motive power being produced by the explosions of the

Chapter 3: Next Steps

gas in the cylinders.

First, - To have you ask him how many explosions per minute he gets in each cylinder; second, - whether he has any water jackets on the cylinders; third, - how many revolutions he obtains from the propellers when the engine is delivering its full power to them. Please also note whether he transmits the power from the engine shaft to the propellers by means of bevel gears, and if so, what is the size of the gears.

As I said above, I think the man's claim to having flown is fraudulent, and am anxious to get the above information, which, if you can obtain for me without any serious inconvenience to yourself, I will appreciate very much….

Very truly yours,
Chas. M. Manley

Mr. F. W. Hodge,
Albemarle Hotel,
Atlantic City, N.J." [240]

Manley would later famously attempt to pilot Langley's failed invention, "the Aerodrome," in October and December of 1903, nearly losing his life in the process. Manley also became known for the development of a lightweight engine, interestingly enough, in light of the aforementioned gathering of information on Whitehead's engine. Manley is credited, to this date, with development of "the first internal combustion engine specifically designed for an aircraft" by Smithsonian.

Considering Charles Manley's protests in several parts of the letter that Whitehead's (competing) flying machine (which Manley never saw) could not possibly have flown, it is notable that he was so extremely interested in gathering details which could only have been used to further his and Langley's own experimentation. To this day, the Smithsonian and other US government agencies laud Samuel P. Langley and Charles M. Manley nearly as if they had invented the airplane – which Smithsonian virtually claimed Langley had, through the early 1940's, angering Orville Wright, considerably, for 20 years.

Perhaps one of this group is the "Philadelphia connection" who enticed Whitehead to go to Atlantic City, in the first place.

Newspapers from the region covered Whitehead's flying machine display in Atlantic City, which was to have a demonstration on the beach, according to the following article, in *The Daily Union*, of that city. It is not known whether that demonstration ever occurred.

(partial transcript)

Young's Ocean Pier
"Perhaps the two things which attract the greatest amount of interest on Young's Pier today are the tiny little boat in which Captain Andrews and his young bride will attempt to cross the billowy Atlantic, and the big flying machine of Prof. Whitehead. Both of these unique contrivances -- one intended to sail through the water, the other to navigate the air -- are novel and so different from anything that has hitherto been exhibited that unusual attention is centered in them….The flying machine will be on exhibition throughout the weekend and it is probable that Prof. Whitehead will give a practical demonstration of its workings on the beach …"
[Note: the rest of the article does not pertain to Whitehead]

(end of transcript)

FIRST FLYING MACHINE FACTORY

"No. 22" Improved Design

In early October 1901, an enthusiastic Gustave Whitehead established the world's first airplane factory in order to produce more of his flying machines, with the help of his new backer, Herman Linde (also known as Hermann Linde, a German immigrant, Shakespearean actor, painter, and art collector from New York). Prior to this date, as early as August Whitehead may have moved his shop from his home at 241 Pine Street to this new location. But with Linde's promised infusion of funds, the newest and most progressive "factory" in Bridgeport was established. The humble assortment of wooden buildings was located on Cherry Street, in Bridgeport, near the northeast corner of Cherry and Hancock Streets, across from the Wilmot & Hobbs manufacturing company. Whitehead and Linde wanted to produce an improved, stronger flying machine made with steel tubing rather than bamboo, with a more powerful motor; attempt a roundtrip flight to New York City; begin a commercial service that could transport up to six persons; and sell airplanes to people in a manner similar to cars, for $2000 each. It is certain that neither of the men understood that, while their goal was eventually to be attainable, it would occur only in future decades, building on the pioneering breakthroughs of Whitehead and others, through collective efforts and sacrifices. Sadly, Gustave, for all his revolutionary work and enthusiasm, would not be amongst those who accomplished viable commercial flights. Nevertheless, he had opened the door and led the way to realize that objective.

During this period, Whitehead began to be more careful to keep his inventions protected from the public eye. No admittance to the shop was allowed. A wire fence was erected to keep people out. Day and night shifts of mechanics were described. A local newspaper, the *Naugatuck Daily News*, less than 30 miles away, reported confirmed details which could only be known through direct interview, on November 18th:

> **"Whitehead's Flying Machine**
> *Bridgeport Inventor Now Has Fifteen Men Working for Him.*
>
> Bridgeport, Conn., Nov. 18. – Gustave Whitehead, the flying machine inventor, backed by New York capital, has leased a machine shop in the western part of this city where a force of 15 machinists are at work manufacturing a permanent flying machine for publicly [public] demonstration purposes. Whitehead says he will manufacture his inventions in this city on a large scale this winter and expects to be able to put several of them on the market next spring. The model machine has a seating arrangement to accommodate six persons. This style of a machine will be made to sell for $2000.
>
> The identity of the capitalists who are backing the enterprise is a secret, as is much of their plans. Admittance is refused to the many curious person who daily apply at the shop for the privilege of witnessing the manufacture of the steel flying machine. Whitehead himself is not the frank and talkative man he was a few weeks ago and firmly adheres to a determination to say nothing for publication until such a time when he can fulfill his promise to flying his machine to New York [C]ity.
>
> Whitehead's machine shop is well equipped and the mechanics at work in it are personal friends with whom he formerly worked in the factory of the Wilmot & Hobbs Manufacturing Company, as an engineer. It has steam power, which is used 20 hours each day. Half of the help works in the daytime and the other at night. They alternate weekly. Up to date over $10,000 has been spent by Whitehead's backers who appear to be men of wealth. They visit the shop frequently but no one but Whitehead himself knows their identity."[241]
>
> Parts of the machine are being made by other firms in this city. Whitehead has a new motor which he proposed to use in his invention which can be operated, he believes, with any of those now used in the various styles of automobiles."

Chapter 3: Next Steps

However, the initially amicable partnership with "secret sponsor" Linde would last only a few more months – at most, into the early spring, due to many disagreements and subterfuge by Linde, who did not understand the realistic costs of such an endeavor, nor the time it would take to be accomplished. Linde eventually attempted to obtain the means to produce the airplanes without Whitehead, later related to researcher Stella Randolph by Mrs. Whitehead, which caused the final blow, leading to termination of the relationship. [242]

One of the main disagreements appears to have been about design ideas and safety. Linde, who was, at best, an art dealer and actor who recited entire plays to audiences all around the nation, and at worst, insane, apparently began to dictate exactly how the new flying machines should be designed, though he had no background to do so. One of Linde's unfounded, dangerous pet ideas was the use of motors utilizing gunpowder as the motive power. Whitehead's assistant, mechanical engineer Anton Pruckner reported they'd experimented with gunpowder engines, resulting in partially blowing up the shop on Pine Street, at one point – undoubtedly making Whitehead, his wife, and the neighbors quite unhappy.

The January 26, 1902 edition of the *Bridgeport Sunday Herald* ran a large, feature article on page four, with an update concerning the status of the world's first flying machine factory in Bridgeport, followed by announcement of Whitehead's application to the World's Fair aerial contest and a treatise by Gustave Whitehead on his discoveries about flight. Very significantly, as aforementioned, *the Herald also reconfirmed that Whitehead had been flying with power, during the previous summer.* Regarding the Whitehead – Linde partnership venture, the factory, and "No. 22'," the Herald informed its readership, as follows: *(emphasis added)*

"BRIDGEPORT'S FLYING MACHINE FACTORY
Whitehead and Herman Linde Delving Into the Difficult Problem of Aerial Navigation. The Great Obstacle in the Way of Success is to Get a Motor That is Both Sufficiently Light and Adequately Powerful. Experiments With Gunpowder, Carbide Calcium and Kerosene Generators.
(*Bridgeport Sunday Herald*, Jan. 26, 1902)

WHEN THE FLYING machine tourney opens at the St. Louis Exposition, Connecticut will be represented. In Bridgeport two men are working to perfect air ships that will not only fly but be of some use from a commercial point of view. These men are Gustave Whitehead and Herman Linde. Until a week ago Friday they were associated in building one airship but owing to a misunderstanding they had about methods and plans of development they separated and now each one is building a flying machine embodying his own ideas.

The ideas of the two men are quite dissimilar in many respects regarding the style or kind of a machine that will be most practicable for navigating the air. The motor for the machine is the hard problem to solve. The motor must weigh as little per horse power as possible and still be strong enough to be safe and secure.

Linde is at present developing a gun powder motor. The power is obtained from exploding the powder by contact with a strip of platinum made red hot by an electric current generated by fastening one end of the platinum strip to a copper pole and the other end to a zinc pole. There is great power in the motor but it is said to be dangerous.

Whitehead is at present working on a kerosene motor. *He has a calcium motor, which he used in his experiments last summer when flying,* but he is not satisfied with it. He also has ideas for a gun powder motor, but he says that the gun powder motor and the carbide calcium motor are dangerous. The kerosene motor, if brought to a condition of perfection, will be one of commercial utility as kerosene is cheap, can be bought anywhere and it is safe.

Whitehead has already received letters from the St. Louis exposition aerial committee to participate in the tourney and he fully intends to have a machine ready for that great occasion.

Gustave Whitehead: "First in Flight"

Herman Linde now occupies the flying machine factory in the West end of Bridgeport, back of the Wilmot and Hobbs plant, alone. He has several machinists working for him. Whitehead is working at his home on Pine street. He has prepared specially for the Herald the following article on aerial navigation: …"[243]

Linde was undoubtedly eager to invest and make money right away off the attractive venture. As time went on, it became apparent that neither of the two men was anticipating the actual costs or difficulties involved with such an ambitious project. In a time when skilled factory workers earned one or, at most, two dollars a day - working ten hours daily, six days a week often producing far less than a hundred dollars. The costs of building an airplane (and establishing a factory) could reach easily into the thousands: occasionally, for other aspiring aeroplane inventors, such as Smithsonian's Samuel Pierpont Langley, between fifty and a hundred thousand dollars and even, as with Hiram Maxim, up to a million dollars in capital investment.[244] Squabbles over Linde's far more limited funds did not take long to erupt between Linde and Whitehead, leading to eventual legal action in the spring against Linde for, literally, a few extra dollars charged to Linde's account at the local lumber company, which occurred in late November.

The Frank Miller Lumber Company filed suit in April 1902, to try to collect $60 that the highly excitable Linde did not wish to remit[245]; after having made a partial payment, he claimed he'd cancelled the agreement to furnish materials to Whitehead. Mr. Linde denied during the trial that he'd had an agreement with Whitehead, despite evidence to the contrary, in the form of a letter to the lumber company, and an account opened jointly, in both of their names. Linde claimed his agreement with Whitehead, executed in October 1901, was only to provide $1,000 (though he told the court he'd invested $6,000 total), which he further claimed expired when the new plane was not completed during his prescribed, brief time period. By November 20, 1901, $110 worth of lumber was furnished to Mr. Whitehead, whereupon the tight-fisted Linde only paid $76. The lumber company said Linde had never notified them not to provide Whitehead with more materials. It seems Linde was unable to fund the experiments and from his performance in court, we can surmise that he also had problems telling the truth. There is no evidence he actually invested $6,000, though this was not pertinent to the case against him. Developing a commercial aeroplane was going to cost more than $76 in materials! Two of the local Bridgeport newspapers - rivals of the *Bridgeport Sunday Herald,* the largest newspaper in the state, which ran long exclusives about Whitehead - reported on Linde's predicament, while taking a moment to poke fun at Whitehead for his lofty flight ambitios.[246]

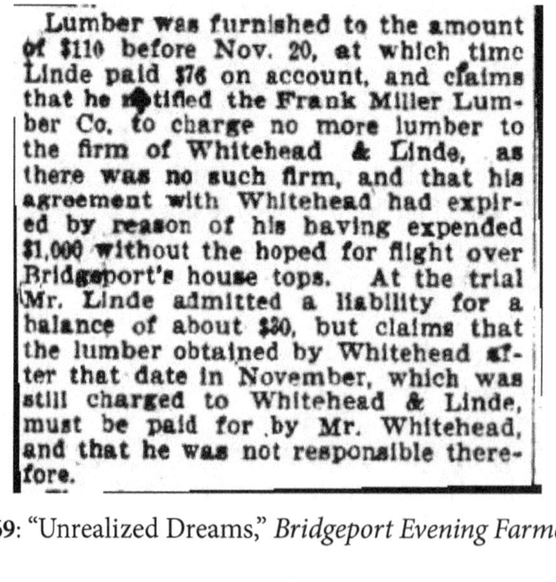

> Lumber was furnished to the amount of $110 before Nov. 20, at which time Linde paid $76 on account, and claims that he notified the Frank Miller Lumber Co. to charge no more lumber to the firm of Whitehead & Linde, as there was no such firm, and that his agreement with Whitehead had expired by reason of his having expended $1,000 without the hoped for flight over Bridgeport's house tops. At the trial Mr. Linde admitted a liability for a balance of about $30, but claims that the lumber obtained by Whitehead after that date in November, which was still charged to Whitehead & Linde, must be paid for by Mr. Whitehead, and that he was not responsible therefore.

Figure 69: "Unrealized Dreams," *Bridgeport Evening Farmer,* April 5, 1902

Chapter 3: Next Steps

Linde began to back out as Whitehead's sponsor before the end of November according to his court testimony[247], with evidence the relationship continued into January and at most, the spring of 1902, according to Whitehead, who published some limited information about a January 1902 split in the *Bridgeport Sunday Herald*.[248] Later, interviews conducted by Stella Randolph with Whitehead's wife, Louisa, revealed that Linde was trying to steal Whitehead's flying machine plans[249]; likely with the anticipated equivalent of $5 million at stake in the upcoming St. Louis World's Fair aerial competition as a prime motivation. The *Bridgeport Evening Post* carried an article on May 19, 1902 revealing that Herman Linde, an art critic and "famous Shakespearean," who'd claimed a lucrative art deal that went bad, "is the person who at one time backed up Mr. Whitehead of this city in his efforts to construct a flying machine"… "Mr. Linde is now at work on a flying machine of his own in the West End of this city."[250] The *Bridgeport Daily Standard* of August 2, 1902 reported that Linde had closed the shop he'd funded on Cherry Street, across from Wilmot & Hobbs, when he parted with Whitehead.[251] Apparently, Mr. Linde wished for a very fast return off a minimal investment, but this was not to be possible, particularly when the technology being developed, to attempt to build an airplane to transport people distances as far away as New York was to be the first of its kind in the world, sought after for thousands of years. The jump from success in a lightweight airplane with a single pilot, flying short distances, to being able to develop practical applications was to be long and arduous, though neither man apparently knew this, and it might be said, "how could they?" It is only with hindsight developed over a hundred years that we can see how long that would take. But practical applications of aeroplanes seemed to be right around the corner to many inventors, hard at work, during the early years of the 20th century. Locked out of the factory, Whitehead soon had to continue on alone, with whatever funds he could pull together, for the next six months.

Mr. Linde is worth examining from the perspective of the type of unfortunate, opportunistic sponsor Gustave Whitehead unknowingly attracted and had to deal with, at this juncture. Herman Linde, who traveled about the country's major cities for four decades, was well known for his work in the arts, an art collector, art critic and instructor, notable for his remarkable memory, oratory powers, and Shakespearean recitations in cities throughout the United States. He would eventually move to the west, where he eventually died, after a tumultuous life, including a stint in a Denver county insane asylum. This followed an arrest in 1906 for what was described to be a "trivial" incident in a New York newspaper upon his death [252] but derived from threatening the life of President Theodore Roosevelt's wife. In 1906, the Secret Service considered Herman Linde to be "a lunatic of a dangerous type."[253] [254] The record shows a number of legal cases and lawsuits involving Linde, who seemed to operate out of New York until 1906. Most involved claims he had been defrauded of money or goods by artists or clients, or causing a public scene of one sort or another. In one case, there was a ruckus at an auction involving Linde, who said he'd bid higher than another bidder for a piece of artwork.

In 1892, the same Herman Linde showed how unsavory he could be, both in public and in court - the latter he would repeat again, ten years later, in Bridgeport. Linde's real name was revealed as Henry Lindner in the *Washington Post* article, providing his professional name as "Herman Linde," describing him as an artist and public speaker. He was placed on trial for blocking the path of and lewdly staring at - consequently, insulting - a sixteen year old girl in Washington, DC, the daughter of a military man. Upon telling her father what happened, he approached Linde and confronted him. Linde called him a liar, and was struck by the father. Linde was fined $25 for insulting the girl. His defense was that he was admiring her figure.

> "The defendant, who is a German, *was very excited in his manner, even in court, and counsel frequently referred to this*, as well as to the fact of the sharp eyes of the defendant."[255]

In November 1901, Herman Linde was described as being from Pittsburgh, PA, in the account of one case where he sued the estate of a gentleman who had not paid $6000 for paintings Linde had ostensibly delivered the previous August. Linde later died in abject poverty, in Denver, CO, in April 1909, while claiming to own

Gustave Whitehead: "First in Flight"

$500,000 worth of paintings allegedly stored in New York, but refusing all purchase offers.[256]

An early photo [257] [258], newly evaluated, is now known to show part of Whitehead's Cherry Street shop at right, from the period likely taken in October 1901 – evidenced by the clothing and activities of the men, the condition of the ground, the design of the bat-winged monoplane, and location. In the distance, behind, with the smoke stack and multiple buildings, is Wilmot & Hobbs' manufacturing plant, at the northwestern corner of Cherry and Hancock. Newspapers reported that Whitehead began his agreement with Herman Linde on October 1, providing the funds to build the factory, which began in a modest building.

Figure 70: Cherry Street shop, 1901 "First Airplane Factory," with "No. 22" prototype
Courtesy of Missouri History Museum, St. Louis

This previously unidentified action shot preserves this vital moment in history for all time, revealing the world's first airplane factory workers, including machinist Anton Pruckner, wearing shop aprons, seen working on the first successful airplane design. The factory was reported by local newspapers to be producing multiples of an improved version of Whitehead's "No. 21," or what might better be described as the early prototype of "No. 22."

Chapter 3: Next Steps

Figure 71: Gustave Whitehead, fall, 1901 at Cherry Street shop
Whitehead is pictured third from left at rear of "No. 22."

Figure 72: World's first airplane factory workers #1

Figure 73: World's first airplane
factory workers #2

Figure 74: World's first airplane factory workers #3,
Anton Pruckner leaning over plane.

**The world's first airplane factory workers, in Bridgeport, Conn, fall, 1901.
At right may be "Mr. Miller," factory foreman,** later described by John Whitehead.

© Susan Brinchman, 2015

Gustave Whitehead: "First in Flight"

The worker at far left has cord in hand, sewing the wing fabric to a wing rib, while the man to his left holds it steady. Whitehead is viewed, at far back, third from left, holding the brim of his cap against the bright, early afternoon sun. Six workers in all, five with shop aprons, pose for the photograph, some appear to inspect and work on the plane. A young Anton Pruckner is seen leaning over the wing, smiling. He was about age 20 then (see portrait of Pruckner at Figure 38). He worked with Whitehead on "No. 22" 's new, more powerful engine, leaving at the end of 1901 for a temporary job in NJ. Two men are seen at right, wearing suits (first from right and third from right). The first man wears a shop apron also. The third man from right appears to be a businessman – perhaps it is Herman Linde [aka Henry Lindner], Whitehead's sponsor, in October seen below, looking expectantly and fondly, at what seems to bear promise in being the world's first prototype of a commercial airliner.

Figure 75: fits description of actor Herman Linde, Whitehead's NY sponsor

The second unidentified "suited man," seen in Figure 74 (at right), and at far right in the original photo, could be an associated party from New York, frequently visiting the Cherry Street shop, with Mr. Linde to check on progress, fresh from visiting the machine shop, protecting his suit with an apron. Articles of the era refer to multiple sponsors, which may account for this additional "gentleman" in a suit. The building at far left seems to be an outhouse for the workers.

"There is nothing pretentious about Whitehead's factory. In fact, one might easily pass it without notice. It is only about forty feet long and about fifteen feet wide and is rudely constructed of boards. In it, however, is some valuable machinery, and Whitehead says the place is big enough for the present. Adjoining it is a diminutive engine house about fifteen feet square. In this little shop a dozen men are working on the day force and five at night." (NY Evening Telegram, Nov. 19, 1901)

Chapter 3: Next Steps

The plane's billowing wings, seemingly flapping in the breeze, are tied down to stakes, one is seen in the ground at left. The fuselage is barely visible, beneath the wings, at center. The rudder appears to be crumpled, or not yet assembled, while the propellers, motor, and wheels are noticeably absent, not yet added to this particular machine. Leaning against what appears to be the sidewall of the "factory" building, is an oval shaped object with slatted boards – it also might be the early prototype of an enlarged fuselage being developed to accommodate six persons, as described in interviews with Whitehead. Previously this was thought to be a boat used to help retrieve the flying machine when it lands in water.

The roof of the shop reveals a skylight, also visible in rows on the roofs visible in a sketch of the multiple buildings identified as Gustave Whitehead's "flying machine factory" on Cherry Street, which appeared in the January 26, 1902 *Bridgeport Sunday Herald* article (see below).

Figure 76: Cherry Street shop, 1901 "First Airplane Factory," photo #2
Photo courtesy of Fairfield Museum, O'Dwyer archives

Whitehead's "No. 22" powered plane pictured on Cherry Street. *Note: this is the "sister" photo (taken a few minutes apart) of the photograph sent to the Louisiana Purchase Exposition Company in January 1902, shown above. This photo previously thought to be located at Black Rock harbor, being inspected for damage, now is revealed to be at the site of the new aeroplane factory. Sponsor Herman Linde may be pictured third from the right, in the dark suit, leaning over the flying machine.*

Figure 77: Cherry Street shop, 1901 "First Airplane Factory," photo #3
Another view of the world's first "flying machine factory."
Probable young Junius Harworth at fence.
Photo courtesy of Fairfield Museum, O'Dwyer archives

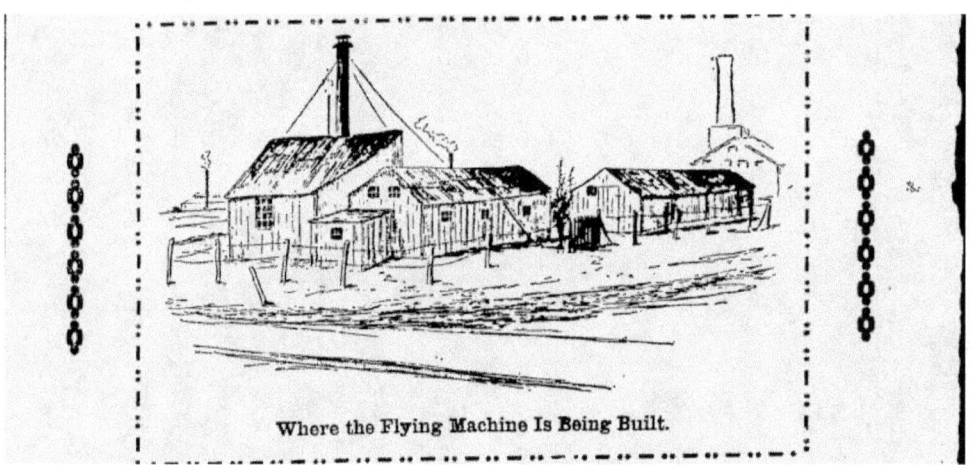

Figure 78: *Bridgeport Herald* **illustration of first airplane factory**

"Flying Machine Works" illustrates and announces first airplane factory in the world, in Bridgeport, CT, Nov. 17, 1901

The full article, below, provides a look at the heady anticipation of what the two partners thought, at the outset, that Whitehead's vision of commercial flight could bring to the world.

Chapter 3: Next Steps

BRIDGEPORT HERALD

VOL. 9, No. 581.   BRIDGEPORT, CONN. SUNDAY, NOV. 17, 1901.   PRICE FIVE CENTS.

THE LARGEST CIRCULATION IN THE STATE.

FLYING MACHINE FACTORY
THE LATEST OF
BRIDGEPORT'S INDUSTRIES

Gustave Whitehead, Inventor of Only Practical Air Ship, Engaged in Building Soaring Carriages Which Will Be Placed on the Market in Spring and Sell For About the Same Price That a High Grade Automobile Brings. Night and Day Forces Working. Fifteen Mechanics and Two Engineers Employed at the Flying Machine Works.

ADMITTANCE TO SHOP REFUSED.

New York Man of Money Backing the Project and Already $10,000 Has Been Placed at the Disposal of the Inventor. A Good Family Machine With Seating Capacity For Six Will Cost About $2,000. Inventor Whitehead Will Fly From Bridgeport to New York.

Figure 79: *Bridgeport Herald* **front page feature Flying Machine Factory #1**

WILL USE NEW MOTIVE POWER.

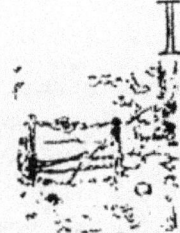

IF THE PLANS OF his financial backers mature, and the indications are that they will, Gustave Whitehead, the flying machine inventor, will shortly experience the pleasure of having his product manufactured on a large scale, and Bridgeport will win the distinction of possessing the most unique and modern industry in the whole civilized world.

Upwards of $10,000 have already been expended by the capitalists who have interested themselves in Mr. Whitehead, believing as he does himself, that the problem of aerial navigation has been solved. It would be foolhardy to presume that Mr. Whitehead could succeed in obtaining such an amount of capital without first giving those possessing it some assurances that his invention had reached the state of perfection.

flying machine modelled after the one in which Mr. Whitehead made two successful flights recently as described in the Herald at the time. It was with this machine that Mr. Whitehead demonstrated the practicability of his invention during the season in Fairfield.

Since that time two more flights have been made for the benefit of the New York capitalist, whose identity is kept a secret. The new machine is to be a permanent affair and when completed, Mr. Whitehead proposes to make good the assertion that he will fly to New York city and return in it. Mr. Whitehead secured capital through the extensive newspaper advertising which he was subjected to recently.

After the first flying machine is completed and publicly exhibited, it is proposed to begin the manufacture of them in Bridgeport immediately. They can be made with accommodations to six people to sell for $2,000. A variety of motor power can be utilized in the flying machines as are now used in the several types of automobiles, but it is likely that a carbide motor will

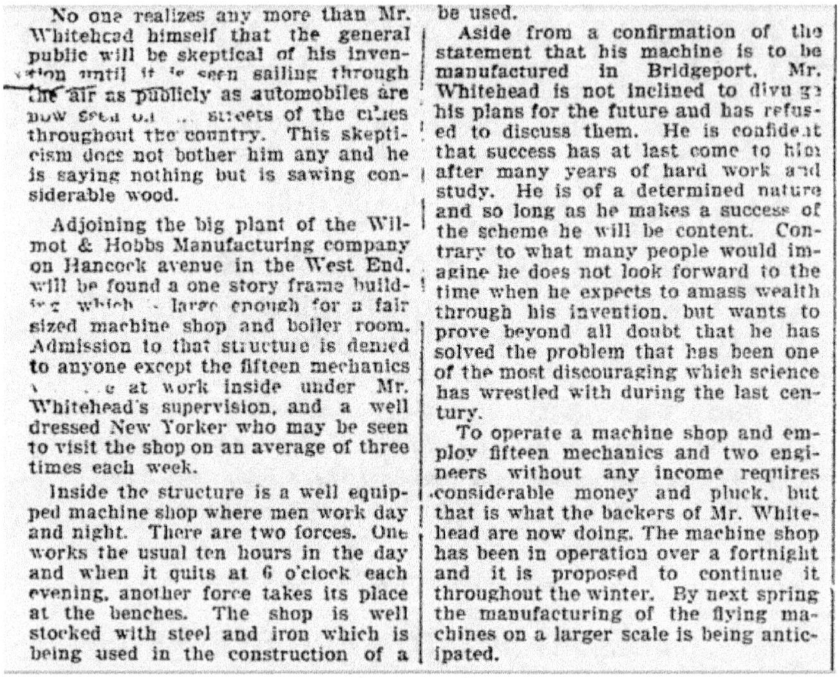

Gustave Whitehead: "First in Flight"

> No one realizes any more than Mr. Whitehead himself that the general public will be skeptical of his invention until it is seen sailing through the air as publicly as automobiles are now seen on the streets of the cities throughout the country. This skepticism does not bother him any and he is saying nothing but is sawing considerable wood.
>
> Adjoining the big plant of the Wilmot & Hobbs Manufacturing company on Hancock avenue in the West End, will be found a one story frame building which is large enough for a fair sized machine shop and boiler room. Admission to that structure is denied to anyone except the fifteen mechanics who are at work inside under Mr. Whitehead's supervision, and a well dressed New Yorker who may be seen to visit the shop on an average of three times each week.
>
> Inside the structure is a well equipped machine shop where men work day and night. There are two forces. One works the usual ten hours in the day and when it quits at 6 o'clock each evening, another force takes its place at the benches. The shop is well stocked with steel and iron which is being used in the construction of a be used.
>
> Aside from a confirmation of the statement that his machine is to be manufactured in Bridgeport, Mr. Whitehead is not inclined to divulge his plans for the future and has refused to discuss them. He is confident that success has at last come to him after many years of hard work and study. He is of a determined nature and so long as he makes a success of the scheme he will be content. Contrary to what many people would imagine he does not look forward to the time when he expects to amass wealth through his invention, but wants to prove beyond all doubt that he has solved the problem that has been one of the most discouraging which science has wrestled with during the last century.
>
> To operate a machine shop and employ fifteen mechanics and two engineers without any income requires considerable money and pluck, but that is what the backers of Mr. Whitehead are now doing. The machine shop has been in operation over a fortnight and it is proposed to continue it throughout the winter. By next spring the manufacturing of the flying machines on a larger scale is being anticipated.

Figure 80: *Bridgeport Herald* **front page feature Flying Machine Factory #2**

Whitehead's Flying Machine Factory described, November 1901
First Airplane Factory in the World[259]

(transcript)

"Flying Machine Factory, The Latest of Bridgeport's Industries" (*Bridgeport Sunday Herald*, Nov. 17, 1901. p. 1)

"WILL USE NEW MOTIVE POWER.

IF THE PLANS OF his financial bakers mature, and the indications are that they will, Gustave Whitehead, the flying machine inventor, will shortly experience the pleasure of having his product manufactured on a large scale, and Bridgeport will win the distinction of possessing the most unique and modern industry in the whole civilized world.

Upwards of $10,000 have already been expended by the capitalists who have interested themselves in Mr. Whitehead, believing as he does himself, that the problem of aerial navigation has been solved. It would be foolhardy to presume that Mr. Whitehead could succeed in obtaining such an amount of capital without first giving those possessing it some assurance that his invention had reached the state of perfection.

No one realizes any more than Mr. Whitehead himself that the general public will be skeptical of his invention until it is seen sailing through the air as publicly as automobiles are now seen on the streets of the cities throughout the country. This skepticism does not bother him any and he is saying nothing but is sawing considerable wood.

Adjoining the big plant of the Wilmot & Hobbs Manufacturing company on Hancock avenue in the West End, will be found a one story frame building which is large enough for a fair sized machine shop and boiler room. Admission to that structure is denied to anyone except the fifteen mechanics who

Chapter 3: Next Steps

are at work inside under Mr. Whitehead's supervision, and a well-dressed New Yorker who may be seen to visit the shop on an average of three times each week.

Inside the structure is a well-equipped machine shop where men work day and night. There are two forces. One works the usual ten hours in the day and when it quits at 6 o'clock each evening, another force takes its place at the benches. The shop is well stocked with steel and iron which is being used in the construction of a flying machine modelled after the one in which Mr. Whitehead made two successful flights recently as described in the Herald at the time. It was with this machine that Mr. Whitehead demonstrated the practicability of his invention during the season *[sic: summer]* in Fairfield.

Since that time two more flights have been made for the benefit of this New York capitalist, whose identity is being kept a secret. The new machine is to be a permanent affair and when completed, Mr. Whitehead proposes to make good the assertion that he will fly to New York and return in it. Mr. Whitehead secured capital through the extensive newspaper advertising which he was subjected to recently.

After the first flying machine is completed and publicly exhibited, it is proposed to begin the manufacture of them in Bridgeport immediately. They can be made with accommodations for six people to sell for $2000. A variety of motor power can be utilized in the flying machines as are now used in the several types of automobiles. But it is likely that a carbide motor will be used.

Aside from a confirmation of the statement that his machine will be manufactured in Bridgeport, Mr. Whitehead is not inclined to divulge his plans for the future and has refused to discuss them. He is confident that success has at last come to him after many years of hard work and study. He is of a determined nature and as long as he makes a success of the scheme he will be content. Contrary to what many people may imagine he does not look forward to the time when he expects to amass wealth through his invention, but wants to prove beyond all doubt that he has solved the problem that has been one of the most discouraging that science has wrestled with during the last century.

To operate a machine shop and employ fifteen mechanics and two engineers without any income requires considerable money and pluck, but that is what the backers of Mr. Whitehead are now doing. The machine shop has been in operation now over a fortnight and it is proposed to continue it throughout the winter. By next spring the manufacturing of the flying machines on a larger scale is being anticipated."[260]

(end of transcript)

Whitehead's new, improved plane, "No. 22", the factory, and the flights of August 14th, 1901, are all described in *The Evening World*, a New York newspaper, and the *New York Evening Telegram*, on November 19, 1901.

Figure 81: **Evening World announces new airplane factory**

(Transcript)

Bridgeport, Conn., Nov. 19 -- There is building in a little shop in this city an airship that the inventor says will certainly fly. His name is Gustave Whitehead and he has already travelled more than a mile through the air in a ship of his own invention. This ship has been improved upon and the new machine is said by the inventor to be as near perfect as it can be with the facilities at hand...His machine will also run on land and through the water...

The new machine is built like a boat. Projecting from the side are gigantic wings and in the rear is a fan-shaped arrangement like the tail of a bird. There is an engine in the boat that operates the wings and rudder. The power will be generated by calcium carbide, which is fourteen times stronger than gasoline.

Whitehead says that his engine, which weighs only twenty-five pounds, will generate thirty-horse power. Rubber-tired wheels for use on land will be attached to the bottom of the body of the machine and a propeller for use in the water will be added.

The section in which the machinery is placed weighs 150 pounds. Instead of canvas, sheet steel, so thin it weighs less than eight ounces to the square foot, will be used for the wings and fan-shaped tail.

Whitehead asserts that he has solved the mystery of flying in the air with the wind or against it. He will soar like a bird, he says, and teach others to soar. he has capital back of him and expects to be ready to experiment with his new machine in a short time..."[261]

(end of transcript)

Chapter 3: Next Steps

The original interview was conducted at his shop by a New York Telegram reporter, as reported in a lengthier article in November 1901[262].

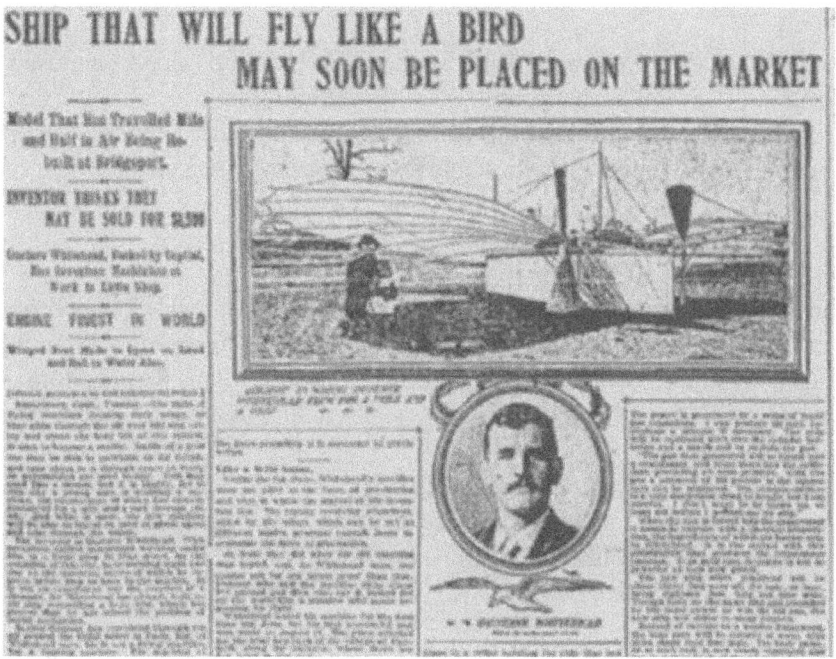

Figure 82: Evening Telegram Announces "No. 22" and new factory

THE EVENING TELEGRAM – NEW YORK, TUESDAY, NOVEMBER 19, 1901
(*transcript*)

SHIP THAT WILL FLY LIKE A BIRD MAY SOON BE PLACED ON THE MARKET

Model That Has Traveled Mile and Half in Air Being Rebuilt at Bridgeport.

Gustave Whitehead, Backed by Capital, Has Seventeen Machinists at Work in Little Shop.

ENGINE FINEST IN WORLD

Winged Boat Made to Speed on Land and Sail in Water Also.

[SPECIAL DISPATCH TO THE EVENING TELEGRAM.]

BRIDGEPORT, Conn., Tuesday.–."... in this city a young man is building a machine, the counterpart of which has already journeyed for a mile and a half through the air. And what is more, the new machine will be able to travel on land at great speed and also through the water.

The inventor is Gustave Whitehead. With seventeen skilled machinists working under him in a little shop in Pine Street, *[sic: actually, on Cherry Street, one block away from Pine Street]* on the outskirts of this city, he is working night and day on the machine, the likes of which he expects before long to have in the market. It is not an experiment nor has the creation of a dreamer, for Whitehead already built an

Gustave Whitehead: "First in Flight"

air ship resembling a huge bird, which has proved that he has solved the problem of aerial navigation.

... The machine of Whitehead ... will soar through the air...

"This new machine will be the twentieth I have made," Whitehead said as he mused in his work to-day, and talked about the invention that promises to make him famous for all time. Eighteen of them were failures, through some small fault that I could not fathom at the time, but the last one I made rewarded my years of effort and accomplished what I have so long been trying to solve.

Will Astonish World.

"The new one I am making now will be far better than the last one. For I have profited by my mistakes and, when completed, it will astonish the world. It will have the finest engine ever made, one I invented and constructed myself, and its power, considering the weight, will be far greater than that of any engine in existence.

"Since I was a boy, going to high school in Augsburg, Germany, where I acquired some knowledge of mechanics and engineering, I have had the idea of a flying machine in my mind and then I made up my mind that I would someday be like the birds I was so fond of watching. After leaving school I went to sea and sailed around the world five times.

"I remember once watching the big condors flying off the South American coast and trying to understand how they did it. I used to study the gulls too, as they would soar against the wind with outstretched planes moving apparently without the slightest effort.

"Now I understand how they did it, for I have done the same thing myself. I am the only man who has ever risen from the ground and have flown through the air. Money? No, I do not believe I will ever be rich. At least I do not think or care to think about that. When I make my machine perfect so I can fly about at will, I shall be satisfied. My new machine will do that better than the old one, but, of course, there will always be room for improvement. Besides flying through the air, it will run along the ground on four big rubber tired wheels and will also sail through the water.

Mile a Minute.

"I expect my new machine to attain a speed of fifty or sixty miles an hour through the air and about forty miles an hour on the ground. The little propeller astern, which will be arranged so it can be connected with the land engine, will drive the machine through the water at a speed of something like fourteen miles an hour. The power will be generated by calcium carbide, which is fourteen times as powerful as gasoline."

With all his knowledge, Whitehead is a modest man. When I surprised him in his shop, he at first refused to talk about his invention at all, saying he would rather wait until the new machine was completed.

*[**AUTHOR'S NOTE:** the above may explain the repeated reports that Whitehead would not discuss his flights, throughout his life. He may have done so for several reasons, including ridicule from those who would not believe, and modesty, in focusing on future goals, rather than what had been accomplished.]*

Chapter 3: Next Steps

He declared, however, there was no secret about what he was doing and to prove it pointed out a window and said:--

"There is the machine that I flew in. You can go out and look at it. It is abandoned now as junk for the new one I am making will be much lighter and stronger and will contain better material. The old one taught me my lesson, and that was enough for it to do."

It was with a look of pride that Whitehead gazed upon the curious creation that had moved through the air like a thing of life. The machine, which weighed three hundred and fifty pounds when equipped for flying, resembles a canvass boat with big wings of canvas spread over bamboo poles, and a canvass, fan-shaped tail like that of a bird. The framework of the boat is of wood painted blue, and a bowsprit projects from the bow just as in a regular sailboat. Underneath it are four wooden wheels .... The sail area of the old machine is 130 feet. The idea of operation is simple, even if it did take years to think it out. After running along the ground until a good rate of speed is attained ...[six-foot,] twin blade propellers, [located] .... [of the boat for-]ward, are started revolving at great speed and the sails or wings are unfolded.

The rush of air striking the outstretched wings raises the machine from the ground just like a flat stone thrown with one's arm ... keeps moving upward until the force propelling it is overcome by gravitation.

Like a Wild Goose.

Unlike the flat stone, Whitehead's machine does not yield to the force of gravitation and that is where the marvel of his invention lies. The rapidly revolving propellers, aided by the wings, which can be set at different angles, generate enough force to overcome the force of gravitation. At least they did when the old machine was tested, and, as Whitehead says, one cannot ask for any better proof than that. Persons who saw the machine skim along the ground and then fly, say it looked for all the world like a monster wild goose beginning its flight. Whitehead tested the machine for the first time last June but his first successful test was made on August 14. The place selected for the trial was back of the village of Fairfield, along the highway, where there are few trees in the way.

It was two o'clock in the morning when the great white wings were spread, ready to leap through the air. The first test was made with two bags of sand, each weighing 110 pounds, for ballast, in the ship. Ropes were attached to the machine to keep it from flying away, and then the engine that operated the four wheels were started.

When the machine was going as fast as the men holding the ropes could run, Whitehead shut off the ground propelling engine and pulled open the throttle that started the air propellers. Almost instantly the bow of the ship was lifted and rose at an angle of six degrees. The two men with the ropes were tumbling over the hummocks in the field while Whitehead waved his arms excitedly as he watched his invention rise in the air.

He had set the dial so that the power shut off automatically, and, in a few minutes when the men with ropes were almost exhausted, the ship settled to the ground as easily as a bird without injuring any of the mechanics.

Gustave Whitehead: "First in Flight"

That was only a preliminary test, but it satisfied the inventor. Taking the ship back to the starting point, he threw out the sand ballast and stepped into it himself. The engines were carefully tested and every joint and rod in the structure carefully gone over.

Whitehead was about to risk his life, but his confidence in his ship was so great he had no fear. Settling himself in the ship, he opened the throttle of the ground propeller and was soon bounding along the ground at an alarming speed.

The machine rocked like a ship in a storm as it sped along on its crude wooden wheels, but Whitehead kept his nerve and soon spread the great wings and started the propellers. As he did this the ship rose from the ground. A human being, for the first time in the history of the world, was flying through the air like a bird. Up the ship soared until it was about fifty feet from the ground and making a "chunk, chunk" something like the noise of a threshing machine. Everything was working just as the inventor had planned it should.

But there was danger ahead, for the ship was moving straight at a clump of chestnut trees on a little knoll. Whitehead saw the danger, but seemed powerless to avoid it, as it was too late to rise above the trees, high up on the knoll as they were, and the inventor had not thought of a plan to turn suddenly sideways. To strike the trees meant destruction to the airship and probable death to its solitary passenger. But neither happened. Whitehead suddenly remembered how birds slanted their wings when they turned, and instinctively, he turned a little to one side.

This curved the ship and she turned her nose away from the trees and glided around them as prettily as a steam yacht answers her helm. This gave Whitehead confidence, and he looked back and waved his arms. He had now soared through the air for more than half a mile and, satisfied with what he had accomplished, shut off the power.

Without a slip or any indication of turning over, the ship settled down from a height of about fifty feet and lighted on the ground so gently that her passenger was not even jarred.

Another trial was made later and the ship sailed through the air for a mile and a half without any accident. But all that is in the past, and Whitehead now has his eyes and mind turned to the future. The new ship – but before going into that, it will be interesting to tell something about this remarkable man who has conquered the eternal force of gravitation.

Whitehead is only twenty-seven years old, and he was born in Bavaria. To prove that he is an American at heart, however, aside from speaking excellent English, he dropped his real name, Weiskopf, [Weisskopf] about six months ago, and adopted the same he now uses. He came to New York a few years ago and, while working in a humble way, began making models of flying machines.

They were ... successful. ... More machines were made there, but Whitehead could not make them fly. From Buffalo he went to Pittsburgh, Pa., where he kept on working and trying. He made a machine in Pittsburgh which, as he says, was more or less successful, but briefly flew. Intent on improvement he flies. About a year and a half ago he came to Bridgeport.

As he said to-day, he had no means to build the new machine he had in his mind then, but instead of

Chapter 3: Next Steps

giving up, he took a position as night watchman and worked day-times in a cellar building the ship that has crowned his efforts with success.

His savings were meager, and he used all on the machine, but the future looks brighter now, as Whitehead has a man with capital backing him. Who the man is Whitehead refuses to say, and he was equally non-committal in talking about his plans for the future. But he admitted that his machine would be put on the market in a few months perhaps and said it was possible that the price would be as low as $1,500 or $2,000.

Common as Automobiles.

"I have no doubt flying machines will be as common as automobiles in a few years," Whitehead said, "and before you and I are old men there will be more travelling through the air than on land or water. At present it seems impossible that air ships will be able to carry heavy cargoes or even many people. I say it seems improbable, but it is not impossible.

"It is not safe nowadays, when so many wonderful things are being invented, to say anything is impossible. I am not prepared to say something is impossible except perpetual motion. I have wasted no time trying to solve that problem, for it is beyond the power of man."

While Whitehead was talking he opened a closet and took out a polished steel cylinder a little more than a foot long and about four inches in diameter.

"That weighs only about a pound and a half," he said, "and it is worth its weight in gold. Two of those will be used in the new engine I am building to operate the air propellers. That steel was made to order in England and there isn't any better in the world. I have carefully considered aluminum, but decided steel was better, as it is much stronger in proportion to its weight."

Whitehead became more interested as he talked and told a great deal about his new air ship that was interesting.

"The engines will be the finest in the world," he declared. "The one that will operate the air propellers will weigh only twenty-five pounds, but will generate thirty horsepower. Isn't that a triumph of mechanical skill? This engine, which will be about four feet long, will be placed across the bow of the boat, projecting over each side just as the engine did in the old boat."

To show just how the engine would be placed, Whitehead walked into the old ship and showed where the engine had been. As he did this he looked at the old engine lying on the ground and smiled.

"That isn't like the new one will be," he said, "but I built that old one all myself in a cellar. I think I have a right to be proud of it. No, the weight of the engine forward does not overbalance the ship. That matter of balance was one of the most difficult problems to solve.

Thirty Feet Over All.

"Anybody who knows anything about a bird knows that its greatest weight is at the front, where the breast are. The engine to propel the ship on land will be in the bottom of the boat. It will weigh about fifteen pounds and will be of about twelve horse power.

"The ship will carry about twelve pounds of calcium-carbide, enough to run it all day. The power is generated by a series of rapid gas explosions. I can produce 150 such explosions in a minute if necessary. The ship will be equipped with two dry cylinder batteries and a spark coil to explode the gas.

"The gas thus generated will be forced into a compressor, and from there into the cylinders, producing an even pressure. With the gas, a pressure of 500 pounds to the square inch can be produced. Yes, calcium-carbide is a very dangerous thing to handle, but I am careful. I don't want to be blown up, at least not before I perfect my air ship."

When the gas is forced into the compressor it comes in contact with a chemical preparation, the ingredients of which are known only to Whitehead: It is the contact with this preparation that produces the tremendous pressure. It is said that dynamite is not as powerful as this new power.

The new ship when completed will be about thirty feet over all the body, or boat, being eighteen feet long and four wide. Though built on the same plan and propelled by the same power as was the old one, the new ship will differ in many respects.

Instead of canvass on a wooden framework, the boat part will be entirely of wood, with sides about four feet high. The boat, pointed at each end, is now nearly completed and lies in a shed back of the machine shop.

It will weigh 150 pounds, but Whitehead says that will not be too heavy. Instead of canvass wings and tail, the inventor says he intends to use sheet steel made as thin as the most skilled workers in Pittsburgh can possibly make it. This will be more durable than canvass and will hold more steadily in the wind. The sheet steel, Whitehead calculates, will weigh less than eight ounces to the square foot. The fan shaped tail will be ten feet long, and, like the sails, made of sheet steel. With all the steel used in its construction, Whitehead declares the new ship will weigh not much more, if any, than the old one.

"One of the chief reasons men have not been able to fly," Whitehead said as he looked meditatively at the parts of his new engine, "has been that they could not make an engine light enough. My engine will create a power greater in proportion to its weight than the muscles of a bird's wings, but in a bird the brain that directs the muscles weighs less than an ounce. If a man could use only his brain without the heavy body that goes with it, flying would not be so difficult."

Whitehead declares that Santos-Dumont has not accomplished anything remarkable in his air ship.

"The only new thing about it," he said, "is that he uses a gasoline motor. The balloon, La France, in 1900 made five successful trips out of seven, returning to its starting place. Santos-Dumont has nothing more than a balloon, a floating machine, I call it. A flying machine, like a bird, must have a greater specific gravity than the air.

Best in Heavy Wind.

Chapter 3: Next Steps

"Santos Dumont did not fly around the Eiffel Tower, but floated around. Any great speed with his machine is impossible, as the big gas bags offer too much resistance to the air. I do not believe he can make any head-way against a wind blowing fifteen miles an hour.

"My machine is entirely different in that respect, as it will fly better in a heavy wind than in light airs. It will fly in any direction too, just as a bird does, regardless of the wind, and will make fast time, even directly against it, soaring like a bird.

"Yes, there will be some danger in learning to sail my air ship, but I do not think it will be any more difficult than learning to ride a bicycle. After a person can ride well, it becomes second nature, and one learns to balance it instinctively.

"It is just the same with an air ship. One can control it easily, if he keeps a cool head, and he will soon realize that it is almost part of him. When one has mastered the art, he will be able to handle my ship as easily as one does a checkerboard."

There is nothing pretentious about Whitehead's factory. In fact, one might easily pass it without notice. It is only about forty feet long and about fifteen feet wide and is rudely constructed of boards. In it, however, is some valuable machinery, and Whitehead says the place is big enough for the present. Adjoining it is a diminutive engine house about fifteen feet square. In this little shop a dozen men are working on the day force and five at night."

(end of transcript)

Gustave Whitehead's brother, John, arriving at Bridgeport from California, at the end of March or early April 1902, described the scene at the factory, in letters written 33 years later from Eagle Bay, British Columbia, where he'd moved in 1911:

"My brother had been associated a few months before my arrival at Bridgeport with a Mr. H Linde, they had about 4-6 aeroplanes of the same type as flew before under construction in a small shop near the crossing of Pine St. and Hancock Ave., Bridgeport, Conn. They never completed them as they had a falling out over something or another."[263]

Later that fall, in another letter to researcher Stella Randolph, John writes,

"End of March I arrived at Bridgeport and found my brother living at 241 Pine Str. He had already broken with Mr. Linde but I could see the little shop they had used in starting to construct a few Aeroplanes after the model my brother claimed he flew in, for I could see two bodies, the same shape as the machine described in the N.Y. Herald standing on the outside of the building."[264]

John was not present for the flights of the summer of 1901 and early 1902, though his brother told him of these, explaining that his airplane could have gone further if the "motor had not broken down beyond repairs." John Whitehead gave a detailed description of the aeroplane he saw in Gustave's yard, which appears to be "No. 22'", as "No. 21" and "No. 22" would have looked nearly identical, visually, except for a strengthened frame, improved steering apparatus, and increased motive [engine] power. The frame John viewed was of wood. The lightweight steel frame envisioned by Whitehead had not yet come to fruition, but this description includes modifications that we know were being made to "No. 21", starting the first week following its August 14th, 1901 flight[s]. John describes an improved, joint steering mechanism involving controls for the wing tips and a tail with both a horizontal and vertical rudder.

> "As I remember after 33 years the shape, size of Machine and Motor and material build thereof was as follows [:]. The main body was the shape of a flat bottom (row) boat about 18 feet long, 3 ½ ft wide at the middle, walls about 3 ft high, stern and bow painted, bottom build of light wood […] skeleton from of wood covered with canvass, wings extending about 20 ft from body on each side at body side about 10 ft wide, narrowing toward tips, when spread was held firm with rope on extended bowsprit, from each rip to bottom of body [ ] from each rip to a sort of mast in [contour] of body. Rudder was a combination of horizontal and vertical fin-like affair, the [principle] the same as in up to date Aeroplanes. For Steering there was a rope from on[e] of the foremost Wing tip to the one affixed running over a [pulley] in front of operator a lever was connected to [pulley] the same [pulley] controlled also the tailrudder at the same time. For Ground transportation to get a running start the Machine was resting on 3 small [Bicycle] wheels 2 in front 1 in back. The Motor of said machine was a 4 cylinder 2 cycle motor, an opposed type, resembling a 2 cycle motor built by the Van Stucken Co at Bridgeport for Speed boats.
>
> As my Brother never had much backing, therefore had to earn money for his experiments and had to work at his hobby in spare time this motor was sort of crude, [more so] as the internal combustion engines was just in its infancy in fact there was nothing light enough to be suitable for aeronautical experiments… Cylinder of Motor was made of gas pipe 4 inch diameter, 5 inch stroke, piston of cast iron cylinder head and bottom was of steel plate (in pairs for 2 cylinder on each side Heads and bottom was held together by Steel rods (studs) connecting rods of Steel rods. The peculiarity of this motor was it had no crank case as an ordinary 2 cycle motor, but had longer cylinder and dependable one it crankcase compression on the lower side of the cylinder under the piston it looked more like a steam engine, than a gas motor. The Connecting Rods were directly connected to propeller shaft. [Propeller] was constructed of Spruce wood was about 8 feet long and 18-20 inch at its widest. Was made in a very modern fashion by placing say about 6 spruce board of the required length on top of each other then bore a hole for the shaft then spread the boards on top each about an inch or so farther from the last to get the required width then shape them [smooth] an varnish them."265

The modifications to "No. 21," seen in the plane John viewed, indicate that in April 1902, Gustave Whitehead had, in his yard, an improved version of "No. 21," which certainly could be designated as the next model, "No. 22,'" though without all its formerly envisioned developments, due to a lack of funds. Gustave was reported by assistants, such as Anton Pruckner, to use parts (or the whole) of previous flying machines to save on construction costs. This would explain why the plane in Whitehead's yard would have been at the same time, the former "No. 21" as well as the current "No. 22." With the split between Whitehead and Linde, and the takeover of the factory by Linde, his resources had dried up, and Gustave would have been left with only the improved "No. 21" to modify and work upon, alterations having started in late August 1901.

John explained that (due to his late arrival) he never saw that particular machine fly, and appears to have confused some of the 1901 flights with the early 1902 flights which he had heard of from his brother and read about in the newspapers Gustave showed him, but not seen. In subsequent letters, John clarifies that Gustave described his recent flight successes to his newly arrived brother, who'd been separated from him for decades. John was skeptical at first, as would have been natural. This, however, so hurt Gustave's feelings, according to John, Gustave would later be reluctant to review his past experiments with his brother, something John later regretted.

Chapter 3: Next Steps

"In the first days of my arrival at Bridgeport in April 1902 my Brother related to me some of his experiences of his flights of this machine he had in possession at that time, but as he found me skeptical about his flight and I liked to wanted to be shown, he been sensitive feeling hurt because I did not believe in his accomplishment outright, shut up like a clam and even in later days confided in me not much of his former experiments."[266]

However, John believed emphatically that the plane flew, "but in the light of later experiences I have absolutely no doubt it was able to demonstrate the possibility of dynamic flight."[267] John's drawing of the aeroplane he viewed in Gustave's yard, enclosed with his letter, confirmed the changes.

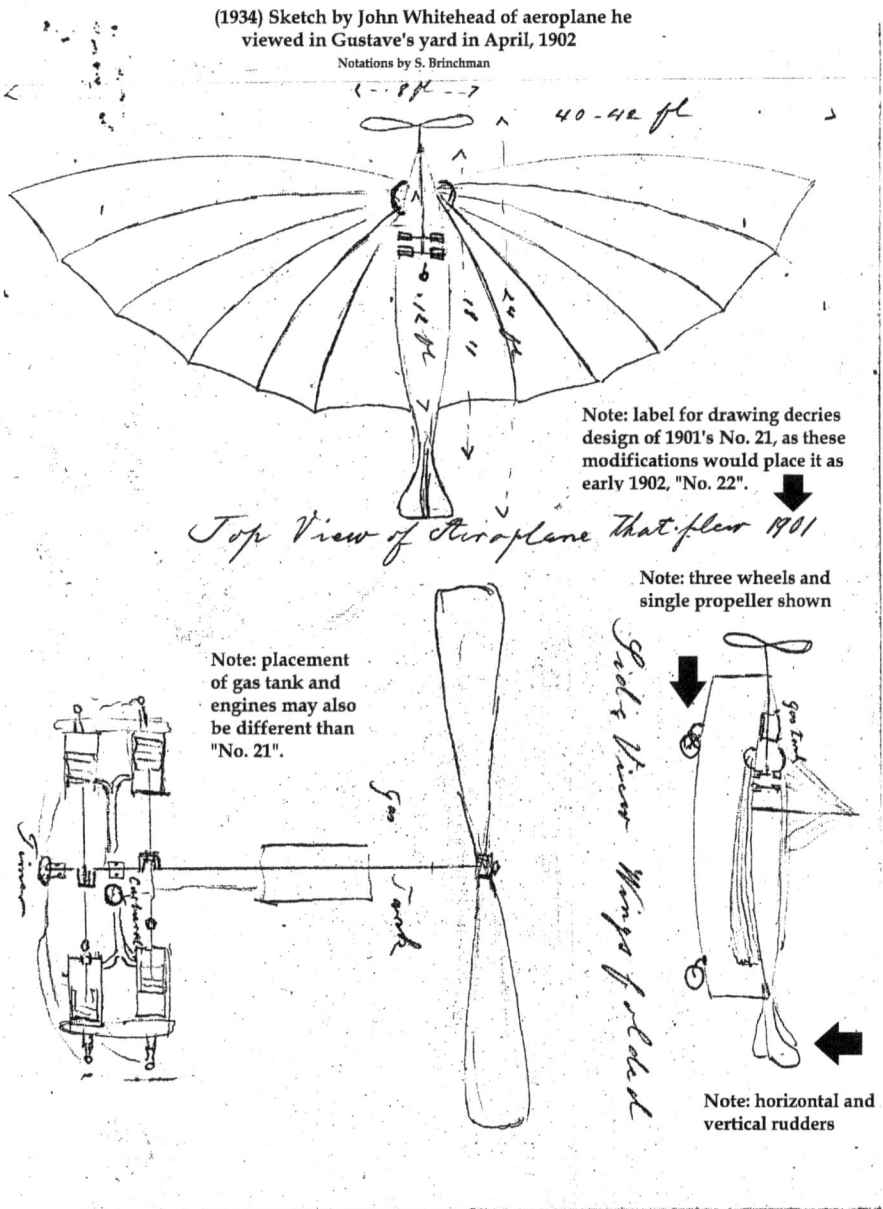

Figure 83: Sketch by John Whitehead of the likely "No. 22,'" seen April 1902

Gustave Whitehead: "First in Flight"

Significantly, John's description is followed up with a detailed explanation of why Gustave was not able to build a new motor for the previously successful aeroplane, which, he also said had been left out in the weather – "we did not consider it safe to use."[268] A new flying machine and motor was necessary to build. Consistent with Gustave's previous comments, that his goal was to produce a commercially viable heavier-than-air flying machine in which multiple passengers could travel distances, the two brothers, joining forces even though John had no known experience with flying machines, made the decision to change the aeroplane's basic design, to "build a bigger plane of different type than the original one, a biplane in front with a longer shipshape body and two small foldable wing attached to back part of body."

This pivotal decision has generated much controversy in the past half-decade, as prominent historians, also considered Wright-spokesmen, have ridiculed Whitehead for giving up a reportedly successful design for one that might have been less successful (or, as they claim, didn't fly). As it is said, "hindsight is 20-20." The brothers decided to change the design with reasons that must have made sense to them, determined to unlock the secrets to a *practical* flying machine, which "all the world" was seeking. Practical meant strong enough to be commercially viable – carrying passengers and cargo. In doing so, they left behind Whitehead's "No 21" and "No. 22" aircraft designs which are, literally, the archetype for all successful airplanes to follow. Of course, in the spring of 1902, Gustave and John could not have foreseen this. It may be assumed that the brothers Whitehead felt that certain of the components used in the "No. 21," made larger and strengthened, with additional design features, would provide the elements necessary for a larger, practical flying machine. They would never, however, have the ability, time, or funding to fully develop future models to fly as successfully as the "No.'s 21" and "22." The secrets of flight were being unlocked, but it was to be a longer process, taking decades and multiple designs by a handful of talented inventors, before a safe and reliable commercial airplane would be developed. Gustave Whitehead was, quite simply, the first to be successful at powered flight. Whitehead solved the secret of flight; he led the way for others to build on his inventions.

In the same letters, John illuminates the extent of the brothers' funding problems and activities in the late spring and summer of 1902. John was working at a low-paying factory job which was typically six days a week for ten hour shifts. Gustave had taken on the building of a 40 (or 60) horsepower lightweight gas motor for a customer in Fresno, California, and lightweight engines for several other customers. Not knowing what the materials might cost, Gustave built the engines but made little or no profit, thus causing him not to have the money to build a new engine and aeroplane for his own experiments.

The newspapers noted that John was present at Bridgeport in August 1902, planning on entering the upcoming World's Fair aerial contest with his brother, Gustave. However, John soon left for California for more lucrative work, after the funds he brought were depleted and jobs in Bridgeport were not providing sufficient pay. He returned a year later, in the fall of 1903, upset to learn that their joint plans for registering patents for a wing-warping mechanism had instead been applied for by Beach and Whitehead, without asking John - but were rejected by the US patent office.

After John returned, when the brothers finally built a larger aeroplane with a 40 horse, 4 cylinder 4 cycle gasoline motor weighing about 100 lbs. for their new model, they found they had not sufficient power to raise [the] machine. Further tests, including pulling the plane by a Locomobile Car to determine the thrust needed, revealed that for "No. 23," they'd need an 80 horsepower engine. Later, John says, he and his brother built a 200 horsepower 8 cylinder, 4 cycle V-shaped engine that weighed about 500 pounds. That engine, which took six months to build, according to other witness testimony, John explained, had been sunk in Long Island Sound by a backer of Whitehead's (Stanley Y. Beach), when Beach insisted on testing it on his speedboat. [269]

In a letter to Randolph on September 3, 1934, John explains:

"At my coming to Bridgeport I had a few savings a little over a hundred Dollars, My Brother left

Chapter 3: Next Steps

by Mr. Linde, mostly through jealous rivalry. Mr. Linde was also a Helicopter crank or called at those days, and I came to an agreement, after compromising on our own past ideas as to Flying machines, we decided to build a flying fish type aeroplane, designed together an improved xxxxxxxxxxxx's incorporating a joint control of Wing tips and both horizontal an[d] vertical rudder, we made a fair sided model of body with wings and tail, flew it as a kite had also a photo taken of same. We intended to take out patents on same, but as we never could raise the money we postponed time after time to make application. Meanwhile my brother working on that 60 horsepower motor for that Fresno lighter than men Hill or something was his name and I working in a different shop at low wages could hardly support myself, my Brother's family and materials for this motor in a few months we both was broke and that motor barely complete, that had to be shipped to Fresno, before it could be tried in my Brother's former Aeroplane….being discouraged by proceeds of events and the slow acquisition of funds I went out West to, as I thought, earn money faster [than] I could in Bridgeport, but could not succeed, so in fall of 1903 returned to Bridgeport."[270]

Problems Surface

"*Whitehead Flew High*" and "*Unrealized Dreams*" are articles, both published by Bridgeport, Connecticut newspapers in April 1902, which poke a bit of fun at Gustave Whitehead, while reporting on a court case against Herman Linde by the local lumber company. Linde, Whitehead's former impatient, excitable sponsor, was a man soon to be also an "inpatient" incarcerated in an insane asylum, considered very dangerous by the Secret Service, for threatening President Roosevelt's wife.

It appears, from the description in "*Whitehead Flew High*" article, that during court proceedings it was learned that Linde invested $1,000 in lumber toward the project to build passenger airplanes to New York City, and was dissatisfied that the high flight to New York had not yet been accomplished within several months. Later, Linde refused to pay the full bill to the lumber company, trying, instead, to have Whitehead billed for a paltry remaining amount. The article's title "*Whitehead Flew High That Is Financially But Not Actually*" is not referring to whether his flights of summer, 1901, occurred, but rather, on the promised future flights to New York City. Flying short distances were considered impractical, and merely part of Whitehead's experimentation. What the public, the media, Whitehead, and Linde wanted was "practical" flight, that which could easily be navigated and carry numerous passengers and freight to distant locations. Unfortunately for all concerned, this was "not to be" for at least three decades, following the combined, cumulative work of many more inventors, including Gustave Whitehead.

(transcript)

    April 5, 1902

"Whitehead Flew High
That Is Financially but Not Actually — That Is, to Say as Yet He Hasn't
Linde Tired of Putting up Ducats.
Millers Lumber Co. Brings Him into Court — Says He Ordered Brakes Down
(*Bridgeport Post*, April 5, 1902)

    The Frank Miller Lumber Company summoned Herman Linde before Justice John S. Pullman yesterday to show cause why he should not foot a bill which Gustave Whitehead, *the widely known flying machine inventor,* had contracted. [emphasis added by author]

Gustave Whitehead: "First in Flight"

Many months ago Mr. Whitehead intending to carry on his extensive experiments, sought the assistance of men with money. His enthusiastic descriptions of what he hoped to do interested Mr. Linde who promptly paid $1,000 to the venture.

This fund, although not large, enabled Mr. Whitehead to do considerable experimenting. Lumber was necessary in the work and Mr. Whitehead went to the Frank Miller Co. to get it. He told them that Mr. Linde was back of him and would be all right.

The lumber firm was a bit skeptical on flying machines and made some inquiries. At the City National bank it learned that Mr. Linde was all right, so an account was opened with the firm of Linde and Whitehead.

Up to Nov. 20, $110 worth of lumber was purchased. Then the company began to inquire about payment XXX. Linde received a letter. He went around and found out how things were. He paid $76 on account and then, so he says, told the lumber people not to let the firm of Linde & Whitehead have any more on account, as the thousand dollars was used up.

But the inventor wanted more lumber and he ran up a bill for $38 more. When this was presented Mr. Linde refused to pay. He acknowledged the $X4 balance due, but he would not pay the new amount.

Upon the trial the defendant put in his statement that he had ordered that the company not to trust the firm of Linde & Whitehead any more. But this was denied by the plaintiff. The company held that it had not received notice of any kind and had filled Mr. Whitehead's order the same as before.

Before the Justice, Hill & Hill appeared for the plaintiff. William K. Dewitz for the defendant. Justice Pullman reserved his decision.

Mr. Linde is now of the opinion that inventors are very expensive business." [271]

(end of transcript)

The *Post* article, above, shows Linde to be a liar, according to the lumber company, which states Linde had never indicated to them that the funds should be "cut off." Whitehead has not flown high to New York as promised, but is still held in high esteem – nothing in the article attacks his efforts, which are referred to as "extensive experimentation." The article merely points out that inventing airplanes is expensive business, which Linde was not ready for – readers will note that other experimenters, far less successful than Whitehead, spent hundreds of thousands to millions.

In another local article of April 5, 1902, the *Bridgeport Evening Farmer*, Whitehead appears to be ridiculed for not making good on his flight goals, without taking into consideration that the goals being referred to by Linde are the flights to New York City. No one in the world had yet flown as far as it was to New York City – or any flights past those made by Whitehead the previous summer - and one could certainly not accomplish this without proper funding and extensive trials. If Whitehead is to be criticized, it would be for thinking the next steps to accomplish practical flight would be easier than he anticipated.

The two articles taken together show conclusively that the ridiculing of Whitehead is based on a couple of local newspapers taking a court case against Linde and doctoring it up to make the news more titillating for their readers. The *Bridgeport Evening Farmer*, which chose to present the "court story" title as "*Last Flop of the*

Chapter 3: Next Steps

Whitehead Flying Machine," is editorializing at its worst, ignoring the more mundane facts regarding lumber customer Linde, who would not pay his small bill at the lumber yard after just a short time, and then quit supporting Whitehead altogether, who was at work building a number of the bird-like "No. 22" flying machines, following in the footsteps of the "bird-like, boat-shaped" "No. 21." It is very noteworthy that, in later years, the same newspaper, the *Bridgeport Evening Farmer*, supported Whitehead's successful 1901 flights, and that he was a famous airplane inventor and builder of excellent lightweight motors, well known nationally as well as regionally.[272] Whitehead *had* invented and flown the first powered airplane, humble as it appeared. However, no one could have realized it then, as we can see below.

"UNREALIZED DREAMS
Last Flop of the Whitehead Flying Machine"
(*Bridgeport Evening Farmer*, April 5, 1902)

There was both an amusing and an interesting trial before Justice J. S. Pullman yesterday afternoon, which might be called the "Last Flop of the Gustave Whitehead Flying Machine." The case came before Justice Pullman on an action brought by the Frank Miller Lumber Co., against Herman Linde, to recover on a lumber bill to the extent of about $60.

It seems that in October 1901, Herman Linde, the defendant, made some agreement with Gustave Whitehead, the flying machine man, whereby he was to back Mr. Whitehead to the amount of $1,000, the said amount to be expended upon an airship then under construction. Mr. Linde gave Mr. Whitehead a letter authorizing him in Linde's absence to procure necessary materials for the air ship on Linde's credit, the latter stating that Linde's total [liability] in connection therewith was to be $1,000, and referred to the City National bank as to Linde's credit. This letter was presented to the Frank Miller Lumber Co. and after reference to the bank, an account was opened by them under the name of Whitehead and Linde.

Lumber was furnished to the amount of $110 before Nov. 20, at which time Linde paid $76 on account, and claims that he notified the Frank Miller Lumber Co. to charge no more lumber in the firm of Whitehead & Linde, as there was no such firm, and that his agreement with Whitehead had expired by reason of his having expended $1,000 without the hoped for flight over Bridgeport's house tops. At the trial Mr. Linde admitted a liability for a balance of about $20 but claims that the lumber obtained by Whitehead after that date in November which was still charged to Whitehead and Linde, must be paid for by Mr. Whitehead, and that he was not responsible therefore.

The plaintiffs claim they were never notified to stop furnishing lumber to Whitehead and charging it as they had heretofore done, and as Whitehead's asset consists chiefly of unrealized dreams, they preferred to hold Linde with his bank account, responsible rather than Mr. Whitehead.

Messrs. Hill & Hall represented the plaintiffs in the case. Attorney William V. Devitt appeared for the defendant. The decision of the justice was reserved.

Mr. Linde made a somewhat excitable witness. Every time Attorney Hill referred to the firm of Whitehead & Linde, the witness would jump up and state that there was no such firm in existence nor never had been. He never would answer the questions of the opposite attorney whenever that individual mentioned the name of Whitehead in connection with his own.

The trial recounts the breaking away of a partnership that blasts local hopes of the realization of the flying machine by Mr. Whitehead. Mr. Linde had faith in Mr. Whitehead to the extent of $6,000. That amount of money went away in experimenting and there is yet no airship. This will be a blow to some of the New York daily papers who have been printing long accounts of the airship and which were amply illustrated. It appears that Mr. Whitehead made a failure of some kind of a boat. After the failure

Gustave Whitehead: "First in Flight"

he constructed another, which Mr. Linde thought was a boat similar in all respects to the failure. This made him angry, hence the dissolution, and the unrealized dreams of an airship."[273]

This little known article, from a small newspaper in Bridgeport, CT, pertains to a falling out with one of his earliest sponsors, often used by Whitehead detractors such as Smithsonian NASM's head curator, who obtained it from an earlier Wright supporter and Whitehead critic, in the 1960's. The criticisms of Whitehead within the article's last paragraph are based on the court testimony of the unsavory, mentally incompetent Linde, in order not to pay a trifling bill (part of a pattern we see with Linde in examining his conduct over decades). These must be dismissed as counter to the statements of multiple eyewitnesses to Whitehead's flights the previous summer. The fact that the *Bridgeport Evening Farmer* later supported Whitehead's earlier 1901 flights is more than enough proof of the above article as simply poorly informed editorializing.

Gustave Whitehead - and the world at large - expected great things from flight. A practical aeroplane was sought, to achieve transportation and other uses of the sort we now enjoy. Flying short distances of an eighth of a mile, a half mile, or mile and a half, all said to be accomplished by Whitehead on August 14, 1901, and his claimed longer flights of January 1902, circling over Long Island Sound, whetted the appetite of both the inventor and the public for more.

These accomplishments were not seen as important events in history when they occurred, but merely as experimental steps to the final outcome only to transpire through the efforts of many inventors. Whitehead was struggling to accomplish effortless, practical flight, and his early accomplishments were the first small steps of mankind toward this goal. Recognition for those significant early successes should widen, as well as the later successes in development of the art of flying by all who participated, as we look back on them with the advantage of a century having passed. Let us honor them all, including Whitehead, with our recognition, for their combined struggles have blessed us with technologies that enable relatively effortless travel and will take us to the planets and beyond.

Chapter 4

A NEW GOAL: THE WORLD'S FAIR AERIAL CONTEST

Very early in 1902, a new incentive emerged for Gustave – the goal of participation in the nation's first aerial contest [274] and exposition at the St. Louis World's Fair. Initially planned for 1903 to celebrate the 100th anniversary of the Louisiana Purchase, the Fair would showcase the technological accomplishments of mankind in the previous hundred years. Its planners deliberately set about to stimulate solutions to "the problem of aerial navigation" amongst inventors in the several years prior to its opening, in order to reveal them during the Fair. The attractive prizes offered for the best airship of any type influenced Whitehead's focus and designs during the next three years, January 1902 - December 1904, leading to his attendance and an exhibition at the World's Fair. The exposition, for a variety of reasons, did not exert the most positive influence on Whitehead, but it can shed light on much of what transpired during those years. The St. Louis World's Fair of 1904 is an important aspect of the Whitehead history to examine carefully, as Wright-oriented historians have oftentimes commented on Whitehead's limited participation there, oftentimes taking a critical tone.

The Louisiana Purchase Exposition Company, organizers of the upcoming World's Fair, intended to both showcase and stimulate the technological development of the growing nation, entering the 20th century. In mid-January 1902, at the direction of Frederick J.V. Skiff, Director of Exhibits, meetings were held by the Exposition's organizers to discuss and plan "aeronautic events," including an international "Aerial contest," the first of its kind, to be held over a period of months during the height of the Fair. With a budget of $200,000 (equivalent to $5.5 million dollars in 2015) and prizes totaling $150,000, news coverage of the upcoming aeronautical competition was expected to help advertise the Fair, drawing contestants and excited crowds from all over the world. "It was the first real prize money of any consequence ever offered in the interest of aeronautics. The airplane was then practically unknown." [275] The Fair's organizers wanted to awe their visitors with ongoing aerial displays, utilizing the latest technologies. Officially known as the Louisiana Purchase Exposition, this colossal exhibition would ultimately open its gates to a throng of 200,000 should-to-shoulder visitors on April 30th, 1904, ending on December 1st of the same year. It would be popularly called "the St. Louis World's Fair of 1904" and the "Universal Exposition," attracting 20 million attendees in 7 months, and costing $40 million. The US population stood at 75 million, at the time.

The aerial contest was to be held with immense monetary prizes, with a top prize initially announced in the press as $200,000, though actually $150,000, later pared down to $100,000 [the equivalent of $2.75 million in 2015]. The grand prize would be awarded "for aeronautic achievement considerably beyond anything yet attained". [276] Winning any of these would end Whitehead's money and sponsor woes. It would fund his experiments to accomplish his dream of practical flight. He'd have enough money to open up his own factory. Truly, this was an opportunity that would guide his inventive efforts, through the end of the Fair in December 1904.

Whitehead's close acquaintance with "a local," Stanley Yale Beach, Science American's Aviation Editor, would have allowed him to keep abreast of opportunities, in addition to those gleaned from the New York and Bridgeport newspapers.

In the aftermath of the falling out that began in late November with his short-lived sponsor, the opportunist, Herman Linde, Gustave changed his focus from planning a commercial flight to New York, to entering and winning the aerial competition at the Fair. This turning point may explain his experimentation with various designs from early 1902 through the end of 1904. It may also explain Whitehead's final separation from Herman Linde in the spring of 1902, after his sponsor was caught trying to steal Whitehead's designs for himself. This was just when the "ante" suddenly went up, as the massive Fair prizes became public and Gustave Whitehead's application became known.

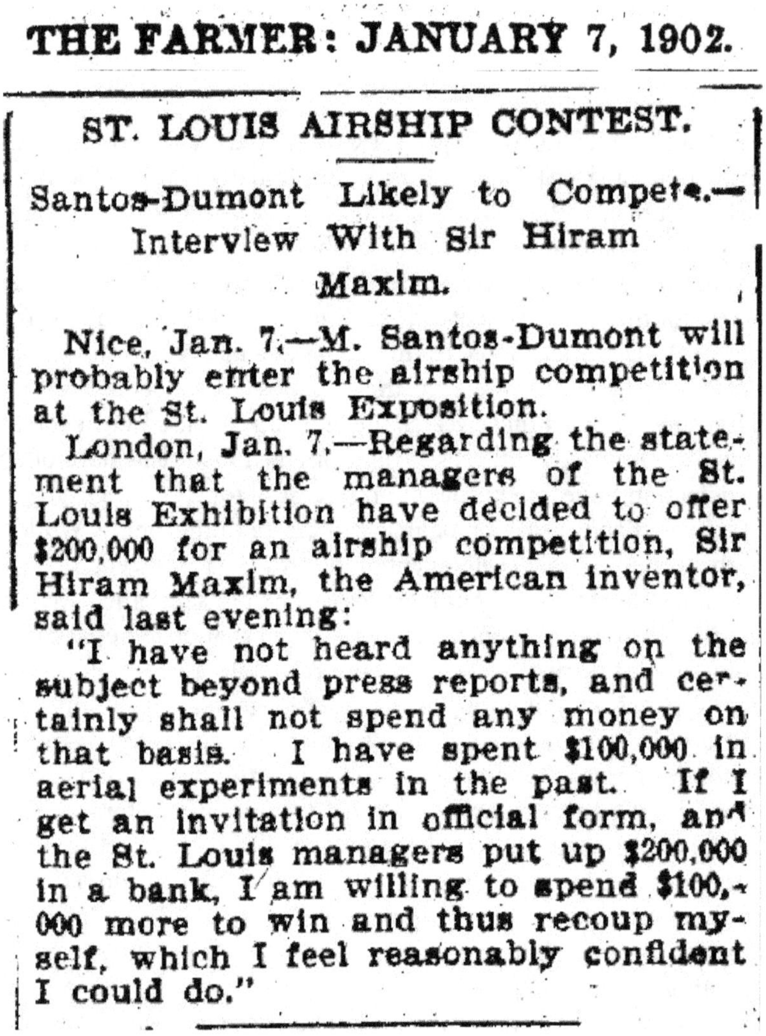

THE FARMER: JANUARY 7, 1902.

ST. LOUIS AIRSHIP CONTEST.

Santos-Dumont Likely to Compete.—
Interview With Sir Hiram
Maxim.

Nice, Jan. 7.—M. Santos-Dumont will probably enter the airship competition at the St. Louis Exposition.

London, Jan. 7.—Regarding the statement that the managers of the St. Louis Exhibition have decided to offer $200,000 for an airship competition, Sir Hiram Maxim, the American inventor, said last evening:

"I have not heard anything on the subject beyond press reports, and certainly shall not spend any money on that basis. I have spent $100,000 in aerial experiments in the past. If I get an invitation in official form, and the St. Louis managers put up $200,000 in a bank, I am willing to spend $100,000 more to win and thus recoup myself, which I feel reasonably confident I could do."

Figure 84: Bridgeport Farmer, Jan. 7, 1902 announces aerial competition at St. Louis Exposition
(Courtesy of the Bridgeport Public Library newspaper archives, Bridgeport, CT)

Above, on p. 7 of the *Bridgeport Farmer* of January 7, 1902, a brief article announced an airship competition at the St. Louis Exposition that Gustave Whitehead undoubtedly viewed and became immediately interested in. If Whitehead did not find the article on his own, he surely would have had any number of people in the community, who knew of his well-advertised flying exploits either by sight, ear, or reading about him in the local newspapers, bring it to him. Three days after this article appeared in Bridgeport, Whitehead's letter to the Louisiana Purchase Exposition Company, planners of the fair and its aerial competition, was in the mail.

WHITEHEAD FIRST ENTRANT

On January 10th, 1902, an enthusiastic Gustave Whitehead mailed a letter of inquiry to the Louisiana Purchase Exposition Company, becoming the first entrant for its newly announced aerial competition. In his letter, Whitehead reportedly stated he'd made a long flight the past June with his "No. 21" airplane, enclosing three photos of his flying machine. Formal mention of Whitehead's application, prominently featured in the World's Fair Bulletins of both February and June 1902, suggests that his letter did mention a flight claimed for the previous June.

The first formal entry in the aeronautic tournament of the Louisiana Purchase Exposition was made by Mr. Gustave Whitehead, of Bridgeport, Conn., who is now making improvements in an aeroplane flying machine in which he has already made flights. It is made of bamboo and silk, the body 3x3 feet and 16 feet long, with great wings, operated by a double compound high-pressure engine of twenty-horsepower. The entire weight is 280 pounds. This machine, last June, with an operator on board, made a safe and successful flight to a distance of one and one-half miles.

Figure 85: GW First Applicant, World's Fair Bulletin (Feb. 1902)

(transcript)

"The first formal entry in the aeronautic tournament of the Louisiana Purchase Exposition was made by Mr. Gustave Whitehead, of Bridgeport, Conn., who is now making improvements in an aeroplane flying machine in which he has already made flights. It is made of bamboo and silk, the body 3x3 feet and 16 feet long, with great wings, operated by a double compound high-pressure engine of twenty-horsepower. The entire weight is 280 pounds. This machine, last June with an operator on board, made a safe and successful flight to a distance of one and one half miles." (World's Fair Bulletin, Feb. 1902, p. 21.)

(end of transcript)

The prospects were daunting – competition with all other types of air ships, with powered dirigibles already able to travel great distances and high altitudes - as were the underlying realities, undoubtedly unknown by Whitehead at the time. The alluring prizes beckoned, heavily advertised in newspapers and magazines. According to a number of witnesses and local newspaper coverage, Gustave Whitehead had successfully flown on multiple occasions during the summer of 1901. He knew he was on the right track to "completely solving the problem of aerial navigation," to be able to fly about "at will," as do the birds, which was the mantra of the day. His first successes, "No. 's 21 and 22" he considered to be "toys" that would not pass muster for commercial use nor competition at the Fair. Test flights and continuous experimentation to develop and attempt to improve his designs were to consume Whitehead over the next three years.

The three photos accompanying his letter included two taken of "No. 21" in the spring and summer of 1901, and one newly identified as an early prototype of "No. 22." These three previously known photos of Whitehead's plane on the ground first surfaced as having been sent to the exposition committee in the early 1980's, discovered by Major O'Dwyer in correspondence with Missouri archivists. Whitehead's original letter, or even a copy of it, has not yet been located - however, a flurry of newspapers reported his application, nationwide.

THE BOSTON SUNDAY GLOBE-JANUARY 19, 1902.

BRIDGEPORT MAN ENTERED.

Gustave Whitehead Wants to Compete in a $200,000 Airship Contest at St Louis in 1903.

ST LOUIS, Jan 18—The first formal entry into the world's fair airship contest for a $200,000 prize was made today by Gustave Whitehead of 241 Pine St, Bridgeport, Conn, who in a letter to director of works Taylor says that: he has been working on the problem of the dirigible balloon for the last 10 years, *and achieved a one and one-half mile flight on June 3, 1901.* He states that he has a large force of men engaged in making a new and improved airship, which will be his 21st machine, and he expects to make a still better one for 1903.

He asked that his name be entered on the list of competitors, and that a copy of rules and conditions to govern the contest be mailed to him at once. [277]

Another article with similar wording ran in the January 19, 1902 Boston Globe's sports section, while not referring to an operator on the flight, the "mile and a half" distance is mentioned. An error, calling the Whitehead flying machine "a dirigible" was introduced, which came to be repeated as the report was disseminated via the Associated Press.

BRIDGEPORT MAN ENTERED.
Gustave Whitehead Wants to Compete in a $200,000 Airship Contest at St. Louis in 1903.

St. Louis, Jan. 18 - The first formal entry into the world's fair airship contest for a $200,000 prize was made today by Gustave Whitehead of 241 Pine St., Bridgeport, Conn., who in a letter to director of works Taylor says that he has been working on the problem of the dirigible balloon[278] for the last 10 years, and has achieved a one and one-half mile flight on June 3, 1903..."[279] [Note: Whitehead had *not* worked on dirigible balloons, but rather, development of "heavier-than-air flying machines" for the past decade.]

Gustave Whitehead was *not* working with dirigible [lighter than air] aircraft, but with "heavier-than-air" flying machines, including wind-powered gliders and engine-powered flying machines. There is some evidence, however, that he did sell lightweight engines for use in dirigibles.[280] According to the reports of his application to the contest, Whitehead stated that he made a powered flight in June perhaps a preliminary momentum flight

Chapter 4: New Goal: The World's Fair Aerial Contest

from one of the many local hilltops where he was known to conduct experiments. Two months later, a flight of 1.5 miles from level ground in Stratford, Connecticut was attested to by his young assistant Junius Harworth, in an affidavit signed in 1934. There is no further information about the flight in June allegedly mentioned in the letter to the Aerial Committee. However, virtually all those who knew Gustave and were later interviewed, stressed his honesty and integrity. Due to Whitehead's own minimal documentation, and the early lack of interest by governmental historians and their staff (actually his competitors at the time) we do not have all the details for each flight. Following his sudden, early death, much of what existed went to the town dump, sent by a struggling family that did not yet comprehend Whitehead's place in history. As a result, we do not have all correspondences and the exact details of each one of his many reported flights. We do know that he was flying throughout the summer of 1901, and that his exacting system took at least six weeks, working through various stages, to the final end result – manned, powered flight taking off and landing on level ground. According to newspaper articles in early June his "No. 21" plane, after repairs that took a month, was ready to fly.

Whitehead received this letter back from the Aerial Committee, written on January 16, 1902, published in the *Bridgeport Sunday Herald* on January 26th:

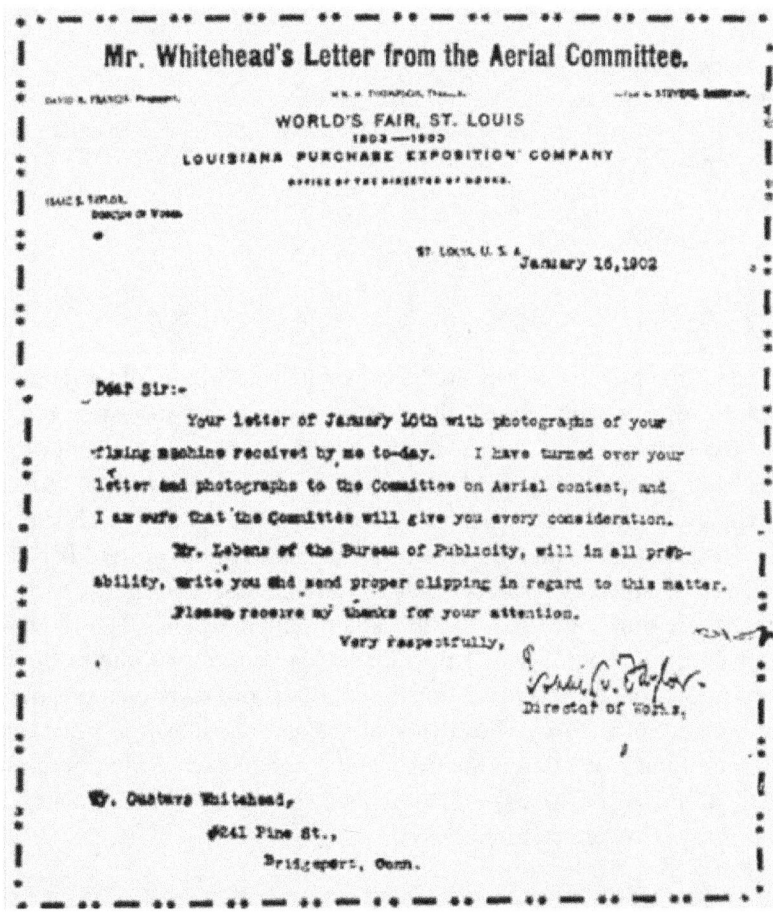

Figure 86: St. Louis Exposition Aerial Committee letter to Gustave Whitehead

**Whitehead's response from the Aerial Committee was published
in the** *Bridgeport Sunday Herald* **of January 26, 1902.**

Gustave Whitehead: "First in Flight"

(transcript)

"January 16, 1902

Dear Sir,

Your letter of January 10th with photographs of your flying machine received by me to-day. I have turned over your letter and photographs to the Committee on Aerial contest, and I am sure that the Committee will give you every consideration.

Mr. Lebens of the Bureau of Publicity will in all probability write you and send proper clipping in regard to this matter.

Please receive my thanks for your attention,

Very respectfully,
(Isaac Taylor) *(signature)*
Director of Works

Mr. Gustave Whitehead,
       241 Pine St.,
              Bridgeport, Conn."

(end of transcript)

    A scattering of national press then reported that Whitehead had made a flight of "a mile and a half" on June 3rd, 1901, "with the operator on board … It has done so several times since with safety. This is the first machine of its kind that has ever risen in the air with a human being on board in an upright course." [281]

    Confirmation of the contents of Whitehead's letter has not been possible to make; his letter to the Exposition authorities apparently no longer exists (*curiously vanished* from the public record, along with those of all other applicants). The photos he sent still remain in the Fair archives at the Missouri History Museum in St. Louis, first identified and obtained by researcher Maj. William J. O'Dwyer in the early 1980's – his copies are at the Fairfield Museum. These show several of Whitehead's monoplane, "No. 21." The first, from the pre-flight, development stage taken in the spring of 1901 (most likely March or April due to the bare trees and heavier clothing worn by those photographed), was made during a photo shoot taken in a vacant lot along Cherry Street by Stanley Yale Beach; the second is an overhead shot of the aeroplane as it appears on a wooden deck, first published in the *NY Sun* on June 9, 1901; and the third is the one of two newly interpreted photographs of an early version of "No. 22'," at the site of the second Whitehead shop and world's first airplane factory on Cherry Street, in the early fall of 1901. They are pictured below.

Chapter 4: New Goal: The World's Fair Aerial Contest

Figure 87: GW and "No. 21" in 1901, photo #1 of 3 sent to Fair officials (Jan. 1902)

No. 1 of 3 photos sent by Whitehead to the Louisiana Purchase Exposition Company in January 1902.
Photo used with permission of Missouri History Museum, St. Louis.
Sister photo below, from O'Dwyer collection

Above, photograph of "the Condor," Whitehead's "No. 21" monoplane, taken spring, 1901 by Stanley Yale Beach. #1 of 3 photos sent to the Louisiana Purchase Exposition Company on Jan. 10, 1902, with his letter of inquiry. The same photo appears to be identical to the one published in the October 1901 issue of the Illustrirte Aeronautische Mitteilungen, in Germany – also sent to them by Whitehead. It also appears to be over-exposed above the wings, as evidenced by a near duplicate now in the O'Dwyer /Whitehead collection at the Fairfield Museum (see Fig. 88).

Figure 88: 1901, Sister-photo to Figure 87

In photo above, not sent to the Exposition company, there are bare-leafed trees and buildings above the lines of the aeroplane.

Figure 89: "No. 21" in 1901, photo #2 of 3 sent to Fair officials (Jan. 1902)

No. 2 of 3 photos sent by Whitehead to the Louisiana Purchase Exposition Company in January 1902.
Photo used with permission of Missouri History Museum, St. Louis.

Above, Whitehead's second photograph of his "No. 21" monoplane, the second of three photos sent to the Louisiana Purchase Exposition Company, Jan. 10, 1902, with his letter of inquiry. This photo was also published in the (NY) Evening Telegram, Nov. 19, 1901, part of a series of photos that began to appear in New York newspapers, in June 1901.

Chapter 4: New Goal: The World's Fair Aerial Contest

Figure 90: "No. 22" in fall, 1901, photo #3 of 3 sent to Fair officials (Jan. 1902)

No. 3 of 3 photos sent by Whitehead to the Louisiana Purchase Exposition Company in January 1902.
Photo used with permission of Missouri History Museum, St. Louis

Above, is a newly identified photograph of Whitehead's early prototype of the "No. 22" monoplane, taken in the fall of 1901 by an unknown photographer (possibly Stanley Y. Beach) at "the Cherry Street shop," also the world's first airplane factory, across from the Wilmot & Hobbs factory, seen in the background. This photograph of "No. 22" was sent to the Louisiana Purchase Exposition Company, Jan. 10, 1902, with his letter of inquiry.

EARLY PLANNING OF AERONAUTICS AT THE FAIR

The theme of the World's Fair was to be "man in his full twentieth century development," which tied in perfectly to showcasing current developments in aeronautics, offering a means to bring international aeronautical inventors together, and stimulating solutions to aerial navigation that inventors, in 1902, appeared to be close to finding.[282] Its planners announced, in the World's Fair Bulletin of February 1902, in a two page article entitled "Aerial Navigation: $200,000 Appropriated for an International Tournament at World's Fair," that, "taking note of recent great achievements in aerial navigation, [it] has unanimously decided to devote $200,000 to a great aerial navigation contest at the World's Fair in 1903." In addition to the publicity they knew would be generated, the planners hoped to use enormous financial incentives to stimulate "a solution to the problem of aerial navigation" that the world was waiting for – fully opening the doors to mass travel in the skies, upon the "universal highway," to be revealed during the Fair.

The article provides a glimpse into the prevailing perceptions of "the state of the art of aviation in 1902," by "the educated." It includes comments that likely refer, obliquely, to the recent accomplishments of two famed aeronauts – Gustave Whitehead and Alberto Santos-Dumont, both in their mid-twenties, concerning their respective recent experimentation with marginally navigable, powered flying machines and dirigibles. However, labeled "Distinguished Aerialists Interested in World's Fair Airship Tournament," Hiram Maxim, Samuel Pierpont Langley, and Octave Chanute [the latter both Committee advisors] were pictured front and center of the article with Santos-Dumont [all were direct competitors of Gustave Whitehead, at that date]. Santos-Dumont became world famous in October 1901, winning a prestigious prize for his sensational, semi-controlled, powered flight made with a dirigible at the Eiffel Tower, in Paris. Santos-Dumont, expected to draw massive crowds, later made a series of demands to reduce the distance (from the original fifteen down to six miles) and speed (from twenty five miles per hour to a mere ten) required to win the grand prize, even when he was the only official contestant.

Figure 91: Distinguished Aerialists – World's Fair Bulletin, Feb. 1902
Courtesy of the University of Missouri, MU Libraries
(Above) Illustration of four "distinguished aerialists" then indicating an interest in competing at the "Airship Tournament" from "Aerial Navigation" [283]

The Wrights, unknowns just beginning to experiment with box kites and gliding at Kitty Hawk during the previous summer, in February 1902, still at work in Dayton building and selling bicycles, were not mentioned at all. This eminent group dubbed "distinguished aerialists" (despite their inability to successfully invent and fly a powered heavier-than-air flying machine), would all remain competitors, jostling for recognition of their contributions to early flight, with elevated reputations exceeding Whitehead's, even into future centuries. The sincere efforts of all these often-named "scientists and engineers" like Langley, Chanute, and later, the Wrights, did not ultimately earn them the right to the title of "first," for their efforts to produce powered flights either failed or came too late, *after* Whitehead. Each contributed to the collective effort to produce the solution for "aerial navigation" which we now enjoy, building on the footsteps of countless other inventors. The personal

Chapter 4: New Goal: The World's Fair Aerial Contest

influence and wealth of these four men readily surpassed Whitehead's, who was by contrast, an impoverished German immigrant. The tendency to emphasize this "upper crust of aeronautics" would continue throughout the planning of the Fair's Aerial Contest, giving insider preference to these "big-names," rather than to Whitehead or many other applicants.

Langley and Chanute, both aware of Gustave Whitehead's successes, and considered top experts in the field of aeronautics – despite a failure to fly all but gliders or models - had been named as consultants for the tournament, with some input into rules and regulations. Just months earlier, Langley's assistant had been hard at work gathering Whitehead's design ideas in Atlantic City. In June 1901, Chanute advised his mentored friends, the Wrights, that Gustave Whitehead had an excellent, powerful, lightweight engine they might wish to take a look at. As consultants to the Exposition's Aerial Committee, Chanute and Langley both knew Whitehead was the first applicant for the contest, with his claims of powered flight in 1901, and had undoubtedly seen the photos he sent to the Committee of his "No. 21" flying machine.

THE AERIAL CONTEST

The World's Fair Bulletin of February 1902 reveals the status quo concerning flight in 1902, allowing us to see what these entrepreneurial businessmen, intent on getting the oft-mentioned "problem of aerial navigation" solved, were thinking. [emphasis added]

> "The Executive Committee of the Louisiana Purchase Exposition, taking note of recent great achievements in aerial navigation, has unanimously decided to devote $200,000 to a great aerial navigation contest at the World's Fair in 1903. In apportioning this money as between prizes and necessary expenditures, and also in defining the conditions of the contest, distinguished scientists and aeronautic experts will be consulted, and there is reason to believe that the rules of contest will be so satisfactory as to bring to St. Louis all of the dirigible balloons and flying machines in the world that have made or can make, a successful voyage in the air. *It is not improbable that the liberal offer of the Exposition Company will greatly stimulate the designing and construction of such machines, and perhaps enable some to obtain the means of perfecting incomplete ones.* The contest will certainly be one of the most interesting and attractive events of the World's Fair, and *the World Congress of Aeronauts, brought together to witness it, may end in the long sought solution of a problem "as old as Adam ..."*
>
> ....The problem of aerial navigation was haunting the mind of man....Of late years, men of the highest scientific attainments, formed into associations for the purpose of experimenting upon and working towards it, have made such progress in the construction of successful flying machines that *the whole world appears now to be on the tiptoe of expectation, prepared for the advent of an ocean line of air ships at any moment.* The costly automobile requires very costly improved roads for its successful use, the railroads are far apart, and their trains must stop at stations far apart. So every resident of the rural districts has occasional dreams of possessing in the future an individual airship of his own, in which he can fly anywhere like a bird, regardless of roads, trees, fences, rivers, or houses. ... Many aeronautic experimenters have held that the only successful airship will be one that, like the bird, supports and propels itself by its own mechanical power. These have thought that the problem could be solved by machines with weight properly proportioned to a power sufficient for both elevation and propulsion by its own flying appliances, such as wings, screws [*propellers*] or aero-planes, wedged forward by screws. A part of the power of this machine will be derived from the modeling of its surfaces, so as to extract from the air the recoil or resistance necessary to elevate and carry it forward.
>
> ...recent progress has been made, encouraging hopes of complete success. The number of dirigible balloons and of flying machines proper that have made more or less successful aerial flights

is large enough to inspire aeronautic circles with much confidence... it is hoped that in this way, the material wanted and the missing link necessary to perfect the machinery of completely successful aerial navigation, will soon be supplied.

The newspapers of Europe and American for a year past have been teeming with reports of airship feats [Author's note: again, likely including the well-covered Whitehead accomplishments which appeared in at least 100 newspapers worldwide], balloon races, and long distance balloon voyages."[284]

The bulletin further noted that by February 1902, it had heard from "a score of aeronauts who had written in regard to the World's Fair Association in regards to the big tournament in 1903. *Most of them think they have solved the problem of successful aerial navigation or are near the solution of it.*"

Up until that time, ballooning and later, dirigible flights, had enjoyed popular successes in the past century and could fly considerable distances. By 1901, dirigibles had begun to somewhat successfully add motorized power, to aid in navigation. Those organizing the World's Fair knew these rarely seen displays would entertain and draw crowds. They designed the competition primarily for balloons and dirigibles, though they would accept all types of aircraft - including categories to include flying machines and ambitious kite demonstrations.

Expected demonstrations at the Fair were described, such as one by Prof. Carl E. Myers in his "Sky-Cycle," "a dirigible balloon operated with aeroplanes," originally powered by foot-operated pedals and hand cranks, said to be 'heavier-than-air,' and his aerial torpedo, also "heavier-than-air, sustained and aided by aeroplanes," which ostensibly could already "carry five or ten passengers 800 miles" at "20 miles per hour for forty hours without renewal of supplies." Myers had already demonstrated his Sky-Cycle at the St. Louis Exposition of 1900, pedaling his small dirigible eight to ten feet above the arena floor for fifteen minutes, on its opening night, to the great delight of spectators. " [285] [286]

According to Prof. Myers, quoted in a Popular Science article in April 1901, "With practice acquired by use of the Sky-Cycle, and with some indicated variation in structure and equipment, *including a light auto-motor engine of best type,* there should be no great difficulty in accomplishing an overland transcontinental journey by two or three persons with this type of air craft in less time than the same trip could be made by the same party on the ground."[287] Octave Chanute mentioned, in a subsequent letter to Wilbur Wright on July 3, 1901, that Prof. Myers was thinking of installing a Whitehead Motor in his Sky-Cycle. Professor Myers later became "Superintendent of Aeronautics" at the Fair, through August 25, 1904, when he was relieved of his duties, in part, for being both an entrant and judge for the grand prize event.[288] Myers intended to use his Sky-Cycle, perhaps with a Whitehead Motor, to compete for the grand prize at the Fair[289].

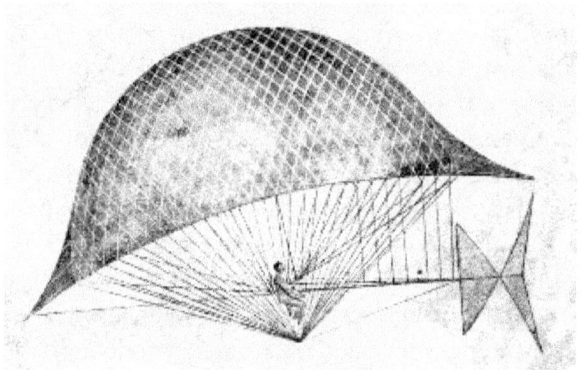

Fig. 6. Myers's Sky-Cycle (I).

Figure 92: Professor Myer's Sky-Cycle 1

Chapter 4: New Goal: The World's Fair Aerial Contest

Fig. 7. Myers's Sky-cycle (II).

**Figure 93: Prof. Myer's Sky Cycle 2
Illustration from article by Cochran, Popular Science, April 1901.**

One of the anticipated demonstrations was to be by Prof. Carl Myers, appointed as the first World's Fair "Superintendent of Aeronautics." Myers may have used a Whitehead Motor in his 1901 sky-cycle.[290]

The World's Fair planners envisioned the Aerial Contest as a means to generate international publicity for the Fair, and attract large paying crowds to excitedly view hundreds of unprecedented aerial feats they anticipated would result. Over the next 2 1/2 years, a tumultuous series of events resulting from the Aerial Committee's ever-changing decisions and mistakes led to far fewer competitors and aerial displays than the initial planners visualized. In the end, according to the authoritative "History of the Louisiana Purchase Exposition"[291], published in 1905, *only $1,000 in Aerial contest prize money was actually paid out.* $45,864 was the "total cost of the aeronautic feature of the Exposition," out of $200,000, with $150,000 touted as prize money in much of the Fair's publicity, right up through the end. Considering the average worker then made $400-$500 a year[292], and poverty level was a yearly income of $600 or below in 1902[293] , prizes involving thousands of dollars, especially hundreds of thousands, were a very strong incentive, indeed – particularly for inventors like Gustave Whitehead, envisioning commercial applications and production in large factories. Inventors were trying to find a way to enter the contest and win the prizes offered, right up through the fall of 1904, when the realities of the impossible requirements became more apparent and their hopes began to unravel.

Ultimately, with many questionable changes occurring to the rules and regulations, especially to win the grand prize of $100,000, Gustave Whitehead's aeroplane-style flying machines which reportedly flew ½ to 1.5 miles at best, at an elevation of 5-200 feet, would have been directly competing with gas-filled, powered dirigibles that already flew hundreds of miles, and to elevations of thousands of feet. His aircraft would have had to fly a 15 mile L-shaped course over the fairgrounds, three times, at 20 mph, starting at the point of intersection, changing direction at the end points for each of the five and ten mile "legs" (see diagram). Even with Octave Chanute, mentor to the Wrights, as a consultant to the Aerial Committee helping plan the contest, aeroplane-style heavier-than-air flying machines, in their earliest infancy at that time, were no match for the far more maneuverable, long-distance-capable "gas-bag" dirigibles. Or was this by design?

Figure 94: Aerial Contest course
The Grand Prize course at the World's Fair "Airship Contests," with the starting point
at A1 (the intersection), buildings all along it.
Willard Smith, overseer of the contest, Chief of the Transportation Department, is pictured.
This course was not designed for fledgling heavier-than-air aeroplanes.
Courtesy of the University of Missouri, MU Libraries

By April 1902, the Exposition's Aerial Committee, headed up by Willard A. Smith, Chief of the Department of Transportation, had received over 100 applications from prospective competitors for the "aerial tournament." Gustave Whitehead's application was submitted months before the competition's Rules and Regulations were announced.

CHANUTE, THE WRIGHTS, WHITEHEAD, AND THE FAIR

Communications between Octave Chanute and the Wrights concerning the upcoming Fair shed light on the conditions leading up to the aerial contest, revealing Whitehead as a known competitor and source of lightweight engines. The stakes were so high that information concerning successful inventions were considered fair game.

Chapter 4: New Goal: The World's Fair Aerial Contest

On February 7, 1902, Wilbur wrote to Octave Chanute (now consultant for the World's Fair aerial competition) ridiculing press accounts of flying machines (like Whitehead's) that allegedly had "completely solved" the problem of aerial navigation, built in cellars and "other secret places" in order to win what he referred to as the "aeronautical contest" at St. Louis. Whitehead's plane had been widely publicized as having been constructed mainly in his cellar. This is evidence Wilbur was aware of the Whitehead flight claims.

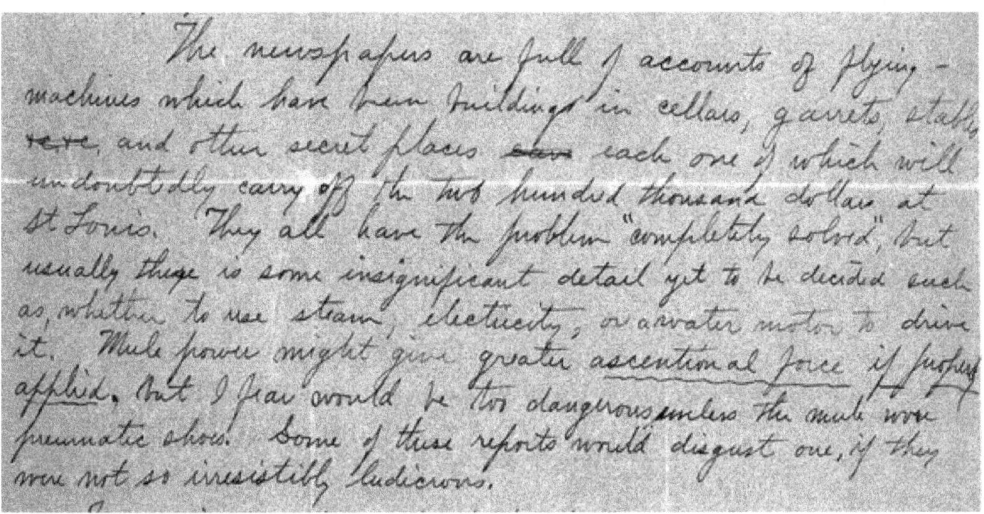

Figure 95: Wilbur Wright's 1902 letter to Chanute shows he knew of Whitehead

(transcript)

"The newspapers are full of *the accounts of flying machines which have been building in cellars,* garrets, stables, etc. etc. and other secret places each one of which will undoubtedly carry off the two hundred thousand dollars at St. Louis. They all have the problem "completely solved," but usually there is some insignificant detail yet to be decided such as, whether to use steam, electricity, or a water motor to drive it. Mule power might give greater ascentional force if properly applied, but I fear would be too danger unless the mule wore pneumatic shoes. Some of these reports would disgust one, if they were not so irresistibly ludicrous."

(end of transcript)

The Wright brothers were in frequent communication with their mentor, Octave Chanute, while he was providing expertise to the World's Fair aerial contest planners. The Wrights investigated the World's Fair regulations and prospects of winning the upcoming Aerial Competition with his "insider" help, even making a visit there to inspect the field. They'd be up against powered balloons (dirigibles) that could fly hundreds of miles, leaving from an enclosure with a thirty foot high fence built to protect the dirigibles from winds. At the time, the Wrights were having trouble flying twenty feet. Without the winds of Kitty Hawk to provide the initial lift to their "Flyer 2," to compete at the Fair was a hopeless endeavor for them, from the start. Their original "Flyer" had only flown several hundred feet the previous December based on their own reports. The Wrights' communications with Octave Chanute often referred to Willard A. Smith, Chief of the Fair's Department of Transportation, providing the historic record with a closeup view of considerations concerning the regulations and conditions of the Aerial Competition for flying machines[294], that would have also pertained to Whitehead. [*emphasis added*]

Gustave Whitehead: "First in Flight"

Jan. 18, 1904
Dear Mr. Chanute,

....We are at work building three machines with which we shall probably give exhibition at several different places during the coming season. We may decide to enter one at St. Louis, and have written ~~to them~~ for copy of their revised rules & regulations. When these come we will give the matter serious consideration, and if we find that *the objectionable feature of the original rules* have been eliminated we may decide to make a try for it. Otherwise we will see what we can do elsewhere than inside the Fair Grounds, if we go to St. Louis at all.

Yours truly
Wilbur Wright

Feb. 13, 1904
Dear Mr. Chanute,

Your two letters of January 6 received. Also copies of rules and map of Exposition grounds, and several newspaper clippings for which we thank you. We have a letter from Mr. Smith giving an interpretation of the rules on the points we talked about when you were in Dayton. I see that in one of the papers you sent us, *Santos Dumont is quoted as saying the distance is to be from twenty to thirty miles*. Do not the rules say plainly that the distance specified in the rules is the <u>total distance</u> traveled? in <u>Fifteen to twenty-five Kilometers?</u> It surely can not mean twice this distance.

Orville and I are intending to go down to St. Louis next week, if we can arrange to see Mr. Smith there at that time, and inspect the grounds and surroundings.

Yours truly
Wilbur Wright

March 1, 1904
Dear Mr. Chanute,

Your letter of Feb. 15 has been received. I wonder if Captain Farber has any real conception of the difficulties he would have had to surmount in order to have been the first to "take this step."

Orville and I went down to St. Louis last month and took a look at the aeronautical grounds and surrounding country. We were not expecting ideal conditions, but we found things even less favorable than we anticipated. I do not know that this would be serious danger to life, but much of the ground over which the course must be laid out is such as to make forced landing almost inevitable. It would probably be necessary to win the prize in their trials or not at all. As there are no consolation prizes for flying machines, like those provided for the airships. It is a tough proposition. However, when we get out again with our machine, and have fully tested its reliability for long flights, we will see whether it will pay to enter. The conditions are such that we wish to know that we will win before we finally decide to go for it.

If we enter, it will be for the purpose of winning; not for the purpose of seeing how close ~~even~~ we can come to it.

....

Yours truly
Wilbur Wright

Chapter 4: New Goal: The World's Fair Aerial Contest

March 29, 1904
Dear Mr. Chanute,

  Your letter of 19th inst. (instance) is read with interest. My calculations based on a comparison of the #6 and #7 give Santos Dumont a speed in still air of between 24 and 25 miles an hour. There will be a loss in starting, landing and making turns, but nevertheless with everything working perfectly he ought to be able to make the St. Louis course at an average speed of 18 3/4 miles an hour. I think 20 miles would have been beyond his limit about nine times out of ten, unless the conditions at St. Louis prove superior to these in Paris. The changes in the rules do not affect us one way or the other but we approve of them because we would like to see someone known down that prize...

  .... This reminds me that you once spoke of desiring to exhibit your multiple wing and oscillating wing machines at St. Louis. I had intended to see to having them completely packed before we left camp last fall, but our hurried departure prevented. We have been so busy ever since that the matter escaped our minds. Shall we arrange to have them sent to St. Louis at once?

  ...

  Yours truly
  Wilbur Wright

April 10, 1904

Dear Mr. Chanute,

  We recently wrote Mr. Smith asking that the words "starting point" be interpreted as including the entire aeronautical enclosure, and he writes that this will be considered. As this gives the entire enclosure for starting, and the entire enclosure together with a fifty yard strip outside the fence for landing. The conditions are thus made much less severe than if more strictly interpreted. The only question now is whether we can make sure that the engine will run twenty minutes under full load without any serious risk of making a single stop in their trips.

  ...

  Yours truly
  Wilbur Wright

April 14, 1904
Dear Mr. Chanute,

  .... Mr. Herring would seem to have a cinch on the St. Louis prize for flying models, if he can substantiate his claims published in the Boston Journal.

  (more descriptions of working on Flyer #2)
  ...

  Yours truly
  Wilbur Wright

Gustave Whitehead: "First in Flight"

May 27, 1904
Dear Mr. Chanute,

... Can you find out whether entries in St. Louis Contest <u>positively</u> close June 1st? If so we would be glad to know by telegraph. We wish to enter but not just yet.

(describes failed trials of May 24, 26)

Mon. - not enough wind, "only a hundred feet of track," "unable to obtain supporting speed."

On Wed. we again took it out but were driven in by rain.

Again on Thursday we took it out and again the rain compelled us to take it in, but in the afternoon we again took it out. Once more a rain came up but before we made a start. The engine was not working right but this was no time to see what the trouble was then. *The machine rose six or eight feet but the power was insufficient and it came down....*

... If Mr. [Willard] Smith is in St. Louis please inform me.

Yours truly,
Wilbur Wright

June 2, 1904
Dear Mr. Chanute,

We thank you for so kindly obtaining the information we desired. We had also written Mr. Smith but were uncertain whether we would reach him promptly. We have made repairs in our machine and expect to be ready for trials on Thursday of this week. After a few flights we will know better what we will wish to do about entering at St. Louis. I have written Mr. Smith that we wish to test the machine before taking up the matter of entering the race.

The newspaper reports seem to indicate that Santos Dumont had made no flights as yet, but only shop tests of the machinery. He will probably not sail for America without a thorough trial of his new system of hanging his engine below the car, as that would seem doubtful whether he does much flying at St. Louis before August. Is his shed finished?

The fact that we are experimenting at Dayton is now public, but so far we have not been disturbed by visitors....

...

Yours truly
Wilbur Wright

June --, 1904
Dear Mr. Chanute,

(discussion of Santos-Dumont and his 60 hp motor) "he should have little difficulty getting inside the 15 mile limit, as it would require less than half the power necessary for 20 mi."

We certainly have been "Jonahed" this year, partly by bad weather and partly by being compelled to use pine spars in our wings which cause breakage difficult to repair quickly....

Chapter 4: New Goal: The World's Fair Aerial Contest

.... we took a trial last week but make an awkward start and struck the ground after about 60 ft. This machine is entirely new, including engine and machinery. We are using the old screws.

...

Yours truly
Wilbur Wright

The Wright brothers, falsely reported in the media as *flying three miles* in December 1903, were then asked to participate in the aerial contest. They wisely declined, for their fledgling Flyer could not possibly fly the Fair's prescribed courses, as could no other heavier-than-air flying machine of that time. The Wrights, unlike Whitehead, who had far fewer resources, went to St. Louis to view the location, but did not enter the Aerial Competition because they knew it was not feasible for them to win. It might have proved quite an embarrassment, as they were having trouble just getting off the ground, back in Dayton, Ohio, without the winds of Kitty Hawk, in the spring of 1904. Their investigations of the fairgrounds had to be only to save face, at that point.

NEWS OF WHITEHEAD AND THE FAIR

News of the aerial competition went round the globe, with anticipation high, based on the ambitious initial planning of the Fair's Aerial Committee. A Scotland newspaper reported the following, on April 19, 1902, prominently mentioning Gustave Whitehead's projected participation, with his "mechanical bird," actually "No. 22'," representing one class of airship, while calling it what was familiar, a "balloon."

"The Great Flying Machine Contest: 'A Huge Silken Bird to Compete'"

"If the promoters of the St. Louis World's Fair succeed in their endeavors, the two distinct classes of airships will be tested and contrasted simultaneously. *Among the new airships is one invented by Mr. Gustave Whitehead, of Bridgeport, Conn. In design, the craft is a kind of mechanical bird.* The balloon rises from the earth by means of power supplied by a 20-horse-power engine. The machine has four wheels upon which it rests, and when it is started these wheels are given rapid motion, the wings being tilted so as to lift it from the ground. When the airship is "off" energy is applied to powerful propellers, which maintain the speed, and the craft continues to sail upwards like a huge bird. The machine is built of wood and bamboo, and the covering is silk. The body is 16 feet long, 3 feet wide, and 3 feet deep. On each side are great wings, or aeroplanes, stretched tightly on a bamboo framework. The engine drives the propellers at a speed of 700 revolutions per minute. The propellers are 6 feet in diameter, and when running at full speed have a forward thrust of 365 pounds. The entire weight of Mr. Whitehead's airship is 280 pounds. Trial trips have been made and these have gone through without accident.... [More entrants and their airships are described.]

It is anticipated that a hundred or more aerial machines will enter the proposed airship races at the Exposition. As it is impossible to handicap large and small balloons, the suggestion has been thrown out that 1200 cubic feet should be the dimensions of contesting balloons or airships. The machine must be under perfect control. All movement must be made without letting out gases while descending or throwing out ballast while ascending. As to speed, it should not be less than 60 miles per hour." [295]

On the same date, in the Deseret Evening News, a Salt Lake City, Utah newspaper that kept abreast of developments in aeronautics, Gustave Whitehead was described as "strong competition" for Alberto Santos-Dumont.

Gustave Whitehead: "First in Flight"

Not So Easy For Santos-Dumont
Brazilian Airship Navigator Will Have Strong Competition at the World's Fair
St. Louis, April 15th.

"Santos-Dumont, the "Wizard of the Air," who is now en route to St. Louis to confer with world's fair officials on the subject of the air races to take place during the progress of the Louisiana Purchase exposition, may find warmer competition among the American aeronauts than he anticipates at this time. Many *American Inventors*, with plenty of money to back them up, are laying plans to dispute the Brazilian's title to being the "all of it" when it comes to navigation in the clouds. The dirigible airship is M. Santos-Dumont's special hobby, and his sail around the Eiffel Tower, and the later successful flights over Monaco bay, have no doubt created a general impression that he will probably have an easy time of it walking off with the $200,000 prize offered by the Louisiana Purchase exposition for this sort of flying machine. That impression is an erroneous one. There are others, and there are Americans among them. When the airship races at the world's fair are over, M. Santos-Dumont and those who expect to see him an easy winner may find themselves on the wrong side of the guessing contest. They may have another guess coming…[describes several contenders]

Inventor Gustave Whitehead, of Bridgeport, Conn., is also working on a dirigible airship with the intention of meeting Santos-Dumont in the balloon race at the world's fair. Whitehead recently conducted a series of trial tests with his machine at Charles Island, Milford. He is elated over the success of the trials. He asserts that he made a complete circuit in the air, covering an area of about a quarter of a mile, returning to within 50 feet of the starting point, when the machine descended and dropped lightly to the sandy shore.

"The flights were a complete success," said Whitehead. "I had a kerosene motor, which worked perfectly. I steered the machine by running one propeller faster than the other, and there was not a hitch of any kind. I have much faith in this kerosene motor, which is the lightest I have ever used. It is of forty horse power and weighs but 120 pounds. I am now planning to fulfill the promise I made some years ago to get to New York in May. I will accomplish it if my machine breaks down a dozen times in the attempt."[296]

Gustave Whitehead's Aerial Competition application generated national excitement, through the summer of 1904, during which time he, and his brother John, newly arrived in April 1902 to help him, busily discussing a variety of designs – perhaps in futile hopes of developing an aircraft that might fly the required 15 mile circuit at the Fair. He and John were determined to win the $100,000 prize, described in an interview in August 1902. Some newspapers even referred to him as "Prof. Whitehead." The Middletown (CT) Penny Press had this to say, in early August 1902:

Soar Through Skies
Whitehead Confident His Machine Will Fly

"The Bridgeport Standard says that *Gustave Whitehead*, of 241 Pine Street, is again at work on his flying machine, after a few weeks of enforced rest, due to his inability to secure funds to conduct certain experiments. Capital is now furnished by his brother, John Whitehead, until recently a resident of California. John Whitehead is a successful prospector, and has made a fortune in gold mining. Since Gustave Whitehead and Herman Linde had their disagreement last spring, after which Mr. Linde withdrew all support from Whitehead, the latter was in a quandary for a while. He did not have the funds necessary to continue his work … The brothers are working together and are confidant of participating

Chapter 4: New Goal: The World's Fair Aerial Contest

in the contest for the $100,000 prize [worth $2.8 million dollars in 2014] offered by the Louisiana Purchase exposition for the best dirigible balloon, airship or flying machine. Whitehead said: "I have just completed a new motor, which I propose to use in my flying machine during the experimental flights which we will make within two or three weeks. We are now planning to enter the competition in St. Louis at the exposition next year....If I do not appear publicly before then I will most certainly be at the exposition and enter the contest for the prize. A prize is also offered for the lightest motor in proportion to its power, and I will also try for that prize, which is $2500 [worth $70,000 in 2014] ... My brother has been interested in flying machines for several years ... and is willing to provide me with all the funds necessary to conduct experiments and complete a machine which he can take to St. Louis. He understands aerostatics[297], and is more help to me than anyone else I ever had working for me. We will be able to make good before a great while." "[298]

The Chicago Tribune, in a 1903 article entitled "*Inventors Turn to Aerial Navigation: Americans Native Pride Aroused by Leadership of Foreign Competitors,*" informed its readers about Gustave Whitehead and other aspiring *American Inventor*s working towards winning at the Fair. They pictured Whitehead's 1903 triplane glider being launched by men pulling it with ropes, into the wind.

"*...Whitehead Relies on Wheels,*" "*With Gustav Whitehead of Bridgeport, Conn., experimenting with the idea of motor driven aeroplanes has been carried out to a practical issue. He shares with Gathmann the belief in motor power and wheels as a means of propulsion in the air rather than the winged vehicles of Prof. Langley, and his invention, with which he has already made successful experiments, promises to hold an important place in fair competition.* He is engaged in making some improvements in his machine, which he confidently expects will bring him far greater success than he has secured."[299]

Whitehead was considered to be "a well-known aeronaut" in the early years of the 20th century, compared to Octave Chanute, in this article from the *Sheridan Weekly Sun* April 21, 1904, p.3 which references the then-popular Cassell's Magazine:

"**A Gliding Machine.**
Two Foreign Aeronauts Have Devised a New Sport

The well-known aeronauts, Profs. Octave Chanute and Gustave Whitehead, says Cassell's Magazine, have endeavored to test the possibility of flight by means of what is termed "gliding" machines or kites.
    The apparatus consists of two long sheets of white canvas running horizontally with each other, and joined at each end by two uprights. The canvas is enclosed, as it were, in a frame of strong wood, made more rigid by a number of cross sections. Attached to the lower part of this machine are two "arms" for the use of the aeronaut when in mid-air, while a tail completes the apparatus. By running a little way along the ground the kite is made to lift the operator in the air and carry him some little distance. Astonishing as it may seem, glides of. 300 feet, 500 feet, and even 800 feet and more are often attained. These glides are invariably done down a steep slope or hill. After a flight the operator can alight without discomfort. A considerable amount of practice is required, however, before anyone can hope to become a good glider, the slightest little thing upsetting one's equilibrium. Prof. Whitehead has gone so far as to attach a small cycle motor to his machine, which enables him to skim over the ground for a longer distance than would otherwise be the case."
    Cassell's reproduces an interesting photograph of the glider, supplied by Prof. Chanute.[300]

Figure 96: Chanute glider

[Author's note: This triplane glider lithograph, pictured above, looks nearly identical to a photo of Gustave Whitehead's May 1903 triplane glider, on its way to becoming a flying machine with a motor and additional modifications (see Fig. 101). Note the use of lithographs in newspapers, a widespread practice during this time period.]

AERIAL COMPETITION PROBLEMS

The Aerial Competition's planners had not yet released their final Rules and Regulations in April 1902 - these were under lively discussion at multiple meetings that began in January and continued through June 1902, finally being released to the press – and then revised again and again, right through the end of the Fair, several years later.

A grand prize of $100,000 was initially being offered, with a set of subsidiary prizes based on speed, distance, and even for the lightest, most efficient engine. The engine competition stimulated Whitehead's interest – and indeed, he reportedly did display an engine there, according to Octave Chanute[301], and brought his plane, according to at least one associate[302], to the Fair. The rules and regulations would be revised often enough to conceivably exasperate and even eliminate prospective competitors. For an inventor like Whitehead, trying to keep up with the latest revisions of a set of rules designed to favor powered lighter-than-air airships and their wealthy owner-contestants, and ultimately, the Louisiana Exposition Company, would have been most frustrating and eventually, disheartening.

Santos-Dumont, investing heavily with both time and money, visited the Fairgrounds several times and brought his specially built "No. 7" air ship from France in late June 1904. The one man in the world anticipated to attract hundreds of thousands to the fair and expected to win the grand prize, he negotiated it to be increased to $150,000 [the equivalent of $4,000,000 in 2015[303]]. During the night, days before a July 4th demonstration he was to give, his balloon was ostensibly slashed "by vandals," when its guard was engaged in several coffee breaks, making it impossible to fly – and *perhaps making it possible for the Fair's planners not to have to pay out the grand prize,* after attracting crowds to the Fair with its publicity. The perpetrator of this crime was never identified, though Santos-Dumont was inexplicably accused by Fair security, at one point, of slashing his own dirigible,

Chapter 4: New Goal: The World's Fair Aerial Contest

causing him to pack up and indignantly leave for Paris on June 30th, never to return to the Fair. As barely any prize money was ultimately awarded ($1,000 in all), one might consider whether there was ever a plan to really pay any of what was promised – and if the money to pay it even existed, where did it go, in the end? Not to have to pay out the equivalent of $4 million would be a likely incentive. The "for-profit" Louisiana Purchase Exposition Company and its Aerial Contest Committee members would be the ones to answer that question, and they are long gone –the complete records of the Contest are not to be found in the public record, though all else that occurred at the Fair seems to be. Examination of the records that do remain shows constant decision-making by the Aerial Committee leading to fewer and fewer contests, with impossible criteria paving the way to non-payout of the highly publicized prize monies, while making excessive demands of aeronaut exhibitors and contestants who would be entertaining the massive paying crowds they drew to the Fair. It is clear that "inner circle" conflicts of interest and questionable behavior on the part of the planners was rampant. It seemed to be, not surprisingly, "all about the money"… which it appears the Company was suddenly short of, as it headed into dismantling of all the buildings and paying its debts, when the fair ended.

The final contests, held in September - December 1, 1904 emphasized the favorite of those then involved with early aviation – the dirigible balloons and popular attempts at building "man-carrying kites." Accommodations and rules that favored balloons above other types of aircraft such as powered flying machines, which were in their infancy, overtook the Aerial Committee for the Exposition. Negotiations and arrangements became unstable and even, chaotic, as the competition approached. The World's Fair Bulletins described the Fair's "Aeronautical Concourse," as a 12 acre field surrounded by a dangerous thirty foot fence - ostensibly erected to shield from winds - that the airships could barely clear. It was quite muddy, in part due to not being "seeded" (with grass) in time, with the main buildings (called "stables," though later might be referred to as "hangars") set up to house airships. Even in late June 1904, these became filled with "a sea of mud" when it rained, due to late installation of sewers. Whitehead's flying machine would have had no runway, a high fence preventing ascent, an impossibly long course in the midst of buildings and fairgoers, and no rules under which he could possibly hope to win.

Concerns were expressed regarding the costs of going to St. Louis from all parts of the world and transporting aircraft there. Some contestants were demanding that the Exposition pay, though this was not forthcoming. Complaints were made by prospective competitors that the prescribed courses, even for experienced balloonists and dirigible owners, were seemingly so impossible that the large prizes would never be paid out, but be "safe" for the Fair's planners "to keep." Only a handful were left who wished to enter and paid the refundable $250 entrance fee, though virtually none were technically said to be considered qualified to compete, under the planners' far too ambitious "Rules and Regulations."

Rules for the competition were drafted after a meeting of a panel of "world renowned experts in aeronautics" held on April 21, 1902 at the request of Fair officials, revised, and then finalized on September 4, 1904, based on what even dirigibles might have trouble accomplishing, leading to increasing criticism.

THE EIGHT MAJOR CONTESTS

In all, eight major contests were planned, in the final announcement carried in the St. Louis Republic on September 4, 1904, with a total of $135,000 in prize monies offered.

These were:
1. The Grand Prize Contest
2. Pilotless Flying Machine Contest
3. Glider Angle Contest
4. Glider Stability Contest
5. Altitude Contest

Gustave Whitehead: "First in Flight"

6. Endurance Contest
7. Long Distance Contest
8. Washington Monument Contest[304]

The Grand Prize Contest held everyone's attention, as its unprecedented prize of $100,000 was a strong incentive, with plans for second, third, fourth, and fifth place winners, and prizes that ranged from $3500 to $1500, respectively. Whitehead would have been discouraged upon hearing what the final decision for the contests was to be, in early September 1904. It was too much to expect, too soon, for any flying machine, including his, the "first to fly," able to cover a distance of a half mile and possibly up to a mile and a half in a clear, open space, but certainly not above the heads of fairgoers, hemmed in by a few square miles of tall buildings – especially in a soft, muddy field with no takeoff runway space.[305]

Interestingly, there was also a pilotless flying machine contest for $2500 that had to go a mile on a straight course and return back to its starting point. There were two glider contests, one for "a vertical angle most acute with the horizon" that would "advance against the wind" or in a "calm"; another for altitude, for "the aeronautical vessel which attained the greatest altitude after ascending"; an endurance test - for the aeronautical vessel which remained in the air for the longest duration; a long distance test for traveling the furthest distance at the fairgrounds; and the Washington Monument Contest – requiring travel for at least 500 miles, landing near the Washington Monument in Washington, DC.

Competing with dirigibles in these sorts of contests would be a losing proposition. Prospective applicants had to prove their aircraft was not dangerous and could be flown with safety, and that they'd flown a mile, returning in a circuit, paying the $250 grand prize entrance fee – to be refunded when they showed up and occupied their reserved space in the airship building at the Aeronautical Concourse. Out of 97 persons and companies that indicated an interest in the Contest, 44 listed their aircraft as "air ships"; 23 as "aero-planes"; 3 as "flying machines"; 10 as balloons; 12 as "kites" and 1 as a "gliding machine." *Only eight parties eventually paid the fee, with four of the eight being returned - two of these clearly did not meet the criteria of the competition.*[306] It is unknown exactly why Gustave Whitehead decided, in the end, not to compete, but there were growing reasons not to, by September 1904.

The Motor Contest, described in the Rules and Regulations of the Aeronautic Competition (Revised), March 1904, set out a first prize of $2,500 and a second prize of $1,000 …

"offered for the air-ship motors other than the exact machine winning the grand prize, having the least weight and greatest efficiency in proportion to their power. There are no limitations as to the kind of type, but the motor must have a minimum capacity of one-brake horse-power and shall not exceed a maximum of 1000 brake horse-power. The weight of the motor is to include all appurtenances (tanks, water, etc.), and fuel, or its equivalent, for a run of one hour. It must be so constructed that it can be attached to an apparatus for making a brake test. The first test will cover one hour's run to determine power and the second test a continuous run of ten hours for ascertaining the reliability and durability of the apparatus. One prize of $3,000 for a successful attempt to drive an air-ship motor by energy transmitted through space, either in the form of electric radiation or in some other form of electrical energy, to an actual amount of one-tenth of a horse-power at the point of reception and at a distance of at least a thousand feet. The test must be made on the Exposition grounds by experts satisfactory to the jury [judges]. [307]

However, in a decision recorded in the Minutes of the Aeronautical Contest Committee of October 21, 1904, the prizes for the (lightest, most efficient) motor contest *were withdrawn*, just as many other prizes were

Chapter 4: New Goal: The World's Fair Aerial Contest

not paid out *"in view of the failure of the contestants to meet the* [Note: unreasonable] *conditions of the contest."* [308]

CRITICISM OF THE RULES AND REGULATIONS

Criticism of the Fair's rules for its aerial contest were rampant. As the Fair drew closer, many formerly enthusiastic contestants dropped out, with good reason.

While St. Louis Fair historian James J. Horgan, PhD reported that Gustave Whitehead had paid his fee "early on," [309] there is no verification of this. It is quite likely that Gustave Whitehead, like Leo Stevens, described as the "prominent New York aeronaut" of a dirigible, eventually opted out of the contest, as participating would be pointless, as Stevens explained in a letter to the *Scientific American* in early March 1904 ....[310]

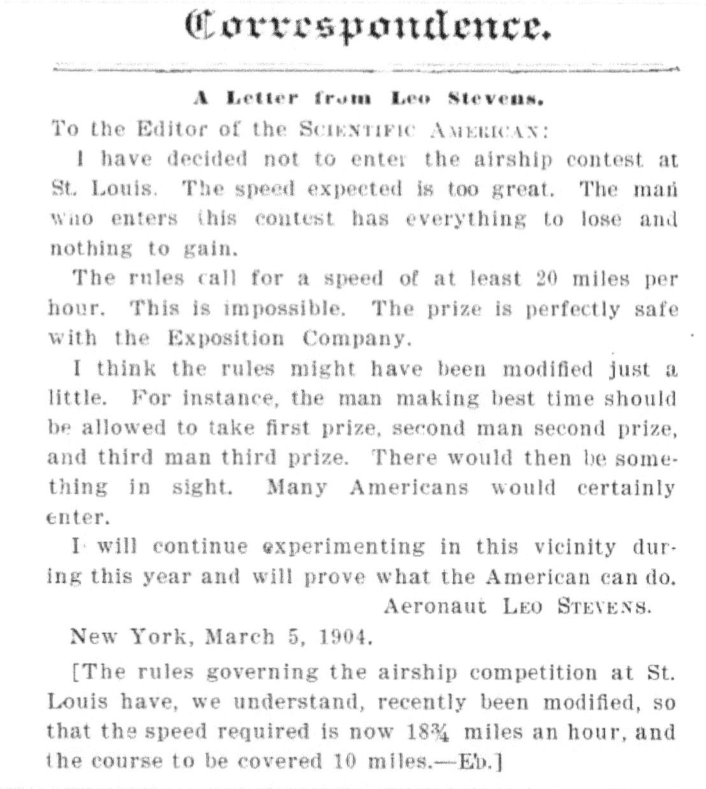

Figure 97: Leo Stevens Letter to the Editor re: World's Fair contest

(transcript)

"A Letter from Leo Stevens.
To the Editor of the *Scientific American*:

I have decided not to enter the airship contest at St. Louis. The speed expected is too great. The man who enters this contest has everything to lose and nothing to gain.

The rules call for a speed of at least 20 miles per hour. This is impossible. The prize is perfectly safe with the Exposition Company.

I think the rules might have been modified just a little. For instance, the man making best time should be allowed to take first prize, second man second prize, and third man third prize. There would then be something in sight. Many Americans would certainly enter.

I will continue to experiment in this vicinity during this year and will prove what the American can do.

Gustave Whitehead: "First in Flight"
Aeronaut Leo Stevens.

New York, March 5. 1904

[The rules governing the airship competition at St. Louis have, we understood, recently been modified so that the speed required is 18 ¾ miles per hour and the course to be covered 10 miles. –ED.]"

(end of transcript)

Two and a half years of multiple design efforts and countless, scarce, precious dollars had gone into the Whitehead brothers' effort to compete at the World's Fair of 1904. As previously noted, John even had to leave for a year during this time to try earning more money in California to subsidize their experiments. It had been a chance at winning major funding that would not only pay the household bills but would fulfill the dream of a large, unencumbered sum, to be used for funding Whitehead's future flying machine experiments. Not being able to compete had to be very disappointing for Gustave and his brother John, his family, friends, and assistants.

Prospective competitors had planned to spend up to $100,000 to develop "airships" for the contest. The Fair's organizers did, indeed, stimulate the development of aviation through their unprecedented prize announcements. Flying machines, however, would not fly those distances, with the degree of control required, for at least another decade.

Cosmopolitan published its perspective in an article from a section of its World's Fair guide, called "*The Five Great Features of the Fair*," published in September 1904, written by a journalist, John Brisben Walker, who'd attended the fair. He commenting on the incompetence of those who planned the aerial contests.

> "*Perhaps the greatest single feature of the Fair is that the very intelligent body of men composing its directorate and management should have been bold enough and broad enough to devote a single item of one hundred and fifty thousand dollars to exploiting aerial flight,* the very idea of which was considered so chimerical at the time of the Chicago Fair [11 years before, in 1893] that only one scientist in the country dared approve of an investigation of the subject. *When every other feature of the St. Louis Fair has been forgotten, this one fact will go down into history and be recalled to the eternal credit of the men who favored the idea of so liberal an expenditure.* It is a great misfortune that, after the management had proved itself so broad-minded, *the execution of its plans could not have been placed in the hands of someone competent to carry them out properly. Mistakes have characterized this branch of the work at every turn. I don't even know the name of the man to whom this department was committed but certainly he could have had but a very dim idea of his subject. If, instead of making crude rules, and expending money on enclosures and gasplants, he had been a man who comprehended what he was about, the world would have secured different results.*" [311]

The guide continued on with its viewpoint about the ridiculousness of the contest and the stupidity of those engaged in the inventing, lending another revealing look at the current thinking of the time:

"Great Inventions and Discoveries: The Aeroplane

The aeroplane will not reach the expected development at the St. Louis Exposition, owing to the fact that persons in charge of the expenditure of the one hundred and fifty thousand dollars appropriated had no knowledge, apparently, of the matter, and approached the subject from the standpoint of the racetrack. We can imagine that they were estimable gentlemen who knew all about Missouri race-tracks, and could have but one idea, that of "a good run for our money." Add to this that the men wealthy enough to engage in the expensive work of aerial construction have been stupidly indifferent to what is involved in its accomplishment. Yet nevertheless there is the certainty of ultimate success if the necessary steps are

Chapter 4: New Goal: The World's Fair Aerial Contest

pursued with one-tenth the care taken in the development of the automobile." [312]

Smithsonian Secretary, Samuel Pierpont Langley's Advice for the Aerial Competition

Consultant to the Aerial Competition, the Smithsonian's Samuel P. Langley, gave his wise but largely ignored advice, on May 31, 1902 – that a successful heavier-than-air flying machine basically "doesn't exist" and should not be made to compete with those traditionally referred to as "lighter than air" – in the balloon or dirigible category, that the heavier than air flying machines were "absolutely untried" and should be considered separately, not "placed on the same footing in your contest." However, he also said that he realized "it may be unavoidable."

While it was true that Langley's efforts to produce a flying machine had failed - even after his assistant, Manley, sent an emissary to record the details of Whitehead's reputedly successful machine when it was displayed in Atlantic City in September 1901 - he does imply that one inventor has succeeded in going beyond a hundred yards, though he says, not in "carrying a man." Whether Langley's letter refers to what he believes about Whitehead, or to himself (he had produced a smaller model that made unmanned, powered flights), its main message is that the aeronautic competition's planners should consider having "a competition of flying machines between themselves or balloons between themselves" [or] "the best method" being "fixing a condition, as you have done, which will make speed the dominant factor, but I would rather see a speed of 25 miles an hour than 20." He further advises that no machine or balloon "can land on a 'point,' " and that the landing area must be made larger, such as "a circle at least 100 yards in diameter." It appears that the Aeronautical Committee followed Langley's advice to the degree that there was some separation of the classes of aircraft, in that there was a gliding competition planned, though no informed, separate trials, rules or regulations for the various types of powered aircraft. Perhaps the planners followed Langley's "plan B," which was to make speed the dominant factor.

Considering the flights would be made high overhead of the crowds and along a lengthy, prescribed course, while being safely executed, this all but eliminated the class of powered heavier-than-air flying machines Whitehead and a number of others were experimenting with. Whitehead's designs were so novel that the Aerial contest planners and their consultants, had no foundational understanding to bring to the table in considering the upcoming contest. Octave Chanute, a consultant who should have been recognized as a voice of reason, in addition to Langley, concerning the needs of flying machines in general, was apparently not heeded. Whitehead's plane and six to eight foot propellers would never have been able to takeoff and fly over the heads of thousands of people, avoiding buildings. The competition planners' focus was mainly on drawing crowds, and for this, they solicited world famous dirigible aeronauts like Santos-Dumont.

Smithsonian's Samuel P. Langley displayed his aerodrome in the government building, but did not enter a contest. Sir Hiram Maxim, of London, announced his intention to compete[313] and began to build a new heavier-than-air flying machine for that purpose, spending $75,000[314], but had to withdraw his interest, due to continuing ill health.

THE CALIFORNIA ARROW AND THE WHITEHEAD MOTOR

The Baldwin airship, mentioned above, was an "arrow-shaped" dirigible. Arthur Boltzmann, a highly regarded Austrian journalist, and reportedly an expert early balloonist, was covering the World's Fair for a Vienna newspaper. Boltzmann wired his "eyewitness report" as an "original dispatch" to a well-respected newspaper, "Luftschiffer Zeitung" *revealing that, during his visits to the various shops of the airship competitors, he had personally seen Captain Thomas Baldwin's balloon with a "Whitehead motor made in Bridgeport, Conn., USA"* installed. The California Arrow, a prize-winning dirigible that participated in the competition, reportedly used a Whitehead engine for all or some of the upcoming competition, even though it has been claimed that its engine was made by Curtiss.[315] Whitehead had been making and selling engines for at least three years by this time, said

Gustave Whitehead: "First in Flight"

to have started out selling engines for dirigibles, according to the *Bridgeport Evening Farmer* of June 20, 1910:

"Gus Whitehead, as his friends best know him, is one of the most expert engine builders in the world. He has succeeded in turning out engines whose efficiency in proportion to their weight is marvelous. *Years ago he was building engines for dirigible balloons.*" [316] [emphasis added]

Arthur Boltzmann was present at the Fair with his father, Professor Ludwig Boltzmann, a physicist from the University of Vienna, who lectured at an academic congress the afternoon of September 24, 1904, on "The Relations of Applied Mathematics."[317] Professor Boltzmann had long been a proponent of the coming age of flying machines, predicting in the mid-1890's that attaching a lightweight engine to a glider was the most likely route to initial success. [318]

Here is the full translation of Arthur Boltzmann's "original dispatch," so we may experience the scene on the Aeronautic Concourse through his eyes, a similar sight to what Gustave Whitehead was to undoubtedly experience within a month; Boltzmann's account also mentions Chanute and Langley aircraft present on this date, though Whitehead's exhibits had not yet arrived:

"From the World's Fair in St. Louis (Original Dispatch)
St. Louis, 25 September (1904)

In short words I want to here share what I have seen and heard at my visit to the World's Fair in St. Louis.

In the corner lying opposite to the main entrance of the Fairgrounds is the Aeronautic Concourse, which is surrounded by a high fence; on the great, empty square Marines temporarily stationed at the World's Fair drill every morning, and with difficulty haul the landing-guns through the soft, muddy ground, and it seems as though people had picked the area specifically for this purpose.

In the afternoons it is customary for the tethered balloon to go up (a round type balloon). As empty as the area seems from outside, things are quite lively in the gigantic Balloon-House. In one hangar M. Francois, a member of the Paris Aero Club, and M. Contour are assembling their steerable balloon-airship which was built in Paris. The equipment of the long gondola is presently being reconstructed, it consists of wooden poles of square cross-section which are fastened to one another with screws. The motor, still half in the crate, has likewise been brought along, and was made by the firm Prosper Lambert, of Nanterre. It is a four-cylinder. M. Francois gave its power as 30 H.P. The balloon envelope, made in Lachambres shop, is still on the way.

In the second hangar Mr. [Benbow], from Montana, is working on a steerable balloon. His gondola equipment consists of a net of steel pipes, the motor has already been installed, likewise the power take-off to the two screws, which are supposed to rotate in opposite directions, right next to each other, on the same shaft. The cigar-form balloon for this is also in the same hangar, inflated. Next to it lies a round balloon, half inflated, which will be used for free ascensions as opportunity permits.

In a neighboring shed, Mr. Baldwin from San Francisco has set up his workshop. The gondola equipment of his airship is built of wooden poles of triangular cross-section. *The Whitehead Motor, from Bridgeport, Conn., U.S.A., has already been installed, and at the moment they are working on the screw, which is fastened to the end of the long shaft.* His balloon is next to all this, still packed in its crate. It too is from San Francisco.

Chapter 4: New Goal: The World's Fair Aerial Contest

In the last section I caught sight of a very nicely built gliding machine of Chanute. This has two surfaces over one another, a vertical and horizontal steering, both at the rear. The flier places his armpits over two parallel poles which run toward the rear from under the under-surface. The machine is completely built of wood; only the connections are of short lengths of iron piping. The wood ribs, covered with blinding-white smooth material, form the surfaces.

Mr. Avery, a student of Chanute, intends to use the machine in the Aeronautic Concourse, and in the following manner: The machine is to be tied to a long cable, and then wound up on a winch driven by an electric motor. The machine, pulled along by this means, should with the help of this horizontal speed, raise up and then glide down from the desired height. I saw the electric motor and cable already there.

In the Building of Government I saw two smaller aeroplanes by Langley, both driven by gasoline engines, and they were different from the Chanute machines [in] that their two surfaces were located behind one another.

I was assured that competitions would begin in the first half of October.

Arthur Boltzmann"[319] [320]

It is part of the public record that Roy Knabenshue, pilot of the California Arrow, experienced the same serious engine trouble several times with a motor and had to be repaired more than once, during crucial moments of its flights. "An accident to the motor rendered the big fan propellers useless and curtailed his command of direction ..."[321]

Interviewed about the engine problems during his flights, Knabenshue said, "The only trouble was that the exhaust cap blew off. I lost the cap twice, and each time the motor stopped dead and I was at the mercy of the wind..."[322] The November 1904 World's Fair Bulletin described the problem as deriving from a chain slipping from a wheel that went to the two propellers, caused by the speed of the motor, which was described as "electric."[323] "On October 31, Knabenshue made the most successful flight of the season, ascending to a height of 2,000 feet, going Southwesterly over the Exposition and returning in 37 minutes to the point of starting, the first achievement of the kind in America." [324] The "Baldwin flights" were considered "the hit" of the Fair; and the only ones rewarded with prize money.

Figure 98: Baldwin's "Arrow" at World's Fair may have had Whitehead Motor
Courtesy of the University of Missouri, MU Libraries

© Susan Brinchman, 2015

Gustave Whitehead: "First in Flight"

> ### BALDWIN'S "ARROW" IN FLIGHT.
>
> The airship contests at the Exposition, of which much had been expected, were a disappointment, as none of the entries qualified, which would seem to indicate that the art of aerial navigation has not progressed in America as it has in France. Though development is less rapid in this country up to this time, a very gratifying exhibition was made at St. Louis by the Baldwin airship, which made several ascensions and showed dirigibility under favorable conditions, but it was not manageable when the wind blew at a greater velocity than eight miles an hour.

Figure 99: No Aerial Contest entries qualified.
Courtesy of the University of Missouri, MU Libraries

The published Boltzmann report [325] must stand as an accurate, primary source record of a neutral, experienced journalist and informed aeronaut on the scene, regardless of evidence or speculation that Baldwin may have left California for St. Louis with a Curtiss engine. A letter from the Curtiss Museum to Roger Post of Flight Journal, 1998 mentions a negative at the Curtiss museum labeled in handwriting, "Engine No. 1, California Arrow, World's Fair, St. L 1904." Perhaps the Whitehead Motor was "Engine No. 2"! [326]

WHITEHEAD PREPARES FOR THE FAIR

As details of the requirements for the St. Louis Exposition's Aerial Contest became known, Gustave Whitehead incorporated these into his designs and flight experiments, with a focus on improving control. The contest was designed to improve navigation of airships and would require flying circuits with controlled turns in the air, starting and stopping at the same location. Several of his significant early flights during the mid- to late winter of 1902, experimenting successfully with making rudimentary circuits, are described in detail in the next chapter.

Working steadily on improved flying machines, including a lightweight triplane intended for use at the Fair, Whitehead made progress, but without his brother John, who'd gone back to earn more money in California, from fall, 1902 – fall, 1903. Gustave Whitehead's latest aeroplane was documented in trade and scientific journals, as well as newspapers and magazines. One trade journal was doubtful whether the new Whitehead triplane could handle the additional weight of the fuselage and pilot.

"Gustave Whitehead's New Machine"

From *The Aeronautic World*, May 1903

"This improved machine, which somewhat resembles in appearance the Herring Chanute multiple glide, is clearly shown, minus the screw propellers in the illustration below. It is equipped with three superposed concavo-convex aeroplanes, arranged 10 inches apart, measuring 18 feet long by 6 feet wide, which afford a total aero-surface of 300 square feet, while the tail or rudder offers horizontally and vertically 80 square feet of surface.

The motive power is a marvelous 12 horsepower gasoline motor of the two cycle, two cylinder type, specially designed by Whitehead for the purpose. It is built entirely of steel for strength and lightness, and is designed for high speed and high compression, and complete, weighs with propellers, only 45 pounds. This air-cooled motor occupies a floor space of only 6 inches, with a height of 16 inches, and

Chapter 4: New Goal: The World's Fair Aerial Contest

consumes only 2 1/2 gallons of oil for a run of 12 hours.

...The two propellers, which are arranged in front, one on each side of the body and six feet apart. They measure 4 feet 6 inches in diameter and when revolving in opposite directions exert a pulling or drawing effect on the machine and not the pushing effect as utilized by steamships. This method of drawing into the air by means of propellers placed near the front of machine has been found to act much more effectively in aerial craft than like propellers placed near the stern and exerting a pushing effect.

The machine, which is securely stayed from every point with steel wires, will be first tested without the body and as a simple glide, but it is not quite clear as to what such a demonstration will lead, as the weight will be about 79 pounds, and this for a man to run with at top speed so as to launch himself on the air may prove a somewhat difficult undertaking. The aero-surface is so great that light puffs of wind may cause it to tilt and flutter about considerably and thereby shift its center of gravity and otherwise still further increase the difficulty.

Those who, like Mr. Whitehead, have tested similar ideas experimentally, know how difficult it is to handle such a craft during a breeze...

The construction of a practical flying machine is simply a mechanical difficulty, which should and will be shortly overcome, but it will require the skill and ability of a mechanical and scientist, and a man of sound general knowledge and good judgment. Among the chief points for consideration are lightness, strength, great self-contained power and perfect stability. Of course, there are many other points, but they can undoubtedly be surmounted." [327]

Figure 100: Bpt Standard Article Whitehead 9.1.1903
BRIDGEPORT'S SANTOS DUMONT.
Captions: WHITEHEAD FLYING TEN FEET from the Ground.

Gustave Whitehead: "First in Flight"

FRONT VIEW OF WHITEHEAD'S FLYING MACHINE READY TO START
Sept. 1, 1903

This set of photos in the *Bridgeport Daily Standard's* "The World of Sport," of September 1, 1903 (Fig. 100) shows Whitehead flying a triplane glider, entitled "Bridgeport's Santos Dumont." The short caption reads, "Gustave Whitehead of 241 Pine street, this city, is the inventor of a flying machine which he will enter in the competition for the $100,000 cash prize for the best dirigible balloon, airship or flying machine at the St. Louis exposition next year. He has devoted 20 years of his life to the study of aerial navigation and says he is confident that his machine solves the problem of aerial navigation."[328] The photos used to illustrate this article were first seen in a *Bridgeport Sunday Herald* of May 31, 1903, "Herald Man Makes a Trial Trip"[329], with credit given to the *Herald* photographer who took the pictures.

Front of Aeroplane, Showing Operator in Position.   12 H. 1
EXPERIMENTS WITH THE WHITEHEAD AEROPLANE.

Figure 101: Whitehead Triplane 1903 First Tested As Glider

Photos as seen in *Scientific American* September 19, 1903, showing Whitehead triplane without engine and propellers, being tested first as a glider.
Same photos published earlier in in *Bridgeport Sunday Herald* of May 31, 1903 and *Bridgeport Daily Standard* of September 1, 1903.

The *Scientific American* of September 19, 1903 confirmed Whitehead had designed, built, and attached a lightweight, two cycle gasoline motor to this triplane, successfully flying it – this was three or more months before the Wrights reported powered flights at Kitty Hawk. The motor was air-cooled, with "numerous loops of aluminum wire fastened to the two cylinders in order to radiate the heat…it is designed to run at speeds of from 1,000 to 2,500 R.P.M. It develops 12 horse power at the latter speed, and its weight complete is but 54 pounds, or 4 ½ pounds per horse power, which shows it to be one of the lightest gasoline motors ever built… in actual

Chapter 4: New Goal: The World's Fair Aerial Contest

tests, when mounted on the aeroplanes, [by elimination of a large wire-spoked crank case] the total weight of the motor [was reduced] to 47 ½ pounds… By running with the machine against the wind, after the motor had been started, the aeroplane was made to skim along above the ground at heights of from 3 to 16 feet for a distance, without the operator touching, of about 350 yards [Note: 1050 ft.]. It was possible to have traveled a much longer distance without touching terra firma, but for the operator's desire not to get too far above it. Although the motor was not developing its full power, owing to its speed not exceeding 1,000 R.P.M., it developed power sufficient to move the machine against the wind… Making the propellers pull, instead of push the machine, aids greatly in maintaining its stability…Having proven that a less powerful motor will do the work, Mr. Whitehead is now constructing one of 6 horse power which will weigh between 25 and 30 pounds…Besides this smaller two-cylinder motor, he is also constructing a four-cylinder one, of 10 horse power, which he expects will not exceed 40 pounds in weight, aluminum being used as far as possible in its construction. This is to be used on an improved aeroplane with which the inventor hopes to be able to rise vertically in still air, travel horizontally, and descend vertically again. This is the desideratum of the aeroplane flying machine. "[330]

Figure 102: Two-Cycle Whitehead Motor, Sci Am (1903)

Gustave Whitehead: "First in Flight"

Gliding Near the Ground Against a 15-Mile-an-Hour Wind.

Figure 103: Gliding near ground, Sci Am (1903)

The photos above are of Whitehead's 1903 2 cycle gasoline engine, used on this triplane with a set of propellers added, for successful recent flights (*Scientific American*, Sept. 19, 1903, p. 204).

Gustave Whitehead worked all the next year on improving his gliders, adding power for their next phase as aeroplanes, and his lightweight engines. He was planning to be present in St. Louis for the Fair, sometime after early October 1904, according to an article in the *Bridgeport Daily Standard* of October 1, 1904.

Figure 104: Gustave Whitehead shows he can fly ½ mile, Bpt. Daily Standard (Oct. 1, 1904)

(transcript)

"GUSTAVE WHITEHEAD SHOWS THAT HE CAN FLY FOR AT LEAST HALF MILE"

Exhibits Photographs in Window of a Main Street Store Which Indicate that His Aeroplane Principal is a Good Foundation Upon Which to Base Plans for His Flying Machine.

If anyone doubts that Gustave Whitehead has been able to fly a limited distance at least, with his aeroplane, such doubt can be dispelled by viewing the photographs of his flight in the

Chapter 4: New Goal: The World's Fair Aerial Contest

south window of Lyon & Grumman's hardware store on Main street.

> There are two pictures in the window showing Whitehead in his aeroplane about 20 feet from the ground and sailing along. Of course he has not perfected his invention but says that he has frequently flown over a half a mile. There are people who believe that Mr. Whitehead is all that the newspapers have represented him to be. The photographs show that he has the ability to make short flights.
>
> Whitehead is still calculating upon taking part in the flying machine competition at the St. Louis fair. There is "$100,000 to be awarded to the man who exhibits the best dirigible balloon, flying machine or air ship and Whitehead thinks that he has a chance to win it. His dream is to get money enough to build a big experimental plant so that the problem of aerial navigation can be solved.
>
> Whitehead has had his trials. He has been backed by capital at different times but only for short periods. He never loses confidence and rebuffs only make him more enthusiastic. He says he expects to see the problem solved in his day and that if he doesn't accomplish it someone else will.

(end of transcript)

The *Bridgeport Standard* affirms that the Gustave Whitehead flight photographs show he has the ability to make short flights. Given that Whitehead was then in competition for the equivalent, in today's money, of nearly $2.8 million dollars at the Fair, he may well have asked the Standard to refrain from publishing those (now lost) photos, but to invite the local community to see them in person. Why they didn't publish the photos has always been a mystery. The competition for the enormous prizes at the Fair may help explain why, during this critical period, photos of Whitehead's powered planes may not have been published, just as those of the Wrights were withheld for five long years.

The local article shows, *even at that late date*, in October 1904, Whitehead did not understand the Rules and Regulations of the Aerial Competition – nor the conditions or course he must fly, which were both completely unsuitable for his powered flying machines and gliders. To compete for the Grand Prize, Whitehead would have also had to pay $250 as an entrant fee, prove he'd flown a mile, and believe he'd be able to meet the unsuitable requirements for the contests. It is unknown how the previous flight criteria was to be authenticated, as this does not appear to be part of the historic record. By the time the aerial contest was to be held, its coordinators seemed more interested in *disqualifying* inventors, than in holding competitions that might be won, or qualifying anyone who might need to be paid for winning a prize.

As of the same date, October 1, 1904, "the Grand Prize, Gliding Contests, Kite Contest and Motor Competition" were "yet in force," with Octave Chanute named as one of the seven international judges.[331] Whitehead Motors were already on sale, bought by aeronauts and inventors, and gaining a positive reputation for their light weight and power, as described earlier, with a Whitehead Motor reportedly installed in the California Arrow independently of Whitehead's presence, in late September.

By November 11th, 1904, newspapers carried reports that Whitehead had developed a successful triplane with a box-like movable rudder at the rear and puller propellers in front, which had made short flights of up to 1/3 of a mile, at heights of 50 to 75 feet, with the ability to turn in midair, powered by a lightweight 10 HP gasoline engine, weighing 46 lbs., immediately behind the operator, who hung between the two lower wings (or aeroplanes) by straps, at the "point of equilibrium."[332]

FLYING MACHINES AT THE FAIR

Figure 105: Avery flies Chanute glider at World's Fair

William Avery, as he prepares to launch a Chanute biplane glider, the only "heavier-than-air" flying machine to fly at the Fair, St. Louis World's Fair, 1904.
Bennett's *History of the Louisiana Purchase Exposition*[333]
Courtesy of the University of Missouri, MU Libraries

In addition to the dirigibles and balloonists that participated in the fair's Aerial Competition during the summer and fall of 1904, William Avery, of Chicago, made the only true heavier-than-air (non-balloon-based) flight at the Fair, in a Chanute biplane glider, called "Chanute's gliding machine." The unpowered glider made a first flight of five feet in elevation, for 166 yards (propelled by attendants who ran alongside, to give it momentum). In all, the Chanute glider made 46 flights during the next month. Using equipment to propel it into the air, the glider attained elevations of 30 feet, similar to some of Whitehead's flights in Connecticut, but for distances of only up to 100 feet. On September 18, 1904, Wilbur Wright wrote to Octave Chanute, "Mr. Avery has taken on a very difficult task in attempting to make glides of 400 feet under such conditions as must be encountered at St. Louis. If he fails, it will be no discredit to him, if he succeeds, he will be worthy of the highest honor…"[334] Avery was "the only man to fly a "heavier-than-air" machine at the Exposition."[335] The demonstration of Chanute's glider shows the degree of difficulty in attaining even limited distances and elevations from level ground achieved at that time by Whitehead's competitors with heavier-than-air machines – particularly within the conditions at the St. Louis World's Fair.

Chapter 4: New Goal: The World's Fair Aerial Contest

WHITEHEAD AT THE FAIR

Gustave Whitehead may have arrived at the exposition as a hopeful contestant or exhibitor, in October or November 1904. He would have then learned of the realities of the grounds and last minute changes in contests, which must have been felt as a crushing blow. In the end, Whitehead did not participate in the "Aerial Competition." He'd spent nearly three years in development of gliders and heavier-than-air flying machines of the aeroplane type, in high hopes of winning the Grand Prize, or several of the still lucrative, lesser prizes, for the aerial contest or the lightweight motor competition at the Fair.

Figure 106: East Entrance of the Transportation Building
This is where it is possible Whitehead's motor and photographs were displayed.[336]
Courtesy of the University of Missouri, MU Libraries

Figure 107: Aerial View of Transportation Building, World's Fair 1904
Balloon view from the Aerial Concourse to the Transportation Building (west entrance) at the Fair, with the Pike (amusement park) to its left. Photo by F. P. Stevens [337]
Courtesy of the University of Missouri, MU Libraries

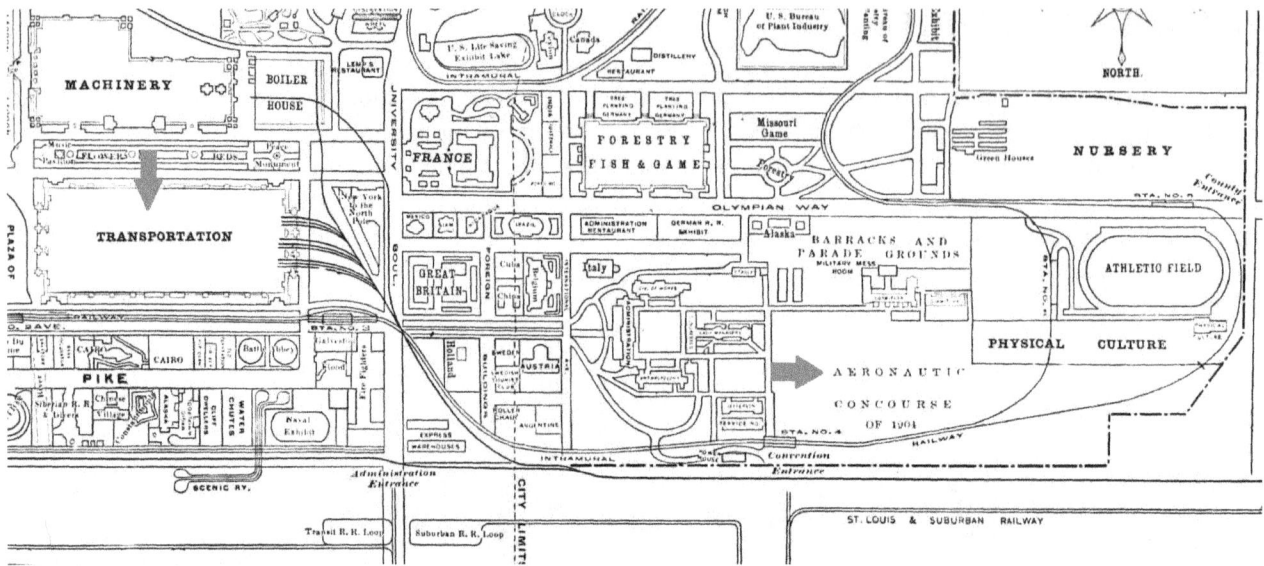

Figure 108: Map of World's Fair Transportation Building and Aeronautic Concourse

Map of Northwestern corner of Louisiana Purchase Exposition (World's Fair) of 1904, showing Transportation Building at left and Aeronautic Concourse at lower right.[338]
Courtesy of the University of Missouri, MU Libraries

    The Transportation Palace, the largest exhibit hall, covered 15 acres. It would have been the most probable location for Whitehead's engine exhibit, within its display of "aerial artifacts." The exhibit included everything pertaining to airship construction, including examples of aeroplanes, propellers, and instruments used in the art."[339] [340] The Department of Transportation oversaw the Aerial Competition at the Fair.

    To exhibit at the St. Louis World's Fair of 1904 was to be considered on the cutting edge of technology and achievement. The Fair, which cost $40,000,000 just for construction, located on a 1200 acre site, was considered to be "the greatest show the mind of man ever conceived and the like of which will probably not be attempted for a hundred years to come."[341]

    Whitehead is known to have attended and exhibited at the St. Louis World's Fair, displaying at least one of his light-weight, self-built engines, according to his associate John Lesko and Octave Chanute. One of his aeroplanes may also have been exhibited there, according to Lesko[342] most likely within the Aeronautic Exhibits located at "the Aeronautic Concourse, west of the Administration building."[343] "The aeronautic concourse was on the plateau west of the Administration building and embraced about twelve acres, surrounded by a fence thirty feet high. Within the enclosure was an aerodrome, or balloon house."[344] There was also an aeronautic section displaying "Illustrations of modern airships and a report of their flights."[345] "Whitehead and His Flying Machine" is one of the few aeronautical photos illustrating the aerial portion of the Fair in Volume 2 of the Universal Exposition of 1904[346], considered to be "the standard primary narrative of the 1904 St. Louis World's Fair and its official final report"[347], published in 1913.

Chapter 4: New Goal: The World's Fair Aerial Contest

WHITEHEAD AND HIS FLYING MACHINE.

Figure 109: Whitehead and his flying machine (1901), from official World's Fair report 1913
Illustration of "Whitehead and His Flying Machine" included in the final official report of the World's Fair of 1904, published 1913. This was one of the three photos sent in with his application, in January 1902. The photo was very likely on display at the Fair, in the aeronautic section, as evidenced by its sole inclusion in the standard Fair reference, above.

According to all available records, Whitehead was, in the end, never able to compete in any contest at the World's Fair of 1904. It is unknown whether he was able to attend the brief International Congress of Aeronauts, a meeting of high ranking "experts" on aeronautics held at the Fair – though not one of those presenting had invented or flown a successful powered aeroplane. According to the St. Louis Republic, eminent scientists and professionals in a wide range of academic fields were invited, worldwide, to attend and present at various "International Parliaments," referred to as "Congresses," at the expense of the St. Louis Exposition Company. It was anticipated that, while together, these distinguished experts, many of them renowned professors from the most prestigious universities and institutions, worldwide, esteemed for "lines of original research, the builders of the last quarter century's great epoch of progress and foremost exponents of modern science and art"[348], might share knowledge and formulate even more solutions to benefit the mankind.

Certainly, the Aeronautics Congress meeting would have interested Gustave Whitehead, but he didn't have the status of the others named as presenters. It began on October 4, [349] and closed the next morning, on Oct. 5th, [350] despite many other academic congresses being held during the Fair for far longer. Presided over by Prof. Woodward of Washington University, those assembled were told that "the main object of the congress was to demonstrate that progress in aerial navigation was possible, and the purpose of the congress was to learn, through the failure and experiments of others, and a comparison of notes and results, that success cannot be hoped for except through careful study and scientific investigation." Professor A. F. Zahm, Willard Smith, Superintendent of Transportation (for the Fair) and Lt. Colonel Capper of Great Britain were amongst those presenting the first day. The next morning, Major B. Baden-Powell (President of the British Aeronautical

Gustave Whitehead: "First in Flight"

Society) spoke regarding efforts to build man-carrying box kites, Walter F. Reid (England) presented regarding fabric sought to contain hydrogen gas, and Captain von Tschudi (of Berlin) lectured about German advances in aeronautics and balloon mapping and photography.[351] Prof. A. L. Rotch of Milton, MA was "amongst those" attending.[352] At the Engineering Congress, Octave Chanute gave a talk on the efforts of the fair's planners to stimulate improvements in aeronautics. [353]

Interestingly, a letter from Wilbur Wright to Octave Chanute, written on October 5, 1904, indicates that he'd (falsely) read in the newspapers that the Aeronautic Congress had been abandoned (though its brief existence testifies to a letdown from the originally lofty expectations). Wilbur further noted, confirming the obvious, "It seems that every aeronautical feature of the exposition has been a failure so far," noting there might have been more chance of success "if the conditions attached to the various prizes had been less exacting… In the gliding and flying model classes, as well as in the grand competition, the minimum requirement was so severe as to exceed all records of human attainment under similar condition. The natural tendency was to discourage entries."[354]

Gustave Whitehead, the humble inventor of the first aeroplanes to fly with power, *was* not invited to present at the St. Louis Exposition's Aeronautical Congress, but *was* able to exhibit at least one motor, and possibly an aeroplane, with photos of his successful 1901 "No. 21" and "No. 22" flying machines already in the hands of the Aerial Committee, which were likely displayed. A lightweight Whitehead Motor may also have powered Baldwin's acclaimed dirigible flights over the fairgrounds and potentially, even Myer's SkyCycle.

Future historians would wonder why Whitehead didn't stick with his original design for the "No. 21" monoplane, whose structure so closely resembles the eventual development of modern aircraft. Preparing for the Aerial Competition at the World's Fair of 1904 provided strong incentives to Whitehead and other inventors of that period to come up with heavier-than-air flying machines to compete with dirigibles and in his mind, become more practical for commercial purposes, at the same time. The World's Fair Aerial Contest strongly influenced Whitehead's designs. However, the changes he made over a three year period could not keep up with dirigibles, nor with the incredibly difficult requirements to carry off a prize.

Gustave brought back a souvenir cup from his time at the Fair, as a gift to one of his teenaged helpers, John Lesko, who grew up to be an prominent business owner in Fairfield. Lesko later donated the cup to Major O'Dwyer's Whitehead collection, in the 1960's, following several interviews. It is now a Whitehead artifact, on display at the Gustave Weisskopf museum, in Leutershausen, Germany.

There were pros and cons concerning the first great aerial contest held in the United States. The contests and outcomes imagined at the beginning fell short of the planners' original ambitious plans. With few contestants, only $1,000 prize money actually paid out, and solutions for "the problem of aerial navigation" merely creeping closer to realization, overall, many were frustrated with the results. However, there were positive benefits, even with the disappointments. The Exposition's aeronautical tournament, the first of its kind in the world to offer large prizes for a wide variety of air ships and flying machines, drew large, paying crowds. The St. Louis World's Fair Aerial Competition opened the door to competitive efforts which would help fund increasingly successful flight experiments by many inventors, worldwide, with the development of what were to become wildly popular aerial contests in St. Louis, throughout the United States and beyond, within a decade. [There were other benefits, as well.]Following the close of the Exposition, Chief Willard Smith, of the Department of Transportation, in charge of all transportation exhibits and the air show, described the progress and culmination of the aeronautical exhibitions::

"The newspapers had prepared visitors to expect a great showing, by publishing accounts of successful attempts made by inventors in several places of America, until small doubt was left in the minds of the masses that at the St. Louis Fair might certainly be seen several crafts sailing at will and under perfect control, competing for the honor and reward that were held forth. At one time announcement was made

Chapter 4: New Goal: The World's Fair Aerial Contest

that no less than ninety-two contestants had filed their application of entry, but as it came to be known that the requirements were less experimental than practical and that the governing rules made it necessary that to win the prizes contestants must sail over a prescribed course, execute certain movements, and return to the starting point within a specified time, the list of entries diminished so rapidly that when the date set for the flights arrived, not a single inventor had fulfilled the conditions necessary for the eligibility to compete for the prizes…No one really qualified for the contests, but a factitious showing was made by four inventors, Viz.: Baldwin, Berry, Benbow, and Francois…."[355] Baldwin's ship [dirigible] was measurably successful in that it made several ascensions under the direction of [Knabenshue] … these flights were very interesting to the multitude and the sight was a delightful one to behold."[356]

Recognizing the progress made toward solving the problem of aerial navigation, and the possibility, if not the probability of remarkable achievements in the air, the Exposition offered a grand prize of $100,000 to the airship which should make the best record over a prescribed course, marked by captive balloons, at a speed of not less than twenty miles an hour, in addition to which there were other prizes, aggregating $50,000 for balloon races, altitudes attained, and for distances of flights made by aeroplanes.

Several entries were expected … but while a half dozen balloons were brought upon the grounds, none of the applicants fully qualified under the rules and the results of the contests were disappointing. Successful flights were made, however, by the Baldwin airship, which served to attract immense crowds to the grounds, and while speed and control of the ship showed no improvement over air navigating crafts that have made successful ascensions, in France, particularly, there was the interest of novelty in Baldwin's flights that has greatly stimulated efforts of inventors in this country to devise a commercially practicable, steerable, and safe air-sailing vessel. *In this respect the advertised airship contests at the Louisiana Fair may be said to have been highly beneficial, even though disappointing the enthusiasm of the millions who had expected a perfect demonstration* ("Transportation Exhibits," "Louisiana and the Fair" Smith, Willard; Buel, J.W., PhD , 1905).

The most positive side, as noted above by Chief Smith, was the stimulation of efforts by inventors in this country "to devise a commercially practicable, steerable, and safe air-sailing vessel." Gustave Whitehead was certainly one of those expending effort, but his decision to change to different designs would lead to negligible improvements, by 1904. Whitehead had already reached his zenith – having already made the first flights with power, using a design that others would return to, building airplanes far into the distant future. Clearly, criticisms of Whitehead for not competing and winning prizes at the World's Fair of 1904 are misplaced. Yet he would continue to work on new designs, following his dream of developing commercial aviation, and making more witnessed flights, up through 1911. His early designs, shared with so many, did make it into the future, adding to the solutions for aerial navigation, collectively leading to successful flight, which has changed the world.

Chapter 5

OTHER NOTABLE WHITEHEAD FLIGHTS

SIGNIFICANT 1902-1904 FLIGHTS

On January 17th, 1902, Whitehead reportedly took his "No. 22" out to make some extended flights over Long Island Sound. The extended flights were later confirmed by his associate Anton Pruckner, and published in the *American Inventor* of April 1902 in several letters to the editor, sent by Whitehead. Thought to occur within a few months of those January flights, Whitehead later reported more modest successes at Milford, CT. These flights may be considered in preparation for the World's Fair aerial contest, as it was known that flying a circuit was to be required, beginning from a location and returning to the exact starting point, making a turn in the air.

First Circuit: January 17, 1902

By this time, according to an article in the *Bridgeport Sunday Herald* of January 26, 1902, the partnership between Linde and Whitehead had been broken. Whitehead was not sharing information regarding the development of his new plane with Linde, prior to its trials in mid-January. After the fiasco with Mr. Linde, and his application to enter the World's Fair Aerial competition, Whitehead was increasingly more protective of his inventions, hoping both to obtain patents and win the St. Louis World Fair's grand prize. But by April Whitehead's public announcement, sent earlier during the winter to the *American Inventor* in a Letter to the Editor, was published. It informed other inventors that he'd successfully flown the improved "No. 22" plane two times, on January 17, 1902, including making the *first circling flight in the world*. These flights reportedly occurred at Lordship Manor, Stratford, Connecticut, supported by statements from Anton Pruckner, Whitehead's mechanic, whose testimony decades later asserted he'd heard of these flights from multiple persons who'd seen them, and from Gustave Whitehead, who'd told him about it, when he returned from working a short while in New Jersey. Pruckner explained that the new, powerful engine they'd developed since the "No. 21" had flown in the summer would have been strong enough to accomplish the flights. [357] [358]

Whitehead's letters to the editor of the *American Inventor* described these long flights, a few months afterwards. The first was described as a two-mile, straight-line flight and the second, a seven mile circling flight, at an estimated altitude of 200 feet. These apparent flights took place during the daytime hours, as Whitehead indicated when the day was at a close, they returned home. Whitehead reported them in a trade journal purposefully selected to announce the news. He wrote, "*I do not care much in being advertised except by a good paper like yours.*"[359] Though he had authored an article in the *Bridgeport Sunday Herald* in January

1902, explaining his views concerning aerial navigation, published nine days after the flights[360], he, like the Wrights after him, was not always eager for local publicity explaining all he was doing. Whitehead's primary focus was always the development of what he considered to be a practical plane. Secondarily, starting in January 1902, he became interested in competing for what he thought would be a $100,000 (+) prize at the upcoming aeronautical competition at the World's Fair in St. Louis, expected to be held in 1903, at that time.[361] Junius Harworth said Gustave Whitehead didn't want crowds chasing his aircraft and getting in the way, as they had, on other occasions. At times, he seemed cognizant of the risk of losing his inventions to others. On occasion, being legally unsophisticated, unlike the Wrights, Gustave seemed eager to share what he'd learned.

Whitehead's assistant, machinist Anton Pruckner, said of this report, "I personally know the facts as stated in Mr. Whitehead's letter to the Editor of the *American Inventor*, and published in the issue of April 1, 1902, to be true." This was also stated in a letter to Ms. Stella Randolph dated March 17, 1937.[362] Pruckner stated in an affidavit in 1963 that "[he] knew that the flight took place because of talk by those who had seen it and because Whitehead himself told [him] he made it." Pruckner further stated, "When I arrived back from Elizabethport, N.J., where I worked for a short time, I heard about the long 7-mile flight over the water.[363] I believe Whitehead made that flight, as his aircraft did fly well and with the bigger engine we had built, the plane was capable of such a flight. Whitehead was of fine moral character, and never in all the long time I was associated with him or knew him did he ever appear to exaggerate. I have never known him to lie; he was a very truthful man. I believed him then when he said he flew and I still believe that he did what he said. I have no reason to believe otherwise. I saw his aircraft fly on many occasions and I see no need to disbelieve this particular event." [364]

Junius Harworth insisted that Whitehead's January 1902 flights *had* taken place and drew a set of plans to detail flying machine "No. 22" for Stella Randolph, Whitehead researcher, in the 1930's.[365] In a letter to Randolph, dated January 27th, 1935, Harworth explained that he'd also assisted Whitehead in writing the letters to the *American Inventor*, helping him "rewrite" phrases in English on his own "common school pad with blue lines."[366] Harworth, who would have been fourteen in May 1902[367], also mentioned that his own mother was German. This may have assisted in Harworth's communications with Gustave, who spoke understandable English but with a noticeable accent[368], according to those who knew him.

Figure 110: *American Inventor* **Whitehead flight article**
Photo courtesy of Fairfield Museum, O'Dwyer archives

Chapter 5: Other Notable Whitehead Flights

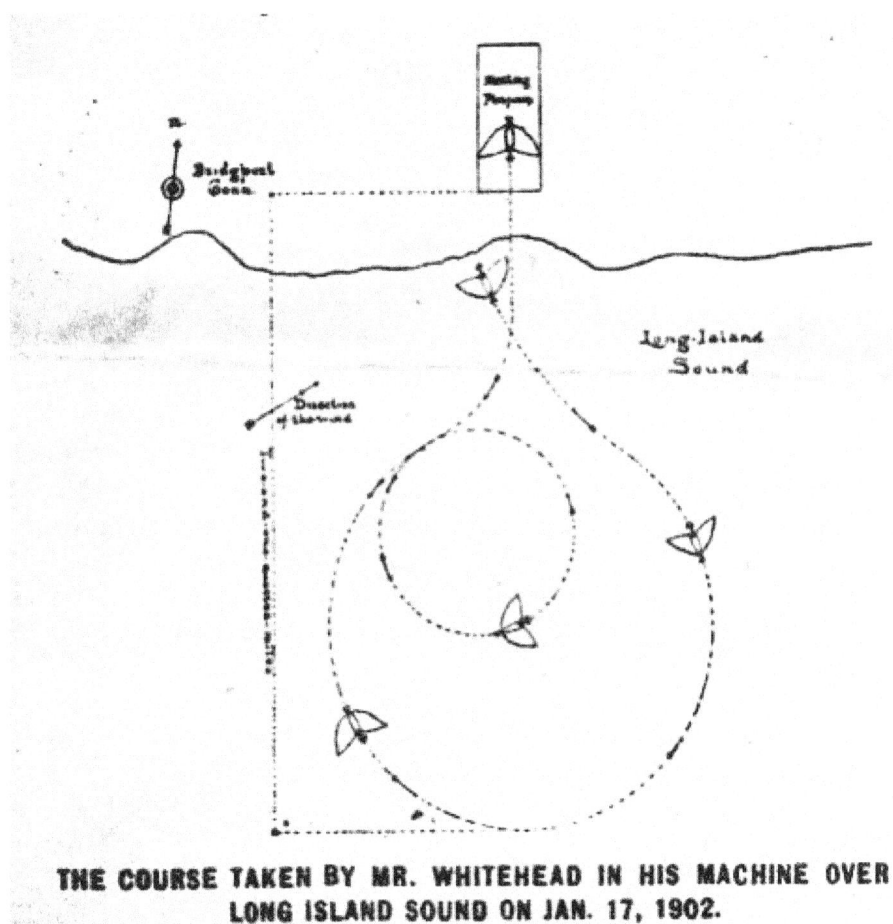

Figure 111: Circular route of January 17, 1902 flight

Photo courtesy of Fairfield Museum, O'Dwyer archives
**Sketch of the 7 mile flight of Jan. 17, 1902 over Long Island Sound,
sent in by Whitehead to the** American Inventor**'s editor
Location: Lordship, in Stratford, Connecticut, USA**

"I enclose a small sketch showing the course the machine made in her longest flight, January 17, 1902." (Gustave Whitehead)

From Whitehead's Letter to the Editor, "*American Inventor,*" April 1, 1902:

"*This new machine has been tried twice, on January 17, 1902.* It was intended to fly only short distances, but the machine behaved so well that at the first trial it covered nearly two miles over the water of Long Island Sound, and settled in the water without mishap to either machine or operator. It was then towed back to the starting place. On the second trial it started from the same place and sailed with myself on board across Long Island Sound. *The machine kept on steadily in crossing the wind at a height of about 200 feet, when it came into my mind to try steering around in a circle. As soon as I turned the rudder and drove one propeller faster than the other the machine turned a bend and flew north* with the wind at a frightful speed, but turned steadily around until I saw the starting place in the distance. I continued to turn but when near the land again, *I slowed up the propellers and sank gently down on an even keel into the water, she readily floating like a boat.* My men then pulled her out of the water, and as the day was at a close and the weather changing for the worse, *I decided to take her home until Spring.*

The length of flight on the first was about two miles, and on the second about seven miles. The last trial was a circling flight, and as I successfully returned to my starting place with a machine hitherto untried and heavier than air, I consider the trip quite a success.

To my knowledge it is the first of its kind. This matter has so far never been published.

I have no photographs taken yet of "No. 22" but send you some of "No. 21" as these machines are exactly alike, except the details mentioned. *"No. 21" has made four trips, the longest one and a half miles, on August 14, 1901.* The wings of both machines measure 36 feet from tip to tip, and the length of the entire machine is 32 feet. It will run on the ground 50 miles an hour, and in air travel at about 70 miles. I believe that if wanted, it would fly 100 miles an hour. The power carried is considerably more than necessary.

Believing with Maxim that the future of the air machine lies in an apparatus made without the gas bag[369], *I have taken up the aeroplane and will stick to it until I have succeeded completely or expire in the attempt of so doing.*

As soon as I get my machine out this Spring I will let you know. To describe the feeling of flying is almost impossible, for, in fact, a man is more frightened than anything else.

Trusting that this will interest your readers, I remain,

Very truly yours,
Gustave Whitehead."

The *American Inventor*'s editor wrote to Whitehead requesting more information and confirmation. Whitehead's reply:

"Editor, *American Inventor*

Dear Sir:

Yours of the 26th received. Yes it was a full-sized flying machine and I, myself, flew seven miles and returned to my starting point.

In both the flights described in my previous letter, I flew in the machine myself. *This, of course, is new to the world at large, but I do not care much in being advertised except by a good paper like yours.* Such accounts may help others along who are working in the same line. As soon as I can I shall try again. *This coming Spring I will have photographs made of Machine "No. 22" in the air and let you have pictures taken during its flight.* If you can come up and get them yourself, so much the better. I attempted this before, but in the first trial the weather was bad, some little rain and a very cloudy sky, and the snapshots that were taken did not come out right. I cannot take any time exposures of the machine when in flight on account of its high speed.

Chapter 5: Other Notable Whitehead Flights

I enclose a small sketch showing the course the machine made in her longest flight, January 17, 1902.

Trusting this will be satisfactory, I remain,

Yours truly, Gustave Whitehead"

The following is the editor's note in response:

"Newspaper readers will remember several accounts of Mr. Whitehead's performances last summer. Probably most people put them down as fakes, but it seems as though the long-sought answer to the most difficult problem Nature ever put to man is gradually coming in sight. The Editor and the readers of the columns await with interest the promised photographs of the machine in the air. The similarity of this machine to Langley's experimental flying machine is well shown in the accompanying illustration, reprinted from a previous issue. Mr. Langley, it will be remembered, was the first to demonstrate the possibility of mechanical flight."[370]

Milford Circuit 1902

Following his successes with "No.'s 21 and 22," Whitehead began to prepare for the upcoming St. Louis World's Fair by flying at Charles Island, Milford, 10 miles east of his Pine Street home and shop. The experiments appear to have occurred sometime in the late winter of 1902. Charles Island, at the mouth of Milford Harbor, was about three miles east of his flying fields at Lordship, in Stratford. The exact date of this flight was not provided, though it was said to be "recent," in a widely distributed Associated Press report published in mid-April 1902. The Milford flight experiments should not be confused with the January 17th, 1902 flights, as these were separate events, evidenced by the separate several news releases and the length of the reported circuits. Milford, however, appears to have been the site of a second series of flight experiments for "No. 22,"" over Long Island Sound.

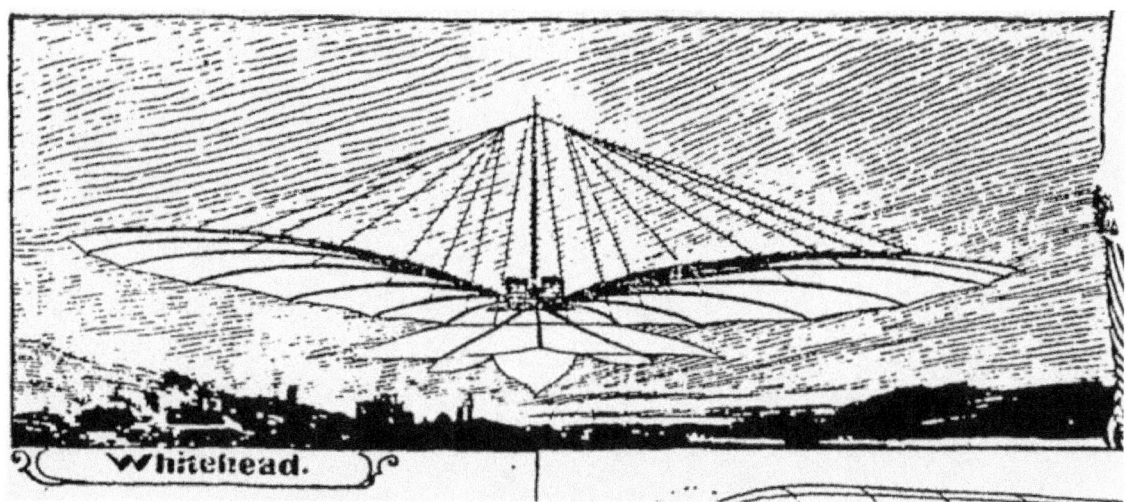

Figure 112: 1902 Milford flight illustration
The Deseret Evening News sketch of the Condor, the Whitehead plane that had recently flown.[371]

The Salt Lake City newspaper reported, on April 19th, 1902:

Gustave Whitehead: "First in Flight"

"Inventor Gustave Whitehead of Bridgeport, Conn., is also working on a [*] airship ... Whitehead recently conducted a series of trial tests with his machine at Charles Island, Milford. He is elated over the success of the trials. He asserts that he made a complete circuit in the air, covering an area of about a quarter of a mile, returning to within 50 feet of the starting point, when the machine descended and dropped lightly to the sandy shore.

"The flights were a complete success," said Whitehead. I had a kerosene motor, which worked perfectly. I steered the machine by running one propeller faster than the other, and there was not a hitch of any kind. I have much faith in this kerosene motor, which is the lightest I have ever used. It is of forty horse power and weighs but 120 pounds ..." [372] This article was widely carried in the Associated Press across the nation, from Connecticut, to New York, to Colorado Springs, the St. Paul, Minnesota, and beyond.

[Note: the original text incorrectly says "dirigible" (gas-filled) airship. Whitehead did not develop dirigibles or "gas-bag" airships, as he did not believe they had a viable, commercial future.]

As with other news stories concerning Whitehead, "recent" could mean anytime in the past six or more months. Did Gustave decide to take his plane out one more time, before the weather destroyed his creation? Did it make it through most of the winter? We do not have this information. He stated in his second letter to the editor of the *American Inventor*, written during the winter, "As soon as I can I shall try again." In the Associated Press report about Milford, Whitehead was said to have flown "a circuit" of 1/4 mile, returning back to his point of origin, within fifty feet. This flight was conducted near and possibly, over, the water, in keeping with his desire to practice near soft sandy soils and the waterfront. This route also followed Count D'Esterno's recommendations, a predecessor whose designs were similar to those used by Lilienthal and Whitehead. The boat-like fuselage of Gustave's "No.'s 21 and 22," could safely land in water and be towed to shore. In the lengthy article of January 26, 1902, written by Gustave Whitehead, published in the *Bridgeport Sunday Herald*, he declared,

"Man will ... learn the science of the birds by practicing over *water*, so in case the operator gets upset, he will not get hurt and his flying machine may be but little injured: for if he gets once the hang of it, so to speak, he may be enabled in a very short while to manage it with perfect safety ..."[373]

Chapter 5: Other Notable Whitehead Flights

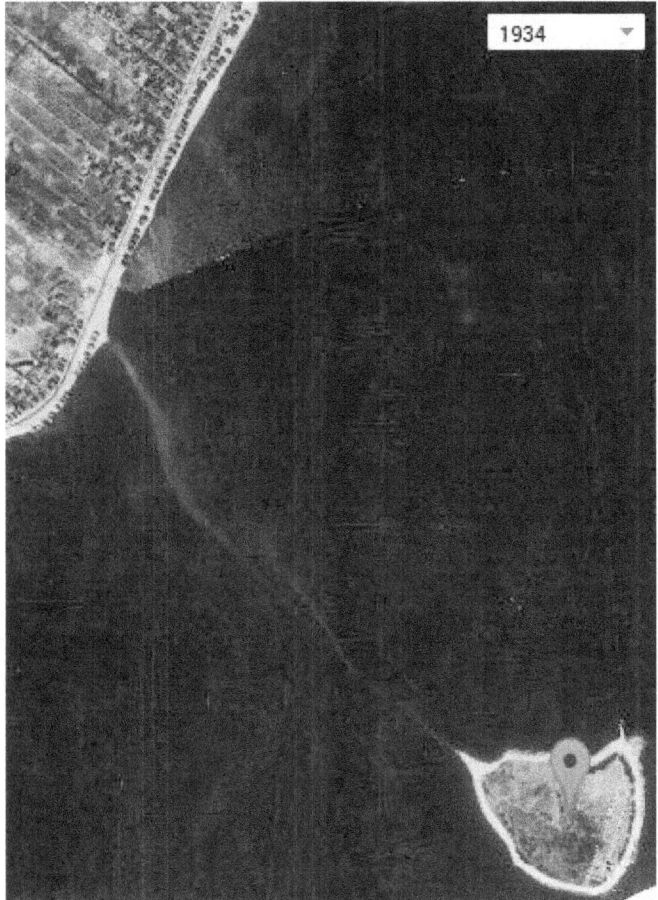

Figure 113: Milford flight route to Charles Island (1902)
1934 Aerial photo of Milford, CT, at left, with Charles Island, a sandy spit of land in its harbor, at lower right, where Whitehead reported making a flight that was a "1/4 mile circuit" in early 1902. At low tide, a sandbar is present along the line seen connecting Charles Island to the beach at Milford.
Photo courtesy of CT State Library

Tragically, due to the aforementioned squabbles that began in November and continued into the early winter, causing the loss of sponsor Herman Linde, Whitehead reverted back to use of his Pine Street shop, but was said to have had no funds to build a shed or "cover" for "No. 22'," which had developed a broken motor, and eventually, by the time Gustave's brother, John Whitehead, arrived in early April the motor needed major repairs and the plane had become so "deteriorated" that it was considered unsafe and could not fly again. At the time, Gustave experienced a number of setbacks with his engine sales to others, due to pricing them too low and not ending up with a profit, thus he and John were without the funds to complete an engine for his own flying machine. [374] Linde had taken over the airplane factory after conflicts about the alleged discovery of his plans to steal Whitehead's design and build without him; impatience with development timelines, costs and design disagreements. However, without Whitehead it did not flourish and the 4-6 aeroplanes being built previously at the factory were not completed. [375] [376] [377]

"My brother had been associated for a few months before my arrival with a Mr. H Linde, they had about 4-6 Aeroplanes of the same type as flew before under construction in a small shop near the crossing of

Pine Str. and Hancock Avenue. Bridgeport, Conn. They never completed them as they had a falling out over something or another…[378]

"End of March I arrived at Bridgeport and found my brother living at 241 Pine Str. He has already broken with Mr. Linde but I could see the little shop they had used in starting to construct a few Aeroplanes after the model my brother claimed he flew in, for I could see two bodies, the same shape as the machine described in the N.Y. Herald standing on the outside of the building."[379]

With the arrival of his brother John in spring, 1902, who had some small amount of money to invest and partner with Gustave, after a few months delay in putting together the funding, they began to work, this time putting their ideas and talents together.

John reported, "As his original plane was left out in weather, for want of cover the material deteriorated and we did not consider it safe to use plane again…" [380]

Their plans involved building a "bigger plane of different[s] type than the original one, a biplane in front with a longer shipshape body and two small foldable wing[s] attached to back part of body." They designed and built a new "40 horse 4 cylinder 4 cycle gasoline motor for same weighting about 100 lbs. but found we had not sufficient power [to] the raise [the] machine."[381] The new flying machine was being built with their eyes on the $100,000 prize to be offered at the upcoming St. Louis World's Fair.[382] [383] Of note, in his letter of August 6, 1934, to Stella Randolph, rather than going into detail on every feat, John Whitehead referred her to the many newspaper "clippings" of 1901-1903 about his brother for more information on his accomplishments and aeroplanes, indicating that he believed them to be accurate.[384] Having left for California again in fall of 1902, John was really only present during his brother's most successful early years, up through fall, 1903, for a small number of months, after the early flights had been made.

EARLIER FLIGHT EXPERIMENTS, 1894-1900

Prior to the successful, sustained, powered flights of August 14, 1901, Gustave had been hard at work for at least six years, carrying out a sequential series of experimental steps to develop a viable, powered aircraft , adapting proven elements of Otto Lilienthal's successful basic gliding design. In the years when the Wrights had been building bicycles, with little thought of flight, Whitehead was already flying gliders and conducting powered flight experiments. With every spare minute and cent he could gather, Whitehead was designing and redesigning, testing and building aircraft, with one goal in mind - to invent and fly a successful, *practical,* powered, flying machine. Against all odds, through his vision, his genius and persistence, and an uncanny ability to marshal very modest resources to use for his inventing, Gustave finally began to succeed.

During the summer of 1901, Gustave Whitehead made a number of preliminary shorter, controlled, powered "street flights" and other practice flights in his "No. 21" heavier-than-air flying machine, much closer to home, in Bridgeport's West End. His many shorter flights appear to have been considered inconsequential, both by Gustave Whitehead and the general public, though they were noteworthy enough to be included in local and national news at the time, and began world records for successful powered flight, surpassing that now credited to Orville and Wilbur Wright. Whitehead focused on the sustained, powered, manned flights that occurred on level ground as the prelude to development of commercial flight.

1900- 1901 Connecticut Flights

Preliminary, *unmanned* tests in early May 1901 led to an accident that required repairs through the month of May according to several media interviews published in early June. Experiments in the repaired plane

Chapter 5: Other Notable Whitehead Flights

were set to begin, with June experiments referred to, over the next year.

Whitehead reported that his first tests of the flying machine were in June 1901 - in an interview with the *Evening Telegram* - New York, Tuesday, November 19, 1901. "Whitehead tested the machine for the first time last June but his first successful test was made on August 14." What Whitehead considered "successful" was entirely personal. He had a set plan to achieve manned, controlled, sustained flight on level ground, preferably rising vertically, without need for "a running start"[385], which could ultimately transport people and materials long distances. "Partial successes" for Gustave Whitehead would later be considered a series of "firsts" in the history of the world and aviation. He would modestly refer to some of his early successes as "flying more or less," or "not practical" and his early models as a means to learn more, but never as an end product. The *Scientific American* of September 19, 1903, would later affirm that Whitehead conducts his flights "unlike Chanute and Lilienthal" by "flying near to the ground"… still working on solving "the problem of rising from it quickly at will, and descending gently whenever and wherever he wishes." This long-sighted desire would lead to experiments with many kinds of flying machines in short succession, including some of the earliest known prototypes for powered monoplanes, biplanes, triplanes, and helicopters. Some were built from parts of prior models, to save money, according to Anton Pruckner, Whitehead's machinist and assistant[386], while others co-existed during the same time period, with multiple projects underway.

On January 10th, 1901, Gustave Whitehead sent his aforementioned letter of inquiry to the Louisiana Purchase Exposition Company (planners of what came to be known as "The World's Fair of 1904"), subsequently becoming the first entrant for its newly announced aerial competition. In his letter, Whitehead reportedly stated he'd made a long flight the past June with his "No. 21" airplane, enclosing three photos of his flying machine. The World's Fair bulletin of February 1902, appears to quote from Whitehead's letter to them, "This machine, last June with an operator on board, made a safe and successful flight to a distance of one and one half miles." [387]

The *New York Sun* of June 9, 1901, referenced earlier, published a long article about Gustave Whitehead's invention and his *unmanned* flying experiments of May alluding to tests being made shortly.

> "Last November [Whitehead] began work on the present machine which was completed several weeks ago and is now undergoing repairs made necessary by an accident which happened at the machine's trial flight on May 3 last. These repairs are nearly completed and at an early date the flying machine again will be tested. When and where the test will be made Mr. Whitehead will not tell, because he does not want to be bothered with a crowd…[Whitehead is quoted as saying,] 'I do not know just when the next experiment will be made, but it will be soon.'" [388]

The previous tests, in May were said to be held starting in a street at the top of a steep hill, which he did not want to name so that he might use the location again for his next set of experiments – perhaps, these were held in June.

> "It is a good fifteen miles distant … is out Fairfield way.[389] The road is hilly but the machine climbed the hills all right."

> "We started the machine on the crest of a hill and from right in the middle of the road. With the under motor it got a good momentum and began to rise from the effect of the aeroplane wings." [390]

With 220 pounds of sand ballast in the unmanned plane, on its second test of the day, it rose up to an estimated elevation of higher than forty feet, clearing the treetops, for a distance of "a full half-mile," then slanted downward into a tree upon landing. Therefore, it is possible that a lengthy part-momentum driven flight, motor driven, from a hilltop, was again made in June possibly that time, manned - much as powered hang gliders

Gustave Whitehead: "First in Flight"

make flights today. Perhaps he did succeed with a sustained, powered flight from a hilltop in June 1901. If so, Gustave Whitehead would not have been satisfied with that performance, not reflecting his concept of "true flight." However, this type of experiment would fit with the sequential, systematic steps Whitehead had utilized for the previous four years, as he worked towards powered flight from essentially level ground, where he might fly "at will," using only the power of his engines, taking off and landing where he wished. That lofty goal *would* be achieved several months later, succeeding beyond the efforts of all other "heavier-than-air flying machine" inventors, albeit in a limited fashion, on August 14, 1901[391].

With a short gap between interviews and publication, it is possible that Gustave Whitehead, who rarely missed a weekly chance to experiment, did make preliminary flights of some nature, in early June. that later appeared in news interviews, intermittently. How long these were and where they occurred has not been corroborated by any eye witnesses, which certainly can be laid at the feet of the Whitehead research beginning over thirty years later. Witnesses were later located who did attested to half mile flights in both Fairfield and Stratford, and a mile and a half flight made at Stratford, CT in August 1901. Whether Gustave Whitehead made any sustained, manned, powered flights in June 1901 is not possible to determine, at this writing, though it was feasible that these occurred on hilly ground.

In all, 17 witnesses contacted by researchers described seeing powered flights in the years 1901-1903, all of which preceded those of the Wrights; 13 of these mentioned 1901 as a year they observed the flight(s). At least hundreds, and likely, thousands of potential witnesses were never located, primarily due to the Whitehead research starting three decades later, and lack of funding. Even so, there is compelling evidence that Gustave Whitehead made a number of preliminary flights in the streets of the West End of Bridgeport and some adjoining areas, in 1901. For a more complete listing of witness statements, see Appendix, and Chapter 6.

There were no specific months given by eyewitnesses for the preliminary test flights - the younger witnesses were interviewed decades later and could give only the year and an estimate of whether it was summer, due to not being in school. According to witness Junius Harworth, these occurred close to Whitehead's Pine Street shop and home, in the West End of Bridgeport, Connecticut. According to observer Junius Harworth, Whitehead made hopping flights along the Bridgeport Gas Co. property, from Howard Ave., easterly to Wordin Ave.; turning around at the eastern end of Pine Street, the plane made additional hopping street flights, returning to Howard Ave.[392] [393] Joe Ratzenberger, Thomas Schweikert, and Alexander Gluck reported powered flights along Cherry Street. John McColl, and Louis Lazay reported powered flights at the old circus grounds in the West End. Mary Savage described a flight over the neighborhood and down to the harbor, below, that would have occurred in 1901-1902.

The street flights were witnessed by numerous persons and at times, crowds of people. Schools[394] and factories in the area were said, by a number of witnesses, to have been "let out" in order to allow their occupants to view the historic flights that were a source of wonder to a public not accustomed to even *the idea that man could fly*. 1901's summer flights in Bridgeport, Connecticut could easily be credited as the first successful powered flights in the world, brief as they were. After all, Orville Wright was credited with an *estimated* 120 foot flight[395], no higher than 10 feet from the ground, said to have occurred on December 17, 1903. In May 1904, the Wrights were testing their newly built "Flyer 2" at Dayton, Ohio, and without the strong winds at Kitty Hawk, after three days' trials, were only able to get no lift on the first two days, and on the third day, flew 12 feet, with a sudden drop to the ground. [396] [397]Whitehead easily went beyond that distance each time he flew - starting three years earlier.

Chapter 5: Other Notable Whitehead Flights

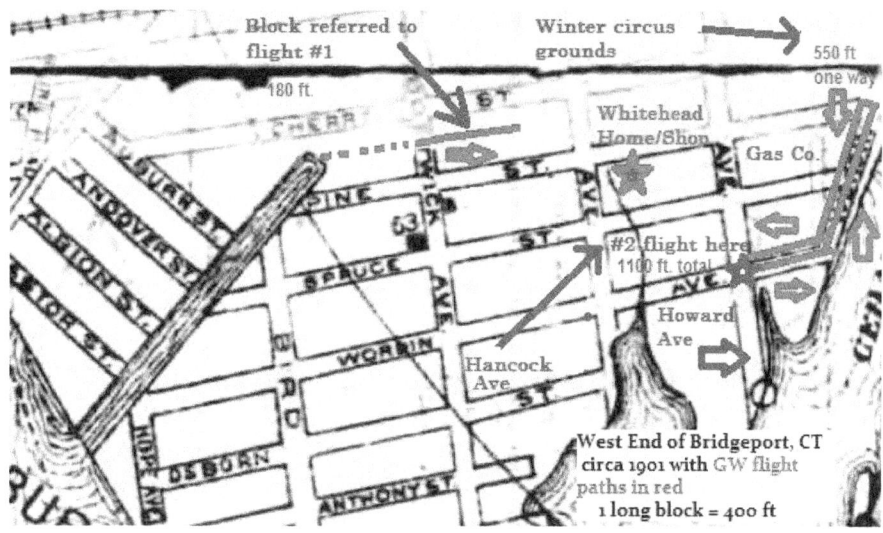

Figure 114: West End Flight Paths (1901-1902)

Specifics and locations (pictured above) for several of the Gustave Whitehead early street flights of 1901 in Bridgeport, CT were provided by several witnesses (see below):

1. A street flight for a distance of 175-180 feet, rising to an elevation of 30-40 feet, in a "folding-wing" plane "driven by a gasoline motor," was conducted by Whitehead around 1900, off Bostwick Avenue in a vacant lot by the circus grounds, near the St. Stephen's School in [the West End of] Bridgeport, Connecticut..[398] "The block was bounded by Cherry, Bostwick, Hancock, and Pine streets."[399] *[Author's note: the earliest this flight could be is 1901]*
2. In the summer of 1901, Harworth, an assistant, reported Whitehead's "No. 21" "made its first attempt at flight … from Howard Avenue east to Wordin Avenue," turning around at the east end of Pine Street, and flying a hop back to Howard Avenue. Then the plane "was pushed west to Hancock for another brief flight" [in Bridgeport's West End].[400] [401]

Other powered flights in Bridgeport are mentioned for 1901, such as one from the sloping hill at the old Gilman estate, on Fairfield Avenue, between Orland and Ellsworth Streets, to the circus lots, at a distance of 1000 ft.[402], with an elevation of 3-5 ft.[403] [404]It appeared that "the take-off site was on the north side of Fairfield Ave., just slightly east of Ellsworth."[405] Another flight of a Whitehead monoplane "of about four hundred feet," at an elevation of 6 feet, was reported for September or October of 1901, at Tunxis Hill Road, near the Mountain Grove Cemetery in Bridgeport, Connecticut.[406] One more occurred in 1901 [likely the late fall], near the Whitehead shop on Cherry Street, Bridgeport, traveling 300 feet at a height of 15 feet.[407] One notable, sustained, nighttime flight in the West End of Bridgeport, 1901-1902, was witnessed by Whitehead's close neighbor, Mary Savage, her husband, and many from the entire neighborhood. It began in the middle of the night from his Pine Street shop, being pushed along by volunteers to get it started, then catching the wind and with its noisy engine, flying over the neighborhood down to the harbor, a half mile away.

A daytime quarter mile flight in 1901, one of a series viewed on that day at Fairfield Beach, occurred in the neighboring town of Fairfield. Multiple witnesses were present, including Frank Lanye, a man who did not know Whitehead personally, but had traveled from Waterbury, Connecticut, about thirty five miles away, to see him fly, having heard about his experimentation. No month was provided, though it likely occurred in the late summer or sometime in the fall, as considerable success was met.[408] Whitehead flights commonly known to have occurred on Fairfield Beach were confirmed by Waldo, editor of the *Bridgeport Post*, in the 1930's.

Others related accounts of flights they were sure had occurred in the summer of either 1901-1902. Joe Ratzenberger, a police officer at the time he was interviewed, told of a July or August 1901 or 1902 test of a motorized folding-wing plane, built by Whitehead, that began a flight on a lot between Pine and Cherry Streets, flying to Bostwick Avenue, [Bridgeport, CT] at an elevation of 12 feet.[409] A further test occurred right outside the Pine Street shop, in the summer of 1901-1902; the plane left the ground and a group of children followed it.[410]

1899 Pittsburgh Flight

Before moving to Bridgeport, Connecticut in early fall or summer, 1900, Gustave lived in Pittsburgh, Pennsylvania for a period of time that may have ranged from 1-2 years, where he worked as a coal miner. In his off-hours, Whitehead was engaged in developing and testing important predecessors of the "No. 21" flying machine. The US Census of June 1900 reveals that Gustave Whitehead, using his fully Americanized name, was then living on Bates Street, in the modest immigrant neighborhood of Oakland, in Pittsburgh. He reported being out of work 6 months during the past year. The Census, taken in June 1900, showed a neighborhood populated by Hungarians, Germans, Irish, and English families. Many of them rented rooms from building owners, as did the young Gustave and his wife, Louisa, living with their year and a half-old daughter, "Rosie," born in October 1898. Both Gustave and Louisa reported they could read, write, and speak English. We can be sure that the 25 year old Gustave, who was quite predictable, made very good use of his unemployment, which would have been an ideal time to work on his flying machines. Little information is known about these years, though it is likely he landed sponsors for his inventions during this time, as without that type of help, he would not have been able to support his growing family of three, nor work on his aircraft.

A newspaper article from 1899 confirms that Whitehead was, indeed, conducting heavier-than-air flight experiments in Pittsburgh with an earlier model of the "No. 21," in which he made practice flights at Bridgeport - and shortly after - sustained flights at Fairfield and Stratford, Connecticut, two years later.

> Pittsburg has produced the latest apostle of "Darius Green," in the person of a Mr. Whitehead, who has invented a flying machine. Unlike the scientific models of the day, Mr. Whitehead's machine has wings and wheels, and on the ground looks like a huge bird. When Mr. Whitehead gets his machine in operation he expects to present an appearance as imposing as that of a Pittsburg politician at a state convention.

Figure 115: Whitehead in Pittsburgh article (1899)

The Scranton Tribune, Dec. 11, 1899 shows Gustave has been at work on an original flying machine archetype of the "No. 21" in Pittsburgh. [411]

According to the affidavit of Louis Darvarich, made on July 19th, 1934, in April or May of 1899, Whitehead reportedly also made at least one historic manned, powered flight[412] with a predecessor to the "No. 21" design,

Chapter 5: Other Notable Whitehead Flights

near Bates Street, in Oakland, where he lived and conducted flight experiments. Darvarich, His friend and assistant, was seriously burned in the attempt, leaving a lifelong scar on his leg. Whitehead and his bird-like plane may have traveled down the street pictured below, pushed by volunteers, just twelve years before this photo was taken. According to Charles Ritchey, the Pittsburgh Press had published a picture of Whitehead's plane[413], but searches conducted from the 1930's through the 1970's did not produce the article, however it may be that they were searching during the wrong months, due to the later correction Darvarich made to the time of year that the flight occurred.

Figure 116: Bates Street, Whitehead in Pittsburgh (1899)
Bates Street in the early 1900's, where the Whiteheads rented rooms during his "Pittsburgh flight experimentation period." The Whitehead home was located amidst those pictured at left.
Photo courtesy of Historic Pittsburgh, Pittsburgh City Photographer Collection, University of Pittsburgh.[414]

Likely by design, this neighborhood was near the sprawling Schenley Park, a large open space with an elevation of 912 feet, where the enterprising young Whitehead also tested and demonstrated his aircraft.

On October 4, 1934, Darvarich wrote to Whitehead's daughter, Rose Rennison, his account of the occurrence, but this time, he indicated he thought that the flight occurred in late fall.

"Dear Mrs. Rennison,

The following are answers to Miss Randolph's questions:

1. I lived on Bates Street. I have forgotten the number.
2. & 3. I have forgotten the owners name but I do remember it was on Oakland, the second or third house from the dry bridge.
4. A horse and buggy were nearby and I was taken to the hospital in that.
5. The plane was destroyed. Some parts of it were kept to build a new plane.
6. It was in the late fall about three o'clock in the afternoon.
7. The plane was started from the top of a hill. It was only pushed a short way. The down grade was a means of starting without much pushing.
8. No attempts were made before this time to try and fly the plane.

Gustave Whitehead: "First in Flight"

I hope that these notations will greatly help Miss Randolph. …

Sincerely yours,
Louis Darvarich"[415]

Witnesses interviewed from this area of Pittsburgh, in the 1930's, reported a Whitehead flight of 1/2 mile, in a steam-powered, manned flying machine, at an altitude of 20-25 feet, which ended in a fiery crash against a new, three story, brick apartment house, at the second floor level. The flight accident occurred on the O'Neil estate[416], according to witness Martin Devine[417], on the corner of Bates and Wilmot Streets, shown on this 1900 map of the area:

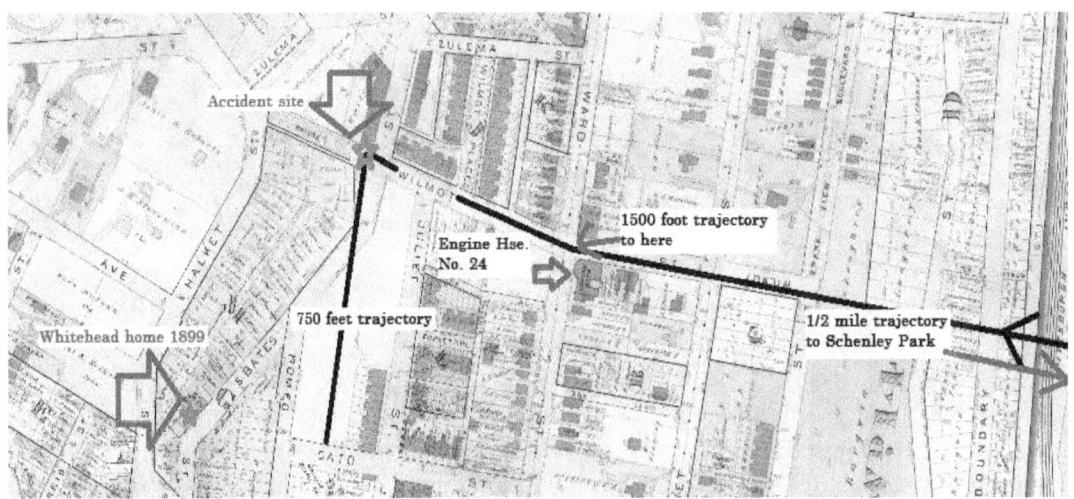

Figure 117: Whitehead Pittsburgh flight trajectories

Various flight trajectories are shown above for the reputed 1/2 mile flight that ended with an accident against the O'Neil apartment building, at the second floor.

Figure 118: Whitehead Pittsburgh crash site (1899) 1
*May 23, 1911. Top right, view of apartment building at Wilmot and Bates Street.
Photo courtesy of Historic Pittsburgh, Pittsburgh City Photographer Collection,
University of Pittsburgh[418]*

Chapter 5: Other Notable Whitehead Flights

Photos taken at the Wilmot and Bates Street intersection, Pittsburgh, PA. *Above and below, the three story apartment building at the top right of the photographs may be the one Whitehead and his assistant flew into, at the second floor level, in 1899.* An examination of available photos shows it to be there in 1908 as well, see below. At left is likely "the dry bridge" referred to by Darvarich, as a landmark near where he lived, three doors down.[419]

Figure 119: Whitehead Pittsburgh crash site (1899) 2
"Bates Street Wall" (with apartment building at top right). March 25, 1908.
*Photos courtesy of Historic Pittsburgh, Pittsburgh City Photographer Collection,
University of Pittsburgh*[420]

Whitehead's assistant and passenger, Louis Darvarich [later changed to *Darvarich*], working to fire the boiler which powered the plane, was severely injured. This attempt may well represent the first manned, powered flight in the world, even though it ended unsuccessfully in a serious crash, due to Whitehead's inability to avoid a building. It also represents the first powered airplane flight with a passenger onboard, and perhaps, the first copilot.[421]

**Figure 120: Louis Darvarich, Whitehead's Pittsburgh Assistant
Louis Darvarich, first passenger on a powered flight (1899)**
circa 1936

© Susan Brinchman, 2015

Gustave Whitehead: "First in Flight"

The Pittsburgh flight is thought to have occurred near Engine House No. 24, located at the corner of Wilmot and Ward Streets. Wilmot Street is currently known as "Boulevard of the Allies." According to Mr. William Burns, his father, a fireman there, told him about the plane. The origin of the flight has thus far been unknown, but the map above provides various trajectories for possible flight paths down open spaces and the city streets, with the 379 acre Schenley Park[422] a half mile away from several directions. Whitehead's house on Bates Street was one block from this accident site, as was the Engine House No. 24, on Wilmot Street. There is little information on the tests that occurred there before the ill-fated flight, as not many witnesses could be located by the 1930's, when the research began in earnest. Stella Randolph, a part-time writer-researcher, conducted those investigations when she was able to get time off from her job as a secretary, which wasn't often. Her funding was limited; it was during the post-Depression years. Ms. Randolph did a remarkable and persistent job, she gathered the people and statements she could find, given such short opportunities. Some of her research was conducted in person and some, via telephone and written communications.

Witnesses explained that, following the flight accident, the Pittsburgh police forbade Whitehead to fly anymore in the city, thus eventually forcing him to relocate, to Connecticut and Bridgeport's West End. In Connecticut, Gustave would find work, perhaps friendlier police, a Hungarian-German neighborhood, and lots of open space with hills, close by.

A Mr. Johns saw Whitehead's plane at the corner of Louisa and McKee Streets where it was being prepared for a flight. Martin Devine said that this spot was the site of "most of the experiments," indicating, along with others interviewed, that there were multiple tests being made in Pittsburgh, as well. Both locations are one to two blocks from Bates Street.

In Pittsburgh, the resourceful young Whitehead put together a formula to develop the world's first airplane on a very modest budget. Only 25 at the time of his alleged flight in Pennsylvania in 1899, the young Gustave worked at physically demanding, low-paying jobs by day or night. He conducted experiments in his off-hours during the week and on Sundays, used every spare penny and very likely finding sponsors for his work, living in a Hungarian and German neighborhood where could gain the assistance of coworkers and friends. He rented rooms for his small family near streets and an assortment of open spaces and wide streets where he conducted test flights and public demonstrations. We cannot help but admire this young man's single-minded determination and successes, which culminated, within just a few years, in developing the world's first successful, manned, powered flying machine.

1897 New York, New Jersey Flight Experiments

"The Flying Condor" and the "Soaring [Gliding] Machine"

Several years before his 1899 flight experiments in Pittsburgh and four years before his successes in the summer and fall of 1901 in Fairfield County, Connecticut, Gustave was very actively engaged in the prolific development of precursors to his 1901 - 1903 flying machines.

During a press conference held on October 4th, 1897, in New York City, Gustave Whitehead, then aged only 23, announced that, over a period of years, he'd invented forty-two "airships," displaying two of his latest, in his yard at No. 130 Prince Street.

On October 5th, the *New York Herald* covered the story, reporting that Whitehead explained he'd been experimenting with both soaring machines (gliders, without power) and flying machines with power, describing soaring experiments from high elevations. He believed that he had developed a powered solution to "aerial navigation" that would work, eventually, on level ground, which he called the "flying condor," under construction in his yard, nearly completed.

"With the gliding machine out in the yard," he said, "I'll have to start from an elevation before sailing.

Chapter 5: Other Notable Whitehead Flights

With this more elaborate machine [the Condor], I'll be able to rise from the level ground by the motive power alone in a calm or high wind." He described "the air ship" to have "four movable wings" shaped like those of the condor, "in pairs, twenty feet from tip to tip...connected by a frame of steel, which runs on bicycle wheels that are necessary in starting or alighting...The horizontal tail [rudder] will extend twenty feet to the rear and is shaped like the tail of a condor. It is also movable and can be folded up. The operator [pilot] has the management of the tail [rudder]. By sliding his body from side to side on a sliding frame he can change the centre of gravity to maintain his balance and steer the machine from right to left...Before landing the operator will slacken the speed and lift the tail [rudder]." Whitehead spoke of his plans for the plane not to rise more than six feet from the ground. He expected, with a new 3 horsepower, gasoline motor he'd had built (which was not yet paid for, and required a sponsor), that the aircraft might travel at 50 miles per hour. The weight of the Condor and the engine were each about 50 pounds, and he believed the machine "would bear a weight of from 600 to 800 pounds." He described plans for testing the "soaring machine" (glider) without the motor.

His other airship, a soaring machine (also referred to in the article as a "gliding machine"), was 16 feet long by 4 feet wide, weighing 12 pounds, had three aeroplanes [wings], one above the other [a triplane glider], of red cotton cloth, with a bamboo framework. That machine was built like a box-kite, but shaped like a car. "It can also be fitted with a motor of 3 horsepower, operating two propellers, one at each end of the framework, or simply as a soaring machine [glider], without motive power [without a motor]." [423]

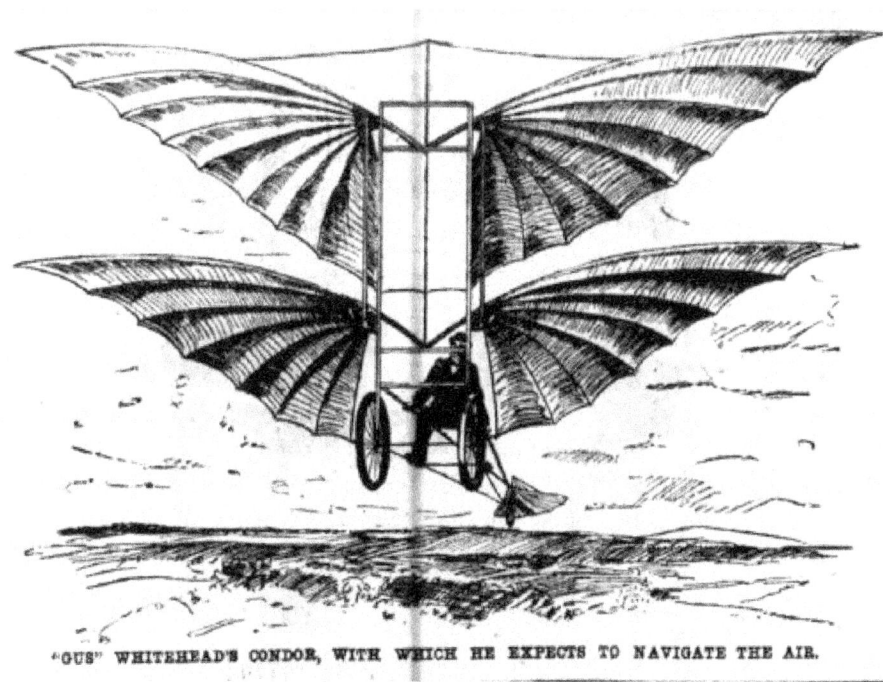

Figure 121: Whitehead's Flying Condor (1897)
Above illustration is from "Whitehead's Flying Condor," an article in the *New York Herald*, Oct.5.1897.p.12

Figure 122: Whitehead's Triplane (1897)
"Gus" Whitehead and The Airship He Has Constructed
The second airship displayed to the New York press
From the New York Herald, October 5, 1897, p.11

The New York press picked reported the story on October 5th, entitled, "New Airship Ready for Flight," describing Whitehead's plans to make a demonstration Sunday at "Highbridge" "if the weather is favorable." They mentioned Whitehead's association with "Otto Lilienthal, the German aeronaut" and that for twelve years, he'd constructed forty-two airships, studying the albatross and condor while traveling the world, and constructing the new airship patterned after the same proportions of the condor's wings and body.[424]

The *NY World* also ran the story on October 6, though incorrectly calling Whitehead "August Whitehead," describing the new 20 foot long flying machine, "the Condor," and also the soaring machine, which Whitehead said he intended to test the following Sunday near "High Bridge." The article reported that Whitehead had soared [gliding from a high point] five miles.[425] Whether he actually soared five miles, or even said that he did, has been a point of contention. Suffice to say that soaring experiments were likely underway during this period of time.

The *NY Times* described the upcoming demonstration of the box-kite-like triplane glider that could be fitted with a motor and propellers, and the Condor, which Whitehead said could "sail with, against, or across the wind." [426]

1894-1896/97 Massachusetts Flight Experiments

Gustave Whitehead entered the United States in 1893, according to the 1900 and 1910 US Censuses. Shortly after, in about 1894, he began to live in Boston, Massachusetts to work with building meteorological kites at Blue Hill (Weather) Observatory in Milton, Massachusetts. Blue Hill Observatory is described as "the

Chapter 5: Other Notable Whitehead Flights

foremost structure associated with the history of weather observations in the United States," known for its pioneering work with "kite soundings into the atmosphere" in the 1890's (a period when Whitehead worked for them) and is still active to this day.[427] In January 1895, the Boston Aeronautical Society was formed. Its members conducted experiments with "soaring machines" (gliders), and emerging aircraft technologies at Great Blue Hill and surrounding areas near Boston. "The Society's objective was for members to engage in, and support basic aeronautical research and experimentation. The Society's Constitution stated that its goal was to 'encourage the work of aeronautical experimenters and their study of heavier than air aerial machines and to advance the science of aerodynamics.'"[428] Whitehead, known as "Gustav Weisskopf," began to work for the Boston Aeronautical Society (BAS) as a mechanic. He helped produce several Lilienthal-style gliders, one of which worked for short distances at low elevations, and a "human-propelled" ornithopter, which did not work.[429] [430]Albert B. C. Horn, his co-worker, thought that if Whitehead had weighed less, the glider might have been more successful![431]

This period, when Whitehead was between 19 and 22, gave the new American arrival, "Gustav Weisskopf," his first jobs in building early aircraft at the foremost aviation facility in the country, at the time, where they paid him to actively engage in experimentation with heavier-than-air machines. Whitehead (Weisskopf) found himself surrounded by influential "aeronautical experimenters," such as E. B. Millet, publisher and President of the Boston Aeronautical Society, Harvard's Professor William H. Pickering (astronomer), Albert A Merrill (bank manager, accountant, lecturer on aeronautics), and James Means (author of "The Problem of Manflight" 1894, and publisher of *Aeronautical Annuals*), all on its Executive Committee. While there, "Gustav Weisskopf" also came to the attention of Octave Chanute, soon to be the Wrights' mentor. This must have been a dream job for the young Gustav, who'd been intrigued by the idea that man could fly from early childhood. At some point, either before or after going to work at Blue Hill, Whitehead said he had known and worked with Otto Lilienthal, the famed builder of gliders, whose theories and structure influenced Whitehead's future No.'s 21, 22, and their predecessors. Working at Blue Hill's hallowed grounds was undoubtedly an important step toward Gustave Whitehead's prolific, successful future, with increasingly more successful inventing periods, soon to follow. From Blue Hill and the greater Boston area, now known as Gustave Whitehead, he moved to New York City, to work as part of a "Scientific Kite Team" for toy manufacturer Edward I. Horsman, a member he'd met in Boston. For more information on this time period, see *History by Contract* by O'Dwyer and Randolph, the earlier Stella Randolph books on Whitehead, and the research papers of O'Dwyer and Randolph, with some limited online information, at this writing (see Resources at end of book).

Gustave Whitehead: "First in Flight"

Chapter 6

KEY TESTIMONIES

Eyewitnesses

Gustave Whitehead was an inexhaustible inventor of flying machines, said to have produced scores of aircraft of various designs during his two decades of inventing.[432] He flew often and in a variety of favored locations in Fairfield, Bridgeport, Stratford (Lordship Manor), Milford, and Easton, Connecticut. His flights were witnessed by many - watching his test flights was a favorite past-time of the primarily Hungarian immigrant neighborhood, of which he and his wife were popular members.

Whitehead would typically use models, followed by a succession of gliding experiments, tethered and untethered; then he eventually placed his own lightweight engines in the machines, which were tested unmanned by being towed, in flight with auto-shut off, or tethered to a pole. Later, un-manned, then manned powered flights were conducted, in streets, on flatlands, beaches, hills, or above Long Island Sound's shallow waters with power, close to the ground to avoid accidents till he was sure the plane could fly well. Whitehead's most successful years occurred in 1901-1903. Other flights occurred during this time and at least several beyond, up through 1911, including some shorter "hops," and low-flying flights deliberately made close to the ground, to avoid injury. Witnesses have reported viewing approximately 25 manned, powered flights during in the period 1901-1902, some with multiple eyewitness statements. Several articles appeared reporting photos of Whitehead in successful powered flight; one indicated that flights went on through at least 1904[433], and other witnesses stated they'd seen Whitehead in powered flight, as late as 1911.

There are also several undated accounts by eyewitnesses who watched Whitehead fly at varying elevations, in the early years of the century.

The following are descriptions of some of the 47 key witness statements for various stages of the work and flights of Gustave Whitehead; half of these describing flights a variety of powered "flying machines." Witness affidavits and statements were gathered by Stella Randolph (1934-1937); Dr. John B. Crane of Harvard University (1935-37); Attorney K.I. Ghormley, hired by C.D. Hudson, Randolph's publisher (1948); and Major William J. O'Dwyer (USAF, ret.) with members of the Connecticut Aeronautical Historical Association (1960's - 1980's). Had Gustave Whitehead's flights been documented by historians at the time they occurred, without a doubt, hundreds of adult witnesses would have been available to produce testimony.

Gustave Whitehead: "First in Flight"

1899 - 1902 Flights

27 eyewitnesses reported that Gustave Whitehead made *powered airplane flights* during the period 1899 to 1911. [434] Some of these individuals gave testimony to more than one powered flight on the same day and/or on different dates. 18 eyewitness reports of powered flights were gathered for the period 1899 -1902. Two of these flights ended in a crash. Powered flight eyewitness reports were determined through direct references to the engine or the sound of the engine; flights being made during a particular time period by "No. 21" (a powered airplane); and flights made starting from level ground. This is not thought to be the total number of powered flights made, due to the large number of varied flight experiments, with and without power, known to be conducted by Whitehead during the period 1899 - 1911, and the lapse of time in gathering witness statements, making it more difficult to find the hundreds of eyewitnesses known to have existed.

Affidavit of Louis Lazay (Toolmaker, interviewed 1936 & 1948)
Louis Lazay reported viewing a Whitehead flight at a distance of 175-180 feet, rising to an elevation of 30-40 feet, in a "folding-wing" plane "driven by a gasoline motor," around 1900, off Bostwick Avenue, in a vacant lot by the circus grounds, near the St. Stephen's School in Bridgeport, Connecticut..[435] When interviewed by Attorney Ghormley in 1948, Lazay "stated positively that he saw Whitehead's plane in the air ... and that it traveled a block." Lazay was "14-15 years old at the time... The block was bounded by Cherry, Bostwick, Hancock, and Pine streets."[436]

Affidavit of John Lesko (Undertaker, interviewed 1934, 1936, 1963)
John S. Lesko, resident of Bridgeport, Connecticut, a well-respected, prominent businessman, stated that he was present in September 1901 when Gustave Whitehead made a successful series of 50 foot hops, 4 feet in elevation, in a monoplane called "The Bird," "propelled by a four-cylinder gasoline engine."[437]

Lesko reported another successful flight in August of 1902 on Fairfield Avenue in Bridgeport, and again at Gypsy Spring, a location in Fairfield's Tunxis Hill section. Lesko, whose family owned a horse and wagon used often to transport the Whitehead plane and give it a start, said, "Gypsy Spring was a part with a steep hill that would give the plane a good start. Mr. Whitehead used to construct the planes as gliders first, then put motors into them..."[438]

During a taped interview conducted by W. O'Dwyer and E. Hildes-Heim on December 17, 1963,[439] in which Lesko provided extensive details on Whitehead's flying activities for several years, he further indicated that the longest hop he observed, in about 1902 - 1903, was approximately 80 feet and that its elevation was about 5 feet. Mr. Lesko was about 12 - 13 years old at the time of this observation.

Affidavit of Alexander Gluck (File Clerk, interviewed 1934)
Alexander Gluck reported viewing, as a child, a 1901 or 1902 Whitehead flight "for some distance," at an elevation of 4 or 5 feet. "The machine used by Mr. Whitehead was a monoplane with folding wings. I recall its having been pushed from the yard back of the residence where the Whitehead family then lived, 241 Pine Street, Bridgeport Connecticut, which was opposite my residence at the time. The plane was set in motion in the street in front of the house and when it flew was propelled by an engine...I believe it was in summer or fall..."[440]

Affidavit of Frank Lanye (US Navy Veteran, interviewed 1968)
Frank Lanye [pronounced Lan-yee], of Waterbury, Connecticut, was interviewed on tape several times by Captain William J. O'Dwyer. The first occasion was March 30th, 1968, the second interview occurred on June 15, 1968, with Smithsonian Curator Paul E. Garber, Connecticut Aeronautical Historical Association (CAHA) President Don Richardson, and CAHA Founder Harvey Lippincott present. Lanye didn't claim to have known

Chapter 6: Key Testimonies

Whitehead, nor to have any technical information - he just stated, "All I did was watch him fly." Lanye reported being an adult eyewitness, with his friends, to multiple flights, one being at least 1/4 of a mile. He also stated that other flights on the same date were longer, and some shorter. He could not remember the exact number of flights that occurred on that day. Mr. Lanye believed the flights occurred in 1901 because he associated it with just having been discharged from the Navy. He and some friends from Bridgeport went to watch Whitehead fly at Fairfield Beach.[441] Mr. Lanye also reported being present to watch Whitehead fly on subsequent occasions. During this time period, he was about 24-25 years old. [442] [Note: The well-known, highly respected editor of The *Bridgeport Post*, Charles Waldo, later reported to Stella Randolph, Whitehead researcher in the 1930's, that it was "common report" (common knowledge) that Fairfield Beach was a site where Gustave Whitehead had flown.[443] The *Bridgeport Post* was a major newspaper in the vicinity, now still in existence, at this writing, as "The *Connecticut Post*."]

Affidavit of Michael Werer (Machinist, interviewed 1934)
Michael Werer stated that in September or October of 1901, he witnessed a folding-wing Whitehead monoplane flight "of about four hundred feet," at an elevation of 6 feet, at Tunxis Hill Road, near the Mountain Grove Cemetery in Bridgeport, Connecticut.[444] Mr. Werer was about 30 years old in 1901.

Affidavit of Joe Ratzenberger (Police Officer, interviewed 1936)
Police officer Joe Ratzenberger signed a sworn affidavit that when he was an older teenager, in July or August of 1901, he and his friends were at hand when a motorized folding-wing plane, built by Gustave Whitehead began a flight on a lot between Pine and Cherry Streets, flying to Bostwick Avenue, at an elevation of 12 feet. He recalled the flight clearly, and having hung on the back of the plane, being carried into the air, till "being driven away" by Whitehead's assistants. He remembered the motor making noise, its boat-shape, and wheels. In addition, he remembered Whitehead testing additional planes in his backyard, flying them in a circle, attached to a pole, and being told by his friends of another flight in Black Rock, a section of western Bridgeport, where the plane had landed in the water near "Sandy Beach."[445] Mr. Ratzenberger, born in 1885, was about 16 at the time of these observations.

Affidavit of John Ciglar (Clerk, interviewed 1936)
John Ciglar reported remembering "distinctly" being witness[446] to a summertime flight attempt on Pine Street in Bridgeport, in 1901 or 1902, where a motorized Whitehead bi-plane flew at an elevation of 12 feet for a distance of 30 feet, but fell to the ground and burst into flames. [447] According to the Federal Census of 1900, John Ciglar was born in 1891 and would have been 10-11 in 1901-1902.

Affidavit of John Fekete (Machinist, interviewed 1948)
John F. Fekete, an adult witness who'd previously lived at 241 Pine Street, in the same apartment building as Whitehead, was interviewed by attorney K. I. Ghormley, of C. D. Hudson publishers, in 1948.[448] He stated he'd worked with Gustave Whitehead in 1901 through 1903. Fekete said he was present in May or June of 1902 at Sport Hill (on the Fairfield and Easton border), when a Whitehead plane made a successful flight at an elevation of 30 feet for a distance of 200 feet, landing without damage. "The flight started with a downhill run of about 15 feet. Whitehead then turned on the engine..." Fekete said that Whitehead told him he became "thoroughly frightened" once in the air, then shutting off the engine and landing. A Mr. Roth (owner of the farm where the flight occurred) and Mr. Cignay, his helper, were also present. Fekete told Attorney Ghormley that the Whitehead drove the plane there "on its ground wheels under its own power" from Pine Street, Bridgeport (6 or 7 miles away) using a gasoline motor. Fekete and Mr. Roth left after Whitehead from Pine Street in a wagon and arrived ahead of the airplane at Sport Hill. Fekete further stated he'd helped build the engine, which had batteries, not

Gustave Whitehead: "First in Flight"

a magneto; having "personally made the crankshaft" for the flying machine. He also told Mr. Ghormley that he thought Whitehead was "a very good machinist."

Affidavit of Elizabeth Papp Koteles, (Shop Owner, retired; interviewed 1965 and three times in 1974)
Mrs. Koteles was a married woman and an adult when she saw Whitehead fly.

(1901 or 1902) "I, Elizabeth Koteles, declare and testify that I witnessed one of the experimental tests of an aircraft built and designed by the late Gustave Whitehead, during that period of my life when my husband and I lived as neighbors to Mr. Whitehead on Pine Street, Bridgeport, CT.

It was during our early married life and after we had moved from Hancock Avenue that Whitehead also moved into the Pine Street area. Shortly after his arrival he began to build aircraft and engines in his rear yard. His rear yard bordered our yard. These were homes we rented from landlords.

One day, not long after Whitehead had built his airplane, and as close as I can recall it was around 1901, my husband asked me to walk with him up to Tunxis Hill, to watch Whitehead fly his airplane.

The location of the experiment, as I now understand it to be, was in the Gypsy Springs section of that hill in the general park area of Villa Park. The area where the aircraft was tested was on the level portion, mid-hill…We stood at the side of the road and looked over the stone wall into that field. The craft was just behind the wall. I can only recall one of the men present was Gustave Whitehead who occupied the aircraft. There were at least two other men whom I cannot at this date identify or recall by name. The craft lifted off the ground during one experiment to an elevation of approximately 4-5 feet, and I doubt it was over 6 feet. It flew for a distance of approximately 150-250 feet before landing. There was no damage to either the aircraft or Mr. Whitehead… Mr. and Mrs. Whitehead were customers in our store. They were nice people. Very nice … In response to your question, "Was the ground level?" I can recall it was level and that the ground was smooth, like a park field, and covered with grass."

Harvey Lippincott, President of CAHA, was present for this interview. He said that Ms. Koteles noted it was in 1901-1902, when she was about 21 years old, and that she also mentioned how the engine sounded, "It go cajunk, cajunk, cajunk and make hissy noises." This appeared to describe the engine used in "No. 21."[449]

Jesse Davidson, of the American Aviation Historical Society, was present for the interview on February 2, 1974, which took place with Mrs. Koteles to determine the above. These are some of his comments: "She readily identified Gus Whitehead who was holding his baby daughter Rose in his lap plus three other people sitting in front of the machine. Among other photos shown to her, Mrs. Koteles was able to pick out and identify certain areas where Gus Whitehead conducted his backyard work shop activities on both the machine and the engine. At that time she lived with her husband on Pine Street, Bridgeport, Connecticut, between 1900 and 1906. After studying the photos of aircraft "No. 21", she said she remembered the machine very well and even helped a bit by sewing a piece of fabric to one of the wings. She nodded knowingly as she studied the airplane photos from different angles…I asked Mrs. Koteles if she saw the machine actually get off the ground. She replied, "Yes, but it only go up a very short distance and come right down again…" When she was asked how high the plane went, we pointed to the ceiling (about 8 feet high), she said, "No that's too high, lower." I then pointed to the fireplace and asked if the machine rose that high. She thought for a moment and said, "About as high as mantelpiece." We estimated the height of the mantelpiece to be about 5 to 5 1/2 feet high. This meant the flight had trajectory. We then asked Mrs. Koteles to pick out a spot from where she was standing in front of the picture window and point to a place where the machine came down. ….I asked if he flew as far as across the road from her house. She

Chapter 6: Key Testimonies

replied that she thought it was a bit farther than that. You then pointed to a mail box on the other side of the street. Mrs. Koteles studied the distance a little while and then said: "Maybe that far or a little more." At that point both of us, and I believe, Harvey Lippincott estimated the distance to be between 150 and 175 feet." When Mrs. Koteles was asked what year she witnessed this particular flight, she said, "1901-1902." [450]

During the interview, Mrs. Koteles kept insisting he didn't fly, "he just went up and came down." The flight she described was further by 30-50 feet than the so-called "first" flight credited to Orville Wright in the Smithsonian and at Kitty Hawk, and it was 1-2 years earlier.

In 1965, Mrs. Koteles was interviewed by her grandson Stephen Link[451], concerning her observation of the Whitehead flights. She was then 84 years old. The interview was tape recorded, the following is from the transcript, used with permission of Stephen Link. Mrs. Koteles reported that she lived right next door to Whitehead and that she'd gone to Wheeler Park to see him fly. Her description uses the term "they," possibly indicating a passenger flight involving her brother and Whitehead, who was known to occasionally take other people (one at a time) during his powered flights.

Stephen: Did you ever see the plane yourself?
Elizabeth: Oh sure! We went to see it when they fly.
Lot of people went to see it when they fly.
Stephen: Did you ever actually see it get up in the air?
Elizabeth: Well sure, we were all there!
Stephen: No , but I'm saying...Did YOU ever see it with your own eyes ... ACTUALLY IN THE AIR FLYING?
Elizabeth: Why sure, I saw them when they went up and I saw them when they came down.
Stephen: About how far did they go?
Elizabeth: Oh, not very far. They just went up and then they came down. Other people watching them. We were all there!
Stephen: How old were you when this happened?
Elizabeth: Oh, me, I was married. (** she was married at age 18)

Mrs. Koteles further described how her brother Bert Papp had worked with Whitehead on at least one plane when he was an older teenager, that he was a mechanic and Whitehead asked him to help. She said that there was "a lady who gave them money...some rich lady." She recalled that the material used for the wings was "some real fine stuff...it looked like silk." Mrs. Koteles contributed portions of her wedding gown to be sewn into the wings of "No. 21", and was one of the neighborhood women who volunteered to sew fabric for the plane. [452] She indicated her brother only worked for a time with Whitehead but then had to stop, that Bert became busy with his job.

Thomas Schweikert (Silk Weaver, interviewed 1936)
Schweikert reported witnessing a Whitehead flight in Bridgeport, CT, on Cherry Street, very close to Whitehead's home. The flight was for a distance of 300 feet, at an elevation of 15 feet. This was on level ground. Schweikert reported that this occurred when he was a boy, playing in a lot at the time of this flight.

Affidavit of Louis Darvarich (Engineer, interviewed 1934, *also known as Darvarich, as Louis Darwarics in 1902, and Louis Darvareich in 1910* [453]) This witness testified to both a significant attempt of 1899 and a successful flight in 1902. Darvarich (aka Darvarich, Darwarics, Darvareich) participated as boiler-man in a 1899 manned, powered flight by Whitehead, of 1/2 mile in Pittsburgh, at an elevation of 20-25 ft., ending in a crash against the upper second floor of an apartment building.
Darvarich was born in 1878, was 21 at the time of the 1899 flight in Pittsburgh.

Gustave Whitehead: "First in Flight"

(*Flights of 1899*) Louis Darvarich, an aide, coworker, and friend of Whitehead, made a sworn affidavit reporting participation in a street flight with him in April or May of 1899, for a distance of 1/2 mile, at an elevation of 20-25 feet, in Pittsburgh, Pennsylvania. The flight ended by striking a three story building and scalding Mr. Darvarich, who was onboard firing a boiler. Mr. Darvarich showed the severe scars from the burns he received on that date to a newspaper reporter in the 1930's.[454] The Pittsburgh flight was discussed with and scars on his legs were also shown to Fairfield police officer Andy Tuba, nephew of Louise Tuba Whitehead, in the 1930's. [455]

In 1964, Major Robert Del Buono of the 9315th Air Force Squadron (retired) interviewed Mr. Darvarich's widow and brother-in-law, Mr. Franko, in Miami, Florida, and several other of their relatives, about Gustave Whitehead. The interview was tape-recorded and transcribed. Mr. Franko said that he'd flown in one of Whitehead's gliders near King's Highway (Fairfield, CT) and knew Darvarich in Pittsburgh. Mr. Franko explained that his family (his parents, his sister, and he) had also come from Pittsburgh to Bridgeport, around the same time as Mr. Darvarich did. He said that Darvarich then stayed at his home, in Bridgeport. Mrs. Darvarich said she'd briefly gone up in a Whitehead airplane as a young woman, during one of its trials in Pittsburgh.

> Maj. Del Buono: Did you ever see him fly in Pittsburgh?
> Franko: Yeh. That's where he was flying! He was flying when he went into the house.
> Maj. Del Buono: He had a steam engine?
> Franko: Yeh. He had steam engine in airplane --
> Maj. Del Buono: He had a steam engine in an airplane and he crashed into a house with it! That's when?
> Franko: 1900 or 1898 or 1899
> Maj. Del Buono: He came to Bridgeport when? In 1900?
> Franko: 1901 [1900?]
> Maj. Del Buono: Then if he flew a plane in Pittsburgh, then in other words that would be before 1900.
> Franko: Yeh...
> Maj. Del Buono: We were hoping to find someone who had seen him fly in Pittsburgh.
> Franko: They are all gone. No one is living....
> Maj. Del Buono: Now, in Pittsburgh -- was that the only time he had flown, when he crashed into the house?
> Woman: My sister could tell you about that. (Discussion of seeing the sister that day)
> Maj. Del Buono: Now your brother-in-law from Pittsburgh that flew with him [Whitehead], his name was...
> Franko: Louis Darvarich.
> Maj. Del Buono: Did he come to Bridgeport?
> Franko: They came together.
> Maj. Del Buono: Now did Darvarich fly with him anymore in Bridgeport, do you know?
> Franko: He didn't work with him anymore.
> Maj. Del Buono: Now Darvarich -- who was he -- he's married to your wife's sister?
> Franko: Yeh.
> Maj. Del Buono: Now how many of his airplanes, or gliders did you see of his?
> Franko: I only saw three of them.
> Maj. Del Buono: ... Did you ever see the one with three wings?
> Franko: Yeh. I saw that.
> Maj. Del Buono: What did he do, pull the airplane right through the streets?
> Franko: Yes...
> Maj. Del Buono: Well, what about the wings? Did you have trouble with the wings hitting trees anywhere

Chapter 6: Key Testimonies

or did he take them apart -- take the wings apart?
Franko: I don't know. I know he took them out there [to Kings Highway, Fairfield]...There were lots of people , you know, pulling from all sides.
Maj. Del Buono: Well, do you remember seeing any of the planes fly?
(The voice of a different woman -- Seems to be Louis Darvarich's widow): I'm the one. I remembered ... in fact the _____ and my husband talked that they tried it out one Sunday, but they didn't have no gauge or something on it, and it went up about six feet high -- the plane, and it then came down.
(Other woman): That's in Pittsburgh.
(Second woman): That was in Pittsburgh.
Maj. Del Buono: Well, was that when they crashed into a building or something?
[(Darvarich's widow):] They didn't crash into a house. It was a landing. An open space, and cracked. And I must have been in it...because that is just about after we got married. And of course, I was young and eager. I remember that. I went up.
Maj. Del Buono: You went up with them?
[(Darvarich's widow):] I went up but they came down. They didn't crash, you know. But they didn't have a gauge or something like that, and that's what caused it. Otherwise, they would have succeeded in going up higher. And that's all.
Maj. Del Buono: Now that's where, in Pittsburgh or Bridgeport?
[(Darvarich's widow):] Pittsburgh.
Maj. Del Buono: And did you move to Pittsburgh with them then?
[(Darvarich's widow):] Not then. I moved to Bridgeport the same year, I know it was in August.
Maj. Del Buono: What year was that?
[(Darvarich's widow):] Sixty three-- 63 years ago.
Maj. Del Buono: In 1901?
[(Darvarich's widow):] Sixty three or something like that, because my daughter wasn't born, and she'll be 63 next month. [*Author's note: that means it had to be about the year 1900.*]
Maj. Del Buono: Now when you came to Bridgeport did your husband still work with Mr. Whitehead?
[(Darvarich's widow):] No. My husband didn't. He worked for Winston (?) Brothers here as a blacksmith, shoeing horses, and a care-taker....After that, I don't know what they done. My husband wasn't interested anymore...My husband gave it up.[456]

Darvarich's widow, explaining what occurred after much passage of time, provides us with vital information - there were additional flight trials in Pittsburgh (not surprisingly, for Whitehead's custom was to make many), and that her husband did not fly with Whitehead again after his serious accident, also not surprisingly, for the experience had to have been traumatic, particularly for those times.

The Pittsburgh flight reported by Darvarich that burned his legs was confirmed by several other witnesses (Marty Devine - later, a fireman - who arrived at the scene of the crash immediately afterward and recalled the hospitalization of someone on the airplane and had read of the flight in the newspapers; William Burns, who was told of the airplane by his father, a fireman; and Charles L. Ritchey, who recalled reading about the crash in the local papers, as well as being present for an anchored test of the engine in Schenley Park, Pittsburgh, PA).[457]

Attempts to locate the reported newspaper accounts of the airplane crash and hospital records for treatment of Mr. Darvarich's injuries have been unsuccessful to date, though efforts are being made to locate them. Hospital records for one key medical facility had been reported lost for the years in question. These are all still being sought.

The local police were said to have been very unhappy with Whitehead's street flights in Pittsburgh, helping prompt him to leave for Bridgeport in 1900, with Mr. Darvarich.

Gustave Whitehead: "First in Flight"

(*Flight of 1902*) Mr. Darvarich reported seeing another flight, this time in 1902, in Bridgeport, Connecticut, where he and the Whitehead family had moved, and where he is listed in the Bridgeport City Directory from 1902 through 1904, under "Louis Darwarics," residing close to Whitehead, at 259 Pine Street [1902]. The airplane was described as "a monoplane with folding wings" that had been built by Whitehead at his 241 Pine Street residence. [Author note: This may have been a test of the "No. 22" airplane built by Gustave Whitehead, flown in January 1902.] Darvarich said he worked with Whitehead until 1912.[458] His wife reported that he never again flew with him, following the accident in Pittsburgh, however.

Junius Harworth (Engineer, provided affidavit in 1934)
Harworth (aka Junius Horvath) reported a flight of 1 1/2 miles at an elevation of up to 200 ft., in the morning hours on August 14, 1901 in Lordship, Stratford, CT. Harworth was 12 years old at the time of the flight. Harworth became a prolific source of information concerning Gustave Whitehead, in later years, until his death in 1962, as he was said to have spent over a decade with him.

Cecil Steeves (Stockbroker, interviewed 1936 and 1966)
Steeves witnessed a powered flight in Bridgeport, from the Gilman estate to circus lots, distance 1000 ft., elevation 3-5 ft., in 1901. Mr. Steeves was born in Jan. 1887, and would have been 14 1/2 years of age in the summer of 1901. He was interviewed by Randolph in 1936, signing an affidavit to witnessing the above flight. He later wrote, in a letter to the Connecticut Aeronautical Historical Association (CAHA), December 20, 1965, "I thought it might be of interest to you to know that I actually witnessed Mr. Whitehead fly his plane a greater distance than the Wright Brothers and the flight took place in Bridgeport, Connecticut in the year 1901. A rope was tied to the nose of the plane and three men pulled the plane by running down a grassy slope on the old Gilman Estate. After running about 200 feet, the plane was airborne and Mr. Whitehead flew the plane across Fairfield Avenue to what at that time was called "the old circus lot." I watched this flight while standing on Fairfield Avenue." During an interview on January 2, 1966 with Captain William J. O'Dwyer and Albert E. Burr, member of the CAHA (present as observer) Steeves described himself as a "close friend and neighbor" of Whitehead. Burr said, "He was very emphatic that the monoplane #21 was powered by steam and was fired by either gas or acetylene... He described very graphically a flight which left the Gilman estate from a long sloping field. After crossing Fairfield Ave he landed in the old circus lot, a flight of about 700 feet in length and approximately thirty feet high. After the interview we took Mr. Steeves in O'Dwyer's station wagon and he retraced the exact location... He also pointed out to use the spot where he stood during that particular flight." Steeves was described by Burr as having "a clear, keen mind," instilling confidence in him. O'Dwyer described Cecil Steeves as "one of the most clear-headed witnesses to Whitehead's early flights." He placed his hand on a bible, very eager to swear that all of his testimony was true and fact. O'Dwyer had cautioned Steeves that it was "absolutely essential to be accurate and factual, without exaggeration, because of [the] historical significance."[459]

Anton Pruckner (Engineer and Journeyman Machinist, interviewed 1934, 1963, 1964, 1966)
Pruckner, an adult eyewitness, signed an affidavit to witnessing a flight of 1/2 mile that occurred on August 14, 1901 in Lordship, Stratford, CT. Extensive interviews were held with Mr. Pruckner and his wife, in the 1960's, with a Hungarian interpreter present to ensure accurate communications. Paul Garber, Head Curator at Smithsonian, was present for the final interview in 1966.

Excerpts from interview with Anton Pruckner, conducted by Harvey Lippincott and Captain O'Dwyer, Nov. 13, 1963[460] at the home of Mr. Pruckner, who was age 80 and ten months at the time, born in Jan., 1883.

    Mr. Pruckner heard about the January 1902 flights over Long Island Sound from his associates and Whitehead within a year of the event (as he had gone to Elizabethport, New Jersey to make more money for a

Chapter 6: Key Testimonies

time, earning $2.75 a day). Anton was an adult at the time, about 19-20 years old in 1901/1902. He began as a boarder on Pine Street, meeting Whitehead there for the first time in 1900.

Anton Pruckner also witnessed and participated in experimental multiple (undated) shorter, pre-flights over Seaside Park with the "No. 21" flying machine, or its predecessor ("No. 20"), and assisted in building multiple lightweight aeroplane engines with Whitehead, using various types of motive power, such as gunpowder, steam, gasoline, etc.

Mr. Pruckner described driving the plane, which he called "the bird," from Hancock Avenue down to Seaside Park during early morning hours when there wouldn't be too many people out and around, as it was dangerous, especially with the propellers going, once they'd begin the experiments. He said there were barely any cars on the streets at that time. He described Whitehead and himself, during that period, as "always experimenting." He said he flew the "No. 20/21" plane alone, several times, describing how both he and Whitehead as "shaking" and barely able to know what to do, once up in the air. "You didn't know, some time, what you're doing, when you get up there, no joking. Some times, we was shaking … No joking, It was some time shaking." Pruckner said that before the one and a half mile flight, Whitehead made about half a dozen flights, that he'd "keep on trying."

> [Pruckner] … we didn't have any place to fly, you know. So he have to go to Seaside Park, and from the bank right on the water, over the water, see. Well, when we drop on the water, nobody got hurt. About the same time, we rowed back again…I was couple times in it. You just go, if you drop down, okay, let's go and row it back. That's all you can do.
> [Lippincott] How far were *those* flights?
> [Pruckner] Oh, there was no more than about, say, 75, 80 feet. … [the location was] right around where the bathing pavilion is now. I think that's the place.

Mr. Pruckner described the takeoff location as straight and level, with just a little rise at the beach, going down the beach. [Author's note: there are no dunes at the edge of Long Island Sound in the area of Seaside Park, the land is often just a foot or two above sea level.]

Pruckner also confirmed, during this interview, being present for "the mile and a half flight" in 1901.

Statement of Mrs. Mary Savage (Homemaker, interviewed 1964)
Mrs. Mary Savage [originally, Jusewicz], an adult eyewitness, lived at 353 Pine Street with her husband Peter, very close to Whitehead's house and shop, when he lived at 241 Pine Street. She described, to Major William J. O'Dwyer, Whitehead researcher, with her son, Joe, present, in 1964, how "terribly loud" sounds were heard, like "blasting motor noises," every day "for hours on end." She further described watching Whitehead make numerous "short hops" into the air. But one day, he did far more than that - the plane flew about 1/3 to 1/2 mile.[461]

Mrs. Savage reported that about 3:00 in the morning, there was a "terrific noise." She thought it was Whitehead's flying machine. Her husband went outside on the front porch and confirmed that a flight was being attempted, with men pulling the plane. As it came closer to sunup, the plane became airborne. Mrs. Savage said, "We saw it fly all over the neighborhood" up to about 50 feet in the air. After a period of time where it looked like it was out of control, the powered flying machine flew over the houses and down the hill to Seaside Park, which was on Long Island Sound. It landed in the harbor "rather hard," with "slight damage." She said that Gustave Whitehead was not hurt.[462] [463]

In 2013, Mary's granddaughter, Jean Savage Collins, confirmed in an affidavit that her father, Stanley Savage, had told her when *she* was about 12 years old, that her grandmother, Mary, [his mother] had seen Gustave Whitehead fly his airplane. *This affidavit has been added to the Fairfield [CT] Museum and Library Gustave Whitehead and William J. O'Dwyer Collections.* The date of the Whitehead flight Mary Savage and her husband observed was not provided, but a check of the Bridgeport City Directories confirms that the Savage [Jusewicz] and Whitehead [Weisskopf] families both lived on Pine Street during the years 1903-1906, with a possible year's lag in being included in the directory, placing them there in 1902.[464] It is likely that this flight occurred closer to 1902-1903, during part of Whitehead's early, prolific flying period.

Gustav Peschel (Mechanic)
Peschel witnessed powered flight test experiments on Tunxis Hill, in Fairfield, in 1901-1902. He was a teenager at the time.

William London, a Town Selectman, viewed a plane after its flight in January 1902, Lordship (Stratford); he'd also heard about flights on that date from others. Mr. London was born in 1858, and would have been 44 years old in 1902.

1903 – 1911 Flights

The total number of manned, powered flights reported during this period in eyewitness statements[465]: 15-17, including multiple flights witnessed by individuals, and those which occurred during established flight periods, with some overlap between 1901-1902. This is not thought to be the complete number of Gustave Whitehead's powered airplane flights; it is merely a record from witness statements for some of Whitehead's flights, obtained years later. *Detractors have falsely accused Whitehead of not continuing to make powered flights during this period.*

John Havery (Machinist, interviewed 1948)
Mr. Havery told Attorney Ghormley, an interviewer, that in approximately 1905 [when he was 12 years of age] he'd seen a Whitehead flight "at least 10 feet in the air," for a distance of several hundred feet, at "the old Circus grounds between Cherry and Bostwick streets." [466]

Edward Bradtmuller, Painter, viewed flight in 1907, distance of 200 ft., elevation 10 ft. Mr. Bradtmuller was born in 1894, and would have been 13 years old at the time.

Mary Kopasci viewed multiple flights from 1905-1908 in Fairfield. She was born in 1867, and would have been 38 - 41 years old at the time.

Frederick Szur, Toolmaker, viewed multiple flights from 1905-1908 in Fairfield. Mr. Szur, born in 1886, would have been about 19-22 at the time.

Clarence Crittendon, a carpenter and an adult at the time, watched Whitehead fly out over Long Island Sound at Seaside Park, circle around and return to where he took off, during the period 1908-1911.

Raymond J. Keefe, GE Plant Supervisor, undated, as a boy, found a Whitehead plane in the Mountain Grove Cemetery, in the Tunxis Hill area, which was fenced in, with no way to be there except landing from a flight.

John A. McColl, Bank Vice-President, undated, saw a plane in the air near the old circus grounds in Bridgeport. Mr. McColl was born in 1870, so he would have been an adult over the age of 30 at this sighting, which would likely have been during the period 1901-1905.

James Verzaro, Jr., was present for (undated) powered flights at Orr's Castle, Tunxis Hill, Fairfield; these involved

Chapter 6: Key Testimonies

short hops, 3-4 ft. in elevation. He recalled the loud noise from the engines. He was a boy at the time.

Jeanette Virelli Bacon is possibly the very last living witness interviewed, who turned up in *"The Hou*r," a Norwalk, CT newspaper, in late 1999[467]. As a child, she'd seen the flight of a Whitehead aircraft that went up over Washington School, on Villa Avenue (in Fairfield's Tunxis Hill area, southeast of Tunxis Hill Park and northwest of Mountain Grove Cemetery, where Whitehead's plane had been viewed by Raymond J. Keefe - see above - inside the fenced area). This would be estimated to be in the period 1903-1911, as those were the years that Ms. Bacon, born on August 20, 1899, would be old enough to remember what she saw and during the time when he was making flights in that locale. In this case, it is unknown whether what she saw was a powered flight or a glider. Mrs. Bacon, who lived on Ridgeview Avenue, in the Tunxis Hill neighborhood of Fairfield, CT, less than two miles from where she'd witnessed a Whitehead flight, died at the age of 102, in 2001.

11 of the 27 witnesses who viewed a powered Whitehead flight were confirmed to have been adults at the time of the flights (over the age of 18); 7 were confirmed as teenagers (12-17 years old); and 7 were youths - boys up through 11 years old. Of the 5 witnesses arriving just after a flight, 1 was a known adult, 1 a teen, 1 a youth, and the ages of 2 are unknown. At the time that research began on Whitehead, three decades after the flights, many of the adult witnesses had left the area or died. Those who'd witnessed the flights as adults, teenagers, or children had indelible memories of the-then-astonishing flights. Eyewitnesses who testified to multiple researchers that they'd seen the flights were sincere and vehement about what they'd seen - oftentimes up through the last days of their old age - and contrary to the statements of Whitehead detractors, did not receive payment for their affidavits or statements. Their families also have reported in a number of instances that these witnesses earnestly described the flights they'd seen to their children and grandchildren, desiring that Gustave Whitehead be given proper credit for his achievements.

All documentation for these witness affidavits and statements are publicly available in the O'Dwyer / Gustave Whitehead Research archives at Fairfield Museum, Fairfield, CT; the Gustave Whitehead Collection at the Connecticut State Library, Hartford, CT; the Stella Randolph Gustave Whitehead History of Aviation Collection at University of Dallas, TX, and the Gustav Weisskopf Museum in Leutershausen, Germany. Transcriptions of many of the affidavits are available online at Gustave Whitehead websites such as www.gustavewhitehead.org, overseen by a relative of Whitehead at the time of this writing. A table of key witnesses is available online at this writing at www.gustavewhiteheadinfo.org, in the Master Witnesses File at the Fairfield Museum and the Connecticut State Library Gustave Whitehead Research Collection, Hartford, CT., and in Appendix E of this book.

A final reiteration concerning witnesses - Whitehead flew often and in front of crowds for a period of approximately ten years. The number of potential witnesses is in the hundreds, if not more. Diaries from the period and additional documentation, including the potential for more photos, are expected to surface with increased public awareness.

SCIENTIFIC AMERICAN ON EARLY FLIGHTS

Stanley Yale Beach, Aviation Editor for the *Scientific American* and son of its owner, reportedly direct descendant of William the Conqueror and Elihu Yale, founder of Yale University[468], published half a dozen significant Whitehead articles in that noteworthy magazine, *five different times crediting Whitehead as "first to fly,"* describing his work and flights, especially those of 1901, in a very positive manner. Beach pointedly referenced Whitehead's successful powered flights of 1901 in his articles in *Scientific American* from 1903-1908,[469] up until the time of his "falling out"* with Whitehead (*to be covered in the next section). These are as follows: (*emphasis added*)

Gustave Whitehead: "First in Flight"

Scientific American June 8, 1901, p. 357

This article describes the "No. 21" as it was being prepared for a manned, free flight, describing the aeroplane as "inherently stable." Beach also wrote, "He built [an engine] of 20 horsepower to drive the two propellers of his new monoplane and one of ten horsepower to propel it on the ground."

Scientific American, Sept. 19, 1903, p.204 (see entire article at the end of this chapter)

Beach wrote this article, crediting Whitehead with recently flying along the ground surface, up to 16 feet in the air, with a motor-driven aeroplane of his own construction, a triplane. The date is still three months ahead of the Wrights' flights at Kitty Hawk.

Scientific American, Jan. 27, 1906, pp.93-94

The Aero Club of America's Exhibit of Aeronautical Apparatus

"This exhibit was the most complete of its kind ever held in any part of the world, for all types of flying machines, balloons and airships were represented … Besides these very complete exhibits of apparatus, the walls of the room were covered with a large collection of photographs showing the machines of other inventors, such as Whitehead, Berliner and Santos-Dumont; and other photographs showing airships and balloons in flight … *A single blurred photograph of a large birdlike machine propelled by compressed air and which was constructed by Whitehead in 1901 was the only other photograph besides that of Langley's machines* of a motor-driven aeroplane in successful flight. In order to at least partially substantiate their claims, it would seem as if aeroplane inventors would show photographs of their machines in flight …*"

[*Author's note – Langley's photo was of a scale model]

Scientific American, Nov. 24, 1906, p.379

Santos Dumont's Latest Flight

"…In his enthusiasm, the Brazilian aeronaut forgets also that at least three experiments in America (Herring in 1898, *Whitehead in 1901* and the Wright brothers in 1903), Maxim in England (1896), and Ader in France (1897) *have already flown for short distances with motor-driven aeroplanes,* and yet no really practical machine of the kind has as yet been produced and demonstrated." (p. 378)

Scientific American, 15. Dec. 1906, p.447

The Second Annual Exhibition of the Aero Club of America

"The body of the framework of Gustave Whitehead's latest bat-like aeroplane was shown mounted on pneumatic-tired, ball bearing wire wheels … Whitehead also exhibited the 2-cylinder steam engine which revolved the road wheels of his former bat machine, *with which he made a number of short flights in 1901.*"

At the bottom of the next page, the 1901 Whitehead engine is displayed in a photograph from the exhibition, as are two additional motors and a propeller.

Chapter 6: Key Testimonies

Scientific American, Jan. 25, 1908, p. 54

The Farman Aeroplane Wins the Deutsch Archdeacon Prize

"In view of the above-mentioned facts, while giving to M. Farman the credit for first publicly demonstrating that it is possible to fly in all directions, both with, against and across a light wind, we nevertheless wish to recall to the *Aeronautical World* the fact that *to America belongs the credit of producing the first successful motor-driven aeroplane, and that to such men as* the Wright brothers, A. M. Herring, and *Gustave Whitehead – men, who under the tutelage of Lilienthal and Chanute, have begun with gliding flight and gradually worked their way forward to the production of a self-propelled aeroplane in all its details, including the gasoline motor – belongs the real credit of having produced the first successful heavier-than-air flying machines.*"

The *Scientific American* carried a full page article about Whitehead in September 1903, three months *before* the Wrights conducted their experimental powered "hops" at Kitty Hawk. *The article then credits Whitehead with recently flying along the ground surface, up to 16 feet in the air, with a motor-driven aeroplane of his own construction*, a triplane. The article, without a byline, is credited to Stanley Yale Beach, the *Scientific American* Aviation Editor who lived in Lordship, where Whitehead was known to fly.

Stanley Beach knew Whitehead, photographed him on many occasions, and several years later, signed onto a patent with Whitehead for his self-leveling, bat-winged soaring machine (a type of glider that was developed into a large biplane), with Beach's father financing some Whitehead-built Beach designs.

Beach sought Orville Wright's friendship, influence, and business in later years. Beach was increasingly affiliated, from 1906 on, with those who were squarely in the Wright "camp." [470] When Orville's position as "first in flight" was threatened, in the latter half of the 1930's, by Whitehead researcher Stella Randolph's publications, Beach was prevailed upon to come to the rescue by Wright proponents and did [471], producing a jointly written, never published or signed "Whitehead Statement," later used by Orville Wright and all later Whitehead detractors, to denounce the Whitehead flight claims. Following Stanley Beach's notorious late life, highly publicized, unfortunate mental health problems which led to serious personal and financial crises, Beach turned against Gustave Whitehead - more than a decade after Whitehead's death. He was "put up to" writing an unsigned, never-published, collaboratively edited, negative Whitehead statement by several highly placed friends of Orville Wright, in which he denied that Whitehead had ever flown.

The *Scientific American* of September 19, 1903, contains this article, which illustrates some of the steps and mathematical calculations Gustave Whitehead engaged in during the invention of his powered planes. First, he would make a model and/or glider, testing the glider sufficiently, then he'd add a lightweight engine he'd build or have built for him. He tried to take these steps as safely as possible, for most of the test flights, cognizant of the dangers involved and people who had been killed in the course of aerial experimentation, such as Otto Lilienthal. Whitehead came up with a variety of designs, some of his own, but increasingly using those of others, his sponsors, who hired him to produce airplanes for them. One recurrent theme with Whitehead was the creation of a "practical plane" (one that had commercial potential) that could rise and descend (land) vertically. He was not alone in both of these concepts, for this was mentioned by others of his era. With no protected airports or runways, establishing suitable places for takeoffs and landings was difficult at best. Whitehead did not consider his earlier successful designs to be practical for the uses he so strongly envisioned. He continued to strive, with his limited funding, to invent and produce designs for a practical plane that would rise vertically. In this article, by Stanley Yale Beach, aviation editor for the *Scientific American*, we view photos with descriptions of a triplane glider soon to be motorized, the process, and the thoughts of Gustave Whitehead on this subject, several months before the Wrights "flights" at Kitty Hawk.

Gustave Whitehead: "First in Flight"

Scientific American **SEPTEMBER 19, 1903:**

EXPERIMENTS WITH MOTOR-DRIVEN AEROPLANES [472]

"Our Illustrations depict experiments with an aeroplane carried out recently by Mr. Gustave Whitehead, of Bridgeport, Conn., who has been studying the subject of mechanical flight for upward of fifteen years. In one of the pictures is shown a lightweight, two cycle motor, which was used on the aeroplane in a recent experiment.

Unlike Lilienthal and Chanute, Whitehead does not attempt to soar by jumping off a hill or precipice. *He is content, on the contrary, with flying near the ground, if he can only solve the problem of rising from it quickly at will, and descending gently whenever and wherever he wishes.*

The method of soaring used by Mr. Whitehead consists in running with the aeroplane against the wind, preceded by an assistant who draws it with a rope when it leaves the ground. When sufficient speed is attained, the operator, *by tilting the aeroplanes slightly upward, can leave the ground and skim along in the air,* as shown in one of the photographs. The trimming of the aeroplanes, both longitudinally and transversely, is accomplished by the operator shifting the position of, his body, and the proper trimming necessary to keep from taking a plunge is quite a delicate matter. A puff of wind striking the aeroplanes harder on one side than on the other can also easily upset their transverse stability, unless the operator is quick to counteract it.

**Figure 123: Sci Am Whitehead Triplane Glider (1903)
Gliding Near the Ground Against a 15-Mile-an-Hour Wnd.**

Chapter 6: Key Testimonies

**Figure 124: Sci Am Whitehead Triplane Glider, rearview (1903)
Rear of Aeroplane, Showing Pyramidal Rudder.**

**Figure 125: Whitehead Triplane Glider w/operator (1903)
Front of Aeroplane, Showing Operator In Position.**

After practising [practicing] considerably at balancing the aeroplanes when drawn by, a man, Mr. Whitehead at length designed and built a light-weight, two-cycle gasoline motor for propelling them; This motor is of the air-cooled type, and has numerous loops of aluminum wire fastened to the two cylinders in order to radiate the heat. The inventor says that he has found *aluminum* to be much better for this purpose than copper, which is the metal generally employed. The cylinders of the motor have a 4-inch bore and a 4 ⅝-inch stroke, and it is designed to 'run' at speeds of from 1,000 to 2,500 R. P. M. ,

It develops 12 horse power at the latter speed, and its weight complete is but 54 pounds, or 4½ pounds per horse power, which shows it to be one of the lightest gasoline motors ever built. Over 100 pounds compression is employed, the sole compression space being the small dome on top of each cylinder, in the top of which is seen the sparking plug. The motor, being of the two-cycle type, is valveless, with the exception of light aluminum check valves, through which the gas passes before making its entrance into the sheet-steel crank case (which is divided by a central partition) through the holes seen in its side. Splash lubrication is employed in the crank case, and oil is fed to the cylinders from two oil cups. A 25- inch wire wheel was used as a flywheel, and carried fan blades for assisting in cooling the motor. Its dimensions are 18 inches high by 12 inches long by 8 inches wide, and in the experiments made with it, a two-bladed propeller 4⅝ feet in diameter was fastened on the motor shaft and revolved at a speed of 1,000 R. P. M. As the motor has four disk flywheels inside its crank case, the large wire-spoked one is not absolutely necessary, and in actual tests, when mounted on the aeroplanes, the motor was found to work equally well without it, thus reducing the total weight of the motor to 47½ pounds.

Figure 126: 12 H. P., two-Cycle Motor with Wire Flywheel; Weight, 54 Pounds.

EXPERIMENTS WITH THE WHITEHEAD AEROPLANE

The three aeroplanes are spaced 3 feet apart and are 16 feet long by 5 feet wide. They are made up of

Chapter 6: Key Testimonies

spruce wood frames, covered with muslin, and are suitably braced with diagonal wires. There is a space in the center of the lower one for the operator, who hangs from the two forward uprights and keeps the apparatus in trim by shifting his body. A rigid, pyramidal-shaped rudder projects from behind. After ascertaining, by loading himself with sandbags, that the aeroplanes were capable of lifting the extra weight of the motor and propeller, the motor was attached to the two longitudinal projecting rods of the lower aeroplane, and carried the propeller in front of it on its crank shaft. *By running with, the machine, against the wind; after the motor had been started, the aeroplane was made to skim along above the ground at heights of from 3 to 16 feet' for a distance, without the operator touching, of about 350 yards.* It was possible to have traveled a 'much longer distance without touching terra firma, *but for the operator's desire not to get too far above it*. Although the motor was not developing its full power, owing to its speed: not exceeding 1.000 R. P. M , it developed , sufficient to move the machine against the' wind. The total thrust, or, in this case, pull of the propeller was found to be 280 pounds, while all that is needed to keep the machine in the air, according to the dynamometric measurements made when it was drawn by a man, is a pull of 28 pounds. Making the propellers pull, instead of push the machine, aids greatly in maintaining its stability.

Having proven that a less powerful motor will do the work, Mr. Whitehead is now constructing one of 6 horse power which will weigh between 25 and 30 pounds. He intends to drive two 4½-foot propellers with this; by means of bevel gears, giving the proper speed reduction for obtaining a speed of 600 to 800 R. P. M. of the propellers. Besides this smaller two- cylinder motor, he is also constructing a four-cylinder one, of 10 horse power, which he expects will not exceed 40 pounds in weight, aluminum being used as far as possible in its construction. *This is to be used on an improved aeroplane with which the inventor hopes to be able to rise vertically in still air travel horizontally, and descend vertically again.*

This is the desideratum [eventual goal] of the aeroplane flying machine [to rise and descend vertically]."
(1903 *Scientific American*)

Gustave Whitehead: "First in Flight"

Chapter 7

LATER YEARS

1904 - 1908 FLIGHT EXPERIMENTS

More Flights in the West End of Bridgeport

Additional witnesses were located who reported Whitehead 'street flights' in powered biplanes, up through 1908 [473] and beyond. One such witness was Mary Kopacsi, who said, "During the years 1905, 1906, 1907, and 1908, I saw Gustave Whitehead make airplane flights at Villa Park in the West end of Bridgeport at an altitude of three or four feet above the ground. I also saw him make many similar flights along State Street, most of which took place around sunset. In my judgment, his flights were from 7-100 yards *[Author's note: 21-300 feet]* in length without touching the ground. The airplane was a biplane - two wings - one above the other ..." The above statement was also signed by Frederick Szur, who acted as interpreter and who has lived at Pine Street since early in 1905, having moved there from another city. *The authenticity of these early street flights seems unquestionable.*" (John B. Crane, PhD, Professor of Economics, Harvard University, *"Did Whitehead Actually Fly?"* from the *National Aeronautic Association Magazine*, December 1936)

A Tunxis Hill Flight

Another witness, Edward Bradtmuller, of Ridgely Avenue, Fairfield, a neighbor of Whitehead's (after 1906, when Whitehead moved there), gave this account of seeing a biplane flight:

"I recall his building the aircraft on his property across the street from where I presently live. At that time, however, there was nothing other than fields here. I lived up the street further and across from Mr. Suelly. Mr. Suelly was a machinist and worked at Bullard's along with Gustave Whitehead. They built this bi-plane in the back yard of his old house and in front of the shop that has since burned down. I can recall seeing them go up and down the street, of course then it wasn't a street like now, it was just an open area. I distinctly saw the plane fly and would estimate it to be over 10 feet in height and for a distance of a few hundred feet at a time...(11 October 1964, affidavit, witnessed by William J. O'Dwyer, Captain, USAF)[474]

Flight Experiments with Whitehead Associate and Aeronaut Howard Booth

Figure 127: *Bridgeport Herald* **article Nov.22, 1908, GW to Outdo Wrights** [475]

Chapter 7: Later Years

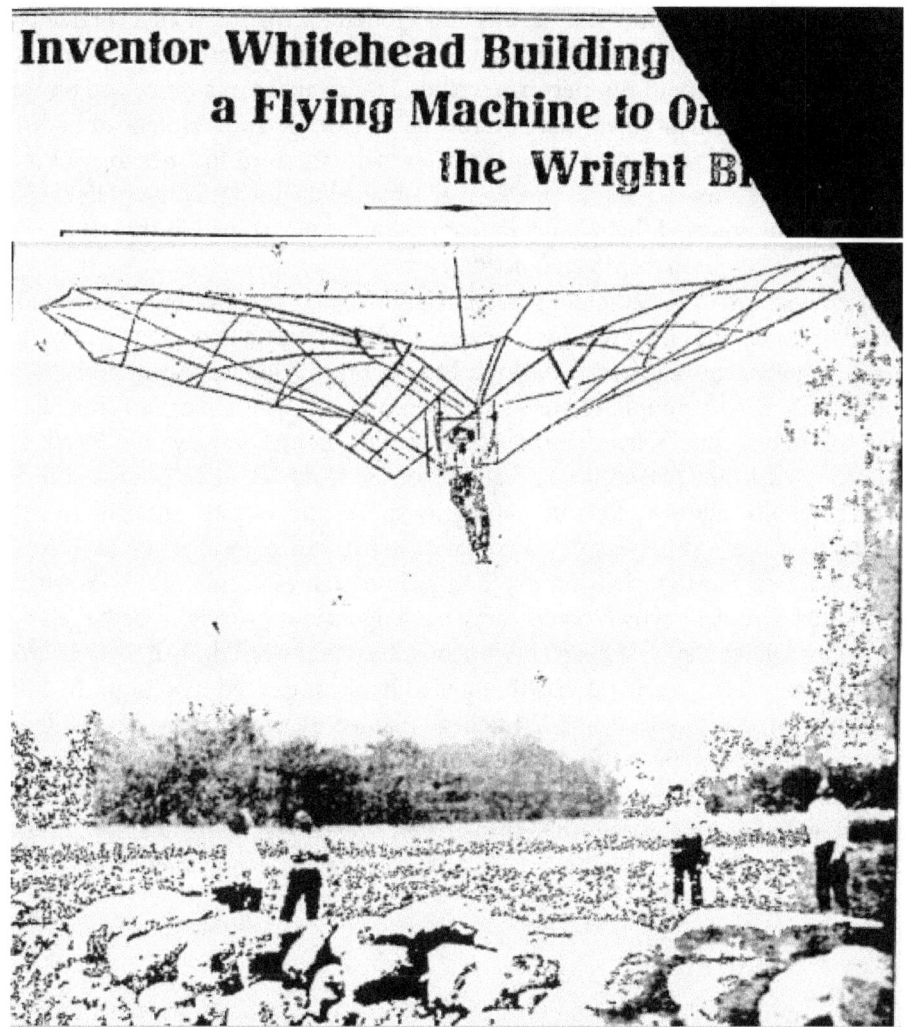

Figure 128: *Bridgeport Herald* **photo/sketch of 1908 glider**

In addition to being an informative scene, helping us understand Whitehead's activities in 1908, the above photo also shows that, even in 1908, *the Bridgeport Herald*, long criticized for not doing the impossible -taking a *night* photo of Whitehead's flight of August 14, 1901 - still did not have proper, high end technology to always produce perfect photos in their newspaper, even when taken in the daytime.

In a little-known *Bridgeport Sunday Herald* article of November 22, 1908[476], entitled "Inventor Whitehead Building a Flying Machine to Outdo the Wright Bros.," Whitehead and "aeronaut" Howard Booth were depicted as co-inventing a powerful but lightweight 50 horsepower engine for a new Whitehead flying machine, 40 feet long by 30 feet wide, that could hold two passengers, modeled after a huge bird, that "always alight[s] right side up." The article notes that the Whitehead machine will have an advantage over the Wright aeroplane, which had recently taken a nose dive, causing the death of a passenger. Booth and Whitehead reportedly had conducted extensive, successful trials aggregating 47 miles, with a smaller glider based on this design near "Orr's Castle," a hilly region in Fairfield, and were poised to conduct more tests with the engine attached, using either one or two propellers. If they did not succeed, they'd try additional designs similar to the Wright plane, but with a device attached that prevented instability. Mr. Booth described the Wright brothers' plane as "a fine machine, but a very dangerous one" that he and Mr. Whitehead intended to improve upon. Stanley Yale Beach, aeronautic

Gustave Whitehead: "First in Flight"

authority and *Scientific American* Aviation Editor, was interviewed for the story. He expressed confidence in the flying machine, having watched it from the street and taken it to some trials at the flying field at the Morris Park racetrack, where it unfortunately could not perform well due to breakage of a brace rod on the journey on the way there, in Beach's car. Booth mentioned that several years prior, he and Whitehead had tried a helicopter, but it was unsuccessful and they reverted to the present model - the bird-like design.[477] Specific information on the success of the initial Whitehead-Booth powered aeroplane has not yet come to light, but at least several reports do exist of successful powered flights during that period, as mentioned in this section. It was to later be developed into the Beach-Whitehead Aeroplane of 1909.

A week earlier, *Scientific American* had run an aviation article mentioning Whitehead's latest glider, in its November 14th, 1908 issue. The glider had just been exhibited at Morris Park, New Jersey, the previous week, though it was unable to perform well there, due to "a broken brace rod," according to the *Bridgeport Sunday Herald* article, above, published a couple of weeks later. In March 1908, Gustave Whitehead had received a shared patent[478] for this glider, with *Scientific American* Aviation Editor Stanley Yale Beach (*see Appendix C*), a fact may have contributed to the reason it was featured in the story with two photos. The glider design was noted for its inherent stability, allowing for safe gliding by sports enthusiasts, rather than risking lives due to accidents. The design, typical of Whitehead developmental steps, was to become the basis for a large, powered commercial aeroplane, which was to have been much safer in design than that of the Wrights. The idea was to build a practical powered aeroplane which could carry passengers and or freight, be large and strong, but not deadly and unruly to control. Stanley Yale Beach became involved in the building of the powered aeroplane with Gustave Whitehead, the following year, and was thought to have influenced its design. In 1909, the aeroplane failed to fly, and Beach blamed Whitehead, and Whitehead blamed Beach. In 1934, when talking by phone with Stella Randolph, Beach claimed he'd been the inventor, and Whitehead, merely his mechanic. But by 1939, Beach would, once again, blame Whitehead for its failure to fly, though this was undoubtedly related to its size and not understanding the amount of power needed when upsizing an aircraft. (*see Chapter 8: FAQ: Why did Whitehead's much larger aeroplanes fail to fly?*)

Chapter 7: Later Years

Figure 129: *Scientific American*[479], **Whitehead glider at Morris Park, NJ (Nov. 14, 1908)**

(transcript)

"THE FIRST OPEN-AIR EXHIBITION OF THE AERONAUTIC SOCIETY.
Scientific American, November 14, 1908[480]

On Election Day, Morris Park, which has been the scene of many horse and automobile races, was opened as an aeronautic ground by the Aeronautic Society. The society's first exhibition was held in the afternoon in conjunction with the championship motor-cycle races …. and while nothing novel happened in the aeronautical line, three were some very fast motorcycle races and some interesting experiments with gliders.

A considerable number of inventors were present with models of their apparatus. They were invited to place their models upon the lawn in front of the grand stand, where they could be inspected by the spectators. One of our photographs shows some of the apparatus as it was displayed upon the lawn....The lower pair of photographs which we reproduce illustrate an improved type of aeroplane, which was invented some three years ago by Gustave Whitehead, of Bridgeport, Conn., and which has since been patented both in the United States and abroad. This machine, owing to its long triangular body with a bow at the forward end and a tail at the rear, is far more stable when in the air than is the Chanute double-surface machine. The foldable wings resemble those used by Lilienthal, with whom Whitehead at one time experimented in Germany. The main feature of the machine is the central body portion. A glider of this type can be made to lift a man when it is towed by another man against a fifteen or twenty- mile wind, and once it is well up in the air, the rope can be cut, and the machine will always alight on a level keel. Should it start to plunge downward, it will immediately right itself automatically. The aviator does, not have to balance it by kicking out his legs, and it is possible to tow one of these machines behind an automobile with perfect safety to the man hanging from it."

(end of transcript)

Side view of Whitehead glider in free flight.   Front view of Whitehead aeroplane making a glide.
THE FIRST OPEN-AIR EXHIBITION OF THE AERONAUTIC SOCIETY.

Figure 130: Side view of Whitehead glider in free flight. Front view of Whitehead aeroplane making a glide. *Scientific American* **(Nov. 14, 1908)**

Above, Fig.128 shows an illustration of the latest Whitehead glider which was exhibited at the Aeronautic Society's first exhibition, on "Election Day," the first week in November 1908. The article was published a week later, on November 14th. These photos were said to be taken near Orr's Castle at Tunxis Hill, previously that year (note most of the leaves still on trees and men not wearing jackets, circa September or October 1908)

Chapter 7: Later Years

Figure 131: Transporting 1908 glider to Morris Park

Stanley Yale Beach transporting Whitehead glider with wings folded, possibly to Morris Park, New Jersey, from Tunxis Hill, Fairfield, CT, circa fall, 1908 (possibly the early morning of November 14, 1908).[481] Note S. Y. Beach, Howard Booth in rear seat, G Whitehead standing beside Beach, with milkman in background.
Photo by John Slezsak.
Courtesy of Fairfield Museum, O'Dwyer/Whitehead Research Collection

Figure 132: Stanley Yale Beach and Gustave Whitehead (Nov. 1908)
Enlargement from Fig. 131
Stanley Yale Beach (left), Gustave Whitehead (right) in closeup
(Courtesy of Fairfield Museum, O'Dwyer/Whitehead Research Collection)
© Susan Brinchman, 2015

Figure 133: Howard Booth and Stanley Beach (fall, 1908)
Stanley Yale Beach at far right, Ridgely Avenue Whitehead home in background.
Howard Booth, aeronaut, at far left.
(Photos courtesy of Fairfield Museum, O'Dwyer-Whitehead Collection)

Figure 134: Aeronaut Howard Booth at left, at GW's house (fall, 1909)
(Courtesy of Fairfield Museum, O'Dwyer/Whitehead Research Collection)

Above, two previously unidentified visitors stand to Stanley Beach's left at Whitehead's Tunxis Hill shop and home, circa 1908. Man at far left is now known to be Aeronaut Howard Booth, who worked with Whitehead from 1906-1908; also, he is Beach's mystery automobile passenger, pictured below. *Photo by John Slezsak*

Figure 135: Aeronaut Booth in Beach's car, on way to Morris Park (Nov. 1908)
Aeronaut Howard Booth on his way to Morris Park, NJ, in the morning, to demonstrate a Whitehead glider.
(Courtesy of Fairfield Museum, O'Dwyer/Whitehead Research Collection)
Photo by John Slezsak

Chapter 7: Later Years

Above, Beach-Whitehead associate, recently identified by this author as Aeronaut Howard Booth, sitting in back of Beach's automobile thought to be leaving for a November 3, 1908, in the early AM [note milkman in distance] to transport the Whitehead glider to the Aeronautic Society's Morris Park, New Jersey, for a demonstration on Novembr 3, 1908. The glider had performed well locally, at Tunxis Hill, aggregating 47 miles in flight without a mishap. At the park, Aeronaut Booth "mounted the glider" towed by a powerful automobile [belonging to Beach, above] at 25 mph, only to find that damage had occurred en route. That ended their chances on that date. [482]

Figure 136: Howard Booth sketch in the Herald (Nov. 22, 1908)

Howard Booth, aeronaut and inventor, worked with Whitehead from 1906-1908, first, on a helicopter prototype and then, a successful glider with inherent stability. They intended to provide the glider with power, to "outdo" the Wright brothers, whose aeroplane was known to be inherently unstable, and therefore, quite dangerous - having already killed a man and harmed Orville severely. Stanley Beach was associated with the builders during the 1908 period, watching their efforts, with half ownership in the glider's patented design with Whitehead, ultimately hiring him to build a large Beach-Whitehead aeroplane, based on the earlier gliders.

Figure 137: Gustave (left) and brother John (right) at Ridgely Avenue home (1908)
(Courtesy of Fairfield Museum, O'Dwyer/Whitehead Research Collection)
The Whitehead brothers, pictured beside the Beach-Whitehead V-shaped glider at Ridgely Avenue in Tunxis Hill, circa 1908. Gustave Whitehead appears at left, assistant

Gustave Whitehead: "First in Flight"
and sometime partner, his brother, John Whitehead, at right.

Figure 138: Early morning milkman, Tunxis Hill (1908)
(Courtesy of Fairfield Museum, O'Dwyer/Whitehead Research Collection)
Photo by John Slezsak

Above, a local milkman drives his wagon up Tunxis Hill, behind Beach's automobile, similar to the commonplace, early morning scene described by Richard Howell at the Fairfield half-mile flight, in August 1901.

Figure 139: Large monoplane glider towing test, Lordship, CT (1908)
(Courtesy of Fairfield Museum, O'Dwyer/Whitehead Research Collection)

Gustave Whitehead with largest of his monoplane gliders, patented March 1908. Test not powered, towed with Stanley Yale Beach's car, to determine ground speed and horsepower needs.

Chapter 7: Later Years

Figure 140: Whitehead runs alongside large monoplane glider towing test, Lordship, CT (1908)
(Courtesy of Fairfield Museum, O'Dwyer/Whitehead Research Collection)

A Flight at Seaside Park

Clarence Crittendon was interviewed on February 15, 1964 by Captain William J. O'Dwyer and E. Hildes-Heim, CAHA member. Mr. Crittendon recalled watching a powered flight occur over Seaside Park, Bridgeport, CT, *after* the period 1908-1910. The flight was for a distance of 100-200 feet out over the water heading west, circling south, and returning east, back to where he started from, landing hard "shaking up the craft quite badly"; approximately a three minute flight, skimming over the ground. It occurred where the baseball diamonds were located at the time of the interview, next to PT Barnum's statue, at Seaside Park.[483] This is a flat area, popular with Gustave Whitehead, as it was an open space that accessed Long Island Sound, which he flew over in his boat-like aircraft to enhance safety.

In the years following his successful flights of 1901-1902, Gustave often worked with sponsors to build flying machines to compete for lucrative prizes. These types of jobs were undertaken with an eye for a rapid return on the sponsor's investment. Successful, non-infringing designs had to be invented and a product developed for use often with a short timeline. In retrospect, we might say that the basic elements of flight were locked up under expanding patent language, during this latter period, with the Wright brothers, amid the suits of infringers, widely covered in the newspapers. Whitehead was not sued, perhaps as his flying machines were sufficiently different, but none could be successfully developed for commercial use, which was his goal.

Gustave Whitehead: "First in Flight"

A FALLING OUT WITH STANLEY YALE BEACH (1909)

A newly discovered series of local newspaper articles describes the 1909 Beach-Whitehead aeroplane, pictured below, revealing the later time period when Beach became involved financially with Whitehead, and how their usually positive relationship began to deteriorate, as the two men were apparently incompatible, in terms of business. Following the establishment of the Aero Club of America and its offshoot, the Aeronautical Society of New York, it became fashionable for its members to portray themselves as inventors and aeronauts, rather than promoters of aeronautics. The enterprising Stanley Yale Beach, from a very prominent family, recipient of his father's trust fund, editor of the *Scientific American* and a founding member of the Aeronautical Society, became convinced he could invent and fly an aeroplane, build multiple copies in a factory he'd establish, and fly them for profit at air meets. Beach had need of becoming wealthy, independent of his family – having compelling personal reasons which would surface in coming decades. Unfortunately, the aspiring aviator and inventor Beach, who began to sponsor Whitehead, was not destined to become airborne, though for a couple of years, Beach was featured in a notable number of news and magazine articles. Sadly, Stanley Beach, a talented and informed aviation editor, was to eventually spiral downhill, having increasing business mishaps, financial, family, personal and finally, mental health difficulties over his remaining lifetime, into the 1950's.

    By March 10, 1909, Gustave Whitehead's relationship with Stanley Yale Beach, with whom he shared a glider patent granted in 1908, had begun to sour. The *Bridgeport Standard* reported that Beach demanded Whitehead conduct a dangerous powered flight demonstration on a Sunday for Beach's friend, when the plane didn't even have the cloth needed to cover the framework. Whitehead did not want to disturb the neighbors, nor, undoubtedly, have anyone die in a rash attempt to fly the unfinished flying machine. Interestingly, Gustave Whitehead describes his systematic testing period as taking six weeks. We are also shown how Whitehead is mistreated at the hands of yet another wealthy, spoiled, illogical, non-mechanical sponsor who takes the beleaguered, impoverished inventor to court when the backer can't have his way. Inevitably, these types of frequent legal assaults broke Whitehead and his family down financially and undoubtedly, emotionally.

    In 1934, Beach pompously claimed to Stella Randolph that he was "the inventor" and Whitehead was merely "a mechanic and machinist hired to work with him." He told Randolph that the experiments, starting in 1908 or 1909, involving a glider, then a monoplane with a motor that didn't fly, and building an 8 cylinder motor that worked successfully in a boat, cost about $10,000. [484] In his later alleged "Beach-Whitehead Statement," crafted with a couple of prominent Wright supporters in 1939, this expenditure for building multiple flying machines would be *misleadingly made to sound like it spanned ten years, rather than just a few*, and that Whitehead's airplanes never left the ground, thus contradicting his own earlier articles in the *Scientific American* through 1908. The cost of *all* Beach's experiments, including three Bleriot-style monoplanes built by others, may have been included in that sum. Beach's alleged critique of Whitehead was used first by Orville Wright, in 1945, to whom it was given, *and ever since,* by Smithsonian curators and Wright supporters even at this writing. It is used to erroneously bash Gustave Whitehead for what we will see were design errors on Beach's part and which occurred from 1908, at the earliest, and ended in 1910. Thus, Beach's alleged portions of the unsigned, unpublished, so-called "Beach-Whitehead Statement" penned in 1939 to disparage Whitehead's accomplishments, will be shown to be completely without merit.

WHITEHEAD WOULDN'T DISTURB NEIGHBORS.

Says Stanley Beach Wanted Him to Operate Flying Machine Motor on Sunday and He Refused.

His refusal to operate his flying machine on Sunday and thereby disturb the peace of Lenox Heights, is the reason Inventor Gustave Whitehead gives for the business difficulties between himself and Stanley Y. Beach, one of the editors of the Scientific American. Since Mr. Beach asked for a temporary receiver for the partnership and Judge Curtis of the superior court advised the parties to get together, efforts have been made to adjust matters but nothing has yet been agreed upon.

Would Disturb Neighbors.

Whitehead declares that Beach came to his workshop on Lenox Heights last Sunday with a friend and wanted the airship to be sent on a trial. Whitehead refused to make a trial on Sunday. He said the big motor makes an explosion like a Gatling gun and would be very disturbing to the neighbors on Sunday.

Beach Insistent.

The inventor says Beach insisted on a trial and attempted to start the machine himself. In order to block this, Whitehead took off the timer. Then Beach seized two propellors. A wordy war followed and the next day Beach started legal proceedings against the inventor. Whitehead says the machine is all ready for flight with the exception of a canvas covering which must be put over the frame work. He explains that the trial will take about six weeks, however, because the flights must be made at different distances above the ground, gradually grower higher.

Attorney William A. Redden represents Whitehead and Judge E. K. Nicholson is counsel for Beach.

Figure 141: Whitehead Beach Problems – Neighbors - Bridgeport Standard (1909)

Gustave Whitehead: "First in Flight"

(transcript)

"*Whitehead Wouldn't Disturb Neighbors.*
Says Stanley Beach Wanted Him to Operate Flying Machine Motor on Sunday and He Refused.
(*Bridgeport Standard*, March 10, 1909, p. 1)

His refusal to operate his flying machine on Sunday and thereby disturb the peace of Lenox Heights is the reason Inventor Gustave Whitehead gives for the business difficulties between himself and Stanley Y. Beach, one of the editors of the *Scientific American*. Since Mr. Beach asked for a temporary receiver for the partnership and Judge Curtis of the superior court advised the parties to get together, efforts have been made to adjust matters but nothing has yet been agreed upon.

Would Disturb Neighbors.
Whitehead declares that Beach came to his workshop on Lenox Heights last Sunday with a friend and wanted the airship to be sent on a trial. Whitehead refused to make a trial on Sunday. He said the big motor makes an explosion like a Gatling gun and would be very disturbing to the neighbors on Sunday.

Beach Insistent
The Inventor says Beach insisted on a trial and attempted to start the machine himself. In order to block this, Whitehead took off the timer. Then Beach seized two propellers. A wordy war followed and the next day Beach started legal proceedings against the inventor. Whitehead says the machine is all ready for flight with the exception of a canvas covering which must be put over the framework. He explains that the trial will take about six weeks, however, because the flights must be made at different distances above the ground, gradually growing higher.

Attorney William A Redden represents Whitehead and Judge E. K. Nicholson is counsel for Beach."[485]

(end of transcript)

Just four days after the *Bridgeport Standard* coverage of the Beach-Whitehead falling-out, on March 14th, 1909, the *New York Times* predicted that the large Beach-Whitehead aeroplane, with its "long, boat-shaped body" would be competing at Morris Park, New Jersey, a few months later. The Times showed a prominent photo of the aeroplane, featured on the first page of its "Part Four, Sporting News Section," under the headline, "Two Latest Productions of American Aviators," followed by an article entitled, "New Aeroplanes for Early Flights." The photo, and description below shows Gustave Whitehead and Stanley Beach incorporated some of the design elements of successful commercial airplanes of the future, though their late alliance ultimately did not lead to a machine destined to fly in 1909.

Chapter 7: Later Years

Figure 142: Beach-Whitehead Biplane NYT (1909)

"New Aeroplanes for Early Flights"
(*New York Times*, March 14, 1909)

"… The second machine is the joint product of Stanley Y. Beach, one of the active members of the Aeronautic Society, and Gustave Whitehead. It embodies some decidedly novel ideas, and after being tried out at Bridgeport, Conn., where it was built, it will be taken to Morris Park, Where Mr. Beach intends to make a number of flights during the coming season … The appearance of these … new machines so early in the season is simply another indication of the widespread interest being taken in aeronautical matters, giving creditable assurance that the coming season will witness successful flights of more heavier than air machines than has ever been seen before…

The Beach aeroplane is entirely different in appearance from anything of the kind hitherto constructed. It combines some of the features of the Wright machine and the Bleriot monoplane, but its distinctive characteristic is a triangular longitudinal body with a bow like a boat, this idea being original with Mr. Whitehead and for which a patent [*] has been granted. Experiments made with a glider constructed on this principle showed that it gave the aeroplane excellent longitudinal stability while increasing the transverse stability, making it unnecessary to box in the ends of the main planes with vertical partitions.

The machine is built on a rectangular fame mounted on four wheels and covered to form a platform at the front end. The moto and operator are located on this platform beneath the lower main plane. The triangular body is above this lower main plane, carrying at its read end the horizontal rudder, while twin vertical rudders are placed on each side near the rear. This triangular body spreads into a tail at the rear and is also fitted with a par of wings about two-thirds of the distance back from the front end.

Two eight-foot propellers are mounted on the front edge of the planes on either side of the triangular body. They are driven by a rope from the motor and run in opposite directions. The *bow of the triangular body is made of sheet metal,* and the cooling water from the engine is sprayed over it on the inside, collecting at the bottom, thus forming a combined radiator and a tank. The steering is by a wheel operating the rear pair of wheels or the running gear, and the vertical rudders, while the horizontal rudder is operated by a lever at the side of the aviator.

The length of the main plane is forty feet, and the triangular body has the same length. It weighs, ready for flight, including operator, about 1,200 pounds, the surfaces thus being required to lift about two pounds to the square foot. The motor, which was designed and built especially for the machine by Mr. Whitehead, is a four-cylinder, four-cycle engine weighing 275 pounds, fitted with concentric valves and capable of developing fifty horse power. Ignition is by means of a single coil storage battery, and a distributor."[486]

[*Author's note: see Appendix for Whitehead-Beach Patent.]

On March 17th, a second article surfaced in the *Bridgeport Standard*, describing the same V-shaped aeroplane as if it was entirely Whitehead's idea, sponsored by Beach, that was now ready for trials. In this article, Gustave Whitehead praised Beach. This on-again, off-again relationship would continue for the next several years, making "good fodder" for amusing newspaper articles, but undoubtedly causing great strain on Gustave Whitehead and his family. Gustave needed to continue to work, and Beach had the money to help him survive, for the time being.

(Transcript)

"This Flying Machine Will Soon Be Ready
Gustave Whitehead of This City Has Completed One Which Will Have Trial at Greenfield Hill
Stanley Y. Beach is Helping Him
Machine is So Simple that Anyone Can Learn to Operate It Says Investor – Expects Aeroplane Will Soon Be as Numerous as Automobiles.
(*Bridgeport Standard*, March 17, 1909)

With capital furnished by Stanley Y. Beach of Stratford, editor of the *Scientific American*, Gustave Whitehead, the flying machine inventor, has perfected an aeroplane, the final private trials of which will be made in a few days at Greenfield Hill. It is claimed that the Whitehead invention is superior to that of the Wright Bros. in several ways, chiefly in stability provided through devices which have just been patented at Washington.

The Whitehead aeroplane is the result of three years of constant study and experiment and every feature of its mechanism has been demonstrated by models. Whitehead has already flown in his machine, which is not an experiment. Mr. Beach and some of his friends have ridden in it and they are enthusiastic over its success.

Has 70 Horse Power Engine

The aeroplane is equipped with a 70 horse power four cycle engine of Mr. Whitehead's own invention. It weighs about 275 pounds and has a number of novel features, one of which is inlet valves inside of the exhaust valve. The machine, full rigged, has a surface measurement of 1500 square feet and the aeroplanes aggregate weight is 1200 pounds, providing considerably less than one pound to the square foot. The body is triangular, has an eight foot propeller on either side, revolving in opposite directions, with two horizontal rudders and two vertical rudders for steering. It is driven very much like an automobile and like all aeroplanes is equipped with wheels to run along the ground for a distance before it ascends in the air. Automobile wheels are used.

Chapter 7: Later Years

Great Automatic Stability

The aeroplane has an automatic stability feature for which great claims are made. Whitehead has demonstrated by experiments with models that the stability feature is possessed with an unusual degree and in this particular, it is tenfold superior to the Wright Bros. invention which has made so many successful flights. He says that it is impossible for his machine to upset and if there is any tendency in that direction the machine will right itself instantly.

He says that safety of aeroplanes and feels confident that it is only a question of a very short time when the use of aeroplanes will be general for their construction has progressed so far that their safety has been demonstrated.

Flying Machine Factory Soon.

"We will have a private trial before the end of the week," said Mr. Whitehead yesterday. "After that we will give the newspapermen a demonstration and a ride if they wish. My machine is a success and we are planning now to form a company to manufacture them. My idea is to have a factory erected in Bridgeport and to make the aeroplanes for the general public the same as automobiles are made."

"My machine is so simple that anyone can learn to operate it within a couple of hours and use it without danger. It will be no more difficult to operate than an automobile. The cost will not be great and I am not dreaming when I say that very soon the use of the aeroplanes will be common about Bridgeport. The capital is available and there is nothing to delay us."

At It for 15 Years

Whitehead has been studying the subject of aerial navigation for 15 years. For five years he worked in Baltimore and for ten years he has been at work in this city. He is an expert machinist and toolmaker and during his application to the problem he has made 65 models, having tried all kinds of aerial navigation with dirigible balloons, boat and cigar-shaped flying machines, and aeroplanes, the last mentioned form of airship being the easiest to fly in;.

At Greenfield Hill, where he lives *[Author's note: this is incorrect]*, he has a fully equipped machine shop, with lathes operated by a gas engine and a costly equipment. He keeps two machinists at work with him all the time and they are regularly employed working the same number of hours they would in a factory. They are enthusiastic over the aeroplane and having ridden in it themselves, are confident that Whitehead has finally been successful.

Praises Editor Beach

Whitehead said yesterday that Stanley Y. Beach was deserving of a large share of the credit for the success of the machine. "I had the ideas," he said, "but could not work them out without capital, which he furnished. Three years ago we met and I explained to him my idea and he placed confidence in me. He gave me financial support, and it was through the means placed at my command that I have been able to build this aeroplane. He obtained patents for me and I feel that he is deserving of great credit for what he has done."[487]

(end of transcript)

Gustave Whitehead: "First in Flight"

Whitehead was known to live in *Tunxis Hill* at the time of this article, *not Greenfield Hill* (both in Fairfield), which must have been reported in error. Whitehead flew at Mill Hill, near Greenfield Hill, and may well have made flights at Greenfield Hill itself, as the many steeply elevated areas in the region often became his flight locations, as did level areas, such the local beaches.

The patent referred to in the article is the "G. Whitehead Aeroplane Patent" applied for on Dec. 20, 1905, granted on March 10, 1908, consisting of an aerial navigation system that will maintain equilibrium in flight, which can sustain considerable weight. It consisted of a V-shaped body with tail and single set of wings extending "outwardly and upwardly" from sides.[488] At least partially influenced by Stanley Yale Beach, this design evolved from a type of hang-glider to a monoplane, by 1908 [489] and later, a biplane in 1909. [490] *The "Beach-Whitehead" Patent may be viewed in the Appendix.*

The above "St. Patrick's Day" article from the *Bridgeport Standard* of March 17, 1909 is particularly significant in that it was locally written and taken from obvious interviews, confirming that Gustave Whitehead and Stanley Yale Beach began their formal business relationship approximately three or four years earlier. This was much later than Whitehead's 1901-1903 most prolific flying period, when Beach had covered his progress as Aviation Editor for the *Scientific American*. These articles precipitated the beginning of several major falling-outs between the two men, both of whom had a reputation for wanting things "their way." By June 1909, lengthy descriptions emerged of a fiasco involving both Whitehead and Beach at the Morris Park, NJ aviation and Arlington meets, a larger falling out which occurred with Gustave Whitehead over disagreements concerning design differences for a flying machine that would not fly, after which Beach took legal action against Whitehead. This provided additional incentive for Beach's later retaliatory backlash against Whitehead's legacy in 1939, then fostered by Wright supporters, following the publication of Stella Randolph's book, "Lost Flights of Gustave Whitehead."

Figure 143: Beach-Whitehead Biplane – no wing coverings (circa Mar. 1909)

Beach-Whitehead biplane, circa March 1909, shown above, without covering for the wings and fuselage. Beach took Whitehead to court because he wouldn't attempt a flight on a Sunday with the aeroplane in this condition, above. Whitehead's first self-built home now on Ridgely Avenue in Tunxis Hill, at right. Whitehead stands at left. Below, the same machine with canvas covering over framework, described as having a sheet metal bow, circa late April 1909.

Chapter 7: Later Years

Figure 144: Beach-Whitehead Biplane with coverings (April 1909)

The April 1909 issue of *Aeronautics*, an emerging trade journal, covered the Beach-Whitehead aeroplane story[491], using nearly identical language to that of the *New York Times* article, of March 14th, adding that "a light float-feed carburetor is used." The machine was also described as "about completed, and the tests of the propellers to determine their thrust will be made in a few days." It included this photograph of the plane, which mysteriously appears in Fig. 143, without the canvas. Someone likely painted in the canvas for the magazine's deadline, to show it as it might look near completion.[492]

Figure 145: Beach-Whitehead Biplane, *Aeronautics*, April 1909

Gustave Whitehead: "First in Flight"

On May 16, 1909, a prominent local newspaper, the *Bridgeport Herald*, which had carried the exclusive eyewitness report in August 1901, concerning Whitehead's record-setting, half mile flight of the smaller monoplane, "No. 21," reported that Whitehead's latest flying machine was soon to be seen in a public exhibition. Since the inventor was widely known to be experimenting and making modest flights in the region for nearly a decade, the article was matter-of-factly presented.

WHITEHEAD FLYING MACHINE TO BE PLACED ON EXHIBITION
(*Bridgeport Herald*, May 16, 1909)
"Gustave Whitehead's flying machine, which has been in process of construction in a field on the Tunxis Hill road in Fairfield for the past year, will be moved this morning to West End park, where it will be placed on exhibition and the public will be enabled to get a good look at it. Mr. Whitehead is still experimenting on the machine, and expects to have things in such shape that he will be able to make an ascent some time this week."[493]

On May 23, 1909, the *New York Times* reported that a new machine constructed by Stanley Y. Beach and Gustave Whitehead would likely be amongst competitors for $1,000 in an upcoming "aerial carnival" later in the week sponsored by the West Hudson Aero Club at Arlington, New Jersey. The contest required a mile long flight, with a prize of $500 "for the machine showing the best construction, even if it did not get off the ground."[494] The Beach machine, as the Beach-Whitehead biplane was most often becoming known, would be featured in quite a number of news articles, through the spring.

Meanwhile, the May 27, 1909, the *Evening Statesman* of Washington reported that Stanley Beach was simultaneously developing a monoplane called the Beach-Hillman monoplane, with a balloon aeronaut, a Mr. Hillman, famous at the time for making 750 ascents in a balloon. This monoplane, not built by Whitehead, which had a 50 h.p. engine, appears to be the one to have gone over the cliff and crashed, at Lordship, in September of the following year.[495]

A June 6th article in the *New York Sun* explained that a major altercation between Beach and Whitehead occurred, apparently over Beach's choice of design for the Beach-Whitehead biplane (pictured above) before the "Arlington aerial carnival" meet and afterward. Whitehead took off with the engine and Beach had him jailed. It is noteworthy that Beach is described as the inventor, supporting the fact that Whitehead had been hired to build Beach designs at this juncture. Their failure can only be laid at Mr. Beach's feet. Beach, later interviewed by Stella Randolph in the mid-1930's, insisted that Whitehead worked for him and that he, Beach, was the inventor. Then, in 1939, after years of recognizing Whitehead's early, pre-Wright flights from 1903-1908, as author of numerous pro-Whitehead articles in the *Scientific American*, while he was its Aviation Editor, Beach claimed Whitehead's designs had never flown, despite his investment of 10,000. The truth was, Whitehead's own, early designs had made successful flights, but later, he could not make those designed by Beach fly – particularly a monstrous aeroplane that weighed far more than anything Whitehead had previously constructed. (See Chapter 8: Frequently Asked Questions: "Why did Whitehead's much larger aeroplanes fail to fly?")

"MONOPLANE OR TRIPLANE
Perfectly Lovely Airship That Would Not
Fly Causes Trouble for Inventors
(June 6, 1909, *New York Sun*)

At the Arlington aerial carnival, only one prize of $500 was awarded and that went to Morris Bokor for the best-constructed machine. Now Stanley Y. Beach, another inventor who arrived with a monoplane after the judges' decision is contesting the award on the grounds that according to the rules governing the contest, the decision was to have been given at sunset and that the award was made early in the day. But for a disagreement with Gustav[e] Whitehead, with whom Mr. Beach collaborated in the building of the machine, he would have been there on time. In the first place, Mr. Beach and Mr. Whitehead constructed a biplane. It had all the good points of a first class air ship except that it would not fly. It made splendid circles around the Morris Park track on wheels but it steadfastly refused to soar in the air as the inventors had believed it would.

Then a dispute arose. Mr. Beach insisted that it could have been a monoplane, while Mr. Whitehead maintained that the mistake had been in not making it a triplane. Mr. Beach was firm in his conviction, and without the consent of the other inventor went to work and converted the biplane into a monoplane. After he had finished the machine, to his dismay he found the engine was missing and so was Mr. Whitehead. He traced Mr. Whitehead to Bridgeport Conn where he had taken the engine. Mr. Whitehead was persistent in his refusal to give up the engine, unless Mr. Beach would agree to construct a triplane. Mr. Beach took the law in his hands and had Mr. Whitehead arrested and thrown into prison. Then there came a sudden change of mind on the part of Mr. Whitehead who said if Mr. Beach would have him released he could take the engine and build any kind of a plane he chose. However, repentance came too late to get the machine to Arlington in time for the $500 prize ..."[496]

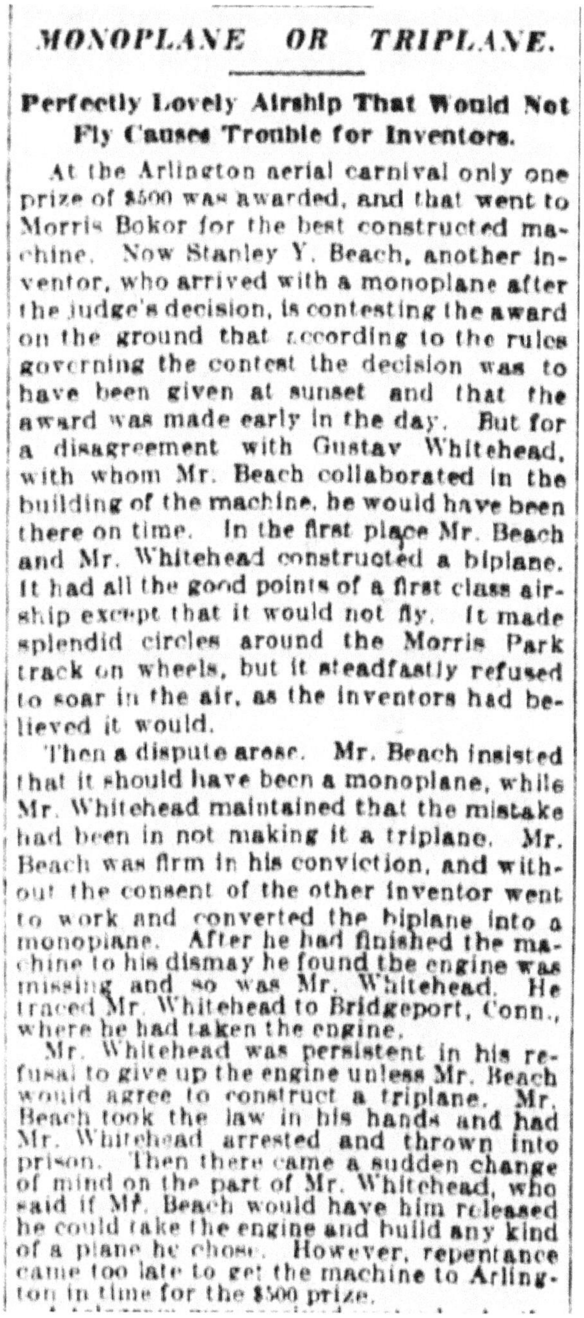

An end of the year, a *New York Sun* tongue-in-cheek article reveals that at the end-of-May meet at Arlington, NJ, Beach and Whitehead had a semi-final "parting of the ways," with Beach going elsewhere to build his next flying machine design, a monoplane that failed testing. The experiment was conducted at Morris Park[497], an old racetrack rented by the newly formed Aeronautic Society as a machine shop and testing location for its members to develop aeroplanes, following its 1908 breakup from the primarily dirigible-promoting Aero Club of America. The unsuccessful, non-Whitehead "Beach Flier," as his new monoplane was dubbed, was also exhibited at the Aero

Figure 146: Beach-Whitehead design dispute (June 1909)

New York Sun article describes Beach-Whitehead design disagreements, landing Whitehead in jail. (June 6, 1909)

Gustave Whitehead: "First in Flight"

Show at Madison Square Garden, in the fall of 1909[498].

As this aeroplane was larger and heavier than anything attempted before, by Whitehead, it was experimental and, unfortunately, failed. (see   Ch. 8: WHY DID WHITEHEAD'S MUCH LARGER AEROPLANES FAIL TO FLY?)

"AIRSHIPS THAT DIDN'T FLY"
(*New York Sun*, Dec. 5, 1909)

"Stanley Y. Beach and Gustave Whitehead built an aeroplane with which they hoped to win the $500 prize offered by the promoters…It proved a perfectly good aeroplane with the exception that it failed to fly. Thereupon the inventors fell out. Aeronaut Beach was convinced that the mistake was in making the machine a biplane. He insisted it should have been a monoplane. Aeronaut Whitehead was satisfied that the whole trouble was that they had not built a triplane. Aeronaut Beach took matters into his own hands, demolished the biplane and constructed a monoplane. When he had finished it he looked about for the engine and found that it was missing. Then more trouble started.

His partner, disgusted, had seized the engine. Mr. Whitehead vowed that he would never, never give it up until Mr. Beach consented to build a triplane. He kept his vow for a week but then his resolution broke down. He sent for his former partner and told him he could have the engine and build a monoplane or any other type he wanted to.

The engine arrived and Mr. Beach tried out his next scheme, and still his invention showed no birdlike tendency. It is housed at Morris Park and occasionally its inventor takes it out and runs it around the track on wheels …"[499]

A late 1909 article appeared in the "*American Review of Reviews*" entitled "*The Flying Machine of Today*" by Stanley Yale Beach. It was replicated in the *Nebraska State Journal* of November 14, 1909, explaining the state of the art, according to Beach, at the time, considered an expert on aviation efforts, due to his position at the *Scientific American*, if not at inventing or flying. In the article, Beach predicted, unlike Whitehead, that "the aeroplane" would "ultimately lead the automobile as a vehicle of sport." He generally described the types of monoplanes, biplanes, triplanes, and multiple-surface machines and their steering mechanisms then in use. For the past several years, Stanley Beach had presented to illustrious members of the early aero clubs on the topic of aviation and flight; his family's *Scientific American* Cup Trophy awarded to famed aviators such as Glenn H. Curtiss, since the spring of 1907. Beach was influential -- though not always thought well of -- an associate through his editorship and inner core aeronautical club affiliations with the Wright brothers, G. H. Curtiss, Alexander Graham Bell, Augustus Post, Earl Jones, Captain T. S. Baldwin, William Hammer, to name but a few. Beach was present for virtually all important flying meets and events during this period. Starting in the next decade of the new century, however, growing personal and family problems impacted Beach's ability to maintain his reputation and job at the magazine.

Beach's numerous *Scientific American* articles on Whitehead's early successes, and his later business association and falling-outs with Whitehead in the spring of 1909, as well as the embarrassment of his public ridicule in the newspapers due to aviation-expert Beach's failures to fly, sheds light on future comments he made about Whitehead. Stanley Beach's critical statement made three decades later, prompted and edited by key Wright defenders to seem even worse, was used by Orville Wright and his inner circle of supporters, virtually all "Whitehead detractors," and later, Smithsonian curators, up through the present date, to deny Whitehead's legacy as first in powered flight. The cleverly crafted so-called "Beach-Whitehead Statement," seeded in their soured relationship and Beach's own failures, would ultimately indirectly impact American aviation history, as those same individuals who designed the Statement with Beach also designed the label for the "Wright Flyer,"

Chapter 7: Later Years

three years later. The Flyer's label cemented credit for Orville and his flying machine as "first in flight," through what many consider to be a scurrilous legal agreement between Orville Wright's heirs, the United States and the Smithsonian in 1948, to obtain the famous Wright artifact, now the most popular exhibit at the Smithsonian. This "Contract" will be examined in future chapters.

On Thursday, August 19, 1909, the Wright brothers had filed their first patent lawsuit, "against the Aeronautic Society on the ground that the public exhibition of the Curtiss machine now owned by the society constitutes an infringement of their interests." [500] The patent suit would shortly extend out to many others, including Glenn Curtiss, with the Wrights' ultimate goal being to control world aviation, and have those who profited by it pay them a pricey royalty. The suit would eventually necessitate broad interpretation of the Wrights' patent rights, through vigorous, aggressive establishment of the claim that theirs was "a pioneer invention," that they were the inventors of the aeroplane, and to include use of "all horizontal surfaces" on any flying machine. The Wrights used every device available, including use of a subrosa Wright Company employee named William J. Hammer, who credited Wilbur Wright (not Orville) in the *World Almanac of 1911* with first flight, by arrangement with Wilbur and Orville. Hammer then testified as an expert witness on their behalf in key patent proceedings, entering the document into the court record, falsely denying he had any affiliation with the Wright Company other than testifying as an expert witness.[501]

It has been widely recognized that the Wright patent suit stifled further experimentation in America for the next decade, though not in other countries, like France and other parts of Europe, where their legal systems did not allow the Wright interests to prevail. In America, after August 19, 1909 and in the next several years, it became apparent to all, that to attempt to profit through building and selling or exhibiting and flying aeroplanes using the successful principles of flight, including the use of horizontal surfaces, meant you could become one of the growing number of unfortunate Wrights' patent suit targets. This was the beginning of the end for Whitehead's inventing efforts, in addition to the mounting, expensive legal problems he encountered with the impatient, wealthy, "aristocratic" members of the aero clubs who lived in Fairfield County, Connecticut and greater New York City, as they began to hire him to build their designs.

1910-1915 HELICOPTERS, LAWSUITS, FINAL INVENTIONS

The 1910 census for Gustave and Louisa Whitehead of Fairfield, Conn. was located by this author with some difficulty, due to it being misfiled in the national database, under the name incorrect last name transcription of "Whiteker." On the 16th of May 1910, Gustave was living "East of Mill River," with his growing family, in Lenox Park, Fairfield; his immediate neighbors were trades people and laborers - frequently, Hungarians. He resided in the increasingly comfortable but modest, self-built home there, with his wife of 12 years, Louisa, and their four children: Rose, age 12 (born in New York) and the rest of the children, Charles, age 11, Lilly, age 5, and Nelly, age 1, born in Connecticut. Gustave was then 36 and Louisa, 34. Gustave and Louisa were listed as immigrating to the United States in 1893 and 1894, respectively. Gustave's ancestry is recorded as "German," and Louisa's as "Aus. (Magyar) Hungarian." His citizenship status is categorized as "alien" vs. naturalized. Whitehead's occupation was that of a machinist working at "on his own accord" in his own shop. Louisa does not have an occupation listed. Both speak English, and can read and write. They owned their own home and had a mortgage.[502]

A further glimpse of Whitehead in the 1910-1911 period is provided by Wilfred Walsh, an eighteen year old hired to make parts for a helicopter project. On November 30th, 1966, Walsh, then in his 70's, was interviewed by Harvey Lippincott, President of the Connecticut Aeronautical Historical Association, about his employment with Whitehead. Walsh described Whitehead as a genial, quiet, no-nonsense sort of fellow, always busy - running to go somewhere or get some materials, a person he felt in awe of. He described conversations between Whitehead and Stanley Yale Beach, a frequent visitor to "the shop," then located behind Whitehead's Ridgely Avenue home in the Tunxis Hill section of Fairfield. On one occasion, according to Mr. Walsh, *Whitehead complained to Beach that he'd flown before the Wright brothers, but didn't get any credit.* Walsh said Beach accepted this statement at the time; he didn't deny it.[503]

During 1910, Stanley Beach was in and out of Whitehead's life as an interested and influential person and sometime employer. When Beach was demonstrating his planes, Whitehead was there, at least some of the time. When Whitehead obtained sponsorship or work on aeroplanes or helicopters, it was invariably with aviation-minded friends of Stanley Beach.

Figure 147: Stanley Beach's Flier - Monoplane (1910)

Above, one of Stanley Yale Beach's Bleriot-style monoplanes[504], of similar design as the Bleriot aeroplane which crossed the English Channel[505], was one of three owned by Beach, following the breakup with Whitehead. His 1910 flight trials and troubles with several monoplanes brought Whitehead back in the picture as an bystander and later that year, he again built an engine for Beach.

The *Bridgeport Evening Farmer* reporting on a recent failed trial of Stanley Beach's monoplane on the damp, soggy ground at Beach's duck farm, on February 1st that "Gus Whitehead, the well-known expert engine builder and aeronautic engineer, was among the spectators, and he was not hesitant in declaring the craft would not do. He and Beach recently had a misunderstanding that brought them into the courts."[506] Onlookers were unhappy that the plane failed to fly, and some jeered, "Fake!" at Beach, who vowed to keep trying. Four days later, the *Farmer* reported another try, with hundreds watching, that yielded clouds of smoke and flame arising from the engine, and a mishap with the propeller.

Beach was roundly ridiculed by the *Bridgeport Sunday Herald* Feb., 6, 1910, for taking this plane out on "Fresh Pond" in Lordship, a section of Stratford where Beach lived, skidding around on the ice, but not becoming airborne, with Whitehead observing. It is worthwhile to note that the Herald's editor at the time, Dick Howell, was the eyewitness journalist to Whitehead's flight nine years earlier, on August 14, 1901. The amusing account was illustrated with cartoons.

"Mr. Beach quickly impressed the spectators with the fact that he is an accomplished tinkerer. Under the skillful hand of Mr. Beach, the aeroplane was made to do everything but fly.… "

The article further provides background for some of the late 1909 troubles between Beach and Whitehead over the recent machine Beach had Whitehead build, which also failed to fly.

"One of the most sympathetic spectators of the series of ground flights was Gustave Whitehead. Mr. Whitehead has an aeroplane which flies similarly to Beach's machine. He and Beach had some trouble

Chapter 7: Later Years

over the Whitehead machine because Beach advanced him some money to carry on his experiments but finally announced that the machine was no good and demanded his money back."[507]

Lee S. Burridge announced, on March 29th, 1910, the building of a large shed at Mineola, Long Island, to be ready by April 15, for the aeroplanes and flying machines belonging to his fellow Aeronautical Society members, who would also have an acre to fly over, "1,000 feet would be steam-rolled for a starting point."[508] It was becoming "the thing to do" for the wealthy aeronautical club members to develop and own flying machines. Burridge would soon be hiring Gustave Whitehead to build him a helicopter.

In July 1910, in front of a large crowd of summer colony onlookers and Beach family and friends, the aspiring aviator and inventor, the former Whitehead customer, Stanley Yale Beach, bailed out of his "new" *non-Whitehead-built* Bleriot monoplane, just after launching, as it neared a cliff overlooking the beach near Point-no-Point at Lordship Park, part of Stratford, CT. The accident considerably damaged the flying machine, which had a 50 h.p. engine in it, also not built by Gustave Whitehead. Neither the plane nor the engine was made by Whitehead. Beach had set a goal of flying across Long Island Sound.[509] Attached to the monoplane was a gyroscope, to help balance it. The development of a gyroscope to help automatically stabilize and navigate an aeroplane became a passion for Beach, whereas Whitehead's designs were inherently stable, without need of an external device.

By early September 1910, Stanley Yale Beach, needing a lightweight motor for one of his three independently built monoplanes owned in the past year, once again, approached Gustave Whitehead to provide one. Whitehead agreed, and the two were reunited in a business endeavor, for the time being, at least.

"BEACH AND WHITEHEAD RECONCILED"
(*Bridgeport Evening Farmer*, Sept. 2, 1910)

"Burying the hatchet that has for more than a year been brandished with no little bitterness, Stanley Yale Beach, aeronautic editor of - the *Scientific American* and Gustave Whitehead, expert engine builder, have joined forces again and Whitehead has constructed an engine which Beach plans to install in a monoplane for the Harvard-Boston aero meet Sept 3 to 13. Mr. Beach heads the Scientific Aeroplane Co. of Stratford, a Connecticut corporation that has existed for several months. It is proposed to build machines and to furnish exhibition flights for fairs and other amusement enterprises.

The new motor Whitehead has just finished for Beach develops 30 h. p. and .weighs only 180 pounds. It Is a four cylinder, two cycle engine with distinctive features. Beach expects to be in the competitions for the $5,000 prize offered for amateur aeronauts. Mr. Beach expects to attempt a flight at Lordship park this afternoon."

A 1910 Beach monoplane, *built by a person other than Whitehead*, failed to fly later in the year, and eventually was wrecked when it went over a cliff at the beach in Lordship, Stanley Beach jumping out at the last minute, escaping with just a few bruises and scratches. A third monoplane, somewhat smaller, was built in France, and shipped to Beach, where he received it with grand plans to win prize money at air meets with prizes up to $80,000. One of the Beach monoplanes made several hops, but not much else. By 1912, Stanley Yale Beach would file for bankruptcy.[510]

Figure 148: "Whitehead's Effort 1910" photo 1 by Arthur K. L. Watson

Figure 149: "Whitehead's Effort 1910" photo 2 by Arthur K. L. Watson

"Whitehead's Effort, January 1910," above, a set of photos so labelled in a photo album belonging to Arthur K. L. Watson, son of an influential local family and Beach associate. Watson's father sponsored Whitehead for a short while. Whitehead continued with a version of the Beach-Whitehead biplane into 1910. Note single propeller design change. Eyewitness reports of brief Whitehead powered flights up through 1911 have been gathered by researchers, over the past 80 years. Photo albums discovered by then-Captain William J. O'Dwyer, US AF (ret.) emerged in early 1963.

In July 1910, Gustave Whitehead was reported to have sustained a serious crash in one of his flying machines. The *Boston Post* described it as follows, in an article carried in many newspapers, nationwide:

Chapter 7: Later Years

"MONOPLANE WRECKED IN A BRIDGE CRASH

Bridgeport, Conn., July 12. – Gustave Whitehead, a local aviator, had a narrow escape from serious injury today when he lost control of a monoplane in which he was attempting an ascent and the machine crashed into the side of a bridge, hurling him out and rendering him unconscious, but not seriously injuring him. The machine was wrecked."

In October 1910, Gustave Whitehead "the aeronautic engineer of Holland Heights" in his "machine shop" was engaged in building a flying machine made of "hollow steel tubing, using "wing-like devices which will feather" for Buffalo Jones, "ranchman, scout, huntsman, friend of Roosevelt, and inventor," using a device similar to a "water motor …recently displayed in the current running beneath Ash Creek bridge" and used on Mr. Jones' ranch for a windmill. Mr. Jones "says he only wants to be convinced that his scheme is impractical before he is willing to abandon it." [511]Jones had invented this machine and hired Whitehead to build it, similar to the agreement between Beach and Whitehead.

Starting in 1910, through 1911, Whitehead would again attempt a helicopter for a new sponsor - *ominously, a close associate of Stanley Yale Beach and William J. Hammer*. Whitehead's helicopter sponsor was the influential Lee S. Burridge, typewriter inventor, aviation enthusiast, and tycoon. Burridge helped found the Aeronautic Society in June 1908, with consulting engineer (and Wright promoter) William J. Hammer, *Scientific American* Aviation Editor and Whitehead-sponsor Stanley Y. Beach, part of a group of nine defecting from the Aero Club of America's aviation committee. Burridge was elected the Aeronautic Society's first President, serving from 1908-1909. The Society wanted to take more practical action to "push aviation to the front," especially concentrating on heavier-than-air machines, vs. lighter-than-air "ballooning," in America. In 1910, Burridge was the current Vice-President (1910) of the Aeronautical Society of New York, which had grown, in the first six months, from 9 to 150 members. It was comprised of mainly wealthy members who began to build heavier-than-air flying machines of various types, hiring aeronauts to pilot them and compete for prizes. Some, like Stanley Y. Beach, wished to begin building airplanes and marketing them. Starting in 1908, the Aeronautic Society rented Morris Park Racetrack in New Jersey, providing a shop with tools, sheds, machinery and large grounds, to encourage and support inventors of aeroplanes.

William J. Hammer, close associate of Burridge and Beach, was also a founder on the board of the Aeronautic Society. He had been working to promote the Wrights to the aero clubs, and helping them, behind the scenes, for years, to help them win their patent lawsuits. In May 1910, Hammer became an official, subrosa Wright Company employee. One of his tasks was to solidify the Wrights in the eyes of the court as "first in flight," to advance their patent rights as owners of a "pioneer invention" (see Appendix). Hammer frequently testified for the court on behalf of the Wright brothers, denying he had any other relationship but as their expert witness. He had already worked closely with Thomas Edison as his assistant, for years, and was familiar with patent wars as Edison had gone through a similar process. He began years before the first suit was brought forth, to help prepare his friends, the Wrights for "patent wars." Hammer was undoubtedly aware of the Whitehead flights which had been widely publicized, and had to see him as a threat to the title, "first in flight." Whitehead, whose early flights had made him famous, world-wide, in 1901, was not even mentioned in Hammer's "*Chronology of Aviation*," a summary of aviation statistics which credited Wilbur Wright as "first in flight" when it was first published in 1911's *World Almanac*. Since Whitehead was the only credible threat to the title, and much skullduggery was occurring behind the scenes to help the Wrights win their patent suits, it is not unthinkable that Burridge and Hammer may have cooked up a plan to oust Whitehead from the aviation scene entirely. Many of the Hammer communications with the Wrights were left out of their papers, donated to the Library of Congress, after being culled by Orville. *But William J. Hammer did not eliminate his copies of their communications.* These are currently hidden away at Smithsonian, under lock and key, providing a view the world has not yet seen, of what was done to help the Wrights became established as "first in flight," to help with their patent suits.[512] With all that

Gustave Whitehead: "First in Flight"

has been written about Wilbur and Orville, it is most telling that William J. Hammer's function has not been revealed. Gustave Whitehead undoubtedly had no idea what he was getting into, working for core members of the Aeronautical Society – but he was about to find out. *At the very least*, Burridge was Stanley Beach's friend, and Beach and Whitehead were at odds.

Burridge would ultimately sue Whitehead for not inventing a working helicopter quickly enough (in less than a year) for an upcoming competition that Burridge had set his sights on, *even though none had yet been successfully developed anywhere in the world.* The helicopter Whitehead invented did raise up on its restraints, up to four feet during tests, according to Harworth and local news articles. Whitehead indicated he needed time to develop a more powerful engine. This was not to be, for the curiously impatient Burridge would not wait. Gustave was not as adept at business arrangements as he was at inventing, it seems, for he made verbal agreements that came back to haunt him legally, time and again – or in Burridge's case, was said to have made. In addition, in 1910, since the Wright patent suits were in full swing, and the Aeronautical Society needed tools for their members' own flying machine shop, located at Morris Park, New Jersey, it is at least a possibility that this was a setup. When Lee S. Burridge became Whitehead's customer on the heels of the very public falling out with Stanley Yale Beach, the whole enterprise may have been a trap that Whitehead unknowingly stepped into.

The resulting cruel lawsuit Lee Burridge initiated in 1912, by early 1914 callously appropriated the helicopter and most of his tools, equipment, and contents of the workshop Whitehead had painstakingly developed, and was the source of his income, in payment for the debt, which was likely spent on materials for the helicopter and engines. In short, the lawsuit, starting in 1912, ruined Whitehead, striking the final blow for his aviation endeavors. It also humiliated him and helped break him financially. He later was to have been brought into the Wright patent lawsuit by the Curtiss defense attorney, possibly to testify regarding his own "first flights," but at the last minute, the judge determined it was not to be.

A local newspaper article from the *Bridgeport Evening Farmer*, previously unseen by modern eyes, describes portions of the debacle, which began with great vision and enthusiasm. This long, feature article, which appeared on page 1, reveals Gustave's changing attitude towards aeroplanes, in favor of a helicopter prototype which could be vertically launched, potentially solving the problem of not yet having airfields established for flying. Gustave's concern for engines that will not fail is based on wanting the pilot to live, something the wealthy but impatient Burridge seems not to either care about or understand.

"FLYING MACHINE THAT WILL
REMAIN STATIONARY IN MID
AIR IS WHITEHEAD'S CREATION

Holland Heights Engine Builder with Millions at His
Command, Is Perfecting Brand New Type of Craft
(June 20, 1910)
(emphasis added)

Picture a bumble bee magnified hundreds of times, capable of lifting much weight; stretch your imagination still further and imagine 60 such large creatures combining their strength to lift a big steel and aluminum ribbed frame from the ground, and then imagine 60 more, trained to do the bidding of a master, pulling the craft, free from the ground, hither and thither, and you have an idea of the unique flying machine that is now being completed at a cost of thousands of dollars in the machine shop of Gustave Whitehead in Holland Heights.

Nearer than ever before appears the realization of the dream of Whitehead, the German mechanical expert, the best part of whose life had been spent in striving to solve the problem of aerial

Chapter 7: Later Years

navigation. Satisfied that the aeroplane is an impractical device to make aerial navigation of utility, Whitehead has taken up the helicopter idea.

Backed by a multi-millionaire member of the Aero Club of America whose identity Whitehead is bound not to disclose, he has already spent thousands in purchasing the equipment for his machine. Fast it is nearing completion. By the middle of July if nothing goes amiss Whitehead expects to step into his car, turn a lever and ascend to any desired height. Then he will turn another lever and start forward. Speeding, backing, turning sideways, ascending or descending as he wishes these are the stunts that Whitehead will demand of his creation.

Gus Whitehead, as his friends best know him, is one of the most expert engine builders in the world. He has succeeded in turning out engines whose efficiency in proportion to their weight is marvelous. Years ago he was building engines for dirigible balloons. *Back in 1901 he made a flight in an airship of the aeroplane type, out near Fairfield beach, when he soared through the air for one eighth of a mile and astounded the few who were privileged to witness the unheralded trial.*

Whitehead's life for the past decade had been little else than a series of hardships and privations. Occasionally he obtained a listener as he unfolded his dreams of aerial navigation. Once in a while he would obtain a financial backer. But his headstrong persistency in carrying out his own ideas has almost always resulted in his losing the support of his partners and he has found himself time after time with a half-finished flying machine on his hands. No -less than half a hundred such has he built time after time, and each has brought its lesson.

Whitehead became convinced nearly a year ago that the aeroplane is impracticable. It is useless, he points out, to have such a device on your hands if you must first go by train along your proposed route to pick out suitable landing places en route. He knew that if one is to build a high fence many yards in diameter about a condor or an eagle, the bird is just as much a prisoner as if in a solid steel cage. The bird must first run over the ground to gain momentum before it can use its aeroplane wings to soar from the ground.

He watched big birds in flight, then he watched the humming birds that gathered in the flower garden near his little home in Holland Heights, and he decided at once that the humming bird is the model that must be followed in the construction of the airship.

Whitehead gained his knowledge of aeronautics not so much from books as from practical experience, though he has read practically everything that has ever been written about aerial navigation. He tested a certain type of helicopter and found -under certain conditions it would develop a pull of 25 pounds. This he adopted as his type.

But what good, he argued, are any amount of helicopters if your motor goes bad? Suppose you are one thousand feet or more above ground, what are you going to do when your spark, or your gas, or something else goes wrong? You're going to fall just as sure as Isaac Newton's apple.

So Whitehead decided it was safer to have a couple of engines available. He has completed one engine of a new type, which he calls the Whitehead motor, a four cylinder two cycle engine, which develops 100 horse power. The other is nearly finished. These are to be installed in the flying machine. Eventually he will probably have eight engines of 25 horse power each, five of which would suffice to sustain the machine. He plans to have 60 propellers, each developing a pull of 25 pounds to lift the machine and 60 to drive it forward or backward. The propellers have been turned out at the Fairfield Aluminum foundry. Each is ball bearing, and the transmission is made upon a silk cord capable of bearing 1,500 pounds. The silk cord, Whitehead says, is the most efficient means of transmission. "When you're walking," argues Whitehead, "you may feel a slight pain in your leg. You limp, favoring the limb. You have been warned that something is wrong. Maybe the pain disappears. II it grows worse you stop, perhaps for liniment, perhaps to rest. That's the way with a helicopter machine with eight engines. If one of the engines goes wrong, the others are sufficient to sustain the machine. If two fail, you take Warning and descend, because when the third one goes bad, you can't fly any more. The first engine break down is like the pain that reaches the man who walks. It's a warning. The second break means danger, and the third means that you must descend or take desperate chances.

Whitehead's engine cylinders are drilled out of solid bars of nickeled steel. The frame of the machine is made of steel, bronze and aluminum. The propellers are of aluminum. With the capital that has recently been placed at his disposal he has built and equipped a modern machine shop on his little piece of land in Holland Heights and three experts are working every day hurrying the machine to completion.

Whitehead's dogged persistency, despite his seemingly overwhelming obstacles has been at times almost pitiable. With none but his faithful little wife and his children to cheer him in his toil, he has spent every cent he could make from his engine building
in fashioning out model after model of aeroplane and eventually of helicopter. At times he has deprived himself of the absolute necessities of life to buy fuel for his engine or material for his devices. Finding it too expensive to pay house rent he gathered a little money, built a story and half house in Holland Heights and here he slapped together a few rude timbers to form the skeleton of his workshop.

Now the little home has been supplanted by a modern two story house, and the machine shop has grown to imposing proportions. Inside the shop glistening and bright are the parts of the airship and the framework, like the skeleton of some antediluvian monster, awaits the installation of the motors to speed away."[513]

Figure 150: Whitehead's Helicopter (1911)

A closeup of Whitehead's 1911 helicopter, under construction in Holland Heights behind his Ridgely Avenue house (today's Tunxis Hill).

Chapter 7: Later Years

Figure 151: Whitehead's 3rd shop and helicopter at Ridgely Ave. (circa 1910-1911)
Photo courtesy of Fairfield Museum, O'Dwyer archives

During this period, Whitehead, gifted in mechanical aptitude and engineering, though not in business, increasingly made errors that impacted him financially. According to a current family member, her father told her his grandfather, Gustave was said within the family to be "too trusting, as was the family," in those days. He was described as "an open, trusting" individual who often made verbal arrangements, and each time, this seemed to cause difficulties when dealing with "businessmen" who were far more calculating than he was. [514]Time and again, he found himself in court over disagreements with sponsors who would then confiscate the work he'd engaged in with their money. In addition, in later years, his wealthy aeronautic club member sponsors appeared to frequently be those who wished to make a quick profit and self-aggrandize, portraying themselves as the inventors. The demands they made of Whitehead to produce quick results were neither realistic nor safe, following these would place him and anyone in the airship in danger. Eventually, with the major upset with Aeronautical Society members Stanley Yale Beach and Lee S. Burridge, by 1915, Whitehead found himself "at the end of the line" – finished with his dreams; for all purposes, finished with his aeronautical pursuits. The Wright patent suits had also made it clear that anyone attempting to build an aeroplane using any of the features that would cause it to be successful (as they claimed ownership of all of these) would be sued. Whitehead just couldn't afford to lose the last home he had placed his family of four children in. The decline of the inventor may painfully be seen in these surviving documents.

From February 29 through March 4, 1911, the *Bridgeport Evening Farmer* covered a story, unearthed during the research for this book, concerning a prospective aerial contest involving Whitehead and another aviator. On February 29th, *the Farmer* announced that "Whitehead May Fly on Saturday," describing him as an expert builder of gasoline engines, who expressed an interest in competing in a local aeroplane contest with "Aviator Frank Paine" at Seaside Park, for "half of the purse" in prize money. The funding had been raised by "Professor Atlas," using an aeroplane entirely "built in Bridgeport," every inch, even to the smallest particle, furthermore it is made on designs of Mr. Whitehead's own invention, and even the engine was made in Bridgeport, at Mr. Whitehead's shop."[515] An article on March 1st from the same newspaper, telling its readers that "Mr. Whitehead has put his monoplane in shape" … it is "a flying machine" which is "a very small, very light monoplane, something on the type of a Lilienthal glider. It has an extremely powerful engine mounted on it and Mr. Whitehead's chief concern is that the engine may prove too powerful for it... He said he would not make any foolish promises … If I fly, well and good; if I don't, why then I'll take my machine home and say nothing." The ground at Seaside Park was to be "rolled down" to smooth it for the prospective flying machines.[516] On March 4th, the Farmer ran a front page feature article on the contest, which was to have been "from Seaside Park to Steeplechase" but which ended in a serious accident, wrecking Paine's flying machine and sending him to the hospital. The Farmer interviewed Whitehead, who was unable to make the flight attempt following the mishap.

> "Gustave Whitehead, who was scheduled to take part in today's festivities until the unfortunate accident to Paine set the plans all awry, said to the Farmer today that he will attempt to make a flight some time next week, not at Seaside Park, but in some other, more , suitable part of the city. So long as his machine is all in trim, he feels that he may as well give it a whirl before putting it away again. "Those things are part of the risk of the business," said Whitehead, in referring, to Paine's accident; "his machine was not powerful enough to surmount those trees at the park."[517]

Once again, it appears that Whitehead had missed a chance to make some substantial money for his family. He'd have even worse problems in the coming year.

Figure 152: Whitehead – Burridge in Court, article (1912)

Chapter 7: Later Years

(*transcript*)

"Whitehead, Who Builds Airships
Appears In Court"
Bridgeport Evening Farmer (May 8, 1912)

"Gustave Whitehead, the well known Airship builder, was in the Superior court this morning as defendant in a suit brought against him by Lee S. Burridge, a wealthy New York resident. Burridge claims Whitehead failed to deliver a rotary motor according to the terms of a contract.

It is alleged that Whitehead had a conference with- Burridge 'in New York, and received $260 upon condition that if the motor was not completed as agreed upon, Whitehead was to pay Burridge the sum of $1,250 which had previously been advanced.. The motor was not completed and suit was brought for $1,500. Whitehead admits having a conference with Burridge but says .he did not agree to have the motor completed within a certain time.

Judge Burpee reserved decision."[518]

(*end of transcript*)

Notably, the article verifies that Whitehead is well known in the region as an "airship builder." The amount Whitehead was ordered to pay is equivalent to $31,288 in 2015 dollars.

"Whitehead Must Pay $1,240.27:
Judge Burpee Finds Against
Airship Builder in Suit
Brought By Lee S. Burridge"
(May 14, 1912)

"Gustave Whitehead, the local inventor who has experimented a great deal in building airships, must pay $1,240.27 to Lee S. Burridge of New York, according to a decision handed down today by Judge Burpee of the Superior court. Burridge claimed Whitehead failed to complete a motor as he 'agreed and therefore bound himself to pay $1,250.

It was alleged that in July 1910, Burridge loaned Whitehead $1,000 while the inventor was working on the motor. Later he loaned Whitehead $250 with the understanding that Whitehead could keep the $1,250 if the motor was complete in three weeks, but if the motor .was not complete and ready for use in that time Whitehead must pay the; entire amount. Burridge said the inventor did not complete the motor. He asked for $1,600 damages."[519]

The financial burdens kept spiraling downhill. Just a few months earlier, Gustave and Louisa had been sued by another person after borrowing a sum of money equal to a bit more than a year's salary, which they also found they could not repay in time. They had been sued in March 1912, for that.

"AIRSHIP INVENTOR
SUED FOR $500"
(*Bridgeport Evening Farmer*, March 12, 1919)

"Sheriff Ellwood yesterday served papers in a civil suit brought by Elmer F. Blank against Gustav and

Gustave Whitehead: "First in Flight"

Louise Whitehead for $500. The case is returnable at the Court of Common Pleas at the April session. The papers allege the non-payment of a loan made to the defendants by the plaintiff. *The defendant [Gustave Whitehead] is well known throughout this section and attained national reputation by inventing an airship a few years ago.*"[520]

In the Fairfield, Connecticut Town Hall archives, the following documents showed a prior attachment of the personal property of Gustave Whitehead held against his debt to Lee Burridge, incurred during the building of a helicopter engine.

"Know All Men By These Presents:
That I, Gustave Whitehead, of the Town and County of Fairfield in the State of Connecticut, for the consideration of Twelve Hundred Fifty Dollars ($1250.) received to my full satisfaction of Lee S. Burridge of the City, County, and State of New York, do hereby bargain, sell, transfer and convey unto Burridge, the following articles of personal property, Viz:
One (1) helicopter flying machine known as my make "xx";
One (1) Lathe, Lucius W. Pond, Mfr., Worcester, Mass;
One (1) Shaver, Bliss & Williams, Brooklyn, New York, makers;
One (1) Hack-saw machine, one other Lathe built by Windsor Mfg.
Co., Windsor, VT.
One (1) Emery Wheel Machine, one other Lathe also mfd. by Lucius
Pond;
One (1) Planer, Thayer, Houghton & Co., Worcester, Mass. Mf'r's.

One Otto gasoline engine with fly wheel, also all pulleys, belting, shafting therewith and corrected thereto, together with one four cylinder motor, and all parts thereof same being a motor for flying machine, all situate in my shop and shed on the premises of Louise Whitehead in the Town of Fairfield" (p. 123)

".... whereas the said vendor is justly indebted to the said vendee in the sum of Twelve Hundred Fifty ($1250.) Dollars, as evidenced by his promissory note and agreement of date herewith, payable to the order of the said vendee, with interest, said agreement calling for the completion of a certain motor as more particularly described therein....if said note and agreement shall be well and truly paid and kept according to its tenor, then this deed shall be void, otherwise to remain in full force and affect."

(8th day of October A.D., 1910) (p. 124)

A later document shows that the helicopter was finally remanded to Burridge by early February 1914. By May 1914, the Whiteheads were out of their home on Ridgely, purchasing a new piece of land at Alvin Street in May 1914, where they shortly after commenced to construct their final home together. Gustave must have named the street "Alvin Street" using an Americanized version of his middle name, "Albin."

"Feb. 7, 1914
Lee S. Burridge vs. Gustave Whitehead
Superior Court
Fairfield County

Chapter 7: Later Years

This may certify that the attachment on one certain flying machine known as a "helicopter" in the above entitled action, is hereby released.

Lee S. Burridge
by Edward K. Nicholson
his attorney.

A true copy of the original
Received for record Feb. 9, 1914.
at 9:07 o'clock A.M.
ATTEST: xxxxxxxxxxxx"
(Town Clerk.) (p. 8)

Lee Burridge died one year later, leaving an estate in the amount of $94,000, valued at $2,271,070 in 2015 dollars. It is quite obvious that Mr. Burridge did not need to destroy Gustave Whitehead as a person and his means of making a living. Burridge's actions were soon to be judged by a higher authority.

From this period forward, Gustave Whitehead experienced severe financial troubles, never again to work as actively on his aeronautic inventing. The records show one more plane built and exhibited in 1915, in New York. He worked on automobile engines and invented several additional devices, unrelated to aviation, sporadically. His home was listed in the local business directory in his teenaged son's and wife's name, likely due to legal issues. During the period of World War One, being German had to have presented difficulties for Gustave, as some Germans found themselves discriminated against, and feared deportation. The Connecticut Military Census of March 3, 1917 lists Gustave Whitehead living in Fairfield, occupation as machinist, with no other trades, aged 43, height 5' 9," weight 175 lbs., married, with 6 people dependent on him for support. He answered "no" to being a citizen of the United States, and "no" to taking out his first papers (to become naturalized). His nationality was listed therein as "Brazil," with no military service in any country. The census lists Whitehead as having a disability, "1 eye" problem (*of indecipherable type*), can drive a car, operate a steam engine, experience with high speed gasoline engines, and is a good swimmer.

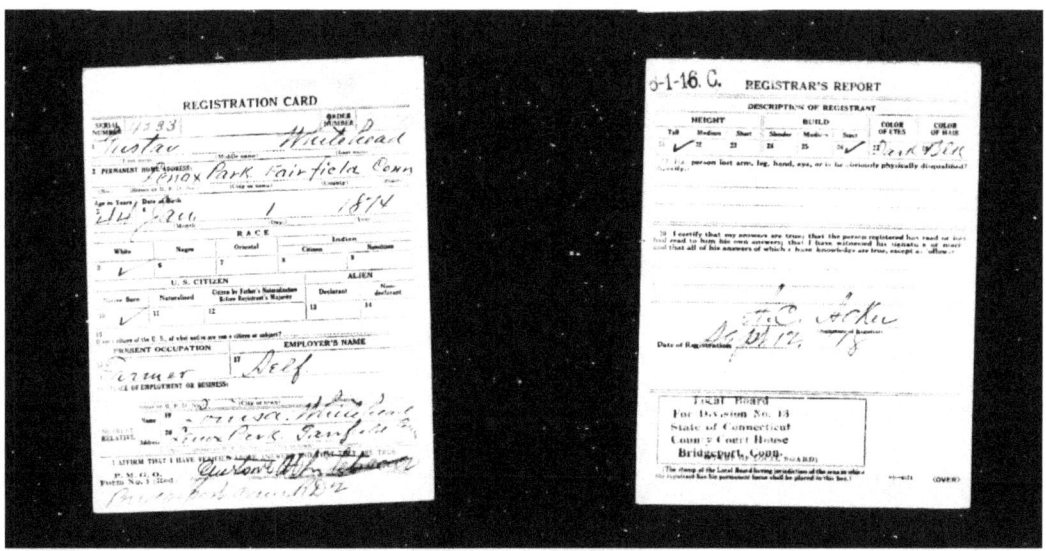

Figure 153: Draft registration documents for Gustave Whitehead, 1918

Gustave Whitehead: "First in Flight"

Whitehead's draft registration card from September 12, 1918 spells his first name in the German manner, "Gustav," showing his occupation to be that of a self-employed farmer. He was described as living in "Lenox Park" (the original name for the Alvin Street, Holland Hill area now called Tunxis Hill), "native-born" (the safest answer, undoubtedly), aged 44 years, height was tall, his build, stout, with dark eyes and black hair. Louisa Whitehead, his wife, is listed as Gustave's nearest relative.

The Whiteheads do not appear to have been included in the 1920 census, though it is possible that it was misfiled under another name, as was the 1910 census. It is also possible that Gustave Whitehead became increasingly concerned about repercussions to residing in the United States for over three decades, adopting it as his country, but without becoming naturalized, with the war breaking out and anti-German sentiment rampant. Fear of deportation or other possible negative outcomes might have driven the Whiteheads to avoid the census.

The local business directory of 1923 again lists Gustave as a machinist, living at Alvin Street, near Lenox Road, where he resided through his death in 1927. The 1927 directory lists no occupation. A newspaper ad seen in the *Bridgeport Telegram* of August 25, 1923, on page 23, shows Gustave Whitehead listed amongst those involved with the International Bible Student Association giving lectures on the aftermath of the Great War, seen by them as creating chaos in the world, leading to Armageddon. Whitehead, with family members still in Germany, must have been quite upset during and after the war. During the early 1920's, a visiting, now grownup associate, Junius Harworth, wrote Stanley Yale Beach that he was shocked and saddened to find Gustave Whitehead a mere shadow of his former self.

With increasing health conditions, including a blinded eye pierced by a stray piece of metal at work, and heart problems which culminated in an untimely death at age 53, in 1927, Whitehead gradually disappeared into history, for most of the next 90 years.

Chapter 8

FREQUENTLY ASKED QUESTIONS

WHITEHEAD DESIGNS - WHY DID THEY CHANGE?

Gustave Whitehead formulated a lifelong habit of continual experimentation with flight. He was unafraid to try a large number of approaches to what he envisioned as experiments leading to practical, manned, powered flight, in accordance with his goals, which included commercial airplane development and competition at the St. Louis Exposition of 1904 (also known as the World's Fair of 1904).

Upon arriving in Bridgeport, Whitehead soon began improving his bat-like "No. 20" machine, constructed and flown in Pittsburgh, Pennsylvania in the spring of 1899, though it ended in a crash against a building, the flight said to be for half a mile.[521] He began to construct an improved, but similar monoplane, "No. 21", in late 1900, readying it for unmanned test flights by May short manned hops through July and a longer set of sustained flights in August 1901. Following this success, and several more reported flights, Whitehead began improvements using a similar bat-like monoplane design for "No. 22", which purportedly made two sustained flights over Long Island Sound in Jan. 1902; the longest, allegedly, a circular flight of 7 miles. That plane was destroyed by the winter weather, and No.'s 23 and 24 followed, by December 1903, described in the *Aeronautical World* issue of that date.

The enormity of what Whitehead had accomplished with his first manned, powered flights did not seem to be recognized, especially by Whitehead, himself. His inventions, even his successes, were looked upon as a series of experiments. He was never satisfied, as what he visualized flight should be was never to be accomplished in his short lifetime, though virtually all of it was to occur in the future.

Contributing factors to the changes in design over time, and the gradual decline of Gustave Whitehead's success in flying appear to be related to his belief, confirmed by those who worked with him on the planes, that his successful model, the bat-like machine, or "The Bird" as he called it at times, was not commercially practical, nor was it able to lift off and land vertically or be easily navigated, as he imagined it should. New designs were necessary.

> In talking with a Herald representative Mr. Whitehead said:
>
> "I will never give up trying to make a flying machine that will be practicable and of commercial value. It is easy to make flying machines that will fly, but they are toys and of no practical use.

Figure 154: Whitehead will never give up practical, commercial flying machine (1903)
Bridgeport Sunday Herald, **May 31, 1903**

In May 1903, Whitehead said, "It is easy to make flying machines that will fly, but they are toys and of no practical use." He does not appear to focus on the fact that no one else through that date had been successful, in the history of the world, in creating and flying powered airplanes. For him, inventing was about practical success with commercial applications - being able to transport people to distant places. To accomplish this, he'd have to develop a design with enough lift to accommodate a group of passengers.

As Whitehead increased the power of his engines, he also changed the design of his planes. A prolific inventor; as early as spring, 1902, he was working on an early helicopter prototype, according to Junius Harworth[522], one in 1906 with Howard Booth, and another helicopter developed from 1910 to 1911, built for a customer, Lee Burridge. At the start of this project, in 1910, Whitehead, always the visionary, was interviewed by the *Bridgeport Evening Farmer*, referencing design changes due to difficulties in an era with no airports or places for suitable horizontal takeoffs or landings …

> "Whitehead became convinced nearly a year ago that the aeroplane is impracticable. It is useless, he points out, to have such a device on your hands if you must first go by train along your proposed route to pick out suitable landing places en route."[523]

When Whitehead set his sights on competing at the St. Louis World's Fair of 1904's Aerial Competition and exhibitions, he had to change his designs to be able to follow the ever-changing, stringent rules and regulations crafted by the contest's planners – requiring overly optimistic navigational controls to allow tight circuits and long distances, eventually shown to be basically unsuited for any airships of the era – especially heavier-than-air flying machines.

Gustave Whitehead was also unable to pursue his own designs to the extent that was needed, lacking the funds. Significantly, once the Wright brothers' patents were granted, well understood from the press at the time, Whitehead could have been included in the infringement lawsuits *for use of his own inventions, necessary for flight*. Stanley Yale Beach, Aviation Editor for the *Scientific American*, was available on a regular basis. Whitehead would have received updates about the granting of the Wright patent and its impact on other inventors. Whitehead's brother John has indicated that his brother Gus was upset when he read about the Wright brothers' flights, losing a lot of his motivation to invent on his own. The news of the Wrights' flights, which were exaggerated at first, also impacted the motivation of his assistant, Anton Pruckner.[524]

John described Gustave's feelings about the Wright patents, the first obtained in May 1906, but filed on March 23rd, 1903 and expanded to several others, for an automatic stabilizer (Feb. 1908), yaw control (Feb. 1908), vertical rudders (Feb. 1908), and a mechanism to flex the rudder (July 1908).[525] John Whitehead said,

> *"My brother was surely bitter when he heard that the Wright Bros. got a patent on the very ideas we intended to patent and was told we had to demonstrate the possibility first. Perhaps they got them rightly*

Chapter 8: Frequently Asked Questions

after proving them a success. After the Wright Bros first demonstration [likely 1908, at Le Mans, France] *my brother became very er[r]atic in his further work pertaining to Flying Machines in fact he only finished and tried only one machine while I was just in Bridgeport up to spring 1911. I have given you some details of this machine in my former letter."*[526] [Author's note: this would likely have been the Beach-Whitehead biplane, from the period 1908-1909]

From then on, the world's first successful airplane inventor would most often work for others, building lightweight engines to sell, and flying machines often not entirely of his own design. There are sporadic reports of successful powered flights at low altitudes, for short distances, up through 1911.

Major William J. O'Dwyer, US AF (ret.) world authority on Whitehead for 45 years, had this to say about his designs:

"Whitehead eventually dropped his monoplane and tried bi-planes, tri-planes, gliders, etc... being influenced by the successes which now engulfed him, by other pioneers. Yet none of his work is so meaningful as his monoplane series. In our minds, he was one of the more brilliant men of his day and a Nostradamus of the aircraft era."[527]

O'Dwyer further adds, "This craft ["No. 21", incorporating past designs and continuously modified] offered more practical application capabilities than any other known or tried. His convictions are today's realities. We have seen the bi-plane and tri-plane evolutionary steps retire into antiquity."

Designs Timeline:

1895-1899 Designed and experimented with large kites and an assortment of aircraft, including an ornithopter and gliders in Boston, gliders in New York and finally, a powered flying machine in Pittsburgh. Heavily influenced by designs of Lilienthal and Count d'Esterno.

April/May 1899 Pittsburgh, Pennsylvania - Using steam-driven (No. 19 or 20) monoplane, first manned flight with passenger, 1/2 mile, ended in crash 20 feet high against a building (reported by passenger Louis Darvarich).

1901 Bridgeport, Connecticut built "No. 21," bat-winged powered monoplane, successful shorter manned flights summer of 1901 in Bridgeport, sustained higher altitude flights on August 14, 1901 in Fairfield and Lordship (Stratford, CT) - up to 1.5 miles distance (reported in *Bridgeport Sunday Herald*, Aug. 18, 1901 and by witnesses Anton Pruckner and Junius Harworth, and in local and regional newspapers following these flights).

August - Oct. 1901 New shop and then factory formally set up to build bat-winged powered monoplanes with sponsor Linde (reported in multiple local and regional newspapers).

1902, Winter. Lordship (Stratford, CT) long, sustained circling flights over Long Island Sound in "No. 22", improved bat-winged powered monoplane (reported by multiple associates of Whitehead and Whitehead in his letters to *American Inventor*, April 1902). Later, briefer (1/4 mile) circuitous flights during winter or early spring, 1902 at Milford, CT.

1902 First helicopter attempted (according to Junius Harworth)

1902 – December. Working on biplane with movable wings and adjustable aeroplane surfaces, altering angles using levers with compressed air for steering a circular course; rudder likewise moved by compressed air controlled by levers (announced in the *Aeronautical World* of December 1902, and according to Gustave's brother, John).

Gustave Whitehead: "First in Flight"

1903-1904 Triplane glider with motor and propellers added, flew successfully, reported in *Scientific American*, Sept. 19, 1903 and *Bridgeport Daily Standard*, October 1, 1904. Being developed for World's Fair of 1904.

1902-1906 Built and flew monoplane, biplane, and triplane gliders and aeroplanes, with and without power (documented by multiple witnesses, news accounts, and in photos). In 1904 it was reported that his 1903 powered glider had flown, by multiple newspapers, including the local *Bridgeport Daily Standard* of Oct. 1, 1904. The *Sheridan Sun* reported, on April 21, 1904, that *Cassell's Magazine* ran an article that included a description of Whitehead making successful flights in a powered triplane glider.[528]

1905 G. Whitehead Aeroplane Patent applied for (Dec. 20, 1905), *granted on March 10, 1908*, consisting of aerial navigation system that will maintain equilibrium in flight, and to sustain considerable weight. V-shaped body with tail and single set of wings extending "outwardly and upwardly" from sides.[529] Thought to be influenced by Stanley Yale Beach, this design evolved from an early, inherently stable hang glider to a monoplane, by 1908 [530] and later, a biplane in 1909. [531]

1907-1911 Built, flew, and attempted flights with powered monoplanes and biplanes (documented by multiple witness reports of flights, news accounts, and in photos - no photos survived of flights). V-shaped fuselage, *larger flying machines being attempted, but failed.*

1908 Built and attempted flights with patented Albatross glider / monoplane prototypes with and without single engine and propeller (stationary photos available) but no specific information on its success with power, although witnesses do report viewing short flights during this period.

1910-11 Built and accomplished short tethered (4 ft.) elevation of 60-bladed helicopter, unmanned (documented by witnesses). News accounts, and photos exist showing helicopter on ground. Required a more powerful engine which Whitehead was not allowed to develop before being foreclosed upon.

1915 Entered an airplane at Hempstead, Plains, NY, the last time his inventing is seen in the public record.[532]

WHY DID WHITEHEAD'S MUCH LARGER AEROPLANES FAIL TO FLY?

Figure 155: Lightweight monoplane "No. 21" made flights of up to 1.5 miles (1901)

Chapter 8: Frequently Asked Questions

Figure 156: Beach-Whitehead Biplane exponentially larger and heavier (1909)

In the later years, particularly during the 1907-1909 period, when Gustave Whitehead and Stanley Yale Beach, his latter-day sponsor, were attempting to develop a larger commercial-style aeroplane, suitable to transport people and freight, he was unable to construct a final product which could successfully fly, beyond minor hops. The final plane design, impacted by Beach's influence, was large and cumbersome. It appearing much like more modern airplanes, but could not make successful flights comparable to Whitehead's earlier (and lighter) powered aircraft. It has been said that if Whitehead really flew earlier, his later planes would have been improved and flown even more successfully. Wouldn't they? The answer is, "No," due to simple scaling laws well known today, but apparently unfamiliar to those involved in early aviation.

The author posed this question to aerodynamics expert Joe Bullmer, who worked for the US Air Force at Wright-Patterson AFB in Dayton, Ohio, as an aircraft performance engineer, for most of 31 years. Mr. Bullmer has a Master's Degree in Aeronautical Engineering from the University of Michigan. He has an understanding of technical aspects of very early aircraft, including those of the Wright brothers, gained through investigations for his book, *The WRight Story*.

Q: Why wouldn't Whitehead's much later, heavier aircraft fly?

[Author's note: emphasis added]

A: (Bullmer): "You could say there are three major segments to aircraft design, *aerodynamics (including flight control), structures, and propulsion*. These three major design areas are affected in different ways by *upsizing* a vehicle.

If a shape is made twice as big in its lengths it becomes four times as big in area and eight times as big in volume. For instance, to make a cube like a dice twice as big in all its dimensions you'd have to place another like it next to it. Then you'd have to place two more alongside of those, and finally four more on top of those four. So to make the shape twice as big it would entail four times the area on any side and eight times the volume. Any shape, even an airplane, follows this rule in a general sense. Aerodynamic forces, both lift and drag, are proportional to the areas of an airplane. So since doubling the vehicle's lengths increases its areas by a factor of four, aerodynamic forces on it will increase by roughly the same amount.

Making it twice as big in its lengths will result in it having roughly four times the surface area and eight times the volume. This increase in volume, and the corresponding increase in carrying capacity, necessitates roughly eight times the structure and structural weight given the same materials. Actually achieving this can become quite difficult in complicated things like aircraft when structural shapes start intruding on the spaces required for other shapes.

The effects of *upsizing on power* can be even more complicated. A vehicle whose structure and payload weights have been increased by a factor of eight obviously must develop eight times the lift. But, as we just saw, its areas, including wing areas, have only been increased by a factor of four. To develop the extra lift required it will have to fly faster. Unfortunately, flying faster to double lift also results in doubling drag. So now, with four times the area and twice the drag just due to speed, the thrust required to push the airplane through the air is increased by a factor of eight.

But for propeller airplanes the power problem is even worse than that. Power is actually thrust times speed. Horsepower required is the thrust required to overcome drag times the speed at which the vehicle is flying. We just saw that the thrust required was eight times as much but, on top of that, the speed was increased, actually by about 40 percent. *The result is that the horsepower increase required to propel an airplane whose size in all dimensions has been doubled is roughly a factor of eleven!*

Of course, these are general arithmetic rules and many factors can mitigate these requirements to some degree. But *in the earliest days of flight, those involved in aviation, including both Whitehead and the Wrights, didn't realize the true implications of making vehicles bigger or faster."*[533]

WHY ARE THERE GAPS IN THE HISTORICAL RECORD?

Much of history is pieced together from what survived after it happened, using all available primary sources (first-hand evidence: people with direct knowledge, a document or recording created by or with such a person - including interviews, witness statements and affidavits, original documents from the era, in-person newspaper interviews, statements and letters written by Whitehead, photos taken at the time, etc.). We identify reliable secondary sources (sifting through second-hand evidence: what people wrote and said about Whitehead who were *not* on the scene or who may have repeated what appeared elsewhere, newspaper articles based on Associated Press reports, or books using primary sources that discussed what happened).

At the time of his flights, Whitehead was not intent on gaining fame or recognition. He was conducting experiments in flight, leading up to the development of a practical, commercially viable airplane. At times, as did other inventors, such as the Wright brothers, Whitehead would avoid public displays for a variety of reasons, including safety and securing privacy for his unpatented inventions.

The *Bridgeport Sunday Herald* eyewitness account is singularly most important as a primary source document, as it was written and published within days of the first flight by a reporter who was on the scene. Subsequent authentic articles based on in-person interviews with Whitehead or containing Whitehead's letters or statements that appeared in Bridgeport, CT and New York newspapers, the *Scientific American*, and trade journals such as the *American Inventor* and the *Aeronautical World* are invaluable primary sources. Statements by immediate family members and his associates, those who lived in the neighborhood and worked with him or observed flights are valuable primary sources. Many of these were authenticated further as sworn affidavits.

It must be remembered that Whitehead died early, and unexpectedly, at the age of 53. Evidence has been found that he kept some plans and other records of his experimentation. His family reported disposing of much of what existed after his death - before the first researcher arrived, seven years later - at the town dump, not realizing its historic value. In addition, Whitehead's last shop was destroyed in a fire.

Chapter 8: Frequently Asked Questions

We are indebted to Stella Randolph and Major William J. O'Dwyer, USAF (ret) for obtaining and preserving witness statements, obtaining affidavits and locating what artifacts and records *were* left, starting in the 1930's (Randolph), and extending into the 1960's through the 1980's (O'Dwyer). These activities were conducted while a number of witnesses were still alive, though decades later.

However, the entire record could have been obtained, from the beginning, had our nation's historians been interested in documenting what Whitehead was accomplishing, rather than engaging in their own aviation projects or self-aggrandizement. Historically, Whitehead researchers have been subjected to attacks by those who should be helping to preserve history. Those with information who have sought to turn it over to the Smithsonian for evaluation have been met with ridicule and rejection. Junius Harworth, Whitehead's associate for 14 years, reported having spoken at length with Ernest La Rue Jones, US Army Aviation Historian, and Smithsonian Aviation Curator Paul Garber about Whitehead; even filing design plans with Jones for Whitehead airplanes "No.'s 21 and 22," which subsequently were placed in Garber's care. Yet Garber later denied having the plans.[534] A current search of Smithsonian archives online produces not one file on Whitehead or Harworth. Where are the notes from these contacts? Where are the plans Harworth submitted? It is unknown whether others also contacted Smithsonian about Whitehead on their own, and met with failure or dodges. Interviewed on CBS' "60 Minutes" in 1987, a then-young Peter Jakab, still a present-day curator at the Smithsonian, explained laughingly that a 98 year old woman had written him saying she'd been a passenger in Whitehead's plane.[535] He didn't accept the statement, wasn't convinced by it, nor, did it appear, did he follow up on it. This type of mindset has been present for 112 years at the Smithsonian. As it turns out, Whitehead did take passengers on his planes, even in the earliest years. Where is that letter? Where are others that might have been sent? Where is the photo evidence that Smithsonian unreasonably demands? Is it, as some think, within the walls of Smithsonian's archives?

The book, "*History by Contract*," co-authored by O'Dwyer and Randolph, published in 1978, thoroughly documents the dodges and maneuvering by Smithsonian's curators as they strove mightily to avoid any proof Whitehead might have flown prior to the Wrights, avoiding examination of the historic record, though they were charged with doing so.

A great deal of what might have been preserved has been lost through the passage of time - some items thrown out, others lost in fires, still others disappeared through carelessness, accidental or deliberate negligence. Even that which *has* been gathered is now scattered in separate archives - one must travel to Texas, Connecticut, or Germany to try to obtain access to the archival records concerning Whitehead, gathered by Randolph and O'Dwyer. Despite long-term plans to establish one central file at the Connecticut Aeronautical Historical Association (CAHA)'s headquarters in Windsor Locks, CT, this was not ultimately successful. It should be noted that Randolph's archives are not fully accessible to the public at the University of Texas at Dallas, in what proves to be a revealing embarrassment for that venerable institution. During Randolph's and O'Dwyer's respective lifetime[s], their research was openly made available to each other, additional Whitehead researchers and interested parties, the Connecticut Aeronautical Historical Association, and offered to the Smithsonian repeatedly, for decades. O'Dwyer's files are fully accessible to the general public for study, located at the Fairfield Museum, in Fairfield, CT. There is currently only one Gustave Whitehead (Gustav Weisskopf) museum; it is in Leutershausen, Germany.

All of Whitehead's flights were not covered in local news, there were so many that occurred on a regular basis, in 1901-1903, in particular, when the media was notified, it likely became "old news." Some of the flights were considered quite modest and impractical, therefore, not newsworthy – something the Wrights ran into for years. All possible witnesses were not located and statements taken, as decades passed before this was undertaken. If certified witness statements had been taken at the time of each of the witnessed flights, we would have had many hundreds, or even thousands, to work with, as Whitehead flew over entire neighborhoods, at times, and performed demonstrations for crowds.

Yet, thanks to the research conducted to date, despite all problems encountered, enough evidence remains to show Gustave Whitehead succeeded with powered flight on numerous occasions, several years before the Wrights, and went on to successfully, if modestly, fly his other powered aircraft designs though at least 1911.

WHY WASN'T WHITEHEAD RECOGNIZED FROM THE BEGINNING?

Current day

Dr. Tom Crouch, a Smithsonian Senior Curator for the National Air and Space Museum, is a native of the Wrights' hometown, Dayton, Ohio; educated at Wright State University. In April 2013, Dr. Crouch published his position on Whitehead online, entitled "The Flight Claims of Gustave Whitehead"[536], where it resides on the Smithsonian website at this writing, two years later. Taking a look at his brief explanation helps illustrate "the Smithsonian attitude and culture" when it comes to Whitehead, which I must point out, once again, is a direct threat to Orville Wright's title of "first in flight" and the Smithsonian's ownership of the Wright Flyer. Crediting Whitehead could also undermine all the misinformation pumped out to the public about the Wrights history. It could harm book sales, too, for certain Smithsonian curators, including Dr. Crouch, have been hard at work writing and selling books about the Wright brothers for thirty years, increasingly glorifying them, a profitable bandwagon many other historians have been quick to join. In providing the Smithsonian position, your author's responses are contained within brackets [ ].

Dr. Crouch gives the following reasons *why he thinks* Whitehead's flight claims are false, which reveal he doesn't know the facts in Gustave Whitehead's history, nor does he understand how the inventor worked or thought:

[*emphasis added*]

1. ***Questionable* news articles reported Whitehead's flights.**

[Author's note: the most prominent local sports editor was an eyewitness and other 2 other Bridgeport newspapers confirmed the flights of summer, 1901, as did those in neighboring towns and cities]

2. **Much testimony for and against the claims**

[Author's note: Actually it was only one questionable person's denial vs. 18 trustworthy eyewitnesses, any other testimony against did not come from contemporaries present in 1901-1902]

3. **"A supposed photo of "No. 22" in the air" not seen since 1906**

[Actually, the photo was taken in 1901, of "No. 21" in flight – last seen in 1906, its viewing at an Aero Club of America exhibition documented in the *Scientific American*]

Dr. Crouch goes on to explain that "supporters of the claims have been arguing in favor of Whitehead for many years, while the critics, like me [Crouch], have been *vigorously refuting their evidence*" [Author's note: apparently, "playing defense"]. Then he provides examples of why he doesn't believe Whitehead flew, which further illustrate his own confusion. He criticizes Whitehead for having built two gliders in 1897, which he showed to reporters. Dr. Crouch implies one is a copy of the Chanute-Herring triplane hang glider of 1896, and the other, a "bat-like" winged machine "that would have been much more frail than the sturdy, braced triplane wings." Dr. Crouch then explains that in 1901-1902, Whitehead "claimed' he flew later versions of that bat-winged prototype: the first, claimed on August 14, 1901, flown for a half mile, and the second "later claimed to

Chapter 8: Frequently Asked Questions

have flown "Number 22, a heavier version of his basic design with a metal structure, for flights of two and seven miles over Long Island Sound." [Note: there is no evidence that Whitehead used a metal structure to accomplish those flights, as "No. 22" began in stages, ending prematurely with a broken engine, ruined by weather, by spring, 1902.] Then, quite *amazingly*, without further explanation, Dr. Crouch makes *the leap* to say, "They ["No. 21" and 22] represent a step *backwards* from the trussed beam structure of his Chanute-Herring glider"*[my emphasis], though in the next breath, he asserts the triplane glider is obsolete, just one or two years later.* In the next paragraph, Dr. Crouch moves on to cite a September 1903 *Scientific American* article; he interprets it, explaining Gustave Whitehead had gone on (in 1903) to build a new version of the Chanute-Herring triplane hang glider, which Dr. Crouch now says is "eight years old and obsolete", asking why Whitehead would resort to this, if he had flown successfully in the bat-winged monoplanes, No.'s 21 and 22. Then he poses the question, "Why did Whitehead not call the attention of the readers of the *Scientific American* to his claim to have flown a very different powered machine over considerable distances less than two years before?" The illogical question hangs, and is not answered by Dr. Crouch. Perhaps your author should point out that Gustave Whitehead *was not writing the article*, and that the *Scientific American* Aviation Editor who was writing it, Stanley Yale Beach, went on to credit Gustave Whitehead's early flights in 1901, numerous times through 1908 in the *Scientific American* (until the point they'd had a major disagreement). Lastly Dr. Crouch makes the incredible, unsupported assertion that "over the next decade, Whitehead would continue to build aircraft for other enthusiasts. *Not one of those powered machines ever left the ground.*" He concludes with his oft-repeated mantra, "*either Whitehead had somehow forgotten the secrets of flight, or he had never flown a powered machine at all*," ending with a statement criticizing Whitehead for not keeping records of his experiments, noting that the Wrights kept "detailed notebooks, letters and photographs …," then displays the "famous Wright photo" at the bottom of the article, showing Orville entering his failed flight at an altitude of 18 inches, and "rests his case," having given the entire analysis one page.

One hardly knows where to begin. It is obvious that Dr. Crouch is not aware of the actual facts concerning Whitehead, which is troubling, since Smithsonian certainly has the resources to have fully investigated his history, a cry that has gone out directly to them, over the past 52 years (but alas, there is the Contract standing in the way), and before that, by Junius Harworth and others who knew or researched Gustave Whitehead, for the preceding three decades. Yes, Gustave Whitehead was experimenting with a bat-winged monoplane for at least five years – and which finally worked well in 1901, four years into that progression. But Gustave considered it to be "a toy," too impractical for commercial uses, like transportation of people and goods, and troublesome to use, when launching using wheels, in an era with no airports. It also would not be able to meet the unfolding criteria (requiring far more maneuverability) of the World's Fair Aerial Committee to win the grand prize, which he sought from 1902-1904.

The current cursory Smithsonian analysis reveals that its curators do not understand that, unlike the Wrights, Gustave Whitehead was an astonishingly prolific inventor, who worked on and flew multiple flying machines in rapid succession and even simultaneously, during the same period. He tried out many different designs, for his own reasons, which were appropriate and made sense to him, at the time. It seems presumptuous to attempt to impose our current day suppositions on historical figures without, at least, an attempt to understand why they thought and acted as they did, within the context of their own personal realities. Gustave was limited by finances, also, and he didn't have the hindsight we do, today, to know that his "bat-winged" aeroplane design would rise much further - into the future as an early prototype, in so many ways, of today's aircraft. That does not mean he did not fly before 1903, or that he didn't make some modestly successful powered flights all the way through to 1911, according to witnesses! Whitehead's flights are *better* documented than those of the Wrights; their documentation was not produced till long afterward, in 1908 and beyond. It was *all self-generated*, by two legally-minded men, who wished to completely control and profit from all aeroplane manufacture and flight, worldwide. This book covers much of what Gustave Whitehead did and thought, and why it made sense to him, something the Smithsonian has never been interested in, though they were, literally, begged to do investigate Whitehead's history, for decades.

Gustave Whitehead: "First in Flight"

In taking this position, clearly, Senior Curator Crouch *dismisses the very sincere eyewitness accounts of 18 Connecticut residents* whose testimonies, most under oath, stated they'd seen Whitehead fly before December 1903. He is discounting the early *Scientific American confirmations of these early flights,* and local Connecticut media support which is published in this book – much of which has been available for three decades. Instead, Dr. Crouch apparently uses the statement of one questionable eyewitness with a grudge, James Dickie, who denied the flight of August 14, 1901, only after 37 years, as his sole source of evidence. Dr. Crouch does not mention the standard Smithsonian fare for denying Whitehead's claims: Orville Wright's "The Mythical Whitehead Flight" article of 1945; the contrived "Beach-Whitehead Statement" of 1939 which provided content for Orville's writings; the Smithsonian –Wright Agreement of 1948, written by those contriving the previous two (all of which are covered in this book); or the 1970's unpublished monograph by a London historian hired by Smithsonian to attack Whitehead's "flight claims," *though these are all lurking just beneath the surface, comprising the sum total of the evidence the venerable institution has historically used against Whitehead.* He does not mention that the Whitehead replicas/reproductions have successfully flown up to a half mile, but those of the Wright Flyer won't leave the ground.

The usual fare from Smithsonian is the question, *"Did Whitehead forget how to fly?"* One might respond, *"Have Smithsonian's curators forgotten how to investigate history?"* The bottom-line is that Smithsonian's curators cannot prove Whitehead didn't fly before the Wrights – and they should certainly not approach the subject with that objective in mind. "The Smithsonian Institution was created by Congress in 1846 as 'an establishment for the increase and diffusion of knowledge.' " [537] Basically, one might ask, how has it investigated Gustave Whitehead, before diffusing knowledge, and if so, where is the information coming from? Where is the proof of such investigations?

The information presented in this book may be used to help the Smithsonian take a more serious look at Gustave Whitehead and credit him for his earliest flights, which preceded those of the Wrights. If the Wright Flyer must revert to the heirs, as some have pointed out, it was *second* in flight, after all. Since it is not entirely original and some question whether it is, at all, a reproduction of the Flyer could replace it. A Whitehead "No. 21" reproduction could grace the National Air and Space Museum entrance quite well – and bring in even more visitors – in fact, it could even be *flown* on special occasions, not possible for the Wright Flyer or any of its copies. It is likely that an appropriate title can be thought of for both. Whitehead was "first in successful powered, sustained flight." The Wrights weren't first, but they did help develop a practical airplane, later in the decade, as did the also-greatly-maligned Glenn Curtiss, and many others, who should all be recognized correctly, finally.

A brief overview of Smithsonian-Whitehead activity:

1901 – 1940

Smithsonian, the nation's bastion of historical information, was intent on feathering its own nest during the time Whitehead was making his early flights, and this attitude persisted for the next half century, through the end of the 1940's. Secretary Samuel P. Langley, head of the Smithsonian at the time of Whitehead's pre-Wright flights, was a direct competitor of Whitehead, many thousands of government dollars were funneled into Langley's attempt to produce the first viable airplane for the US Army. Langley's staff noticed Whitehead's flight claims, but rather than examine these in a professional manner, in September 1901, a "spy" was sent to view his plane, on display in Atlantic City, to gather details which might be helpful to Langley and his assistant, Manley, for his own project. The Smithsonian didn't even formally recognize the Wrights' claim to "first in flight" till 1948, as it continued to laud Langley's efforts and failed plane, until that time. Gustave Whitehead's successful flights were written about in at least two hundred media outlets of the early 1900's, but faded away in public memory, by at the end of the first decade of the new century. His accomplishments and recognition were

Chapter 8: Frequently Asked Questions

replaced by media coverage of the practical development of the aeroplane by the Wrights and many others, with strategic public promotion of the Wrights in place.

Stella Randolph and a professor of economics at Harvard who specialized in the aviation industry, Dr. John B. Crane, both asked Congress - and Randolph additionally wrote the President of the United States - to request Congressional or other hearings to examine the Whitehead evidence for first flight, in the late 1930's. These hearings never occurred while living witnesses were still available. Dr. Crane's examinations concluded that short successful powered flights by Whitehead undoubtedly occurred in the period before the Wrights flew.[538] He penned Louise Whitehead, wife of Gustave,

> "I have written to Dr. Zahm, head of the Library of Congress, Aeronautics Branch, telling him that I am convinced your father (sic) [husband] made short flights."

1940 – present

In the 1940's, Dr. Albert Zahm, a governmental expert in the aviation field, and again, Dr. John Crane, wrote that more inquiry was necessary. No official investigations were made. Junius Harworth was in direct communication with Paul Garber, founder of the National Air Museum, sending him information and drawings of Whitehead's flying machines, described in letters to Stella Randolph, through 1962, when Harworth did. Where is that information now? Garber told Harworth, it had been "lost"[539]. In the 1960's, 1970's, and 1980's requests for Smithsonian and Congressional inquiries by Major William J. O'Dwyer, USAF (ret) were made, along with requests for nullification of the *Smithsonian-Wright Agreement of 1948*, seen as a major stumbling block to nonbiased evaluation. In the 1960's, Smithsonian's then-Assistant Director, Paul Garber even participated in one interview of an important Whitehead flight witness and assistant, Anton Pruckner, but afterward, Garber was, for a short while, only willing to credit *later dates* Whitehead had flown (On June 7th, 1968, in a Smithsonian National Air and Space Museum weekly staff meeting, Harvey Lippincott reported that Garber said Whitehead was an aviation pioneer worthy of recognition and that *he could* credit him with 1903-1908 flights, even though the witness had described *pre-1903 flights*, perplexing the researchers, till they learned about the Contract-factor, in 1976, which would preclude recognition prior to Dec. 17, 1903.) Smithsonian's crediting of Whitehead never happened, formally, though, and over the years, have used words like "hoax" and "fraud" referring to his flight claims. In 1968, Smithsonian's Director, S. Paul Johnston, sent a letter to Maj. William J. O'Dwyer, Whitehead researcher, denying that a mandate to endorse anyone's accomplishments existed and stating that Smithsonian was entirely objective[540]. Randolph repeated her request for a Smithsonian hearing in 1978, joining with O'Dwyer, in their coauthored book, *History by Contract.* No hearings occurred. In the 1980's, the state of Connecticut requested hearings, none occurred. In the 2000's, requests for nullification of the *Smithsonian-Wright Agreement of 1948* [541] has been made by this author to the Smithsonian Board of Regents, which includes the Chief Justice of the Supreme Court, Vice President of the United States, and members of Congress[542]. Silence was the reply.

There has been no indication that the Smithsonian has any interest in changing the status quo, despite mountains of evidence available. The Smithsonian (and all its affiliated museums and research facilities), under a legal contract (signed in 1948) to deny all other contenders for "first flight" in order to maintain the Wright Flyer as an exhibit, has denied Whitehead for 112 years with biases and dodges of various sorts. It is no wonder that the state of Connecticut, some world authorities on early aviation, and independent experts, as well as the Governor of CT, and members of the CT State Legislature, are not waiting for Smithsonian's approval. Many have concluded Whitehead was "first in powered flight," based upon voluminous supportive information, increasing in quantity over the past 80 years; with the previous and most recent research evidence and findings now presented in this book. It will be up to the citizens of America and beyond, to take a look at the evidence,

© Susan Brinchman, 2015

and decide what *they believe* occurred, and undoubtedly there will be discussion for a long time to come, on this topic. Ultimately, perhaps in another time yet to come, Whitehead will receive "his due": worldwide recognition as "first in powered flight," including at the Smithsonian.

DID WHITEHEAD CONDUCT SCIENTIFIC EXPERIMENTATION?

While not a scientist by training, Gustave Whitehead was systematic in his approach to the problem of flight, from the time of childhood through adulthood, when he captured, tethered, and studied the flight of birds[543]. He employed methods that involved careful analysis of what had been attempted before by others as well as his own experiments, as evidenced by books on the topic of flight and artifacts found in his shop and home, given to Stella Randolph, researcher, in the 1930's. He sketched, drew up plans, conducted mathematical analyses planned his improvements with his assistants, built experimental models, then gliders, testing these extensively from hilltops and sloping fields. Finally, Whitehead would add power, in the form of lightweight engines he constructed, carefully testing the resulting heavier-than-air powered flying machine first unmanned, towed, tethered, and then in free flight manned, in short hops on streets and in fields close to the ground, that increased in distance and elevation, over a period of about six weeks. To conserve materials, he often used components from older models for the new ones. Whitehead built and experimented with various types of engines including those using gas, kerosene, and steam. He even set up, with Junius Harworth, his young assistant, "a power plant in a barn to test the efficiency of propellers and fans of various sizes"[544] and a "wind-wagon" used to test engines and propellers. Gustave Whitehead was systematic and methodical, which undoubtedly contributed to his successful first flights.

DID THE WRIGHTS VISIT WHITEHEAD?

This question has been hotly contested by supporters of the Wrights, over the past 80 years, and vehemently denied by Orville Wright. Whitehead's contemporaries say *the Wrights did visit* the increasingly famous Whitehead, and took away information that may have been used in the construction of their own flying machine or engine.

Whitehead flew numerous times in the coastal and nearby towns of Fairfield County, Connecticut, USA, starting in August 1901, before the Wrights "flew" in Dec., 1903. His success was carried in a hundred or more newspapers and trade journals internationally. According to witnesses and Whitehead himself, both Wilbur and Orville Wright came to his shop several times, learning about Whitehead's "secrets of flight" in the years before their own powered flight attempts at Kitty Hawk. Octave Chanute, the Wrights' mentor, knew of Whitehead and referred the brothers Wright to him as an excellent source for a lightweight motor. Stanley Yale Beach, Aviation Editor for the *Scientific American*, having met and written about both Whitehead and the Wrights, was another likely potential link for information to flow back and forth between the three inventors, and perhaps, for a visitation. Inventor Simon Lake was a good friend of the Wrights, who lived in Connecticut, nearby. It has been said that they visited Lake, and went to see Whitehead.

Octave Chanute, expert for the World's Fair Aerial Competition and chief mentor and advisor to the Wrights, first heard of Gustave's aeronautical work during Whitehead's employment with the Boston Aeronautical Society at the Blue Hill Meteorological Observatory, when Chanute donated $50, in the summer of 1896, towards the construction of an early Whitehead glider. In June 1901, Chanute became aware of Gustave Whitehead's lightweight engines from Carl Myers, a balloonist, and also, undoubtedly from the press coverage for "No. 21," including an early June issue of the *Scientific American*. Chanute recommended that the Wright brothers investigate Whitehead's engine for future use in their box-kite-based glider, in a letter to Wilbur Wright, on July 3, 1901.

Chapter 8: Frequently Asked Questions

"I have a letter from Carl E. Myers, a balloon maker, stating *that a Mr. Whitehead has invented a lightweight motor* and has engaged to build for Mr. Arnot of Elmira 'a motor of 10 I.H.P. to weigh with supplies for 2 hours and accessories about 30 lbs. as estimated'... Mr. Myers talks of applying it to his Skycycle."[545]

Wilbur wrote Chanute back, indicating interest in the Whitehead engine, and in the same letter, admitted that he and Orville actively seek out and utilize the ideas of others in their own invention. In his response to Chanute, written on July 4, 1901, Wilbur made two very significant points pertaining to Whitehead. *Wilbur shows great interest in the Whitehead engine Chanute referred the brothers to.*

"*The 10 horse power motor you refer to is certainly a wonder* if it weighs only that, thirty lbs with supplys [supplies] for two hours, as the gasoline alone for such an engine would weigh some ten or twelve lbs thus leaving only 18 or 20 lbs for the motor or about two lbs. per horse power. *Even if the inventor miscalculates by five hundred per cent it still would be an extremely fine motor for aerial purposes.*"[546]

In the same reply to Chanute, the competitive, secretive Wilbur also explains how he feels about reliability and discretion concerning workers he is poised to employ and in general. He *adds that his brother and he naturally do incorporate what they learned from others in their own work.*

"We of course would not wish our ideas and methods appropriated bodily, but if our work suggests ideas to others which they can work out in a different line and reach better results than we do, we will try hard not to feel jealous or that we have been robbed in any way. On the other hand we do not expect to appropriate the ideas of others in any unfair way, *but it would be strange indeed if we should be long in the company of other investigators without receiving suggestions which we could work out in such a way as to further our work.*"[547]

Irreconcilably with the Wrights' famed, future legal stance taken against those who were accused of "stealing design ideas," Wilbur has explained that he wouldn't even mind if others appropriated aspects of the Wrights' own inventions – perhaps to justify his explanation, given 'in the same breath', of how the Wrights exploit the ideas of others.

Written on the same page as his discussion of the Whitehead engine, it is not hard to imagine that the Wrights set their sights on Whitehead as early as July 1901, following Chanute's communications about his lightweight, powerful engines and prominently placed press coverage of the Whitehead flight experiments in May and June 1901. Articles and insider information leading up to the World's Fair activities would have informed them further.

Cecil Steeves, an eyewitness and close acquaintance of Gustave Whitehead as a teenaged helper, recalled the Wrights' visit to Whitehead, in the early 1900's. He related the event in a taped interview conducted by then-Captain William J. O'Dwyer, USAF (ret) on Sunday, Jan. 2, 1966, when Mr. Steeves was nearly 80 years of age. Steeves was first interviewed by Whitehead researcher Stella Randolph in 1936, when he was 49. He asserted both times that the Wrights did indeed visit Whitehead's shop, around 1901. Steeves, born in Jan. 1887[548], was approximately 14 - 15 years old at the time of "the visit," old enough to understand and recall it, years later.

"Mr. Whitehead then moved his shop to Cherry Street, where he continued to do his experimenting ... It was here that the Wright Brothers visited Mr. Whitehead during the early 1900's coming from Ohio and under the guise of offering to help finance his inventions, actually received inside information that aided them materially in completing their own plane. I was at the shop with him when they arrived and waited outside while they talked inside. After they had gone away Mr. Whitehead turned to me and said, "Now that I've given them the secrets of my invention, they will probably never do anything in the way of financing me." [549] [550]

On January 2, 1966, Cecil Steeves was interviewed by then-Capt. William J. O'Dwyer (USAF), Whitehead researcher. Present was Albert E. Burr.

"[O'Dwyer] – I would like to have you, with the sincerest effort you can make, describe what you had been talking with us about earlier today, "the fact that the Wright brothers were here." What age were you at that time? And could you recall anything about that visit that you claim was connected with their journey here to Bridgeport?

[Steeves]. – I can start right off by saying that I know the Wright bros. were here because I saw them. You can't take that from me. I was on vacation at the time, and I was visiting with Whitehead in his shack on Cherry Street. This was sometime in late August I would say.

[O'Dwyer] – About what year was it, Mr. Steeves?

[Steeves]. – I can't recall whether it was 1900, late, or 1901. I don't recall.

[O'Dwyer] – It was right after the turn of the century?

[Steeves]. – That's right. It was very, very dull; it had been raining; it was a very wet day. I was visiting Whitehead, who was going over one of his drawings and he was talking at this particular time about this drawing. I was very much interested likewise as I took a profound interest in mechanics. A knock came at the door. Whitehead opened the door, and the shorter, stockier of the Wright brothers said, "Mr. Whitehead?" And he said, "Yes?"

And he said, "We are the Wright brothers. Did you get our message?"

Whitehead said, "Yes. I did. But I didn't expect you to come." He said "We are here to talk to you about the proposition we sent you." (I believe there may have been a telegram sent to Whitehead at that particular time. Either a telegram or a letter.)

[O'Dwyer] – They had sent a message that they were coming?

[Steeves]. – Sent a message announcing that they were coming.

[O'Dwyer] – Did they have anyone else with them?

[Steeves]. – No.

[O'Dwyer] – Just the two of them?

[Steeves] – Just the two brothers. And after they went inside I immediately walked out and I stayed out there only about three feet away from the shack until they left, which was about three-quarters of an hour later. And they said, "All right, Mr. Whitehead, you will hear from us. We must get that six o'clock train for New York." Those were the exact words that they said. They said, "We are in a hurry." So they walked away very, very fast. I imagine they came from the railroad station on the trolley car and went back on the trolley car. They had to walk up to State Street to get the lift out of here.

Whitehead said, "Now that I have shown them how I am going to fly they won't give me one dollar."

[O'Dwyer] – Do you know whether they ever came back again?

[Steeves] – Not to my knowledge. I don't know. Maybe they did.

Chapter 8: Frequently Asked Questions

[O'Dwyer] – Now, you heard the name Wright brothers from them?

[Steeves] – Yes.

[O'Dwyer] – Now, I am not trying to confuse you, I am only doing something other people have done to me. Different researchers and historians I have encountered thought it was possible, because this was 1901, or 1900 or in that vicinity, right up to even 1903 --- that is – a range of three or four years, just in a matter of speaking, for discussion – Is it possible that the name Wittemann Brothers could have been the name that was used rather than the name Wright brothers?

[Steeves] – No. After that I saw many photographs of the two men published in magazines and newspapers. They were the same two.

[O'Dwyer]. Now again, you said you are 79 years old.

[Steeves]. That is right.

[O'Dwyer]. Trying to do some quick arithmetic here – 1900 you were about 14 years old. What year were you born?

[Steeves]. About 1887. [*Author's note: January 30, 1887*]

O'Dwyer. Then you were about 13 or 14 years old. [*Author's note: 14 ½ in August 1901.*] So I would say that you were reasonably old enough. You were not a child.

[A. Burr]. At 14, I can recall many things. Very clearly!

[Steeves] The words I have expressed are the words that I heard.

[A. Burr] The very closest to the words that you can recall?

[Steeves]. That is right.

…(further discussion)

[Steeves]. ….he did have other people that were in the newspaper game, reporters and so forth [visit]…

[O'Dwyer] You did see some of his plans. Would you say that he was working on plans before the Wright brothers were there. He had some plans he was going over. Do you recall – you said you were interested in the plans – Do you recall what those plans were?

[Steeves]. At that particular time he was drawing up a motor which he thought would be ideal for his plane.

[O'Dwyer] Did he ever mention – did you hear outside the shop any of the conversation?

[Steeves]. I could not….

(*further discussion*)

[O'Dwyer] we do know on the other hand, no less than 3 or 4 people who have sworn that they were here and met him…

(*further discussion*)

[O'Dwyer]. For the record, and stepping out of my every day character as a civilian, in the stature and position which I hold in the Air Force, and as a Captain in the Air Force, I'd like to have you place your hand on this holy Bible, this is our family Bible, and I'd like to have Mr. Al Burr as witness that Mr. Steeves did put his hand on this Bible and will swear to the testimony which he just gave. Will you put your hand on the Bible please, your left hand, and raise your right hand. Do you swear, Mr. Steeves, that the testimony you just gave that Orville and Wilbur Wright were the ones who entered the shop of

Gustave Whitehead: "First in Flight"

Gustave Whitehead in the years or approximately 1900-1901 is true to the best of your knowledge and ability?

[Steeves]. I wish you'd use the word "shack" instead of "shop."

O'Dwyer. I will go [with] that. Call it a shack.

[Steeves]. – I do.

O'Dwyer. So help me, God.

[Steeves]. So help me, God.

[O'Dwyer]. This is important, Mr. Steeves. Because …

[Al Burr]. It is a very important little ceremony.

[O'Dwyer]. I don't think this should be taken lightly.

[Steeves]. I'm too old a man to try to tell falsehoods.

[O'Dwyer] No this is not the case. I didn't feel that you would tell a falsehood. It is this, that someday, someone who is going to be sitting down … They respect acts like this. They are simple acts but they say an awful lot.

[Burr] Hmm.

[O'Dwyer]. I feel that people who listen to a tape or tape recording have to rely on something, and when you get someone to swear on a Bible that this is the truth then you don't sit back and challenge it too easily.

[Burr]. Yeh." [551]

Albert E. Burr, a member of the Connecticut Aeronautical Historical Association (CAHA), was invited to be present during the interview with Steeves, "to verify the interview and evaluate Mr. Steeves as a witness." He noted in a letter to CAHA President, Harvey Lippincott, written the same day as the interview, that the taped session lasted 1 1/2 hours and that Mr. Steeves "had a clear, keen mind" that instilled confidence in him. Steeves said during the interview that he was associated with Whitehead in 1901, as he lived nearby, but he moved later to Trumbull.[552]

> "Mr. Steeves remembers very distinctly a visit made by the Wright brothers to Whitehead's shop, before 1903. In recalling this visit he claimed he met and spoke with both of these men and he described their physical characteristics in detail...I believe this entire interview was very sincere and unbiased....Mr. Steeves took an oath with his hand on the Bible and was very eager to swear that all of his testimony was true and fact[ual]. He had been cautioned by Captain O'Dwyer prior to the tape recording that it was absolutely essential for all statements to be accurate and factual and without exaggeration because of the historical significance."[553]

The time period for Whitehead's second shop at Cherry Street was short - it opened at the earliest, sometime in the summer of 1901, most likely later in August after his flight of August 14th, through early-January 1902, when a falling out with Whitehead's fall and winter sponsor, Herman Linde, caused him to be locked out of the shop, which was, by then, a factory. It is possible that the factory closed a bit later than that date – at latest, very early spring, 1902.

Another eyewitness, Anton Pruckner, can place the Wrights at Whitehead's shop no later than the end of 1901, as he only worked with Whitehead through late 1901, during that early period.

Chapter 8: Frequently Asked Questions

"Anton Pruckner was working in Whitehead's shop the day the Wrights visited. "How did you know they were the Wrights?" he was asked. He replied, simply, "They had to introduce themselves." The meeting took place outside the shop, according to Pruckner's recollection, and he went about his work, unmindful of what the Wrights and Whitehead discussed. Pruckner also said the Wrights visited more than one time."[554]

"I can also remember very clearly when the Wright brothers visited at Whitehead's shop here in Bridgeport, before 1903. I was present and saw them myself. I know this to be true, because they introduced themselves to me at the time. In no way am I confused, as some people have felt, with the Witteman brothers who came here after 1906. I knew Charles Witteman well. The Wrights left here with a great deal of information."[555] (Anton Pruckner, Oct. 30, 1964)

Figure 157: Pruckner identifies (1901) photo

Identifying the photo above, Pruckner stated in 1936:

"It was taken on the then vacant lot on Cherry St. across from the Wilmot and Hobbs Company (now the American Tube and Stamping Company) [1936] where later a small shop was built in which Gustave Whitehead pursued his construction of airplanes. It was at this shop that he was visited on several occasions by the Wright brothers, Orville and Wilbur, during the period between 1900 and 1903. I believe the time of their visits was actually prior to 1902 because I left Bridgeport for two years, going sometime in 1902. Upon my return I again worked with Gustave Whitehead at times with his experiments. Picture No. 25 shows the shop which was constructed on Cherry Street where the Wright Brothers visited..."[556] (Anton Pruckner, Jan. 3, 1936)

Junius Harworth was present during one Wrights' visit, looking in through the shop window with curiosity. John Lesko said Harworth had told him of it.[557]

"Julius [aka Junius] Harworth attested to this [Wright] visit. In a letter to aeronautical historian Erik Hildes-Heim of Fairfield, dated August 7, 1961, Mr. Harworth said Mr. Whitehead gave the [Wright] brothers his plans for moving an elevator and rudder in the rear of the plane. Mr. Whitehead, Mr. Harworth wrote, had not used this yet and had been planning it for use in one of his future craft."[558]

These were eyewitnesses with affidavits and recorded interviews who had seen the visits first hand; and

Gustave Whitehead: "First in Flight"

we shall hear how Whitehead related the same to a neighbor. However, Orville Wright, when asked about going to Whitehead's shop, denied it. He said in a letter to Fred L. Black, dated Oct. 19, 1937, that he'd never been in Bridgeport till 1909, "and then only passing through on the train."[559] We must consider Orville's record when it came to telling the truth - after all, in order to be considered "first in flight," it appears that he may have nudged brother Wilbur out of the way for the "glory." It is not well known that Orville spent much time culling many of the Wright brothers' correspondences and documents in his final years; they were incinerated in February 1948, according to provisions in his will, less than a month after his death.[560]

What did Whitehead say later about the Wrights' visit and his own inventions? Mrs. Clarence Crittendon of Fairfield, Connecticut, a neighbor of Whitehead's, interviewed on October 11, 1964, and signed an affidavit stating the following:

> I, Mrs. Crittendon recall Mr. Whitehead talking to me one morning... I said, "I hear you have an aeroplane," He said, "Yah." I said, "Don't you fly it?" He said, "Well, when someone takes what you have worked all your life on, " and I said how did that happen? Then he said he wrote someplace and the Wright Brothers came to see him. **He said something about some patents, and his losing his rights to some of his inventions.** He said he didn't have any money at the time and wrote the Wrights asking for help. They came out here and took some papers away with them. Mr. Whitehead said he also visited somewhere, I can't recall where, but he did say he visited the Wrights, and they had an engine that was his design and were using it. He said it is the same as mine...I would classify Whitehead as a genius. He should get credit for things that were never credited to him, but which he did do."[561]

The date of Mrs. Crittendon's discussion with Whitehead is unclear, but it had to be during the period after the patent suits (1908) had been filed, as he mentions losing his rights to his inventions. During that period, Whitehead was using drastically different designs, such as an aeroplane with a v-shaped fuselage and helicopters. If an inventor used wing-warping or eventually, even horizontal plane surfaces, he'd be in danger of patent infringement charges from the Wrights.

Octave Chanute, Sept. 1, 1909, to Earl Jones:

> "With the Wrights stating, 'So long as there is any money to be made by the use of the products of our brain, we propose to have it ourselves ...' they initiated similar action against other aviation pioneers in Europe and the United States, virtually all of whom are technically guilty of infringement. Though they usually ignored amateur builders or 'inventors', they mercilessly attacked those who built machines for profit ... their profit."[562]

Other inventors were trying to devise a work-around to this problem, devising ailerons as one solution. Then the courts determined that these also were covered by the Wrights' patent. Confusion reigned. The Wrights believed that all successful aviation was due to them, so anyone who profited from flight must pay them. The brothers tried to control all aviation, worldwide. Those who competed for prize money without a license approved by the Aero Club of America at meets sanctioned by the Wrights, could be sued or not allowed to compete, in the first place.[563] No one could design and sell airplanes that utilized the basic control methods that would cause them to work - no one, except the Wrights or their authorized agents. This could have been one reason for Whitehead's change of designs during this period, which were less successful, in addition to the demands of his sponsors. He'd have been prevented from using his own inventions - the long sought solutions responsible for causing his early aeroplanes to fly were no longer his to use. Inventing new systems apart from using wing-warping and horizontal surfaces wouldn't be feasible. This situation continued until June 14, 1910, when a US

Chapter 8: Frequently Asked Questions

Court of Appeals in New York ruled dissolved temporary injunctions against the main defendants, Curtiss and Paulhan, and allowed them and others to operate their flying machines at exhibition meets until the cases were decided. This did not protect new infringers from being named. [564] In this atmosphere, and with pending patent lawsuits that were top news, Whitehead may well have felt reluctant to use his original system for controlling and stabilizing his flying machines.

Whitehead's brother, John, also confirmed that he was upset about the Wright patents, obtained in later years, but first filed in March 1903. He said,

> "*My brother was surely bitter when he heard that the Wright Bros. got a patent on the very ideas we intended to patent and was told we had to demonstrate the possibility first. Perhaps they got them rightly after proving them a success. After the Wright Bros first demonstration my brother became very er[r]atic in his further work pertaining to Flying Machines in fact he only finished and tried only one machine while I was just in Bridgeport up to spring 1911*. I have given you some details of this machine in my former letter."[565]

Gustave Whitehead had much to learn about protecting his inventions – his lack of business acumen, being oblivious to his own original accomplishments, and lack of money undoubtedly caused him not to focus properly on his original invention, to give away his original ideas to others, including, possibly, the Wright brothers, and not gain the protection of patents for his powered aeroplane. This does not detract from being "first in flight," as there is overwhelming evidence that Gustave Whitehead, though being unable to acquire rights through patenting his inventions, did make the world's first sustained, powered flights.

WHAT WAS MRS. WHITEHEAD'S INVOLVEMENT?

According to Whitehead's associates, Louisa Tuba Whitehead helped sew fabric onto the wings[566] for days on end, along with her husband and other women in the neighborhood, who pitched in. [567] [568] She undoubtedly had hopes of success that included being able to live more comfortably - their dreams of improving their own lives were dashed time and again with legal and business problems, and frequent financial difficulties. Louisa worked when it was possible, to supplement the family income. According to her grandson, she also made braided rugs and sold them. John Whitehead, brother of Gustave, wrote researcher Stella Randolph in 1934, " … he would take the last cents in the house, borrow money, or go in debt, to buy material for a flying machine. He had quite a few disputes with his wife about that."[569] There is some indication, through the statements of Junius Harworth that "Mrs. Whitehead often opposed her husband in his untiring work." Louisa reportedly did not go out of the home to view his flights, undoubtedly tending to her babies and perhaps more than a little worried about injuries as well as finances. Harworth also mentions that Mrs. Whitehead, not always pleased with the flying machine ventures, very seldom came into the shop - though she would stop in to bring a hot cup of coffee at times - let alone coming out to the street or fields to witness any events.[570]

Mrs. Anton Pruckner was interviewed about Mrs. Whitehead, in 1964.

"(O'Dwyer): You were quite friendly with Mrs. Whitehead?

Mrs. P: Oh yes, they were very nice people.

O'Dwyer: What were they, next door neighbors?

Mrs. P: No, no, no. They were living on Tunxis Hill, and we were living on Scofield Ave.

O'Dwyer: Oh, yes. Did you ever know if she sewed fabric on the wings?

Mrs. P: Well, I didn't see that but I heard about it. She was working on it.

Gustave Whitehead: "First in Flight"

O'Dwyer: Did she ever discuss anything about her husband's works at all?

Mrs. P: No. One time she was kind of excited because nothing went through [as] she thought ... when she was working so hard on [it]."[571]

When interviewed by Stella Randolph in the 1930's, Mrs. Whitehead and her children indicated that despite the difficulties and financial problems encountered during Gustave's inventing periods, he had provided two self-built homes for his family on large multiple lots with a cow, chickens, a garden and fruit trees. There had been a warm family relationship, and he was recalled with love. [572]

There can be no doubt that to be married to Gustave Whitehead was a challenge unlike anything other wives had experienced. Mrs. Whitehead stayed with and supported her aeronaut husband, took work outside the home to help out, even helped sew countless wings full of fabric, while raising four children in financially challenging and confining circumstances [their flat in Bridgeport, in 1901-1906 reportedly consisted of two small rooms: a kitchen and bedroom]. Gustave was looked upon by some as "crazy" for his belief that man could fly. Police were involved at times, over noise, property or safety disputes. Property was taken away in court. Through all this, she loved Gus and raised a happy family. That, in itself, can be considered an achievement. Perhaps she, too, never realized the impact of what her husband (and she) had accomplished. This author watched the pride and joy on the faces of Gustave and Louisa's three grown daughters, when in August 1964, a large headstone was erected on the gravesite of their father Gustave, in the pauper's section of the cemetery, who was then being officially recognized as the "Father of Connecticut Aviation" in a special ceremony.

Wives and family members are often not witnesses to historic events and yet we accept them, on the basis of the evidence. When we consider that other Wright family members were not witnesses to the "flights" of the Wrights at Kitty Hawk, this has not been used to disparage their "historic record." So it was, likewise, with Mrs. Whitehead. With regards to the children, daughter Rose was a young toddler during the early flights in 1901-1902, and would been neither present nor remembered it if she was. Son Charles was about six months old in the summer of 1901, and his other two daughters, Lillian and Cornelia (Nell), were born in 1905 and 1909[573], past his most prolific period. Within the family, his "first flights" were not recognized for their historic importance, as they did not lead to lasting, practical, or commercially viable results for Gustave. They, like all those of their era, were focused on those who made flying a financial success, were better funded and able to further the art of flying. His family like most of the media and the community at large, did not focus on the important early contributions that Gustave Whitehead had made to accomplish the first viable powered flights of mankind, inventing new flight technologies that the later work of others were based on, in part, till much later.

Louisa Whitehead is one of the heroes of this account, for she withstood many trials and tribulations while successfully raising a beautiful family that loved each other. With her as his wife and helpmate, Gustave was able to accomplish what no human had: a succession of powered, manned flights of the first successful airplanes the world had ever seen.

Chapter 9

FUNDING AND FINANCES

Gustave Whitehead received funding for his active fifteen-year inventing period from a variety of sources. Newspaper accounts and associates interviewed later describe a string of sponsors who came along mostly to make a quick profit and reluctant to provide as much time or financing as was needed, leading to legal action in the courts on several occasions. Coworkers at the nearby factories and other workplaces became investors and/or helpers. At one time, he was known to have planned (and may have offered) a "purchase of shares" in his projects[574][575]. This may have led to ill feeling with those who invested and did not receive a return on their investment, amongst these, possibly, the recalcitrant eyewitness and Whitehead "partner" to the "first flight," Dickie.

The neighborhood he lived in contained many people who were willing to volunteer to build; assist in physically moving the plane from place to place, as needed: women to sew fabric for the wings[576], and on least one occasion, the community took up a collection of their meager savings to help Gustave with costs. In 1901-1902, Whitehead had been financed by Miller and Linde, as aforementioned. Starting in April 1902, some funding came from his brother, John, who'd worked as a prospector in California and volunteered to help through the first decade of the century, on and off, when he was available[577][578]. In the latter years of Gustave's waning inventing period (thought to be 1908-1911) he was least partially sponsored by the wealthy, prominent fathers of a local photographer, Arthur K. L. Watson and aviation editor Stanley Yale Beach, who'd covered Whitehead's inventions since 1901 in that magazine. Beach's father owned the *Scientific American*. In 1911, Whitehead built a helicopter prototype for Lee S. Burridge, who, as we have seen, turned around and cruelly sued Whitehead, taking all his tools and contents of his shop, for not producing an operational, flying model fast enough (there were none at the time!). There is ample evidence that Gustave Whitehead was building designs then not entirely of his own making, undoubtedly while trying to avoid being named as in a Wright patent lawsuit in those later years of the first decade of the 20th century.

Whitehead was also at least partially self-financed throughout the years, earning money at various jobs he held, using what extra he could take out of his budget for the planes. He built lightweight engines, gliders, aeroplanes, and helicopter prototypes for others from about 1901 – 1912, to help pay for his own inventions and earn a living for his family.

Importantly, in the early, more successful years before Whitehead had a large family, he was able to self-finance and find a few sponsors who gave him more freedom - the designs were his own, as a result. Whitehead had primarily funded the previous flying machines that led up to the successful flights. He had various day, and at times, night, jobs such as being a coal miner (in Pennsylvania), and in Bridgeport, Connecticut- a coal truck driver, night watchman, or mechanic, but this was only to pay the bills and to be able to work on "flight." His "main" job and life mission was to design and build what he considered to be a practical airplane – first, designing and flying models; then gliders; and finally, full scale flying machines, powered by his own self-built lightweight engines. Members of his family worked when they were able to do so, as every extra penny Whitehead had went into his flying machines, a number of those who knew him attested, including his brother, John.

> "I know he would take the last cents in house, borrow money or go in debt to buy material for a flying machine. He had quite a few disputes with his wife about that." [579]

The family lived very sparingly in the early years. He did eventually own four lots in the Tunxis Hill area and built two modest homes there for his family to live in, in later years. One still remained, through April 2014, as it appeared in Whitehead's lifetime, on Alvin Street, in Fairfield, Connecticut, when it was allowed to be torn down, for want of a piece of land to move it to, amidst international media coverage, and the state of Connecticut's promise to fund its restoration, move, and maintenance.[580] [581]

Whitehead's attitude about becoming wealthy through his efforts was unpretentious. Money and fame were not what he was after. In 1901, several months after his successful August 14th flights, the *New York Evening Telegram* reported Whitehead as saying, "Money? No, I do not believe I will ever be rich. At least I do not think or care to think about that. *When I make my machine perfect so I can fly about at will, I shall be satisfied.*" [582]

In the 1930's, Charles Waldo, editor of the *Bridgeport Post*, said of Whitehead, who he'd known earlier, when he was a reporter, "Let Whitehead earn two dollars and a half - enough to purchase a block of steel, and he was off on his favorite hobby of constructing airplanes."[583]

Sponsors came and went, rapidly, in part due to problems concerning a desire for a quick return on their money or other business arrangements and disagreements, which it appears, happened with regularity. A sponsor with both money and patience who would allow Whitehead to invent using his own designs did not seem to appear much after 1902. As his family grew, he sought more backers - there was an intermittent string of these that seemed to last long enough to build at least one or part of one "flying machine." Some tried to appropriate Whitehead's ideas, like Linde, who was caught attempting to get one of the mechanics he employed to learn about Whitehead's designs, quit, and work directly for Linde.[584] The types of sponsors Whitehead found appear to have been a drawback, as many of the later ones, including Stanley Yale Beach[585], and Lee S. Burridge, prominent members of the Aero Club and Aeronautical Society, wanted significant input on the designs, which was a matter of contention, certainly a deterrent to successful production of a practical airplane. Several disagreements led to legal action and reclamation of the planes, engines, or equipment. Whitehead, as a result, was often described by those who knew him as "short of funds" for his inventions. He never was funded to the extent necessary to fully develop his ideas.

Another problem in locating potential funders was that Whitehead was working on flight at such an early period that it was before people even accepted the idea that man could fly. Junius Harworth related a time when Whitehead was ridiculed by wealthy members of a local country club,

> "... After the photos were taken [1902], a group of club members came across the links to view the machine, they laughed at it and said, "*Mr. W was crazy, as man could never fly.*" They were not interested and were angry because the machine had made deep ruts in the turf, later, the police arrived and told us to get off the links."[586]

In May 1964, during a radio interview with WICC in Connecticut, Anton Pruckner, Hungarian immigrant and longtime associate and mechanic for Whitehead, said,

Chapter 9: Funding and Finances

"... we couldn't make a job perfectly because we didn't have the money to do that, and we couldn't get anybody too interested in it, because they would say, 'Oh that's something - you can't go up and see -- God.' Flying up, you know. That's what people said...We tried to interest many of them for a little backing, a little money, etc. All of them ... you know, money fellows, but impossible to make them interested in it."[587] [588]

One way Whitehead was able to save money was to use parts from earlier planes in the later ones. Anton Pruckner explained, " He was very quiet. He never complained. If he didn't succeed, he never complained, so he'd keep on going and going, build another one." Pruckner described how Whitehead would reuse parts on these later models, "A lot of them he used. A lot of them he didn't. Whatever he wanted to change, he'd throw away, and put a new one in there, make a new style one...There was a lot of times we couldn't afford it. Didn't have the money to buy it. Some time we went to work. Work for a couple of weeks, have some money together." The wages that Anton (and likely Whitehead, as well) earned, in the early years of the century, ranged from $1 (10 cents an hour) to $2.75 a day, for ten hours of labor. Pruckner also stated that Whitehead had never paid him a cent,[589] yet he'd been willing to work on the inventions for a number of years, on weekends and summer nights.[590] It is important to note that flying machines each could range in cost from $1200 to millions of dollars, when built by other inventors, including the Wrights, Maxim, Langley, and others. The daunting cost of materials was an ever-present factor limiting progress, but one which Whitehead was determined would not stop him from flying. For labor, at least with his prototypes, Whitehead had inspired (and put to work) a small army of skilled immigrant volunteers.

"Financial troubles, failure to develop the helicopter, which he believed to be the only practical type of airplane, marked the rest of his career and he died before --he believed-- he had achieved success."[591]

Nevertheless *Gustave Whitehead had succeeded* in being the first human being to invent, build, and fly an airplane; he pointed the way to hundreds of key inventors who read the periodicals describing his advanced, successful methods, sharing his secrets of flight as far away as Europe, seven years before the Wrights would reveal their technical feats.

Whitehead's success had been achieved with the help and support of Bridgeport, Connecticut's West End immigrant community of Hungarians, Germans, and Polish people, who welcomed him and his family, tolerated noise and unusual occurrences at all hours of the day and night. They accepted, helped, and believed in him. Gustave, a man who'd been orphaned before he was thirteen, had found a new family of supporters and together, without riches, they succeeded, by pooling their resources, in accomplishing the age-old dream of mankind, *successful human flight*. We owe Gustave, his family, and that vibrant community of immigrants our thanks, for the gift of flight we enjoy today might not have been, if not for all of them.

Gustave Whitehead: "First in Flight"

Chapter 10

WHITEHEAD HISTORIC SITES

WHERE WHITEHEAD FLEW

The following is an incomplete list of all the flights and places Gustave Whitehead flew, due to the delays in obtaining witness statements. It is known that all witnesses could not located, for entire factories, schools, and neighborhoods watched him fly and the statements began being gathered three decades later, when many witnesses had moved or died. Whitehead's successful flight experiments continued for a 15 year period, beginning around 1896 and continuing through 1911. New information continues to come forward. Recently, the author spoke to a woman whose family owned a farm on Mill Hill, above Southport, in Fairfield. When she was a child, her older relatives showed her where Whitehead had flown in the Mill Hill area, telling her the story of how it happened. An older resident of Fairfield has conducted some research identifying Burr Street in Greenfield Hill as an area where Whitehead is thought to have conducted flights. One thing is certain – there were many locations ideal for Whitehead's flight experiments, in and around coastal eastern Fairfield County. Whitehead made good use of most of them.

Pre-1900
See Chapter 5, *Earlier Whitehead experiments (1895-1901)*

1900-1902
Eyewitnesses reported numerous powered Whitehead aeroplane flights in parts of Fairfield County, Connecticut, in 1901, 1902, and up through 1908. The flights were made in open fields, on gentle hills and beaches, and over Long Island Sound, a large saltwater body of water located between Long Island, NY, and Connecticut. The first powered flight in the world, now credited to Gustave Whitehead[592], made on August 14, 1901 "in a long lot at the back of Fairfield"[593] likely occurred on a raised pastoral field called "Turney Farm," near the Ash Creek entrance by Fairfield Beach, off Turney Road, a location close to the present day South Benson marina in Fairfield. Several additional flights of that date were said to made at Lordship Manor, Stratford[594], where there was plenty of open space and a beach. Two flights on January 17, 1902 were reportedly also made "on the sea beach" at Lordship Manor, out over the waters of Long Island Sound[595] [596] [597]. Whitehead made additional flights at Seaside Park[598] (as early as 1901, according to Anton Pruckner, his mechanic and assistant),

a grassy open space with hard-packed, sandy soil on Long Island Sound in Bridgeport, CT [599] [600]. Other flights were reported near the Pine Street [601] [602] [603] [604] and Cherry Street [605] [606] [607] areas of Bridgeport where Whitehead had his shops, and again, at Lordship Manor[608]. In Bridgeport, a witness, Cecil Steeves, described "a trial flight near the Gilman estate located on Fairfield Avenue, between Orland and Ellsworth Streets."[609] Another witness, John Lesko, gave testimony concerning flights on Fairfield Avenue, the Wordin Estate at the foot of Spruce Street, and on St. Stephen's Street in Bridgeport. [610] [611] Additional flights took place from Tunxis Hill[612] in Fairfield (Gypsy Springs / Lenox Hill, also named general park area of "Villa Park"[613]; area where there was a long flat, grassy piece of land). Whitehead flew near and over beaches, including Fairfield Beach, where planks were laid upon the sand to run along [614] [615], and out over Long Island Sound in areas which may be seen in coastal Bridgeport, Stratford (Lordship) Black Rock[616], Fairfield, and Milford (Charles Island).[617] [618] [619]

1903-1905

Clifford Connor reported seeing a Whitehead powered "type of biplane" fly in 1903, watching it with his classmates[620], location unknown to this author. Oliver Cole described the powered flight of a biplane at the hill below Orr's Castle, in the current Tunxis Hill area, at an altitude of ten feet, which then crashed and broke into bits.[621]

Figure 158: Orr's Castle, Whitehead flying site
Whitehead's old flying grounds at Orr's Castle, Tunxis Hill, Fairfield, CT
Pictured June 2013
Photo courtesy of C. Lautier

Figure 159: Whitehead glider flight near Orr's Castle, Tunxis Hill, Fairfield, CT (1908)
Nov. 22, 1908 Bridgeport Herald article[622], photo by Bridgeport Herald photographer

1906-1911

During 1906, Whitehead was in the process of relocating his family and shop to nearby Holland Heights (Tunxis Hill), a neighborhood on the hilly eastern border of Fairfield, not far from the West End of Bridgeport. He increasingly flew on the hills in his new neighborhood, which were his former flying grounds some of the time, prior to that period.

John Havery, an eyewitness, saw a flight of a Whitehead aeroplane with a single propeller, at least ten feet in elevation, for a distance of several hundred feet, in 1905 at "the old circus grounds," in Bridgeport, between Cherry Street and Bostwick Ave.[623] The flight of a biplane occurred on Ridgely Avenue, south of Tunxis Hill, at a height of ten feet, and for a few hundred feet in distance.[624] Flights also took place from nearby locations in the vicinity of Orr's Castle (see Fig. 152, above)[625][626][627][628] where there was a hill and large open field; at Holland Heights[629][630]; at Wheeler Park; and Sport Hill, on the border of Easton and Fairfield[631][632]. Mari Kopacsi and Frederick Szur both reported viewing flights from 1905-1908 (throughout each of these years) at Villa Park, in the West End of Bridgeport, at an altitude of three or four feet above the ground; also along State Street, in Bridgeport, often at sunset. A biplane, for a distance of about 75-100 yards, made the flights "without touching the ground."[633]

Figure 160: Heavy Beach-Whitehead Biplane control center, by Ridgely house (1909)

Figure 161: Orr's Castle top left, viewed from Marlborough Terr. (1908)
Photo by John Slezsak, 1908.
Courtesy of Fairfield Museum, O'Dwyer archives.

Above, scene at Tunxis Hill's uppermost plateau, in Fairfield, CT, 1908. A later model, V-shaped fuselage Whitehead aircraft being transported by then-sponsor Stanley Yale Beach. Whitehead stands behind Beach on the back side of the car. Taken on lane later to become Marlborough Terrace, where Whitehead lived, 1906-1914. Orr's Castle seen at top left, on hill. Glider tests made in field at left, below Orr's Castle (1901-1906+). A milk wagon is seen going up Tunxis Hill Road.

Chapter 10: Whitehead Historic Sites

Figure 162: Whitehead at Brooklawn Country Club (1910)

(Above) Gustave Whitehead pictured with checkered blanket, in Tunxis Hill, on grounds of Brooklawn Country Club, January 1910.
Photos courtesy of Fairfield Museum, O'Dwyer archives.

Figure 163: Beach-Whitehead Biplane at Tunxis Hill, Brooklawn Country Club (Jan. 1910)

Stanley Yale Beach's design for a biplane, built with Whitehead's help, at same photo shoot as above, labeled "Whitehead's Effort" in photo album of Arthur K. Lyons Watson, pictured in automobile, above.
Photos courtesy of Fairfield Museum, O'Dwyer archives.

© Susan Brinchman, 2015

Gustave Whitehead: "First in Flight"

Figure 164: Map of Whitehead's main flying grounds (1901-1911)

WHITEHEAD SHOPS

1900-1905

Whitehead's first shop was located at 241 Pine Street in the West End of Bridgeport, from late 1900, on and off through 1905. Always resourceful, the 27 year old Gustave used a modest shop he built in the yard with $300 given to him by his first sponsor, Mr. Miller[634]; his own kitchen (one of two rooms in the flat), and the basement of his home, to build "No. 21," the world's first successful airplane.

Junius Harworth, who lived next door, formerly a young helper of Whitehead's, recalls the shop in detail, in 1934: "Mr. Whitehead's first machine shop in Bridgeport was built in front of his home and up next to the fence that bounded the church garden. Besides myself [Julius Horvath] assisting, there was Mr. Bert Papp, Charles Galambosh, John Kedves, and Wargo. It was about thirty feet long and twelve feet wide, had a peaked, slanting roof covered with tar paper. The entrance was on the long side, nearest his house. The equipment in the shop consisted of a six foot lathe, a large wall type drill press, and a smaller bench drill. Power was furnished by a vertical, single cylinder Otto gas engine, having a 30 inch fly wheel and used dry cells for ignition...Later we secured a magneto to replace the cells. I recall fastening this magneto to the floor, back of the Otto, and Whitehead showed me how to splice a rope or cloths-line sailor fashion for an endless "belt" which we put over the small pulley of the magneto and the large flat surface of the flywheel. For the winter, I secured a small "chink" stove from the laundryman next door and it was a common occurrence to find several visitors seated around this stove with their wet shoes on the iron edge for drying...On one side of the shop was a long bench, had a large vise attached and there was a large assortment of mechanics and carpenters tools at hand. We had to have a small forge and we constructed a hand crank operated windmill, all boxed in and with a stove pipe at the exit end, this we placed under the "chink" and answered very well for heating pieces of iron. For an anvil I brought a large piece of iron from the forge shop on Wordin Ave. and we used up several files to put it in shape for smithing."
[635] Whitehead's first job in the shop was to alter his steam engine, "wrecked somewhat" in the Pittsburgh flight experiments. Harworth went on to describe how when the kerosene ran out for the shop lamp, they'd go into the kitchen to finish up work soldering the engine, using the kitchen lamp[636]. This shop was where they hand-built the wooden propellers. The fuselage, or "carriage" as Whitehead referred to it, was constructed in the basement of the home, away from prying eyes. They cleverly built it so it could be brought up from the cellar in pieces, and assembled in the small yard.

Chapter 10: Whitehead Historic Sites

Figure 165: Whitehead's first shop at 241 Pine Street (June 1901)

Whitehead's 1st modest shop in Bridgeport, CT, with "No. 21" assembled outside in yard, having been built in the basement, kitchen and shop.

Later, as early as August 1901- winter / spring, 1902, a second shop was built and used on Cherry Street opposite the Wilmot and Hobbs factory (later American Tube and Stamping Company)[637]. In 1964, Charles Whitehead described it as follows: "My dad ... moved it to a large lot (large at that time)... located between Bostwick Ave. and Hancock [-] are running parallel [-]. The other boundaries are Pine Street and Cherry Street I believe ... I'm sure the shop is not standing anymore."[638]

Figure 166: Whitehead's 2nd shop, "The First Airplane Factory in the World"

Above, Whitehead's 2nd shop, pictured on Hancock Ave. and Cherry Street,
near Pine Street, Bridgeport, CT
circa October/November 1901
Photo courtesy of Fairfield Museum, O'Dwyer archives

© Susan Brinchman, 2015

Gustave Whitehead: "First in Flight"

Figure 167: Whitehead's 2nd shop at northeast corner of Cherry and Hancock, in West End 1 (fall, 1901-1902)

The Wilmot and Hobbs factory and office on Hancock is pictured in the background. These two photos were recently identified as Whitehead's second shop, with "No. 22."

Figure 168: Whitehead's 2nd shop at northeast corner of Cherry and Hancock, in West End 2 (fall, 1901-1902)

Chapter 10: Whitehead Historic Sites

When that shop was closed, within 6-8 months (at the latest), due to disagreements with a sponsor, attempts to steal Whitehead's ideas, and subsequent loss of the sponsor's funds, Whitehead returned to building his flying machines at 241 Pine Street. In 1906, Whitehead moved his family and shop to a home he built on Ridgely Avenue, in Tunxis Hill, or "Holland Heights" as it was then known, a few miles northwest of Pine Street, on the eastern side of Fairfield, CT.

1906-1913

Figure 169: Whitehead's 2nd shop at Ridgely Ave. (1910-1911)

Whitehead's 3rd and final shop, with helicopter at [Ridgely Ave. and] Marlborough Street home on Tunxis Hill Fairfield, CT, where helicopter parts were found, later strewn in the lawn.
circa 1910-1911
Photo courtesy of Fairfield Museum, O'Dwyer archives

The Ridgely Avenue shop as described by Wilfred Walsh, who'd been a paid employee of Whitehead in 1911: the shop was "very small" and "packed in" including a lathe, upon which Walsh made parts including "bushings" for a helicopter project during at least one of several summers. He was provided with a little satchel of tools to use. There were no other people in the shop except for Gustave Whitehead, sporadically there to check on his work or provide directions, and a frequent visitor, Stanley Yale Beach. To get to the shop, Walsh had to "trudge" up a steep hill from the "end of the street car." This became tiresome to Walsh, even though he indicated it was a great pleasure, at the time, to have the opportunity to work in an early aviation shop on that project.[639]

Whitehead's children loved to tell their children and grandchildren (Whitehead's great-grandchildren) how, scattered across this field, their yard, were helicopter parts, which the children and grandchildren later gathered and sold for scrap metal, to buy ice cream.[640]

Charles Whitehead, son of Gustave, recalled the Ridgely home and shops several times, for researcher Randolph,

"... We lived in Fairfield on what was know[n] at that time as Ridgely Ave which runs off of Tunxis Hill Rd. My dad built part of that house and he also build [built] a large shed which he used for housing his

Gustave Whitehead: "First in Flight"

planes, later using it to house his Helicopter which he worked on. He also built a large machine shop. In it he had several machines such as lathes, shapers, planners [planers] etc., for constructing his machines and motors. As to whether these buildings are still standing I do not know as I left Conn in 1947. We sold that place to a Charles Phillips... We lived at this place from about 1906 to 1914."[641]

(Through a letter Rose Whitehead Rennison sent to Stella Randolph in 1968, for the purpose of providing information for a Whitehead museum then being planned by CAHA (nonprofit parent organization of the current New England Air Museum in Windsor Locks, Connecticut)[642]:

I am enclosing a drawing Charles made of the old homestead or rather, the placing of the buildings, on the plot.... Geese were mentioned in the future plans for the museum – I would like to state that Pa also built an octagon pigeon house on this place – about 4 or 5' tall placed on a telephone pole in the yard. The pigeons would fly down to feed and many times would light on our shoulders. (Pretty picture?) GW [Gustave Whitehead] sure loved anything that had wings. At one time he raised canaries on Pine Street.

... Built in the summer of 1906. 2 rooms – latr [later] addition 2 rooms upstairs and 2 rooms at front of house, 1 up and 1 down living room. Addition not finished inside just 2 x 4 studding and sheathing outside. Wood shingles on roof. Clap boards for siding outside.[643]

Whitehead later relocated to another home he built with his son, Charles, on Alvin Street in Fairfield, where he also built a shop, but at which "no work was done on airplanes," according to Charles.[644] Both locations were very close to favorite flying locations. Alvin Street was to be his last move.

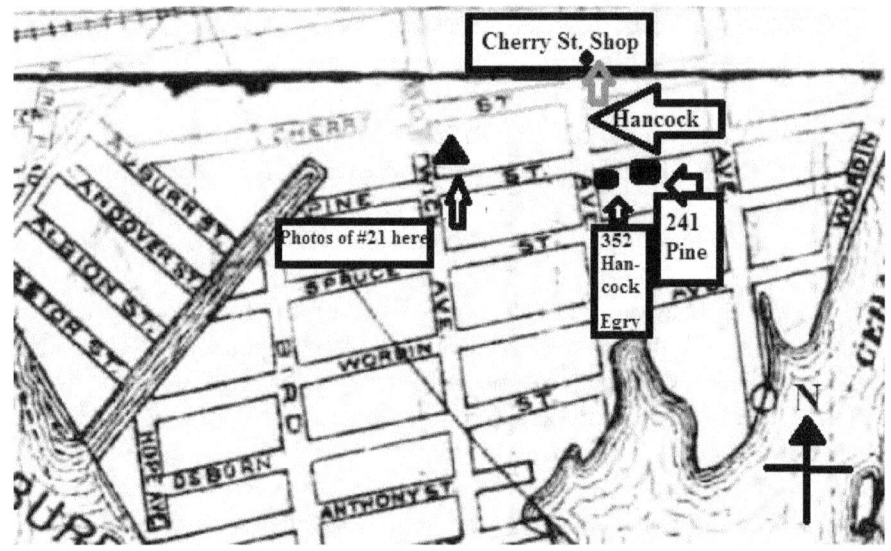

Figure 170: Whitehead home and shop locations 1901-1906

Above, Bridgeport City Map for the year 1900[645], with Whitehead home and shop locations on Hancock, Pine, and Cherry Streets. Location at left, on Bostwick Ave and Cherry Street is the place photos of "No. 21" were taken.[646] Whitehead's second shop was located on the northeast corner of Hancock Ave. and Cherry Street, across from the Wilmot and Hobbs office on Hancock Avenue.

Chapter 10: Whitehead Historic Sites

WHITEHEAD HOMES

1900- 1905

The circumstances were humble, indeed, under which this brilliant inventor and his family lived, with nothing but his own internal desire to succeed in flight, despite crushing challenges. Their living conditions illustrate what a truly remarkable feat it was for Gustave Whitehead to invent and fly the world's first airplane. He did receive support from many he met in the hard-working immigrant neighborhood in Bridgeport's West End; this may be the factor that made success possible.

Gustave Whitehead's first home in Connecticut was located at 352 Hancock Street in Bridgeport, owned by Mrs. Julius Egry. Gustave first rented alone, as he had just arrived in there in approximately late summer or fall of 1900; his rent included both room and board. We receive the following details from a description by Junius Harworth, written in 1934. According to Junius, Mr. Egry spoke German. "His room at the Egry home was very modest, merely had a bed, bureau, and chair in it."[647]

A few weeks before Christmas, according to Harworth, his wife and child arrived from Pittsburgh, Pennsylvania. The family then moved to a two-room flat nearby, at 241 Pine Street, Bridgeport, renting the lower rooms on the east end of the building, having the benefits of both a yard and a basement. The immediate neighborhood was primarily occupied by Hungarian, German, and Polish immigrants who labored in the nearby factories. This worked well for Gustave, who spoke German, and his wife Louisa, who spoke Hungarian.

The Pine Street apartment was directly adjacent to the home of then-Julius Horvath, aged 12 in the fall of 1900 (later, Americanized as Junius Harworth), a young man who would spend many years as an assistant and protégé to Whitehead. It was also located right next to the Hungarian Reformed Church. The building the Whiteheads rented in had formerly been a barn that was remodeled into four two-room flats. "This house had a front porch about two thirds length and several steps up. A central door opened up into a hallway that extended to the rear of the house and doors lead left and right to the rooms. These apartments were rather very small, each with a kitchen having an iron sink, a small wood-burning stove, table, old fashioned cupboard, and several chairs. ...One window faced the back yard of a trucker and the window on the east faced the garden plot of the minister of the Reformed Church." [648] The second room was the bedroom, described as likely having "scarce space." [649] The Whiteheads rented here, according to the Bridgeport Business Directory, from 1901 up through 1906, during the most productive, successful period of Gustave's inventing years.

1906-1914

Whitehead later built several homes in the vicinity where he liked to fly, at Tunxis Hill, Fairfield, near the Brooklawn Country Club. The first was a modest home on Ridgely Avenue, built in the summer of 1906, where the Whiteheads lived until 1914. The Ridgely Avenue home may well be one of the most significant historic home sites still standing in the world, home to the recognized Connecticut's "Father of Aviation," first in powered flight - the first inventor of the airplane and his family. The hilly terrain immediately surrounding these homes is the site of America's earliest testing ground for successful powered flight.

Whitehead's Tunxis Hill homes: Whitehead's first self-built home still stands, located on the corner of Ridgely Ave and Marlborough Terrace. His last (self-built) home at 184 Alvin Street has recently been demolished. Tunxis Hill Park was location of many of his glider and powered plane flights. The entire neighborhood consisted mostly of open fields, with few houses or roads, in October 1906, when Whitehead relocated his family and shop there. Just to the north was the Brooklawn Country Club and fairway, still in existence, where Whitehead took several of his planes for photo sessions.

Figure 171: Whitehead's first self-built home in "Holland Heights," now Tunxis Hill

At right is Whitehead's original, self-built home on the corner of Ridgely Ave. and Marlborough Terrace, in the Tunxis Hill neighborhood of Fairfield, CT.

Above photo by John Slezsak, circa 1908. In left, rear, the home of Whitehead's immediate neighbor and sometime assistant, Andrew Suelli, is shown. Stanley Yale Beach, Aviation Editor of the *Scientific American*, and sponsor of Whitehead during this period, appears at far right with two companions, the man at left, is Howard Booth, an "aeronaut " who worked with Whitehead for a time.

Figure 172: A Whitehead shop at Ridgely Avenue (circa 1908)
Left to right: brothers Gustave and John Whitehead.

Chapter 10: Whitehead Historic Sites

Figure 173: Whitehead home and a shop (1908)
Ridgely Ave. shop at left, Whitehead home at right with glider, circa 1908

The Whitehead's Ridgely Avenue home consisted of two lots (240 and 251).

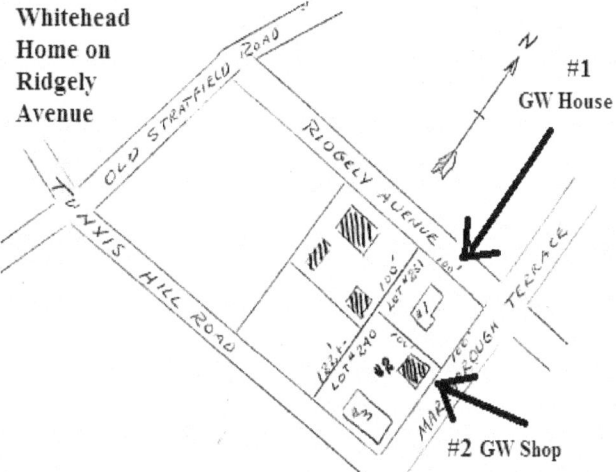

Figure 174: Diagram of two lots owned by Gustave Whitehead 1906/7-1914

Map of two lots where the Whitehead's first home and shop were located on Tunxis Hill, drawing by Maj. William J. O'Dwyer (US AF), Whitehead researcher
Courtesy of Fairfield Museum

While living on Ridgely Avenue for the next eight years, Whitehead created "a large proportion of his aeronautical machines and engines." After leaving Bridgeport, he continued experimenting with gliders, monoplanes, biplanes, and triplanes, selling some of these commercially. At least several witness attest to having seen Whitehead flights during this period. At Ridgely Avenue, he began work on a number of practical aircraft engines that he designed and sold, including several to famed aviation pioneer Charles Wittemann, known as "The Father of Commercial Aviation" in the USA. Wittemann spent a week there with Whitehead, building an engine, and who carried his engines in his catalogue. Here, Whitehead built what may well be Connecticut's first helicopter. [650] The Ridgely Avenue home and surrounding land is a significant site for both aviation and state history.

Figure 175: Whitehead with his 1911 helicopter, on Ridgely Avenue property. Whitehead's helicopter, circa 1910-11, built at Ridgely Avenue.

This may be Connecticut's first helicopter. It reportedly raised up on the ropes tethering it, but could not yet make manned flights, when the sponsor sued him for needing more time. At that time, there were no working helicopters anywhere.

Photo courtesy of Fairfield Museum, O'Dwyer archives

In June 1914, Whitehead began construction to build his family a second and final home at 184 Alvin Street [consisting of 4 lots] in Lenox Heights (Lenox Park, Tunxis Hill), Fairfield, CT, obtaining a deed recorded in his wife Louisa's name on June 27, 1914, where he lived till his death on Oct. 10, 1927.

Charles Whitehead remembers,

"He sold his property on Ridgely Ave. about Jan., 1914 … It was about June 1914 when we bought property at Alvin St and we started to build our house at Alvin St."[651]

1914-1927

During the final decade and a half of his life, Gustave and his family enjoyed this lovingly self-built second home on Alvin Street in Tunxis Hill, a stone's throw from some of his favorite flying locations, at a

Chapter 10: Whitehead Historic Sites

higher elevation. Gustave Whitehead died here at the age of 53, in 1927, staggering from the driveway, where he was lifting an engine out of a car, to the porch, and then into his living room. He expired before help could be obtained, from a massive heart attack. Louisa Whitehead and their son Charles owned this home until September 30, 1944, when it was sold. [652].

The Alvin Street homestead, pictured below, though considered a significant historic building by the state, despite funding available to preserve it and weeks of international public outcry, was issued a demolition permit by the Town of Fairfield during the writing of this manuscript. Shortly thereafter, the house was torn down, in late April 2014. Thus, for want of what may be called "*political will*" the final, self-built home of Gustave Whitehead, "first in powered flight," was lost to the ages, as has his legacy, thus far, in our history books. Proof that the home was 100 years old, an important factor in saving the home while land was located to move it to, was resting but a few hundred feet from the Fairfield Town Hall, in the Fairfield Museum's O'Dwyer/Whitehead archives, left untouched by those who approved and issued the demolition permits.

Figure 176: Whitehead's last home, where he died, on Alvin Street, in 1927

**Whitehead's self-built, final home at 184 Alvin Street
pictured in 2013 before its demolition in April 2014, following weeks of protests.**
Photo courtesy of C. Lautier of Stratford, CT

On October 10, 1927, at the age of 53, Gustave Whitehead succumbed to a heart attack that struck when lifting an engine out of a car in his driveway, pictured above. Stumbling up the porch steps, he went into his living room, where he died before help could be obtained.

Planning is underway to further identify, map, and place monuments and markers at these historic sites.[653]

WHITEHEAD'S GRAVESITE

Figure 177: Gustave Whitehead headstone, erected 1964

Above, Whitehead's headstone, installed August 15, 1964 by the Connecticut Aeronautical Historical Association (CAHA) in a large ceremony to honor Gustave Whitehead as" Father of Connecticut Aviation."

Location: Lakeview Cemetery, Bridgeport, CT.
Photo by Edward Collins, used with permission.

Text of the headstone reads:

GUSTAVE WHITEHEAD
JAN. 1, 1874   OCT. 10, 1927
FATHER OF CONNECTICUT AVIATION

ON AUG. 15, 1964 THIS HEADSTONE WAS ERECTED BY THE CONNECTICUT AERONAUTICAL HISTORICAL ASSOCIATION AS A TRIBUTE TO THE EFFORTS AND GENIUS OF GUSTAVE WHITEHEAD, AVIATION PIONEER, INVENTOR, DESIGNER AND BUILDER OF MANY EARLY AIRCRAFT AND ENGINES. WHITEHEAD CONSTRUCTED THE FIRST AIRPLANE IN CONNECTICUT, A STUDENT OF THE GERMAN AERONAUTICAL PIONEER OTTO LILIENTHAL, HE CLAIMED TO HAVE SUCCESSFULLY FLOWN HIS NUMBER 21 AND 22 AIRPLANES AT FAIRFIELD, BRIDGEPORT, AND LORDSHIP DURING 1901 AND 1902.

Chapter 10: Whitehead Historic Sites

This large headstone, commemorated Gustave Whitehead's contributions to aviation and hailing him as "Father of Connecticut Aviation," prior to the intensive additional research and interviews, over the next two decades, that would firmly establish Whitehead as "inventor of the airplane," bringing international recognition a half century later. It was donated by Robert C. Kohn, President of Honeyspot Monument Works of Bridgeport, replaced the pauper's grave marker "No. 42" previously at the site, since 1927. An official ceremony, attended by an overflow crowd of 150 people, was held on the clear, beautiful afternoon of August 15, 1964, which was 63 years and one day after Whitehead's flight of August 14, 1901.

The commemoration of 1964 included many honored guests, especially Whitehead's relatives, including his three daughters, "Mrs. Rose Rennison, Mrs. Lilian Baker, and Mrs. Nellie Kuster[er]…and grandson Robert Whitehead … [A]lso present were [Anton Pruckner] of Fairfield, one of Mr. Whitehead's early associates, John Lesko, of Bridgeport, who assisted Whitehead on many of his flights, and Stella Randolph, of Washington, D.C., the sole biographer of Whitehead…Officials of Bridgeport, Fairfield, and Stratford paid tribute to Mr. Whitehead's contributions" and acknowledged his importance to the aviation industry, "lifting him from the unknown."[654]

Also in attendance were several famous air pioneers, including one who worked with Gustave Whitehead in the first decade of the century - Charles Wittemann, who verified Whitehead's ability to produce aircraft engines and is on record attesting, after examining photos and data, that Whitehead's "No. 21" "was capable of stable flight." Witteman had worked with Whitehead in his shop making a helicopter engine, and bought Whitehead engines to fly his own planes, in 1908-1909, offering at least one in his well-known catalogue. [655]Famed aviation pioneer, Clarence Chamberlain, also attended. In 1927, Chamberlain became a "world endurance" record-setting pilot for Wright Aeronautical Company, amongst other notable credits. In an earlier visit to the area, Witteman referred to Whitehead as "a genius and extremely fine mechanic and designer."[656] Whitehead researchers O'Dwyer and Randolph, members of the Connecticut Aeronautical Historical Society (CAHA), [parent organization now running the New England Air Museum], members of all military services, and many elected officials. Mayor Tedesco, of Bridgeport, spoke, "It is my firm conviction as Mayor of Bridgeport that Gustave Whitehead flew the first airplane in the world." [657] The Town Manager of Stratford, Richard Blake, mentioned the town's plans to erect a landmark* in Lordship where a Whitehead's flight was said to have occurred, "adding that the town of Stratford is indebted to Gustave Whitehead for his contribution to the aviation industry, which is the life-blood of Stratford." Master of Ceremonies, CAHA's founder and director, Harvey Lippincott, described "the unveiling of a historic site marker* at the Wordin avenue exit of the Connecticut Turnpike…close to the site of Whitehead's home on Pine street and Hancock avenue."[658]

After the formal ceremony, the large crowd relocated to Whitehead's grave, "a few hundred feet away," where a wreath was placed on the new headstone by Mayor Tedesco, and the stone was dedicated. "An honor guard from Westover Air Force Base, Mass. Stood at attention while Taps was played by a lone bugler and Gustave Whitehead at last received the recognition which he had never known in life."[659]

A *Bridgeport Post* article noted that [in 1964] CAHA was convinced that Whitehead deserved credit as an aviation pioneer, and at that time "hails him as 'the father of aviation in Connecticut.'"[660] CAHA would go on, interviewing and gathering the testimony of numerous still-living, eyewitnesses through the 1970's, to eventually convince Founder and [by then] President-Emeritus, Harvey Lippincott, that Whitehead had definitely made short flights that predated those of the Wrights.[661]

[*Interestingly, no historic markers have yet been placed, nor have any local schools, airports, or parks been renamed to honor Gustave Whitehead, the inventor of the airplane, though planning for a goodly number by local officials and residents has occurred sporadically for the past fifty years, continuing into the present time.]

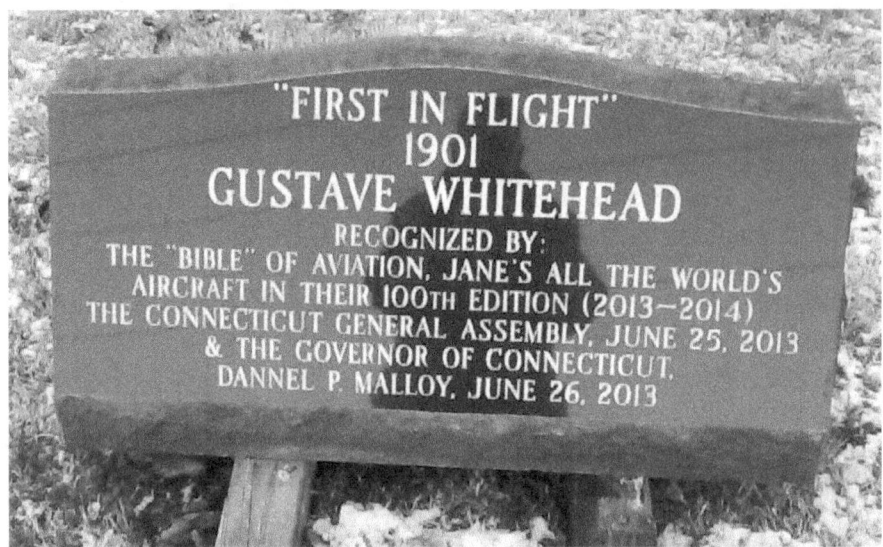

Figure 178: Gustave Whitehead's supplementary "footstone," erected 2014

In 2014, a local Stratford, Connecticut historian, Susan del Bianco, thoughtfully conceived of and made the arrangements for a supplementary headstone, above, adding the growing international recognition of Gustave Whitehead as "First in Flight."
(Photo by Edward Collins, used with permission.)

"FIRST IN FLIGHT"
1901
GUSTAVE WHITEHEAD
Recognized by
The "Bible" of Aviation, Jane's All the World's Aircraft in their 100th edition (2013-2014). The Connecticut General Assembly, June 25, 2013 & the Governor of Connecticut, Dannel P. Malloy, June 26, 2013.

The new, supplementary headstone was placed December 27, 2014, at the foot of Gustave Whitehead's gravesite at Lakeview Cemetery, attended by Whitehead family member, Ken Kusterer, and a number of other members of the Kusterer family, including Gustav Weisskopf Kusterer, his namesake and great-great grandson, and Whitehead's great-grandsons Jim and Ronald Kusterer.[662] Also in attendance were Ms. Del Bianco and Andrew Kosch, construction team-member and pilot for the Whitehead "No. 21" "replica," built in 1986 and successfully flown a number of times. Mr. Kosch is a local teacher who has made countless presentations about Gustave Whitehead's history for local residents, displaying the replica at countless events for the past thirty years. The headstone was designed and donated by Carl Salvaggi, owner of Carl's Monuments, of Bridgeport, Connecticut.[663]

Gustave Whitehead's modest obituary, issued by a local newspaper the day he was buried in a pauper's grave at Lakeview Cemetery, with only a number to mark his grave, read:

"Gustave Whitehead, well-known local resident, died Monday evening at his home, 69 Alvin street. He is survived by his wife and four children, Charles, Mrs. J. W. O. Rennison, Mr. C. O. Baker and Miss

Chapter 10: Whitehead Historic Sites

Nellie Whitehead. Mr. Whitehead was a member of the International Bible Students' association. Funeral services were held this morning at 10:30 o'clock at Lakeview cemetery. A member of the Bible Students' association officiated."

Even in death, shortly after Lindberg had crossed the Atlantic in an aeroplane, the local newspapers, as well as his own family and the local community, did not seem to recognize the importance of Whitehead's past achievements. He was long-forgotten for what seemed at the time to be his very modest accomplishments of 1901-1903, in trying to produce "a practical flying machine." All eyes, even then, were on the desired airplane capabilities of the future, rather than "firsts" that seemed of no consequence. It would be nearly a decade more before it began to be realized that Gustave Whitehead's experiments, which never produced lasting fame or fortune during his lifetime, represented the "first powered flights" of mankind.

Gustave Whitehead: "First in Flight"

Chapter 11

LEGACY

THE "FIRSTS"

"For aviation is a century-long evolution, not the work of any one nation or generation. All well versed historians of aeronautics surely must admit that much."
(Dr. Albert F. Zahm, 1945)

Gustave Whitehead accomplished what no human had before. In 1901, with a plane and engine that he designed and built, he made a sustained, powered flight of a half mile. He lengthened that distance later the same day by flying one and a half miles. This was no anomaly in the history of flight, as Whitehead not only flew first but shared his knowledge and designs with others who further developed a practical airplane. Here are his accomplishments and "firsts," which clearly illustrate his contributions to "flight."

In 1945, Albert Zahm[664], (Guggenheim Chair of Aeronautics at the Library of Congress, 1929-1946[665]) commented on Whitehead's legacy, in his book, *Early Powerplane Fathers*:

"From the accredited reports it appears that Mr. Whitehead accomplished

1. The first high flight
2. The first long flight
3. First closed-circuit flight
4. First flight over and landing on water
5. First with passenger
6. First with internal-combustion engine.

All at a time when no other plane on earth was making any sustained hops at all. This seems a glorious record which, if officially accepted, should receive distinguished recognition from city, state, and nation. Further inquiry, especially by an unbiased professional committee, would seem warrantable." [666]

Albert Zahm was emphatic that the Wrights did not invent the first plane to fly, did not fly first, nor did they patent wing-warping or other elements of their plane first. Dr. Zahm credited Whitehead with "First to Fly with Petrol Power," the name of the chapter in his book devoted to him. He was particularly impressed with the long flights made by Whitehead's "No. 22" over Long Island Sound in 1902, in addition to his flights on August 14, 1901.

Zahm also wrote another commentary on Gustave Whitehead, *"Man's First Practical Power Flight: Gustave Whitehead America's Father of Flying"* (by A. F. Zahm)[667]:

"The first long curvilinear power flight of man was made by Gustave Whitehead at Bridgeport, Connecticut, on January 17, 1902. Seated at the boat of his twin-tractor amphibian monoplane, "No. 22", he taxied down the beach, took off and flew 200 feet high over Long Island Sound in a loop 7 miles long, and landed nicely on the water at his starting point. His practicable speed was 50 miles an hour on land, 70 in the air; his control, comprising with [of] fixed dihedral wings, movable elevator and rudder, was satisfactory for pioneer use. A 40 horsepower kerosene compression-ignition engine weighing 120 pounds complete drove 6-foot twin airscrews [propellers], giving a stable thrust of 508 pounds; it could run a week continuously without heating or other trouble. The inventor's previous plane "No. 21", like "No. 22" but using acetylene, had flown 1.5 miles on August 14, 1901.

Such in Brief is the story published by Whitehead in the *American Inventor* of April 1, 1902. It shows two photographs of the airplane and two diagrams outlining the control mechanism and course of flight. That account was credited by the acting editor, C. H. Clandy. Later it was confirmed by Whitehead's skilled assistants, in formal affidavits now filed in the Library of Congress.

If these documents be approximately correct they have immense historic interest. The main question is whether Whitehead reported the facts as he observed them. He could not be gravely mistaken; for obviously it is immaterial whether he flew 7 miles or 1 mile, 200 feet or 10 feet high, 70 miles an hour or any less amount. If he flew round a long circle in his own craft driven by a compression-ignition engine, he was much the greatest airplane developer the world had yet seen. If he tells the truth*, he must, as inventor pilot, be entitled to the following claims:

1. The first power flight worldwide
2. The first circular flight in the world,
3. The first fast, high, or long flight
4. The first flight with an internal-combustion engine,
5. The first amphibian flight
6. The first practically controlled flight"

*We must recollect that there are multiple witnesses to Whitehead's flights of 1901-1902, more added a decade after Dr. Zahm's death, which occurred in 1954.[668]

A list of firsts

Whitehead accomplishments that may be considered "firsts*," expanded from lists first compiled by Stella Randolph, Whitehead's original researcher [669] [670]:

- First known manned, powered and controlled flight in a "heavier-than-air craft," worldwide in an aircraft he designed and built
- First to fly in a complete circle
- First passenger flight
- First night-time flights
- First true "aeronaut"

Chapter 11: Legacy

- First to make a successful powered night flight
- First training program for airplane pilots (he trained his assistants to fly)
- First use of movable rudders and forms of wing-warping in successfully flown aircraft
- First to design and fly a roadable "aero-car-boat" aircraft
- First powered successful seaplane
- First rubber-tired wheels used on successful airplane
- First to master launching plane using wheels and propellers
- First to design and build first powerful, lightweight gasoline engines for powered flight (1, 2, 3, 4, 6, & 8 cylinder engines)
- First to *sell* powerful, lightweight gasoline engines for powered flight
- First air-cooled engine in powered flight
- First airplane propelled on ground by engine
- First airplane with folding wings
- First use of aluminum propellers
- First to use lightweight metals for airplane construction
- First to design individually controllable propellers
- First to design two-place aircraft
- First to experiment with aircraft in Pennsylvania and Connecticut
- First to publicly advertise multiple passenger aircraft
- First to build a concrete runway for aircraft
- First to design and use a concrete-laying machine in Connecticut

*Biographer and researcher Stella Randolph notes most of these firsts were accomplished prior to December 17, 1903, in her book "Before the Wrights Flew."

WHITEHEAD'S MAIN ACCOMPLISHMENTS

- "First-in-Flight": first successful manned, powered and controlled flight in a "heavier-than-air craft" in the world, with his August 14, 1901 "No. 21" "Condor" aeroplane [671]
- Developed first inherently stable airplane
- Developed first successful flying boat, the precursor to the hydroplane
- World record for speed, duration, and altitude (1901-1903)
- Development of forms of wing warping, use of a movable rudder, and other means of control before the Wright patent was taken out
- Developed and flew first successful aerocar
- Developed and flew first successful aeroplane using wheels and ground engine to launch
- Developed and flew first successful aeroplane that used opposing propellers in front (later referred to as tractors)
- Provided a vision and example to others that flight was possible
- Developed multiple aircraft, with early successful designs that demonstrated flight was entirely possible
- Shared his findings openly with contemporary inventors in person, during press conferences, in trade journals, through letters to the editor, and in press interviews
- Designed and built lightweight engines for commercial use, some of which powered aircraft that flew successfully, such as those sold to aviation pioneer Charles Wittemann

Gustave Whitehead: "First in Flight"

Chapter 12

KITTY HAWK REVISITED

> **Wrights**
> Dec. 17
> 1903
> 3 attempts,
> 1 hop
> < .2 mi.
> w/ control problems
> and damage

KITTY HAWK "FIRST" FLIGHTS

"[The Wrights] were first to fly at Kitty Hawk, but they were *not first to fly*."
(Albert F. Zahm, PhD, 1945. Director Aerodynamical Laboratory, US Navy, 1916-1929; Director of Aeronautics Division, Library of Congress, 1930-1946)

The Wright brothers' first powered flights at Kitty Hawk occurred two years, four months, and three days *later* than those of Whitehead.

According to records, the Wrights took off in windy conditions (that appear to a number of observers to be necessary for the flight to have occurred) and did not show control over the plane. Each one of the four flights of that date, according to Orville's own words, ended without control and three ended with damage. "Each of the four flights was marked by an instability in pitch; the nose, and consequently the entire aircraft, would slowly bounce up and down. On the last flight, hard contact with the ground broke the front elevator support and ended the season's flying."[672]

Only the last flight was measured, by self-report, the first three were estimated[673]. Orville's first flight, now recognized by Smithsonian today, not only was a failed flight, but its distance was not measured, only estimated. Estimation of the distances flown by Whitehead has led to criticism by some historians - yet, both estimation and self-reporting has been deemed acceptable for the Wrights, particularly as the Wright Flyer was being given to the Smithsonian for $1 in 1948, under contract for this recognition.

From "How We Made the First Flight: Flight" by Orville Wright, published in "*Flying*," December 1913 and *The Aero Club of America Bulletin*, December 1913 [Author's note: when Wilbur was dead, having expired from typhoid fever in May 1912, Orville gave himself the credit his more capable brother had earlier received, for first flight].

[*emphasis added, below*]

The First Flight (by Orville Wright)

"Wilbur, having used his turn in the unsuccessful attempt on the 14th, the right to the first trial now belonged to me. After running the motor a few minutes to heat it up, I released the wire that held the machine to the track, and the machine started forward in the wind. Wilbur ran at the side of the machine, holding the wing to balance it on the track. Unlike the start on the 14th, made in a calm, the machine, facing a 27-mile wind, started very slowly. Wilbur was able to stay with it till it lifted from the track after a forty-foot run. *One of the Life Saving men snapped the camera for us, taking a picture just as the machine had reached the end of the track and had risen to a height of about two feet.* The slow forward speed of the machine over the ground is clearly shown in the picture by Wilbur's attitude. He stayed along beside the machine without any effort.

The course of the flight up and down was exceedingly erratic, partly due to the irregularity of the air, and partly to lack of experience in handling this machine. *The control of the front rudder was difficult on account of its being balanced too near the center. This gave it a tendency to turn itself when started; so that it turned too far on one side and then too far on the other. As a result the machine would rise suddenly to about ten feet, and then as suddenly dart for the ground. A sudden dart when a little over a hundred feet from the end of the track, or a little over 120 feet from the point at which it rose into the air, ended the flight.*

As the velocity of the wind was over 35 feet per second and the speed of the machine over the ground against this wind ten feet per second, the speed of the machine relative to the air was over 45 feet per second, and the length of the flight was equivalent to a flight of 540 feet made in calm air. *This flight lasted only 12 seconds, but it was nevertheless~ the first in the history of the world in which a machine carrying a man had raised itself by its own power into the air in full flight, had sailed forward without reduction of speed and had finally landed at a point as high as that from which it started.* [Author's note: this statement is contrary to the records Orville had approved, in William J. Hammer's "Chronology of Aviation." Note lack of control and very brief hop. "Chronology of Aviation," approved by the Wrights, and entered into their patent lawsuit as evidence of their purported "pioneer invention" (cite) shows that the first three flights were "attempts" and not successful.[674] Finally, note the attempts by Orville to overstate the estimated distance of his flight, from 120 feet to 540 feet, by "factoring in the wind."]

With the assistance of our visitors we carried the machine back to the track and prepared for another flight.

The Second and Third Flights

At twenty minutes after eleven Wilbur started on the second flight. The course of this flight was much like that of the first, very much up and down. The speed over the ground was somewhat faster than that of the first flight, due to the lesser wind. The duration of the flight was less than a second longer than the first, but the distance covered was about seventy-five feet greater.

Twenty minutes later the third flight started. This one was steadier than the first one an hour before. I was proceeding along pretty well *when a sudden gust from the right lifted the machine up twelve to fifteen feet and turned it up sidewise in an alarming manner. It began a lively sidling off to the left.* I warped the wings to try to recover the lateral balance and at the same time pointed the machine down to reach the ground as quickly as possible. The lateral control was more effective than I had imagined and *before I reached the ground the right wing was lower than the left and struck first.* The time of this flight was fifteen seconds and the distance over the ground a little over 200 feet.

Chapter 12: Kitty Hawk Revisited

The Fourth Flight

Wilbur started the *fourth and last flight* at just 12 o'clock. The first few hundred feet were up and down, as before, but by the time three hundred feet had been covered, the machine was under much better control. The course of the next four or five hundred feet had but little undulation. However, *when out about eight hundred feet the machine began pitching again, and, in one of the its darts downward, struck the ground.* The distance over the ground was measured and found to be 852 feet; the time of the flight was 59 seconds. *The frame supporting the front rudder was badly broken,* but the main part of the machine was not injured at all. We estimated that the machine could be put in condition for flight again in a day or two."[675]

WRIGHTS' FLIGHT PROBLEMS

The famous photo lauded by Smithsonian as "proof of flights by the Wrights on Dec. 17, 1903, shows the Wrights' plane no more than two feet above the ground for the first, *unsuccessful* flight of the day, by Orville. This was an out-of-control hop. There was no control, the plane lifted erratically *only to 10 feet* and it crash-landed within 12 seconds, at a distance *estimated* to be 120 feet. Only the last flight out of four was measured, the others were estimated, according to the Wrights' records. There are no photos of the Wright aeroplane in successful flight, none clearly airborne. *This photo proves nothing, showing that a photo of Whitehead's plane is not needed to compete with this one.*

[Author's note: Billed as: *"The first manned flight in history: December 17, 1903. At 10:35 a.m., Orville Wright takes off into a 27 mph wind. The distance covered was 120 feet; time aloft was 12 seconds. Wilbur is seen at right. Picture was taken with Orville's camera by John T. Daniels."*][676]

FIRST FLIGHT OF THE DAY BY ORVILLE:
The famed photo is of an unsuccessful attempt and only proves the plane lifted off the ground several feet at most. The photo cannot be considered "in-flight."
Duration of flight: 12 sec
Distance: 120 feet (estimated by Wrights)
Altitude: 8-10 feet

FLIGHT TWO BY WILBUR:
No in-flight photo
Duration of flight: 12 sec
Distance: 175 feet (estimated by Wrights)
No altitude given

FLIGHT 3 OF THE DAY, BY ORVILLE:
Unsuccessful attempt, no in-flight photo
Duration of flight: 15 sec
Distance: 200 feet (estimated by Wrights)
Altitude: 12-14 feet
[Author's note: this is also very brief, unsuccessful flight, 12-14 ft., crash landing.]

FOURTH FLIGHT OF THE DAY, BY WILBUR: Called "successful," though it too, landed with damage. No in-flight photo has been authenticated.
Duration of flight: 59 sec
Distance 852 feet (measured and self-reported by Wrights)
(No altitude given)   Elevator damaged on landing

© Susan Brinchman, 2015

Gustave Whitehead: "First in Flight"

WRIGHTS' FLIGHTS LESS SUCCESSFUL

The first three flight attempts of December 17th, 1903 and (4th) last flight (which may or may not be considered successful as it also landed with damage) cannot compare with Gustave Whitehead's successful flights of 1901-1902.

> "Between 10:35 a.m. and noon on December 17, 1903, the brothers made four flights. The first and second were 12 seconds, then 15 seconds on the third, and the final, long flight lasted 59 seconds. Distances covered were 120 feet, 175 feet, 200 feet, and 852 feet. Altitudes ranged between about 8 to 14 feet."[677] (Smithsonian)

These flights were far shorter and at much lower altitudes than the successful ones attested to by the Whitehead witnesses, two years earlier. The Wrights' longest (and only) flight of December 17, 1903 was the fourth, Wilbur's, and it was one-third the distance of Whitehead's first flight of August 14, 1901, which was 1/2 mile. Whitehead's flight also showed more control, as there was no damage. Compared to Whitehead's longest flight of August 14, 1901, said to be 1.5 miles, Wilbur's flight of December 17, 1903 was one-tenth the distance. Whitehead flew from 50 to 200 feet in altitude, while The fourth flight has no altitude recorded, but it would appear that it was just as close to the ground as the others, which were under 15 feet.

In 1913, Orville agreed that William J. Hammer's "Chronology of Aviation," published in 1911 in the World Almanac of that year, and reprinted and widely distributed in 1912, was the best treatment of "their work" so far. The Chronology *did not credit Orville with first flight,* because both of his flights and Wilbur's first were considered NOT to show they had power or control. However, Wilbur was gone, having died in May 1912, and Orville began seeking the credit for first flight, becoming upset when anyone claimed even close to that title. His lifelong crusade for the recognition he couldn't get with the more dominant brother Wilbur alive, culminated in the trade that was made in November 1948 – the Wright Flyer for $1, in exchange for recognizing Orville posthumously as "first in flight," as long as the Smithsonian wished to keep the aeroplane. (See Appendix of this book for all documents substantiating this statement.)

The Smithsonian, to this day, *recognizes Orville's flight* as first in the world (first of the day), per their contract made with the Wright executors. The flight was *self-reported, a flight of only 12 seconds, 8-10 feet above the ground and for an estimated maximum distance of 120 feet, a tiny hop that ended with damage!*

The flights at Kitty Hawk were witnessed by "John T. Daniels, W. S. Dough, and A. D. Etheridge, from the Kill Devil Life Saving Station. W. C. Brinkley of Manteo, and Johnny Moore from Nags Head."[678] No affidavits were taken.

In May 1904, the Wrights attempted to provide *thirty* reporters with a demonstration of their flying feats in Dayton, OH. After two days of failure attributed to both wind and engine trouble, and one attempt that raised the plane off the ground a few feet for 60 feet, the press left, with several writing disparaging articles.[679]

WRIGHTS' WITNESS STATEMENTS

In early 1906, while their "invention" was still several months from being covered by an approved patent, the Wrights provided a list of 17 witnesses to the *Scientific American* regarding their "historic flights." In March the Aero Club of America, after receiving a statement from the Wrights describing details of their flights of the past three years, including " that of a "man-carrying motor flyer, which, on the 17th day of December 1903, sustained itself in the air for 59 seconds ... a distance of 852 feet"[680] and the names of witnesses to their flights, endorsed them[681]. *Ten of the eleven witnesses referred only to flights conducted late in 1905. There is no mention of anyone who acknowledged being present for the flights at Kitty Hawk.* The *Scientific American* and Aero Club endorsement, therefore, *was not based on being "first in flight,"* but "for developing an aeroplane type of flying

Chapter 12: Kitty Hawk Revisited

machine that many times has carried a man safely through the air at high speed and continuously over long distances."

No member of the Aero Club had witnessed the Wrights fly, or even interviewed a witness. The endorsement was made entirely on the Wrights' statement[682] sent with the encouragement of their new friend, Consulting Engineer William J. Hammer, formerly a Thomas Edison assistant. Stanley Yale Beach, Aviation Editor for the *Scientific American*, another prominent member of the Aero Club, relates the following in his article in the *Scientific American*, "*The Wright Aeroplane and Its Performance*" of April 7, 1906:

"According to the statement sent to the Aero Club of America recently by Messrs. Orville and Wilbur Wright (which statement is, by the way, the first authoritative one made by the brothers in their own country), they have already solved the problem of the century, mechanical flight, with their motor-driven, man-carrying aeroplane...

...The Wrights refused [earlier] to make a statement, and they gave the names of but a few persons who had seen them fly. With the communication recently sent by them to the Aero Club, however, they sent a list of names of seventeen men who were eyewitnesses of their experiments.

In order to dispel any lingering doubt regarding the flights, the reported accounts of which the leading German aeronautical journal, Illustrirte Aeronautische Mitteilungen, characterized as "ein amerikanischer 'bluff,'" a list of questions was sent to the seventeen witnesses. In all we received eleven replies.

To the first question, on what date or dates did you see the aeroplane fly ... *ten of the witnesses agreed, however that they had seen the aeroplane fly in the autumn of 1905*, the majority in the month of October."[683]

Figure 179: Sci American - Wright witnesses only for later flights in 1905

The article does not mention the date that the 11th witness saw a Wright plane fly, but it is clear that witness statements were not taken nor necessary for the eventual acceptance of the Wrights as "first in flight."

GAINING RECOGNITION AS FIRST IN FLIGHT – WHO WAS REALLY "FIRST"?

Recognition of "first in flight" was engineered by William J. Hammer. The Wrights' early recognition stemmed from their development of a more practical airplane in the years following 1903, not for being first with a sustained, powered, aircraft with control. They did not achieve partial control until after 1905, and killed many pilots with their unstable aeroplanes in the following ten years.

"The Chronology of Aviation," written by William J. Hammer (secret Wright employee) and Hudson Maxim, published in the World Almanac 1911, distributed widely as a booklet, and entered into the Curtiss patent suit court records as evidence by the Wrights' attorney, approved by Orville Wright in 1913, *gave Wilbur credit for "first flight" [despite the lack of control and landing problems],* not Orville, whose two attempts failed. This was commonly accepted during Wilbur's lifetime (he died in 1912).[684]

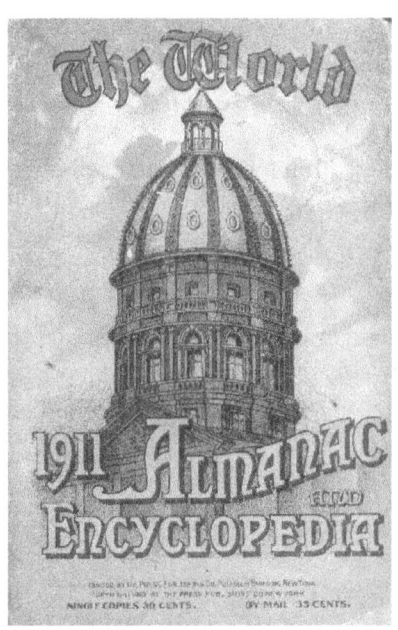

Figure 180: World Almanac 1911 documented Orville's 1903 flights failures

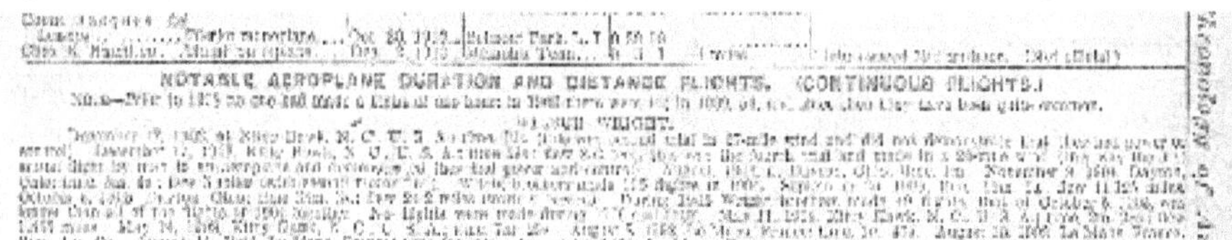
NOTABLE AEROPLANE DURATION AND DISTANCE FLIGHTS. (CONTINUOUS FLIGHTS.)

WILBUR WRIGHT.

ORVILLE WRIGHT.

Figure 181: World Almanac's "Chronology of Aviation" shows Orville's flights failures

Chapter 12: Kitty Hawk Revisited

Transcript from the "Chronology of Aviation," World Almanac, 1911, p. 437

NOTABLE AIR DURATION AND DISTANCE FLIGHTS
Approved by Orville Wright 1913
Coauthored by secret* Wright employee William J. Hammer
[*to be covered in "Hidden History of Gustave Whitehead and the Wrights Series]

Dec. 17, 1903: At Kitty Hawk
Orville Wright (first attempt) "did not demonstrate that they had power or control"
(third attempt) "did not demonstrate that they had power or control"
Wilbur Wright (2nd attempt) "did not demonstrate that they had power or control";
(4th trial) "first actual flight by man in an aeroplane and demonstrated they had power and control"[685]

Albert F. Zahm, PhD, director of the Aerodynamical Laboratory of the U.S. Navy and Guggenheim Chair of Aeronautics at the Library of Congress, a contemporary and critic of the Wrights for four decades, lambasted them for their claims of "first in flight" and for their patents and treatment of other aviators. He commented in an undated essay,

> "All the World" can of course say *the Kitty Hawk machine was the first to fly from a monorail launching track, aided by a wing-holding assistant*, as reported in 1903. It was not the first powerplane invented or patented; not the first designed with aileron or wing-warping control; not the first to taxi or make sustained flight with a pilot." [686]

Now, in its 100th anniversary edition, Jane's All-the-World's Aircraft agrees with Zahm, in effect, crediting Whitehead with the first powered, manned, sustained, controlled flight in all the world.

LITTLE KNOWN FACTS ABOUT KITTY HAWK

The Wright Brothers were more than two years later in "flight" than Whitehead, so they cannot be "first."

The Wright Brothers and Whitehead both had a means of steering using the wings. Both had systems requiring shifting the position of the pilot. Both had wires connected to wing tips and rudders. Whitehead also used the propellers to steer successfully, alternating power.[687]

The Wright Brothers flew at a much lower altitude than Whitehead's notable flights in 1901 and 1902. The Wrights flew very close to the ground. (The Wrights flew between 2-14 ft. in altitude; Whitehead flew 50-200 ft. in altitude.)

The Wright Brothers flew much shorter distances than Whitehead's notable flights in 1901 and 1902 ; 1/3 the distance, at best. Wilbur Wright's longest distance on Dec. 17, 1903 was 852 ft., while Whitehead's shortest distance of Aug. 14, 1901 was 2640 ft.

The Wright Brothers' plane was not in control on during all four flights, per the descriptions by Orville in "How We Made the First Flight" (flights #1, 2, 3, 4) and per William J. Hammer's "Chronology of Aviation" (#1, 2, 3) approved by Orville. If there was a means to control it, as is claimed, it certainly did not work.

The famous photo of "the first flight" shows the first attempt, with Orville at the helm, which is a failed attempt and only shows the plane about 2 feet off the ground. Yet Smithsonian challenges Whitehead's flights, in part for not (now) having an in-flight photo for the 1901-1902 flights.[688]

Gustave Whitehead: "First in Flight"

The December 17, 1903 photos of the Wrights' "flights" were not released until 1908, five years later.[689]

The Wrights made no public displays of their flights till 1908, in France.[690]

A full public description of these flights was not provided by the Wrights till 1906, more than two years later.[691]

The Wright Flyer replica was unable to fly at the Centennial celebration at Kitty Hawk, as there was very little wind[692], while several Whitehead replicas, built to test Whitehead's designs by several separate teams, had no problems flying at all during the past 27 years, with or without wind.[693] [694]

The Wrights' 1903 plane did not take off under its own power. It needed a strong wind to lift off the ground or a catapult to launch it into the air without the strong wind and dunes. "Without the winds of Kitty Hawk, it was a problem getting enough airspeed to fly. So the brothers devised a catapult system to help launch the aircraft."[695]

Documentation for the first flights of the Wrights is through their own words, and the story does change over time about who gets the credit (Orville or Wilbur), especially after Wilbur's death in 1912.

The Wrights took till 1905 to further develop the art, the beginnings of a practical plane, which is acknowledged, although others were also doing so by then...[696]

Orville finally gained credit, years after Wilbur died, for the purported "first flight" even though he agreed in 1913 that the "Chronology of Aviation" was accurate, and that Wilbur's flight was the only "success" of the day.

The Wrights gained credit for first flight with the American public through a subrosa employee, William J. Hammer, previously chief engineer to Thomas Edison, who successfully promoted them as first, to assist in their lawsuits, as a "pioneer invention" [first, completely new invention] was necessary to allow a broad interpretation of the patent, and allow a world monopoly on the only designs necessary for flight, [more on this in coming Series].

SMITHSONIAN-WRIGHT "CONTRACT" CREDITING ORVILLE DESIGNED BY PROMINENT WHITEHEAD DETRACTORS

The Smithsonian has been bound by "a Contract" signed with the Wright executors, since November 1948 requiring recognition of Orville's failed flight as "first" or suffer loss of the Wright Flyer as an exhibit.[697] The Contract, called an "Agreement" by Smithsonian, was unearthed by Major William J. O'Dwyer, Whitehead researcher, in 1976, with the help of Connecticut's then-Senator Lowell Weicker, Jr.. From 1963 through 1976, Major O'Dwyer had noticed peculiar behavior on the part of Smithsonian curators, a tendency to avoid any discussion of flights that might have occurred prior to 1903. He was tipped off that the contract had been loudly cited by a Wright executor, in a meeting with museum directors, when a curator mentioned he wanted to change the legend on the Flyer.[698]

After a number of attempts, using the newly minted Freedom of Information Act, Major O'Dwyer was finally able to obtain a signed copy of the formerly secret "Wright-Smithsonian Contract," as it is now referred to. Further information about Whitehead and the process in uncovering the Contract is detailed in "History by Contract," a book coauthored by O'Dwyer and Randolph, published in 1978. The book sold enough copies (some of which remain in circulation, though out of print) to alert the aviation historian community that the Contract existed (and still exists at this writing).

Recently, in 2013, various news media outlets have seized upon the existence of the Contract as evidence of an inappropriate conflict of interest[699]. There have been a number of calls for its abrogation, or nullification.[700] Thus far, Smithsonian's curators defend and minimize the contract, calling it "a healthy reminder"[701] of

Chapter 12: Kitty Hawk Revisited

Smithsonian's past sins of partiality to its own Secretary Langley for the some of the laurels for first flight. Students of Whitehead's history know that Orville Wright and the Smithsonian were well aware of Whitehead as a contender for first in flight up through the time that the Contract was crafted in 1948, and therefore, it included wording that makes it impossible to impartially examine oR acknowledge Whitehead as first in flight. Critics state that if it was only written so Langley couldn't receive credit, his name could have been mentioned. But the Contract is far broader than that - no earlier successful plane or aviator may be recognized, or the Wright Flyer returns to the heirs.

Required labeling on Wright Flyer per the Smithsonian-Wright Contract:[702]

"The Original Wright Brothers' Aeroplane
The world's First Power-Driven Heavier-than-Air Machine
In Which Man Made Free, Controlled, and
Sustained flight
Invented and Built by Wilbur and Orville Wright
Flown by Them at Kitty Hawk, North Carolina
December 17, 1903
By Original Scientific Research the Wright Brothers Discovered The Principles of Human flight
As Inventors, Builders and Flyers They Further Developed the Aeroplane
Taught Man to Fly and Opened the Era of Aviation
Deposited by the Estate of Orville Wright."

(Required labeling)

"The first flight lasted only twelve seconds, a flight very modest compared with that of birds, but it was nevertheless the first in the History of the world in which a machine carrying a man had raised itself by its own power into the air in free flight, had sailed forward on a level course without reduction of speed, and had finally landed without being wrecked. The second and third flights were a little longer, and the fourth lasted 59 seconds covering a distance of 852 feet over the ground against a 20 mile wind."

Wilbur and Orville Wright

(From Century Magazine, Vol. 76 September 1908, p. 649)"[703] [704]

A never-before-known, direct connection between denying Whitehead flew first and the designing of the "Contract"[705] with Smithsonian, including the label on the Wright Flyer, has been "unearthed." This is a game-changer that establishes exactly how Whitehead's claim was deliberately, secretly, and effectively denied, all these years. It involves plotting behind the scenes, by Smithsonian curators and influential friends of Orville Wright, to provide Orville permanent credit that he did not deserve, without regard for historical facts. It worked for 70 years.

From 1935 through 1937, Stella Randolph, Whitehead's first researcher and original biographer, wrote a series of articles and a book about Gustave Whitehead's flights, which predated those of the Wright brothers. Her writings received national attention, to the dismay of Orville Wright and his supporters.

Following the death of Wilbur Wright in 1912, Orville, previously considered "the lesser brother," worked unceasingly to establish his role in first flight. Until the date of Wilbur's death, it was Wilbur who'd been credited with being first, established in the publication of the *World Almanac of 1911*. Orville's flights of December 17, 1903 had been openly admitted as failures, by both brothers. Whitehead had been ignored, as the data and article had been put together by a secret, subrosa employee of the Wrights, Thomas Edison's former right-hand engineer, William J. Hammer. Hammer was hired by Wilbur Wright to promote the brothers as first in flight, amongst other duties. Hammer would go on to perjure himself as an independent expert during the Wright patent trials, where the World Almanac article was entered as evidence that the Wright brothers deserved "pioneer inventors" status. In the popular mind and the media, following Hammer's PR campaigns that began in 1906, and with the support of the New York aero clubs, the Wrights were seen as "first in flight."

Once Randolph began to publicize the earlier flights of Whitehead, friends of the Wrights organized to stamp out the claims wherever they appeared. They began to use their considerable influence to attempt to stop the Whitehead information from getting out the public, as if it was heresy. News of Whitehead's credit was spreading like wildfire in Hollywood, in syndicated magazine articles nationwide, on a very popular coast-to-coast radio show, in ads on NYC subway cars, an article in the *Reader's Digest*, and with a Harvard professor of transportation who called for a Congressional hearing on the topic. Friends of Orville felt these had to be controlled.

Major Lester D. Gardner and Earl Nelson Findley, two of the most influential Wright supporters, openly discussed their mutual campaign to credit Orville and wipe out Whitehead's claim in letters that they wrote, back and forth, from 1939-1946. Both Gardner and Findley were widely recognized in aeronautical circles of the era, particularly for their close relationships with Orville Wright. Major Lester D. Gardner was the original publisher of the journal *Aviation and Aeronautical Engineering*, and founder of the Institute of the Aeronautical Sciences (IAS), located in New York City, in 1932. Its first honorary fellow was Orville Wright. Earl Findley was the first editor of US Air Services magazine. Findley formerly was a reporter and editor for the *New York Times* who became very close to the Wright brothers and the Wright family, for the rest of his life.

In 1939, Major Lester D. Gardner and Earl Findley orchestrated and co-produced the so-called "Stanley Yale Beach Whitehead Statement," which denounced that Whitehead could ever have flown, now available at the Library of Congress (also, see Appendix of this book).

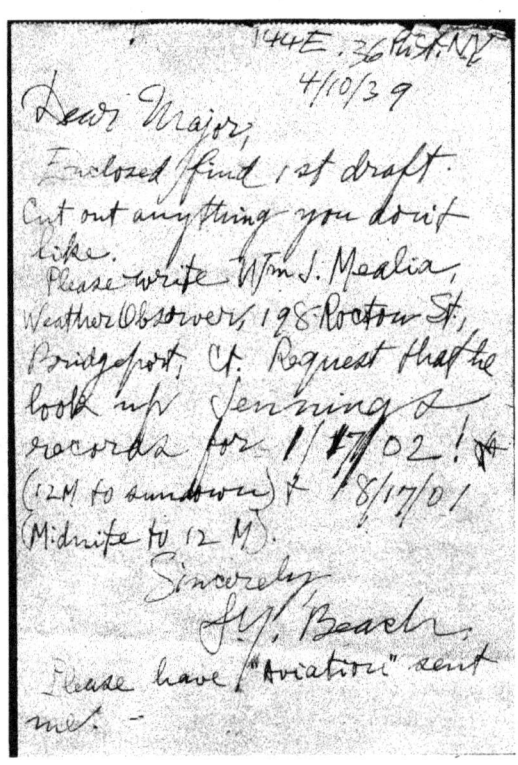

Figure 182: Stanley Beach wrote Maj. Lester Gardner to check weather records

Chapter 12: Kitty Hawk Revisited

Stanley Yale Beach, former Aviation Editor and supporter of Whitehead flights through 1908, was influenced to write a negative statement on Gustave Whitehead in 1939, and he wrote Major Lester Gardner to ask him to "cut out anything he doesn't like" in the Beach statement which Gardner and Findley solicited. The draft is profoundly edited by two individuals, in addition to Beach, one is Gardner, the other, Findley. Letters back and forth clearly show this.

The heavily edited Beach statement drafts looked like this (pages 1 & 2 of 6):

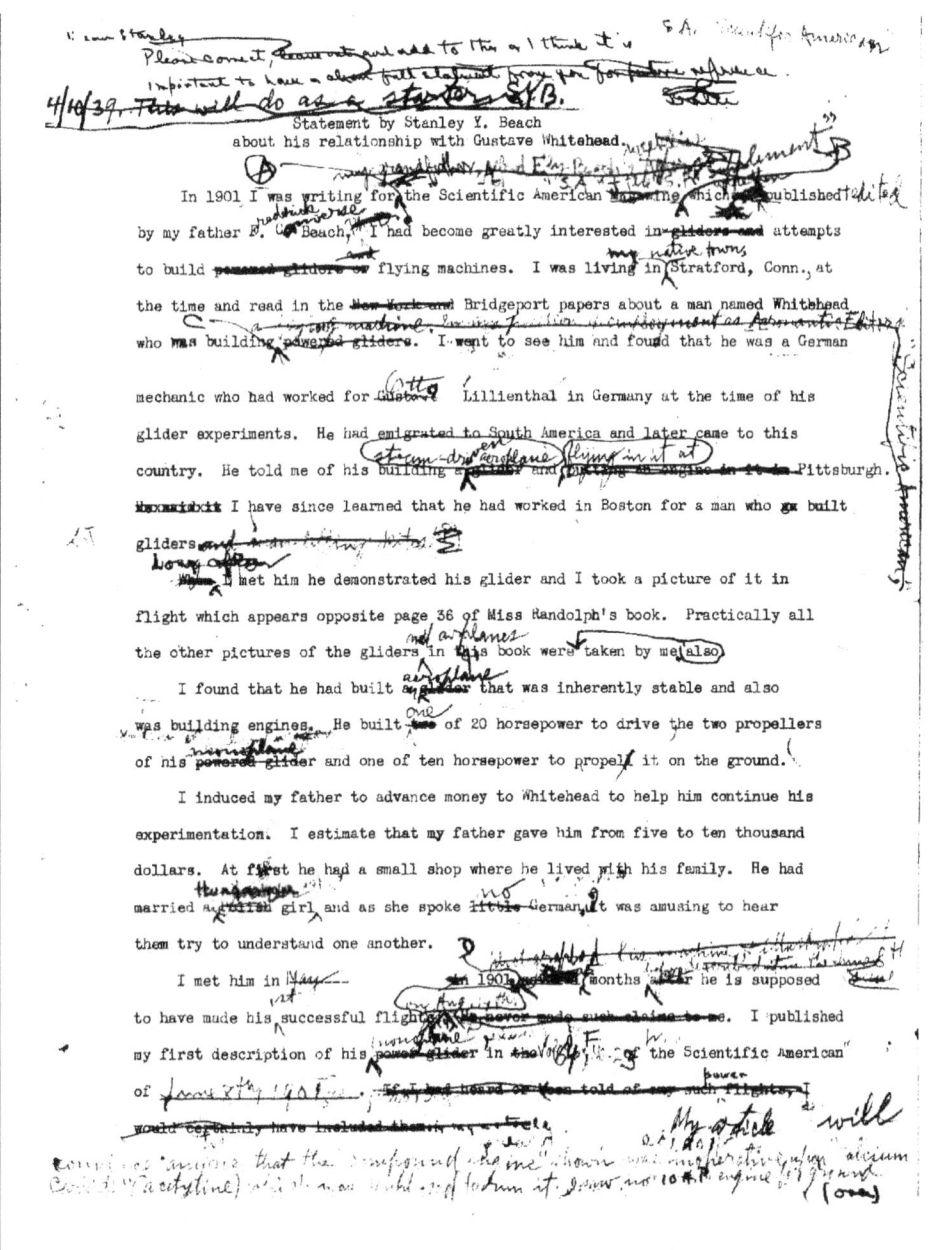

Figure 183: Beach Whitehead Statement draft edited by Gardner, p. 1

Beach Whitehead Statement Draft 1 (p. 1 of 6) with heavy edits including Gardner's.

© Susan Brinchman, 2015

Gustave Whitehead: "First in Flight"

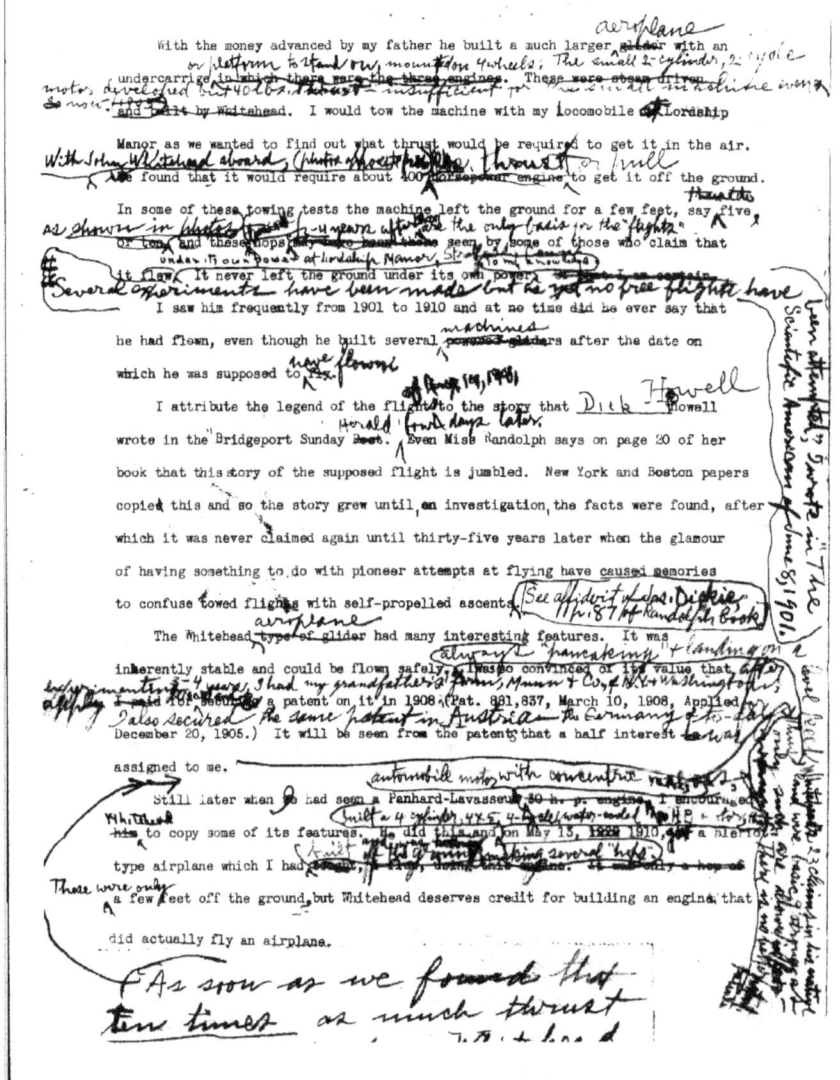

Figure 184: Beach Whitehead Statement draft edited by Gardner, p. 2

Beach Whitehead Statement Draft 1 (p. 2 of 6) with heavy edits including Gardner's.

Major Lester Gardner (LDF) wrote Earl Findley on April 11, 1939, after he'd received the final draft. He said, "I have just received the statement from Stanley Beach…If you knew him you would know what a job it was to pry this out of him. I could not edit it as I would have wished, but you could do so by omissions in any article you write." Then Gardner proceeded to express concern that Stella Randolph, in her book "Lost Flights of Gustave Whitehead" (1937) talked about an early visit to Whitehead's shop from the Wright brothers. He wants Findley to look into it. Also, Gardner mentions Randolph used a Wright quote in her 1935 *Popular Aviation* article, without a citation, "Man will never fly in a thousand years" and asks Findley to read it. Gardner and Findley became a "tag-team" to defend Orville's desired position as first in flight and attack Whitehead researcher Randolph and supporters. They would continue this through 1948, culminating in the legal contract requiring Orville to receive the credit for first powered flight, to the exclusion of Whitehead, their nemesis, his brother Wilbur, and all others.

Chapter 12: Kitty Hawk Revisited

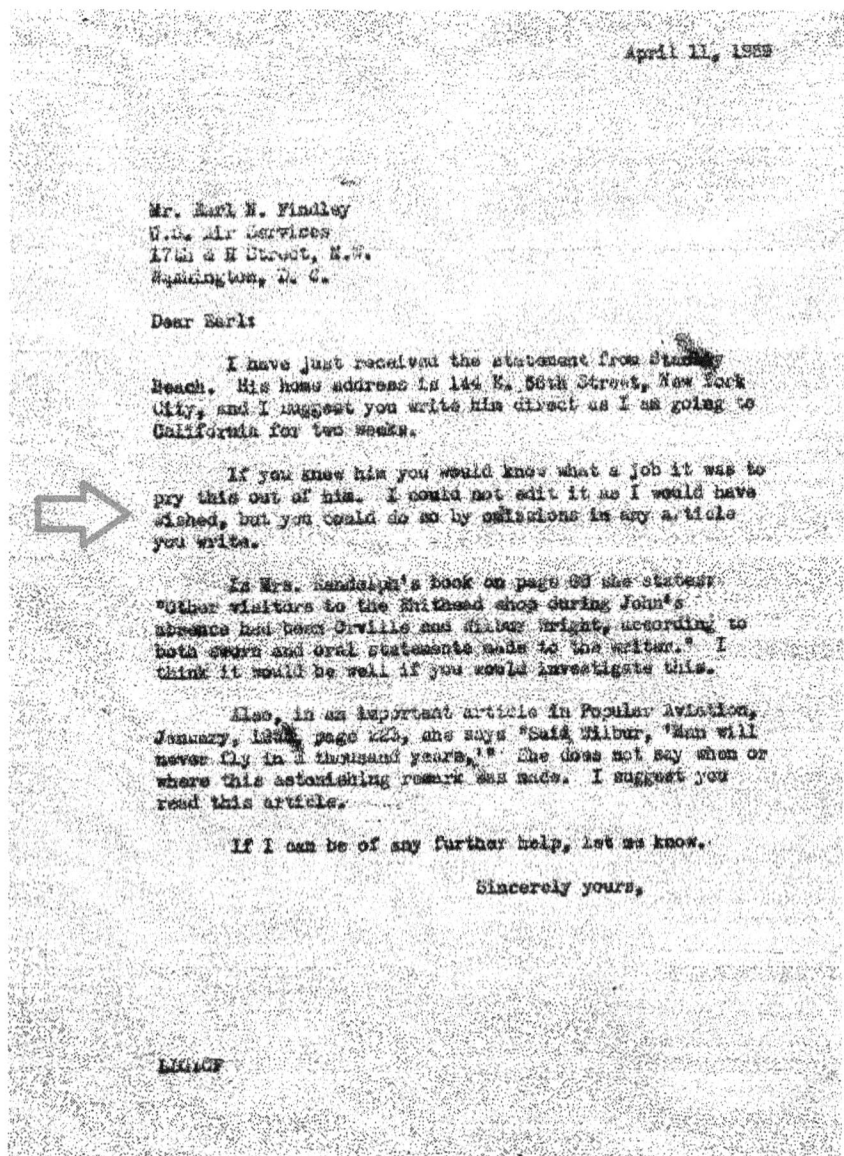

Figure 185: Maj. Gardner writes Earl Findley suggesting edits to Beach-Whitehead Statement

Gardner wrote Findley about the final Beach statement, revealing how to best use it and that he couldn't edit it fully as he wished, but "Findley can."

Both Gardner and Findley became recipients of a piece of cloth from the Wright Flyer as a token of esteem afterward (perhaps, thanks for their dogged support) from Orville.

The unpublished and unsigned Beach statement was then deliberately provided to Orville Wright, influencing him to use it as the basis for his "The Mythical Whitehead Flight" article of 1945, published in Findley's US Air Services magazine. Orville's negative Whitehead article, denying Whitehead or his plane could ever have flown is still the "playbook" for denying Whitehead, used by Smithsonian curators through the present date.

Just a few years later, Gardner and Findley, who vowed to salvage Orville's title and to destroy Whitehead's claims, have now been revealed as key consultants, invited by the Smithsonian curator, Paul Garber[706], to design

Gustave Whitehead: "First in Flight"

the final details of the *Smithsonian-Wright Agreement of 1948* (aka "the Contract"), following Orville's death in January 1948. This direct connection to the creators of the denouncement of Whitehead and their subsequent influence on "the Contract" was never before known, outside of the inner circles in Smithsonian, where the documents are kept. Others who worked on the label included Wright family members; Orville's longtime secretary, Mabel Beck; Fred C. Kelly – the Wrights first biographer and trusted, old friend; and the Smithsonian curator, Paul Garber, described as "very loyal to Orville." The Wright Flyer label was designed by highly biased individuals based on what they felt Orville would have wanted, and what would secure credit for the first flight. No historical investigation was conducted to make the label accurate. This is clear from the correspondence and transcripts included in the Smithsonian archives concerning the planning of the Contract.

This is the required wording for the Wright Flyer* exhibit that resulted from the biased group's efforts, which attempts to "cement" the credit for first flight for Orville, who had just died earlier that year.

"The Original Wright Brothers' Aeroplane

The World's First Power-Driven Heavier-than-Air Machine

In Which Man Made Free, Controlled, and

Sustained Flight

Invented and Built by Wilbur and Orville Wright

Flown by Them at Kitty Hawk, North Carolina

December 17, 1903

By Original Scientific Research the Wright Brothers Discovered The Principles of Human Flight"

[and]

"The first flight lasted only twelve seconds, a flight very modest compared with that of birds, but it was nevertheless the first in the history of the world in which a machine carrying a man had raised itself by its own power into the air in free flight, had sailed forward on a level course without reduction of speed, and had finally landed without being wrecked. The second and third flights were a little longer, and the fourth lasted 59 seconds covering a distance of 852 feet over the ground against a 20 mile wind.

Wilbur and Orville Wright
(From Century Magazine*, Vol. 76 September 1908, p. 649)"

Orville and his sister Katharine wrote the Century Magazine article without Wilbur, crediting Orville, when Wilbur was out of the country for an extended period. By the time Wilbur returned, it had been published. Orville credited himself, rather than Wilbur, then, and later, as first in flight. This is a matter of record, per the correspondences concerning this article in the months leading up to September 1908, located in the Papers of Wilbur and Orville Wright at the Library of Congress.

The *Smithsonian-Wright Agreement of 1948*, allowed Smithsonian to obtain the Wright Flyer for $1 from the Orville Wright estate. The agreement, often referred to as "the Contract," essentially requires Smithsonian and all its affiliates, to recognize the Wright Flyer as the first airplane that flew with power, and Orville Wright as the first successful aviator. Required labels on the exhibit and required placement in the Smithsonian are included. If the Contract is broken, the Wright Flyer, the most popular exhibit at the Smithsonian, returns to the heirs. The Contract, originally kept secret from the public, was learned of and obtained by Major William J.

Chapter 12: Kitty Hawk Revisited

O'Dwyer (USAF, ret.), with the help of then-Senator Lowell Weicker, Jr., in 1976. [The Contract is available in Appendix A of this book.]

The communications between Gardner and Findley concerning Whitehead's claim as first in flight were very clear – they wanted to stamp out that claim and worked on this for 11 years following the publication of Stella Randolph's book. They were in a position to do so, behind the scenes. Letters received and sent between Gardner, Findley, Beach, and Orville Wright, amongst others, are located at the Library of Congress, in their Gustave Whitehead collection, and the Earl Findley and Lester Gardner sections of the Papers of Wilbur and Orville Wright archives. Interestingly, and obviously by design, *none of these appear on the public listing online*, but they are there. Who at the LOC decided that these should be hidden from the public?

Their efforts worked, too, quite effectively, for the past (nearly) seven decades. Exposing the Gardner – Findley involvement in the development of the *Smithsonian-Wright Agreement of 1948* "the Contract" *exposes "the agreement" with Smithsonian for what it was – a means to deny Whitehead a claim on first flight.* Smithsonian National Air and Space Museum (NASM) curators and Wright supporters cannot continue to maintain that it was developed solely to fend off old Smithsonian claims that its former Secretary, Samuel P. Langley, built "the first plane capable of flight," which had so angered Orville in 1928.

Below is a letter sent in August from Smithsonian's Assistant Secretary, naming Gardner and Findley as parties to the ongoing process to determine the wording of the Wright Flyer exhibit labels, which continued through Sept. and Oct. of 1948. Additional documents obtained include transcripts of conversations and letters between the principal parties.

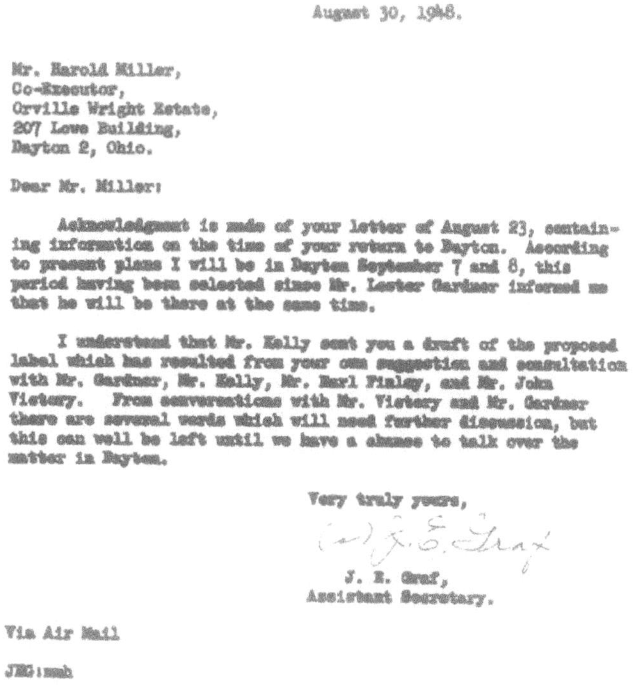

Figure 186: Asst. Secretary Smithsonian confirms Gardner and Findley planning label on Wright Flyer crediting Orville.

"Dear Mr. Miller [husband of Orville Wright's niece Ivonette; co-executor, Orville Wright Estate],

Acknowledgement is made of your letter of August 23, containing information on the time of your return to Dayton. According to present plans I will be in Dayton September 7 and 8, this period having been selected since Mr. Lester Gardner informed us that he will be there at the same time.

I understand that Mr. Kelly sent you a draft of the proposed label which has resulted from your own suggestion and consultation with Mr. Gardner, Mr. Kelly, Mr. Earl Fin[d]ley, and Mr. John Victory. From conversations with Mr. Victory and Mr. Gardner there are several words which will need further discussion, but this can well be left until we have a chance to talk over the matter in Dayton." (J. E. Graf, Asst. Secretary, Smithsonian, Aug. 30, 1948)

> Major Lester D. Gardner,
> 251 West 101st Street,
> New York 25, N.Y.
>
> Dear Lester:
>
> Herewith is the carbon of the August 24, 1948, draft of proposed label for the Wright airplane as tentatively agreed to as a basis at your and Mr. Kelly's meeting with Dr. Wetmore, of the Smithsonian. There are still some points for improvement. I suggest the following:

Figure 187: Letter confirming Lester Gardner's involvement with development of Wright Flyer labels (part a).

"Major Lester D. Gardner [Whitehead detractor]

Dear Lester:

Herewith is the carbon of the August 24, 1948 draft of proposed label for the Wright airplane as tentatively agreed to as a basis at your and Mr. Kelly's meeting with Dr. Wetmore, of the Smithsonian. There are still some points for improvement. I suggest the following:

I thoroughly enjoyed my frequent meetings with you recently and congratulate you on the opportunities that are now yours for further constructive contributions." (J. F. Victory)

….. (letter continues to end):

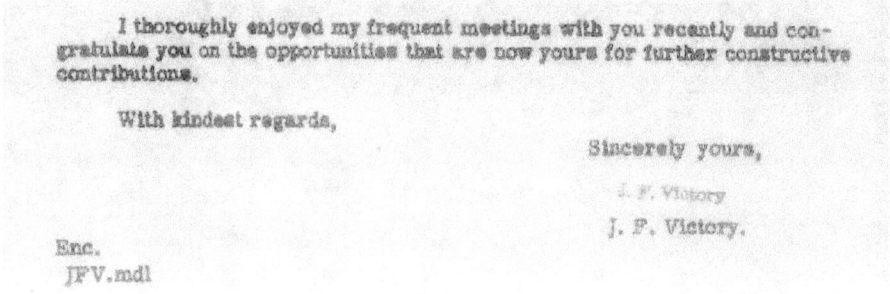

Figure 188: Letter confirming Gardner participation (part b).

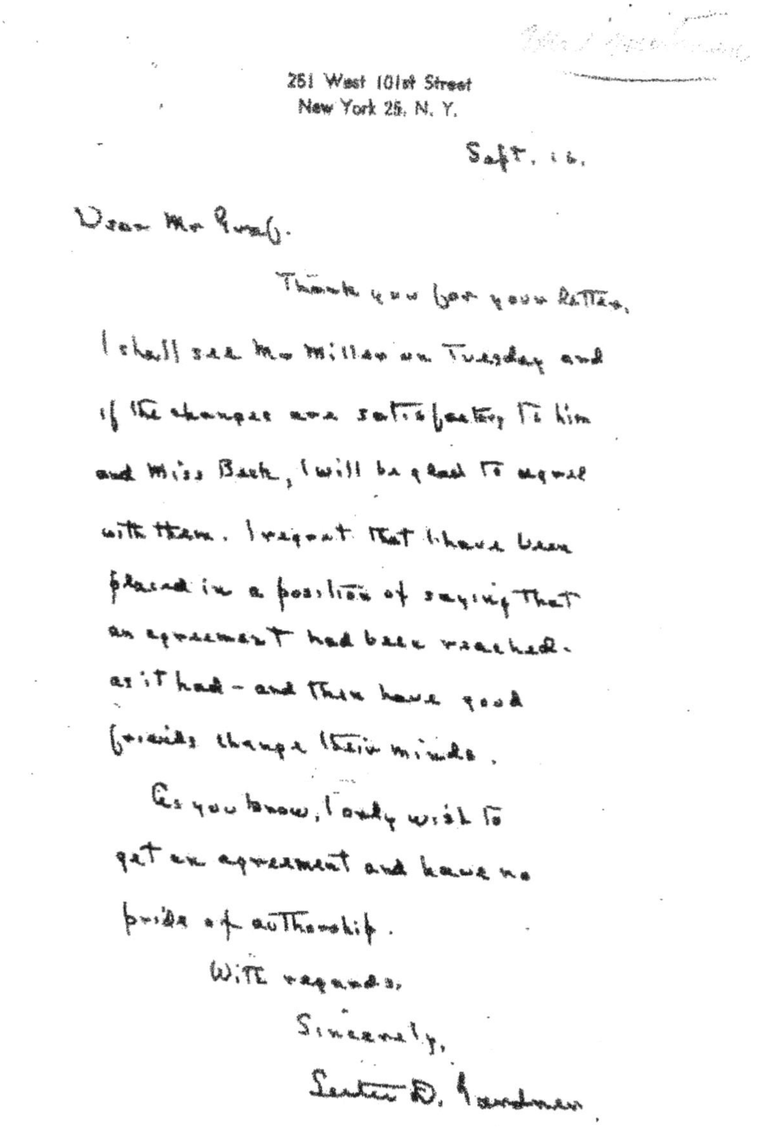

Chapter 12: Kitty Hawk Revisited

Figure 189: Gardner confirms working on label and agreeing to changes

Lester Gardner replies to a letter from Smithsonian Asst. Secretary Graf that he will see Mr. Miller (co-executor of O. W. estate) on Tues. and if the changes [to the labels] are satisfactory to him and Ms. Beck [Orville Wright's secretary] he will be glad to agree with them.

Sept. 16 [1948]

"Dear Mr. Gard.,

Thank you for your letter. I shall see Mr. Miller on Tuesday and if the changes are satisfactory with him and Miss Beck, I will be glad to agree with them. I *repeat / resent* [unclear] that I have been placed in a position of saying that an agreement had been reached - as it had - and then have good

Gustave Whitehead: "First in Flight"

friends change their minds.

> As you know, I only wish to get an agreement and have no pride of authorship.
>
> With regards,
>
> Sincerely,
>
> Lester D. Gardner"

Earl N. Findley described some of *his* meetings re: the label, below, in a transcribed discussion with Paul Garber of the Smithsonian. Findley tried to downplay his importance within the group in determining the Wright Flyer label.

Transcript of conversation between Mr. Findley and Mr. Garber, September 15, 1948

Transcript of talk between Findley and Paul Garber, heading.

continued...(Findley to Garber:) So the next day I was at lunch with three men and on the way out there was Victory, Kelly, and Gardner; and they said "Oh come back a minute- just come back a minute." So, I sat down and they hauled out of their pockets various sheets of paper in pencil of this and that and the other...saying this will be the top line and thus and so and thus and so. Well I said that sounds pretty good; you know how you can sit down at a table with your hat in your hand and I just figured that the English sounded pretty good, but then they go off to Dayton and have a conference with the Millers, etc., I guess, and various people like that. I understand from Miss Beck she made some suggestions along about in May. So I feel like a fish out of water on the thing; I feel like I don't represent anybody, except myself.

Mr. Garber: You represent Orville Wright as one of his friends.

Mr. Findley: What I mean is - not as far as these people are concerned.

Figure 190: Transcript of Paul Garber telling Earl Findley he represents Orville in the label planning.

Paul Garber, key founder and a first curator of the Smithsonian National Air Museum (1946) ***reminded Findley he is there to represent Orville Wright***, due to his close relationship. It is very important to note that Findley had sent Orville a telegram on July 14, 1945, three years before, where **he asks Orville to help him "dynamite" the Whitehead claim** that appeared in the *Reader's Digest* of July 1945, below.

The "offending" *Reader's Digest* article in the column, "The Man Who Knows Everything First," condensed from "*Liberty*" by Mort Weisinger, contained the following statement:

Chapter 12: Kitty Hawk Revisited

"It was during one of these programs that Kane presented Charles Whitehead, of Bridgeport, Conn., as "the son of Gustave Whitehead, the first man to fly a heavier-than-air machine -- two years, four months, and three days previous to the Wright flight at Kitty Hawk." This was such a sensational claim that it cost Kane several hundred dollars to convince skeptics. At his own expense, he mailed out thousands of photostated newspaper clippings describing in detail a half-mile, motor-controlled made by Gustave Whitehead, a Bavarian, on August 14, 1901. These were supplemented by copies of 11 affidavits of eyewitnesses."

Originally published in "Liberty Magazine," this *Reader's Digest* column entitled "Firsts" had mentioned Gustave Whitehead claims recently covered in a coast-to-coast radio show featuring Whitehead's son, Charles. Findley became upset and worked with Orville to correct this "problem." Later, Findley ridiculed the *Readers Digest* editors and even mentioned trying to get them to retract the statements.

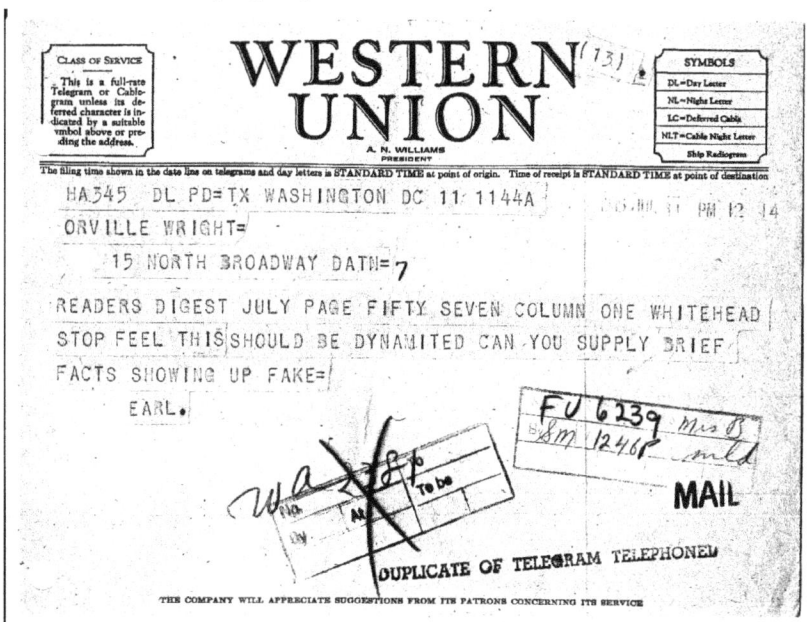

Figure 191: Telegram from Findley to Orville about "dynamiting" the July 1945 *Reader's Digest* **pro-Whitehead article**

Earl Findley writes his good friend Orville Wright about the July 1945 *Reader's Digest* article giving credit to Whitehead for first flight. Findley wishes to "dynamite" it. Asks O. W. to help use "facts" which Findley and Gardner had supplied him with in the so-called *Stanley Yale Beach Whitehead Statement* that Findley and Gardner had edited heavily.

What evolved out of that suggestion was Orville's inaccurate attack on Whitehead, "*The Mythical Whitehead Flight*" article published in Findley's magazine, *US Air Services*, in August 1945:

Orville Wright's heavily biased, misleading article was part of a scheme to discredit Whitehead, orchestrated by Findley and Gardner, from 1939-1945. Orville's article is introduced by Findley, referring to the *Reader's Digest* of July 1945, p. 57, writing, "we were astounded to read therein the following..." [quotes the article verbatim crediting Gustave Whitehead as first to fly a heavier-than-air machine]. He also references one other time when *Reader's Digest* mentioned Wrights were not the first to fly. Then he says, "… we asked the first man in the world to fly ... to give us the facts." Orville's article attacks Whitehead's claim to flight based on the following:

He says the *Bridgeport Herald* story is mythical because it was withheld for four days, and had a witch on a broom theme in the artwork. Orville credits the story to Richard Howell, the sports editor of the Herald. He said that four people were supposedly present, one of them Howell, and that James Dickie, one of the other witnesses, denied being there or knowing the other witness, [Dickie held a grudge against Whitehead, but this is not mentioned]. Then, he describes how a man named John Dvorak, who'd gone to have an engine built at Whitehead's shop in 1904 (and who'd highly praised Whitehead in the newspapers then) in 1936 said Whitehead was incapable of building a satisfactory motor and called him "delusional." Lastly, Orville cited Stanley Y. Beach's statements, crafted with Gardner and Findley, denying that Whitehead had ever flown [contrary to Beach's own articles in *Scientific American* from 1903-1908].

Earl Findley, in a letter to Orville on November 30, 1945, describes Whitehead supporters including Dr. Albert Zahm, very unpleasantly, as follows: **"Zahm is still not the only ——- in the woodpile, but several snakes in the bull-rushes as well"** [see below]. Findley further lambasts Zahm, who has been improperly blamed for the Whitehead claims, by telling him that the new Librarian of Congress wishes to find a younger man to take the place of Zahm…, then stating, "They couldn't get a worse man than Zahm, even if they offered a reward of a million dollars for him. There isn't any."

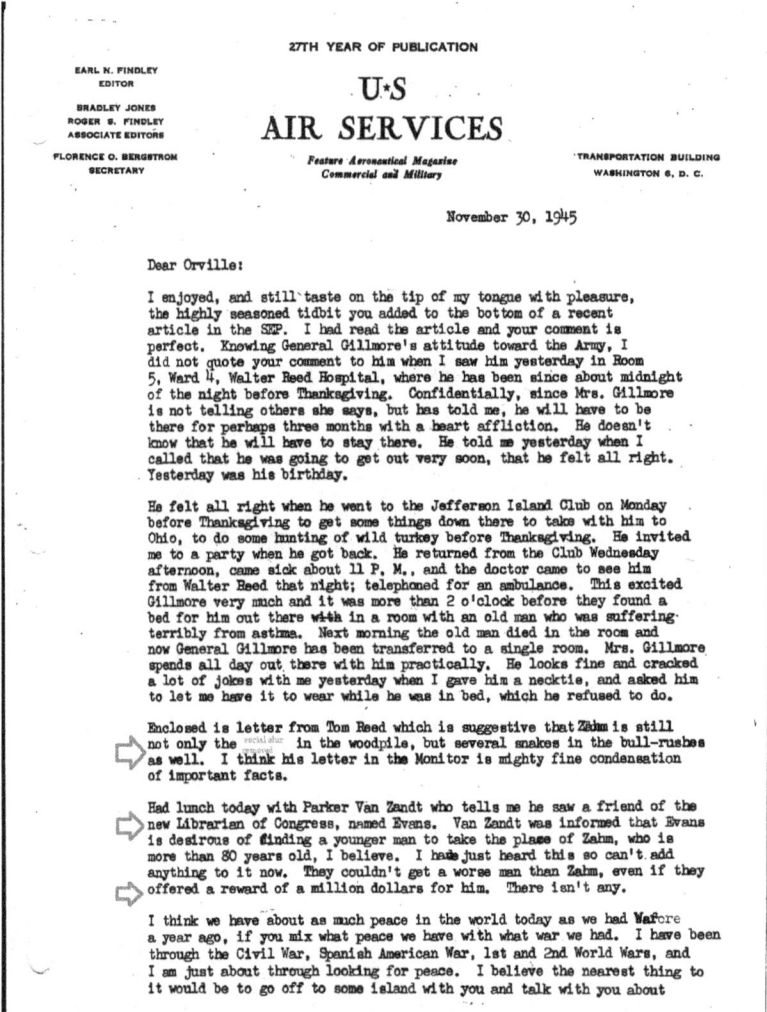

Figure 192: Findley write Orville blaming Dr. Albert Zahm for Whitehead claim (Nov. 1945)
Findley wrote Orville crudely criticizing Dr. Albert Zahm of the LOC, using an offensive racial slur.

Chapter 12: Kitty Hawk Revisited

Zahm has been unfairly blamed for the Whitehead claims. Censored for current-day audience.

Dr. Albert Zahm, professor of physics, was a highly esteemed national authority on early aviation, a chief of the Aeronautical Division of the U.S. Library of Congress, and a longtime *critic* of the Wrights, who'd published a treatise called *Early Powerplane Fathers* in 1945 that came close to crediting Whitehead for pre-Wright flights. Dr. Zahm wrote in May 1944, "It is technically possible, humanly very credible, that in 1902, Whitehead flew with petrol power." Earl N. Findley was not only very angry at all the Whitehead supporters, including Dr. Zahm, but spent a decade trying to destroy the Whitehead claim to first flight and exact retractions. When he got his chance to develop a label that would forevermore credit Orville for first flight, it was the culmination of those efforts.

These are the missing links that show "the Contract," with *the required Wright Flyer's misleading label* was directly aimed at denying Whitehead a chance for recognition as "first in flight," having been developed by his foremost attackers, within a small, heavily biased group. The above is only a small part of what is available at the Library of Congress and Smithsonian showing decades of collusion resulting in false credit for Orville Wright and the reasons why Whitehead never received credit or even a fair evaluation from the Smithsonian.

Additional Resources for "The Contract":

1. Photocopy (pdf) of the *Smithsonian-Wright Agreement of 1948* **on Fox News' site** (Fox News, Apr.1, 2013)] and in the Appendix of this book.

2. Visit www.historybycontract.org for more information on the *Smithsonian-Wright Agreement of 1948*.

3. Transcript of Conversation between Mr. Findley and Mr. Garber, September 15, 1948 (NASM, Smithsonian)

4. Wrong With Wright: Smithsonian Under Fire For Wright Brothers Contract (Jonathan Turley, April 2, 2013)

Gustave Whitehead: "First in Flight"

Chapter 13

CONCLUSIONS

Over the past 80 years, multiple researchers, experts, and historians felt there was very solid evidence that these shorter flights did take place in 1901-1903+ and it was obvious that they surpassed what the Wrights accomplished in December 1903. Those with the most prominent credentials include:

Economics Professor John B. Crane of Harvard, engaged in writing an "exhaustive book on aviation" in America[707], publicly and privately expressed increasing support for Whitehead flights in 1935[708], 1936[709], 1937[710], and finally, in 1949, with a *US Air Affairs* article Crane wrote. It culminated in crediting Whitehead with "succeeding in making successful airplane flights" prior to the Wrights' flights of December 1903; including several short straight-line flights of up to 300 feet in length near the edge of Bridgeport between 1900 and 1902, as well as longer flights in 1901-1902, including credit for a large circular flight of 1902.[711]

Dr. Albert F. Zahm, "a man of many accomplishments ... professor of mechanics at Catholic University, aerodynamic researcher of note, secretary of the Aero Club of Washington, governor of the Aero Club of America, consulting editor of the *Aero Club of America Bulletin*, and consultant to the National Bureau of Standards"[712], aviation pioneer, professor of mathematics and mechanics, University of Notre Dame, 1885-1892, and chief of the Aeronautical Division of the Library of Congress, 1929- 1946[713], credited Whitehead with having made the first petrol flights, in 1902, in Zahm's publication, *Early Powerplane Fathers*. Zahm wrote, "It is technically possible, humanly very credible, that in 1902, Whitehead flew with petrol."[714] Critics have pointed out that Dr. Zahm was not a devotee of the Wright brothers, unlike the large number they had attracted long after Wilbur's death in 1912 and the settlement of their patent lawsuits a few years later. Dr. Zahm has been falsely accused of attempting to undermine Orville Wright's claim to first flight, but this accusation is without merit, as the record speaks for itself. Zahm knew none of the witnesses and gathered none of the information first-hand. Based on that which was provided to him (which would help convince others) he noted that witnesses had stated Whitehead made early flights during the period 1899 through 1902, though he could not affirm conclusively that these had occurred. Rather, along with a number of other early experts in the 1930's and 1940's, he called for more investigation. Dr. Zahm did feel that the Wrights were not the first to develop the airplane nor "first in flight," however, as he wrote, the Wrights were "first to fly at Kitty Hawk, but not first to fly."[715] Zahm credited William Samuel Henson, a British inventor who patented a power plane in 1842, but never built it, as the true inventor of the airplane; with Clement Ader, of France, as the 'first to fly a powerplane', this status.[716]

Harvey Lippincott (Founder and Director of the Connecticut Aeronautical Historical Association (1959-1970's)), a highly respected Connecticut aviation historian who helped plan and participated in some of the witness interviews, agreed that Whitehead had made powered flights before the Wrights. He stated in a

Gustave Whitehead: "First in Flight"

videotaped discussion in 1981 with Maj. William O'Dwyer, recorded by German filmmaker, H. Spannenberger, that in 1901-1902, "[Whitehead] was in the air, in my opinion … for short flights."[717]

Whitehead researchers, Stella Randolph (first Whitehead investigator in later decades, researched Whitehead 1934-1937) and Major William J. O'Dwyer (researched Whitehead 1963-2008), coauthors of *History by Contract* (1978)[718], both concluded Gustave Whitehead made numerous successful airplane flights prior to 1903, and should be credited with "first in flight."

Paul Jackson, Editor-in-Chief of the century-old *Jane's All the World Aircraft* (2013), often referred to as "the bible of aviation history"[719], announced in its Centennial Issue, on March 2013, that Whitehead was "first to fly," ahead of the Wrights, and was the inventor of the airplane, based on the mountainous evidence accumulated over the previous eight decades.[720] This was followed up in June 2013 with legislation enacted by the state of Connecticut in support of Whitehead being first in powered flight[721], followed by more stringent legislation under way currently, to establish an annual Gustave Whitehead Day on August 14th. At this writing, much contention has broken out between the state legislatures of Ohio, North Carolina, and Connecticut. Backlash has been brought to bear by Wright supporters, upon the parent company of Jane's and Editor Jackson.

For documentation of Whitehead's history, we have relied the extensive comments of his contemporaries, the more dependable local newspaper articles and interviews, the writings of Whitehead published in trade journals or the press, existing photos, and eyewitness accounts.

Like most busy people in his time with a wife and four children, working ten hour days, six days a week at backbreaking jobs, and into the rest of the day or night on his flying experiments, living in a modest, small home, Whitehead apparently did not keep a diary nor a log of his activities. He did not spend his life writing long letters to others on a daily or weekly basis - not that have survived, at any rate. When he died, his wife, Louisa, said she sent most of his belongings related to "flying" to the dump, not realizing their historic value - and probably to be rid of what was reported to be a difficult challenge for all the years of her life with Gustave. Yet the story of Gustave Whitehead's colorful genius has been richly painted, thanks to the painstaking efforts of scores of volunteers interested in uncovering the truth about the flights of Gustave Whitehead, and the surviving accounts in the local newspapers.

Wilbur and Orville Wright, on the other hand, who seemed to document every minute of every day in writing journal accounts or letters – selected to present only what Orville wished to have the public view - were more eccentric. The Wright brothers had no wives or children, and lived a life of isolated luxury by comparison, with even "a cook" to provide their meals, in their father's home, well into adulthood. The Wrights were more sophisticated and even ruthless in business, having already been involved in years of unpleasant legal wrangling and suits related to their "bishop" father's church problems, so they well knew how to maintain and even create documentation to protect their future interests. The Wright brothers and their extended family had plenty of time to write, which seemed to be a nearly obsessive family past time. There was also plenty of time to create illusions and cull from the writings, which is irrefutably known to have occurred. We do not have that sort of alleged minute-by-minute coverage of Gustave's activities, the public being saturated with the so-called Wright documentation, orchestrated to credit Orville Wright as "first in flight" in the latter day Smithsonian version. Indeed, Gustave was not so vain nor greedy as to be building his image over a lifetime – his main objective was neither gold or fame. *In seeking practical flight, that elusive goal, Whitehead made the first powered flights of mankind.* With the mountains of evidence amassed over the past century that indicate Whitehead made multiple powered flights in 1901-1903, there is no credible reason to keep insisting that the Wrights were first.

Critics of Whitehead have, historically, often been closely associated with Wright interests, particularly those affiliated with Smithsonian. Some have stated, in the absence of Wright-like documentation, they believe the "No. 22" didn't exist and that Gustave Whitehead never left the ground in a powered plane. It has been alleged, based on Smithsonian interests and misinformation, that all Whitehead newspaper announcements and stories were based on falsified accounts given to the media to attract sponsors for Whitehead or readership for

Chapter 13: Conclusions

the paper. Whitehead research began more than 30 years after these events took place, so witnesses could not be located for each major Whitehead flight. However, those who were interviewed over the next sixty-five years would be adamant that they'd seen Gustave Whitehead in the air, in both powered airplanes and gliders, and most had a very good idea of the year it occurred, as well as the month or even, the day, often based on relating it to events in their own lives. The very real story of Gustave Whitehead compels us to consider the magnitude of what this humble, orphaned man with no other resources but his own brain and hands, accomplished for the human race, in being first in powered flight.

With current evidence in place, Whitehead is viewed by many, including the state of Connecticut's current legislature and governor, as universally deserving of credit for the first sustained, manned flight with power and control. With additional evidence uncovered by this author to support the first flights of the summer of 1901, it is imperative to broaden recognition of Whitehead's accomplishments.

An aviation trail with markers and monuments, and a virtual tour for Whitehead historic sites should be established in CT, PA, and MA, where Whitehead lived and invented. At this writing, coordinated, preliminary steps are being taken in the towns of Fairfield, Bridgeport, and Stratford, Connecticut to establish this trail.

Whitehead's remaining home should be considered for historic site status, with the surrounding areas where he lived, built planes, and flew designated as historic landmarks. In April 2014, Gustave Whitehead's self-built home on Alvin Street was lost, demolished to make way for a new home to be built on the property, despite clamor from those wishing to preserve it for the ages. Whitehead's previous home on the corner of Ridgely Avenue and Marlborough Terrace currently remains standing.

The descendants of Whitehead should receive posthumous honors and recognition for Gustave Whitehead's achievements, including being "first in powered flight."

The Smithsonian must be required to drop the *Smithsonian-Wright Agreement of 1948* and change the labels to be historically accurate. The Wright Flyer may have to be returned to the heirs or the terms and labels renegotiated, with a label accurately reflecting its place in history.

A neutral and complete evaluation of the Whitehead and Wright evidence must be conducted, if neutral parties May indeed, be found.

Whitehead exhibits noting the state of CT recognizes Whitehead for "the first powered flight" should be established in the Smithsonian and its affiliates. Smithsonian should acquire a Whitehead replica and label it appropriately, as recognized, at the very least, by the state of CT as "First in Powered Flight," with the August 14, 1901 date on it.

A Whitehead museum should be established in CT.

All CT aviation museums should strongly consider the inclusion of Whitehead exhibits, noting that the state of CT recognizes Whitehead as "first in powered flight." This should include the New England Air Museum, run by CAHA, a nonprofit which interviewed many of the Whitehead eyewitnesses. Interviewers included CAHA's founder and President Emeritus, Lippincott, who asserted Whitehead made short powered flights during the 1901-1903 period, throughout the years.

Smithsonian should not be allowed to discriminate amongst aviation museums in its distribution of exhibits or funding, one of the stated reasons why aviation museums are reluctant to acknowledge Whitehead.

The Smithsonian Institution should not be considered the sole authority on history. Its affiliates should not be bound by its dictates nor any of its signed legal agreements pertaining to crediting historical figures in return for profit or benefits.

History books should be revised, reflecting credit for "first successful powered flight" going to Gustave Whitehead, until such time as any other contender's proof is brought forward. If this cannot be done, at least these should state that Whitehead is recognized as first in powered flight in the state of CT, and why.

Smithsonian should receive a full external audit on a regular basis to ensure that the institution and its employees are following its mission and policies.

Gustave Whitehead: "First in Flight"

The US Congress should amend its oversight documents for Smithsonian to include checks and balances so that history must be evaluated in a neutral manner, without politicizing or selling historical recognition for exhibits or other benefits.

The Wrights should be reevaluated by those without conflicts of interest and recognized for their contributions for "improving the art" of aviation.

Chapter 14

GUSTAVE WHITEHEAD TIMELINE

January 1, 1874 Gustav Albin Weisskopf born in Leutershausen, Bavaria, Germany, son of Karl Weisskopf, a carpenter, bridge-engineer and millright[722], and Maria Sibylla Wittmann. Brother John and Leutershausen records confirm this date. (The USA Census of 1900 inaccurately shows birthdate as Oct. 1874.)

Starting from early childhood, Gustav was fascinated with the idea of human flight, believed it could occur. He experimented with kites to learn about air currents and with "little open balloons with cork and candle," which the police and his father were concerned about due to danger of fire - and which Gustav was spanked often for (according to his brother, John).[723] Gustav also studied birds at close range, captured them and tied strings to their feet to observe their flight (even got in trouble with police for this, after neighbors reported him, according to his brother Nicholas).[724]

1886 (age 12) In October Gustav's mother died in son Gustav's arms, following childbirth[725], leaving 6 children.

February 1887 (age 13) First gliding experiment, used a flying suit his grandmother sewed for him, with wings. Gustav's father died in February of that year, from pneumonia, developed after he contracted a cold while traveling on a train [726] [727]; Gustav's brothers and sisters were distributed to different relatives' homes.

Spring 1887 Gustav apprenticed to a bookbinder in Höchst, Germany, then after several months … to a locksmith at Ansbach, Germany, his father's hometown.[728]

Gustav attended "high school," apprenticed to a machinist – at Rudolf Diesel Werke, Augsburg. He studied technical sciences on the side during his machinist apprenticeship, showed unusual talent, building diesel engines at M.A.N. corporation. [729]"Gustav later stated that he "acquired some knowledge of mechanics and engineering," had "the idea of a flying machine in [his] mind," deciding "that [he] would someday be like the birds [he] was so fond of watching."[730]

1888 (age 14) Gustav shanghaied in Hamburg, forced to work at sea.[731]

1889 (age 15) Gustav back in Germany[732]

1889 Otto Lilienthal publishes book "Birdflight as the basis of aviation"[733]

Summer 1890 Gustav Weisskopf registered as living in Höchst, Germany

© Susan Brinchman, 2015

Gustave Whitehead: "First in Flight"

Fall 1890 (age 16) After traveling to Bremen, Germany, Gustav emigrated to Brazil with another family, worked briefly at homesteading, then found work as a sailor in Rio, spending several years as sailor, enduring much hard work and four shipwrecks, two in the New England area; continues bird observations, including watching condors. "After leaving school I went to sea and sailed around the world five times. I remember once watching the big condors flying off the South American coast and trying to understand how they did it. I used to study the gulls too, as they would soar against the wind with outstretched planes moving apparently without the slightest effort." [734]

1891 Otto Lilienthal's first flights

1893 A letter from Gustave reaches brother John Weisskopf and family in Germany, that Gustave "was sailing on a Norwegian bark "Garmund"."

1893 Gustav immigrates to United States from Brazil.[735]

1894 Gustav Weisskopf employed at Blue Hill meteorological station; tests kites[736]

March 19, 1895 Boston Aeronautical Society (BAS) (first aeronautical society in America) founded by James Means, Albert A. Merrill, and William H. Pickering (Astronomer, Harvard), to support basic aeronautical research and experimentation.

E. B. Millet, President. Founding members included Samuel Cabot; Honorary members included Octave Chanute and Samuel P. Langley.[737]

1895 Gustav Weisskopf begins using Anglicized name: Gustave (or "Gus") Whitehead

1894-1897 (age 21-23) **Milton, MA:** Whitehead and Albert Horn hired by A. A. Merrill, at the end of 1894, to work at Blue Hill Observatory; later built several Lilienthal-type gliders as mechanics for Boston Aeronautical Society (BAS); one trial at Blue Hill made short hops[738]

1895 built an ornithopter for BAS at Boston, Mass. which later failed to fly.

Spring 1896 - ornithopter and Lilienthal glider built by Whitehead and Albert Horn, tested at Hemenway Estate, Blue Hill, Canton, Massachusetts. Glider made short, low, and slow flights, flown by Whitehead.[739]

1895 Samuel Cabot (BAS) visits Hiram Maxim and Otto Lilienthal, brings back plans to construct basic Lilienthal glider.

1896 Otto Lilienthal dies in Berlin following gliding accident.

Summer 1896 Gustave Whitehead and James A. Crowell, carpenter, hired by Samuel Cabot to build Lilienthal glider and test at Morris Island, Chatham, MA. Glider failed to fly.

May 31, 1897 Octave Chanute donates $50 "as a contribution to the expenses of testing the Weisskopf apparatus," with letter to Albert A. Merrill (BAS).[740]

1897 "Condor Gus," a Whitehead aircraft with "two pairs of wings," reported in a German aero club presentation to have made artificial flights ["Zeitschrift für Luftschiffahrt" Jan. 1898 (Club News)][741]

May-June 1897 Gustave leaves Blue Hill to live in NYC, works for Edward I. Horsman, a BAS member, as part of his "Scientific Kite Team"; BAS employers regretful as Whitehead leaves, would like to rehire him.

Chapter 14: Gustave Whitehead Timeline

June 15, 1897 NYC Whitehead interviewed by *NY Herald* as he flew a large kite for Horsman Company, had relocated to New York City, employed by Horsman, a toy manufacturer who often participated in the events at Blue Hill. Whitehead was hired to build the world's first model aircraft, be part of a "Scientific Kite Team," operating meteorological, aerial photography, and large demonstration kites, such as multiple box kites supporting an American flag, on the end of a rope 5,000 feet long.[742] Horsman is also reported to have hired Whitehead to develop a man-carrying type kite. [743] In addition, during this period, Whitehead privately built and conducted experiments with a glider and powered flying machine.

October 4-5, 1897 Press conference and private viewing, attended by numerous members of the NY press and dozens of people, at Gustave Whitehead's home, 130 Prince Street, New York City, NY, to introduce his two aircraft, a partially completed biplane with foldable wings, and a newly completed, bright red triplane, to be fitted with a 3 hp, 50 pound gasoline motor, then being built, and two six-foot diameter propellers. Whitehead described as aeronaut, aerostat, inventor, and kite-flier who reported a previous soaring (glider) flight of 4.5 miles, from 2,000 foot mountain, in 22 mph wind.[744] Announced public flight (soaring) demonstration to be held at High Bridge on the following Sunday. International and national press picked up story, ran articles.

Oct. 1897 (age 23) Public flight displays in NYC.

Oct. 6, 1897 Two public soaring flight attempts, first practical test of new triplane[745], from a 125 foot elevation, at the western slope[746] of Jersey Heights (Jersey City, New Jersey) as it descends gradually "to the meadows of the Hackensack (River)" - located at the foot of Nelson Avenue, opposite Snake Hill, in NYC. Viewed by hundreds, created much excitement in neighborhood. The planned longer flight failed, as a strong west wind was required; instead, the wind came from the east. Short hops made halfway down hill and to roadside below, with "wind beating him down," but landing with agility and safety. Stored aircraft on premises of dairy, at edge of the meadows, to wait for strong west wind. Whitehead in company of new friend, Vassil Skaperdas, NY merchant and Greek engineer and airship experimenter, who said he'd seen Lilienthal and Chanute flights. [747]

November 24, 1897 Buffalo, NY. Marries Louise Tuba, met in NYC. Worked in buggy factory in Tonawanda, NY, by day. Continued work on flying machines by night.

1898 Gustave's grandmother, who helped sew the wings for his childhood flying suit, died in Germany. [748]

March 3, 1898 Baltimore, MD. NY World reports Gustave Whitehead made (undated) soaring flight from high elevation (3,000 feet) when living at Baltimore.

Oct. 21, 1898 Rose ("Rosie") Whitehead born. "The first child of Louisa and Gustave was born in Baltimore" (1900, 1910, 1940 Censuses say New York). Later, her married name was to be "Rennison."

Within the year the family had moved to Pittsburg to join with friends."[749] [750]

Relocated to Johnstown, PA, for a few months, following birth of Rose.

1898 moved to Pittsburgh, PA where friends lived.[751]

In PA, Whitehead found work in a coal mine, continued work on airplanes by night, obtaining his first two sponsors - a butcher and an Englishman[752] and meeting a coworker, who became his friend and assistant, Louis Darvarich. Public viewings of flying machine and flight experiments continue in Pittsburgh, in streets, open lots, and at immense, nearby park.

April - May or late fall 1899 Pittsburgh, a powered, manned flight of up to 1/2 mile reported, in a Whitehead

Gustave Whitehead: "First in Flight"

steam-powered monoplane, said to have flown 1/2 mile at 20-30 ft. in height, which ended by crashing into a building above the second floor, resulting in his assistant, Louis Darvarich, being injured and taken to the hospital. Reported by neighbors and in newspapers. (Darvarich, witness) Neighborhood alarmed by his experiments,[753] [754] A letter from Louis Darvarich to Mrs. Rose Rennison, Gustave Whitehead's daughter, for Ms. Randolph, researcher, places the flight as occurring in *late fall* at about 3:00 in the afternoon. [755]

November 1899 Brother John Weisskopf (soon to be "Whitehead") arrives in USA, landing at Baltimore, MD. [756]

Spring 1900 John Whitehead goes to Tonawanda, NY, to find Gustave, who is "gone to parts unknown." John works four months there and then leaves for California.[757]

June 1900 Pittsburgh, PA. (age 25) Gustave, Louisa, and Rosie Whitehead listed on US Census as living on Bates Street in Pittsburgh City, Ward 14, in a rented house. Occupation for Gustave: "machinist," not employed for 6 months. Birth month of Gustave listed as Oct. on this Census, 1874 the year of his birth. Married 3 years.

1899 World's Fair begins to be planned

Summer 1900 Whitehead and Darvarich begin bicycle trip to Bridgeport, CT. They sold their bikes in Scranton and took the train to NY, looking at a flying machine model GW [Whitehead] had built there, before taking the train on to Bridgeport.[758] [759]

Whitehead settles in Bridgeport, eventually works as a coal truck driver and later, a night-watchman (by summer, 1901). Lives first renting room at Egry home on Hancock Street, then rents at 241 Pine Street, both in the primarily Hungarian West End of Bridgeport, where work was available in nearby factories.

1900 City of Bridgeport population 70,996; growth of over 45% in 10 years.[760]

August - late fall 1900 Wife Louise and daughter Rosie (age 2) join Gustave in Bridgeport, living in a ground floor flat at 241 Pine Street. Basement used by Whitehead for plane and engine construction. Sets up first small shop in backyard. He obtained young volunteer helpers. [761] Louise was pregnant with their second child, Charles, soon to be born, in December.

Dec. 17, 1900 Charles Whitehead born in Bridgeport, CT[762]

1900 Whitehead continues airplane building at night, constructing a folding-wing, single propeller airplane, the first constructed in Bridgeport, at 241 Pine St. Obtains sponsor: Miller, uses money advanced for constructing a shop in front of the house the Whiteheads lived in.[763] Subsequently, Miller died, and Whitehead obtained a new sponsor, Herman Linde in fall, 1901[764].

1900 flight in circus grounds - gasoline-motored, folding-wing airplane raised up 30-40 feet in air, distance of 175-180 feet, then landed in a ditch (witness, Louis Lazay).

Early 1900's (between 1901 and 1905) constructs circular runway near what was later St. Stephen's School property[765], near Pine Street. The owner was displeased, as it was built without permission - therefore, the runway was not completed.

1900- early 1901 multiple powered flights of the single-propeller, #20 aeroplane, from Seaside Park, Bridgeport, starting on hard-packed dirt, then flying over Long Island Sound, distances of 150-300 feet, five feet or more in the air (witness, Anton Pruckner)

May 3, 1901 Whitehead tests "No. 21" unmanned, on top of steep hill, middle of street; accident occurs - it

Chapter 14: Gustave Whitehead Timeline

smashes into a tree as it descends. Repairs made for the next month. Andrew Cellie and Daniel Verovi reported as witnesses by NY Sun[766].

June 3, 1901 Gustave Whitehead claimed he flew 1.5 miles on this date, manned, in a letter to the World's Fair Aeronautic Competition authorities, January 10, 1902. Flight, if report is accurate, may have been a manned, powered momentum flight from top of a hill, as with May 3, 1901; if so, preliminary to sorties of virtually level / level ground powered flights in mid-August of 1901, respectively, at Fairfield and Lordship, Stratford, CT.

June 8, 1901 *Scientific American* (SA) reports on Whitehead's progress with #21, in feature article, stating it is nearly ready for resumed flights. Interview may have been made 2 weeks earlier. Photos for article made several months earlier, by Stanley Yale Beach, resident of Stratford, *Sci American's* Aviation Editor (son of owner), and author of this and subsequent SA articles mentioning Whitehead (through 1908).[767]

June 9, 1901 *NY Sun* reports on May trials and that Whitehead is ready to make more flights as repairs are nearly completed. Interview also may have been several weeks prior.

June 16th, 1901: *New York Herald* reports Whitehead is working on his fifty-sixth airplane (#21, as he didn't number the earlier ones).[768]

July 3, 1901 Octave Chanute writes Wilbur Wright about Whitehead's 10 hp lightweight motor for sale and recommends investigating them. Says Carl Myers, famed Skycycle owner, is thinking of installing a Whitehead Motor in his dirigible.

July 4, 1901. Wilbur Wright replies to Chanute saying the 10 hp lightweight [Whitehead] engine sounds like "an extremely fine motor for aerial purposes" and on same page discusses utilizing ideas of others in their designs.[769]

Mid-Summer Trials 1901 Bridgeport, CT Preliminary, powered, short street flights conducted near Pine Street shop and vicinity (on level ground). *Many of these Whitehead flights in Bridgeport exceeded the estimated 120 feet of the flight Orville Wright formerly credited as "first flight," 2.5 years later.*

1901-1902 A middle-of-the night (early AM) a Whitehead powered flight reported by Mary Savage, close-by neighbor, which flew at a height of 50 feet or more, over the neighborhood and down towards Seaside Park, to the harbor (Bridgeport), distance 1/4 mile to 1/2 mile.[770]

Summer 1901 A series of short flights "hops" with machine #21, on Pine Street, at height of five feet off ground. (Junius Harworth, witness)

July/August 1901 or 1902 Powered flight for at least one block (maybe more) at 12 feet above the ground with children who ran and clung to the plane in flight. (Joseph D. Ratzenberger, witness)

1901. Flight experiments with "No. 21" on Tunxis Hill.[771] (witness – Peschel)

1901/2 Summer or fall. When school not in session- powered flight of Whitehead's monoplane with folding wings, four or five feet off ground; flight took place on Pine Street where it was pushed from the backyard of 241 Pine Street. This witness lived across the street. Many children followed the plane.[772] (Alexander Gluck, witness)

Unknown date: On beach at Seaside Park, Whitehead piloted motored airplane towed by automobile, when motor started it "rose from ground, tipped, struck a tree, one of wings collapsed - dropped forty feet" (witness, Edward Prior).

August 1901 Whitehead obtains sponsor/partner A. W. Custead, of Waco, Texas, brief partnership formed.[773][774]

Gustave Whitehead: "First in Flight"

August 12, 1901 (approx.) Successful flight experiments at the "old" W. W. Cameron Trotting Park, Bridgeport, Connecticut [775]

August 14, 1901 Fairfield; Lordship (Stratford), CT. Powered, manned, sustained flights of Whitehead's #21 aeroplane on level ground, self-built in his cellar and shop, a distance of 1/2 mile at a height of 50 feet or more in the air, witness a local newspaper reporter (Richard Howell, of the *Bridgeport Sunday Herald*) who had been invited. Two other witnesses named: James Dickie and Andy Cellie. Exclusive news article appeared on August 18, 1901 in *Bridgeport Sunday Herald*'s sports section; subsequently reported in the Boston Transcript, and the *New York Herald* on August 19th, 1901 and many others, for the following six months

Aug. 14, 1901 Lordship, Stratford, CT. Later in the same day, another series of flights made at Lordship Manor, Stratford, CT - 1/2 mile flight and 1.5 mile flights reported. (+.) (Anton Pruckner, Junius Harworth, witnesses)[776] [777] [778] [779] "The mile and a half flight, made August 14, 1901, occurred at Lordship Manor, now a suburb of Bridgeport and took place somewhere in the vicinity of the site of the present Sikorsky airplane factory."[780] *In very late years, Pruckner thought it might have been at Seaside Park.*

August 23, 1901 Gustave Whitehead announces he has set a goal to fly to New York City from Bridgeport, and begins working on "No. 22".

August 24-September 22nd, 1901 Atlantic City, NJ. Whitehead is paid to display "No. 21" on Young's Pier, Atlantic City, New Jersey. He is visited by FW Hodge, a Smithsonian clerk, upon request of Charles Manley, the Chief Assistant to Samuel Pierpont Langley, Secretary of the Smithsonian, who is also working to develop an airplane for the Army. Agent takes notes on dimensions, etc.[781]

Sept/Oct. 1901 Powered flight of Whitehead's folding wing monoplane, propelled by motor, approx. a 400 foot distance, six feet off the ground, for a half minute, on Tunxis Hill Road near Mountain Grove Cemetery, Bridgeport, Conn.[782] (Michael Werer, witness)

Sept. 1901 Powered by a four cylinder gasoline engine, the flight of Whitehead's monoplane called "the Bird," for 50 foot intervals, four feet off the ground, for a few seconds at a time. Wing ribs bamboo, shaped like "bird's wing." "I understand that this plane was later exhibited at the St. Louis World's Fair." [783] [784](John S. Lesko, witness)

1901 - Whitehead flew a powered monoplane "across Fairfield Ave. and to the old circus lot," a flight of about 700 feet in length and approx. 30 feet high. The monoplane was powered by steam and fired by either gas or acetylene. (Cecil A. Steeves, witness)

1901 Whitehead powered monoplane flight of 150-250 feet, at elevation of 4-6 feet, at Gypsy Springs, Villa Park area of Tunxis Hill, Fairfield, Connecticut. Took off from and landed on level ground. [785] (witness – Elizabeth Koteles)

September 18, 1901 Wilbur Wright gives talk entitled "Some Aeronautical Experiments," related to Kitty Hawk gliding experiments of 1900-1901, for "Western Society of Engineers," Chicago, IL, after being invited by Octave Chanute to be guest speaker. Published in Journal of Western Society of Engineers, Dec. 1901, covered in *Scientific American*, Feb. 22, 1902. [786]

Early Oct. 1901 Cherry Street shop (Whitehead's second shop) set up in Bridgeport, funded by Herman Linde, across from Wilmot and Hobbs factory (or established as second shop in August and turned into factory in early October).

October 1901 Santos Dumont receives world-wide attention - flies powered dirigible over Paris, wins $20,000

Chapter 14: Gustave Whitehead Timeline

Deutsch Prize for aerial navigation, making a round-trip flight of seven miles from St. Cloud to the Eiffel Tower in 29 minutes, averaging 14.5 mph.

Oct. 1901- Spring 1901 Sometime during Cherry Street shop period, Wright brothers visited Gustave Whitehead's shop, according to multiple witnesses.[787]

Nov. 1901 "First airplane factory in the world" established by Gustave Whitehead at Cherry Street, Bridgeport, described widely in newspaper accounts.

Late Nov. 1901 Herman Linde, sponsor, allegedly tells hardware store to stop filling orders for the Linde-Whitehead account.

January 10, 1902 Whitehead writes World's Fair (Louisiana Purchase Exposition Company) authorities to apply to participate in its aerial competition, sending three photos of his flying machine, reportedly claims a 1 1/2 mile flight on June 3, 1901. Becomes first official entrant to World's Fair Aeronautical Contest, held in 1904.

January 17, 1902 Claimed powered flights of Whitehead's #22 aeroplane - one, for two miles, and the second for 7 miles, up to 200 feet elevation, over Long Island Sound, claimed by Gustave Whitehead in letters to the *American Inventor*, not able to be documented through the direct testimony of the multiple assistants. Anton Pruckner, who was in NJ at the time, later said he'd heard about these flights from others who'd seen them. Whitehead said the pictures did not come out right. #22 was reported to have eventually been ruined in winter weather outside; he had no money to build it a shelter. Flights described in subsequent letters to *American Inventor*'s editor, published April 1, 1902.

January 19, 1902 Boston Globe reports St. Louis, January 18: Whitehead is first applicant to World's Fair contest, Whitehead asked for rules and regulations to be sent to him.

January 22, 1902. Whitehead's views on heavier-than-air flying machines and principles of flight, including angles of flight, use of controllable rudder, and wing-warping mechanisms, with airplane factory update, published in large feature article in *Bridgeport Sunday Herald*.

January 23, 1902. World's Fair Aeronautical Contest subcommittee established; begin to plan rules and regulations, scope of contest.

February 1902 World's Fair officials recognize Gustave Whitehead as the first applicant for the Fair's aerial competition in their monthly newsletter, citing his letter of January 10th.

Spring 1902: According to Mrs. Whitehead, after Whitehead discovered a letter to one of his mechanics instructing him to find learn all he could and then work for Linde directly, Linde stopped sponsoring Whitehead, closing his second shop on Cherry Street.[788] Some disagreement on whether this was spring of 1901-1902 but newspaper accounts show Linde with Whitehead at least through Jan. 1902.

April 1, 1902 *American Inventor* publishes several letters to the editor received from Whitehead in past few months concerning extended flights of January 17, 1902 and "No. 22."

Late March/Early April 1902 Whitehead's brother John Whitehead arrives from California to help him as sponsor and worker on the flying machines. This was the first time he'd seen Gustave in over a decade. They'd had very little contact since shortly after their parents had died, as John was being raised in relatively distant foster homes.[789]

Gustave Whitehead: "First in Flight"

April 1902 – Fall 1902 brothers Whitehead working on engines, new designs, and steering mechanisms; wishing to take out patents for steering concept involving remotely operated, joint wing tip and rudder controls but do not have the money to do so. Gustave Whitehead takes on building engines for others, does not make profit. John works at low-paid job.[790]

April 15, 1902 Whitehead's sponsor, Herman Linde is sued by Lyons and Grumman's hardware store for outstanding (small) bill related to Whitehead-Linde purchases.

Mid-April 1902 Whitehead announces in multiple press accounts that he has recently made successful powered flights at Milford, CT's Charles Island, using a 40 hp engine weighing 120 lbs., 1/4 mile circuit, returning to starting point.[791] [792]

April 21-22, 1902. World's Fair Aeronautical Competition Rules and Regulations formulated in preliminary meetings, with help from Santos Dumont, dirigible (powered balloon) aeronaut

May/ June 1901 or (most likely year) **1902** Gasoline powered flight at Sports Hill, Easton, Connecticut - thirty feet in air, distance of two hundred feet, landing with no damage. Initially "the plane was pushed about 15 feet down the hill, then Whitehead turned on the engine, at which time it rose in the air and flew as described." Fekete reported that "Whitehead became thoroughly frightened as soon as he got into the air and shut off the engine, causing the plane to come down." [793][witnessed by Mr. Roth (owner of the farm where it took place), Cignay (worker on the farm), and reported by Mr. Fekete]

1902 Whitehead flew his motorized aeroplane four or five feet off the ground - monoplane with folding wings, flight took place in the street in front of 241 Pine Street, the backyard, where it had been constructed and pushed from.[794] (Darvarich, witness)

June 1902 World's Fair, set originally for 1903, postponed till 1904

1902 – 1904 Whitehead plane experiment flies across a lot at elevation of six to ten feet, crashes and plane breaks up. Wooden struts, box-like, likely a biplane. Location near Orr's Castle, Tunxis Hill.[795] (witness: Oliver Cole)

Summer 1901/1902, July or August Whitehead powered flying machine "rose from ground" elevation 12 feet, "traveled under its own motor power a distance of approximately 30 feet before it fell to the ground and burst into flames. This plane was a biplane and the flight occurred on Pine Street."[796] [Author note: most likely Summer 1902 because Whitehead did not construct a biplane 1901] (witness John A. Ciglar)

August 1902 "Mr. Whitehead flew his folding winged plane … on Fairfield Avenue, and again, a little later, at Gypsy Spring. Gypsy Spring was a part with a steep hill that would give the plane a good start"[797]. (witness – John S. Lesko)

August 1902 Multiple newspapers announce Whitehead and his brother, John, intend to fly in the aerial contest at the St. Louis World's Fair. The brothers combine ideas to design another flying machine, amidst experiencing severe financial problems.

Oct. 4, 1902 Wright brothers change "fixed double rear fin" to rudder linked with wing-warping control.[798]

December 1902 Whitehead article appears in "*Aeronautical World*" describing "No. 24," based on "No.'s 22 and 23"; set for trials by January 1, 1903. The new flying machine described as having two sets of adjustable, angled wings which, in addition to its tail surfaces could be controlled by levers, to help steer and control the airplane with the use of compressed air. Propellers also described as adjustable in flight, with takeoff being accomplished

Chapter 14: Gustave Whitehead Timeline

using wheels and a ground engine.[799]

December 1902 Wright brothers begin propeller experiments and construction of "their 1903 4-cylinder engine" [800]

Fall 1902 Brother John returns to California to raise funds.[801]

Early 1903 Whitehead takes 6 months to build a 200 hp 8 cycle engine intended for use in an aeroplane; its sponsor Stanley Yale Beach insisted on using it on his boat, which caused an accident, losing the engine in Long Island Sound.[802]

Feb. 12, 1903 Wrights conduct first test of their new motor.

March 23, 1903 Wrights apply for patent on their flying machine which includes wing-warping controls. (Patent granted May 22, 1906.)[803]

Sept. 19, 1903 Article in *Scientific American*, Sept. 19, 1903 documents Whitehead making flights with powered triplane, using tractor (puller-style) propellers, at 3-16 feet for about 350 yards, using a 12 hp., 54-pound (24 kg) two-cycle, 12 horsepower (8.9 kW), 2,500 rpm motor (at 1,000 rpm in trials). [804] This engine is the one displayed in the Dec. 1906 2nd Annual Aero Club exhibition in NYC, next to the Wrights' exhibit.[805]

Fall, 1903 Brother John Whitehead returns to Bridgeport from California and finds that Gustave Whitehead and Stanley Yale Beach had recently tried to take out a patent for a steering device without including John Whitehead, but were not allowed to file by the US Patent Office rules which required a demonstration. [806]

December 17, 1903 Wright brothers self-report 4 limited, experimental powered flights of box-kite style flying apparatus at Kitty Hawk, NC, estimated at approx. 6-8 feet in elevation, distances of 100 - 852 feet, with control problems, launched from rail, requiring 22 mph wind. News media misreports distance as 3 miles. Dayton, OH newspaper refuses to carry story, saying distances flown too short to be of public interest.

Jan. 22, 1904 Chanute travels to visit Wrights to discuss rules and reg's for upcoming Aeronautical Competition at the World's Fair.[807]

Feb. 17, 1904 Wright brothers travel to St. Louis to inspect World's Fair grounds for upcoming Aeronautical Competition. The Wrights decide *not* to exhibit a plane at the fair.[808]

March 1904 Whitehead said to still be interested in World's Fair by a major women's magazine

April 1904 The very popular Cassell's magazine runs article about "the well-known aeronauts, Profs. Gustave Whitehead and Octave Chanute, developing a new sport with their triplane gliders, which fly 300 to 800 feet; Whitehead's, with "small-cycle motor," successfully carrying him longer distances. Photo of Chanute glider in article. Illustrated story with hand-drawing carried in Associated Press, nationwide.[809]

April 30, 1904 St. Louis World's Fair (Louisiana Purchase Exposition) opens to 200,000 initial attendees, providing 1500 extravagant exhibition buildings (including 8 principal "grand palaces") on 1200 acres, featuring "the latest achievements" in technology, manufacturing, and science, amongst other areas. The Fair closed on Dec. 1, 1904, seven months later, having been attended by an estimated 20 million people.[810]

May 24 & 25, 1904 Wrights unable to fly due to rain and insufficient wind, in front of press, which castigates them for their failure.

Gustave Whitehead: "First in Flight"

May 26, 1904 Wright trials at Dayton, OH produce what Wright brothers claim is a "successful" flight; launched by traveling along 100 foot track, for (distance of) 30 feet (actually 25 feet)[811], at 12 foot, "in great secrecy," with "but a few" witnesses. Machine dropped to ground, damaging propellers, ending trial.[812]

June-July 1904 Famed Brazilian, Santos-Dumont's dirigible balloon, widely advertised to make public flights on July 4th, is slashed during night by unknown person(s), rendering balloon useless for demonstration flights and competitions, where he was expected to win the grand prize of $100,000. Dumont angrily leaves Fair after being suggested he is perpetrator. Mystery never solved - *however, elimination of Santos-Dumont as a competitor may have saved the St. Louis Exposition Company $100,000, as he was the only person in the world considered capable of meeting the flight course requirements for the grand prize, which he helped the fair planners develop.*

August 13, 1904. Wilbur flies 1,340 feet at Huffman Prairie, breaking *his* own record, set Dec. 17, 1903[813] - *but not Whitehead's*, who flew 1/2 - 1.5 miles (2640 - 7920 feet) during the summer of 1901, three years before this date.

September 1904 World's Fair Aeronautical Competitions officially begin, originally set to be completed by Sept. 30, 1904. Extended through November due to problems with entrants arriving not at all or late, or taking long time to set up equipment and flying apparatus. Due to numerous changes in rules and regulations, many entrants did not meet criteria or stayed away - due to expectation that it looked impossible to satisfy full criteria to win prizes. For example: ever-changing requirements and entrance criteria, criticized in a *Scientific American* Letter to the Editor - including performing for crowds at the Fair by flying over the ornate buildings at the fairgrounds along an L-shaped, 30 mile long circuit along a (one-way) 15 mile route, with turns, landing at the point of takeoff; flying from St. Louis, MO to Washington DC and circling the Washington Monument, then landing in Ohio; gliders making 40 glides in an arena without a hill, etc.; with exacting prerequisite criteria, *leaving the bulk of the large fund of $150,000 for Aeronautical Competition prizes to be kept by the St. Louis Exposition Company*, while attempting to lure famous aeronauts there to compete and draw crowds. *This is exactly what came to pass.*

Exhibitions in the immense "Transportation Palace" included all manner of aviation apparatus, including aeroplane engines. Competition for lightweight, powerful airplane engine said to have occurred. Whitehead's plane [814] [815] and engine(s) said to have been exhibited during the Fair by Whitehead witness John S. Lesko; likely to have been entered in lightweight engine competition.

September 23, 1904 World's Fair, St. Louis, MO. Famed, reliable Austrian journalist reports he viewed a Whitehead aeroplane motor being placed in the California Arrow, a world-famous dirigible owned by Baldwin. The CA Arrow competed at the World's Fair Aeronautical Contest, winning some minor prizes. California Arrow had motor problems during the several months of exhibitions; started out with a Curtiss motorcycle motor. However, Baldwin may have changed it out to a Whitehead Motor, known even then to be superior and lightweight.

Oct/Nov 1904 *(September was to begin Aeronautical Contests)* Whitehead attended St. Louis World's Fair and was said to have exhibited an aeroplane motor and possibly entered the motor contest there. He also took his flying machine, according to John Lesko [816] [817], possibly to exhibit, though is not listed with those who competed[818]. Brings back a collapsible cup for Lesko, now in the Weisskopf Museum, Germany.

October-November 1904 Following several engine problems, California Arrow flies at World's Fair, takes minor prizes, said to be hero of the fair.

October 1, 1904 *Bridgeport Standard* reports two photos of Whitehead in flight, sailing along at a 20 foot elevation, on public display in south window at local Lyon & Grumman's hardware store on Main Street, in

Chapter 14: Gustave Whitehead Timeline

Bridgeport, CT. Reports Whitehead still wanting to compete at World's Fair for $100K prize; his dream: to build a large experimental plant to solve "the problem of aerial navigation." Ongoing challenges with short-term sponsors are not diminishing his confidence that "the problem will be solved in his day" and that "he will accomplish it or someone else will."[819]

Oct. 1, 1904 *Bridgeport Standard* reports Whitehead going to World's Fair soon.

October 4, 1904 Aeronautical Congress held at St. Louis World's Fair.

1904 *Modern Industrial Progress* is published, a book by Charles Henry Cochrane: Whitehead described as a soaring enthusiast using "aeroplanes" (wings) "much after the fashion of Lilienthal" - describes a successful powered (12 hp) Whitehead triplane aircraft with a "four sided rudder" that "assists the steering," and "puller" propellers; "experiments with this machine were sufficiently satisfactory that another is being built."[820]

October 1904, Professor John J. Dvorak, Professor of Physics at the University of Washington in St. Louis, announced publicly, that Whitehead was more advanced with the development of aircraft than other persons who were engaged in the work. [821]

Nov. 11, 1904 Whitehead triplane "aeroplane" reported recently flown; built with spruce, canvas, and steel wires, with "puller" propellers; a 46 pound, 10 hp gasoline engine; and controllable pyramidal-shaped rudder; pilot seated, firmly strapped in between two lower "wings" (or as they referred to them -"aeroplanes") at point of equilibrium. Reports flights of up to 75 feet in altitude, makes turns, and traveled 1/3 of a mile on several occasions; can fly in relatively still air.[822]

Nov. 1904 Octave Chanute makes a number of demonstration flights of a non-powered glider at St. Louis World's Fair, with a hired pilot, using special launching apparatus.

Nov. 16, 1904 Orville Wright makes flights of 1/8, 1/3, 1/2 miles; Wilbur makes flight of 2.5 miles, with 2 1/4 turns, at Huffman Prairie field, Ohio.

Dec. 1, 1904. Last date for competitors in the Aerial Contest at the World's Fair to compete for the grand prize. The massive St. Louis World's Fair ends, with a band playing "Auld Lang Syne," and a as the lights were turned out, in the sky "fireworks sizzled out the words GOOD NIGHT and FAREWELL"[823]; having entertained an estimated 20 million thrilled attendees in just seven months.

1904-1905 Wright brothers work on control of their flying machine in Ohio, using catapult and/or track to launch.

1905 Lillian Whitehead, Gustave and Louise's third child, is born. Later, married name "Baker."

Mid-October 1905 Aero Club of America formed[824].

Dec. 20, 1905, Gustave Whitehead and Stanley Yale Beach applied for patent on No. 21, 22, 23 gliders - patent #881837, glider and stabilizer

Summer 1906 Whitehead builds his first home on Ridgely Ave., Lenox Heights (now Tunxis Hill), Fairfield, CT[825]

1905-1908 Whitehead biplane flights observed on multiple occasions at Villa Park in West End of Bridgeport at altitude of 3-4 feet. Other multiple flights along State Street, around sunset. Distance 75-100 yards (225-300 ft.) without touching ground. [826](witnesses – Mari Kopacsi and Frederick Szur)

© Susan Brinchman, 2015

Gustave Whitehead: "First in Flight"

January 14, 1906 *First Annual Exhibition of Aeronautical Apparatus* sponsored by the Aero Club of America, during the Sixth Annual Official Show of the Automobile Club of America. Stanley Yale Beach, Aviation Editor of *Scientific American*, publishes article on the exhibition, stating *"a single blurred photograph of a large birdlike machine propelled by compressed air and which was constructed by Whitehead in 1901 was the only other photograph besides that of Langley's [scale model]machines of a motor-driven aeroplane in successful flight,"* which had been exhibited at the show, chastising other inventors [likely aimed at the Wrights] for not providing proof of their claimed flights.[827] The Wright brothers exhibited a crankshaft and flywheel from their 1903 "Flyer," later stolen from the exhibit, never recovered.

Feb. 1906 William J. Hammer, influential member and officer of Aero Club of America meets with and **pledges to Wrights that he would like to promote them above all other aviation inventors**

March 1906 William J. Hammer influences Aero Club core organizers and officers to recognize Wrights

April 1906 Stanley Yale Beach writes *Scientific American* article with witness testimony data concerning Wrights' flights of 1905, credits Wrights with first practical airplane.

1906 Whitehead biplane under construction - Stanley Yale Beach ideas incorporated

Nov. 24, 1906 *Scientific American* November 24, 1906, issue *gives Whitehead credit for 1901 short distance flights of "motor-driven aeroplane,"* while stating no practical plane has yet been produced and demonstrated.[828]

December 15, 1906 *The Second Annual Exhibit of the Aero Club of America* in NYC Whitehead exhibits a 6 hp., 35-pound, two-cycle, 1,000 rpm motor, shown in a photo between the Curtiss and Wright engines, as well as a ground engine and propeller. "The body framework of Gustave Whitehead's latest bat-like aeroplane was shown mounted on pneumatic-tired, ball bearing wire wheels and containing a 3'cylinder, 2-cycle, air-cooled motor of 15 horse-power direct connected to a 6 foot propeller placed in front.

This machine ran along the read at a speed of 25 miles an hour in tests made with it last summer. When held stationary, it produced a thrust of 75 pounds.

The engine is a 4 1/4 x 4 of an improved type. Whitehead also exhibited the 2-cylinder steam engine which revoled the road wheels of his former bat machine, *with which he made a number of short flights in 1901*. He is at present engaged in building a 100-horse-power, 8-cylinder gasoline motor with which to propel his improved machine."[829]

In the same issue, on the first page, the Wrights are described as inventors of "the first successful airplane," having" produced an aeroplane which had made a continuous flight, with one of the inventors on board, of over twenty miles at a high speed and under perfect control."[830]

1907 Whitehead builds and successfully flies glider for sponsor Louis Adams

Sept. 1907 Century Magazine article written by Orville and Katharine, wrongly credited to Orville and Wilbur Wright, falsely credits Orville with the first flight, verbiage later included in the label mandated by the Contract with Smithsonian arranged by Orville's executors.

June 1908 Aeronautics magazine reports that S. Y. Beach of the *Scientific American* and Gustave Whitehead took out in March [1908] English patent No. 5312 for "improvements in aeroplanes."[831]

1908 Whitehead designs and builds 75 hp, two-cycle lightweight engine for George A. Lawrence. Whitehead

Chapter 14: Gustave Whitehead Timeline

Motor Works formed, offices in NYC and factory in CT, building motors in three sizes: 25, 40, and 75 hp.[832]

Sept. 8, 1908 Helicopter developer William Kimball wants machine to carry him as easily as a bird would fly. Believes will solve problem of aerial navigation.

1908-1909 Lee Burridge President of Aeronautic Society (of NY), formed in 1908 with Stanley Yale Beach and William J. Hammer and several others, after break with Aero Club of America, due to emphasis by latter on ballooning vs. flying machines.

1908 Aeronautic Society of NY sets up Morris Park (NJ) with toolshed and support for inventors of aeroplanes.

1908 Wilbur Wright makes demonstration flight in France; Wrights release photos of flight at Kitty Hawk for first time

March 10, 1908 G. Whitehead Aeroplane [glider with V-shaped fuselage and birdlike wings], patent No. 881,837 granted with half interest assigned to Stanley Yale Beach. "*Invention relates to aerial navigation*, and its object is to provide a new and improved aeroplane arranged to readily maintain its equilibrium when in flight in the air to prevent upsetting, shooting downward head foremost, and to sustain considerable weight."[833]

1908-1909 Whitehead built lightweight, 2-cycle airplane engines that ran for about 10 minutes, and sold them to noted aviation pioneer Charles Wittemann, available for sale in his catalogue.

1909 Lee Burridge on Board of Directors of Aerial Development Company (Kimball President, Burridge a Director) manufacturing heavier-than-air planes for sale

August 19, 1909 Wright brothers assert they are first in flight with power and control, have patent, sue Aeronautic Society for damages (patent infringement) and seek to stop its exhibition of Curtiss plane; Curtiss is next to be sued

February 8, 1909 Cornelia Whitehead, Gustave and Louise's fourth (and last) child, is born. Later, married name "Kusterer."

1908 - 1909 Whitehead builds large biplane for Stanley Yale Beach, influenced by Beach design, at his home, corner of Ridgely Ave. and Melville Terrace, Fairfield, CT.

Nov. 1909 Beach-Whitehead plane fails to fly at New Jersey meet; Whitehead jailed overnight for refusal to give Beach all materials, Beach sends his helpers to take plane and parts from Whitehead.

1910 Octave Chanute's *"Chronology of Aviation"* credits Wilbur Wright (not Orville) with "first successful man flight in history."

May 14, 1910 Census (age 36) shows Gustave Whitehead living at Lenox Park, in Fairfield, CT "East of Mill River," with wife Louise (age 34), daughter Rose (age 12), son Charles (age 11), daughters Lilly (age 5) and Nelly (age 1); married 12 years; Occupation: Machinist working in his own shop; owns his own house.

January 5, 1910 Wright attorney Toulmin writes Wilbur Wright to tell him that in court case against Curtiss, Judge Hazel decrees Wrights first to make human flight, pioneer inventors, gives broad patent construction as a result, eventually includes all use of lateral (horizontal) surfaces.

Jan. 1910 Whitehead's biplane photo'd by Arthur Kent Lyons Watson "Whitehead's Effort," on the grounds of Brooklawn Country Club, in the Stratfield section of Fairfield, CT, at a golf course fairway, where it ran alongside

Gustave Whitehead: "First in Flight"

Melville Avenue, opposite the present site of Fairfield's High School (formerly Andrew Ward High).[834]

May 19, 1910 Wilbur Wright hires William J. Hammer, Engineer, to be his public relations person and spy, gathering information about patent transgressors for lawsuits, and to help credit Wrights as pioneer inventors.

1910 - 1912 powered flight by Whitehead, 5-10 feet in air, gliding distance about 150 feet, pedaled with bicycle-type wheels to get it started. (Joseph Vecsey, witness)

Spring 1911 Brother John Whitehead leaves Bridgeport for British Columbia.

1910 Lee Burridge becomes Vice President of Aeronautic Society (of NY)

1911 Lee S. Burridge, of the Aeronautic Society, hired Whitehead to design and construct a helicopter with 60 propellers (photo), which did not yet have a motor strong enough to lift it sufficiently to fly, but did, reportedly, lift approximately four feet up on restraints.[835] [836]Rather than allow Whitehead to remedy the situation, Burridge became angry and foreclosed on Whitehead's property, taking his tools, plane parts, and all his shop equipment, making it very difficult to continue inventing. Later, this helicopter fitted with Whitehead motor by Charles Wittemann, which failed to fly.[837]

1911 World Almanac published, crediting Wilbur Wright with first powered flight in its *"Chronology of Aviation,"* written by secret, subrosa Wright Company employee, William J. Hammer[838], and Hudson Maxim, after approval received from Wilbur and Orville.

1912 *"Chronology of Aviation"* by Hammer and Maxim, crediting Wilbur Wright as first in powered flight, published widely in booklet to all members of the Aero Club of America

March 1912 *"Chronology of Aviation"* crediting Wilbur Wright as first in powered flight entered into court records by William J. Hammer, as part of the proof of pioneer invention, necessary for broadest patent rights. Hammer perjures himself by denying any connection with Wrights or Wright Company except for being their expert to make deposition.

1912 Whitehead entered into a competition for a safety device to prevent third-rail train wrecks - he developed a solution, but no prize was received, company denied offering one.

May 30, 1912 Wilbur Wright dies at age 45, of typhoid fever, after a three week illness - thought to have been contracted from shellfish eaten in Boston, while weakened from stress of their lawsuits. Brother Orville blames Glenn Curtiss for Wilbur's death.

January 1914 Whitehead ordered by court to deliver contents of his shop, including tools and helicopter, to Burridge.

Early 1914 House on Ridgely Avenue is either "lost" to debts or sold

June 1914 Whitehead begins building his second home in Tunxis Hill neighborhood, Fairfield, CT, on Alvin Street, the street named after his middle name: "Albin," Americanized.

1915 Whitehead said to have exhibited an aircraft at Hempstead Plains, NY.

1915 Whitehead designed and sold engines and worked in a factory as laborer. At some point a piece of heavy equipment hit his chest and gave him severe problems, including angina, which he continued to suffer with.

Chapter 14: Gustave Whitehead Timeline

Post-1915 Invented and used concrete laying-machine - last known work was laying a concrete road on Long Hill, Bridgeport.

October 15, 1915 Wright Company sold after Orville Wright fails to successfully manage the company, following his brother's death in 1912.

August 14, 1926 25th anniversary of Whitehead's sustained powered flight at Fairfield, Connecticut ignored by the world.

May 20–21, 1927 Charles Lindberg flies solo, non-stop, across Atlantic Ocean, lands at Paris, France; Whitehead celebrates by dancing in his backyard.

1927 Clarence Chamberlain flies non-stop across Atlantic Ocean with first trans-Atlantic passenger, two weeks afterward

October 10, 1927 Whitehead dies of a heart attack, while lifting an engine out of an automobile. He walks onto his front porch and into his home, where he collapsed and expires before help could be obtained. Whitehead died unexpectedly at the age of 53, with only $8 to his name, and the home he had built for his family. He was buried in an unmarked pauper's grave, solely **numbered 42**, which will mark his grave from 1927-1964 at Lakeview Cemetery, in Bridgeport, CT. The marker is currently at the Gustav Weisskopf Museum, in Leutershausen, Germany.

December 17, 1928 25th anniversary of Wright flights celebrated with monument dedication at Kitty Hawk, NC.

1928 Richard Howell writes and publishes book, "*Tales from Bohemia Land*"

1930 Richard Howell, eyewitness reporter for Whitehead's 1/2 mile, Aug. 14, 1901 flight at Fairfield, CT, now Editor in Chief of the *Bridgeport Sunday Herald*, dies at age 60.

1934 Stella Randolph begins Whitehead research, on a tip from Harvey Phillips.

1934-1937 Stella Randolph conducts interviews and gathers information about Gustave Whitehead, for three years.

January 1935. Randolph and Phillips author Whitehead article in *Popular Aviation* magazine.

1937 Stella Randolph's first book on Whitehead is published: *Lost Flights of Gustave Whitehead*. Publisher, Places, Inc.

1935-37 Economics Asst. Prof. Crane of Harvard researches Whitehead in Bridgeport, CT. Crane is working on a book about the history of American transportation.

1937 Crane and Randolph call for a Congressional hearing on the Whitehead evidence of first flight, ahead of the Wrights. Never held.

1939 Orville's close friends (Maj. Lester Gardner and Earl Findley) cajole Stanley Yale Beach to deny Whitehead in "*Beach-Whitehead Statement*" - they help edit his statement. Never published, unsigned by Beach. Letters back and forth between Gardner and Findley describe this project, as they conduct extensive editing on drafts.

February 1941 *Reader's Digest* publishes article "*They Wouldn't Believe the Wrights Had Flown*," describing why newspapers refused to recognize the Wrights had flown on Dec. 17, 1903, at Kitty Hawk. The content, which actually did credit the Wrights, upset Orville Wright, who was busily defending his desired title: "first in powered flight." Circulation: 4,000,000.

1944 Louise Whitehead (widow) moves to Florida, sells house on Alvin Street

July 1945 *Reader's Digest* article *The Man Who Knows Everything 'First'* [839] mentions that radio host Joseph Nathan Kane went on the air in 1940, with "Famous Firsts," presenting "Charles Whitehead of Bridgeport, Conn., ... as 'the son of Gustave Whitehead, the first man to fly a heavier-than-air machine – two years, four months, and three days previous to the Wright flight at Kitty Hawk' ." The article further describes how Kane spent his own money to mail out "thousands of Photostat-ed newspaper clippings describing in detail a half-mile, motor-controlled flight" made by Whitehead on Aug. 14, 1901, "supplemented with copies of 11 affidavits of eyewitnesses." This article further angered Orville, who wrote a letter decrying the two *Reader's Digest* articles and Whitehead's claimed flights to his friend, Earl Findley, published soon after.

1945 Orville's anti-Whitehead treatise, *The Mythical Whitehead Flight* based on *Beach Whitehead Statement*, is published by his close friend, Earl Findley, *US Air Affairs* editor.

1946 Smithsonian National Air Museum established; Paul Garber named Director

January 30, 1948 Orville Wright dies of a heart attack at age 76

Summer/Fall, 1948 Smithsonian labels for Wright Flyer and "agreement" language worked on by Orville's executors, Paul Garber of Smithsonian, Earl Findley, Lester Gardner, and Mabel Beck, amongst a very few others.

November 1948 Smithsonian signs *Smithsonian-Wright Agreement of 1948* to obtain Wright Flyer for $1, contracts to recognize only Orville Wright and Wright Flyer as "first in flight." Public is never notified, the agreement remains "secret," in files at Smithsonian.

August 14, 1961 50th anniversary of Whitehead's sustained powered flight at Fairfield, Connecticut ignored by the world, recalled by Junius Harworth in correspondence with Stella Randolph.

October 1962 Junius Harworth dies of heart attack. Buried in Mountain Grove Cemetery, Bridgeport, Connecticut.

May 19, 1963 Feature article *Whitehead or Wrights? Riddle Evolves Around First Plane Flight* in *Bridgeport Post*, by Ted Bache[840]

Spring 1963 Captain William J. O'Dwyer, (US AF, ret) of Fairfield, CT, finds photos of Whitehead's plane labeled "Whitehead's Effort, January 1910," during research for a construction job. He begins researching Whitehead with his Air Force squadron, most in Fairfield area. Connects very promptly with CAHA (CT Aeronautical Historical Association) in northern CT and begins to locate artifacts and witnesses who knew Whitehead, to interview. They arrange to meet with Stella Randolph in the next year and collaborate by sharing research efforts.

September 1963 At midnight, O'Dwyer meets with Ted Basche, reporter for *Bridgeport Post* and Hal Dolan, Vice-President of CAHA. Hal explains moratorium on Whitehead due to Chairperson of Board "taught to fly" by Orville Wright. Dolan also tells O'Dwyer that Smithsonian is rumored to have a "Contract" involving giving credit to the Wrights and Smithsonian, whereby S. cannot recognize any other pioneer who flew before the Wrights. A non-member of CAHA at that time, O'Dwyer agrees to head up a project on Whitehead. Later, introduced to CT Aeronautical Historical Association (CAHA)'s first President and Founder, Harvey H. Lippincott. Lippincott, soon afterward, has CAHA Whitehead moratorium lifted.

Chapter 14: Gustave Whitehead Timeline

November 1963 Anton Pruckner interviewed.

1963 "Project Find-It" initiated, to interest local residents and school children to uncover Whitehead artifacts and history. Project of WWII AF Squadron 9315 (Retired), with member, Captain O'Dwyer, as chairman.

Early 1964 Enough evidence gathered to establish Whitehead as Father of CT Aviation. O'Dwyer joins CAHA and becomes head of CAHA's *Whitehead Research* and *Air Pioneer Graves* Committees.

August 15th, 1964, in a formal ceremony that included Whitehead's three daughters, his assistant Anton Pruckner, aviation pioneers who'd known him, representatives from all military services, state and local officials, Connecticut Aeronautical Historical Association members, many supporters and researchers, and a large gathering of media, Gustave Whitehead receives a new headstone designating him as Father of CT Aviation by Governor Dempsey, following the efforts of O'Dwyer and CAHA to replace Whitehead's pauper's grave number "42."

1964 Anton Pruckner interviewed.

1964 Paul Garber meets with O'Dwyer; Garber denies there is a contract with Wright executors, he said he'd never have allowed it.[841]

1966 Stella Randolph publishes her second book on Whitehead "Before the Wrights Flew," utilizing the research of O'Dwyer, CAHA, and the AF Squadron.

1966 Anton Pruckner interviewed ten days before he dies. Lives to view second book by Randolph.

August 14, 1968 Gustave Whitehead Day designated by Governor Dempsey of Connecticut, to honor "Gustave Whitehead, Father of Flight."

1974 Eyewitness to a Whitehead powered monoplane flight circa 1901 - 1902, Elizabeth Koteles interviewed 3 times by O'Dwyer et al..

1974 Gustav Weisskopf Museum founded by Stella Randolph, William J. O'Dwyer, and City of Leutershausen, West Germany.

1976 Smithsonian-Wright Agreement (contract) unearthed by O'Dwyer based on a tip from CAHA member, with help of then-Sen. Lowell Weicker, Jr. (later Governor of CT), using the power of his office and the newly minted Freedom of Information Act[842]. Requires Smithsonian to recognize *only* Orville Wright and Flyer as first in flight.

1978 History by Contract published in English, in Germany, coauthored by O'Dwyer and Randolph - the third book on Whitehead. First printing: 1000 copies. 2nd printing: an additional 1000 copies.

1986 "No. 21" "replica" / Whitehead aeroplane reproduction completed by large group assembled with O'Dwyer, tested for airworthiness and flown in Bridgeport, CT.

Sept. 14, 1983 US State Dept. issues press release recognizing Gustave Whitehead as making "the first motorized flight in the history of aviation."

1986 State of CT demands Smithsonian / federal hearing on Whitehead - never held

1989 Stella Randolph dies, at age 96. Her research files eventually go to the History of Aviation Collection at the

Gustave Whitehead: "First in Flight"

Library of the University of Texas at Dallas.

Jan. 1997 Harvey Lippincott, Whitehead researcher and founder of CAHA, then-archivist of the New England Air Museum dies.

Oct. 4, 1997 German replica built and flown 1/2 mile.

Feb. 1998 German replica makes additional flight.

1990's O'Dwyer publishes multiple magazine articles on Gustave Whitehead

1999 O'Dwyer donates 20 linear feet of his Gustave Whitehead files to *Fairfield Historical Society*, Fairfield, CT

August 14, 2001 100th anniversary of Whitehead's sustained powered flight at Fairfield, Connecticut ignored in the USA, celebrated in Leutershausen, Germany, his hometown.

Dec. 17, 2003 Wright replica embarrassingly – but predictably - fails to fly (barely moves) during its much feted Centennial Celebration.

2007 Fairfield Museum opens its doors to the public, established by the Fairfield Historical Society; organizes O'Dwyer/ Whitehead files in its archives.

Aug. 29, 2008 Long described as "world authority on Gustave Whitehead," O'Dwyer dies at age 87, following 45 years of Whitehead research.

March 9, 2013 Jane's All the World's Aircraft announces it recognizes Gustave Whitehead as first in powered flight, ahead of the Wrights.

June 26, 2013 State of CT's Governor Dannel Malloy signs bill into law recognizing Gustave Whitehead as first in powered flight.

Summer 2014 State of North Carolina begins plans to change its "first in flight" license plate.

April 2014 Local politicians and authorities approve Gustave Whitehead's hand-built century old home on Alvin St. to be torn down, amidst world-wide criticism and local protests, despite full funding available for restoration and maintenance through State of CT and a statewide historic preservation nonprofit.

August 2014 CT State Library Archives division establishes "Gustave Whitehead Research Collection."

December 2015 Gustave Whitehead receives supplemental headstone displaying "First in Flight" status, recognized by *Jane's All the World Aircraft* and the state of Connecticut.

January 2015 State of Ohio's legislature considers a bill denying Whitehead flew before the Wrights. Bill is passed in April 2015.

2015 Fourth book on Whitehead published by Susan O'Dwyer Brinchman, M. Ed, revealing new research discoveries explaining direct links of *Smithsonian-Wright Agreement of 1948* with Whitehead detractors, William J. Hammer's secret employment by Wilbur Wright under which he publishes *"Chronology of Aviation,"* crediting Wilbur Wright as first in flight, making the only successful flight of the day, used in their patent suits; and multiple confirmations of Whitehead's summer flights in 1901 by additional local press, in articles never before seen by researchers.

"First to Fly" Endnotes

1. Current editor: Paul Jackson. Past editors, John W. R. Taylor and Kenneth Munson coauthored "History of Aviation." New English Library, London, 1972. Crown Publishers, NY, NY (reprinted 1977).
2. Prolonged, (relatively) lengthy
3. Executive Overview: Jane's All the World's Aircraft: Development & Production. 07 March 2013. http://www.janes.com/article/23191/executive-overview-jane-s-all-the-world-s-aircraft-development-production
4. "weighing more than the air that it displaces, hence having to obtain lift by aerodynamic means (1900-1905) " dictionary.com
5. The Evening Telegram. NY, Nov. 19, 1901
6. *American Inventor*, Letters to Editor from Gustave Whitehead, April 1, 1902
7. Affidavit of Junius Harworth, August 21, 1934 O'Dwyer Gustave Whitehead Research Collection, Fairfield Museum, Fairfield, CT
8. Statement of Junius Harworth on Plans of "No. 21" and "No. 22", Jan. 18, 1936 O'Dwyer Gustave Whitehead Research Collection, Fairfield Museum, Fairfield, CT
9. Howell, Richard (August 18, 1901). "Flying," *Bridgeport Herald*. p. 5 http://news.google.com/newspapers?nid=4p5LGG1h9z0C&dat=19010818&printsec=frontpage&hl=en
10. The Virginia enterprise. (Virginia, St. Louis County, Minn)., 13 Sept. 1901. Chronicling America: Historic American Newspapers. Lib. of Congress. <http://chroniclingamerica.loc.gov/lccn/sn90059180/1901-09-13/ed-1/seq-3/>
11. New York Herald, June 16, 1901, Section 5, p. 3
12. US Census Bureau
13. "Improved Flying Machine," NY Sun, June 9, 1901, page 2
14. Ibid
15. "Beach Whitehead Statement," Gustave Whitehead files, Library of Congress
16. the terms aeroplane and airplane derive from this earlier use, also referred to as aero-planes
17. This ingenious arrangement is the first known instance of the method for modern takeoff of airplanes, in use for over a century – originally pioneered by Gustave Whitehead.
18. Longitudinal static stability is the stability of an aircraft in the longitudinal, or pitching, plane under steady-flight conditions. This characteristic is important in determining whether a human pilot will be able to control the aircraft in the longitudinal plane without requiring excessive attention or excessive strength. (Longitudinal static stability. Wikipedia. accessed 9.18.14)
19. Transverse stability: The ability of a ship or aircraft to recover an upright position after waves or wind roll it to one side. http://encyclopedia2.thefreedictionary.com/transverse+stability
20. Propellers [sometimes referred to as "screws"] turning in opposite directions was a concept later exploited by and

Gustave Whitehead: "First in Flight"

often mistakenly credited to the Wrights.

21 "A New Flying Machine." *Scientific American*. June 8, 1901. p. 357 https://archive.org/details/scientific-american-1901-06-08

22 Anton Pruckner later confirmed that the "No. 21"pilot would sit on a board that was 2" x 1" or 1" x 2," in the cockpit area, where they determined the center of gravity to be located, by suspending the aircraft from large sawhorses and making tests.

23 Interview with Anton Pruckner, Nov. 13, 1963. O'Dwyer Gustave Whitehead Research Collection, Fairfield Museum, Fairfield, CT. p. 27

24 Edward M. House. Wikipedia, accessed 8/29/13. http://en.wikipedia.org/wiki/Edward_M._House

25 "A New Flying Machine." *Scientific American*, June 8, 1901, p. 357 https://archive.org/details/scientific-american-1901-06-08

26 The term "aeronaut," in 1901, referred to one who piloted a balloon, dirigible, or flying machine of any sort.

27 "No. 21" was able to be flown unmanned due to its inherently stable design, landing after its power was cut off with a timed switch.

28 New York Herald, June 16, 1901, Sec. 5, p. 3

29 "Perfecting His Machine." Bridgeport Evening Post Aug. 26, 1901.p.1

30 Letter of Junius Harworth, Jan. 24, 1936. O'Dwyer Gustave Whitehead Research Collection, Fairfield Museum, Fairfield, CT

31 Whitehead's letter to Louisiana Exposition Committee, Jan. 10, 1901. World's Fair Bulletin, February 1902.

32 http://www.gustave-whitehead.com/history/news-reports-1901-2-flights/

33 Ibid

34 "Flying Machine Factory – Latest of Bridgeport's Industries." *Bridgeport Sunday Herald*, Nov. 17, 1901. p. 1. http://news.google.com/newspapers?id=gGwmAAAAIBAJ&sjid=wf8FAAAAIBAJ&pg=2020%2C4857304

35 "Bridgeport's Flying Machine Builders." *Bridgeport Sunday Herald*, January 26, 1902, p. 4. http://news.google.com/newspapers?id=ZO8yAAAAIBAJ&sjid=kQAGAAAAIBAJ&pg=5366%2C372219

36 confirmed as Richard "Dick" Howell by *Bridgeport Sunday Herald*, Herald Magazine, January 30, 1937. p. 4-5

37 Ibid

38 An examination of the *Bridgeport Sunday Herald* in 1901, and all surrounding years, shows virtually 100% of the illustrations to be hand-drawn. http://news.google.com/newspapers?nid=4p5LGG1h9z0C&dat=19010818&b_mode=2&hl=en

39 http://historybycontract.org/?p=197

40 Aviation Bible: Whitehead First to Fly. Burgeson, John. CT Post. March 13, 2013. http://www.ctpost.com/local/article/Aviation-bible-Whitehead-first-to-fly-4348050.php

41 CT lawmakers write Wright brothers out of history as 'first in flight'. NY Daily News. June 27, 2013. http://www.nydailynews.com/news/national/connecticut-lawmakers-wright-brothers-flight-wrong-article-1.1384079

42 http://www.ctpost.com/local/article/Aviation-bible-Whitehead-flew-first-4348050.php

43 Eyewitness confirmed as Richard "Dick" Howell by *Bridgeport Sunday Herald*, Herald Magazine, January 30, 1937. p. 4-5

44 *Bridgeport Sunday Herald* listed Dick Howell as its "Sporting Editor" from 1897 - 1908, in an examination of the newspaper online. In the November 25, 1900 issue, on page 2, column 2, Howell is specifically mentioned as sporting editor of the Herald in an article describing a local boxing exhibition.

45 Richard Howell, *Bridgeport Herald* Editor Dies at 60. Hartford Courant, Hartford, CT. Nov. 25, 1930.

Endnotes

46   Richard Howell, Frontspiece from Tales from Bohemia Land. *Bridgeport Herald* Publishers, Bridgeport, CT. (1928)

47   "First National Aeronautic Show Opens in the Garden," Part Four - Sporting News Section, New York Times, Sunday, Sept. 26, 1909.

48   Howell, Richard (August 18, 1901). "Flying," *Bridgeport Herald*. p. 5 http://news.google.com/newspapers?nid=4p5LGG1h9z0C&dat=19010818&printsec=frontpage&hl=en

49   Research Log Notes of Wm. J. O'Dwyer. The *Bridgeport Sunday Herald* 1900-1912; Category: Aviation. Feb. 7, 1981, page 8. O'Dwyer Gustave Whitehead Research Collection, Fairfield Museum, Fairfield, CT

50   "Bridgeport Statistics." Glimpses of Bridgeport, Conn., Board of Trade. John H. Kane and Frank A Wood, Publishers. Marigold Printing Company. 1898.

51   Mythical Whitehead Flight. Wright, Orville. US Air Services, August 1945

52   Ibid. page 5

53   Ibid. p. 1-6

54   Orchard Street Cemetery, Dover, NJ Transcriptions of Headstones. http://doverhistoricalsociety.com/files/colls/orchardst/oscburials.pdf

55   In 1911, the very popular World Almanac listed Wilbur Wright as "first in flight," in its "Chronology of Aviation," co-authored by a subrosa (secret) Wright Company employee, William J. Hammer. Both Wrights were given credit in the World Almanac for inventing the airplane. This account was later fraudulently entered into the records of the Wright court case against Curtiss, as evidence of their "pioneer invention," by Hammer, the Wright's expert witness, committing perjury when denying he had any other relationship with the Wright Company. The William J. Hammer archives, showing this manipulation of the courts and the public, currently reside - under lock and key -at the Smithsonian's Air and Space Museum.

56   *Smithsonian-Wright Agreement of 1948* http://www.foxnews.com/science/interactive/2013/04/01/contract-between-wrights-smithsonian-decrees-flyer-was-first-plane/

57   "Smithsonian conspiracy to deny Whitehead flew first." gustavewhitehead.info

58   *Bridgeport Sunday Herald*, Herald Magazine, January 30, 1937. p. 4-5

59   "Forgotten Bridgeporter Was First Aviator," Herald Magazine for the Week Ending January 30, 1937. p. 4. American Institute of Aeronautics and Astronautics, Institute of Aerospace Science. Box 126, Folder 1. Gustave Whitehead. Library of Congress, p. 28 (in pdf)

60   "SY Beach Statement." American Institute of Aeronautics and Astronautics, Institute of Aerospace Science. Box 126, Folder 1. Gustave Whitehead. Library of Congress, p. 57 (in pdf)

61   "The 'Who Flew First' Debate." O'Dwyer, William J., Flight Journal. 1998. http://www.flightjournal.com/wp-content/uploads/2013/03/whitehead.pdf?02a977

62   "Gustave Whitehead and the First Flight Controversy." DeLear, Frank. Aviation History. History.net. published online June 12, 2012 http://www.historynet.com/gustave-whitehead-and-the-first-flight-controversy.htm

63   Research Log Notes of Wm. J. O'Dwyer. The *Bridgeport Sunday Herald* 1900-1912; Category: Aviation. Feb. 7, 1981, page 1-16. O'Dwyer Gustave Whitehead Research Collection, Fairfield Museum, Fairfield, CT

64   "Here's Proof from the Files of the *Bridgeport Herald*," Herald Magazine for the Week Ending January 30, 1937, p. 5. American Institute of Aeronautics and Astronautics, Institute of Aerospace Science. Box 126, Folder 1. Gustave Whitehead. Library of Congress, p. 77-78 (in pdf)

65   Richard Howell: Gustave Whitehead Research Log, William J. O'Dwyer, 27 Feb. 1981, Fairfield Museum, Box 4, Series B, SS1 Folder 15

66   From the article, "Down with McGinty: A Banquet, 30 Feet Underwater": "The guests on Tuesday were .... Richard Howell, of the Sunday Herald..." *Bridgeport Sunday Herald*, July 15, 1900, page 5. http://news.google.com/

67   Ibid.

68   "Liquid Air: What It Has Been; What It Is; What It Will Be." *Bridgeport Sunday Herald*, July 8, 1900, page 6 http://news.google.com/newspapers?nid=4p5LGG1h9z0C&dat=19000708&printsec=frontpage&hl=en

69   Research Log Notes of Wm. J. O'Dwyer. The *Bridgeport Sunday Herald* 1900-1912; Category: Aviation. Feb. 7, 1981, page 9. O'Dwyer Gustave Whitehead Research Collection, Fairfield Museum, Fairfield, CT

70   Interview with Francis Brennan, July 10, 1969. Folder 4, Box 4. O'Dwyer Gustave Whitehead Research Collection, Fairfield Museum, Fairfield, CT

71   Whitehead Airplane No. 20 or 21 - Description furnished by Junius Harworth, Jan. 18, 1936. p. 1

72   "No. 21" and subsequent versions were repeatedly described by observers as inherently stable, both in flight and landing.

73   Randolph, Stella. Lost Flights of Gustave Whitehead. 1937. Places, Inc., Wash. DC, p. 18 Ibid p. 12

74   Howell, Richard (August 18, 1901). "Flying," *Bridgeport Herald*. p. 5 http://www.gustave-whitehead.com/history/news-reports-1901-2-flights/1901-08-18-bridgeport-herald-p-5/

75   later theorized by Whitehead researchers to be the next door neighbor, Anthony Suelli , History by Contract, O'Dwyer and Randolph (1978), p. 31

76   "No. 21" was known to be very easily airborne; Anton Pruckner, Whitehead's assistant, asserted in his affidavit of Oct. 30, 1964 that if they were to build a replica, they'd better "hang on well, because it is going to *go up*." This proved to be entirely accurate.

77   propellers

78   Howell, Richard (August 18, 1901). "Flying," *Bridgeport Herald*. p. 5 http://www.gustave-whitehead.com/history/news-reports-1901-2-flights/1901-08-18-bridgeport-herald-p-5/

79   Randolph, Stella. "The Story of Gustave Whitehead, Before the Wrights Flew." 1966. GP Putnam & Sons, p. 94

80   "Dad Barber dies after 30 years newspaper work." *Bridgeport Telegram*, October 22, 1923. p. 1-2, (p. 1 & 10 of 18 in digital version) Ancestry.com. *The Bridgeport Telegram (Bridgeport, Connecticut)* [database on-line]. Provo, UT, USA: Ancestry.com Operations Inc, 2006.

81   Barber, Andrew V. *Bridgeport, Connecticut, City Directory, 1904, p. 34*

82   1900 United States Federal Census for Andrew V Barber. Year: *1900*; Census Place: *Los Angeles Ward 5, Los Angeles, California*; Roll: *89*; Page: *7B*; Enumeration District: *0050*; FHL microfilm: *1240089*

83   Carpenter, Jack. Pendulum. Arsdelon, Bosch, & Co., 1992. p. 120

84   Current Literature. July - Dec. 1909, p. 368 (from Chicago Tribune article) http://books.google.com/books?id=NkNWAAAAYAAJ&pg=PA368&dq=%22chicago+tribune%22+%22original+aviator%22&hl=en&sa=X&ei=VpjRUZW1MqiCyQGr3YGICQ&ved=0CDUQ6AEwAA#v=onepage&q=%22chicago%20tribune%22%20%22original%20aviator%22&f=false

85   Carpenter, Jack. Pendulum. Arsdalen, Bosch, & Co., MA. 1992, p. 120

86   "More Aviation Prizes." New-York tribune., June 08, 1910, Page 3, Image 3. New-York tribune. (New York [N.Y.]), 08 June 1910. Chronicling America: Historic American Newspapers. Lib. of Congress. <http://chroniclingamerica.loc.gov/lccn/sn83030214/1910-06-08/ed-1/seq-3/>

87   Mythical Whitehead Flight. Wright, Orville. US Air Services, August 1945

88   Richard Howell: Gustave Whitehead Research Log, William J. O'Dwyer, 27 Feb. 1981, Fairfield Museum, Box 4, Series B, SS1 Folder 15

89   Child, Frank Samuel. "Fairfield, Ancient and Modern: A Brief Account, Historic and Descriptive, of a Famous

Endnotes

Connecticut Town. Fairfield Historical Society. Fairfield Printing Co., Fairfield, CT. 1909. p.53

90   Howell, Richard (August 18, 1901). "Flying": "Gustave Whitehead's Story.," *Bridgeport Herald*. p. 5 http://www.gustave-whitehead.com/history/news-reports-1901-2-flights/1901-08-18-bridgeport-herald-p-5/

91   "Flying Machine Factory – Latest of Bridgeport's Industries." *Bridgeport Sunday Herald*, Nov. 17, 1901. p. 1. http://news.google.com/newspapers?id=gGwmAAAAIBAJ&sjid=wf8FAAAAIBAJ&pg=2020%2C4857304

92   Flying Machine That Will Remain Stationary in Mid-Air is Whitehead's Creation." The *Bridgeport Evening Farmer*, June 20, 1910, Image 1. p. 1-2. The *Bridgeport Evening Farmer*. (Bridgeport, Conn.), 20 June 1910. Chronicling America: Historic American Newspapers. Lib. of Congress.

93   NY Telegram, Nov. 19, 1901

94   The Post Road was referred to as "the highway" by the President of the Fairfield Historical Society, in 1909, in a book he wrote about Fairfield. (See endnote 97, below.) It was also known earlier as "the King's highway" in Colonial times, as it ran between New York City and Boston.

95   Child, Frank Samuel. "Fairfield, Ancient and Modern: A Brief Account, Historic and Descriptive, of a Famous Connecticut Town. Fairfield Historical Society. Fairfield Printing Co., Fairfield, CT. 1909. p. 20

96   Mapquest map of Turney Farm field, south of Riverside Drive, east of Turney Road. http://mapq.st/9-8UTv1qYw

97   The *Boston Post* Road was originally from an historic old Native American trail called "The Pequot Path"; colonists later improved and used the road to deliver mail and travel between New York and Boston, Mass.

98   "Gustave Whitehead and the First-Flight Controversy," Aviation Magazine http://www.historynet.com/gustave-whitehead-and-the-first-flight-controversy.htm

99   Ibid. p. 121

100   Realty map of Fairfield, Henry Minor, Civil Engineer. Fairfield Realty Co., Bacon Wakeman, 1912. Town of Fairfield, Fairfield, CT

101   Child, Frank Samuel. "Fairfield, Ancient and Modern: A Brief Account, Historic and Descriptive, of a Famous Connecticut Town. Fairfield Historical Society. Fairfield Printing Co., Fairfield, CT. 1909. p. 43

102   http://www.merriam-webster.com/dictionary/macadam

103   Ibid

104   Howell, Richard (August 18, 1901). "Flying": "Gustave Whitehead's Story.," *Bridgeport Herald*. p. 5 http://www.gustave-whitehead.com/history/news-reports-1901-2-flights/1901-08-18-bridgeport-herald-p-5/

105   http://home.hiwaay.net/~krcool/Astro/moon/fullmoon.htm#00

106   *The Washington times*. (Washington [D.C.]), 23 Aug. 1901. *Chronicling America: Historic American Newspapers*. Lib. of Congress. <http://chroniclingamerica.loc.gov/lccn/sn87062245/1901-08-23/ed-1/seq-2/>

107   Letters of Junius Harworth to Stella Randolph. O'Dwyer Gustave Whitehead Research Collection, Fairfield Museum, Fairfield, CT

108   Howell, Richard (August 18, 1901). "Flying," *Bridgeport Herald*. p. 5 http://www.gustave-whitehead.com/history/news-reports-1901-2-flights/1901-08-18-bridgeport-herald-p-5/

109   Library of Congress. NY Sun. June 9, 1901, p. 2, image 2

110   New York Telegram, November 19, 1901, p.10

111   Letters to the Editor, *American Inventor*, April 1, 1902

112   Letter of Junius Harworth, Jan. 24, 1936. O'Dwyer Gustave Whitehead Research Collection, Fairfield Museum, Fairfield, CT

113   Affidavit of Junius Harworth, Aug. 21, 1934 O'Dwyer Gustave Whitehead Research Collection, Fairfield Museum, Fairfield, CT

© Susan Brinchman, 2015

Gustave Whitehead: "First in Flight"

114 Affidavit of Anton Pruckner, Oct. 30, 1964. O'Dwyer Gustave Whitehead Research Collection, Fairfield Museum, Fairfield, CT

115 Author's note: Junius, then known as "Julius Horvath," was born on May 21, 1889, and was 12 at the time of the flights. Anton Pruckner, another witness, a mechanic who worked with Whitehead on the engines and planes, was born Jan. 4, 1883, and was 18 1/2 years of age at the time of these first flights.

116 August 1901. www.sunrisesunset.com/calendar

117 http://www.gaisma.com/en/location/bridgeport-connecticut.html

118 August 1901. www.sunrisesunset.com/calendar

119 NY Telegram, Nov. 19, 1901

120 Letters to the Editor, *American Inventor*, April 1, 1902

121 Ibid

122 Randolph, Stella. Lost Flights of Gustave Whitehead. 1937. Places, Inc., Wash. DC, p. 18 Ibid p. 50

123 Letter of Junius Harworth to Stella Randolph, January 24, 1936. O'Dwyer Gustave Whitehead Research Collection, Fairfield Museum, Fairfield, CT

124 Affidavit of Anton Pruckner, Oct. 30, 1964. O'Dwyer Gustave Whitehead Research Collection, Fairfield Museum, Fairfield, CT

125 Letter of John Whitehead to Stella Randolph, September 3, 1934. p. 2. O'Dwyer Gustave Whitehead Research Collection, Fairfield Museum, Fairfield, CT

126 Pruckner Interview, WICC, May 20, 1964, p. 3. O'Dwyer Gustave Whitehead Research Collection, Fairfield Museum, Fairfield, CT.

127 Pruckner Interview, WICC, May 20, 1964, p. 2. O'Dwyer Gustave Whitehead Research Collection, Fairfield Museum, Fairfield, CT

128 Anton Pruckner Interview, Nov. 16, 1963, p. 5. O'Dwyer Gustave Whitehead Research Collection, Fairfield Museum, Fairfield, C

129 http://www.e-yearbook.com/yearbooks/mit/1929/Page_226.html

130 Anton Pruckner Interview, WICC.May 20, 1964, p. 11. O'Dwyer Gustave Whitehead Research Collection, Fairfield Museum, Fairfield, CT

131 WJOD notes, Anton Pruckner. O'Dwyer Gustave Whitehead Research Collection, Fairfield Museum, Fairfield, CT

132 Gustave Whitehead's airplane (replica) in flight, Oct 4, 1997. YouTube. https://www.youtube.com/watch?v=Ucm80BYUXEE

133 "Perfecting His Machine." Bridgeport Evening Post Aug. 26, 1901.p.1

134 Randolph, Stella. Lost Flights of Gustave Whitehead. 1937. Places, Inc., Wash. DC. p. 46

135 Correspondence re: Andrew Celley, Dec., 1982 and Jan. 1983. O'Dwyer Gustave Whitehead Research Collection, Fairfield Museum, Fairfield, CT

136 NY Sun, June 9, 1901, p. 2, "Improved Flying Machine"

137 Dickie's birthdate was Dec. 20, 1884, per U.S. World War I Draft Registration Card 1917-1918 for James Dickie

138 Randolph, Stella. Lost Flights of Gustave Whitehead. 1937. Places, Inc., Wash. DC., p. 105, 114

139 Comments of Randolph upon Gustave Whitehead, A Report by C. Gibbs-Smith, p. 6. O'Dwyer Gustave Whitehead Research Collection, Fairfield Museum, Fairfield, CT

140 Letter of Stella Randolph to Junius Harworth, March 4, 1937. O'Dwyer Gustave Whitehead Research Collection, Fairfield Museum, Fairfield, CT

Endnotes

141 Letter of Junius Harworth to Erik Hildes-Heim, August 7, 1961, p. 3 O'Dwyer Gustave Whitehead Research Collection, Fairfield Museum, Fairfield, CT

142 Memorandum: Bridgeport Trip re: Gustave Whitehead Flights, K.I. Ghormley, June 21, 1948. WJ O'Dwyer Archives, Fairfield Museum, Fairfield, CT

143 Affidavit of James Dickie, April 2, 1937. O'Dwyer Gustave Whitehead Research Collection, Fairfield Museum, Fairfield, CT.

144 O'Dwyer, William J., Randolph, Stella. History by Contract. 1978, Fritz Majer and Sohn. p. 28

145 Delear, Frank. "First in Flight, Whitehead or Wright?." Aviation History. March 1996

146 *Bridgeport Sunday Herald*, May 31, 1903, p. 4 http://news.google.com/newspapers?nid=4p5LGG1h9z0C&dat=19030531&printsec=frontpage&hl=en

147 Letter of John Whitehead to Stella Randolph, September 3, 1934. p. 2. O'Dwyer Gustave Whitehead Research Collection, Fairfield Museum, Fairfield, CT

148 Letter of John Whitehead to Stella Randolph, Nov. 5, 1934. p. 1. O'Dwyer Gustave Whitehead Research Collection, Fairfield Museum, Fairfield, CT

149 Flying Machine That Will Remain Stationary in Mid-Air is Whitehead's Creation." The *Bridgeport Evening Farmer*, June 20, 1910, Image 1. p. 1-2. The *Bridgeport Evening Farmer*. (Bridgeport, Conn.), 20 June 1910. Chronicling America: Historic American Newspapers. Lib. of Congress. <http://chroniclingamerica.loc.gov/lccn/sn84022472/1910-06-20/ed-1/seq-1/>

150 "Whitehead Must Pay $1240.27." The *Bridgeport Evening Farmer*., May 14, 1912, Page 2, Image 2. Chronicling America: Historic American Newspapers. Lib. of Congress. <http://chroniclingamerica.loc.gov/lccn/sn84022472/1912-05-14/ed-1/seq-2/>

151 Atlas of the City and Town of Bridgeport, CT. Published by G. M. Hopkins, 1888. Historical Collections Department, Bridgeport Public Library.

152 Roer, Mike. Bridgeport Baseball History. http://www.mikeroer.com/bridgeportballparks.html

153 Adapted from http://www.mikeroer.com/bridgeportballparks.html with permission. Original source: Atlas of the City and Town of Bridgeport, CT. Published by G. M. Hopkins, 1888. Historical Collections Department, Bridgeport Public Library.

154 http://www.mikeroer.com/bridgeportballparks.html

155 "Flying Machine Factory – Latest of Bridgeport's Industries." Bridgeport Sunday Herald, Nov. 17, 1901. p. 1. http://news.google.com/newspapers?id=gGwmAAAAIBAJ&sjid=wf8FAAAAIBAJ&pg=2020%2C4857304

156 "Bridgeport's Flying Machine Builders." *Bridgeport Sunday Herald*, January 26, 1902, p. 4. https://news.google.com/newspapers?id=ZO8yAAAAIBAJ&sjid=kQAGAAAAIBAJ&pg=5366%2C372219

157 Ibid

158 Ibid

159 Whole World Panting for a Perfect Aeroplane, New-York tribune., June 12, 1910, Page 5, Image 58, New-York tribune. (New York [N.Y.]), 12 June 1910. Chronicling America: Historic American Newspapers. Lib. of Congress. <http://chroniclingamerica.loc.gov/lccn/sn83030214/1910-06-12/ed-1/seq-58/>

160 Carpenter, Jack. Pendulum. 1992, p. 41.

161 Goldstone, Lawrence. Birdmen. Ballantine Books, NY, 2014. p. 91

162 "How the World Discovered the Wright Brothers." Ackman, Dan. Forbes Magazine. Nov. 18, 2003. http://www.forbes.com/2003/11/18/cx_da_1118wrights.html

163 Wilbur and Orville: A Biography of the Wright Brothers. Howard, Fred. Dover Publications, Mineola, NY. 1987. p. 142

Gustave Whitehead: "First in Flight"

164 Ibid

165 "Perfecting His Machine." Bridgeport Evening Post, Monday, August 26, 1901. p. 1

166 "Unrealized Dreams." "Whitehead Flew High
That Is Financially but Not Actually — That Is, to Say as Yet He Hasn't
Linde Tired of Putting up Ducats. *Bridgeport Post*. April 5, 1902 http://gustavewhitehead.info/gustave-whitehead-unrealized-dreams/
Millers Lumber Co. Brings Him into Court — Says He Ordered Brakes Down

167 *Bridgeport Daily Standard*, Oct. 1, 1904, p.5. O'Dwyer Gustave Whitehead Research Collection, Fairfield Museum, Fairfield, CT

168 Flying Machine That Will Remain Stationary in Mid-Air is Whitehead's Creation." The *Bridgeport Evening Farmer*, June 20, 1910, Image 1. p. 1-2. The *Bridgeport Evening Farmer*. (Bridgeport, Conn.), 20 June 1910. Chronicling America: Historic American Newspapers. Lib. of Congress. <http://chroniclingamerica.loc.gov/lccn/sn84022472/1910-06-20/ed-1/seq-1/>

"Whitehead Must Pay $1240.27." The *Bridgeport Evening Farmer*., May 14, 1912, Page 2, Image 2. Chronicling America: Historic American Newspapers. Lib. of Congress. <http://chroniclingamerica.loc.gov/lccn/sn84022472/1912-05-14/ed-1/seq-2/>

169 "Lost Flights of Gustave Whitehead." Randolph, Stella.. Places, Inc., Wash. DC. 1937. p. 46

170 *The WRight Story*. Bullmer, Joe. CreatSpace, 2009, p. 156-164, "Straight and Level."

171 Ibid

172 http://www.foxnews.com/science/interactive/2013/04/01/contract-between-wrights-smithsonian-decrees-flyer-was-first-plane/

173 Correspondences of May – Sept., 1908. Papers of Wilbur and Orville Wright, Library of Congress

174 Crouch, Tom. "The Flight Claims of Gustave Whitehead." Smithsonian Institution, April 6, 2013. http://blog.nasm.si.edu/aviation/the-flight-claims-of-gustave-whitehead/

175 "Crouch & Lippincott: Gustave Whitehead Discussion." Spannenberger, 1981. Gustav Weisskopf Museum, Leutershausen, Germany. YouTube https://youtu.be/Eu0OB4jBKm0

176 "What role did the Connecticut Aeronautical Historical Association (CAHA) play in the recognition of Gustave Whitehead?." http://gustavewhitehead.info/connecticut-aeronautical-historical-association/

177 *The WRight Story*. Bullmer, Joe. CreatSpace, 2009. P. x (Preface.)

178 *The WRight Story*. Bullmer, Joe. CreatSpace, 2009, p. 156-164, "Straight and Level."

179 inherently stable - having built-in stability, ability to remain level, without nose-diving

180 Beach Whitehead Statement, Gustave Whitehead collection. Library of Congress.

181 http://www.sti.nasa.gov/sscg/08.html

182 Herald Magazine. *Bridgeport Sunday Herald*, January 30th, 1937. p. 5

183 NY Sun, June 9, 1901, p. 2, "Improved Flying Machine"

184 *Scientific American*, June 8, 1901, p. 357 http://archive.org/details/scientific-american-1901-06-08

185 Gustave Whitehead Will Soon Attempt the Trip to New York in His Airship Now Being Perfected.. Boston Daily Globe August 23, 1901.

186 New York Herald, June 16, 1901, Section 5, p. 3

187 NY Sun, June 9, 1901.

188 *Scientific American*, June 8, 1901.

Endnotes

189   Interview with Andy Kosch, Whitehead reproduction pilot and team member, by S. Brinchman, April 29, 2015.

190   "Ship That Will Fly Like a Bird May Soon Be Placed on the Market." New York Evening Telegram, Nov. 19, 1901.

191   Letter from John Whitehead to Stella Randolph, Aug. 6, 1934. O'Dwyer Gustave Whitehead Research Collection, Fairfield Museum, Fairfield, CT

192   Letter from John Whitehead to Stella Randolph, Aug. 6, 1934. O'Dwyer Gustave Whitehead Research Collection, Fairfield Museum, Fairfield, CT

193   Anton Pruckner Interview with WICC, May 20, 1964, p. 12. O'Dwyer Gustave Whitehead Research Collection, Fairfield Museum, Fairfield, CT

194   Ibid p. 5

195   Letter from Paul Garber to William J. O'Dwyer, Nov. 9, 1966. O'Dwyer Gustave Whitehead Research Collection, Fairfield Museum, Fairfield, CT

196   Notes by William J. O'Dwyer, 1960's, entitled 1st Draft, p. 1, Subseries III. CAHA1963-1986, O'Dwyer Gustave Whitehead Research Collection, Fairfield Museum, Fairfield, CT

197   Popular Mechanics, Dec. 1981, "Was Whitehead First?" p. 75

198   CAHA and Whitehead www.historybycontract.org; original footage donated to the Gustav Weisskopf Museum, Leutershausen, Germany

199   Notes by William J. O'Dwyer, 1960's, entitled 1st Draft, p. 1, Subseries III. CAHA1963-1986, O'Dwyer Gustave Whitehead Research Collection, Fairfield Museum, Fairfield, CT

200   "Wright Flyer" p788 Flight 11 December 1953 http://www.flightglobal.com/FlightPDFArchive/1953/1953%20-%201634.PDF

201   NASA, Glenn Research Center "Wright 1903 Flyer" https://www.grc.nasa.gov/WWW/Wright/airplane/air1903.html

202   "Bridgeport's Flying Machine Builders." *Bridgeport Sunday Herald*, Jan. 26, 1902. p. 4

203   The *Aeronautical World*. December 1902. p. 99-100

204   Pendulum. Carpenter, Jack. 1992. p. 125

205   Pendulum. Carpenter, Jack. 1992. p. 280

206   Letter of Junius Harworth, accompanied by blueprints, Aug. 30, 1934, p. 2-3. O'Dwyer Gustave Whitehead Research Collection, Fairfield Museum, Fairfield, CT

207   "Plane Sputters in Re-enactment of Wright Flight." NBC News. (AP) 12/17/2003 8:27:53 PM ET. http://www.nbcnews.com/id/3737728/ns/technology_and_science-science/t/plane-sputters-re-enactment-wright-flight/#.VJLzihbl7Ax

208   Whitehead replicas were "close reproductions" based on detailed information provided by Whitehead in his published descriptions, the descriptions of his assistants who helped build the aircraft, and original photos.

209   https://www.youtube.com/watch?v=Ucm80BYUXEE

210   O'Dwyer, William J., Randolph, Stella. History by Contract. 1978, Fritz Majer and Sohn. p. 49

211   Affidavit of Alexander Gluck. O'Dwyer Gustave Whitehead Research Collection, Fairfield Museum, Fairfield, CT

212   Randolph, Stella. Lost Flights of Gustave Whitehead. 1937. Places, Inc., Wash. DC. p. 33

213   Letters of Junius Harworth to Stella Randolph. January 9, 1959. O'Dwyer Gustave Whitehead Research Collection, Fairfield Museum, Fairfield, CT

214   http://www.wrightstories.com/kittyhawk.html#hflight

215   Ibid

Gustave Whitehead: "First in Flight"

216 http://www.uscg.mil/history/faqs/Wright_Brothers.asp

217 Ibid

218 Letters to the Editor. *American Inventor*. April 1, 1902.

219 Letters of Junius Harworth to Stella Randolph. O'Dwyer Gustave Whitehead Research Collection, Fairfield Museum, Fairfield, CT

220 O'Dwyer, William J., Randolph, Stella. History by Contract. 1978, Fritz Majer and Sohn. Old Picture Series. p. XV - XVII

221 *Bridgeport Daily Standard*, Oct. 1, 1904, p. 5

222 Ibid

223 *Scientific American*, January 27, 1906, p. 93-94 http://archive.org/details/scientific-american-1906-01-27

224 http://www.cnn.com/2013/06/07/travel/wright-brothers-first-flight-fight/

225 O'Dwyer, William J., Randolph, Stella. History by Contract. 1978, Fritz Majer and Sohn. p.94-95

226 Early news and journal articles concerning Gustave Whitehead, collected by O'Dwyer, Randolph, and the Fairfield Historical Society and local libraries are found at the Fairfield Museum, Fairfield, CT, and the Bridgeport and Stratford libraries.

227 Additional archives of Whitehead materials are located at the Library of the University of Texas, Dallas, TX in the Stella Randolph collection, within their aeronautical archives. http://www.utdallas.edu/library/specialcollections/hac/general/Randolph.pdf

228 http://www.fairfieldhistory.org/wp-content/uploads/ODwyer-Gustav-Whitehead-Research-Collection-Ms-B107.pdf

229 "An Acetylene Air-Ship." London St. James Gazette, August 20, 1901, p. 6

230 Ship That Will Fly Like a Bird Will Soon Be Placed on the Market," New York Telegram, November 19, 1901, p.10 http://www.gustave-whitehead.com/history/statements-by-whitehead/1901-11-19-ny-telegram-p-10/

231 "Bridgeport Man's Projected Midair Flight. Gustave Whitehead Will Soon Attempt the Trip to New York in His Airship Now Being Perfected." Boston Daily Globe. August 23, 1901.

232 Will Fly to New York. The Norwalk Hour. August 23.1901. p. 4 http://news.google.com/newspapers?id=Pj8pAAAAIBAJ&sjid=PWYFAAAAIBAJ&pg=4270%2C3327697

233 The Washington times. (Washington [D.C.]), 23 Aug. 1901. Chronicling America: Historic American Newspapers. Lib. of Congress. <http://chroniclingamerica.loc.gov/lccn/sn87062245/1901-08-23/ed-1/seq-2/>

234 "Perfecting His Machine." Bridgeport Evening Post, Monday, August 26, 1901. p. 1

235 Langley's Aero Engine of 1903. Smithsonian Annals of Flight, No. 6. Smithsonian Institution Press, City of Washington (1971). p. 18. http://www.sil.si.edu/smithsoniancontributions/AnnalsofFlight/pdf_hi/SAOF-0006.pdf

236 Ibid. p. 2

237 Letter from C M Manley to F M Hodge, Sept. 20, 1901. O'Dwyer, William J., Randolph, Stella. History by Contract. 1978, Fritz Majer and Sohn. p.116

238 O'Dwyer, William J., Randolph, Stella. History by Contract. 1978, Fritz Majer and Sohn. p.112

239 Interview with Anton Pruckner, Nov. 23, 1963, p. 34. O'Dwyer Gustave Whitehead Research Collection, Fairfield Museum, Fairfield, CT

240 Letter from C M Manley to F M Hodge, Sept. 20, 1901. O'Dwyer, William J., Randolph, Stella. History by Contract. 1978, Fritz Majer and Sohn. p.113-115

241 "Whitehead's Flying Machine." Naugatuck Daily News. Nov. 18, 1901. p. 3

Endnotes

242 Randolph, Stella. Lost Flights of Gustave Whitehead. 1937. Places, Inc., Wash. DC. p. 35

243 "Bridgeport's Flying Machine Factory ." Bridgport Sunday Herald, January 26, 1902, p. 4. https://news.google.com/newspapers?id=ZO8yAAAAIBAJ&sjid=kQAGAAAAIBAJ&pg=5366%2C372219

244 "Maxim Leads Air Company. Grahame-White, Bleriot and Maxim Company with $1,000,000 Capital." *New York Times*. "Sir Hiram Maxim, who has just resigned from the ordnance firm with which his name has been for so long connected, will be the Chairman of a new company to be known as the Grahame-White, Bleriot, and Maxim Company, limited, with a total authorized capital of 200,000 ($1,000,000)."

245 Unrealized Dreams. *Bridgeport Evening Farmer*. April 15.1902.

246 http://gustavewhitehead.info/gustave-whitehead-unrealized-dreams/

247 Ibid

248 *Bridgeport Sunday Herald*, January 26, 1902. p. 4

249 Randolph, Stella. Lost Flights of Gustave Whitehead. 1937. Places, Inc., Wash. DC. p. 35

250 "Mr. Linde's Experience: Had Verbal Promise from Millionaire Huntington but It Was Not Binding." Bridgeport Evening Post, May 19, 1902. p.8

251 *Bridgeport Daily Standard*. August 2, 1902. p. 1, col. 7

252 New York Dramatic Mirror, May 29, 1909, p. 3

253 The Tucumcari news. (Tucumcari, N.M.), 01 Dec. 1906, Image 8. Chronicling America: Historic American Newspapers. Lib. of Congress. <http://chroniclingamerica.loc.gov/lccn/sn93061709/1906-12-01/ed-1/seq-8/>

254 Los Angeles Herald., Nov. 25, 1906, Image 1, Chronicling America, Library of Congress.

255 "An Artist Fined." Evening star. (Washington, D.C.), 03 May 1892. Chronicling America: Historic American Newspapers. Lib. of Congress. <http://chroniclingamerica.loc.gov/lccn/sn83045462/1892-05-03/ed-1/seq-6/>

256 "Worth $500,000; Died in poverty." The free lance. (Fredericksburg, Va.), 01 May 1909. Chronicling America: Historic American Newspapers. Lib. of Congress. <http://chroniclingamerica.loc.gov/lccn/sn87060165/1909-05-01/ed-1/seq-2/>

257 Missouri History Museum, St. Louis Missouri

258 O'Dwyer Gustave Whitehead Research Collection, Fairfield Museum, Fairfield, CT.

259 "Flying Machine Factory, The Latest of Bridgeport's Industries." *Bridgeport Sunday Herald*, Nov. 17, 1901. p. 1

260 "Flying Machine Factory, The Latest of Bridgeport's Industries." *Bridgeport Sunday Herald*, Nov. 17, 1901. p. 1

261 "Bridgeport Man Says His Airship Will Surely Fly." The evening world., November 19, 1901, Night Edition, Page 5, Image 5 http://chroniclingamerica.loc.gov/lccn/sn83030193/1901-11-19/ed-1/seq-5/

262 New York Telegram, November 19, 1901, p.10

263 Letter from John Whitehead to Stella Randolph, Aug. 6, 1934, p. 2. O'Dwyer Gustave Whitehead Research Collection, Fairfield Museum, Fairfield, CT.

264 Letter from John Whitehead to Stella Randolph, Nov. 5, 1934, p. 5. O'Dwyer Gustave Whitehead Research Collection, Fairfield Museum, Fairfield, CT.

265 Letter from John Whitehead to Stella Randolph, Aug. 6, 1934, p. 4-5. O'Dwyer Gustave Whitehead Research Collection, Fairfield Museum, Fairfield, CT.,

266 Letter of John Whitehead to Stella Randolph, September 3, 1934. p. 1-2. O'Dwyer Gustave Whitehead Research Collection, Fairfield Museum, Fairfield, CT

267 Ibid, p. 5

© Susan Brinchman, 2015

268 Ibid, p. 6

269 Ibid, p. 7-8

270 Letter of John Whitehead to Stella Randolph, September 3, 1934. p. 3. O'Dwyer Gustave Whitehead Research Collection, Fairfield Museum, Fairfield, CT

271 "Whitehead Flew High." *Bridgeport Post*, April 5, 1902.

272 Flying Machine That Will Remain Stationary in Mid-Air is Whitehead's Creation." The *Bridgeport Evening Farmer*., June 20, 1910, Image 1. p. 1-2. The *Bridgeport Evening Farmer*. (Bridgeport, Conn.), 20 June 1910. Chronicling America: Historic American Newspapers. Lib. of Congress. <http://chroniclingamerica.loc.gov/lccn/sn84022472/1910-06-20/ed-1/seq-1/>

273 "Unrealized Dreams." *Bridgeport Evening Farmer*, April 5, 1902.

274 alternately referred to as the "aeronautic, aerial, or air ship contest, competition, or tournament"

275 Lambert, Maj. Albert B., "Early History of Aeronautics in St. Louis," Missouri Historical Society Collections, Vol. 5, No. 3, June 1928.

276 Horgan, James. City of Flight: The History of Aviation in St. Louis. The Patrice Press. St. Louis, MI. 2nd edition, Sept. 1990. p. 59

277 " BRIDGEPORT MAN ENTERED.

Gustave Whitehead Wants to Compete in a $200,000 Airship Contest at St Louis in 1903." Boston Sunday Globe 1.19.1902, p. 6

278 There is no evidence Whitehead mentioned dirigible ballooning experiments to Exposition authorities nor that he ever worked on these. In the media of these early days, aeronautical terms were often used interchangeably, or by accident, out of ignorance on the topic. Balloons and dirigibles had been prominent for over 100 years in 1904, reporters confused the terms when describing heavier-than-air flying machines - and to confuse them even further, there was some overlap, when dirigibles added motors, and were then, at times, called "heavier-than-air."

279 "Bridgeport Man Entered: Gustave Whitehead Wants to Compete in a $200,000 Airship Contest at St. Louis in 1903." Boston Globe, Jan. 19, 1902. p. 82.

280 Flying Machine That Will Remain Stationary in Mid-Air is Whitehead's Creation." The *Bridgeport Evening Farmer*, June 20, 1910, Image 1. p. 1-2. The *Bridgeport Evening Farmer*. (Bridgeport, Conn.), 20 June 1910. Chronicling America: Historic American Newspapers. Lib. of Congress. <http://chroniclingamerica.loc.gov/lccn/sn84022472/1910-06-20/ed-1/seq-1/>

281 "Airship Prizes at the World's Fair." Press and Horticulturist. January 31, 1902.

282 Horgan, James. City of Flight: The History of Aviation in St. Louis. The Patrice Press. St. Louis, MI. 2nd edition, Sept. 1990. p. 59

283 World's Fair Bulletin, Feb. 1902, p. 20. World's fair bulletin, v.3 no.04 1901/02. Text collections. The Louisiana Purchase Exposition: The 1904 St. Louis World's Fair. University of Missouri Library Systems, Digital Library, St. Louis, Missouri.

284 World's Fair Bulletin, Feb. 1902, p. 20-21. World's fair bulletin, v.3 no.04 1901/02. Text collections. The Louisiana Purchase Exposition: The 1904 St. Louis World's Fair. University of Missouri Library Systems, Digital Library, St. Louis, Missouri.

285 Horgan, James. City of Flight: The History of Aviation in St. Louis. The Patrice Press. St. Louis, MI. 2nd edition, Sept. 1990. p. 53-54

286 Ibid

287 "Recent Progress in Aerial Navigation." Cochrane, Charles H., M.E.. Popular Science, Vol. 58. April 1901 http://en.wikisource.org/wiki/Popular_Science_Monthly/Volume_58/April_1901/Recent_Progress_in_Aerial_Navigation

Endnotes

288   Horgan, James. City of Flight: The History of Aviation in St. Louis. The Patrice Press. St. Louis, MI. 2nd edition, Sept. 1990. p. 69

289   Ibid, p. 70

290   "Recent Progress in Aerial Navigation." Cochrane, Charles H., M.E.. Popular Science, Vol. 58. April 1901 http://en.wikisource.org/wiki/Popular_Science_Monthly/Volume_58/April_1901/Recent_Progress_in_Aerial_Navigation

291   History of the Louisiana purchase exposition : comprising the history of the Louisiana territory, the story of the Louisiana purchase and a full account of the great exposition, embracing the participation of the states and nations of the world, and other events of the St. Louis world's fair of 1904 (compiled from official sources by Mark Bennitt, editor-in-chief and Frank Parker Stockbridge, managing editor, Universal exposition publishing company, 1905). www.1904faircd.com/Transport

292   http://www.encyclopedia.com/doc/1G2-3406401046.html

293   https://www.census.gov/hhes/povmeas/publications/povthres/fisher4.html#C3

294   Wilbur Wright to Octave Chanute. Papers of Wilbur and Orville Wright. Octave Chanute – Special Correspondences, 1904.

295   The Great Flying Machine Contest: "A Huge Silken Bird to Compete" Falkirk Herald *April 19, 1902* p.7

296   "Not So Easy for Santos-Dumont." Deseret News, April 19.1902, Part 3. p. 17

      http://news.google.com/newspapers?id=Z4wzAAAAIBAJ&sjid=O0oDAAAAIBAJ&pg=1878%2C4488573

297   an aircraft that is lighter than air, such as a balloon, dirigible, or powered airship; or pertaining to aerial navigation or aeronautics

298   Middletown Penny Press Aug. 6, 1902. p. 2 (Middletown, CT)

299   "Inventors Turn to Aerial Navigation: Americans Native Pride Aroused By Leadership of Foreign Competitors," Chicago Tribune, 1903 (unknown date)

300   "A Gliding Machine." Sheridan Weekly Sun, April 21, 1904, Sheridan, Indiana,, p. 3.

301   Crouch, Tom D. A Dream of Wings. NY: Norton and Company, (1981) p. 119

302   Affidavit of John Lesko, Sept. 3, 1964. O'Dwyer Gustave Whitehead Research Collection, Fairfield Museum, Fairfield, CT.

303   http://www.davemanuel.com/inflation-calculator.php

304   Horgan, James J. ,"Aeronautics at the World's Fair of 1904." (1968), p. 15 O'Dwyer Gustave Whitehead Research Collection, Fairfield Museum, Fairfield, CT. Box 4, Folder 48, Series B,

305   "Von Der Weltausstellung In St. Louis (Original Mittellungen)." by Artur Boltzmann. Weiner Luftschiffer-Zeitung, No. 11. 1904. p. 251

306   Francis, David R. The Universal Exposition of 1904, the standard primary narrative of the 1904 St. Louis World's Fair and its official final report., Vol. 1, p. 442

307   Rules and Regulations of the Aeronautic Competition (Revised), March 1904. P.6-7. Missouri History Museum.

308   Minutes of the Advisory Board on Aerial Contests. Oct. 21, 1904, pg. 322X. Missouri History Museum.

309   Horgan, James J. ,"Aeronautics at the World's Fair of 1904." (1968) p. 47. O'Dwyer Gustave Whitehead Research Collection, Fairfield Museum, Fairfield, CT.

310   "A letter from Leo Stevens." Correspondences. *Scientific American* March 26, 1904. p. 251

311   Walker, John Brisben., "The Five Great Features of the Fair," from "The World's Fair ." Cosmopolitan, September 1904. Vol. XXXVII No. 5. , p. 494

312   Ibid, p. 622

313 World's Fair Bulletin, June 1902, p. 7 World's fair bulletin, v.3 no.8 1902/03, University of Missouri Library Collections, Digital Library http://digital.library.umsystem.edu/cgi/t/text/text-idx?c=lex;cc=lex;sid=c9cc0d7ef4e46c8099c0128c47f165f6;q1=Maxim;rgn=full%20text;tpl=home.tpl

314 World's Fair Bulletin, Aug. 1902, p. 9 University of Missouri Library Collections, Digital Library http://digital.library.umsystem.edu/cgi/t/text/text-idx?c=lex;cc=lex;sid=c9cc0d7ef4e46c8099c0128c47f165f6;q1=Maxim;rgn=full%20text;tpl=home.tpl

315 Letter from Major. William J. O'Dwyer to Prof. David P. Daniel, Aug. 16, 1985. O'Dwyer Gustave Whitehead Research Collection, Fairfield Museum, Fairfield, CT

316 Flying Machine That Will Remain Stationary in Mid-Air is Whitehead's Creation." The *Bridgeport Evening Farmer.*, June 20, 1910, Image 1. p. 1-2. The *Bridgeport Evening Farmer*. (Bridgeport, Conn.), 20 June 1910. Chronicling America: Historic American Newspapers. Lib. of Congress. <http://chroniclingamerica.loc.gov/lccn/sn84022472/1910-06-20/ed-1/seq-1/>

317 Zitarelli, David E. "The 1904 St. Louis Congress and Westward Expansion of American Mathematics." Notices of the AMS, Vol. 58, No. 8. http://www.academia.edu/9930717/The_1904_St._Louis_Congress_and_Westward_Expansion_of_American_Mathematics

318 Professor Ludwig Boltzmann was an avid early supporter of and lecturer on aviation in the 1890's; with the view that successful heavier-than-air flying machines would become a reality and that attaching a lightweight engine to gliders held the most promise; encouraging financial support of these efforts in Austria. Prof. Boltzmann corresponded with Lilienthal several years before his death concerning adding lightweight engines to gliders to make them fly. (Dahmen, Silvio R. "Boltzmann and the Art of Flying," 2007. http://arxiv.org/pdf/0706.0008.pdf)

319 Letter from Roseberry of NY State Educational Department to Maj. William J. O'Dwyer, Feb. 15, 1989, contains Boltzmann's Dispatch and explanations. Boltzmann Dispatch discovered by Whitehead researcher, Lt. Col. Walter Prufert, Germany, 1983. Folder 46. O'Dwyer Gustave Whitehead Research Collection, Fairfield Museum, Fairfield, CT

320 "Von Der Weltausstellung In St. Louis (Original Mittellungen)." by Artur Boltzmann. Weiner Luftschiffer-Zeitung, No. 11. 1904. p. 251

321 "Airship a Success." The Evening Argus, Oct.25.1904 p. 15. http://news.google.com/newspapers?id=O5o1AAAAIBAJ&sjid=qKsFAAAAIBAJ&pg=1330%2C6139145

322 "Baldwin.Airship.Lost.in Dark." Spokesman.Review.Nov.3.1904 p.5 http://news.google.com/newspapers?id=3dcUAAAAIBAJ&sjid=trUDAAAAIBAJ&pg=6527%2C5209163

323 "The California Arrow." World's fair bulletin, v.5 no.8-v.6 no.2, 1904, p. 18

324 Bennett, Mark. History of the Louisiana Purchase Exposition, St. Louis, 1905, p.608

325 J.W. Buel, PhD. "Transportation Exhibits" by Willard A. Smith; "Louisiana and the Fair" (St. Louis, 1905). Volume IX . p. 91 . Missouri Digital Heritage website. http://cdm16795.contentdm.oclc.org/cdm/compoundobject/collection/muellis/id/12429/rec/63

326 Letter from Curtiss Museum to Flight Journal, faxed April 1998. P. 1. Folder 46. O'Dwyer Gustave Whitehead Research Collection, Fairfield Museum, Fairfield, CT

327 "Gustave Whitehead's New Machine." Aeronautic World, May 1903. http://gustavewhitehead.org/news_journalism/1903_-_gustave_whiteheads_n.html

328 "Bridgeport's Santos Dumont." *Bridgeport Daily Standard*, Sept. 1, 1903. O'Dwyer Gustave Whitehead Research Collection, Fairfield Museum, Fairfield, CT

329 "Herald Man Makes a Trial Trip." May 31, 1903. p. 4 http://news.google.com newspapers?id=R9UyAAAAIBAJ&sjid=0wAGAAAAIBAJ&pg=6083%2C2257295

330 *Scientific American*, Sept. 19, 1903, p.204 https://ia700804.us.archive.org/29/items/scientific-american-1903-09-19/

Endnotes

scientific-american-v89-n12-1903-09-19.pdf

331 Letter of Willard A. Smith to FJV Skiff, Oct. 1, 1904. Minutes of the Advisory Board on Aerial Contests. Oct. 11, 1904, pg. 3184. Missouri History Museum.

332 "DownEaster Has Airship." Minneapolis Journal, Nov. 11, 1904. p. 14

333 Bennett, Mark. History of the Louisiana Purchase Exposition, St. Louis, 1905, p. 611

334 Page 1 of Octave Chanute Papers: Special Correspondence--Wright Brothers, 1904-1905. http://www.loc.gov/resource/mwright.06008/?sp=1

335 Horgan, James J. ,"Aeronautics at the World's Fair of 1904." (1968). p. 57 O'Dwyer Gustave Whitehead Research Collection, Fairfield Museum, Fairfield, CT.

336 Memories of the World's Greatest Exposition, St. Louis, 1904. p. 11 . Missouri Digital Heritage website

337 Bennett, Mark. History of the Louisiana Purchase Exposition, St. Louis, 1905, p. 125

338 Ibid, p. 124

339 J.W. Buel. Louisiana and the Fair. (St. Louis, 1905) IV. 1438. . Missouri Digital Heritage website. http://cdm16795.contentdm.oclc.org/cdm/compoundobject/collection/muellis/id/12429/rec/63

340 Horgan, James J. ,"Aeronautics at the World's Fair of 1904." (1968). p. 46 O'Dwyer Gustave Whitehead Research Collection, Fairfield Museum, Fairfield, CT.

341 Wandell, H. B., Anell's Annual, 1000 Fact about the St. Louis World's Fair in a Nutshell. May 1903. p. 60. Missouri Digital Heritage website

342 Affidavit of John Lesko, Sept. 3, 1964. O'Dwyer Gustave Whitehead Research Collection, Fairfield Museum, Fairfield, CT

343 Bennett, Mark. History of the Louisiana Purchase Exposition, St. Louis, 1905, p. 577

344 Ibid., p. 607

345 Bennett, Mark. History of the Louisiana Purchase Exposition, St. Louis, 1905, Chapter XVII, Exhibits in Transportation and Aeronautics, p. 575

346 Francis, David R. The Universal Exposition of 1904, the standard primary narrative of the 1904 St. Louis World's Fair and its official final report., Vol. 2, p. 137 http://cdm16795.contentdm.oclc.org/cdm/compoundobject/collection/expo/id/1014/rec/2

347 Missouri Digital Heritage. http://cdm16795.contentdm.oclc.org/cdm/search/collection/expo/searchterm/whitehead/order/nosort

348 "Celebrated Savants of all the Nations to Participate in the Fair." The St. Louis Republic., January 31, 1904, PART IV, Image 31, p. 1. Chronicling America: Historic American Newspapers. Lib. of Congress. <http://chroniclingamerica.loc.gov/lccn/sn84020274/1904-01-31/ed-1/seq-31/>

349 Bennett, Mark. History of the Louisiana Purchase Exposition, St. Louis, 1905. p. 187

350 The St. Louis Republic. (St. Louis, Mo.), 06 Oct. 1904. p. 4, Image 4 Chronicling America: Historic American Newspapers. Lib. of Congress. <http://chroniclingamerica.loc.gov/lccn/sn84020274/1904-10-06/ed-1/seq-4/>

351 Ibid

352 The St. Louis Republic. (St. Louis, Mo.), 04 Oct. 1904, p. 1. Chronicling America: Historic American Newspapers. Lib. of Congress. <http://chroniclingamerica.loc.gov/lccn/sn84020274/1904-10-04/ed-1/seq-1/>

353 The St. Louis Republic. (St. Louis, Mo.), 08 Oct. 1904. p. 4, Image 12.Chronicling America: Historic American Newspapers. Lib. of Congress. <http://chroniclingamerica.loc.gov/lccn/sn84020274/1904-10-08/ed-1/seq-12/>

354 Page 4 of Octave Chanute Papers: Special Correspondence--Wright Brothers, 1904-1905. http://www.loc.gov/resource/mwright.06008/?sp=4

Gustave Whitehead: "First in Flight"

355 Buel, James W., Louisiana and the fair. An exposition of the world, its people and their achievements, volume 9, St. Louis, Missouri : World's Progress Publishing Company (1905). Divison CXXXIII, Automobiles and Airships, p. 3254 – 3255 http://cdm16795.contentdm.oclc.org/cdm/compoundobject/collection/muellis/id/12429/rec/1.

356 Ibid. p. 3256-3257

357 O'Dwyer, William J., Randolph, Stella. History by Contract. 1978, Fritz Majer and Sohn. p. 58

358 Affidavit of Anton Pruckner, Oct. 30, 1964. O'Dwyer Gustave Whitehead Research Collection, Fairfield Museum, Fairfield, CT

359 http://gustavewhitehead.org/news_journalism/1902_-_letters_to_american_.html

360 Bridgeport's Flying Machine Builders. *Bridgeport Sunday Herald*. Jan. 26, 1902. p. 4 http://news.google.com/newspapers?nid=4p5LGG1h9z0C&dat=19020126&printsec=frontpage&hl=en

361 The Exposition, as it was also called, was actually delayed, with the aerial contests held in the summer and fall of 1904.

362 Randolph, Stella. Lost Flights of Gustave Whitehead. 1937. Places, Inc., Wash. DC, p.13

363 from others who had been present

364 O'Dwyer, William J., Randolph, Stella. History by Contract. 1978, Fritz Majer and Sohn. p.54

365 Randolph, Stella. Lost Flights of Gustave Whitehead. 1937. Places, Inc., Wash. DC, p54

366 Letter from Junius Harworth to Randolph, January 27, 1935. O'Dwyer Gustave Whitehead Research Collection, Fairfield Museum, Fairfield, CT

367 the letters to the editor were written in late winter, early spring of 1902, when Harworth was nearly 14 years old

368 In 1902, Whitehead had been in America for 9 years

369 referring to lighter-than-air crafts, such as balloons and dirigibles

370 Letters to the Editor. *American Inventor*, April 1, 1902. http://gustavewhitehead.org/news_journalism/1902_-_letters_to_american_.html

371 The Aerial Sweepstakes at the St. Louis Fair. The Deseret News April 12, 1902. http://news.google.com/newspapers?id=YYwzAAAAIBAJ&sjid=O0oDAAAAIBAJ&pg=3723%2C3855542

372 Not So Easy for Santos Dumont. The Deseret Evening News. Salt Lake City, Utah. Apr 19, 1902. Part 3, page 1. http://news.google.com/newspapers?id=Z4wzAAAAIBAJ&sjid=O0oDAAAAIBAJ&pg=3936%2C4491738

373 Ibid

374 Letter from John Whitehead to Stella Randolph, Aug. 6, 1934. O'Dwyer Gustave Whitehead Research Collection, Fairfield Museum, Fairfield, CT.

375 Letter from John Whitehead to Stella Randolph, Aug. 6, 1934. O'Dwyer Gustave Whitehead Research Collection, Fairfield Museum, Fairfield, CT.

376 Randolph, Stella. "The Story of Gustave Whitehead, Before the Wrights Flew." 1966. GP Putnam & Sons, p. 57

377 *Bridgeport Sunday Herald*, January 26, 1902. p. 4

378 Letter from John Whitehead to Stella Randolph, Aug. 6, 1934, p. 2. O'Dwyer Gustave Whitehead Research Collection, Fairfield Museum, Fairfield, CT

379 Letter from John Whitehead to Stella Randolph, Nov. 5, 1934, p. 5. O'Dwyer Gustave Whitehead Research Collection, Fairfield Museum, Fairfield, CT.

380 Letter from John Whitehead to Stella Randolph, Aug. 6, 1934, p. 6. O'Dwyer Gustave Whitehead Research Collection, Fairfield Museum, Fairfield, CT.

381 Ibid

Endnotes

382 Still Trying to Fly. The Forest Republican. Tionesta, Pa. August 06, 1902, Image 4, Chronicling America, Library of Congress.

383 Soar Through Skies. Middletown Penny Press. August 6, 1902.

384 Letter from John Whitehead to Stella Randolph, Aug. 6, 1934. O'Dwyer Gustave Whitehead Research Collection, Fairfield Museum, Fairfield, CT. p. 7

385 eliminating the need for open spaces and smooth runways, which did not exist at the time

386 Interview with Anton Pruckner (WICC Radio), May 20, 1964, p. 7. O'Dwyer Gustave Whitehead Research Collection, Fairfield Museum, Fairfield, CT.

387 World's Fair Bulletin, Feb., 1902, p. 21.

388 "Improved Flying Machine."The Sun, June 9, 1901.page 2, image 2. Chronicling America, Library of Congress. http://chroniclingamerica.loc.gov/

389 The exact location is unknown, but it may be "Sport Hill," about 11 miles away, northeast of Fairfield's center, on the border of Fairfield and Easton, CT, was one of a number of flying locations for Whitehead, mentioned by witnesses.

390 Ibid

391 Howell, Richard (August 18, 1901). "Flying": "Gustave Whitehead's Story.," *Bridgeport Herald*. p. 5 http://www.gustave-whitehead.com/history/news-reports-1901-2-flights/1901-08-18-bridgeport-herald-p-5/

392 Letters of Junius Harworth to Randolph. O'Dwyer Gustave Whitehead Research Collection, Fairfield Museum, Fairfield, CT

393 O'Dwyer, William J., Randolph, Stella. History by Contract. 1978, Fritz Majer and Sohn. p 49

394 Schools would have been let out in the spring, *first half of June* or in the fall or winter months, to view Whitehead's many practice flights in the area of Pine Street, 1901-1903.

395 unmeasured

396 Letter of Wilbur Wright to Octave Chanute. May 27, 1904. Library of Congress, Papers of Wilbur and Orville Wright, Octave Chanute – Special Correspondence 1904.

397 Reissue of Chronology Commemorating the Hundredth Anniversary of the Birth of Orville Wright. NASA.http://history.nasa.gov/monograph32.pdf. p. 16

398 Affidavit of Louis Lazay, January 4, 1936. O'Dwyer Gustave Whitehead Research Collection, Fairfield Museum, Fairfield, CT

399 Memorandum: Bridgeport Trip re: Gustave Whitehead Flights, K.I. Ghormley, June 21, 1948, p. 5. O'Dwyer Gustave Whitehead Research Collection, Fairfield Museum, Fairfield, CT

400 O'Dwyer, William J., Randolph, Stella. History by Contract. 1978, Fritz Majer and Sohn. p 49

401 Letters of Junius Harworth to Randolph. O'Dwyer Gustave Whitehead Research Collection, Fairfield Museum, Fairfield, CT

402 Ibid p. 50

403 Letter of Cecil Steeves to CAHA, December 20, 1965. O'Dwyer, William J., Randolph, Stella. History by Contract. 1978, Fritz Majer and Sohn. p 306

404 Statement of Alfred Burr, CAHA representative, witness to interview with Cecil Steeves, Jan. 2, 1966. O'Dwyer, William J., Randolph, Stella. History by Contract. 1978, Fritz Majer and Sohn. p 309.

405 O'Dwyer, William J., Randolph, Stella. History by Contract. 1978, Fritz Majer and Sohn. p 49

406 Affidavit of Michael Werer, September 24, 1934. O'Dwyer Gustave Whitehead Research Collection, Fairfield Museum, Fairfield, CT

© Susan Brinchman, 2015

Gustave Whitehead: "First in Flight"

407 Affidavit of Thomas Schweikert, June 15, 1936. O'Dwyer Gustave Whitehead Research Collection, Fairfield Museum, Fairfield, CT

408 Frank Lanye Interview Notes, O'Dwyer Gustave Whitehead Research Collection, Box 5, Folder 13 http://www.fairfieldhistory.org/wp-content/uploads/ODwyer-Gustav-Whitehead-Research-Collection-Ms-B107.pdf

409 Affidavit of Joe Ratzenberger. O'Dwyer Gustave Whitehead Research Collection, Fairfield Museum, Fairfield, CT

410 Affidavit of Alexander Gluck, July 19, 1934. O'Dwyer Gustave Whitehead Research Collection, Fairfield Museum, Fairfield, CT

411 Scranton Tribune, Dec. 11, 1899, page 4, Image 4, Library of Congress, Chronicling America

412 Affidavit of Louis Darvarich, July 19, 1934. O'Dwyer Gustave Whitehead Research Collection, Fairfield Museum, Fairfield, CT

413 "Flying Models Support Pioneer Aviator's Claims." Randolph, Stella. 1968, p. 2. O'Dwyer Gustave Whitehead Research Collection, Fairfield Museum, Fairfield, CT

414 "Bates Street," May 23, 1911. "Bates Street at angle looking toward second angle." Identifier 715.112031.CP. Pittsburgh City Photographer Collection, 1901-2002, AIS. 1971.05, Archives Service Center; University of Pittsburgh.

415 Letter from Louis Darvarich to Rose Whitehead Rennison, Oct. 4, 1934, p. 1-2. Whitehead Family Folder, O'Dwyer Gustave Whitehead Research Collection, Fairfield Museum, Fairfield, CT

416 The Emily O'Neil estate at Bates Street and Wilmot is the most likely site of the flight accident of 1899, misspelled as "O'Neale" in the Martin Devine Affidavit of Aug. 15, 1936. The O'Neil estate was located one block from Whitehead's rented home and one block from Engine Hse. No. 24, whose firemen responded to the accident. Pittsburgh Historic Maps 1900 http://peoplemaps.esri.com/pittviewer/

417 Affidavit of Martin Devine, August 15, 1936. O'Dwyer Gustave Whitehead Research Collection, Fairfield Museum, Fairfield, CT

418 "Bates at Wilmot," May 23, 1911. Pittsburgh City Photographer Collection, 1901-2002, AIS. 1971.05, Archives Service Center; University of Pittsburgh.

419 Letter from Louis Darvarich to Rose Whitehead Rennison, Oct. 4, 1934, p. 1-2. Whitehead Family Folder, O'Dwyer Gustave Whitehead Research Collection, Fairfield Museum, Fairfield, CT

420 "Bates Street Wall," March 25, 1908. Desc.:"A view of the Bates Street wall, Bates Street looking toward Wilmot Street." Pittsburgh City Photographer Collection, 1901-2002, AIS. 1971.05, Archives Service Center; University of Pittsburgh.

421 Affidavit of Louis Darvarich, July 19, 1934. O'Dwyer Gustave Whitehead Research Collection, Fairfield Museum, Fairfield, CT

422 Historic Pittsburgh. East End : from official records, private plans and actual surveys. Volume 1 [1898] -- Wards 13, 14, 22, and 23. City of Pittsburgh Map, East End, Schenley Park, Plate 24. http://digital.library.pitt.edu/maps/20090529-hopkins.html

423 "Whitehead's Flying Condor. Ambitious Designer Says He Will Imitate the Flight of the Great Bird in the Air." NY Herald, Oct. 5, 1897. p. 12

424 "New Airship Ready for Flight: Modeled After a Condor Called a Sure Thing. Inventor a High Flyer. Says He has Constructed Several Machines and Made Numerous Ascensions." New York Press. Oct. 5, 1897.

425 "Hopes to Fly Like a Condor." NY World, Oct. 6, 1897. p. 8

426 "Will Try His Airship." NY Times. Oct. 6, 1897.p.12

427 http://en.wikipedia.org/wiki/Blue_Hill_Meteorological_Observatory. Accessed April 18, 2015.

428 http://www.massaerohistory.org/Boston_Aeronautical_Society.pdf

Endnotes

429 O'Dwyer, William J., Randolph, Stella. History by Contract. 1978, Fritz Majer and Sohn,. p. 99-102

430 http://www.massaerohistory.org/Boston_Aeronautical_Society.pdf, p. 3

431 O'Dwyer, William J., Randolph, Stella. History by Contract. 1978, Fritz Majer and Sohn,. p. 36

432 Randolph, Phillips. "Did Whitehead Precede Wright in World's First Powered Flight?," *Popular Aviation*, Jan. 1935

433 O'Dwyer, William J. (July 1998). "Letters to the Editor: Gustave Weisskopf." *FAI International*. Archived from the original on September 22, 2001. Retrieved May 28, 2011.

434 O'Dwyer Gustave Whitehead Research Collection, Fairfield Museum, Fairfield, CT

435 Affidavit of Louis Lazay, January 4, 1936. O'Dwyer Gustave Whitehead Research Collection, Fairfield Museum, Fairfield, CT

436 Memorandum: Bridgeport Trip re: Gustave Whitehead Flights, K.I. Ghormley, June 21, 1948, p. 5. O'Dwyer Gustave Whitehead Research Collection, Fairfield Museum, Fairfield, CT

437 Affidavits of John Lesko, 1934, 1936, and 1964. O'Dwyer Gustave Whitehead Research Collection, Fairfield Museum, Fairfield, CT

438 Affidavit of John Lesko, 1936. O'Dwyer Gustave Whitehead Research Collection, Fairfield Museum, Fairfield, CT

439 John S. Lesko, Interview Transcript, Dec. 17, 1963, O'Dwyer Gustave Whitehead Research Collection, Box 4, Subseries II, Folder 4 http://www.fairfieldhistory.org/wp-content/uploads/ODwyer-Gustav-Whitehead-Research-Collection-Ms-B107.pdf

440 Affidavit of Alexander Gluck, July 19, 1934. O'Dwyer Gustave Whitehead Research Collection, Fairfield Museum, Fairfield, CT

441 Frank Lanye Interview of March 30 and June 15, 1968, Waterbury, CT. O'Dwyer Gustave Whitehead Research Collection, Fairfield Museum, Fairfield, CT, Folder 13, Box 5.

442 Frank Lanye Interview Notes, O'Dwyer Gustave Whitehead Research Collection, Box 5, Folder 13 http://www.fairfieldhistory.org/wp-content/uploads/ODwyer-Gustav-Whitehead-Research-Collection-Ms-B107.pdf

443 Randolph, Stella. Lost Flights of Gustave Whitehead. 1937. Places, Inc., Wash. DC. p. 36-37

444 Affidavit of Michael Werer, September 24, 1934. O'Dwyer Gustave Whitehead Research Collection, Fairfield Museum, Fairfield, CT

445 Affidavit of Joe Ratzenberger. O'Dwyer Gustave Whitehead Research Collection, Fairfield Museum, Fairfield, CT

446 Memorandum: Bridgeport Trip re: Gustave Whitehead Flights, K.I. Ghormley, June 21, 1948, p. 3. O'Dwyer Gustave Whitehead Research Collection, Fairfield Museum, Fairfield, CT

447 Affidavit of John Ciglar, January 3, 1936. O'Dwyer Gustave Whitehead Research Collection, Fairfield Museum, Fairfield, CT

448 Memorandum: Bridgeport Trip re: Gustave Whitehead Flights, K.I. Ghormley, June 21, 1948, p. 4. O'Dwyer Gustave Whitehead Research Collection, Fairfield Museum, Fairfield, CT

449 Affidavit of Elizabeth Koteles, August 1, 1974, O'Dwyer Gustave Whitehead Research Collection, Fairfield Museum, Fairfield, CT

450 Letter from Jesse Davidson to William J. O'Dwyer, Aug. 23, 1974. O'Dwyer Gustave Whitehead Research Collection, Fairfield Museum, Fairfield, CT

451 Stephen Link is a Yale-trained adolescent psychologist.

452 Whitehead Flew First! "Sure, We All Saw Him Fly" by Steve Link. Magyar News. http://magyarrnews.org/news

453 In 1902 Bridgeport City Directory, Louis Darwarics was listed as a blacksmith employee at Vincent Bros., living at 259 Pine Street. Records from Ancestry.com confirm this is the same individual; this prior last name and another (Louis Darvareich, Census 1910), before it was "Americanized," provides reasons why searches in Pittsburgh, PA

© Susan Brinchman, 2015

Gustave Whitehead: "First in Flight"

hospital records of "Darvarich" as a burn victim following the flight of 1899 were futile in previous years, according to researcher William J. O'Dwyer, Dec. 14, 1982. O'Dwyer Gustave Whitehead Research Collection Box 7, Series C, Subseries Folder 6, "Research Breakthrough." http://www.fairfieldhistory.org/wp-content/uploads/ODwyer-Gustav-Whitehead-Research-Collection-Ms-B107.pdf.

454 *Bridgeport Sunday Herald* Magazine, January 30, 1937, p. 4. Library of Congress Gustave Whitehead files.

455 O'Dwyer Gustave Whitehead Research Collection, Fairfield Museum, Fairfield, CT. Box 7, Series C, Subseries Folder 6. "Research Breakthrough," p. 1. http://www.fairfieldhistory.org/wp-content/uploads/ODwyer-Gustav-Whitehead-Research-Collection-Ms-B107.pdf.

456 Del Buono Interview with Franko. Series II, Box 4, Folder # 9. O'Dwyer Gustave Whitehead Research Collection, Fairfield Museum, Fairfield, CT

457 O'Dwyer, William J., Randolph, Stella. History by Contract. 1978, Fritz Majer and Sohn, p. 39

458 Affidavit of Louis Darvarich, O'Dwyer Gustave Whitehead Research Collection, Fairfield Museum, Fairfield, CT

459 Letter from Albert Burr to Harvey Lippincott (President of CAHA), Jan. 2, 1966. O'Dwyer Gustave Whitehead Research Collection, Fairfield Museum, Fairfield, CT

460 Interview with Anton Pruckner, Nov. 13, 1963. O'Dwyer Gustave Whitehead Research Collection, Fairfield Museum, Fairfield, CT

461 Mary Savage Interview. Letter by William J. O'Dwyer Feb. 13, 1964. O'Dwyer Gustave Whitehead Research Collection, Fairfield Museum, Fairfield, CT

462 Ibid

463 "The Story of Gustave Whitehead: Before the Wrights Flew." Randolph, Stella. GP Putnam's Sons. (1966). p. 117-119

464 Bridgeport City Directories 1903-1906, US City Directories, Ancestry.com

465 O'Dwyer Gustave Whitehead Research Collection, Fairfield Museum, Fairfield, CT

466 Memorandum: Bridgeport Trip re: Gustave Whitehead Flights, K.I. Ghormley, June 21, 1948, p. 4. O'Dwyer Gustave Whitehead Research Collection, Fairfield Museum, Fairfield, CT

467 "Film to Rescue Fairfield Flight Pioneer Whitehead's Experiment." The Hour, Norwalk, CT, Nov. 4, 1999. p. A-9

468 "Appeal Denied in Trust Fund Case." Milwaukee Sentinel, Mar. 10, 1926, p. 17. https://news.google.com/newspapers?id=e19QAAAAIBAJ&sjid=SA8EAAAAIBAJ&pg=2471%2C6302601

469 O'Dwyer, William J. "The Who Flew First Debate," Flight Journal, Oct. 1998. p. 48-55, http://www.flightjournal.com/wp-content/uploads/2013/03/whitehead.pdf

470 Stanley Yale Beach Archives, Yale University

471 Gustave Whitehead Archives, Library of Congress, Box 126. Stanley Yale Beach Whitehead Statement, Draft, and Associated Letters

472 Archived Sci Am, Sept. 19, 1903, page 204. http://ia700804.us.archive.org/29/items/scientific-american-1903-09-19/scientific-american-v89-n12-1903-09-19.pdf (p.8)

473 Crane, John B. "Did Whitehead Actually Fly?" National Aeronautic Assn. Magazine Dec. 1936 [Author's note: Dr. Crane research continued afterward, he supported possibility of flights, and called for a Congressional hearing]

474 Before the Wrights Flew (Randolph, 1966), GP Putnam & Sons, Appendix

475 "Inventor Whitehead Building a Flying Machine to Outdo the Wright Bros.." *Bridgeport Sunday Herald*. Nov. 22, 1908, p. 11. http://news.google.com/newspapers?id=StwyAAAAIBAJ&sjid=7gAGAAAAIBAJ&pg=5441,3764683&dq=whitehead+aeroplane&hl=en

476 Ibid

Endnotes

477 Ibid

478 Gustave Whitehead Patent No. 881,837 filed Dec. 20, 1905, granted March 10, 1908. (see Appendix C in this

479 "The Aeronautic Society's First Exhibition." *Scientific American*. November 14, 1908. p. 338https://archive.org/stream/scientific-american-1908-11-14/scientific-american-v99-n20-1908-11-14#page/n9/mode/2up

480 Ibid

481 "Whitehead Building Flying Machine to Outdo the Wright Brothers" *Bridgeport Herald*, Nov. 22, 1908, p. 67 http://news.google.com/newspapers?nid=2274&dat=19081101&id=StwyAAAAIBAJ&sjid=7gAGAAAAIBAJ&pg=5610,3768536

482 Ibid

483 Affidavit of Clarence Crittendon, Oct. 11, 1964. O'Dwyer Gustave Whitehead Research Collection, Fairfield Museum, Fairfield, CT

484 Stanley Y. Beach Interview. July 17, 1934. O'Dwyer Gustave Whitehead Research Collection, Fairfield Museum, Fairfield, CT

485 "Whitehead Wouldn't Disturb Neighbors." Bridgeport Standard, April 10, 1909, p. 1

486 "New Aeroplanes for Early Flights." New York Times, March 14, 1909, Sporting News Section, p. 1

487 "This Flying Machine Will Soon Be Ready." Bridgeport Standard. March 17, 1909, p. 1

488 O'Dwyer, William J., Randolph, Stella. History by Contract. 1978, Fritz Majer and Sohn, p. 127-132

489 "Inventor Whitehead Building a Flying Machine to Outdo the Wright Bros.." *Bridgeport Sunday Herald*. Nov. 1, 1908, p. 11 http://news.google.com/newspapers?id=StwyAAAAIBAJ&sjid=7gAGAAAAIBAJ&pg=5441,3764683&dq=whitehead+aeroplane&hl=en

490 "Many Members of Aeronautics Society Building Machines." Aeronautics, April 1909.

491 "At Morris Park: Members of Aeronautic Society Building Machines." *Aeronautics*. Vol. IV, No. 4, April 1909, p. 145

492 O'Dwyer, William J., Randolph, Stella. History by Contract. 1978, Fritz Majer and Sohn, Old Picture Series, p. XXII

493 "Whitehead Flying Machine to be Placed on Exhibition." *Bridgeport Sunday Herald*. May 16, 1909, p. 2. http://news.google.com/newspapers?id=fNUyAAAAIBAJ&sjid=4AAGAAAAIBAJ&pg=4124%2C3242780

494 "Aerial Carnival for High Flyers." New York Times, May 23, 1909, p. 3.

495 "Mrs. Hillman Will Fly With Husband." The Evening statesman., May 27, 1909, Page Three, Image 3. The Evening statesman. (Walla Walla, Wash.), 27 May 1909. Chronicling America: Historic American Newspapers. Lib. of Congress. <http://chroniclingamerica.loc.gov/lccn/sn88085421/1909-05-27/ed-1/seq-3/>

496 "Monoplane or Triplane: Perfectly Lovely Airship That Would Not Fly Causes Trouble for Inventors." The sun., June 06, 1909, Page 10, Image 10. The sun. (New York [N.Y.]), 06 June 1909. Chronicling America: Historic American Newspapers. Lib. of Congress. <http://chroniclingamerica.loc.gov/lccn/sn83030272/1909-06-06/ed-1/seq-10/>

497 "Beach Has Combined Two French models, But His Engine Did Not Work."New York Times, Aug. 20, 1909

498 "Flying Machines in the Big Garden." New York Times, Sept. 26, 1909.

499 "Airships That Didn't Fly." New York Sun, Dec. 5, 1909, p. 8.

500 "Wrights Start Suit on Curtiss Airship…Charge Infringed Patents… Aviation Society Officials Say Wrights Cannot Get Injunction and Plan Flight for Willard at Hempstead Today." New York Times, August 20, 1909

501 Papers of William J. Hammer, 1910-1913. Smithsonian Institution.

502 1910 Federal United States Census, Gustave Whitehead ("Whiteker")

503 Interview with Wilfred Walsh, Lexington, MA. Nov. 30, 1966. Harvey Lippincott, A. Magee. O'Dwyer Gustave Whitehead Research Collection, Fairfield Museum, Fairfield, CT

Gustave Whitehead: "First in Flight"

504 "First National Aeronautic Show Opens in the Garden." New York Times, Sept. 26, 1909, Sporting News Section, p. 1

505 "Whole World Panting for a Perfect Aeroplane" New York Daily Tribune, June 12, 1910, P. 5, Image 58 New-York tribune. (New York [N.Y.]), 12 June 1910. Chronicling America: Historic American Newspapers. Lib. of Congress. <http://chroniclingamerica.loc.gov/lccn/sn83030214/1910-06-12/ed-1/seq-58/>http://chroniclingamerica.loc.gov/lccn/sn83030214/1910-06-12/ed-1/seq-58.pdf

506 "Beach Guests Cry Out, "Fake."The *Bridgeport Evening Farmer.*, February 01, 1910, Page 5, Image 5 The *Bridgeport Evening Farmer*. (Bridgeport, Conn.), 01 Feb. 1910. Chronicling America: Historic American Newspapers. Lib. of Congress. <http://chroniclingamerica.loc.gov/lccn/sn84022472/1910-02-01/ed-1/seq-5/>

507 "Stanley Beach's Aeroplane Fond of Ice on Fresh Pond." *Bridgeport Sunday Herald*, Feb. 6, 1910, p. 13.

508 "Shed for Aeroplanes." The sun., March 29, 1910, Page 6, Image 6. The sun. (New York [N.Y.]), 29 March 1910. Chronicling America: Historic American Newspapers. Lib. of Congress. <http://chroniclingamerica.loc.gov/lccn/sn83030272/1910-03-29/ed-1/seq-6/>

509 "Stanley Beach Plunges From Flying Machine As It Dashes Over Cliff at Lordship Park." The *Bridgeport Evening Farmer.*, July 11, 1910, Page 2, Image 2. The *Bridgeport Evening Farmer*. (Bridgeport, Conn.), 11 July 1910. Chronicling America: Historic American Newspapers. Lib. of Congress. <http://chroniclingamerica.loc.gov/lccn/sn84022472/1910-07-11/ed-1/seq-2/>

510 "Has No Assets." The *Bridgeport Evening Farmer.*, February 14, 1912, Page 8, Image 8 The *Bridgeport Evening Farmer*. (Bridgeport, Conn.), 14 Feb. 1912. Chronicling America: Historic American Newspapers. Lib. of Congress. <http://chroniclingamerica.loc.gov/lccn/sn84022472/1912-02-14/ed-1/seq-8/>

511 "Jones' New Devise will Be Watched With Much Interest." The *Bridgeport Evening Farmer*. (Bridgeport, Conn.), 05 Oct. 1910. Chronicling America: Historic American Newspapers. Lib. of Congress. <http://chroniclingamerica.loc.gov/lccn/sn84022472/1910-10-05/ed-1/seq-3/> The *Bridgeport Evening Farmer.*, October 05, 1910, Page 3, Image 3

512 William J. Hammer Collection, NASM archives. http://airandspace.si.edu/research/arch/findaids/pdf/william_j_hammer_collection_finding_aid.pdf

513 Flying Machine That Will Remain Stationary in Mid-Air is Whitehead's Creation." The *Bridgeport Evening Farmer.*, June 20, 1910, Image 1. p. 1-2. The *Bridgeport Evening Farmer*. (Bridgeport, Conn.), 20 June 1910. Chronicling America: Historic American Newspapers. Lib. of Congress. <http://chroniclingamerica.loc.gov/lccn/sn84022472/1910-06-20/ed-1/seq-1/>

514 Phone Interview with Bernice Keeney, great-granddaughter of G. Whitehead, 4.23.2015, by Susan Brinchman.

515 "Whitehead May Fly on Saturday." The *Bridgeport Evening Farmer.*, February 28, 1911, Image 1, p. 1. The *Bridgeport Evening Farmer*. (Bridgeport, Conn.), 28 Feb. 1911. Chronicling America: Historic American Newspapers. Lib. of Congress. <http://chroniclingamerica.loc.gov/lccn/sn84022472/1911-02-28/ed-1/seq-1/>

516 "Atlas Donates His Share To Gus Whitehead." The *Bridgeport Evening Farmer.*, March 01, 1911, Image 1. The *Bridgeport Evening Farmer*. (Bridgeport, Conn.), 01 March 1911. Chronicling America: Historic American Newspapers. Lib. of Congress. <http://chroniclingamerica.loc.gov/lccn/sn84022472/1911-03-01/ed-1/seq-1/>

517 "Paine Purse Returned to Its Givers…" The *Bridgeport Evening Farmer.*, March 04, 1911, Image 1, p. 1-2 The *Bridgeport Evening Farmer*. (Bridgeport, Conn.), 04 March 1911. Chronicling America: Historic American Newspapers. Lib. of Congress. <http://chroniclingamerica.loc.gov/lccn/sn84022472/1911-03-04/ed-1/seq-1/>

518 "Whitehead, Who Builds Airships, In Court." The *Bridgeport Evening Farmer.*, May 08, 1912, Page 2, Image 2. The *Bridgeport Evening Farmer*. (Bridgeport, Conn.), 08 May 1912. Chronicling America: Historic American Newspapers. Lib. of Congress. <http://chroniclingamerica.loc.gov/lccn/sn84022472/1912-05-08/ed-1/seq-2/>

519 "Whitehead Must Pay $1240.27." The *Bridgeport Evening Farmer.*, May 14, 1912, Page 2, Image 2. Chronicling America: Historic American Newspapers. Lib. of Congress. <http://chroniclingamerica.loc.gov/lccn/sn84022472/1912-05-14/ed-1/seq-2/>

520 The *Bridgeport Evening Farmer*. (Bridgeport, Conn.) 1866-1917, March 12, 1912, Image 4. The *Bridgeport Evening*

Endnotes

Farmer. (Bridgeport, Conn.), 12 March 1912. Chronicling America: Historic American Newspapers. Lib. of Congress. <http://chroniclingamerica.loc.gov/lccn/sn84022472/1912-03-12/ed-1/seq-4/>

521 Affidavits of Martin Devine, Aug. 15, 1936; Louis Darvarich, July 19, 1934; Charles L. Ritchey, August 21, 1936. O'Dwyer Gustave Whitehead Research Collection, Fairfield Museum, Fairfield, CT

522 Letter of Junius Harworth, Jan. 24th, 1936, p. 1. O'Dwyer Gustave Whitehead Research Collection, Fairfield Museum, Fairfield, CT

523 Flying Machine That Will Remain Stationary in Mid-Air is Whitehead's Creation." The *Bridgeport Evening Farmer.*, June 20, 1910, Image 1. p. 1-2. The *Bridgeport Evening Farmer.* (Bridgeport, Conn.), 20 June 1910. Chronicling America: Historic American Newspapers. Lib. of Congress. <http://chroniclingamerica.loc.gov/lccn/sn84022472/1910-06-20/ed-1/seq-1/>

524 Interview with Anton Pruckner, Nov. 13, 1963, p. 20. O'Dwyer Gustave Whitehead Research Collection, Fairfield Museum, Fairfield, CT

525 http://www.libraries.wright.edu/special/wright_brothers/pate

526 Letter, John Whitehead, Sept. 3, 1934 p.7. O'Dwyer Gustave Whitehead Research Collection, Fairfield Museum, Fairfield, CT

527 Notes by William J. O'Dwyer, 1960's, entitled 1st Draft, p. 2, Subseries III. CAHA1963-1986, O'Dwyer Gustave Whitehead Research Collection, Fairfield Museum, Fairfield, CT

528 Sheridan Weekly Sun, Sheridan, Indiana., April 21, 1904, p.3

529 O'Dwyer, William J., Randolph, Stella. History by Contract. 1978, Fritz Majer and Sohn, p. 127-132

530 "Inventor Whitehead Building a Flying Machine to Outdo the Wright Bros.." *Bridgeport Sunday Herald*. Nov. 1, 1908, p. 11 http://news.google.com/newspapers?id=StwyAAAAIBAJ&sjid=7gAGAAAAIBAJ&pg=5441,3764683&dq=whitehead+aeroplane&hl=en

531 "Many Members of Aeronautics Society Building Machines." Aeronautics, April 1909.

532 Sources: witness affidavits and interviews with assistants; local newspaper interviews; O'Dwyer Gustave Whitehead Research Collection, Fairfield Museum, Fairfield, CT

533 Interview with Joe Bullmer, aeronautical engineer and author, April 24 & 25, 2015.

534 Letter of Junius Harworth to Erik Hildes-Heim, August 7, 1961

535 **60 Minutes Show – "Wright is Wrong?"** (Complete 11 minute segment from 1987 show with Major William J. O'Dwyer regarding Whitehead, including replica flights, **with commentary posted August 18, 2013**)

536 "The Flight Claims of Gustave Whitehead." Crouch, Tom. Smithsonian National Air and Space Museum. April 6, 2013. http://blog.nasm.si.edu/aviation/the-flight-claims-of-gustave-whitehead/

537 http://www.si.edu/Governance/BylawsPolicies

538 Letter from Dr. John B. Crane, Harvard University, to Mrs. Gustave Whitehead, Nov. 23, 1935. O'Dwyer Gustave Whitehead Research Collection, Fairfield Museum, Fairfield, CT

539 Letters of Junius Harworth, 1934-1962. O'Dwyer Gustave Whitehead Research Collection, Fairfield Museum, Fairfield, CT

540 O'Dwyer and Randolph. History by Contract. Fritz Majer & Sohn, (1978) p. 200-201.

541 www.historybycontract.org

542 http://www.fairfield-sun.com/10380/smithsonian-requested-to-nullify-wright-brothers-first-in-flight-contract/

543 Letter, Junius Harworth, Sept. 22, 1935, p.1. O'Dwyer Gustave Whitehead Research Collection, Fairfield Museum, Fairfield, CT

544 Letter, Junius Harworth, Sept. 22, 1935, p. 2. O'Dwyer Gustave Whitehead Research Collection, Fairfield Museum,

Gustave Whitehead: "First in Flight"

Fairfield, CT

545 Octave Chanute Letter to Wilbur Wright. July 3, 1901. The Wilbur and Orville Wright Papers at the Library of Congress; General Correspondence; Chanute, Octave, 1901, Image 6-7 of 22. http://memory.loc.gov/master/mss/mwright/03/03064/0007.jpg

546 Wilbur Wright Letter to Octave Chanute. July 4, 1901. The Wilbur and Orville Wright Papers at the Library of Congress; General Correspondence

547 Ibid

548 Ancestry.com. Ancestry.com. *1900 United States Federal Census* [database on-line]. Provo, UT, USA: Ancestry.com Operations Inc, 2004. Year: *1900*; Census Place: *Bridgeport, Fairfield, Connecticut*; Roll: *131*; Page: *2A*; Enumeration District: *0015*; FHL microfilm: *1240131*.

549 O'Dwyer and Randolph. History by Contract. Fritz Majer & Sohn, (1978) p. 117

550 O'Dwyer and Randolph. History by Contract. "Affidavit: Cecil A. Steeves - October 10, 1936." Fritz Majer & Sohn (1978) p. 88

551 Cecil Steeve, as tape recorded; Jan. 2, 1966. O'Dwyer Gustave Whitehead Research Collection, Fairfield Museum, Fairfield, CT. Folder 4, Box 4

552 Ibid. p. 118

553 Ibid. p. 121-122

554 Ibid p. 117

555 Affidavit of Anton Pruckner, taken Oct. 30, 1964, History by Contract. O'Dwyer and Randolph, Fritz Meyer and Sohn. (1978) p. 55

556 Affidavit of Anton Pruckner, Jan. 3, 1936. Randolph, Stella. Lost Flights of Gustave Whitehead. 1937. Places, Inc., Wash. DC, p. 85

557 History by Contract. O'Dwyer and Randolph, Fritz Meyer and Sohn. (1978.) p. 123

558 "Whitehead or Wrights? Riddle Evolves Around First Plane Flight." Bache, Ted. *Bridgeport Post*. May 19, 1963, p. C-3

559 Combs, Harry; Caidin, Martin (1979). Kill Devil Hill: discovering the secret of the Wright Brothers. Houghton Mifflin. p. 351. ISBN 0-395-28216-0.

560 Bullmer, Joe. The WRight Story, CreateSpace, Charleston, SC, 2009. p. 263-264.

561 Affidavit of Clarence and Mrs. Crittendon. O'Dwyer Gustave Whitehead Research Collection, Fairfield Museum, Fairfield, CT

562 Carpenter, Jack. Pendulum. (1992) Arslalen, Bosch, and Company.

563 Robie, Bill. For the Greatest Achievement (1993) Smithsonian Institution Press, p. 64

564 Ibid

565 Letter, John Whitehead to Stella Randolph, Sept. 3, 1934 p.7

566 Randolph, Stella. Lost Flights of Gustave Whitehead. 1937. Places, Inc., Wash. DC, p 49

567 "Whitehead Flew First – Sure, We All Saw Him Fly!." Stephen Link. Magyar News, http://magyarnews.org/news.php?viewStory=1213

568 "The Women Who Supported Whitehead's Flights." Martha Matus Schipul. Magyar News, June 30, 2013 http://magyarnews.org/news.php?viewStory=1256

569 Letter, John Whitehead to Stella Randolph, 1934, p. 2. O'Dwyer Gustave Whitehead Research Collection, Fairfield Museum, Fairfield, CT

Endnotes

570 Letter, Junius Harworth, March 8, 1937, p. 2. O'Dwyer Gustave Whitehead Research Collection, Fairfield Museum, Fairfield, CT

571 Interview with Anton & Mrs. Pruckner, transcript. WICC May 20, 1964. p.11 O'Dwyer Gustave Whitehead Research Collection, Fairfield Museum, Fairfield, CT

572 Randolph, Stella. Before the Wrights Flew (1966) G.P. Putnam's Sons., p.l19

573 Whitehead Family Tree. Ancestry.com http://trees.ancestry.com/tree/61676985/family

574 Letter, Junius Harworth, March 17, 1937. O'Dwyer Gustave Whitehead Research Collection, Fairfield Museum, Fairfield, CT

575 Letter of John Whitehead to Stella Randolph, Nov. 5, 1934. p. 1. O'Dwyer Gustave Whitehead Research Collection, Fairfield Museum, Fairfield, CT

576 Letter, Junius Harworth, Jan. 24th, 1936, p. 3. O'Dwyer Gustave Whitehead Research Collection, Fairfield Museum, Fairfield, CT

577 Letter, John Whitehead, Sept. 3, 1934 p.7. O'Dwyer Gustave Whitehead Research Collection, Fairfield Museum, Fairfield, CT

578 Randolph, Stella. Lost Flights of Gustave Whitehead. 1937. Places, Inc., Wash. DC, p.55

579 Letter from John Whitehead to Stella Randolph, Nov. 5, 1934, p. 2

580 Randolph, Stella. Lost Flights of Gustave Whitehead. 1937. Places, Inc., Wash. DC, p. 66

581 "Whitehead House In Connecticut Demolished: Wrecking Ball Applied Despite Weeks Of Protest From Supporters." May 1, 2014. http://www.aero-news.net/index.cfm?do=main.textpost&ID=0683A7CB-4A0A-4E5A-9817-7A18DA8B9495

582 Evening Telegram (New York). Tuesday, Nov. 19, 1901. "Ship That Will Fly Like a Bird May Soon Be Placed on the Market."

583 Randolph, Stella. Lost Flights of Gustave Whitehead. 1937. Places, Inc., Wash. DC, p. 19.

584 Ibid. p. 35

585 Ibid p. 124

586 Letter from Junius Harworth, March 29th, 1935. O'Dwyer Gustave Whitehead Research Collection, Fairfield Museum, Fairfield, CT

587 Pruckner Interview, at WICC, May 20, 1964, transcript, page 3

588 Pruckner Interview, November 23, 1963, p. 21. O'Dwyer Gustave Whitehead Research Collection, Fairfield Museum, Fairfield, CT

589 Pruckner Interview, at WICC, May 20, 1964, transcript, page 7

590 Pruckner Interview, at WICC, May 20, 1964, transcript, page 4

591 "Forgotten Bridgeporter Was First Aviator." *Bridgeport Sunday Herald*. Herald Magazine. January 30, 1937, p. 4

592 Executive Overview: Jane's All the World's Aircraft: Development & Production. 07 March 2013. http://www.janes.com/article/23191/executive-overview-jane-s-all-the-world-s-aircraft-development-production

593 Howell, Richard (August 18, 1901). "Flying," *Bridgeport Herald*. p. 5 http://www.gustave-whitehead.com/history/news-reports-1901-2-flights/1901-08-18-bridgeport-herald-p-5/

594 Affidavit of Junius Harworth, Aug. 21, 1934. O'Dwyer Gustave Whitehead Research Collection, Fairfield Museum, Fairfield, CT.

595 http://gustavewhitehead.org/news_journalism/1902_-_letters_to_american_.html

596 O'Dwyer, William J., Randolph, Stella. History by Contract. 1978, Fritz Majer and Sohn. p.54 http://

Gustave Whitehead: "First in Flight"

gustavewhitehead.org/news_journalism/1902_-_letters_to_american_.html

597 Affidavit of Junius Harworth, Aug. 21, 1934. O'Dwyer Gustave Whitehead Research Collection, Fairfield Museum, Fairfield, CT

598 Statement of Mary Savage. Randolph, Stella. "The Story of Gustave Whitehead, Before the Wrights Flew." 1966. GP Putnam & Sons, p. 117-119

599 Affidavit of Mr. and Mrs. Clarence Crittendon. Oct. 11, 1964. O'Dwyer Gustave Whitehead Research Collection, Fairfield Museum, Fairfield, CT

600 Affidavit of Anton Pruckner. Oct. 30, 1964. O'Dwyer Gustave Whitehead Research Collection, Fairfield Museum, Fairfield, CT

601 Affidavit of John Ciglar, Jan. 4, 1936. O'Dwyer Gustave Whitehead Research Collection, Fairfield Museum, Fairfield, CT

602 Affidavit of Louis Darvarich, July 19, 1934. O'Dwyer Gustave Whitehead Research Collection, Fairfield Museum, Fairfield, CT

603 Affidavit of Alexander Gluck, July 19, 1934. O'Dwyer Gustave Whitehead Research Collection, Fairfield Museum, Fairfield, CT

604 Statement of Mary Savage. Randolph, Stella. "The Story of Gustave Whitehead, Before the Wrights Flew." 1966. GP Putnam & Sons, p. 117-119

605 Statement of John Havery, May 1948. O'Dwyer Gustave Whitehead Research Collection, Fairfield Museum, Fairfield, CT

606 Affidavit of Thomas Schweibert, June 15, 1936. O'Dwyer Gustave Whitehead Research Collection, Fairfield Museum, Fairfield, CT

607 Affidavit of Thomas Schweibert (Schweikert), June 15, 1936. O'Dwyer Gustave Whitehead Research Collection, Fairfield Museum, Fairfield, CT

608 Affidavit of Junius Harworth, Aug. 21, 1934. O'Dwyer Gustave Whitehead Research Collection, Fairfield Museum, Fairfield, CT

609 Affidavit of Cecil Steeves (Oct. 10, 1936). O'Dwyer Gustave Whitehead Research Collection, Fairfield Museum, Fairfield, CT

610 Affidavit of John Lesko, January 4, 1936. O'Dwyer Gustave Whitehead Research Collection, Fairfield Museum, Fairfield, CT

611 Affidavit of John Lesko, Sept. 3, 1964. Randolph, Stella. O'Dwyer Gustave Whitehead Research Collection, Fairfield Museum, Fairfield, CT

612 Affidavit of Michael Werer, Sept. 24, 1934. O'Dwyer Gustave Whitehead Research Collection, Fairfield Museum, Fairfield, CT

613 Affidavit of Elizabeth Koteles. Aug. 1, 1974. O'Dwyer Gustave Whitehead Research Collection, Fairfield Museum, Fairfield, CT

614 Interview with Frank Layne, 1964. O'Dwyer Gustave Whitehead Research Collection, Fairfield Museum, Fairfield, CT

615 O'Dwyer, William J., Randolph, Stella. History by Contract. 1978, Fritz Majer and Sohn. p. 43

616 Affidavit of Joe Ratzenburger. Jan. 28, 1936. O'Dwyer Gustave Whitehead Research Collection, Fairfield Museum, Fairfield, CT

617 Whitehead wrote to the St. Louis World's Fair Aerial Commission on January 10, 1902, that he'd made short practice flights in Milford, near Charles Island, June 1901. There is no witness for these flights but the text of his letter to the Aerial Committee was carried widely in the news in January - April 1902. Deseret News - April 19,

Endnotes

1902 . http://news.google.com/newspapers?id=Z4wzAAAAIBAJ&sjid=O0oDAAAAIBAJ&pg=3936%2C4491738.

618 St. Paul Globe

619 Colorado Springs Gazette. April 20, 1902. Inventor Gustave Whitehead of Bridgeport, Conn., is also working on a dirigible airship ...Whitehead recently conducted a series of trial tests with his machine at Charles Island, Milford. He is elated over the success of the trials. He asserts that he made a complete circuit in the air, covering an area of about a quarter of a mile, returning to within 50 feet of the starting point, when the machine descended and dropped lightly to the sandy shore.

"The flights were a complete success, " said Whitehead. "I had a kerosene motor which worked perfectly. I steered the machine by running one propeller faster than the other and there was not a hitch of any kind. I have much faith in this kerosene motor, which is the lightest I have ever used. It is of 40 horsepower and weighs but 110 (?) pounds. I am now planning to fulfill the promise I made some time ago to fly to New York. I will make an effort to get to New York in May. I will accomplish it if my machine breaks down a dozen times in the attempt." (Colorado Springs Gazette, Colorado Springs, CO, April 20, 1902).

620 Interview with Clifford Connor, June 27, 1987. O'Dwyer Gustave Whitehead Research Collection, Fairfield Museum, Fairfield, CT.

621 Interview with Oliver F. Cole, Summerville, MA, Dec. 2, 1966. O'Dwyer Gustave Whitehead Research Collection, Fairfield Museum, Fairfield, CT

622 http://news.google.com/newspapers?id=StwyAAAAIBAJ&sjid=7gAGAAAAIBAJ&pg=5441%2C3764683

623 O'Dwyer, William J., Randolph, Stella. History by Contract. 1978, Fritz Majer and Sohn. p. 58

624 Affidavit of Edward Bradtmuller, Oct. 11, 1964. O'Dwyer Gustave Whitehead Research Collection, Fairfield Museum, Fairfield, CT

625 O'Dwyer, William J., Randolph, Stella. History by Contract. 1978, Fritz Majer and Sohn. p. 43

626 Affidavit of Joseph Vecsey, Oct. 11, 1964. O'Dwyer Gustave Whitehead Research Collection, Fairfield Museum, Fairfield, CT

627 Affidavit of James Verzaro, Jr., Dec. 21, 1963. O'Dwyer Gustave Whitehead Research Collection, Fairfield Museum, Fairfield, CT

628 http://news.google.com/newspapers?id=StwyAAAAIBAJ&sjid=7gAGAAAAIBAJ&pg=5441%2C3764683

629 Whitehead's Aeroplane. Reading Eagle. Sept. 19, 1903. http://news.google.com/newspapers?id=2b8hAAAAIBAJ&sjid=p5wFAAAAIBAJ&pg=6236%2C5256336

630 Herald Man Makes a Trial Trip. *Bridgeport Sunday Herald.* May 31.1903. p.4. http://news.google.com/newspapers?id=R9UyAAAAIBAJ&sjid=0wAGAAAAIBAJ&pg=6083%2C2257295

631 Affidavit of John Fekete, May 1948. Randolph, Stella. O'Dwyer Gustave Whitehead Research Collection, Fairfield Museum, Fairfield, CT

632 Affidavit of John Fekete, May 1948. O'Dwyer Gustave Whitehead Research Collection, Fairfield Museum, Fairfield, CT

633 Crane, John B., PhD. "Did Whitehead Actually Fly?." National Aeronautic Assn. Magazine, Dec. 1936.

634 Ibid

635 Letter of Junius Harworth, with Bio of Whitehead, Part 1, Oct. 7, 1934 O'Dwyer Gustave Whitehead Research Collection, Fairfield Museum, Fairfield, CT

636 Ibid

637 Affidavit of Joe Ratzenburger. Jan. 28, 1936. O'Dwyer Gustave Whitehead Research Collection, Fairfield Museum, Fairfield, CT

638 Letter to Stella Randolph from Charles Whitehead, Feb. 19, 1964 p. 4 O'Dwyer Gustave Whitehead Research

Gustave Whitehead: "First in Flight"

Collection, Fairfield Museum, Fairfield, CT

639   Interview with Wilfred Walsh, Lexington, MA. Nov. 30, 1966. Harvey Lippincott, A. Magee. O'Dwyer Gustave Whitehead Research Collection, Fairfield Museum, Fairfield, CT

640   Interview with Bernice Keeney, by Susan Brinchman, April 23, 2015.

641   Letter to Stella Randolph from Charles Whitehead, Feb. 19, 1964 p. 3-4 O'Dwyer Gustave Whitehead Research Collection, Fairfield Museum, Fairfield, CT

642   By the time the museum was established, those who'd researched Gustave Whitehead were no longer in charge, and all had received "the big chill" from the Smithsonian and their employers in the aerospace industry, concerning Whitehead replacing the Wrights, thus giving the earlier CAHA founder and president Lippincott and his contemporaries and replacements within CAHA, "cold feet." Whitehead was dropped from their plans for "political" and "economic" reasons. Through the writing of this book, CAHA and their New England Air Museum, are pro-Wright, supportive of Smithsonian's stance, which benefits the museum - giving Whitehead no credit, reversing their position and ignoring the evidence their founders and early members gathered.

643   Letter from Rose Whitehead Rennison to Stella Randolph, March 29, 1968. O'Dwyer Gustave Whitehead Research Collection, Fairfield Museum, Fairfield, CT

644   Ibid p. 2

645   US City Directory for Bridgeport, CT, 1900, Ancestry.com

646   Based on information from Junius Harworth as located in Randolph, Stella. Lost Flights of Gustave Whitehead. 1937. Places, Inc., Wash. DC. Map 1.

647   Letter of Junius Harworth, with Bio of Whitehead, Part 1, Oct. 7, 1934 O'Dwyer Gustave Whitehead Research Collection, Fairfield Museum, Fairfield, CT

648   Ibid

649   Ibid

650   "Report on the Urgent Need and Underlying Requirements to Preserve the Gustave Whitehead Home," William J. O'Dwyer, circa 1968. CAHA folders. http://www.fairfieldhistory.org/wp-content/uploads/ODwyer-Gustav-Whitehead-Research-Collection-Ms-B107.pdf

651   Letter from Charles Whitehead to Stella Randolph (undated, from 1960's). O'Dwyer Gustave Whitehead Research Collection, Fairfield Museum, Fairfield, CT

652   Town of Fairfield, Town Hall, Records Dept., Fairfield, CT

653   Contact the Fairfield Museum in Fairfield, CT, if you would like to sponsor markers or monuments. www.fairfieldhistory.org/

654   "Air Pioneer is Honored." *Bridgeport Post*, Aug.16, 1964. p.2

655   Affidavit of Charles Wittemann, Oct. 15, 1964. O'Dwyer, William J., Randolph, Stella. History by Contract. 1978, Fritz Majer and Sohn. p. 136-137.

656   "Pioneer Hailed by USAFR Group." *Bridgeport Post*, April 17, 1964. p. 42

657   "Air Pioneer is Honored." *Bridgeport Post*, Aug.16, 1964. p.1

658   "Air Pioneer is Honored." *Bridgeport Post*, Aug.16, 1964. p.2

659   Ibid

660   Ibid

661   http://gustavewhitehead.info/connecticut-aeronautical-historical-association/

662   http://wtnh.com/2015/01/04/local-man-gustav-whitehead-credited-as-first-to-fly/

663   "Whitehead grave gets new headstone." CT Post, Saturday, Dec. 27, 2014. http://www.ctpost.com/local/

Endnotes

articleGallery/Whitehead-grave-gets-new-headstone-5981330.php

664 "Zahm received undergraduate and master's degrees from Notre Dame University and a doctorate from Johns Hopkins University. He taught mathematics and mechanics at Notre Dame University (1885-92) and at The Catholic University of America (1895-1908). A principal organizer of the 1894 international conference on aeronautics, he was also an early and persistent champion of the creation of a national aeronautical laboratory. From 1916 to 1929 he was the director of the Aerodynamical Laboratory of the U.S. Navy. He was named Guggenheim Chair of Aeronautics at the Library of Congress, a position that was created for him (1929-1946). He designed and built the first significant wind tunnel in the United States (1901) and was awarded the Laetare and Mendel medals for his significant achievements in the field of aeronautics. An inventor of precise measuring instruments, he was also known for designing the "Zahm shape," making breakthrough discoveries on skin friction and aerodynamic drag, and inventing the airplane control stick." http://archives.lib.cua.edu/vanish/zahm.cfm

665 http://archives.lib.cua.edu/vanish/zahm.cfm

666 Early Powerplane Fathers. Zahm, Alfred. CAZA 25/19 (Box 25, Folder 19). Notre Dame University Press. 1945, p. 32

667 Albert Francis Zahm Papers, CAZA 23/35 (Box 23, Folder 35) University of Notre Dame Archives (UNDA), Notre Dame, IN 46556

668 O'Dwyer, William J., Randolph, Stella. History by Contract. 1978, Fritz Majer and Sohn.

669 Lost Flights of Gustave Whitehead. Randolph. Stella, (1937), Places, Inc. p. 75

670 "The Story of Gustave Whitehead, Before the Wrights Flew." Randolph, Stella, 1966. GP Putnam & Sons, p. 133-134

671 http://www.cga.ct.gov/2013/sum/pdf/2013SUM00210-R02HB-06671-SUM.pdf

672 NASA Wright 1903 Flyer https://www.grc.nasa.gov/WWW/Wright/airplane/air1903.html

673 Wright, Orville. "How We Made the First Flight." Flying (December 1913): 10-12, 35-36

674 William Hammer and Hudson Maxim. World Almanac, 1911. "Chronology of Aviation". p. 437

http://archive.org/details/worldalmanacency1911newy

675 Wright, Orville. "How We Made the First Flight." Flying (December 1913): 10-12, 35-36

676 Renstrom, Arthur George. WILBUR & ORVILLE WRIGHT, A Reissue of A Chronology Commemorating the Hundredth Anniversary of the BIRTH OF ORVILLE WRIGHT • AUGUST 19, 1871 Flight. http://history.nasa.gov/monograph32.pdf

677 Smithsonian website http://airandspace.si.edu/exhibitions/wright-brothers/online/icon/1903.html

678 Ibid. Flight Log.

679 Robie, Bill. For the Greatest Achievement. Smithsonian Institutions Press, p. 18

680 Aero Club of America. March 12, 1906. Hammer Collection R: 53-61

681 "Aero Club Honors the Wright Brothers." New York Times. March 18, 1906, 8:5

682 Ibid p. 16

683 *Scientific American*. April 7, 1906, p. 291

684 William Hammer and Hudson Maxim. World Almanac, 1911. "Chronology of Aviation". p. 437

http://archive.org/details/worldalmanacency1911newy

685 Ibid

686 Albert Francis Zahm Papers (AZA), University of Notre Dame Archives (UNDA), Notre Dame, IN 46556

687 O'Dwyer, William J., Randolph, Stella. History by Contract. 1978, Fritz Majer and Sohn. p 26

688 "The Flight Claims of Gustave Whitehead " Smithsonian Institute. http://newsdesk.si.edu/sites/default/files/2013-

Gustave Whitehead: "First in Flight"

Whitehead-Statement.pdf

689 O'Dwyer, William J. "The Who Flew First Debate," Flight Journal, Oct. 1998. p. 52

690 Robie, Bill. For the Greatest Achievement. Smithsonian Institutions Press, p. 20

691 Ibid, p. 16

692 Press Release: "Mother Nature Just Doesn't Cooperate in Effort to Recreate First Flight." EEA by Ford Motor Company. http://www.countdowntokittyhawk.com/news/12-17release.pdf

693 O'Dwyer, William J. "The Who Flew First Debate:Whitehead Reproductions," Flight Journal, Oct. 1998. p. 54

694 Gustave Whitehead's airplane (replica) in flight, Oct 4, 1997. YouTube. https://www.youtube.com/watch?v=Ucm80BYUXEE

695 Wright Brothers Aircraft. Glenn Research Center. NASA. http://wright.nasa.gov/airplane/powered.html

696 Crane, Dr. John B., "Early Airplane Flights Before the Wrights." Harvard University, Air Affairs, Winter, American Society of Air Affairs, Wash DC (1949)

697 http://www.historybycontract.com

698 O'Dwyer, William J., Randolph, Stella. History by Contract. 1978, Fritz Majer and Sohn. p. 219

699 Smithsonian releases Wright brothers contract detailing 'first in flight' claims http://www.foxnews.com/science/2013/04/01/contract-forcing-smithsonian-to-call-wright-bros-first-in-flight/

700 www.historybycontract.org

701 http://newsdesk.si.edu/sites/default/files/Wright-Contract.pdf

702 http://www.foxnews.com/science/interactive/2013/04/01/contract-between-wrights-smithsonian-decrees-flyer-was-first-plane/

703 http://www.historybycontract.com

704 O'Dwyer, William J., Randolph, Stella. History by Contract. 1978, Fritz Majer and Sohn. p.236-240

705 "Contract Between Wrights and Smithsonian Decrees Flyer Was First Plane." Fox News. April 1, 2013. http://www.foxnews.com/science/interactive/2013/04/01/contract-between-wrights-smithsonian-decrees-flyer-was-first-plane/

706 Transcript of Conversation between Mr. Findley and Mr. Garber, September 15, 1948 (NASM, Smithsonian)

707 The book was never finalized; the new Whitehead information caused Crane to call for Congress to analyze the data and decide who flew first. Years passed and according to his son, with whom the author has communicated, the book was never published.

708 John B. Crane Letter to Mrs. Louise Whitehead, Nov. 23, 1935. O'Dwyer Gustave Whitehead Research Collection, Fairfield Museum, Fairfield, CT

709 "Did Whitehead Actually Fly?." Crane, John B., PhD. Dec. 1937, National Aeronautics Association Magazine. Crane felt there was sufficient evidence for short "momentum" flights 1904-1908.

710 Asks Congress to Decide if Local Man Was First to Invent Airplane. Jan. 18, 1937. Stratford Star, Stratford, CT. Crane asked Congress to examine the research to rule on whether Whitehead flew before the Wrights, based on witness statements he'd taken.

711 "Early Airplane Flights Before the Wrights." Crane, John B., PhD. Air Affairs; Vol. 2, No. 4; Winter, 1949, p. 514-519. American Society of Air Affairs, Washington, DC. O'Dwyer Gustave Whitehead Research Collection, Fairfield Museum, Fairfield, CT

712 SP-4103 Model Research - Volume 1, " The Quest for a National Aeronautical Laboratory: Progress, Preparedness, and Progressivism, 1910-1915." NASA. http://history.nasa.gov/SP-4103/ch1.htm

713 http://archives.nd.edu/findaids/ead/xml/aza.xml

Endnotes

714 "Early Powerplane Fathers," Zahm, Albert F., p. 35, Zahm Archives, Notre Dame University.

715 Zahm, Alfred, PhD. "Conspectus of Early Powerplane Development." Notre Dame Archives. AZA 006 CAZA Albert Francis Zahm Manuscripts. Notre Dame, Indiana.

716 Zahm, Alfred, PhD. "Early Powerplane Fathers." 1945. University Press, Notre Dame, Indiana.

717 http://gustavewhitehead.info/connecticut-aeronautical-historical-association/. Original tape archived at Gustav Weisskopf Museum Archives, Leutershausen, Germany.

718 O'Dwyer, William J., Randolph, Stella. History by Contract. 1978, Fritz Majer and Sohn

719 http://www.ctpost.com/local/article/Aviation-bible-Whitehead-flew-first-4348050.php

720 Executive Overview: Jane's All the World's Aircraft: Development & Production. 07 March 2013. http://www.janes.com/article/23191/executive-overview-jane-s-all-the-world-s-aircraft-development-production

721 CT lawmakers write Wright brothers out of history as 'first in flight'. NY Daily News. June 27, 2013. http://www.nydailynews.com/news/national/connecticut-lawmakers-wright-brothers-flight-wrong-article-1.1384079

722 Letter, John Whitehead to Stella Randolph, Nov. 5, 1934, p.2

723 Letter, John Whitehead to Stella Randolph, Nov. 5, 1934, p.1-2

724 Lost Flights of Gustave Whitehead, p. 26

725 Letter, John Whitehead to Stella Randolph, Nov. 5, 1934, p.1-2

726 Letter, John Whitehead to Stella Randolph, Nov. 5, 1934, p.1-2

727 Letter, Nicholas Weisskopf to Stella Randolph, Aug. 10, 1936. . O'Dwyer / Gustave Whitehead Archives, Fairfield Museum, Fairfield, CT

728 Letter from John Whitehead to Stella Randolph, Nov. 5, 1934. O'Dwyer / Gustave Whitehead Archives, Fairfield Museum, Fairfield, CT

729 Official Transcript, "Fränkische Zeitung Ansbach," Aug. 1952

730 New York Evening Telegram, Nov. 19, 1901, p.10

731 Timetable by Fritz Majer & Sohn

732 Ibid

733 http://www.lilienthal-museum.de/olma/ebiog.htm

734 Ibid

735 1900 U.S. Census, Pennsylvania, Allegheny, Pittsburgh, S.D. 18, E.D. 179, Sheet 16

736 http://www.connecticutmag.com/Blog/Connecticut-Today/August-2013/The-Case-for-Gustave-Whitehead-as-First-in-Flight-Continues-to-Soar-in-Connecticut/index.php?cparticle=2&siarticle=1

737 http://www.massaerohistory.org/Boston_Aeronautical_Society.pdf

738 Letter, Albert B.C.Horn to S.Randolph, Jan. 28, 1936, p.1

739 http://www.massaerohistory.org/Boston_Aeronautical_Society.pdf

740 O. Chanute to A.A. Merrill, May 31, 1897

741 "Zeitschrift für Luftschiffahrt" Jan. 1898, p.27, Bericht des "Wiener Flugtechnischer Vereins"

742 June 15, 1897. New York Herald. p.7

743 "Celebration of Flag Day." NY Herald. June 15, 1897. p. 7, col.1

744 "To Try His Flying Machine: Gus Whitehead , Aeronaut and Kite Flier, Thinks He Can Now Navigate the Air." New York Herald. Oct. 5, 1897. p.11

© Susan Brinchman, 2015

Gustave Whitehead: "First in Flight"

745 "To Try His Flying Machine." Oct. 5, 1897. New York Herald, p.11

746 http://en.wikipedia.org/wiki/Western_Slope,_Jersey_City

747 "Aeronaut Tries His Airship." Oct. 7, 1897. NY Herald. p.15

748 Letter from John Whitehead to Stella Randolph, Sept. 3, 1934.

749 http://gustavewhitehead.org/the_biography.html

750 US Census 1900

751 Lost Flights of Gustave Whitehead, p. 27

752 Letter, Nikolaus Weißkopf to Stella Randolph, June 6, 1936

753 "Lost Flights of Gustave Whitehead." Stella Randolph. 1937. p. 27

754 Affadavit of Louis Darvarich, July 19, 1934

755 Letter from Louis Darvarich to Mrs. Rennison, Oct. 4, 1934. O'Dwyer / Gustave Whitehead Archives, Fairfield Museum, Fairfield, CT

756 Letter from John Whitehead to Stella Randolph, Sept. 3, 1934.

757 Ibid

758 Ibid

759 "Lost Flights of Gustave Whitehead." Stella Randolph. 1937. p. 30

760 US Census Bureau

761 "Lost Flights of Gustave Whitehead." Stella Randolph. 1937. p. 31

762 U.S., Social Security Death Index: Charles Whitehead

763 Lost Flights, p. 32

764 Lost Flights, p. 33

765 Affidavit of John S. Lesko, Jan. 4, 1936. O'Dwyer / Gustave Whitehead Archives, Fairfield Museum, Fairfield, CT

766 NY Sun., June 9, 1901. p. 2 image 2

767 "Beach Whitehead Statement," 1939. Library of Congress, Gustave Whitehead Collection.

768 Lost Flights, p. 34

769 Wilbur Wright to Octave Chanute. July 4, 1901, p. 1- 2. http://www.loc.gov/resource/mwright.06003/#seq-1

770 Randolph, Stella. Before the Wrights Flew., 1966. p. 118-119

771 Interview with Gustave A. Peschell, Aug. 19, 1987 described in letter to H. Betscher by Wm. J. O'Dwyer. O'Dwyer / Gustave Whitehead Archives, Fairfield Museum, Fairfield, CT

772 Affidavit of Alexander J. Gluck. July 19, 1934. O'Dwyer / Gustave Whitehead Archives, Fairfield Museum, Fairfield, CT

773 Boston Transcript, August 19, 1901

774 *Bridgeport Sunday Herald*, August 18, 1901, p.5

775 "Perfecting His Machine." Bridgeport Evening Post Aug. 26, 1901.p.1

776 New York Herald, Aug. 19, 1901

777 Lost Flights, p. 45

778 *Bridgeport Sunday Herald*, Aug. 18, 1901, p. 5

779 Boston Transcript, August 19, 1901

Endnotes

780 1935 - Did Whitehead Precede Wright in World's First Powered Flight?, *Popular Aviation*, January 1935, Stella Randolf and Harvey Phillips

781 *History by Contract* O'Dwyer and Randolph. Fritz Meyer and Sohn. 1978. p. 111-117

782 Affidavit of Michael Werer, Sept. 24, 1934. O'Dwyer / Gustave Whitehead Archives, Fairfield Museum, Fairfield, CT

783 Affidavit of John S. Lesko, Sept. 3, 1964. O'Dwyer / Gustave Whitehead Archives, Fairfield Museum, Fairfield, CT

784 Affidavit of John S. Lesko, Sept. 24, 1934. O'Dwyer / Gustave Whitehead Archives, Fairfield Museum, Fairfield, CT

785 Affidavit of Elizabeth Koteles. August 1, 1974. O'Dwyer / Gustave Whitehead Archives, Fairfield Museum, Fairfield, CT

786 http://history.nasa.gov/monograph32.pdf

787 *History by Contract* O'Dwyer and Randolph. Fritz Meyer and Sohn. 1978. p. 117-123

788 Lost Flights, p. 34

789 Letter from John Whitehead to Stella Randolph, Sept. 3, 1934.

790 Letter of John Whitehead to Stella Randolph, Sept. 3, 1934.

791 Watertown Daily News, April 16, 1902, p. 9

792 Colorado Springs Gazette, Colorado Springs, CO, April 20, 1902

793 Interview with John F. Fekete by KI Ghormley, Esq., 1948. O'Dwyer / Gustave Whitehead Archives, Fairfield Museum, Fairfield, CT

794 Affidavit of Louis Darvarich. July 19, 1934. O'Dwyer / Gustave Whitehead Archives, Fairfield Museum, Fairfield, CT

795 Interview with Oliver Cole. Dec. 2, 1966. O'Dwyer / Gustave Whitehead Archives, Fairfield Museum, Fairfield, CT

796 Affidavit of John A. Ciglar, January 4, 1936. O'Dwyer / Gustave Whitehead Archives, Fairfield Museum, Fairfield, CT

797 Affidavit of John S. Lesko. January 4, 1936. O'Dwyer / Gustave Whitehead Archives, Fairfield Museum, Fairfield, CT

798 http://history.nasa.gov/monograph32.pdf

799 The *Aeronautical World*. December 1902. p. 99-100

800 NASA. http://history.nasa.gov/monograph32.pdf

801 John was present in Bridgeport from April 1902 till sometime after August 1902, left and returned in the fall of 1903. (Letter from John Whitehead to Stella Randolph, Sept. 3, 1934.)

802 Randolf, Stella; Phillips, Harvey (January 1935), *Did Whitehead Precede Wright In World's First Powered Flight?*, *Popular Aviation*.

803 http://history.nasa.gov/monograph32.pdf

804 "Experiment with motor-driven aeroplanes," *Scientific American*, September 19, 1903

805 "The Who Flew First Debate." O'Dwyer, William J. (Maj.) Flight Journal. Oct. 1998. p. 55

806 Letter from John Whitehead to Stella Randolph, Sept. 3, 1934.

807 http://history.nasa.gov/monograph32.pdf p. 15 of 136

808 http://history.nasa.gov/monograph32.pdf. p. 15 of 136

809 "A Gliding Machine: Two Foreign Aeronauts Have Devised a New Sport." Sheridan Weekly Sun. April 21, 1904. p. 3

810 http://mohistory.org/exhibits/Fair/WF/HTML/Overview/

Gustave Whitehead: "First in Flight"

811   http://history.nasa.gov/monograph32.pdf p. 16 of 136

812   "Fall Wrecks Airship: On Trial Trip It Went Thirty Feet and Dropped -- Inventors Satisfied, Though." New York Times. May 27, 1904. p. 1, Col. 6

813   http://history.nasa.gov/monograph32.pdf p. 16 of 136

814   Affidavit of John S. Lesko, Sept. 24, 1934. O'Dwyer / Gustave Whitehead Archives, Fairfield Museum, Fairfield, CT

815   Affidavit of John S. Lesko, Sept. 3, 1964. O'Dwyer / Gustave Whitehead Archives, Fairfield Museum, Fairfield, CT

816   Affidavit of John S. Lesko, Sept. 24, 1934. O'Dwyer / Gustave Whitehead Archives, Fairfield Museum, Fairfield, CT

817   Ibid

818   Horgan, James J., City of Flight. History of Aviation in St. Louis.1984, Chapter III

819   *Bridgeport Daily Standard*. Oct. 1, 1904

820   Cochrane, Charles Henry. Modern Industrial Progress. J. B. Lippincott Co., Philadelphia and London. 1904. p. 97-98.

821   http://gustavewhitehead.org/the_biography.html

822   "Down-Easter Has Airship: A Bridgeport Machinist Uses the Aeroplanes." Minneapolis Journal. November 11, 1904. p. 14

823   http://www.stlmag.com/The-Perpetual-Fair-The-Fair-Lives-on-With-the-1904-Worlds-Fair-Society/

824   For the Greatest Achievement. p. 11-13

825   Letter from Rose Rennison to Stella Randolph, March 27, 1968 (last page is a diagram of Ridgely St. yard, shop, and house, with date built).

826   "Did Whitehead Actually Fly?" Crane, John B., PhD. National Aeronautic Association Magazine, Dec. 1936. O'Dwyer / Gustave Whitehead Archives, Fairfield Museum, Fairfield, CT

827   "*First Annual Exhibition of Aeronautical Apparatus.*" January 27, 1906. *Scientific American*. p. 93-94

828   "Santos Dumont's Latest Flight ." Nov. 24, 1906. *Scientific American*. p. 378-379

829   *Scientific American*. Dec. 15, 1906. p. 447-449

830   *Scientific American*. Dec. 15, 1906. p. 442

831   Aeronautics, Vol. II, No. 6, June 1908, p. 41

   https://archive.org/stream/aeronautics12aero#page/40/mode/2up/search/whitehead

832   Cycle and Automobile Trade Journal Vol. 14, p. 203, Clinton Co., 1910

833   *History by Contract* O'Dwyer and Randolph. Fritz Meyer and Sohn. 1978. p. 129

834   Research Notes Re: Smithsonian NASM Curator, Paul Edward Garber, covering 1964 meeting with William J. O'Dwyer. O'Dwyer / Gustave Whitehead Archives, Fairfield Museum, Fairfield, CT

835   Randolf, Stella; Phillips, Harvey (January 1935), *Did Whitehead Precede Wright In World's First Powered Flight?*, *Popular Aviation*

836   Letters of Junius Harworth to Stella Randolph. O'Dwyer / Gustave Whitehead Archives, Fairfield Museum, Fairfield, CT.(needs date)

837   O'Dwyer, William J. (July 1998). "Letters to the Editor: Gustave Weisskopf." *FAI International*. Archived from the original on September 22, 2001.

838   NASM Archives, William J. Hammer collection http://airandspace.si.edu/research/arch/findaids/pdf/william_j_hammer_collection_finding_aid.pdf

839   "The Man Who Knows Everything 'First'" *Reader's Digest*. July 1945. P. 57

Endnotes

840 "Whitehead or Wrights? Riddle Evolves Around First Plane Flight." Bache, Ted. *Bridgeport Post*. May 19, 1963, p. C-3

841 Research Notes Re: Smithsonian NASM Curator, Paul Edward Garber, covering 1964 meeting with William J. O'Dwyer. O'Dwyer / Gustave Whitehead Archives, Fairfield Museum, Fairfield, CT

842 Ibid

Gustave Whitehead: "First in Flight"

Appendix A

The *Smithsonian-Wright Agreement of 1948*
First obtained in 1976 from Smithsonian Institution by Maj. William J. O'Dwyer, with assistance from Senator Lowell P. Weicker. Available at O'Dwyer / Gustave Whitehead Archives, Fairfield Museum, Fairfield, CT; also published in *History by Contract* O'Dwyer and Randolph (1978)

Also obtained by *Fox News* from Smithsonian Institution, 2013, available at:
Photocopy (pdf) of the *Smithsonian-Wright Agreement of 1948* **on Fox News' site**
http://www.foxnews.com/science/interactive/2013/04/01/contract-between-wrights-smithsonian-decrees-flyer-was-first-plane/

Available at the Smithsonian Institution for viewing, in person. Smithsonian has not placed this legal document online for public access.

1. Cover letter: Smithsonian to Senator Weicker, Aug. 13, 1976
2. Page 1
3. Page 2
4. Page 3
5. Page 4

Gustave Whitehead: "First in Flight"

SMITHSONIAN INSTITUTION
Washington, D.C. 20560
U.S.A.

August 13, 1976

Honorable Lowell P. Weicker, Jr.
Federal Court House
915 Lafayette Boulevard
Bridgeport, Connecticut 06603

Dear Senator Weicker:

Thank you for your further inquiry on behalf of Mr. William J. O'Dwyer of Fairfield with respect to the agreement between the Smithsonian Institution and the executors of the Wright estate.

I am happy to enclose a copy of the signed agreement which is a <u>bona fide</u> xerox copy of the original document that is in the Smithsonian Institution Archives.

Because of its importance it cannot be removed from the Archives, but we would be happy to furnish additional copies. Furthermore, if Mr. O'Dwyer plans to be in Washington, he can arrange to see the document by writing in advance to the Director, Smithsonian Institution Archives, Smithsonian Institution, Washington, D. C. 20560, and stating his interests in this regard.

Sincerely yours,

Margaret Gaynor
Special Assistant
to the Secretary

Enclosure

Appendix A-1

Gustave Whitehead: "First in Flight"

AGREEMENT

THIS AGREEMENT made by and between HAROLD S. MILLER and HAROLD W. STEEPER as Executors of the Last Will and Testament of Orville Wright, deceased, hereinafter called the Vendors, Parties of the First Part, and THE UNITED STATES OF AMERICA, hereinafter called the Vendee, Party of the Second Part, W I T N E S S E T H:

WHEREAS there is included in the residuary estate of Orville Wright the Wright Aeroplane of 1903, invented and built by Wilbur and Orville Wright and flown by them at Kitty Hawk, North Carolina on December 17, 1903, and

WHEREAS it is in the public interest that said plane be preserved for all time and made available as a public exhibit in an appropriate place and under proper auspices, and

WHEREAS the Probate Court of Montgomery County, Ohio, having jurisdiction over the administration of said estate, after full hearing in a proceeding to which all persons and institutions having any interest under the will of Orville Wright were parties and had submitted themselves to the jurisdiction of the Court, has officially found that the known wishes of Orville Wright will be carried out and the highest and best interest of the estate will be served by recognizing the public interest and has accordingly authorized and directed the Vendors to enter into this Agreement,

NOW, THEREFORE, THIS AGREEMENT WITNESSETH:

1. For the consideration hereinafter set forth the Vendors agree to sell and do hereby sell to the United States of America, and agree to deliver to the United States National Museum, Washington, D.C., within the current fiscal year ending June 30, 1949, and subject to the terms of this Agreement, the original Wright Aeroplane of 1903.

2. In consideration thereof the Vendee agrees to pay to the Vendors the sum of One ($1.00) Dollar in cash and to comply with the following requirements:

Appendix A-2

(a) Said aeroplane is to be displayed as a public museum exhibit in the Metropolitan Area of the United States National Capital only, and except as hereinafter provided in paragraph (b) is to be housed directly facing the Main Entrance in the fore part of the North Hall of the Arts and Industries Building of the United States National Museum. It shall never be removed from such public exhibition except as may be required temporarily for maintenance or protection.

(b) If the proper authorities of the Smithsonian Institution or its successors (acting for the United States of America) at any time in the future desire to remove said aeroplane to any other building in the Metropolitan Area of the national capital, such removal shall be permitted on the following conditions:

1. That the substituted building shall have equal or better facilities for the protection, maintenance and exhibition of the aeroplane.

2. That the Wright Aeroplane of 1903 be given a place of special honor and not intermingled with other aeroplanes of later design.

3. That such building be not a military museum but be devoted to memorializing the development of aviation.

(c) There shall at all times be prominently displayed with said aeroplane a label in the following form and language:

The Original Wright Brothers' Aeroplane

The World's First Power-Driven Heavier-than-Air Machine

in Which Man Made Free, Controlled, and

Sustained Flight

Invented and Built by Wilbur and Orville Wright

Flown by Them at Kitty Hawk, North Carolina

December 17, 1903

By Original Scientific Research the Wright Brothers Discovered

the Principles of Human Flight

As Inventors, Builders and Flyers They Further Developed the Aeroplane

Taught Man to Fly and Opened the Era of Aviation.

Deposited by the Estate of Orville Wright.

"The first flight lasted only twelve seconds, a flight very modest compared with that of birds, but it was nevertheless the first in the history of the world in which a machine carrying a man had raised itself by its own power into the air in free flight, had sailed forward on a level course without reduction of speed, and had finally landed

Appendix A-3

without being wrecked. The second and third flights were a little longer, and the fourth lasted 59 seconds covering a distance of 852 feet over the ground against a 20 mile wind."

Wilbur and Orville Wright

(From Century Magazine, Vol. 76, September 1908, p. 649.)

(d) Neither the Smithsonian Institution or its successors nor any museum or other agency, bureau or facilities, administered for the United States of America by the Smithsonian Institution or its successors, shall publish or permit to be displayed a statement or label in connection with or in respect of any aircraft model or design of earlier date than the Wright Aeroplane of 1903, claiming in effect that such aircraft was capable of carrying a man under its own power in controlled flight.

3. The title and right of possession to be transferred by the Vendors hereunder shall remain vested in the United States of America only so long as there shall be no deviation by the Vendee from the requirements in the foregoing paragraph, and only so long as neither the Estate of Orville Wright nor any person having an interest therein is required to pay and does bear without indemnity an estate or inheritance tax, assessed by the State of Ohio, the United States or any other taxing authority, based upon a valuation of property of the Estate which includes said aeroplane at a value in excess of One ($1.00) Dollar.

4. Upon the failure of the Vendee to remedy any deviation from the requirements set forth in paragraph 2, within twelve months after written specification thereof shall have been given to the Smithsonian Institution on behalf of the United States or upon (a) the final assessment of any state or federal inheritance, succession or estate tax whereby the Estate of Orville Wright or any person or persons having an interest therein shall be required to pay a higher tax by reason of a valuation of said aeroplane for tax purposes in excess of One ($1.00) Dollar, and (b) the omission of the United States or others on behalf of the United States within twelve months of written notice of the final assessment by the person assessed to provide for the payment thereof by appropriations or otherwise, title to and right of possession of said aeroplane shall automatically revert to the Vendors, their successors and assigns.

5. In the event of a termination of title in the United States by reason of an omission on the part of the United States to provide for the

Appendix A-4

payment of a tax assessment as aforesaid, the United States shall have an option to repurchase the plane at any time within five years of the tax payment by reimbursing the taxpayer in the amount paid with interest thereon at six per cent from the date of payment. Upon the exercise of such option, this Agreement, in all of its terms, shall automatically again become of full force and effect.

WITNESS the due execution hereof in duplicate this ___23rd___ day of ___November,___ 1948.

         Harold S. Miller (SEAL)
         Harold W. Steeper (SEAL)
         Executors of the Estate of
         Orville Wright, deceased

UNITED STATES OF AMERICA

BY _A. Wetmore_
    Secretary of the Smithsonian Institution

4.

Appendix B

The William J. Hammer Documents

1. Wilbur Wright proposal to hire William J. Hammer as subrosa Wright Company employee, May 19, 1910
2. William J. Hammer acceptance of proposal to be hired, May 21, 1910.

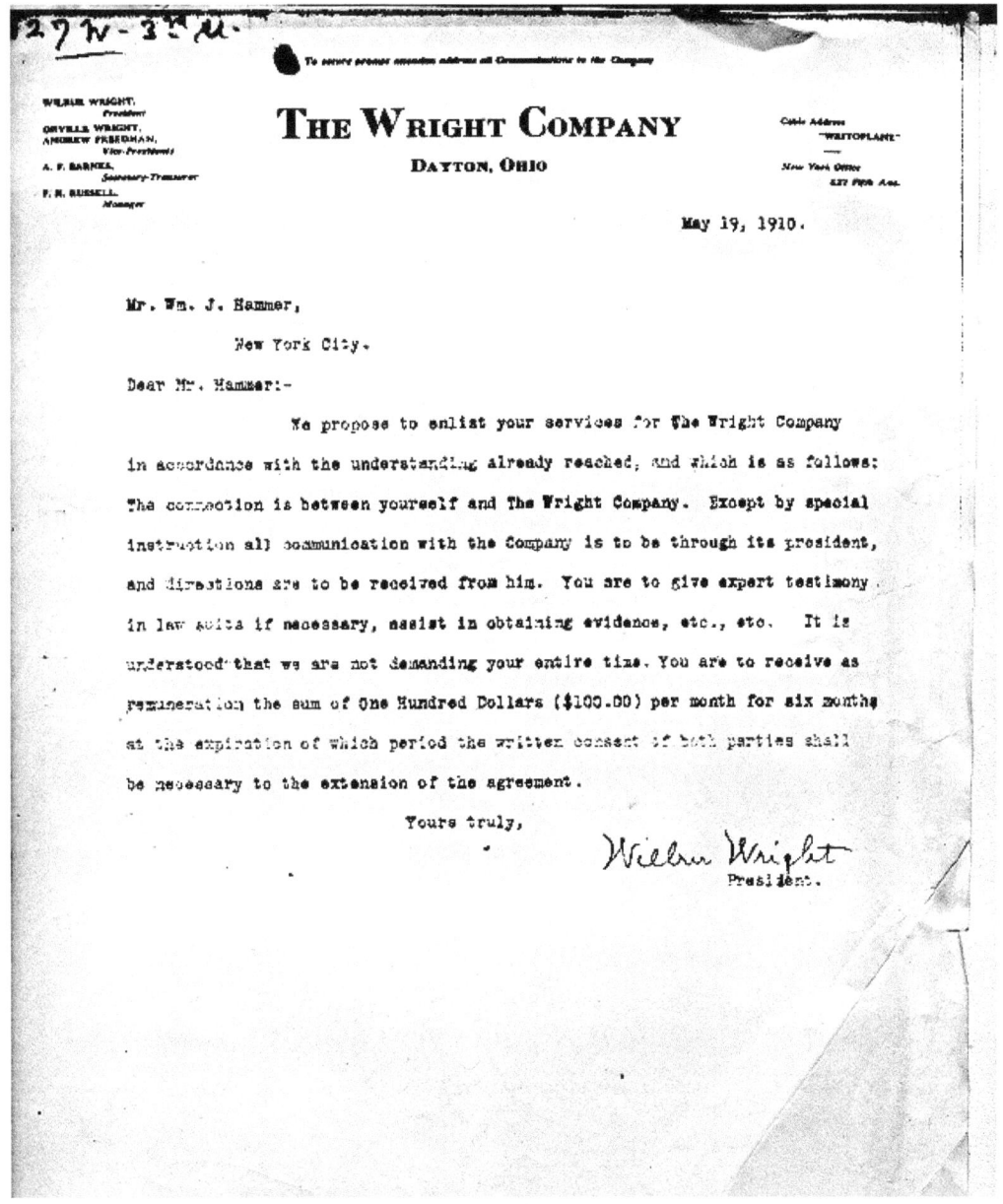

Appendix B-1
Wilbur Wright proposal to hire William J. Hammer, May 1910

OFFICE TELEPHONE, 553 CORTLANDT.
HOUSE TELEPHONE, 2177 BRYANT.

CABLE ADDRESS, "REMMAH NEW YORK."

WILLIAM J. HAMMER,
CONSULTING ELECTRICAL ENGINEER,
1408 Havemeyer Building, 26 Cortlandt Street,
AND
153 West 46th Street,

NEW YORK, May 21, 1910. 190

Wilbur Wright, Esq., President,
    The Wright Company,
       Dayton, Ohio.

Dear Mr. Wright:-

    Your favor of May 19th., received. It is in accordance with the verbal understanding which we have already reached as a result of our last interview of May 13th. and is accepted by me. I have already been laying out certain work and will write you early next week regarding a number of matters, which I believe will be of interest and I will submit certain suggestions which I should like to have your approval of if they accord with your views. I shall also be very glad to receive any instructions or suggestions from yourself and your brother, Orville, which it is needless for me to say will be treated in strictest confidence.

                Very truly yours,

Appendix B-2
William J. Hammer acceptance of proposal to be hired by Wilbur Wright, May 21, 1910.

Appendix B-3
Cover, *World Almanac of 1911*

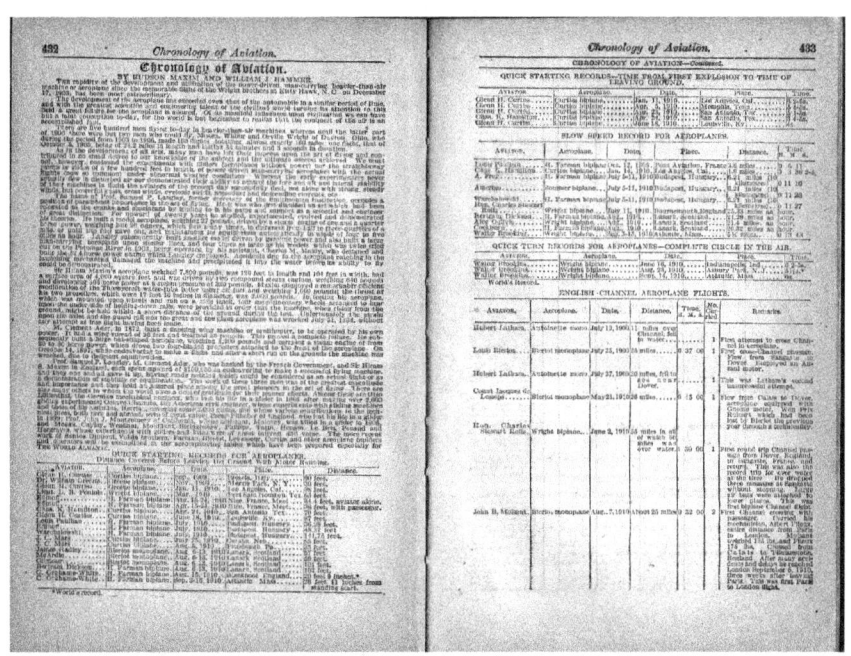

Appendix B-4
"Chronology of Aviation," *World Almanac of 1911*

Gustave Whitehead: "First in Flight"

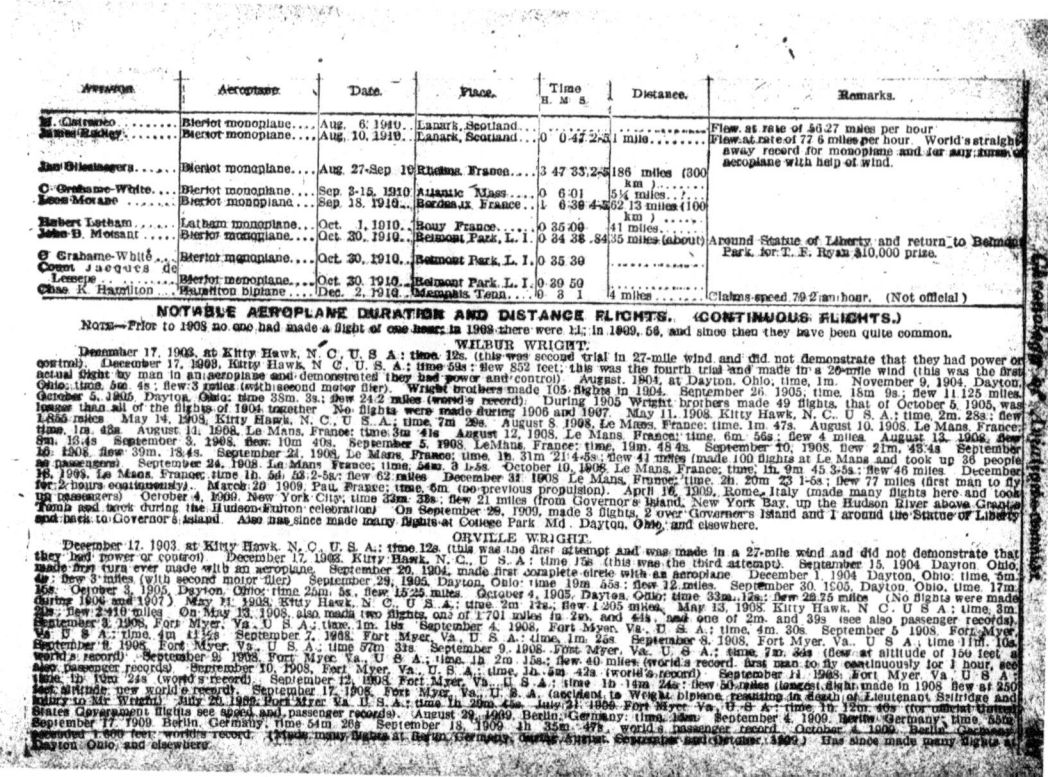

Appendix B-5

Credits for Wilbur and Orville Wright, from the "Chronology of Aviation," by Maxim and Hammer, published within the 1911 World Almanac and approved by Orville Wright in 1913; entered into court documents in patent suits, establishing Wilbur Wright as making, on December 17, 1903, with "the fourth trial" which "flew 852 feet"… "*the first actual flight by man in an aeroplane and demonstrated that they had power and control.*" The Chronology stated that the first three flights were attempts which "did not demonstrate that they had power or control." *This is completely the opposite of the credit given Orville contracted by his executors with Smithsonian, for the first attempt, which Smithsonian now claims had "power and control."*

(Transcript):

NOTABLE AEROPLANE DURATION AND DISTANCE FLIGHTS. (CONTINUOUS FLIGHTS.) (1911 World Almanac, p. 437)

WILBUR WRIGHT

December 17, 1903, at Kitty Hawk, N.C., U.S.A.: time 12s. (this was second trial in 27 mile wind and did not demonstrate that they had power or control.

December 17, 1903, at Kitty Hawk, N.C., U.S.A.: time 59s: flew 852 feet; this was the fourth trial and made in a 20 mile wind *(this was the first actual flight by man in an aeroplane and demonstrated they had power and control).* (emphasis added by Author)

Gustave Whitehead: "First in Flight"

ORVILLE WRIGHT

December 17, 1903, at Kitty Hawk, N.C., U.S.A.: time 12s *(this was the first attempt and was made in a 27 mile wind and did not demonstrate that they had power or control).* (emphasis added by Author)
December 17, 1903, at Kitty Hawk, N.C., U.S.A.: time 15s (this was the third attempt).

The Significance of the *"Chronology of Aviation"* by Maxim and Hammer:

#1 - it shows the flights on Dec. 17th, 1903 were all failures except the last one, which was by Wilbur.
#2 - This invalidates "the famous photo,"
#3 - This invalidates "the Contract" with Smithsonian (that gives Orville credit for first flight - see mandated legend taken from Century mag article that Orville and Katharine wrote when Wilbur was in Europe), and
#4 - it eliminates any mention of Whitehead.
#5 - it credits the Wrights and focuses on them, which was the original purpose as planned ahead of time by Hammer, starting in about 1907. Correspondences flowed back and forth on this, and the final publication was irrefutably proven to have been approved by the Wrights, over and over, in correspondences and in their patent lawsuit, where it was entered as evidence and Hammer says that the Wrights approved it.
#6 – it shows how Orville manipulated history after Wilbur's death, to credit himself.
#7 – it shows how Hammer manipulated history to credit Wrights and ignore Whitehead.
#8 – The "Chronology of Aviation" was entered in as evidence in the patent suits by Hammer, its coauthor and the Wrights' subrosa employee, to solidify the Wrights' claims as first in powered flight, in order to support the patents of a pioneer invention (as opposed to improvement of the art). This allowed support for expansion of the patent language to include "all horizontal surfaces."
#9 – It was the culmination of the systematic efforts by William J. Hammer to promote and credit the Wrights as first in flight, who also influenced the Aero Club of America to recognize the Wrights in March 1906, immediately following its first exhibition (Jan. 1906) where Whitehead was noted by *Scientific American* (Jan. 27, 1906 edition) as exhibiting a photo of his 1901 plane in flight…

The data in this Chronology was all gathered and controlled by William J. Hammer, who had privately pledged to use everything in his power to promote the Wrights. Gustave Whitehead was left out of the Chronology.

Gustave Whitehead: "First in Flight"

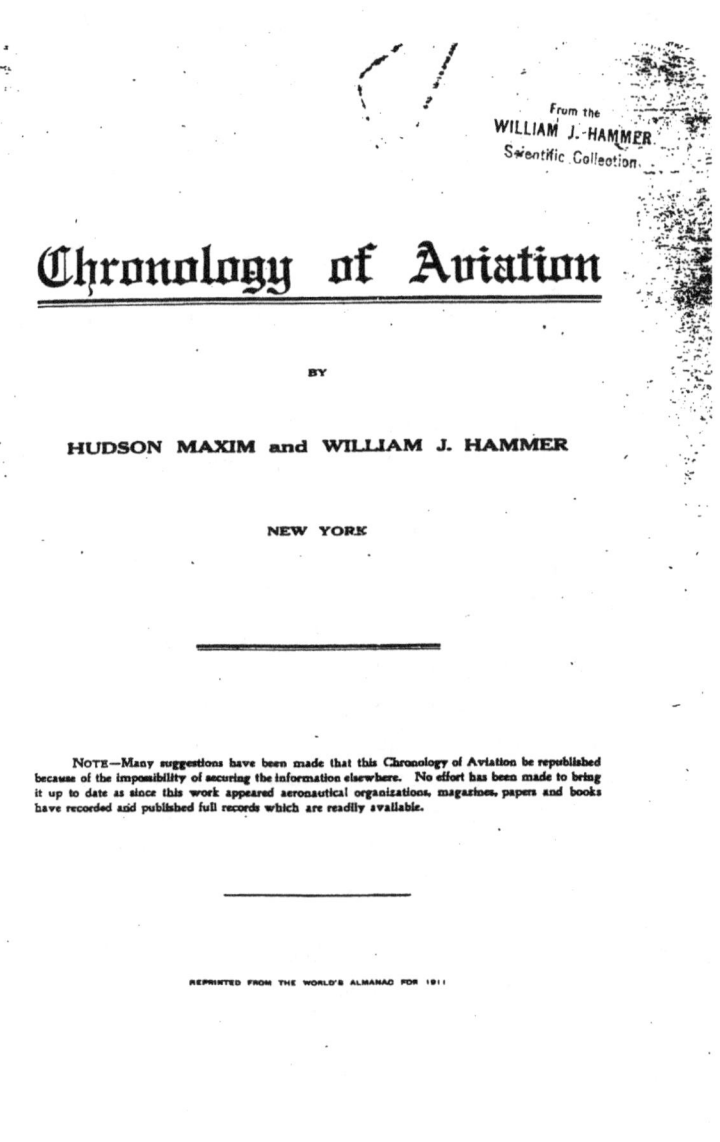

Appendix B-6

Cover of "Chronology of Aviation" Reprinted Booklet, 1912
Distributed to thousands of aero club members by William J. Hammer and entered into Wright patent suit court documents, noting they'd both approved these documents, *crediting Wilbur Wright as "first in flight"… "with power and control"*

Gustave Whitehead: "First in Flight"

NOTABLE AEROPLANE DURATION AND DISTANCE FLIGHTS (Continuous Flights.)

Note.—Prior to 1908 no one had made a flight of one hour; in 1908 there were 11; in 1909, 56, and since then they have been quite common. The following records, while they do not by any means include all of the flights made by the Wright Brothers, cover their most important flights, and they have approved the records here shown.

It must also be borne in mind that the Wright Brothers had made about 2,000 soaring flights with their gliders before they essayed a flight in their power-driven machine. (W. J. H.)

WILBUR WRIGHT.

December 17, 1903, at Kitty Hawk, N. C., U. S. A.; time, 12s. (this was second trial in 27-mile wind and did not demonstrate that they had power or control).
December 17, 1903, Kitty Hawk, N. C., U. S. A.; time 59s; flew 852 feet; this was the fourth trial and made it in a 20-mile wind *(This was the first actual flight by man in an aeroplane and demonstrated they had power and control.)*
August, 1904, at Dayton, Ohio; time. 1 m.
Nov. 9, 1904, Dayton, Ohio; time, 5m. 4s; flew 3 miles (with second motor flyer).
Wright brothers made 105 flights in 1904.
September 26, 1905; time, 18m. 9s.; flew 11 1/25 miles.
October 5, 1905, Dayton, Ohio; time 38m. 3s.; flew 24 2 miles (world's record).
During 1905 Wright brothers made 49 flights, that of October 5, 1905, was longer than all of the flights of 1904 together.
No flights were made during 1906 and 1907.

[CONTINUED ON NEXT PAGE]

ORVILLE WRIGHT.

December 17, 1903, at Kitty Hawk, N. C., U. S. A.; time 12s. (this was the first attempt and was made in a 27-mile wind and did not demonstrate that they had power or control). Note fourth attempt by Wilbur Wright on previous page
December 17, 1903, Kitty Hawk, N. C., U. S. A.; time 15s. (this was the third attempt).
September 15, 1904, Dayton, Ohio, *made first turn ever made with an aeroplane.*
September 20, 1904, *made first complete circle with an aeroplane*
December 1, 1904, Dayton, Ohio, time, 5m. 1s; flew 3 miles (with second motor flyer).
September 29, 1905, Dayton, Ohio; time 19m 55s.; flew 12 miles
September 30, 1905, Dayton, Ohio; time, 17 m. 15s
October 3, 1905, Dayton, Ohio; time 25m. 5s., flew 15.25 miles.
October 4, 1905, Dayton, Ohio; time, 33m. 17s., flew 20.75 miles.

Appendix B-7

Credits for Wilbur and Orville Wright, from p. 11 and 12 of the "Chronology of Aviation" Booklet, by Hammer and Maxim, republished from 1911 World Almanac and approved by Orville Wright the following year; entered into court documents in patent suits, establishing Wilbur Wright as making, on December 17, 1903, with "the fourth trial" which "flew 852 feet"… *"the first actual flight by man in an aeroplane and demonstrated that they had power and control."* The Chronology stated that the first three flights "did not demonstrate that they had power or control."

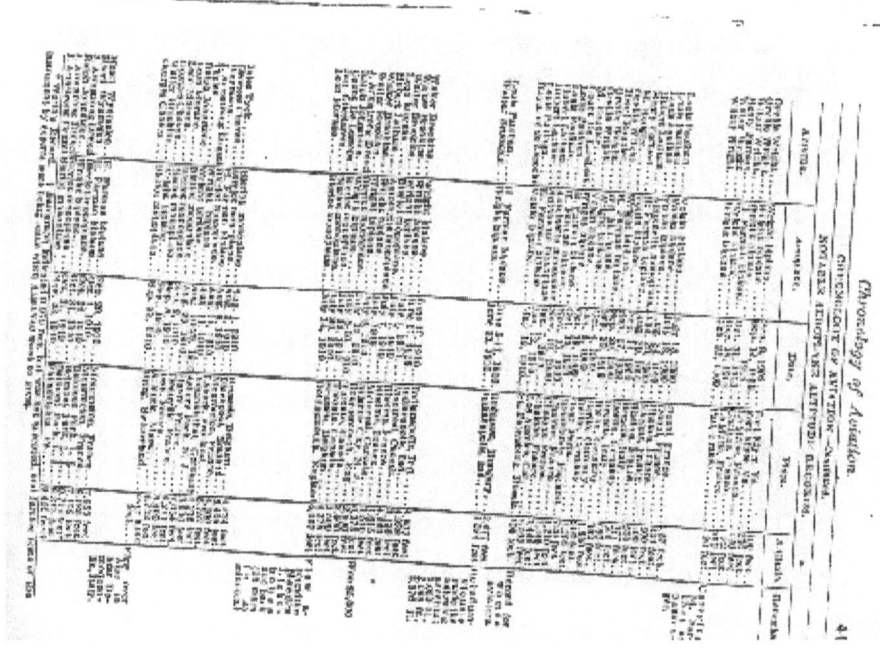

Appendix B-8

The significance of the "Chronology of Aviation" (1912) booklet, distributed to all members of the Aero Club of America, and earlier published (to a wide audience) in the World Almanac (1911) is that: Orville Wright approved the description of the records of the flights of December 17, 1903, as "by far the best record of the early flights that has been published," expressing his appreciation to William J. Hammer in a letter written on July 17, 1913 (see Appendix B-9). This contradicts current flight credit given to Orville Wright by the Smithsonian, as both of Orville's flights on December 17th, 1903 were described as failures, "without power and control," in the Hammer / Maxim "Chronology of Aviation." So, Orville agreed that he'd not had power and control when making those flights on that date, yet he is currently, obviously incorrectly, credited with both.

```
                The Wright Company
                    Dayton, Ohio

                                           July 17, 1915.

Mr. William J. Hammer,
    153 West 26th Street,
        New York, N. Y.

My dear Mr. Hammer:

        Many thanks for the copies of your "Chronolgy
of Aviation".  It is by far the best record of the early flights
that has been published, and I appreciate very much your treat-
ment of our early work.

        I was delayed longer than I expected with some
of my engagements when I was in New York last week, and so did
not get back to the hotel in time to answer your telephone call
before going to the train.  It would have given me much pleasure
to have seen the display of the progress in electric lighting.

                                    Very truly yours,

                                    Orville Wright
```

Appendix B-9

Prima Facie Deposition of Wm. J. Hammer 55

161   Cross-examination by Mr. Newell.

XQ. 43. Are you in any way connected with The Wright Company, the complainant herein?

A. No, not further than that I have been asked to testify in this case.

162

XQ. 44. What was the time you saw your first Wright aeroplane.

A. At the time of the Wright flights at Ft. Myer, Virginia, in the summer of 1909.

XQ. 45. If I understand you, you do not mean to testify of your own knowledge that the Wright Bros., or either of them, were the first to fly in a heavier-than-air machine driven by a motor, do you?

A. I testified to it to my knowledge historically.   163

XQ. 46. Just what do you mean by that?

A. I have testified that I have recently prepared, in conjunction with Mr. Hudson Maxim, a record giving a chronology of aviation embracing various tables and data which was the result of an enormous amount of investigation of the records issued by various aeronautical associations and published by the various aeronautical engineering and other press, and in this connection I have carried on an extensive correspondence and seen personally many of those interested actively in the art and I have endeavored in every way possible, by a study of the subject, to familiarize myself with what has been done in the art and have endeavored to prepare a historical record thereof prior to the work that I did for the World's Almanac of 1911, to which I have referred. I have done considerable work along this line, so that I feel competent to express an intelligent opinion of the historical development of the art.   164

Appendix B-10

From the Prima Facie Deposition* of William J. Hammer, January 16, 1911, at Atty. Toulmin's office in Springfield, Ohio; in the case of The Wright Company vs. Herring-Curtiss Co. and Glenn H. Curtiss; cross-examination by Curtiss' atty, Mr. E. R. Newell (*p. 54-55). At this time, Hammer was a secret employee of the Wright Company, who lied to the court about this (XQ.43, above). Hammer gave testimony about the Wrights being "first in flight" during the Curtiss suit, in order to help secure broader patent rights for them. Hammer further indicated on January 28th, 1911, that the Wrights provided the data for these tables and agreed with his Chronology (*p. 196).

Appendix C

The Whitehead-Beach Patent

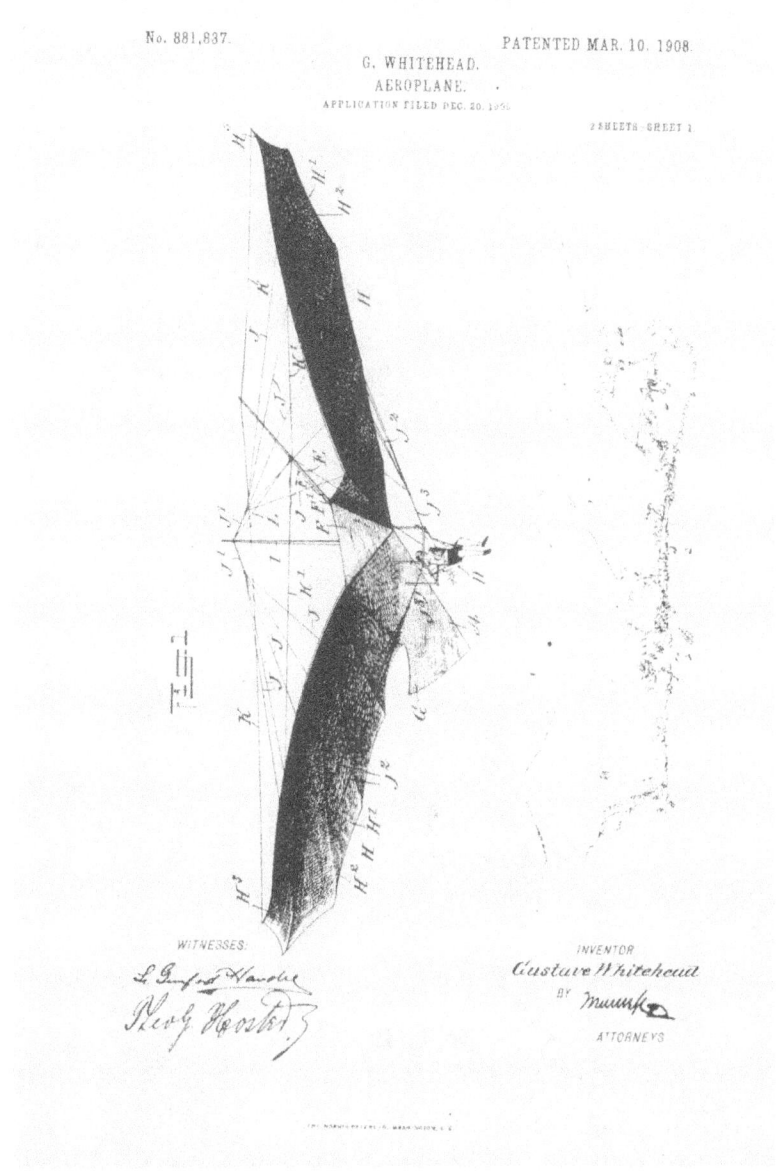

Appendix C-1

Gustave Whitehead Patent No. 881,837 filed Dec. 20, 1905, granted March 10, 1908.

Gustave Whitehead: "First in Flight"

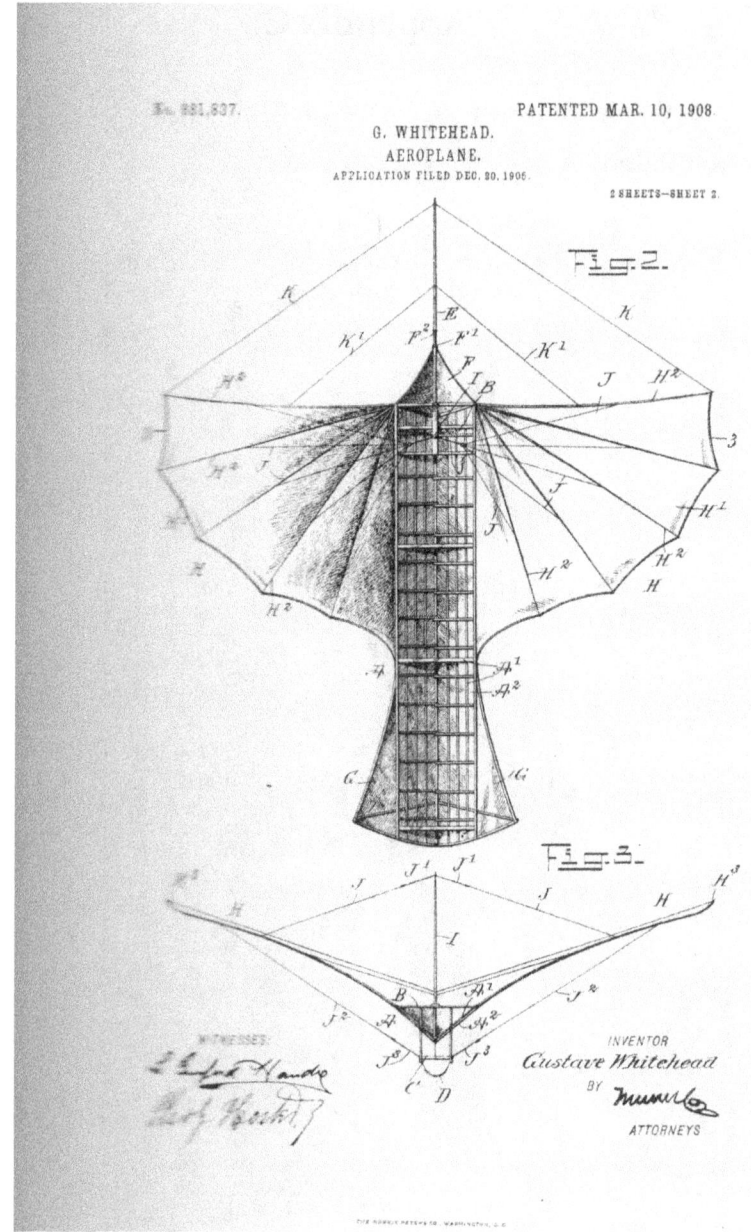

Appendix C-2

Appendix

UNITED STATES PATENT OFFICE.

GUSTAVE WHITEHEAD, OF BRIDGEPORT, CONNECTICUT, ASSIGNOR OF ONE-HALF TO STANLEY YALE BEACH, OF STRATFORD, CONNECTICUT.

AEROPLANE.

No. 881,837.   Specification of Letters Patent.   Patented March 10, 1908.

Application filed December 20, 1905. Serial No. 292,614.

To all whom it may concern:

Be it known that I, GUSTAVE WHITEHEAD, a citizen of the United States, and a resident of Bridgeport, in the county of Fairfield and
5 State of Connecticut, have invented a new and Improved Aeroplane, of which the following is a full, clear, and exact description.

The invention relates to aerial navigation, and its object is to provide a new and im-
10 proved aeroplane arranged to readily maintain its equilibrium when in flight in the air, to prevent upsetting, shooting downward head foremost, and to sustain considerable weight.

15 The invention consists of novel features and parts and combinations of the same which will be more fully described hereinafter and then pointed out in the claims.

A practical embodiment of the invention
20 is represented in the accompanying drawings forming a part of this specification, in which similar characters of reference indicate corresponding parts in all the views.

Figure 1 is a perspective view of the im-
25 provement as it appears in flight; Fig. 2 is a plan view of the same; and Fig. 3 is a transverse section of the same, on the line 3—3 of Fig. 2.

The body A of the aeroplane is trough-
30 shaped; that is, is made approximately V-shape in cross section, and the said body A is formed of a skeleton framework A', covered, at the under side, by a covering A² of canvas or other suitable fabric material. In the
35 front portion of the body A is arranged a reinforcing framework B, from which depends an open framework C for supporting the aeronaut, preferably by the use of a seat D, as plainly illustrated in Figs. 1 and 3. From
40 the framework B extends forwardly a bowsprit E, to which is secured the ring F' of a head F, made of canvas or like fabric material, the ring F' being fastened in place on the bowsprit E by suitable fastening means
45 F² in the shape of ropes or the like tied to the bow-sprit E.

The head F has sides forming continuations of the sides of the body A, and the bottom of this head F is inclined upwardly and
50 forwardly, to terminate in the ring F', in which also terminate the forward portions of the sides of the head F. Thus, the sides of the head F are both inclined toward each other, and also upwardly and forwardly from the forward ends of the body A. The rear 55 portions of the sides of the body A are extended upwardly and outwardly in the same planes containing the sides of the body A, so that the extensions form a tail G, which, with the head F, maintains the aeroplane in 60 proper equilibrium, at the same time preventing the aeroplane from shooting down head foremost in case of contrary winds or the like.

From the upper edges of the sides of the 65 body A extend wings H, slightly curved upwardly and outwardly, as plainly illustrated in the drawings, each of the wings H terminating at its rear end at the beginning of the corresponding side of the tail G, as plainly 70 indicated in Fig. 2. Each of the wings H is formed of canvas or other suitable fabric material attached to ribs H² radiating from the front end of the body A at the top of the sides, as plainly shown in Fig. 2, the outer 75 ends of the ribs H² being curved upwardly, as at H³ (see Figs. 1 and 3), to hold the outer edge of the canvas H' likewise curved upwardly.

In the framework B and that of the body 80 A is secured and erected a mast I, and the several ribs H² of the wings H are connected by upwardly and inwardly-extending braces J, with a single brace J' attached to the top of the mast I. Similar braces J² extend from 85 the ribs H² downwardly and inwardly, to connect with the single brace J³ attached to the suspension means C. Thus the wings H, H are properly braced, both at the top and bottom, to maintain their position relative to 90 the body A of the aeroplane. The foremost ribs H² of the wings H, H extend approximately at right angles to the body A, at the front end thereof, and the said foremost ribs H² are connected by braces K, K' with the 95 bow-sprit E, as plainly indicated in the drawings. A brace L also connects the bowsprit E with the mast I, to give the desired strength to the entire structure, so as to enable the aeroplane to withstand heavy wind 100 pressures without danger of disarrangement of the parts.

By constructing the body A in the manner described and providing the same with the head F, tail G and the wings H, H, a com- 105 plete equilibrium of the aeroplane is main-

Appendix C-3

G. Whitehead patent, p. 1 of 4

tained when in flight in the air, and at the same time the aeroplane is prevented from upsetting or shooting down, head foremost, as the inclined sides of the head F offer sufficient resistance to the air in the descent of the aeroplane that the body A thereof is righted or pushed upward, so as to maintain the body A practically at all times in a horizontal position.

The aeroplane is very simple and durable in construction, and the several parts are connected with each other and braced to such an extent as to form an exceedingly strong and durable structure.

Having thus described my invention, I claim as new and desire to secure by Letters Patent:—

1. An aeroplane provided with a trough-like body terminating in a head and having the rear portions of its sides extended upwardly and outwardly, to form a tail.

2. An aeroplane provided with a body approximately V-shaped in cross section and terminating at its front end in a head, the bottom of which is inclined upwardly and forwardly, and the sides of the head forming extensions of the sides of the body.

3. An aeroplane provided with a body approximately V-shaped in cross section and terminating at its front end in a head, the bottom of which is inclined upwardly and forwardly, and the sides of the head forming extensions of the sides of the body, the head sides and the head bottom terminating at a point lying in a horizontal plane containing the top of the said body.

4. An aeroplane provided with a body approximately V-shaped in cross section and terminating at its front end in a head, the bottom of which is inclined upwardly and forwardly, and the sides of the head forming extensions of the sides of the body, the head sides and head bottom terminating at a point intersected by a horizontal plane and a vertical plane, of which the latter passes longitudinally through the bottom of the said body, and the horizontal plane extends through the top of the body.

5. An aeroplane provided with a body approximately V-shaped in cross section and terminating at its front end in a head, the bottom of which is inclined upwardly and forwardly, and the sides of the head forming extensions of the sides of the body, the sides of the head being inclined toward each other and terminating in a point coinciding with the forward end of the bottom of the head.

6. An aeroplane provided with a body approximately V-shaped in cross section and terminating at its front end in a head, the bottom of which is inclined upwardly and forwardly, and the sides of the head forming extensions of the sides of the body, the sides of the head being inclined toward each other and terminating in a point coinciding with the forward end of the bottom of the head, and a bowsprit attached to the said body and supporting the forward end of the said head.

7. An aeroplane provided with a trough-like body terminating in a head and having the rear portions of its sides extended upwardly and outwardly to form a tail, and wings secured to the said body and extending outwardly and upwardly from the upper edges of the front portions of the sides of the said body.

8. An aeroplane provided with a trough-like body terminating in a head and having the rear portions of its sides extended upwardly and outwardly, to form a tail, and wings secured to the said body and extending outwardly and upwardly from the upper edges of the forward portions of the sides of the said body and between the said head and the said tail.

9. An aeroplane provided with a trough-like body terminating in a head and having the rear portions of its sides extended upwardly and outwardly, to form a tail, wings secured to the said body and extending outwardly and upwardly from the upper edges of the forward portions of the sides of the said body and between the said head and the said tail, a mast rising in the said body, and braces extending from the said mast to the said wings at points between the outer and inner ends thereof.

10. An aeroplane provided with a trough-like body terminating in a head and having the rear portions of its sides extended upwardly and outwardly, to form a tail, wings secured to the said body and extending outwardly and upwardly from the upper edges of the forward portions of the sides of the said body, a mast rising from the said body at a point somewhat in the rear of the front end thereof, and braces extending from the said mast to the said wings.

11. An aeroplane provided with a trough-like body terminating in a head and having the rear portions of its sides extended upwardly and outwardly, to form a tail, wings secured to the said body and extending outwardly and upwardly from the upper edges of the forward portions of the sides of the said body, a mast rising in the said body, a bowsprit extending from the said body and supporting the front end of the said head, and a brace extending from the said mast to the said bowsprit.

12. An aeroplane provided with a trough-like body terminating in a head and having the rear portions of its sides extended upwardly and outwardly, to form a tail, wings secured to the said body and extending outwardly and upwardly from the upper edges of the forward portions of the sides of the said body, a mast rising from the said body

at a point somewhat in the rear of the front end thereof, braces extending from the said mast to the said wings, a bowsprit extending from the said body and engaged by the front end of the said head, and braces extending from the said bowsprit to the front edges of the said wings.

13. An aeroplane provided with a body approximately V-shaped in cross section and terminating at its front end in a head, the bottom of which is inclined upwardly and forwardly, and the sides of the head forming extensions of the sides of the body, the sides of the head being inclined toward each other and terminating in a point coinciding with the forward end of the bottom of the head, a bowsprit attached to the said body and supporting the forward end of the said head, and a suspension means depending from the said body near the front thereof.

14. An aeroplane provided with a trough-like body terminating in a head and having the rear portions of its sides extended upwardly and outwardly, to form a tail, and wings secured to the said body and extending outwardly and upwardly from the upper edges of the forward portions of the sides of the said body, each of the wings consisting of fabric material and ribs radiating from the front end of the body.

15. An aeroplane provided with a trough-like body terminating in a head and having the rear portions of its sides extended upwardly and outwardly, to form a tail, and wings secured to the said body and extending outwardly and upwardly from the upper edges of the front portions of the sides of the said body, each of the wings consisting of fabric material and ribs radiating from the front end of the body, the forward ribs of the wings extending approximately at right angles to the said body.

16. An aeroplane provided with a trough-like body terminating in a head and having the rear portions of its sides extended upwardly and outwardly, to form a tail, and wings secured to the said body and extending outwardly and upwardly from the upper edges of the forward portion of the sides of the said body, each of the wings consisting of a fabric material and ribs radiating from the front end of the body and curved upward at their outer ends.

17. An aeroplane provided with a body approximately V-shaped in cross section and terminating at its front end in a head, the bottom of which is inclined upwardly and forwardly, and the sides of the head forming extensions of the sides of the body, the sides of the head being inclined toward each other and terminating in a point coinciding with the forward end of the bottom of the head, a bowsprit attached to the said body and supporting the forward end of the said head, a mast rising from the front portion of the said body, a suspension means depending from the said body near the front thereof, braces connecting the said mast with the said wings, and braces connecting the suspension means with the said wings.

18. An aeroplane provided with a trough-like body terminating in a head and having the rear portions of its sides extended upwardly and outwardly, to form a tail, wings secured to the said body and extending outwardly and upwardly from the upper edges of the forward portions of the sides of the said body, each of the wings being formed of fabric material and ribs radiating from the front end of the body, a mast rising from the front end of the said body, a bowsprit extending forwardly from the front portion of the said body and supporting the front end of the said head, a suspension means depending from the front portion of the said body, braces connecting the said mast with the ribs of the said wings, and braces connecting the said suspension means with the said ribs.

19. An aeroplane provided with a trough-like body terminating in a head and having the rear portions of its sides extended upwardly and outwardly, to form a tail, wings secured to the said body and extending outwardly and upwardly from the upper edges of the forward portions of the sides of the said body, each of the wings being formed of fabric material and ribs radiating from the front end of the body, a mast rising from the front end of the said body, a bowsprit extending forwardly from the front portion of the said body and supporting the front end of the said head, a suspension means depending from the front portion of the said body, braces connecting the said mast with the ribs of the said wings, braces connecting the said suspension means with the said ribs, and braces connecting the foremost ribs with the said bowsprit.

20. An aeroplane provided with a trough-like body terminating in a head and having the rear portions of its sides extended upwardly and outwardly, to form a tail, wings secured to the said body and extending outwardly and upwardly from the upper edges of the forward portions of the sides of the said body, each of the wings being formed of fabric material and ribs radiating from the front end of the body, a mast rising from the front end of the said body, a bowsprit extending forwardly from the front portion of the said body and supporting the front end of the said head, a suspension means depending from the front portion of the said body, braces connecting the said mast with the ribs of the said wings, braces connecting the said suspension means with the said ribs, and a brace connecting the said mast with the said bowsprit.

Appendix C-5

G. Whitehead patent, p. 3 of 4

4   881,837

21. An aeroplane provided with a trough-like body terminating at its front end in a head and having its rear portion provided with a tail.

22. An aeroplane provided with a trough-like body having a head and a tail, and wings secured to the said body and extending outwardly and upwardly from the sides of the said body.

23. An aeroplane provided with a trough-like body having a head and a tail, and wings secured to the said body and extending outwardly and upwardly from the sides of the said body at points intermediate the said head and the said tail.

In testimony whereof I have signed my name to this specification in the presence of two subscribing witnesses.

                 GUSTAVE WHITEHEAD.

Witnesses:
     S. Y. BEACH,
     J. W. THOMPSON.

Appendix C-6
G. Whitehead patent, p. 4 of 4

Appendix D

The "Beach-Whitehead" Statement

The so-called Stanley Yale Beach Whitehead Statement, never signed nor published, after heavy edits made in 1939 by the "Smithsonian-Wright Contract" collaborators and instigators of the statement, Maj. Lester Gardner and Earl Findley, was provided to Orville Wright for his use. The statement, ostensibly by "Beach," contradicted a much earlier decade of *Scientific American* articles written by Beach, its Aviation Editor, essentially recognizing Whitehead for inventing the airplane. The "Beach Whitehead Statement" inadvertently shows that Whitehead's designs did, in fact make flights, as the patented design is described herein as pancaking upon landing and being inherently stable – removing that telling line on page 7 was obviously missed. It is housed in the small Library of Congress Gustave Whitehead collection.

> STATEMENT BY STANLEY Y. BEACH
> ABOUT HIS RELATIONSHIP WITH GUSTAVE WHITEHEAD
>
> In 1901 I was writing for my grandfather's, Alfred Ely Beach's weeklies "The Scientific American" and the "Scientific American Supplement" which were then published and edited by my father Frederick Converse Beach. I had become greatly interested in attempts to build flying machines. I was living in my native town, Stratford, Conn., at the time, and read in the Bridgeport papers about a man named Whitehead who was building a flying machine. As part of my duties as Aeronautical Editor of the "Scientific American", I went to see him and found that he was a German mechanic who had worked for Otto Lilienthal in Germany at the time of his glider experiments. He had emigrated to South America and later came to this country. He told me of his building a steam-driven aeroplane and flying in it at Pittsburgh. I have since learned that he had worked for the Boston Aeronautical Society where he built gliders.
>
> Long after I met him he demonstrated his glider and I took a picture of it in flight which appears opposite page 36 of Miss Randolph's book. Practically all the other pictures of the gliders and airplanes in this book were also taken by me.
>
> I found that he had built an aeroplane that was inherently stable and also was building engines. He built one of 20 horsepower to drive the two propellers of his monoplane and one of ten horsepower to propel it on the ground.
>
> I induced my father to advance money to Whitehead to help him continue his experimentation. I estimate that my father gave him about ten thousand dollars. At first he had a small shop where he lived with his family.
>
> I met him in May, 1901, photographed his machine, and described

Appendix D-1

S. Y. Beach's Statement
-2-

it in an illustrated article in the issue of the "Scientific American" of June 8, 1901. This was two months before he is supposed to have made his first successful flight on August 14th. I published my first description of his monoplane in Vol. 84, No. 23 of the "Scientific American" of June 8th, 1901. My article will convince anyone that the "compound engine" shown was inoperative upon "Calcium Carbide" (acetylene) which was supposed to run it. I saw no 10 H.P. engine for ground propulsion, nor any boiler for generating steam, although Whitehead was a believer in steam and claimed to have flown at Oakland, suburb of Pittsburgh, Pa., in 1899 with a steam engine.

The gasoline auto had arrived; he was bringing it up-to-date by operating it as an internal-combustion motor on acetylene. I reported what he said -- that it was to run on Calcium Carbide! At that time none had so operated. As it had taken him years to build the "compound engine", it is hardly to be believed that he could construct a boiler and power plant in two months, which he would have to have done in order to fly with his "compound (steam) engine" on Aug. 14, 1901. On Decoration Day he said "Calcium Carbide" was to furnish the motive power. He experimented with steam and it was "out". Highly explosive acetylene was far more powerful and simpler, since all he now had to do was to drip water on "Calcium Carbide". My brief article entitled: "A New Flying Machine", states succinctly all the inventor (who is shown squatting in front of the machine with his child) had to say about it and its motive power, which was sufficient to prove that then he had no practical, operative internal-combustion motor. Hence, we must conclude that the flight of Aug. 14, 1901, like that of Poe's "Steering" balloon supposed to have crossed the Atlantic and to have landed on an island off Georgia (which story

Appendix D-2

Appendix

S. Y. Beach's statement

-3-

my great grandfather, Moses Yale Beach, bought from the post and printed in his newspaper the "N.Y.Sun") was a mere flight of fancy of the Editor-owner of the "Bridgeport Sunday Herald", Richard Howell.

As Automobile Editor of the "Scientific American", I was well informed about steam and gasoline motors. I simply reported photographically and in writing, what I saw and was told. In later years Whitehead told of experiments with Sulphur dioxid having a low boiling point and reverted to steam in talking, but never actually returned to it. Steam probably would have flown his plane, but steam he did not have.

With the money advanced by my father he built a much larger aeroplane with an undercarriage or platform to stand on, mounted on four wheels. The small 2-cylinder, 2-cycle motor developed but 40 lbs. thrust - insufficient for the small machine even. I would tow the machine with my gasoline Locomobile at Lordship Manor, as we wanted to find out what thrust would be required to get it in the air. With John Whitehead aboard, (photos opposite p.36) we found that it would require about 400 lbs. thrust or pull to get it off the ground.

In some of these towing tests the machine left the ground for a few feet, say three to five (as shown in photos) and these towed hops 3 to 4 years after 1901 are the only basis for the "flights" seen by some of those who claim that it flew under its own power at Lordship Manor, Stratford, Conn. It never left the ground under its own power to my knowledge.

"Several experiments have been made but as yet no free flights have been attempted," I wrote in "The Scientific American" of June 8, 1901.

Appendix D-3

S. Y. Beach's Statement

-4-

I saw him frequently from 1901 to 1910 and at no time did he ever say that he had flown, even though he built several machines after the date on which he was supposed to have flown.

I attribute the legend of the flight of Aug. 14, 1901 to the story that Dick Howell wrote in the "Bridgeport Sunday Herald" four days later. Even Miss Randolph says on page 20 of her book that this story of the supposed flight is jumbled. New York and Boston papers copied this and so the story grew until, on investigation, the facts were found, after which it was never claimed again until thirty-five years later when the glamour of having something to do with pioneer attempts at flying have caused memories to confuse towed flights with self-propelled ascents. (See affidavit of Jas. Dickie, p. 87 of Randolph book).

The Whitehead aeroplane had many interesting features. It was inherently stable and could be flown safely always "pancaking" and landing on a level keel. I was so convinced of its value that after experimenting 3 to 4 years, I had my grandfather's firm, Munn & Co., of N. Y. and Washington, apply for a patent on it December 20, 1905 (Pat. 881, 837, March 10, 1908.) I also secured the same patent in Austria--the Germany of today. It will be seen from the patents that a half interest was assigned to me. Thus Whitehead's 23 claims in his native land were basic and strong, as only such are allowed in Germany. There are no better patents.

As soon as we found that ten times as much thrust was required as Whitehead had obtained to get the aeroplane off the ground, he said that this time he'd build a big enough motor.

Accordingly he set to work to make an 8-cylinder, V-type 6 x 8 motor using steel projectile shells for the cylinders surrounded by

Appendix D-4

Appendix

S. Y. Beach's Statement   -5-

copper water jackets. Although of light weight for the 200 H.P. it was supposed to develop, it was much too heavy for his monoplane, so he built a big biplane and installed this engine, driving twin propellers by means of a rope drive. Poised atop "Tunxis Hill" on a Sunday afternoon in 1908 or 1909, it refused to budge. Subsequently, I installed it in a novel "gliding boat." A connecting rod broke and punctured the crankcase off Norwalk.

Still later, when I had seen a Panhard-Lavassar automobile motor with concentric valves, I encouraged Whitehead to copy some of its features. He did this and built a 4 cylinder, 4x5, 4-cycle water-cooled 80 H.P. motor, that on May 18, 1910, at Lordship Manor, Stratford, Conn., got a Bleriot-type airplane which I had built and was testing, off the ground making several hops. These were only a few feet off the ground, but Whitehead deserves credit for building an engine that did actually fly an airplane.

Whitehead's temper got the best of him one with me when I f called to see him. After so many failures and when he had failed to make his aeroplane take off and fly under its own power, we had difficulties over the ownership of the gliders, engines, etc., which my father had paid for. The large aeroplane (glider) was kept on the lawn of my country residence, 1812 Elm St., Stratford, Conn. with its wings folded, and a village humorist told the children it was "Stanley Beach's Flying Machine in which he'd go up and cool off when he got too hot!"

At this period we had the advice of Henry Alonzo House Sr. of Bridgeport, Conn., who was with Sir Hiram Maxim and who actually developed, built, and tested the Maxim machine at Baldwins Park, England in 1895 or thereabouts -- the first lifting of a power-driven

Appendix D-5

S. Y. Beach's Statement

aeroplane. If he had thought or believed that Whitehead was able to build a machine that could fly, he would have supported him generously.

My impression of Whitehead was that he was a good mechanic with a desire to build a machine that would fly. He knew how to build gliders and had a general idea about the requirements of an airplane that would be maneuverable. His idea was to have it inherently stable. To turn it he used a rudder and unbalanced power of two propellers.

Again I say that I do not believe that any of his machines ever left the ground under their own power in spite of the assertions of many persons who think they saw them fly. I think I was in a better position during the 9 years that I was giving Whitehead money to develop his ideas, to know what his machines could do, than persons who were employed by him for a short time or those who have remained silent for thirty-five years about what would have been an historic achievement in aviation.

In conclusion I want to give the pioneer Gustave Whitehead the credit to which I know him to be entitled.

1. He built many gliders and patented an aeroplane that was inherently stable.
2. He built many lightweight engines one of which actually lifted a Bleriot-type monoplane off the ground.

He certainly deserves a place in early aviation, due to his having gone ahead and built extremely light engines and aeroplanes.

The former were marvels of power for their light weight. The 5-cylinder kerosene one, with which he claims to have flown over Long Island Sound on Jan. 17th, 1902, was, I believe, the first Aviation Diesel. It, at least, brought such a flight within the

Appendix D-6

Appendix

S. Y. Beach's Statement
-7-

range of possibility.

As for the patented aeroplane, in the movie thriller "Men with Wings" an inventor like Whitehead takes off and flies successfully in a batlike monoplane that is practically a duplicate of the latter's 1901-1902 machine.

Of my own knowledge, from many experiments and tests, I know that the aeroplane patented by him was inherently stable, laterally and longitudinally, and that it would always make a "pancake" landing instead of a nose dive.

This fact alone would have saved many lives if this slow but safe type had been employed in the early days.

STANLEY YALE BEACH Ph.B.

Appendix D-7

Appendix E

Gustave Whitehead Powered Flights Witnesses List

Witness	Date of Event	Powered Flight	Flight	Location	Affidavit	Statement	Statement/Affidavit/Interview Date
Darvarich, Mary	1899	Y-PF	Y	PA	N	Y	1964
Lazay, Louis	1900	Y-PF	Y	Bridgeport	Y		1936
Lanye, Frank	1901	Y-PF	Y	Fairfield Beach		Y	1964
Schweikert, Thomas	1901	Y-PF	Y	Bridgeport	Y		1936
Conner, Clifford	1903	Y-PF	Y	?	Y		1987
Havery, John	1905	Y-PF	Y	Bridgeport		Y	1948
Bradtmuller, Edward	1907	Y-PF	Y	Fairfield	Y		1964
Darvarich, Louis	1899 (Apr., May), 1902	Y-PF	Y	PA, CT	Y	Y	1934, 1937
Pruckner, Anton	1900, 1901, & later	Y-PF	Y	Lordship, Bpt - Seaside Park	Y	Y	1934, 1963, 1964, 1966
Fekete, John	1901 or 1902, May or June	Y-PF	Y	Sports Hill, Easton		Y	1936 [Crane], 1948
Howell, Richard	1901, Aug. 14	Y-PF	Y	Fairfield		Y	1901
Harworth, Junius	1901, July Aug.	Y-PF	Y	Bridgeport, Lordship	Y	Y	1934, 1934-1962
Lesko, John S.	1901, Sept., 1902, Aug.	Y-PF	Y	Bridgeport, Fairfield	Y Y		1934, 1936
Werer, Michael	1901, Sept., Oct.	Y-PF	Y	Fairfield (Tunxis Hill)	Y		1934
Ciglar, John	1901-1902	Y-PF	Y	Bridgeport	Y		1936
Gluck, Alexander	1901-1902	Y-PF	Y	Bridgeport	Y		1934, 1936 [Crane]
Savage, Mary	1901-1902	Y-PF	Y	Bridgeport		Y	1930's, 1964
Peschel, Gustave	1901-1902?	Y-PF	Y	Fairfield (Tunxis Hill)		Y	1987
Koteles, Elizabeth	1901-1903	Y-PF	Y	Fairfield	Y	Y	1964, 1974
Cole, Oliver	1902-1904	Y-PF	Y	Fairfield (Tunxis Hill)		Y	1966
Kopacsi, Mari	1905-1908	Y-PF	Y	Bridgeport - Villa Park, State St.		Y	1936 [Crane]
Szur, Frederick	1905-1908	Y-PF	Y	Bridgeport - Villa Park, State St.		Y	1936 [Crane]
Verzaro, James Jr.	1907-1910	Y-PF	Y	Fairfield (Orr's Castle)	Y		1964
Beach, Stanley Yale	1908+	Y-PF	Y	Fairfield (Tunxis Hill)		Y - notes on	1934
Crittendon, Clarence	1908-1911	Y-PF	Y	Bpt. - Seaside Park	Y		1964
McColl, John H	undated	Y-PF	Y	Bridgeport		Y	1948
Steeves, Cecil A.	undated	Y-PF	Y	Bridgeport	Y		1936, 1963, 1964

Y-PF = Yes, Powered Flight Observed   Locations of Documents: CT = Fairfield Museum,   TX= U of TX, Dallas

© Susan Brinchman, 2015

Appendix

Location of Documentation	Details	Age	Vocation	Distance	Elevation
CT	saw and participated in short flight in Pittsburgh	adult	homemaker		low
TX	old circus grounds	teen	Toolmaker	180 ft	30-40 ft.
CT	saw multiple plane flights at Fairfield Beach in 1901	adult	Navy veteran	1/4 mile	
TX	Cherry Street flight	adult	Silk weaver	300 ft	15 ft
CT	saw triplane powered flight with his class	youth	Retired		
TX	old circus grounds	youth	Machinist	200 ft	10 ft
CT	biplane flight successful, up and down the street	youth	Painter	200 ft	10 ft
CT, TX, Media Interviews	multiple flights - Pittsburgh; street flights	adult	Engineer	1/2 mile	20-25 ft.
CT, TX, Media Interviews, Letters	multiple flights over Long Island Sound; also flew plane	adult	Mechanic	1/2 mile	50 ft
TX	present for flight at Sports Hill on a farm, other witnesses present	adult	Machinist	200 ft	30 ft.
Media Article, LOC archives	editor/publisher, wrote article about eyewitness to sustained first powered flight	adult	Publisher, Editor	1/2 mile	40-50 ft.
CT, TX, Media Interviews, Letters	multiple flights	teen	Engineer	1.5 miles	200 ft.
TX	Fairfield Ave., Bpt; Gypsy Springs; horse & wagon pulled plane	youth	Undertaker	50 - 80 ft	4 ft.
TX	nr. Mountain Grove Cemetery, Tunxis Hill Road	adult	Machinist	400 ft.	6 ft.
TX	unmanned plane flew, crashed, burst into flames	youth	Clerk	30 ft.	12 ft.
TX	Cherry Street flight longest. Saw airplane flights in 1901 and 1902.	youth	Clerk	60 ft.	15-20 ft.
CT	flew from Pine Street to harbor, over neighborhood	adult	homemaker	1/2 mile	
CT	saw powered flt test experiments, helped carry plane up hill	teen	Mechanic		?
CT [taped interviews, transcripts)	witnessed flight at Tunxis Hill	adult	Grocery Store Ownr	up to 250 ft.	5-6 ft
CT	saw biplane fly 10' elevation Orr's Castle, then crash into bits	youth	Electrical contractor		10 ft
	multiple flights	adult			
	multiple flights	adult	Toolmaker		
CT	near Orr's Castle, Tunxis Hill; lived near GW; knew Davarich also, who told of 2 flts	teen		short hops	3-4 ft
TX	told SR that GW worked for him as mechanic, SYB was the inventor	adult	Sci Am Aviation Editr		
CT	flew over water, circled, returned and landed at Seaside Park	adult	Carpenter	100-200 ft	low
TX	saw plane in air, old circus grounds	teen	VP 1st Nat. Bank		
CT, TX	tethered to pole flights; Gilman estate flight to circus lots	teen		1,000 ft	3-5 ft.

1960's-1980's - O'Dwyer interview   1930's - 1940's (Randolph, Crane, Ghormley)

© Susan Brinchman, 2015

Gustave Whitehead: "First in Flight"

BIBLIOGRAPHY

ARCHIVES:

Bridgeport Public Library Archives

CT State Library

Fairfield Historical Society: Fairfield Museum, Fairfield, CT
    O'Dwyer / Whitehead Research Collection

Library of Congress. Washington, DC
    Gustave Whitehead Collection
    Papers of Wilbur and Orville Wright
    Chronicling America

Missouri State Library
    St. Louis Exposition of 1904

Notre Dame, Indiana
    Albert Francis Zahm Manuscripts

Smithsonian Institution
    William J. Hammer Papers
    Earnest Jones Papers
    Paul Garber Papers
    (Contract) archives

Stratford Public Library Archives

University of Connecticut
    MAGIC Historical Map Collection
    1934 Fairchild Aerial Photography Map Collection

Yale University, New Haven, CT
    Beinecke Rare Book and Manuscript Library
        Stanley Yale Beach Papers, 1911-1948

© Susan Brinchman, 2015

NEWSPAPERS AND JOURNALS: see endnote citations

BOOKS: also, see endnote citations

Aero Club of America, 1916. Kessinger Legacy Reprints
Bullmer, Joe. *The WRight Story.* CreateSpace, Charleston, SC, 2009
Carpenter, Jack. *Pendulum.* Arsdalen, Bosch, & Co., MA, 1992
Goldstone, Lawrence. *Birdmen.* Ballantine Books, NY, 2014
Horgan, James J., *City of Flight. History of Aviation in St. Louis.*1984
Howard, Fred. *A Biography of the Wright Brothers.* Dover Publications, Mineola, NY1987,1988
Lougheed, Victor. *Vehicles of the Air: A Popular Exposition of Modern Aeronautics, With Working Drawings (1909).* Reilly and Britton Co., Chicago, November 1909. Reprinted by Kessinger Publishing
Randolph, Stella. *Lost Flights of Gustave Whitehead.* Washington, DC: Places, Inc., 1937
Randolph, Stella. *Before the Wrights Flew: The Story of Gustave Whitehead.* NY: GP Putnam's Sons, 1966
O'Dwyer, William J. and Randolph, Stella. *History by Contract: The Beginning of Motorized Aviation: August 14, 1901, Gustave Whitehead, Fairfield, Conn..* Leutershausen, Germany: Fritz Majer & Son, 1978
Robie, Bill. *For the Greatest Achievement: A History of the Aero Club of America and the National Aeronautic Association.* Smithsonian Institution Press, Washington and London, 1993.
Zahm, Albert F., *Early Powerplane Fathers, University Press, Notre Dame, Indiana, 1945.* http://archives.nd.edu/findaids/ead/xml/aza.xml

RESOURCES

Books About Gustave Whitehead:

The following are books are out of print but available used, occasionally, on the Internet, on websites such as Alibris.com, Abebooks.com, Amazon.com, and eBay.com. They are also available at the Gustav Weisskopf Museum in Germany, the Fairfield Museum, in Fairfield, CT, the Bridgeport Public Library, Bridgeport, CT, the San Diego Aerospace Museum, San Diego, CA; and the Smithsonian Institute, Washington, DC. [Note: Several key updates to the earlier books about Whitehead are found in *History by Contract* (1978).

Lost Flights of Gustave Whitehead by Stella Randolph, Places, Inc., 1937

Before the Wrights Flew: The Story of Gustave Whitehead by Stella Randolph, GP Putnam's Sons, NY, 1966

History by Contract: The Beginning of Motorized Aviation: August 14, 1901, Gustave Whitehead, Fairfield, Conn. by William J. O'Dwyer & Stella Randolph, Fritz Majer & Son, Leutershausen, Germany, 1978

Websites maintained currently by this author:

www.gustavewhitehead.info
includes more information and supporting documents for *Gustave Whitehead: First in Flight*

www.historybycontract.org

Gustave Whitehead Archives

Note: Witness interview notes, tapes, videos, transcripts, statements and affidavits referenced in the above endnotes are located within the following archives:

The Papers of Major William J. O'Dwyer, USAF (deceased) Whitehead researcher and world authority on Gustave Whitehead 1963 - 2008, are located at the William O'Dwyer - Gustave Whitehead Research Collection, Fairfield Museum, Fairfield, CT, and the Bridgeport Public Library, Bridgeport, CT, USA. Some of Maj. O'Dwyer's correspondences and papers also are available at the Gustav Weisskopf Museum in Leutershausen, Germany. http://www.fairfieldhistory.org/wp-content/uploads/ODwyer-Gustav-Whitehead-Research-Collection-Ms-B107.pdf.

The Papers of Stella Randolph, Whitehead researcher 1934-1937 (deceased), are located at the Stella Randolph – University of TX, Dallas, TX, USA. Please check for restrictions.

Gustave Whitehead: "First in Flight"

Gustav Weisskopf Museum, Leutershausen, Germany research archive established with the assistance of Maj. William J. O'Dwyer (see below).

"Gustave Whitehead Research Collection," State of Connecticut State Library, Hartford, CT, established 2014.

Connecticut Aeronautical Historical Society (CAHA)'s New England Air Museum, Windsor Locks, Connecticut has a Gustave Whitehead file established by Randolph, O'Dwyer, and the CAHA Gustave Whitehead Committee (1960's - 1980's). www.neam.org

Smithsonian Air and Space Museum, Smithsonian Institution, Washington, DC
Smithsonian copied the Gustave Whitehead files of researchers Stella Randolph and Major William J. O'Dwyer for study and research purposes in the 1960's. http://siarchives.si.edu/about/contact-us

Museums/Exhibits

Gustav Weisskopf Museum, Leutershausen, Germany (in southern Germany - Bavaria, close to Ansbach and Nuremberg); has an English online info site. In March 2013, the Gustav Weisskopf Museum was granted 9 million euros by the state of Bavaria, to build a new museum. *The Gustav Weisskopf Museum also maintains a research archive, complete with videos and tape recordings of interviews conducted with witnesses, sent to them by Major William J. O'Dwyer. http://www.weisskopf.de/english-version.html

Discovery Museum, 4450 Park Ave., Bridgeport, CT Whitehead exhibit and 1/4 scale model of "No. 21" plane 203-372-3521.
http://www.discoverymuseum.org/

Fairfield Museum and History Center, Fairfield, CT (call ahead 203-259-1598, to find out when a Whitehead exhibit will be displayed; archival collection available for public viewing and research) http://www.fairfieldhistory.org/

CT Air and Space Center, Stratford, CT (has replica of #21 Whitehead plane that flies, call ahead for exhibit days/hrs) http://cascstratford.wordpress.com/

Whitehead Aviation Trail (in progress)
http://cascstratford.wordpress.com/local-history/gustave-whitehead/whitehead-sites-today/

Additional Information and **Educational Resources** located at **www.gustavewhitehead.info**.

Whitehead researchers Stella Randolph and Major William O'Dwyer view Whitehead's copy of a Chanute book, "Progress in Flying Machines," showing D'Esterno's design elements, used by Gustave Whitehead in his monoplane flying machines. Pictured at 100th anniversary celebration of Gustave Whitehead's birth, in his hometown, Leutershausen, Germany, 1974.
Photo courtesy of Fairfield Museum, O'Dwyer archives

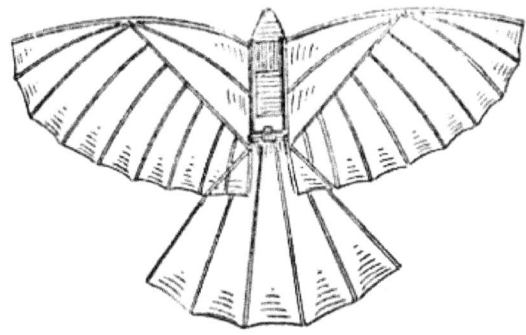

FIG. 44.—D'ESTERNO—1864.

© Susan Brinchman, 2015

Gustave Whitehead: "First in Flight"

Index

9315th Air Force Squadron, 109, 214,
acetylene, 42, 87, 111, 113, 118, 216, 308, 342
Aerial Committee, 121, 151, 157, 159, 160, 165, 169, 186, 271
Aerial Contest, 121, 142, 147, 157, 159-161, 165, 169, 171-173, 176, 181, 186, 189, 257, 264, 344, 347
    entrant fee, 181
aerial navigation,
    problem of, 24, 39, 73, 82, 106, 111, 112, 115, 121, 122, 130, 134, 147, 150, 155, 156, 157, 158, 161, 167, 178. 181. 185-187, 190, 204, 243, 347, 349
Aero Club of America, 34, 48, 89, 106, 108, 220, 238, 247, 253, 255, 270, 280, 311, 314, 315, 333, 347-350
First Annual Exhibition Exhibit of Aeronautical Apparatus, 108, 220, 348
    Second Annual Exhibition, 220
Aeronautic(al) Society,
    New York 231, 232, 235, 238, 241, 247, 249, 251, 253, 254, 257, 284, 349, 350
Aeronautical Society,
    Boston 207, 274, 338
Aeronautics Congress, (World Congress of Aeronauts, 1904) 157, 185, 186
aluminum, 113, 137, 178, 179, 223-225, 254-256, 309
Alvin Street, 260, 262, 264, 296, 297, 300, 301, 304, 335, 350, 352
American Aviation Historical Society, 212
American Inventor (magazine), 63,65,99, 105, 189-192, 194, 265, 268, 308, 343
Ash Creek, 49, 51, 52, 53, 60, 253, 287
Atlantic City, 75, 77, 79, 115-119, 157, 173, 272, 342
August 1901, 24, 38, 68, 74, 77-79, 85, 95, 117, 140, 198, 236, 246, 263, 274, 277, 293, 341
Avery,
    William, 175, 182
Bacon
    Jeannette Virelli, 219

Baldwin
    Thomas, 173-176, 186, 187, 248, 346
bamboo, 25, 30, 46, 66, 86, 93, 95, 96, 120, 135, 149, 165, 205, 342
Barber
    Andrew V., 47
Barnum
    P. T., 30, 31, 77, 78
Bates and Wilmot Streets, (Pittsburgh, PA) 202
Bates Street, 200-204, 340
Beach (Bridgeport)
    Sandy Beach, 211
    Seaside Park 217, 341
Beach (Fairfield) 50-52, 56, 57, 62, 63, 74, 75, 77, 199, 200, 211, 255, 287, 288
Beach (Milford) 195
Beach (Stratford) 51, 63, 65, 66, 287
Beach
    Stanley Yale, 27, 28, 34, 39, 73, 102, 107, 142, 148, 152, 153, 155, 219-221, 229, 230, 233-236, 238-254, 257, 262, 264-267. 271. 272. 274. 283. 284. 290, 291, 295, 298, 315, 341, 345, 347, 348, 349
Beach Whitehead Patent, 241-242,244, 407-412
Beach-Whitehead Statement, 320-325, 330, 351, 352, 413-419
Bell
    Alexander Graham, 248
biplanes, 197, 227, 248, 266, 299
Black Rock, 53, 73, 127, 211, 288
Blue Hill
    Observatory, 206, 207, 274, 338, 339
Boltzmann
    Arthur, 173-176
    Ludwig, 174
Booth
    Howard (Aeronaut) 229, 230, 233-235, 264, 298
Boston Post Road, 49, 57
Bostwick Avenue, 199, 200, 211

Bradtmuller
    Edward, 218, 227
Bridgeport (see first flights - preparatory, street flights, & Chapters 6 & 14)
Bridgeport Evening Farmer
    50, 51, 62, 74, 75, 78, 85, 122, 144-146, 250, 251, 254, 257, 259, 264
Bridgeport Evening Post, 30, 68, 75-79, 110, 115-117, 123
Bridgeport Gas Co, 30, 198
Bridgeport (Sunday Herald)
    Magazine, 38, 39
    Sunday Herald, 33-42, 44, 47-50, 52, 62, 68, 69, 74, 78,81, 82, 85, 94, 99, 102, 110, 112, 113, 121-123, 127, 130, 151, 178, 189, 194, 229, 230, 250, 264, 268, 342, 343, 351
Bridgeport Post, 76, 79, 85, 117, 143, 200, 211, 284, 303, 352
Burr
    Albert E., 216, 276, 278
Burr Creek, 77
CAHA, 91, 98, 210, 212, 216, 237, 269, 278, 296, 302, 303, 335, 352-354
calcium carbide (*also: calcium-carbide*) 25, 30, 45, 87, 118, 132, 134, 138
California Arrow, 173, 176, 181, 346
canvas (*also: canvass*) 25, 30, 73, 93, 95, 132, 135, 138, 140, 167, 240, 244, 245, 347
Cellie
    Andy,34, 40, 42, 68-70, 73, 74, 110, 113, 341
Century Magazine, 88, 90, 91, 319, 324
Chanute
    Octave, 93, 156-164, 167, 168, 173-176, 181, 182, 184, 186, 197, 207, 221, 222, 232, 270, 271, 274, 275, 280, 338, 339, 341, 342, 345, 347, 349
Charles Island (*see Milford*)
Cherry Street, 25, 110, 120, 123-128, 133, 152, 155, 198-200, 211, 213, 275, 276, 278, 279, 288, 289, 293, 296, 342, 343, 349
"Chronology of Aviation," 90, 253, 312, 314, 316m 317, 318, 349, 350, 399-404

Gustave Whitehead: "First in Flight"

Ciglar
   John, 211, 344
circuit(s) (1902) 87, 94, 166, 170, 176, 189, 193, 194, 195, 264, 265, 307, 344, 346
circus grounds, 31, 198, 199, 210, 218, 289, 340
cockpit, 25, 92, 94, 96, 98
Collins
   Edward ("Ed") 11, 13
   Jean Savage 217
Condor, 22, 23, 27, 28, 105, 153, 193, 204, 205, 206, 309, 338
condor(s), 134, 255, 338
Connecticut Aeronautical Historical Association (*see also - CAHA*) 91, 98, 209, 210, 216, 249, 269, 278, 302, 333, 353
Contract (*see Smithsonian-Wright Agreement of 1948*)
control (*see Chapter 2 "Issue of Control"*)
Cosmopolitan, 172
Crane
   John B., 15, 38, 209, 227, 273, 333, 351
Crittendon
   Clarence, 218, 237
   Mrs., 280
Curtiss
   Glenn, 37, 48, 100, 173, 176, 248, 249, 254, 272, 281, 316, 346, 348, 349, 350, 356
Custead,
   W. D. 42, 45, 46, 112, 113, 115, 341
   Waco, Texas, 42, 46, 112, 113, 341
Darvarich
   Louis, (*also, Davarich*), 79, 200, 201, 202, 203, 213-216, 265, 339, 340, 344, 420
Davidson
   Jesse, 212
December 17, 1903, 24, 68, 84, 85, 88-91, 96, 102, 104, 198, 309, 313, 314, 318, 319, 324, 345
Del Bianco
   Susan, 304
Del Buono
   Robert, 214, 215
d'Esterno, Count 93, 194, 265
Devine
   Martin, 202, 204, 215
Dickie
   James, 34, 40, 42, 64, 68, 70-74, 110, 113, 272, 283, 330, 342
dihedral, 92, 98, 308
Easton, 31, 209, 211
   Sport Hill, 289, 344

Ellsworth
   Street, 57, 78, 199, 288
eyewitnesses (*Whitehead* - see Chapters 2, 6, 14, & Appendix E "Gustave Whitehead Powered Flights Witnesses")
   Wright (see Wright witness statements)
factory,
   flying machine (also airplane), 33, 81, 120-133, 139, 140, 152, 155, 195, 243, 265, 278
   Wilmott & Hobbs, 69, 120, 293, 295, 342, 343
Fairfield (*see Chapters 1, 2, 5, 6, & 7*)
Fairfield Avenue, 40, 42, 49, 52, 57, 73, 77, 78, 199, 210, 216, 288, 344
Fairfield Historical Society, 49, 354
Fekete
   John, 211, 344
first flight(s),
   earlier preparatory flights at Bridgeport, 24-31, 75-79, 198 (*see also Chapter 6, Key Testimonies*)
      street flights, 15, 30, 78, 79, 90, 93, 101, 196, 198, 199 (map), 340-342
   "first sustained flight" Aug. 14, 1901 in Fairfield, CT (*see also Chapters 1 & 2*), 23-24, 33-46
      locations & route, 49-63
   later sustained flights of Aug. 14, 1901 at Stratford, CT, 63-68
firsts (*legacy of Whitehead*)
   list of, (*see Chapter 11*)
"Flying" (the *Bridgeport Sunday Herald* article), 33, 37-39, 41, 47, 49, 52, 55, 70, 85
Fountain (Gustave Whitehead Memorial), 79, 80
Franko, 214, 215
free flight, 25, 88-90, 220, 232, 319, 324
Garber
   Paul E., 67, 97, 210, 216, 269, 273, 323, 324, 328, 331, 352, 353
gasoline, 132, 134, 138, 142, 175, 176, 178, 180, 181, 196, 199, 205, 210, 211, 217, 221-224, 257, 260, 261, 275, 309, 339, 340, 342, 344, 347
Ghormley
   K. I., Atty., 70, 71, 73, 209, 210-212, 218
Gilman estate, 199, 216, 288
God, 33, 40, 44, 278, 285
grave,
   Whitehead, Gustave A., 67, 282, 302-304, 308, 351, 353
Greenfield Hill, 242-244, 287

Gustav Weisskopf Museum, (*see Resources, p. 426*)
Gypsy Springs, 62, 212, 288, 342, 421
Hammer
   William J., 90, 107, 109, 248, 249, 253, 254, 312, 314-317, 319, 320, 348-350, 354, 397-403
Hancock Ave, 30, 130, 139, 196, 212, 217, 293, 296, 303
Harvard University, 15, 38, 91, 207, 209, 227, 251, 273, 320, 333, 338, 351
Harworth
   Junius, 30, 60, 63-67, 70, 79, 100, 101, 103, 128, 151, 190, 198, 199, 216, 254, 262, 264, 265, 269, 271, 273, 274, 279, 281, 284, 292, 297, 341, 342, 352
Havery
   John, 218, 289
heavier-than-air (flying machine) 22-24, 40, 46, 51, 88, 89, 99, 101, 105, 142, 150, 156, 158-160, 165, 173, 182, 183, 186, 196, 198, 200, 207, 221, 253, 264, 274, 308, 309, 319, 324, 329, 343, 349, 352
helicopter(s), 84, 143, 197, 230, 235, 249-251, 253-257, 260, 261, 264-266, 280, 283, 285, 295, 296, 300, 303, 349, 350
High Bridge, 206, 339
Hildes-Heim
   Erik, 64, 210, 237, 279
Hillman (Beach-Hillman monoplane), 246
History by Contract, 19, 207, 269, 273, 334 (see Resources)
hoax, 38, 40, 273
Holland Heights, 62, 68, 69, 82, 253-256, 259, 295, 298
Horsman, Edward I., 207, 338, 339
House
   Edward M., 28, 70, 71
Howard Ave, 199
Howell
   Richard "Dick," 33-40, 47-52, 55-58, 60, 62-64, 68, 70, 73, 74, 78, 81, 85, 86, 90, 94, 102, 110
Illustrirte Aeronautische Mitteilungen, 85, 86, 153, 315
inherent stability, 230, 235
inherently stable, 25, 91, 92, 94, 98, 220, 251, 266, 309, 358, 362, 413
Jackson,
   Paul, 334
Jane's All-the-World's-Aircraft, 14, 34, 304, 317, 334, 354
Jones
   Buffalo, 253

Index

Ernest L. R., 71, 269
Keefe
   Raymond, 218, 219
kerosene, 81, 121, 166, 194, 274, 292, 308
Knabenshue
   Roy, 175, 187
Kopacsi
   Mary, 227, 289, 347
Kosch
   Andy, 304
Koteles
   Elizabeth, 212, 213, 342, 353
Lake
   Simon, 39, 274
Lakeview Cemetery, 302, 304, 305, 351
Langley
   Samuel P., 30, 38, 79, 107, 117-119, 122, 156, 157, 167, 173-175, 193, 220, 272, 285, 319, 325, 338, 342, 348
Lanye
   Frank, 199, 210, 211
Lautier
   Charles, 11, 13, 77
Lawsuit(s), Whitehead 85, 249, 254, 264
Lazay
   Louis, 198, 210, 340
Lenox Park, 68, 249. 262. 300. 349
Lesko
   John S., 184, 186, 210, 279, 288, 303, 342, 344, 346
Leutershausen
   Germany, 13, 19, 186, 219, 269, 337, 351, 353, 354, 424-427
lever(s), 96,100, 140, 241, 255, 265, 344
Library of Congress, 38, 68, 74, 253, 273, 307, 308, 311, 317, 320, 324, 325, 331, 333, 413, 423
Lilienthal,
   Otto, 23, 194, 196, 197 206, 207, 221, 222, 232, 258, 265, 302, 337-339, 347
Lindberg
   Charles, 38, 305, 351
Linde
   Herman, 50, 73, 79, 85, 95, 110, 120-124, 126, 127, 139, 140, 143-146, 148, 166, 174, 189, 195, 196, 265, 278, 283, 284, 340, 342-344
Link
   Stephen, 11, 13, 213
Lippincott
   Harvey, 15, 91, 92, 98, 210, 212, 213, 216, 217, 249, 273, 278, 303, 333, 335, 352, 354
London
   William, 218

Lordship, 51, 63-67, 90, 191, 193, 216, 218, 221, 236, 237, 246, 250, 265, 302, 303, 341, 342
   Lordship Park, 251
   Lordship Manor, 64-66, 99, 189, 209, 287, 288
   "Point-No-Point," 251
Louisa and McKee Streets
(Oakland, Pittsburgh, PA), 204
Louisiana Purchase Exposition Company, 127, 147, 149, 153-155, 169, 197, 343
Manley,
   Charles M., 117-119, 173, 272, 342
Maryland, 24
Massachusetts, 24, 110, 115, 338
   (*see Blue Hill*)
Master Witnesses File, 219
Maxim,
   Hiram, 30, 70, 122, 156, 173, 192, 220, 285, 338
   Hudson, 90, 316, 350, 400, 401, 403
McColl
   John A., 198, 218
Milford,189, 209, 265
   Charles Island, 166, 193- 195, 288, 344
   Harbor, 193
   "the spit"195
Mill Hill, 244, 287
monoplane, 66, 92, 93, 124, 152-155, 186, 197, 199, 210, 211, 216, 220, 236-238, 241, 244, 246-248, 250, 251, 253, 257, 263, 265, 266, 271, 299, 308, 340, 341-342, 344, 353, 427
Morris Park, 230, 231, 233, 234, 235, 240, 241, 244, 247, 248, 253, 254, 349
Mountain Grove Cemetery, 73. 199. 211, 218, 219, 342, 352
muslin, 24, 46, 225
Myers
   Carl E., 158, 159, 274, 275, 341
NASA, 87, 92, 94, 99
"navigating the air," 17, 33, 42, 115, 121
New York , (see Chapter 5)
"No. 21" (see Chapters 1, 2, 3, & 6, also see "Condor")
"No. 22", 95, 96, 99, 113, 115, 121, 124-127, 131, 139, 140-142, 145, 150, 152, 155, 165, 189, 190, 192 , 193, 195 , 216, 263, 265, 271, 294, 308, 342, 343
Oakland (Pittsburgh, PA), 200, 201
O'Dwyer
   William J., Maj. (Capt), 11, 13-15, 18-20, 39, 40, 47, 48, 51, 52, 69, 73, 79, 86, 96-98, 107, 109, 110, 127, 128, 150, 152, 153, 186, 207, 209, 210, 216, 217, 219, 227, 237, 252, 265, 269, 273, 275-278, 281, 282, 203, 334, 352, 353, 354
   "Unearthing Smithsonian Contract," 318, 325
O'Dwyer / Gustave Whitehead Research archives (*see Resources, p. 425*)
Old Post Road, 51, 52, 57, 58
old trotting park, 14, 30, 77, 78, 80 (*also see W.W. Cameron Trotting Park*)
O'Neil (*also spelled O'Neal- estate, Oakland, Pittsburgh, PA), 202, 372*
ornithopter, 44, 46, 96, 207, 265, 338
Orr's Castle (Tunxis Hill, Fairfield) 218, 229, 232, 288-290, 344
Whitehead-Beach patent, 242, 407-412
Peschel
   Gustav, 218, 341
photographs (photos) (see Chapter 2 - "Photo Questions")
Pine Street (see Chapters 1, 2, 3, 6, & 10)
police, 62, 63, 103, 204, 215, 282, 284, 337
practicable, 83, 121, 187, 255, 308
   impracticable, 264
practical, 33, 37, 83, 84, 100, 103, 105, 119, 123, 142, 144, 146-148, 167, 177, 186, 187, 190, 196, 220, 221, 230, 253, 255, 263-265, 268. 272, 273, 282, 284, 285, 300, 305, 307, 308, 316, 318, 334, 339, 348,
Pruckner
   Anton, 63, 65-68, 79, 96-98, 118, 121, 124, 125, 126, 140, 189, 190, 197, 216, 217, 264, 265, 273, 278, 279, 281, 284, 285, 287, 303, 340, 342, 343, 353
pulley(s),96, 97, 101, 140, 260, 292
Randolph,
   Stella, 11, 13, 19, 63, 69, 70, 73, 101, 110, 121, 123, 139, 190, 196, 201, 204, 207, 209, 211, 219, 221, 230, 238, 244, 269, 273, 274, 282, 295, 296, 303, 308, 309, 318, 319, 320, 322, 325, 334, 340, 351-353
Ratzenberger
   Joseph D. "Joe," 198, 200, 211, 341
replicas & reproductions, 91, 92, 98, 101, 272, 304, 318, 353, 354
Ridgely Avenue, 68, 227, 234,235, 244, 249, 256, 260, 289, 290, 295, 297-300 (map - 299), 335, 347, 349, 350
Ritchey
   Charles, 201, 215
Riverside Drive, 51, 60
Santos-Dumont,
   Alberto, 41, 138, 139, 155, 156, 162-166, 168, 173, 177, 220, 342, 344, 346
Savage
   Mary (*Jusewicz*), 198, 199, 217, 218, 341

Schenley Park, Pittsburgh, PA 201, 204, 215
Schweikert
   Thomas, 198, 213
Scientific American (*see also Chapter 6*) 25-28, 34, 82, 89, 94, 102, 106-108, 118, 171, 172, 178, 180, 197, 219-225, 230-232, 238, 266, 341, 345, 346, 348
seaplane, 23, 309
silk, 24, 25, 30, 44, 66, 73, 86, 93, 95, 149, 165, 255
Sky-cycle, 158, 159
Smith
   Willard, 160, 164, 185, 186
Smithsonian-Wright Agreement of 1948, 11, 17, 19, 87, 88, 91, 92, 273, 325, 331, 335, 352, 354
   "Contract" (see Chapter 12), 11, 17, 19, 20, 34, 38, 85, 88, 91, 92, 249, 271, 273, 311, 314, 348, 352, 353
   development of, 318-331
Spannenberger, H. 91, 98
St. Louis World's Fair of 1904, (see Chapter 4)
   see also St. Louis Exposition of 1904, 86, 121, 127 & Chapter 4
   Aeronautic Concourse, 174, 175, 184
   Grand Prize, 147, 156, 158-160, 168-170, 181, 183, 187, 189, 271, 346, 347
steam, 73, 87, 120, 140, 161, 202, 214, 216, 217, 220, 261, 265, 274, 292, 340, 342, 348
steering, 25, 30, 45, 94-101, 115, 139, 140, 175, 191, 241, 242, 248, 265, 317, 344, 345, 347
Stevens
   Leo, 171
Stratford (see also Lordship), 90, 110, 151, 189, 191, 193, 198, 200, 209, 216, 218, 242, 250, 251, 265, 287, 288, 303, 304, 335, 341, 342
Suelli, 81, 82, 83, 339
Suelly
   Frederick, 68, 227
Szur
   Frederick, 218, 227, 289, 347
"toy(s)," 83, 150, 264, 271
triplane, 82, 84, 105, 167, 168, 176, 178, 180, 181, 197, 205, 206, 220-223, 246-248, 266, 270, 271, 299, 339, 345, 347
Tuba, Andy, 214
Tunxis Hill (eastern Fairfield), 62, 69, 199, 210-212, 218, 219, 227, 232-236, 244, 246, 249, 256, 262, 281, 284, 288-291, 295, 297-300, 341, 342, 344, 347, 350
Tunxis Hill Park, 219, 297

Turney Creek, 52
Turney field (s), 51-57, 61, 62
Turney's Farm, 49, 51, 52
unmanned tests, 24, 25, 28, 112, 113, 173, 196, 197, 209, 263, 266, 274, 340
unstable (Wright aeroplanes), 91, 96, 98, 235, 316 (see Chapter 2 "Issue of Control")
Villa Park, 212, 227, 288, 289, 342, 347
Waldo,
   Charles, 200, 211, 284
Walsh
   Wilfred, 249, 250, 295
Washington School, 219
Watson,
   Arthur Kent Lyons, 252, 283, 291, 349
Weisskopf
   Gustav, 86, 136, 207, 218, 337, 338
   Kusterer, Gustave Weisskopf, 304
   Museum (Leutershausen, Germany), 13, 19, 186, 219, 269, 346, 351, 353, & see Resources)
Werer
   Michael, 211, 342
West End (of Bridgeport, CT), 14, 24, 25, 30, 57, 69, 77, 81, 85, 122, 123, 130, 196, 198, 199 (map), 204 (Chapter 7), 227, 246, 285, 289, 292, 294, 297, 340, 347
Whitehead,
   Charles, 293, 295, 300, 329, 340, 352
Whitehead,
   John, 67, 73, 109, 125, 139, 141, 166, 195, 196, 235, 264, 281, 298, 340, 343, 345, 350
Whitehead,
   Lillian ("Lilly"), 347
Whitehead,
   Louisa, 123, 200, 204, 249, 259, 262, 281, 282, 297, 300, 301, 334, 339, 340
Whitehead Motor, 46, 158, 159, 173, -176, 179, 181, 186, 255, 341, 346, 350
Whitehead,
   Nelly, 249, 349
Whitehead,
   Rose (Rennison), 28, 72, 201, 212, 249, 282, 296, 303, 339, 340, 349
Whitehead witnesses (*see Chapters 2 & 6*)
witch(es) (as symbol of aviation), 47-49
Wordin Ave, 30, 69, 77, 101, 150, 198, 199, 288, 292, 303
World Almanac of 1911, 249, 253, 314, 316, 317, 319, 320, 350, 357, 399, 400, 404
World's Fair of 1904 (*see St. Louis World's Fair of 1904*)

Wright
   brothers, 23, 24, 31, 38, 39, 84, 87, 91, 99, 104, 161, 165, 216, 220, 221, 229, 235, 237, 248-250, 253, 264, 267, 268, 270, 311, 317, 320, 322, 324, 331, 333, 334, 343-349, & Appendix A & B
   Wilbur and Orville, 85, 88, 249, 400, 403, 423
Wrights visit Whitehead, 274-281
Wright Flyer, 19 34, 87, 89, 90,91, 92, 93, 98, 99, 101, 102, 248, 270, 272, 273, 311, 314, 318, 319, 328, 331, 335, 352
Wright witness statements, 314, 315
W. W. Cameron Trotting Park, 78, 342
Yale University, 423
Zahm
   Albert F., 185, 273, 307, 308, 317, 330, 331, 333, 429

Author's Note: some words occurred too often to list, amongst these were: aeroplane, Bridgeport, Fairfield, flying machine, Pine Street, Gustave Whitehead, and Smithsonian. *See Table of Content and Resources.*

www.ingramcontent.com/pod-product-compliance
Lightning Source LLC
Chambersburg PA
CBHW080722230426
43665CB00020B/2586